HOW
ENEMIES
BECOME
FRIENDS

HOW
ENEMIES
BECOME
FRIENDS

THE SOURCES OF STABLE PEACE

Charles A. Kupchan

A Council on Foreign Relations Book

PRINCETON UNIVERSITY PRESS
PRINCETON AND OXFORD

Copyright © 2010 by Princeton University Press

Published by Princeton University Press, 41 William Street, Princeton, New Jersey 08540
In the United Kingdom: Princeton University Press, 6 Oxford Street, Woodstock,
Oxfordshire OX20 1TW

All Rights Reserved

Library of Congress Cataloging-in-Publication Data

Kupchan, Charles.
How enemies become friends : the sources of stable peace / Charles A. Kupchan.
p. cm. — (Princeton studies in international history and politics) (Council on foreign relations book)
Includes bibliographical references and index.
ISBN 978-0-691-14265-4 (hardcover : alk. paper)   1. Peaceful change (International relations)
2. Peace-building.   3. International relations—21st century.   4. World politics—21st century.
5. National security.   6. Balance of power.   I. Title.
JZ5538.K87 2010
303.6'6—dc22
2009024769

British Library Cataloging-in-Publication Data is available

The Council on Foreign Relations (CFR) is an independent, nonpartisan membership organization,
think tank, and publisher dedicated to being a resource for its members, government officials,
business executives, journalists, educators and students, civic and religious leaders, and other
interested citizens in order to help them better understand the world and the foreign policy choices
facing the United States and other countries. Founded in 1921, CFR carries out its mission by
maintaining a diverse membership, with special programs to promote interest and develop expertise
in the next generation of foreign policy leaders; convening meetings at its headquarters in New York
and in Washington, DC, and other cities where senior government officials, members of Congress,
global leaders, and prominent thinkers come together with CFR members to discuss and debate
major international issues; supporting a Studies Program that fosters independent research, enabling
CFR scholars to produce articles, reports, and books and hold roundtables that analyze foreign
policy issues and make concrete policy recommendations; publishing *Foreign Affairs*, the preeminent
journal on international affairs and U.S. foreign policy; sponsoring Independent Task Forces that
produce reports with both findings and policy prescriptions on the most important foreign policy
topics; and providing up-to-date information and analysis about world events and American foreign
policy on its website, www.cfr.org.

The Council on Foreign Relations takes no institutional position on policy issues and has no affiliation with the U.S. government. All statements of fact and expressions of opinion contained in its pub-
lications are the sole responsibility of the author or authors.

This book has been composed in Times New Roman

Printed on acid-free paper. ∞

press.princeton.edu

Printed in the United States of America

1   3   5   7   9   10   8   6   4   2

For Nicholas and his generation
May they know only peace

CONTENTS

ILLUSTRATIONS

FIGURES

MAPS

TABLE

ACKNOWLEDGMENTS

I began to ponder the central themes of this book about a decade ago, prompted by two emerging trends. The first was the ongoing diffusion of power in the international system. This development begged the question of whether the transition from a unipolar to a multipolar world could occur peacefully. The second was the growing divide between the United States and Europe, a rift that became apparent during the late 1990s and was then brought to a head by the U.S.-led invasion of Iraq in 2003. The resulting acrimony opened the possibility that the political community forged by the Atlantic democracies during the second half of the twentieth century might falter and again fall prey to geopolitical rivalry.

I began to address these changes in international politics in my last two books. In 2001, my co-authors and I published *Power in Transition: The Peaceful Change of International Order*, a volume that explicitly addressed how to manage shifts in global power. I am indebted to my collaborators: Emanuel Adler, Jean-Marc Coicaud, and Yuen Foong Kong. Jason Davidson and Mira Sucharov contributed a chapter, as well as valuable research assistance. United Nations University published the book and provided financial support. I continued my exploration of global change in *The End of the American Era: U.S. Foreign Policy and the Geopolitics of the Twenty-first Century* (Knopf, 2002). This book focused on the changing nature of American internationalism and transatlantic relations, the waning of U.S. primacy, and the onset of a multipolar world.

Both of these volumes helped lay the intellectual foundations for this book. Exploring how and when states are able to manage change peacefully and escape the dictates of geopolitical rivalry led me to the question, at once simple and profound, that is at the core of this work: How do enemies become friends?

My two home institutions, Georgetown University and the Council on Foreign Relations, provided ideal settings for exploring this question. My colleagues and students at Georgetown offered a vibrant community in which to try out new ideas and explore the historical cases. Robert Gallucci, the former dean of the School of Foreign Service, provided consistent encouragement as well as generous research support. My colleagues at the Council on Foreign Relations were similarly helpful and stimulating, offering a venue for testing my analysis and conclusions within the policy community. I am indebted to Council on Foreign Relations president, Richard N. Haass, for his personal and institutional support, and for the thoughtful comments he provided on the draft manuscript.

I was fortunate to receive several external fellowships as I was writing this book. During 2007–2008, I was a fellow at the Woodrow Wilson International Center for Scholars and held the Henry A. Kissinger Chair at the Library of Congress's Kluge Center. I am indebted to both institutions for their support and for providing unique and stimulating settings in which to pursue scholarly research. I thank the directors—Lee Hamilton at the Wilson Center and Carolyn Brown at the Kluge Center—as well as my colleagues at both institutions for their intellectual companionship and input. I would also like to thank the European Commission for providing financial support via a generous grant to the Council on Foreign Relations.

I am indebted to the many individuals who provided assistance with research. My research associates at the Council on Foreign Relations, John Elliott and Joshua Marcuse, not only helped with the historical case studies, but also made significant intellectual contributions to the project. Adam Mount, a doctoral candidate at Georgetown, joined the effort just as it was nearing completion; he helped sharpen the argument and clarify its implications for broader theoretical debates. I also thank the following individuals for their help with research: Jan Cartwright, Caraleigh Holverson, Sabrina Karim, Brian Lowe, Christoph Markson, Jonathan Monten, Parke Nicholson, Alexandros Petersen, Tim Rogan, Conor Savoy, and Brian Thiede.

The Council on Foreign Relations convened a review session to provide feedback on the draft manuscript. I am grateful to G. John Ikenberry for chairing the group. Participants included: Michael Auslin, Michael Barnett, Dale Copeland, Daniel Deudney, Charles Doran, David Edelstein, Patrick Jackson, Charles King, Jeffrey Legro, Robert Litwark, Kathleen McNamara, Abraham Newman, Daniel Nexon, Aviel Roshwald, Stephen Szabo, Samuel Wells, Michael Werz, and William Wohlforth. Rikard Bengtsson, Steven Cook, Magnus Ericson, Arie Kacowicz, Rana Mitter, Magnus Jerneck, Peter Trubowitz, and Hans-Ulrich Yost also provided feedback on the manuscript. I am very fortunate to have benefited from the comments of such generous colleagues.

I presented draft versions of the book at the following universities and institutions: the University of California at Berkeley, the Catholic University of Milan, Cornell University, the Council on Foreign Relations (in Washington and San Francisco), Harvard University, Hebrew University, the Kluge Center at the Library of Congress, Lund University, Oxford University, Princeton University, the University of Texas at Austin, Tokyo University, the University of Virginia, and the Woodrow Wilson Center for International Scholars. I thank the organizers and participants of these seminars for their comments.

Chuck Myers at Princeton University Press has been a pleasure to work with from the outset. He, Debbie Tegarden, Karen Verde, and their colleagues did a superb job of shepherding the book to publication. I would also like to thank my literary agent, Andrew Wylie, for his wise counsel.

Finally, I am profoundly grateful to my family. Nancy Kupchan Sonis, Clifford Kupchan, Sandy Kupchan, and Nicholas Kupchan provided unlimited love, support, and encouragement. My father, S. Morris Kupchan, bequeathed to me so much, including many of the qualities—curiosity, discipline, determination—essential to scholarship. My stepfather, H. Richard Sonis, was a true friend and a man of uncommon decency. Simma Asher was my loyal partner when this book was just getting under way. She is now my wife, a clear sign of her fortitude in putting up with the necessarily idiosyncratic habits of an author at work. Her love, companionship, and applesauce cake helped see me through.

Charles A. Kupchan
Washington, DC

HOW
ENEMIES
BECOME
FRIENDS

CHAPTER ONE

STABLE PEACE

Long before European immigrants came to North America, Iroquois tribes settled the lands that would eventually become upstate New York. These tribes were regularly at war with each other, exacting a heavy toll on their populations. In the middle of the fifteenth century, five Iroquois tribes, aggrieved by the mounting losses, gathered around a communal fire in the village of Onondaga in an attempt to end the fighting. The confederation they forged not only stopped the warfare, but it preserved peace among the Iroquois for over three hundred years. Several centuries later, the Congress of Vienna served as a similar turning point for Europe. The gathering of European statesmen in 1814–1815 not only marked the end of the destruction wrought by the Napoleonic Wars, but also produced the Concert of Europe, a pact that maintained peace among the great powers for more than three decades. Iroquois delegates resolved disputes in regular meetings of the Grand Council in Onondaga, while European diplomats preferred more informal congresses called as needed to diffuse potential crises. But the results were the same—stable peace.

Although the Iroquois Confederation and the Concert of Europe are now historical artifacts, both amply demonstrate the potential for diplomacy to tame the geopolitical rivalry that often seems an inescapable feature of international politics. President Barack Obama appreciates this potential; he entered office determined not only to repair America's frayed relations with traditional allies, but also to use America's clout to address some of the world's most intractable conflicts. In his inaugural address, President Obama asserted that Americans, having experienced civil war and the national renewal that followed, "cannot help but believe that the old hatreds shall someday pass; that the lines of tribe shall soon dissolve; that as the world grows smaller, our common humanity shall reveal itself; and that America must play its role in ushering in a new era of peace."[1]

Obama wasted no time in acting on his words. Two days after assuming

---

[1] http://edition.cnn.com/2009/POLITICS/01/20/obama.politics/index.html.

power, the new administration assigned high-level emissaries the tasks of forging peace between Palestinians and Israelis and bringing stability to Afghanistan and Pakistan. As former senator George Mitchell, Obama's choice for Middle East envoy, stated, "There is no such thing as a conflict that can't be ended. . . . Conflicts are created, conducted and sustained by human beings. They can be ended by human beings."[2] Even with respect to Iran, perhaps America's most intransigent adversary, the new administration arrived in Washington intent on opening a dialogue. The Obama administration clearly believes that enemies can become friends.

The Iroquois Confederation and the Concert of Europe are not alone in demonstrating the potential for diplomacy to produce enduring peace. At the end of the nineteenth century, for example, Great Britain deftly accommodated the rise of the United States, clearing the way for a strategic partnership that has lasted to this day. Not only did the United States peacefully replace the United Kingdom as the global hegemon, but over the course of the twentieth century the liberal democracies of North America and Europe went on to forge a uniquely cohesive and durable political community. Although it formed in response to the threats posed by Nazism, fascism, and communism, the Atlantic community became much more than a military alliance. Indeed, like the Iroquois Confederation and the Concert of Europe, it evolved into a zone of stable peace—a grouping of nations among which war is eliminated as a legitimate tool of statecraft.

It is not simply the absence of conflict that makes a zone of stable peace a unique and intriguing phenomenon. Rather, it is the emergence of a deeper and more durable peace, one in which the absence of war stems not from deterrence, neutrality, or apathy, but from a level of interstate comity that effectively eliminates the prospect of armed conflict. When a zone of stable peace forms, its member states let down their guard, demilitarize their relations, and take for granted that any disputes that might emerge among them would be resolved through peaceful means. To study historical episodes in which states succeed in escaping geopolitical rivalry is to explore how, when, and why lasting peace breaks out.

In investigating the sources of stable peace, this book not only offers a diplomatic road map for turning enemies into friends, but it also exposes several prevalent myths about the causes of peace. Based on the proposition that

---

[2] http://edition.cnn.com/2009/POLITICS/01/23/mitchell.mideast/.

democracies do not go to war with each other, scholars and policy makers alike regularly claim that to spread democracy is to spread peace. To that end, successive Republican and Democratic administrations have pursued robust policies of democracy promotion. Indeed, during the 2008 presidential campaign, influential voices on both sides of the aisle called for the establishment of a "League of Democracies," a new international body that would institutionalize peace among democratic states while excluding autocracies on the grounds that they are unworthy of partnership.[3] So too is thinking within both the academic and policy communities heavily influenced by the assertion that economic interdependence promotes stability. Commercial linkages between the United States and China, Israel and the Palestinian Authority, or Serbia and Kosovo, the prevailing wisdom maintains, promise to serve as fruitful investments in peace, not just prosperity.

This book directly challenges such conventional wisdom. It refutes the claim that democracy is necessary for peace, demonstrating that non-democracies can be reliable contributors to international stability. Accordingly, the United States should assess whether countries are enemies or friends by evaluating their statecraft, not the nature of their domestic institutions. In similar fashion, this work reveals that commercial interdependence plays only an ancillary role in promoting peace; it helps deepen societal linkages, but only after a political opening has first cleared the way for reconciliation. Deft diplomacy, not trade or investment, is the critical ingredient needed to set enemies on the pathway to peace.

These and other insights about how and when states are able to escape geopolitical competition and find their way to durable peace have profound implications for both scholarship and policy. Understanding the phenomenon of stable peace is of paramount theoretical importance. International history is characterized by recurring and seemingly inevitable cycles of geopolitical competition and war. The emergence of zones of stable peace makes clear that conflict is neither intractable nor inescapable, pointing to a transforma-

---

[3] See, for example, G. John Ikenberry and Anne-Marie Slaughter, Princeton Project on National Security, *Forging a World Under Liberty and Law: U.S. National Security in the 21st Century* (Princeton, NJ: Woodrow Wilson School of Public and International Affairs, 2006); Ivo Daalder and James Lindsay, "Democracies of the World, Unite!" *American Interest* 2, no. 3 (January/ February 2007); Robert Kagan, "The Case for a League of Democracies," *Financial Times*, May 13, 2008; and Senator John McCain, address to The Hoover Institution on May 1, 2007, available at: http://www.johnmccain.com/informing/News/Speeches/43e821a2-ad70-495a -83b2-098638e67aeb.htm.

tive potential within the international system. To theorize about stable peace is therefore to advance understanding of one of the most enduring puzzles in the study of global politics: how to explain change in the character of the international system—in particular, the transformation of international anarchy into international society.

The study of stable peace is also of obvious practical importance. Peace might be more pervasive if scholars and policy makers alike knew more about how to promote and sustain international communities in which the prospect of war has been eliminated. Why and how did peace break out among the United States and Great Britain, Norway and Sweden, the founding members of the Association of Southeast Asian Nations (ASEAN), and the nomadic tribes that now constitute the United Arab Emirates? What lessons can be drawn for fashioning zones of peace between China and Japan, Greece and Turkey, or other contemporary rivals? In the Middle East and Africa, regional institutions have the potential to help dampen rivalry and prevent war, but they have yet to mature. What can be done to advance the prospects for stable peace in these regions?

Another priority for policy makers is preserving existing zones of peace, the durability of which can by no means be taken for granted. Following the end of the Napoleonic Wars in 1815, the Concert of Europe succeeded in securing peace among the great powers for over three decades. By 1853, however, Europe's major powers were again at war—this time in the Crimea. The Soviet Union and China forged a remarkably close partnership during the 1950s; by the early 1960s, they were open rivals. The United States enjoyed more than seven decades of stable and prosperous union among its individual states, only to fall prey to a civil war in the 1860s. The United States survived the challenge to its integrity, but other unions have not been as fortunate. The Soviet Union, Yugoslavia, the Senegambian Confederation, Czechoslovakia—these are only a few of the many unions that are today historical artifacts.

The fragility of former zones of peace makes clear that comity among the Atlantic democracies can by no means be taken for granted. Indeed, since the Cold War's end, transatlantic tensions have mounted over a host of issues, including ethnic violence in the Balkans, the invasion of Iraq in 2003, and the ongoing conflict in Afghanistan. Amid the rift that opened over the Iraq war, Europeans began to question whether they could still look to the United States to provide responsible international leadership. In turn, Americans began to question whether they should continue to support European unity, suspecting that the European Union (EU) was gradually transforming itself from a partner into a rival. The Atlantic community is still a zone of stable peace—armed conflict among its members remains unthinkable—but geopolitical competition, even if only in subtle form, has returned to relations between the United States and Europe.

The challenge for contemporary statecraft entails not just preserving existing zones of stable peace, but also deepening and enlarging them. The EU continues to seek more centralized institutions of governance even as it extends its reach to the south and east, exposing new members to its peace-causing effects. ASEAN's membership has also grown, taxing the body's capacity to coordinate regional diplomacy. South America has of late enjoyed advances in cooperation on matters of commerce and defense, but the deepening of regional integration still faces significant obstacles. These experiments in taming geopolitical rivalry are far from complete.

Fashioning stable peace among the great powers is another key challenge. With the European Union, China, Russia, India, Brazil and others on the rise, major changes in the distribution of power promise to renew dangerous competition over position and status. It may well be, however, that shifts in the global balance need not foster great-power rivalry. The history of the Concert of Europe yields important lessons about how to forge cooperation among major powers—but also sobering warnings about how easily such cooperation can erode. Rapprochement between the United States and Great Britain demonstrates that hegemonic transitions can occur peacefully—but it represents the only case of peaceful transition on record.[4] Examining the Concert of Europe, the onset of Anglo-American rapprochement, and other instances of stable peace thus promises to elucidate the opportunities—as well as the challenges—that will accompany the onset of a multipolar world.[5]

---

[4] The end of the Cold War could be considered a case of peaceful hegemonic transition—the transition from bipolarity to unipolarity occurred without major war. However, the transition was effectively accidental. The Soviet bloc collapsed as its satellites defected and the Soviet Union unraveled. The United States was left as the sole superpower. In contrast, Britain deliberately ceded hegemony to the United States as it gradually withdrew from its commitments in the Western Hemisphere.

[5] On the impending transition to multipolarity, see Charles A. Kupchan, *The End of the American Era: The Geopolitics of the Twenty-first Century* (New York: Knopf, 2002); and Fareed Zakaria, *The Post-American World* (New York: Norton, 2008). On the potential durability of U.S.

HOW AND WHY PEACE BREAKS OUT

Two puzzles motivate and guide this study. First, through what pathway do states settle outstanding grievances, dampen geopolitical competition, and succeed in constructing a zone of peace? What is the sequential process through which enemies become friends? Second, under what circumstances do zones of stable peace form? What causal conditions enable stable peace to emerge and endure?

Stable peace breaks out through a four-phase process. Reconciliation begins with an act of *unilateral accommodation*: a state confronted with multiple threats seeks to remove one of the sources of its insecurity by exercising strategic restraint and making concessions to an adversary. Such concessions constitute a peace offering, an opening gambit intended to signal benign as opposed to hostile intent. Phase two entails the practice of *reciprocal restraint*. The states in question trade concessions, each cautiously stepping away from rivalry as it entertains the prospect that geopolitical competition may give way to programmatic cooperation.

The third phase in the onset of stable peace entails the deepening of *societal integration* between the partner states. Transactions between the parties increase in frequency and intensity, resulting in more extensive contacts among governing officials, private-sector elites, and ordinary citizens. Interest groups that benefit from closer relations begin to invest in and lobby for the further reduction of economic and political barriers, adding momentum to the process of reconciliation.

The fourth and final phase entails the *generation of new narratives and identities*. Through elite statements, popular culture (media, literature, theater), and items laden with political symbolism such as charters, flags, and anthems, the states in question embrace a new domestic discourse that alters the identity they possess of the other. The distinctions between self and other erode, giving way to communal identities and a shared sense of solidarity, completing the onset of stable peace.

As to the causal conditions that enable enemies to become friends, stable peace emerges when three conditions are present among the states in question: institutionalized restraint, compatible social orders, and cultural commonality. Institutionalized restraint is a favoring but not necessary condition,

---

primacy, see Stephen Brooks and William Wohlforth, *World Out of Balance: International Relations and the Challenge of American Primacy* (Princeton, NJ: Princeton University Press, 2008).

whereas compatible social orders and cultural commonality are necessary conditions. The causal logic at work is as follows.

States that embrace *institutionalized restraint* possess political attributes that make them especially suited to pursuing stable peace. Governments that accept restraints on their power at home are most likely to practice strategic restraint in the conduct of their foreign relations. The exercise of strategic restraint and the withholding of power reassure potential partners by communicating benign intent and dampening rivalry. The practice of strategic restraint is most pronounced among liberal democracies; the rule of law, electoral accountability, and the distribution of authority among separate institutions of governance serve as potent power-checking devices. Liberal democracy, however, is not a necessary condition for stable peace. Other constitutional orders regularly practice strategic restraint.[6] Constitutional monarchies, for example, institutionalize checks on unfettered power and thus exhibit political attributes favorable to stable peace. Moreover, the cases will reveal that even autocratic states, which lack institutionalized checks on power, at times practice strategic restraint. It follows that whereas the practice of strategic restraint is a necessary condition for stable peace, the presence of institutionalized restraint is not. Accordingly, regime type alone does not determine the suitability of a state for pursuing stable peace.

The emergence of stable peace also depends upon the presence of *compatible social orders*. As the states engaged in building a zone of peace proceed with political and economic integration, the societies involved interact with greater frequency and intensity. If their social structures are compatible, integration reinforces existing political and economic elites—and proceeds apace. If their social orders are incompatible, integration upsets and threatens patterns of authority in one or more of the parties, provoking domestic coalitions that block further advances toward stable peace. The following dimensions of social order are of particular salience: the distribution of political power among different social classes; the distribution of political power among different ethnic and racial groups; the organizing principles of economic production and commercial activity.

The third condition making stable peace possible is *cultural commonality*. Culture refers to an interlinked network of practices and symbols based pri-

---

[6] For elaboration on the relationship between constitutional order and strategic restraint, see G. John Ikenberry, *After Victory: Institutions, Strategic Restraint, and the Rebuilding of Order After Major Wars* (Princeton, NJ: Princeton University Press, 2001), pp. 29–37.

marily on ethnicity, race, and religion. Reciprocal perception of cultural commonality is socially constructed, a product of a changing repertoire of practices and symbols, not a matter of primordial and fixed identities. Peoples that see themselves as ethnically or religiously incompatible can, as the product of reconciliation, eventually come to see themselves as ethnic or religious kin. At the same time, narratives of compatibility and similarity are easier to generate among certain populations than others. The cultural barriers between Protestants and Catholics may be more readily overcome than those between Christians and Muslims. As Britain searched for potential partners in the late nineteenth century, it sought to improve relations with both the United States and Japan. Anglo-Saxon commonality provided a strong sense of cultural affinity between Britons and Americans, a factor that facilitated the onset of lasting rapprochement. In contrast, a narrative of commonality was not readily available between Britons and Japanese. Indeed, a sense of cultural difference ultimately came to stand in the way of a durable partnership between Britain and Japan.

From this perspective, the causal relationship between cultural commonality and stable peace comes close to that of social selection. When searching for potential partners in peace, states are drawn to other states with which a narrative of common heritage is more readily available. Cultural commonality is even more important during the later stages of the onset of stable peace. When elites seek to consolidate stable peace through the generation of a narrative that propagates a sense of communal identity, they have at their disposal preexisting recognition of cultural bonds.

Cultural commonality is no guarantee of compatibility; states sharing a common heritage are often bitter rivals. But it does facilitate the onset of stable peace, both at its onset and its completion. It is also the case that the notion of a common culture is elusive—one that, as mentioned above, is malleable and often the product of political and social construction rather than primordial characteristics. The notion's malleability notwithstanding, the cases demonstrate a strong correlation between perceptions of cultural commonality and stable peace.

THE HISTORICAL CASES

Zones of stable peace can take three different forms—*rapprochement, security community*, and *union*. Rapprochement is the most rudimentary form of stable peace. Long-standing adversaries stand down from armed rivalry, agree to settle their disputes amicably, and ultimately develop mutual expectations of peaceful coexistence. A security community is a more evolved form of stable peace. It is a grouping of two or more states that institutionalize a set of norms and rules in order to manage peacefully their relations. A union is the most mature form of stable peace. It is a grouping of two or more states that merge into a single political entity, minimizing, if not eliminating, the geopolitical consequence of preexisting borders.

Each of these three types of stable peace is examined through an extensive set of historical case studies. Numerous considerations shaped the selection of cases. The empirical chapters examine successful cases as well as failures—that is, historical episodes in which stable peace forms as well as those in which it breaks down.[7] Such variation in outcomes is needed to help identify the conditions under which stable peace takes root and endures. In addition, examining successes and failures enables this book to speak more directly to the policy agenda by offering insight into measures aimed at encouraging new zones of peace as well as at preserving and extending existing ones. The cases were also selected to ensure wide variation on the main explanatory variables—regime type, compatibility of social orders, and cultural commonality—in an effort to isolate the causal role played by these different variables and the feedback mechanisms that exist among them. For similar reasons, the cases exhibit substantial variation across geographic region and historical period.

The successful and failed instances of stable peace examined in this book thus represent a diverse subset of a broader universe of cases.[8] In addition, especially because the literature on this topic is still evolving, preference was given to examining a wide range of cases in less depth rather than examining

[7] I define a case of failure as one in which the parties in question attempt to form a zone of stable peace, but ultimately do not succeed in doing so. In some cases, the parties progress only incrementally toward demilitarized relations, and then abort the process. In other cases, they may succeed in forming a zone of peace, but then experience breakdown at a later point. I define as a success any zone of peace that lasts for a decade or longer. From this perspective, some cases can be coded as both a success and a failure. The Concert of Europe, for example, functioned as an effective security community for over three decades after its inception in 1815, but then broke down after 1848. The United States represents a successful case of union; it endured for over seven decades after its inception in 1789. But it is also a case of failure due to the outbreak of civil war in 1861.

[8] Not only do the historical chapters offer only a representative sample of cases, but the total number of cases as well as language barriers prevented thorough examination of all materials relevant to the selected case studies. The historical summaries presented in chapters 3 through 6 draw on the most authoritative books and articles that pertain to each case, but certainly do not represent an exhaustive examination of all available literature.

a few cases in greater depth. This preference for breadth rather than depth enables the book to probe more effectively similarities and differences across cases and to spot patterns that would emerge only by examining historical episodes that traverse a broad temporal and geographic span. More cases, even if covered in less detail, lend the theory-building enterprise the reliability of a larger sample.

These considerations structure the historical chapters that follow. Chapter 3 contains an in-depth examination of a single case of rapprochement—that of the United States and Great Britain between 1895 and 1906. This extensive case study helps strike a balance between the richness that comes with a close investigation of a critical case and the rigor afforded by a larger set of case studies. As a result of devoting an entire chapter to this single case, rapprochement receives more comprehensive coverage than either security community or union. This bias stems from the observation that it is amid rapprochement that the processes through which states move from rivalry to stable peace are most active and consequential. Along the continuum from anarchy to union, more variance in interstate relations occurs in the transformation from unfettered rivalry to rapprochement than occurs amid the move from rapprochement to security community and/or union. Once rapprochement has been achieved, the advance to security community or union entails a furthering of processes that have already had transformative consequences; much of the work has already been done. In this sense, the "kernels" to understanding stable peace may well be embedded in the core mechanisms that drive rapprochement. Security community and union, more evolved forms of stable peace with more extensive social character, then build on and deepen these core processes.

Careful study of a single case is also necessary to acquire a detailed understanding of the complicated processes through which strategic interaction, domestic politics, and ideational change interact to produce stable peace. Historians have examined the U.S.-British case extensively; the wealth of existing sources makes it an especially attractive candidate for in-depth study. Admittedly, such reliance on this one episode of rapprochement runs the risk that a single case weighs too heavily in the enterprise of theory construction. However, running this risk seems warranted, if not necessary. At this early stage in building a body of theory on stable peace, it is important to capture the richer and more textured insights yielded by close reading of a critical case study.

Chapter 4 contains four additional case studies of rapprochement. Two episodes of successful rapprochement are examined: Norway and Sweden from 1905 to 1935, and Argentina and Brazil from 1979 to 1998. The two cases of failed rapprochement are: Great Britain and Japan from 1902 to 1923, and China and the Soviet Union from 1949 to 1960.

Chapter 5 contains five case studies of security community. The three successful cases examined are: the Concert of Europe from 1815 to 1848; the European Community (EC) from 1949 to 1963; and the Association of Southeast Asian States (ASEAN) from 1967 through the present. The two failed cases are: the breakdown of the Concert of Europe between 1848 and 1853, and the Gulf Cooperation Council (GCC) from 1981 through the present.

Chapter 6 contains five main case studies of union. Three successful cases of union are examined: the Swiss Confederation from 1291 until 1848; the Iroquois Confederation from 1450 to 1777; and the United Arab Emirates (UAE) from 1971 through the present. The two cases of failed union are: the United Arab Republic (UAR) from 1958 to 1961, and the Senegambian Confederation from 1982 to 1989. The conclusion to chapter 6 examines in a more cursory fashion three additional successful cases: the unification of the United States (1789), Italy (1861), and Germany (1871); and two additional failures: the U.S. Civil War (1861) and the expulsion of Singapore from Malaysia (1965). This selection of case studies is summarized in table 1.1.

No single story emerges from examination of these cases. Rather, each instance of the formation or dissolution of a zone of stable peace follows its own unique pathway and takes place amid a unique set of circumstances. Nonetheless, recurring patterns do emerge, both as to how stable peace breaks out and as to the causal conditions that bring it about. The argument summarized above and fleshed out in the next chapter represents a distillation of the complex process that transforms enemies into friends; it is a precise account of none of the cases, but a generic account of all of them. The goal is to locate the common thread that unites the disparate cases, and in so doing to discover the mechanisms and conditions enabling states to escape the imperatives of geopolitical competition. The same caveats apply to the historical cases focusing on the unraveling of stable peace. When a zone of peace unravels, the process through which friends become enemies operates in reverse; narratives of opposition prompt societal separation, which in turn degrades cooperation, ultimately awakening geopolitical competition. And it

TABLE 1.1 Case Studies

RAPPROCHEMENT (Chapters 3 and 4)
Successes
    MAIN CASE (Chapter 3)
        Great Britain and the United States (1895–1906)
    SUPPORTING CASES (Chapter 4)
        Norway and Sweden (1905–1935)
        Brazil and Argentina (1979–1998)

Failures
        Great Britain and Japan (1902–1923)
        Soviet Union and China (1949–1960)

SECURITY COMMUNITY (Chapter 5)
Successes
        Concert of Europe (1815–1848)
        European Community (1949–1963)
        ASEAN (from 1967)

Failures
        Concert of Europe (1848–1853)
        The Gulf Cooperation Council (from 1981)

UNION (Chapter 6)
Successes
        Swiss Confederation (1291–1848)
        Iroquois Confederation (1450–1777)
        United Arab Emirates (from 1971)

Failures
        United Arab Republic (1958–1961)
        Senegambian Confederation (1982–1989)

CONCLUDING CASES
Successes
        United States (1789)
        Italy (1861)
        Germany (1871)
Failures
        U.S. Civil War (1861)
        Singapore/Malaysia (1965)

is the absence of the key causes of stable peace—institutionalized restraint, compatible social orders, and cultural commonality—that explains these cases of failure. Nonetheless, each instance of the collapse of stable peace takes place through its own pathway and occurs under a unique set of circumstances.

Moreover, the following chapters examine only a sample of cases; other instances of the onset and collapse of stable peace may take an altogether different path. Accordingly, this study does not purport to develop and test a determinate model or to make predictive claims about when and where specific zones of peace will form or fail. Rather, it offers scholars a framework and policy makers a guide for addressing how and why enemies become friends and for identifying the conditions that facilitate the emergence and endurance of zones of stable peace.

FROM THEORY TO POLICY

This book addresses dual audiences. It speaks to the mainstream theoretical concerns of scholars, seeking to advance academic debate about global politics. It simultaneously seeks to contribute to ongoing debates within the policy community. In this latter regard, the book develops five principal arguments that have direct implications for the conduct of foreign policy.

First, engagement with adversaries is not appeasement; it is diplomacy. Long-standing rivalries end not through isolation and containment, but through negotiation and mutual accommodation. Under the appropriate circumstances and through skillful diplomacy, enemies *can* become friends. Engagement does not always succeed in bringing geopolitical rivalry to an end—as many of the historical case studies in this book make clear. But it does have the potential to do so. Accordingly, policy makers should give stable peace a chance.

Second, democracy is *not* a necessary condition for stable peace. As mentioned above, the conventional wisdom within the U.S. foreign policy community is that lasting peace is the unique provenance of liberal democracies. The analysis in this book, however, rejects the proposition that liberal democracies alone are suited to fashioning zones of peace. Autocracies are capable of building lasting partnerships with each other as well as with democracies. Accordingly, the United States should base its relations with other states primarily on the nature of their foreign policy behavior, not the nature of their domestic institutions.

Third, the onset of stable peace is about politics, not economics. Academics and policy makers alike often attribute the onset of peace to economic and societal interdependence; societal interaction supposedly clears the way for political reconciliation. In contrast, this book argues the opposite—political reconciliation must come first if societal interaction is to have beneficial geopolitical consequences. Only after political elites have succeeded in taming geopolitical competition do the pacifying effects of economic interdependence make a major contribution to the onset of stable peace. The breakthroughs that lead to stable peace are strategic rather than economic in nature. Diplomacy, not trade or investment, is the currency of peace.

Fourth, compatible social orders are a key facilitator of stable peace, while incompatible social orders are a key inhibitor. Among states with contrasting social orders—aristocratic versus egalitarian, industrial versus agrarian, economically open versus protectionist—the societal integration that follows from political reconciliation threatens privileged social sectors, causing them to block further movement toward stable peace. It follows that policy makers should pay more attention to social order than regime type when assessing the suitability of a potential partner. It also follows that policies aimed at social change and convergence are more likely to promote peace than policies aimed exclusively at democratization.

Finally, cultural commonality plays an important role in determining the potential for and durability of stable peace. Policy makers therefore need to take cultural factors into consideration as they seek to expand existing zones of peace and create new ones. There is nothing primordial or essentialist about cultural dividing lines; societies that see one another as culturally distant can over time come to see one another as sharing a communal cultural identity. There are, however, constraints on the malleability of such identities. The availability of a narrative of commonality gives some zones of peace a greater chance of success than others; states that enjoy a preexisting ethnic or religious commonality will find it easier to construct a shared identity than those that do not. Policy makers should by no means interpret this finding as confirmation of the proposition that different civilizations are destined to clash. But they should recognize that states that enjoy a preexisting sense of common heritage are better candidates for stable peace than those that do not. They should also appreciate the importance that narratives of cultural commonality can play in promoting peace—especially among culturally diverse groupings of states.

The following chapter lays out the book's conceptual foundations in greater detail and explores the causes of stable peace in more depth. Chapters 3 through 6 contain the historical case studies, examining in turn rapprochement, security community, and union. The final chapter draws theoretical conclusions and elaborates on the policy implications of the study.

CHAPTER TWO

FROM INTERNATIONAL ANARCHY TO INTERNATIONAL SOCIETY

THEORETICAL FOUNDATIONS

This book explores the realm of international political life that occupies a middle ground between the anarchy characteristic of international politics and the order characteristic of national politics. This is the realm of *international society.*

As a starting point, this book shares the realist assumption that states reside in a Hobbesian international system whose default equilibrium is one of pervasive geopolitical competition. But it parts company with realism in positing that even if competition is endemic to global politics, it can nonetheless be overcome. As the international system matures, a Hobbesian world can give way to a Lockean world—one in which the practice of reciprocity and the fashioning of political compacts curb rivalry. Thereafter, the international system has the potential to evolve to a Deutschian world—one in which an international society based on communal norms and identities eliminates geopolitical competition and provides a foundation for stable peace.[1]

The logic of international society represents a synthesis of the logics of international politics and that of national politics. In the realm of international politics, each state is self-regarding and sovereign, all embrace oppositional identities, and order, to the extent it exists, emerges from the exercise of power. In the realm of national politics, sovereignty is unitary, identity is common, and order emerges from the institutionalization of power—as articulated by Max Weber and other theorists of the state. International society is located at the intersection of these two realms, containing characteristics of both. In this Deutschian middle ground, states exercise an attenuated form of sovereignty, identity is communal but not common, and order emerges

[1] See Karl W. Deutsch, *Political Community and the North Atlantic Area* (Princeton, NJ: Princeton University Press, 1957).

from the binding and bounding of power rather than its exercise or its institutionalization. In a society of states, the social character of interstate relations overrides the rules of anarchic competition and power balancing—even if it does not entail the mature institutions of governance and the bureaucracy associated with the unitary state. Figure 2.1 presents a conceptual mapping of these different political logics.

International society has been the subject of important scholarly work, much of it part of the so-called English School.[2] In keeping with the tradition of the English School, this book privileges no single theoretical approach. Rather, the analysis is explicitly eclectic and synthetic in nature, seeking to draw insights from multiple paradigms rather than defend any single one. The exploration of stable peace, as many other issues tackled by scholars of international politics, has suffered from the intellectual barriers that accompany theoretical divides. Realist accounts tend to be pitted against liberal ones, and rationalist accounts against constructivist alternatives. As a consequence, insufficient attention has been paid to approaches that cut across paradigmatic boundaries. This study explicitly seeks to transcend these barriers. Because the process under study is a dynamic one—how interstate relations move along a continuum from endemic competition, to halting cooperation, to lasting friendship—theoretical eclecticism is a necessity; at different stages in the onset of stable peace, quite different political and social processes are at work.

At least on the surface, the phenomenon in question represents a prima facie rejection of realism; the emergence of zones of peace confounds a paradigm that posits that international competition is inescapable and conceives of international change exclusively in terms of shifts in the distribution of material power. The inadequacy of a realist approach to stable peace is self-evident; the mere existence of a zone of peace invalidates realism's central

---

[2] Among the main theoretical traditions in International Relations, the English School is the one that has most advanced scholarship about international society. Perhaps the most influential book in this tradition is Hedley Bull, *The Anarchical Society* (London: MacMillan, 1977). For Bull, "A *society of states* (or international society) exists when a group of states, conscious of certain common interests and common values, form a society in the sense that they conceive of themselves to be bound by a common set of rules in their relations with one another, and share in the working of common institutions" (p. 13). Other scholars working in this tradition include Barry Buzan and Richard Little. See Barry Buzan and Richard Little, *International Systems in World History: Remaking the Study of International Relations* (Cambridge: Cambridge University Press, 2000); and Barry Buzan, *From International to World Society? English School Theory and the Social Structure of Globalization* (Cambridge: Cambridge University Press, 2004).

Thinker	International Politics					International Society	National Politics	
	Hobbes			Locke		Deutsch	Weber	
Organizing Principle	Anarchy	Balance of Power	Hegemony	Contingent Cooperation	Rapprochement	Security Community	Federal Union	Unitary State
Character of Sovereignty	Hard Sovereignty					Attenuated or Pooled Sovereignty		Conjoined or Single Sovereignty
Character of Relations	Interstate					Trans-State		Supra-State or Unitary
Source of Order	Order from the Exercise of Power					Order from Binding and Co-binding Power		Order from the Institutionalization of Power
Nature of Identity	Oppositional Identity					Communal Identity		Common Identity

FIGURE 2.1 The Logics of International Politics, International Society, and National Politics

tenets. It is also the case, however, that realist concerns figure prominently in the story that unfolds in the following pages. Indeed, the historical cases reveal that strategic necessity and adjustments to adverse shifts in the material distribution of power initially drive the process of reconciliation that ultimately leads to stable peace.

In contrast to realism, the liberal tradition has begun to map the borderlands between the realms of international politics and international society. A centerpiece of liberalism's research agenda, after all, has been to examine how institutions, international law, ideational convergence, and regime type can tame the international system, mute its competitive incentives, and promote cooperation. Nonetheless, liberalism still adheres to a conceptual framework in which the international system is comprised of self-regarding, sovereign states—even if it submits that instruments are available to induce discrete episodes of international collaboration. The emergence of zones of peace entails a far deeper transformation in interstate relations than that envisaged by liberals.[3] Stable peace is ultimately the product not of the rationalist calculations that predominate in the liberal paradigm, but of societal bonds that endow interstate relations with a social character.

Inasmuch as this book is about profound change in international politics, the constructivist school's insights about the ability of changes in state identity to facilitate transformation of the international system make it a natural theoretical starting point. Furthermore, constructivism recognizes the social character of interstate relations and therefore is well-equipped to theorize about international society. Nonetheless, constructivist accounts of international society often distance themselves too far from the material notions of power that inform realism and liberalism, thereby overlooking the important role played by rationalist conceptions of geopolitical necessity. In addition, many constructivists leave unanswered important questions of when and how changes in state identity take place and make possible the emergence of international society.[4]

---

[3] As Barry Buzan observes, the notion of international society "has some parallels to regime theory, but is much deeper, having constitutive rather than merely instrumental implications." Buzan, *From International to World Society?* p. 7.

[4] In his *Social Theory of International Politics,* Alexander Wendt posits that international anarchy can take three different forms: Hobbesian, Lockean, and Kantian. In broad terms, this perspective is consonant with this book's argument that groups of states can move from a violent Hobbesian setting, through the building of a Lockean compact based on reciprocity, to a Deutschian society characterized by communal identity. (The empirical cases suggest that re-

In seeking to build bridges across theoretical divides—rather than pitting paradigms against each other—this book concentrates on two specific linkages. One is a realist-constructivist synthesis. Here, the central question is the mediating role of perceptions of intent, motivation, political character, and identity in shaping how states react to concentrations of material power. The standard realist account suggests that states balance against other centers of power when they can, and bandwagon when they must. This book embraces this central realist insight. The initial step toward reconciliation is a form of bandwagoning; one state accommodates another because strategic deficiency makes balancing unappealing. This move is motivated by strategic necessity and objective national interests, not intersubjectively constituted meanings.

Nonetheless, constructivist concerns about practice, discourse, and identity are needed to explain why an initial act of accommodation can ultimately result in stable peace. A process that begins with strategic bargaining ends with societal integration and identity change, enabling states to see each other as benign polities. When states see each other as benign, then concentrations of material power, rather than constituting a source of threat, can serve as a vehicle for the spread of shared norms and a magnet around which international society can form. This book thus combines rationalist insights about the role that diplomatic signaling plays in moderating uncertainty with constructivist insights about the role that practice and discourse play in changing identity to explain how the mutual attribution of benignity takes place and contributes to the onset of stable peace.

A synthesis between liberalism and constructivism is the second key linkage explored in this book. The phenomenon under study is not just the absence of war, but a deeper and more durable peace. Liberalism alone is adequate to explain the absence of war; the democratic peace literature contains a wealth of both normative and institutional arguments about the pacific quality of relations among democracies. Exploring stable peace requires a further analytic step, one capable of explaining how polities build societal

gime type is not a necessary determinant of stable peace, hence the preference for a Deutschian focus on communal identity instead of a Kantian focus on republican government.) Nonetheless, Wendt's discussion does little to explain the mechanisms by which states transition between these different forms of anarchy. In subsequent work, Wendt does offer a teleological model of progression through these conditions of anarchy. For further discussion, see note 80 below. Alexander Wendt, *Social Theory of International Politics* (Cambridge: Cambridge University Press, 1999), chap. 6; and Alexander Wendt, "Why a World State Is Inevitable," *European Journal of International Relations* 9, no. 4 (2003).

bonds with each other, embrace communal identities, and, in some cases, merge into a unitary state and enjoy the social solidarity that comes with union. As the process of building stable peace moves from the rationalist to the sociological—from the early stages of signaling benign intent to the later stages of social construction—a liberal-constructivist synthesis is essential.

This inquiry into stable peace is not intended to advance a particular claim about the ontological content of political life, nor does it aspire to theoretical unity. Rather, it draws on a combination of rationalist and sociological processes, and realist, liberal, and constructivist explanations. It simply endeavors to describe the formation of zones of stable peace as accurately as possible.

THE EXISTING LITERATURE ON STABLE PEACE

Despite the subject's theoretical and practical importance, little is known about how and when zones of peace form and endure. The topic has received scant scholarly attention partly because zones of stable peace are uncommon; even in parts of the world where international conflict is rare, such as South America, international tension has been the rule and comity the exception. In addition, scholars have paid insufficient attention to instances of stable peace precisely because they are peaceful and therefore often overlooked. Inasmuch as zones of peace do not draw attention to themselves—they represent non-events or the dog that does not bark—they are chronically understudied. As Thomas Hardy quipped, "War makes rattling good history; but Peace is poor reading."[5]

The main body of literature directly relevant to the study of stable peace focuses on security communities—groupings of states that have succeeded in escaping geopolitical rivalry. The literature on security communities took shape in the 1950s under the guidance of Karl W. Deutsch. He oversaw a multiauthored project, containing numerous case studies, which remains unpublished.[6] The main published product is *Political Community and the North Atlantic Area*, Deutsch's pioneering volume that served as the foundation for

---

[5] Thomas Hardy, *The Dynasts: An Epic-Drama of the War with Napoleon* (London: Macmillan, 1920), p. 71.

[6] Karl W. Deutsch, *Backgrounds for Community: Case Studies in Large-Scale Political Unification*, unpublished manuscript.

future research on security community.[7] Deutsch's agenda was largely set aside during the Cold War, which encouraged scholars to focus on the study of conflict and deterrence rather than cooperative security. As a consequence, the literature on security community did not significantly advance until the collapse of the Soviet Union. Since the Cold War's end, two collaborative volumes have explicitly returned to Deutsch's agenda. Emanuel Adler and Michael Barnett published *Security Communities* in 1998. Two years later, Arie Kacowicz, Yaacov Bar-Siman-Tov, Ole Elgström, and Magnus Jerneck published *Stable Peace Among Nations*.[8] Other authors who have made significant contributions to the literature include Kenneth Boulding, Stephen Rock, and Bruce Cronin.[9] The following chronological overview highlights the main conceptual insights of each of these authors.[10]

Although the notion of security community was initially proposed by Richard Van Wagenen in the early 1950s, it was not until the 1957 publication of Deutsch's *Political Community and the North Atlantic Area* that the concept was developed in a systematic fashion. Deutsch defines a security community as a grouping in which there exists a "real assurance that the members of that community will not fight each other physically." He distinguishes between pluralistic and amalgamated security communities (unions), offering a primarily transactional account of their formation. Communication and economic and social interaction are the primary vehicles through

[7] Deutsch, *Political Community*.

[8] Emanuel Adler and Michael Barnett, eds., *Security Communities* (Cambridge: Cambridge University Press, 1998); Arie Kacowicz, Yaacov Bar-Siman-Tov, Ole Elgström, and Magnus Jerneck, eds., *Stable Peace Among Nations* (Lanham, MD: Rowman & Littlefield, 2000).

[9] Kenneth Boulding, *Stable Peace* (Austin: University of Texas Press, 1978); Stephen R. Rock, *Why Peace Breaks Out: Great Power Rapprochement in Historical Perspective* (Chapel Hill: University of North Carolina Press, 1989); Stephen R. Rock, *Appeasement in International Politics* (Lexington: University of Kentucky Press, 2000); Bruce Cronin, *Community Under Anarchy: Transnational Identity and the Evolution of Cooperation* (New York: Columbia University Press, 1999).

[10] Two other literatures are directly relevant to the study of stable peace: work on unions and on democratic peace. Although I do not survey these literatures, I do draw extensively on them later in this chapter. On unions, see, for example, Murray Forsyth, *Unions of States: The Theory and Practice of Confederation* (New York: Leicester University Press and Holmes & Meier Publishers, 1981). Work on democratic peace devolves from Immanuel Kant," *Perpetual Peace: A Philosophical Essay*, in M. Campbell Smith, trans. and ed. (London: Swan Sonnenschein, 1903). The notion of democratic peace is not synonymous with the notion of stable peace. Democratic peace is about the absence of war. Stable peace runs much deeper; it is about the demilitarization of interstate relations and the elimination of geopolitical competition. Nonetheless, the democratic peace literature does provide rich theoretical and empirical material for studying stable peace.

which security community evolves, with transaction flows and integration incrementally leading to "mutual sympathy and loyalties," a "'we feeling,'" and "partial identification in terms of self-images and interests."[11] Deutsch identifies several conditions that help groupings of states move toward mutual expectations of peaceful change: initial perceptions of a common threat, the presence of a dominant state that takes the lead in promoting integration, compatible values, and responsive and effective institutions of governance.

Although Deutsch presents a primarily transactional and functionalist account of the onset of stable peace, his analysis in several respects does lay a foundation for alternative approaches. His focus on national self-images and the evolution of a "we feeling" broaches the question of changing identities—a matter of central concern to constructivists such as Adler and Barnett. Deutsch also recognizes the role played by substate actors, noting that interest groups inside individual states as well as class-based alliances that span national boundaries help drive forward the process of integration. Finally, Deutsch's study foreshadows the importance of strategic restraint—particularly with respect to major powers. He observes that states are more willing to let down their guard and compromise their autonomy if confident that their stronger partners are prepared to afford them voice and influence in shaping communal arrangements. Deutsch found that pluralistic security communities are easier to attain and preserve than amalgamated ones precisely because they allow their members greater autonomy.[12]

The next major work on zones of peace came over twenty years later with the publication of Kenneth Boulding's *Stable Peace*. Four of the five chapters in the book are drawn from public lectures, making the book more of a reflection on the subject of stable peace than a systematic analysis. Boulding's approach is close to that of Deutsch. His definition of stable peace tracks Deutsch's: "a situation in which the probability of war is so small that it does not really enter into the calculations of any of the people involved."[13] He also agrees with Deutsch that "compatible self-images" and "the rise of travel and communication" are important elements of stable peace.[14] Boulding makes a noteworthy contribution in helping to identify the political dy-

---

[11] Deutsch, *Political Community*, pp. 5, 36.
[12] On substate actors, see Deutsch, *Political Community*, pp. 176–179; on restraint and autonomy, see pp. 30–31, 40, 66.
[13] Boulding, *Stable Peace*, p. 13.
[14] Boulding, *Stable Peace*, pp. 17–18, 63.

namics at work in the early stages of reconciliation. Whereas Deutsch focuses principally on communication and integration as triggering processes, Boulding's work, like the approach of this book, points to the importance of mutual concessions, suggesting that reciprocal accommodation plays a key role in leading the parties "toward compatibility of national images."[15]

Stephen Rock's 1989 book on great-power rapprochement contributed to the study of stable peace in three respects.[16] First, Rock isolates episodes of rapprochement from the broader phenomenon of stable peace, thereby focusing attention on the critical pairings of states that often serve as the core group around which wider zones of peace take shape. Second, he hypothesizes that states whose economies and geopolitical interests are complementary rather than homogenous are best poised to pursue rapprochement. Integration between heterogeneous economies (for example, a producer of raw materials and a manufacturing state) produces mutual gains, while integration between similar economies (for example, two manufacturing economies) leads to competitive clashes of interest. The same logic leads Rock to claim that a naval power and a land power are better suited for rapprochement than two land powers, the latter more likely to have conflicting strategic interests. Third, Rock argues that states are able to engage in rapprochement only when they have similar political systems and ideological orientations. Political similarity promotes a sense of communal identity and affinity, whereas political difference sustains mutual suspicion and ideological rivalry.

In their 1998 book, *Security Communities*, Emanuel Adler and Michael Barnett return to Deutsch's original research agenda, seeking to advance theoretical inquiry into the onset of stable peace and to compile additional empirical material through the inclusion of eight case study chapters.[17] They bring a fresh theoretical lens—constructivism—to the subject, providing them the conceptual tools needed to move well beyond Deutsch's transactional account of security community. In particular, constructivism's core concerns with norms, ideational change, and identity enable Adler and Barnett to explore in greater depth Deutsch's underdeveloped discussion of national self-image and mutual perceptions of we-ness. By focusing on how practices and institutions bring about new understandings of reality as well

[15] Boulding, *Stable Peace*, pp. 112–113.
[16] Rock, *Why Peace Breaks Out*.
[17] Adler and Barnett, *Security Communities*. The following summary draws on chapters 1–2.

as shared meanings and identities, they deepen conceptualization of the so-ciological dimensions of stable peace.

Adler and Barnett also advance exploration of the processes through which security communities form and the conditions that favor their onset. As to the processes that lead to security community, they identify three stages of evolution: nascent, ascendant, and mature. During the nascent phase, states respond to a shared threat or other common stimulus by banding together and interacting with increasing frequency and intensity. During the ascen-dant phase, transactions intensify, norms of multilateralism become institu-tionalized, and these institutions serve as engines for social learning—"an active process of redefinition or reinterpretation of reality."[18] During the ma-ture phase, social networks thicken and the parties come to enjoy mutual trust and a common identity, laying the foundation for dependable expecta-tions of peaceful change.

As to the conditions that facilitate the formation of security communities, Adler and Barnett agree with Deutsch that a common external threat often provides the initial incentive for a group of states to band together. They also support Deutsch's finding that a dominating power usually leads the way, al-though they focus on the ability of a major power to project shared norms and understandings and not only wield material preponderance. Importantly, Adler and Barnett suggest that liberal democracies may be better suited to participate in security communities than other types of polities due to their susceptibility to socialization and their ability to embrace shared norms. They propose that liberal democracy, while not a necessary condition for the formation of security community, may play a prominent role in facilitating the onset of stable peace.

In *Community Under Anarchy*, Bruce Cronin adopts a constructivist ap-proach similar to that of Adler and Barnett. For Cronin, stable peace de-pends on the spread of a transnational identity, which "can transform an egoistic definition of self to one based on membership in a conceptual social group."[19] As the members of such a grouping embrace a transnational iden-tity, they are likely to define their interests in common and to embrace a shared set of guiding norms. Cronin identifies three main conditions that are necessary for a transnational identity to form: a shared characteristic, such as

---

[18] Adler and Barnett, *Security Communities*, p. 43.
[19] Cronin, *Community Under Anarchy*, p. 19.

a common ethnicity, region, or regime type; exclusivity as to the shared characteristic; and a high level of positive interdependence among the states in question. Cronin examines security communities (the Concert of Europe) as well as unions (Germany and Italy), adding to the empirical breadth of his study.

In *Stable Peace Among Nations*, Arie Kacowicz and his co-authors claim a conceptual middle ground between Deutsch's transactional approach and the constructivist account of Adler and Barnett.[20] For Kacowicz, the onset of stable peace results from cognitive learning and the development of a shared normative framework that enables partner states to develop mutual expectations of peaceful change. "Each party learns that it is dependent upon the other to assure its security," leading to "a mutual interest in establishing and maintaining the peace between them. . . . This change in the perception of the national interest means that the parties regard war as an illegitimate instrument for attaining national objectives."[21] Positive consequences follow from building reconciliation, including substantial increases in trade and societal integration. Within this framework, the onset of expectations of peaceful change precedes, rather than results from, societal integration.

As for the conditions that enable this cognitive awakening and the consequent redefinition of national interests, the authors identify the presence of stable political regimes whose behavior is predictable and consistent, mutual satisfaction with the status quo, and open channels of communication. Like Adler and Barnett, Kacowicz and his collaborators see liberal democracy as a factor that facilitates, but is not a necessary condition for, the onset of stable peace.

Realism Revisited

In light of realism's insistence on the pervasive nature of geopolitical rivalry, it should come as no surprise that all of the existing literature on stable peace lies outside the realist tradition. The works just reviewed reside in the liberal or constructivist traditions—and many of them draw on insights gleaned from the literature on the democratic peace. However, one strand of realism,

---

[20] Kacowicz published previous works on the subject, including Arie Kacowicz, *Zones of Peace in the Third World: South America and West Africa in Comparative Perspective* (Albany: State University of New York Press, 1998).

[21] Kacowicz et al., *Stable Peace Among Nations*, p. 25.

although it does not explicitly address the question of stable peace, is none-theless directly relevant. This is the literature on threat perception and state type. Work in this area is rich and broad-ranging; the following is a selective survey intended only to provide a conceptual foundation for a more in-depth discussion later in this chapter.

Balance-of-power logic provides the analytic foundation for realism's insis-tence on the endemic nature of international rivalry. In an anarchic and self-help world, any state that seeks to amass superior power automatically pro-vokes other states to balance in response. Stephen Walt amends this central tenet of the realist canon by proposing that states balance against threats rather than power per se, with perceptions of threat derived from assessment of both capability and intent.[22] Walt does not take full advantage of the con-ceptual opening that resulted from his focus on threats rather than material capability alone; he claims that states base their assessment of intent primar-ily on material variables such as geography and the propensity of states to maintain offensive force postures. But his work does bring the question of intent into the picture, logically raising the possibility that states that perceive each other as having nonthreatening intent might be able to defy realism's insistence on the intractable nature of geopolitical competition.

Others have sought to extend the logical implications of Walt's focus on intent. Walt's student, David Edelstein, for example, examines how states as-sess the intentions of other states and how those assessments in turn shape policy choice.[23] He contends that governments investigate both behavioral signals and domestic characteristics (such as ideology and regime type) in as-sessing intentions. A state sees another polity as benign when its intentions are viewed as complementary to the interests of the observing state, and ma-lign when assessments reveal intentions inimical to those interests.

Edelstein concludes that although states do invest significant time and en-ergy in studying the intentions of others, the uncertain nature of such assess-ments mutes their ultimate impact on the conduct of foreign policy. As Edel-stein writes, "domestic characteristics and behavioral signals are of only limited value as indicators of intentions."[24] Individual leaders and the attri-butes of specific regimes are transient. The behavior of the observed party

---

[22] Stephen Walt, *The Origins of Alliances* (Ithaca, NY: Cornell University Press, 1987).

[23] David Edelstein, "Managing Uncertainty: Beliefs about Intentions and the Rise of the Great Powers," *Security Studies* 12, no. 1 (Autumn 2002).

[24] David Edelstein, "Managing Uncertainty," p. 10.

can also change with little warning. As a consequence, governments of necessity treat benign assessments cautiously. Edelstein notes that states at times pursue cooperative strategies nonetheless, seeking to communicate benign intentions and encourage the target state to reciprocate. But uncertainty about intentions is the norm, making states reluctant to let down their guard lest such assessments prove erroneous.

Edelstein's work opens the door to the possibility that states that perceive each other's intentions as benign should be uniquely cooperative, but he closes that door as a result of his empirical finding that efforts at assessment are regularly compromised by uncertainty. If, however, states had more confidence in their assessments, then Edelstein's insights would have quite significant implications. Under such circumstances, mutual assessments of benign intent would have transformative potential, enabling states to step away from geopolitical competition and begin the transition to stable peace.

The literature on state type provides a useful vantage point from which to further this line of inquiry into the connection between assessments of intentions and stable peace. Authors such as Charles Glaser, Andrew Kydd, Randall Schweller, and Stephen Rock distinguish in their work between status quo states and revisionist states.[25] According to these authors, the principal objective of status quo states is to preserve the existing international order. They seek security, not power. The principal objective of revisionist states is to overturn the existing international order and recast it to their advantage. They are greedy states, seeking to maximize their power, not their security.

If states have the ability to discern whether they are dealing with a security-seeker or a greedy state, then an international system comprised only of security-seekers should be free of geopolitical rivalry. Assuming that status quo states can send signals of benign intent to each other—and that those signals can be reliably received and interpreted—they should be able to avoid strategic competition. Both Glaser and Schweller focus on the signals sent by military policies, including unilateral initiatives, such as procuring defensive as opposed to offensive weaponry, and reciprocal measures, such as arms con-

---

[25] Charles L. Glaser, "The Security Dilemma Revisited," *World Politics* 50, no. 1 (October 1997); Andrew Kydd, "Sheep in Sheep's Clothing: Why Security Seekers Do Not Fight Each Other," *Security Studies* 7, no. 1 (Autumn 1997) ; Andrew Kydd, "Game Theory and the Spiral Model," *World Politics* 49, no. 3 (April 1997); Randall L. Schweller, *Deadly Imbalances: Tripolarity and Hitler's Strategy of World Conquest* (New York: Columbia University Press, 1998); and Rock, *Appeasement in International Politics*.

trol.[26] Kydd enlarges the scope of this approach, contending that "we should not limit our attention to the military realm when considering how states can deliberately convey signals about their motivations."[27] He argues that signals of benign intent can be communicated through a broader range of indicators such as ideology, treatment of minorities, and public statements. Rock capitalizes on these insights in his exploration of the conditions under which appeasement is an appropriate strategy for dealing with an adversary. He concludes that such conditions exist when the appeaser is confident that it is dealing with a status quo state or a state whose aggressive behavior is motivated by insecurity as opposed to greed.

The central insight of this literature is the proposition that status quo states should be able to suspend the security dilemma and coexist peacefully. In arguing that such states can recognize one another as nonthreatening and consequently pursue policies of mutual accommodation, these authors provide an important account of when and how particular groupings of countries may be able to escape anarchic competition. Inasmuch as this literature focuses on how the operation of the security dilemma can be arrested, it offers an explanation not of stable peace, but only of the absence of war. However, this literature need not halt its inquiry with the observation that status quo states can avoid rivalry. If status quo states can suspend the operation of the security dilemma, perhaps they can also make its logic work in reverse, with successive rounds of mutual accommodation leading not just to neutrality, but to friendship and durable peace. The rest of this chapter explores these leads further, building on the literature just surveyed to develop a comprehensive and compelling theory of the origins of stable peace.

DEFINITIONS

A *zone of stable peace* is a grouping of strategically proximate states among which war has become unthinkable.[28] The members of a zone of stable peace

---

[26] Glaser, "Realists as Optimists: Cooperation as Self-Help," *International Security* 19, no. 3 (Winter 1995/96): 68.

[27] Kydd, "Sheep in Sheep's Clothing," p. 140.

[28] The term "strategically proximate" connotes geopolitical interaction. The states in question must either be geographically proximate or be engaged in the same strategic theater. Paraguay and Mauritius may enjoy a state of stable peace; war between them is unthinkable. But this study is not concerned with cases in which the absence of rivalry stems from the absence of con-

succeed in demilitarizing their relationship, thereby eliminating the use of armed force as a legitimate tool of statecraft. The indicators of such demilitarization include: undefended borders and/or the redeployment of forces from contested areas; the absence of war plans against one another; a neutral or positive reaction to mutual increases in defense spending; the establishment of joint political institutions; and evidence that elites, and ultimately publics, have come to see war among the parties in question as extremely remote, if not outside the realm of the possible. The states that comprise a zone of peace renounce the use of force only against each other, not in a universal sense. They may well continue to embrace, both individually and collectively, armed conflict as a tool of statecraft with others. Indeed, zones of stable peace not infrequently entail either implicit or explicit commitments to collective security, meaning that the parties would come to one another's defense in the event of attack.

There are three main types of stable peace: *rapprochement, security community*, and *union*. All three belong to the same family—groupings of two or more states that succeed in escaping the logic of power balancing and significantly muting if not altogether eliminating geopolitical competition. These three types of international society represent stages along a continuum; as the parties move from rapprochement to security community to union, stable peace deepens and matures. Moreover, there are different gradations of stable peace. In some instances, the parties in question significantly dampen security competition, but an undercurrent of geopolitical rivalry remains. In other cases, the prospect of armed rivalry is entirely eliminated. The defining features of rapprochement, security community, and union are as follows.

Rapprochement entails a standing down, a move away from armed rivalry to a relationship characterized by mutual expectations of peaceful coexistence. The parties in question no longer perceive each other as posing a geopolitical threat and come to see one another as benign polities. They do not, however, seek to generate an articulated set of rules and norms to guide their behavior, nor do they come to embrace a shared or common identity. In this sense, the parties succeed in eliminating geopolitical rivalry and entering a nascent type of international society, but they then live comfortably along-

---

tact. Rather, it focuses on cases in which states interact with one another in one or more geopolitical theaters, but nonetheless are able to construct a durable peace.

side each other rather than seeking to expand and deepen the social character of their relations. The states in question define their interests individually, but these interests are deemed to be congruent. They maintain separate identities, but those identities are compatible rather than oppositional. To use a historical analogy, feudal lords have stopped attacking and plundering each other and have learned to coexist peacefully—even if they have not come together to improve their collective welfare through commitments to mutual assistance.

As in rapprochement, the members of a security community come to see each other as benign polities and thereby succeed in escaping geopolitical rivalry. But security community represents a step forward from rapprochement and constitutes a deeper form of stable peace in two respects. First, the members of a security community go beyond peaceful coexistence, developing rules and institutions for managing their relations, resolving disputes peacefully, and preventing power inequalities from threatening group cohesion. Nonetheless, the members of a security community retain significant elements of sovereignty and each is free to pursue its own foreign policy with respect to outside states. Second, the members of a security community enjoy a sense of we-ness or a shared identity. Regulative and constitutive norms combine to give security communities a distinctive social character and help extend predictability and expectations of programmatic cooperation. With the blurring of self/other distinctions, interests come to be defined conjointly rather than individually. To return to the analogy, the feudal lords have forged a league of fiefdoms, promoting their collective welfare and defining their interests communally.

A union is the most highly evolved form of stable peace. The states in question not only see one another as benign, but they merge into a new polity, eliminating their individual sovereignties and minimizing the geopolitical significance of their territorial borders. In so doing, they participate in and consider as legitimate a supra-state realm of political life. In a security community, relations among member states are collectively managed, but each member governs its own domestic affairs and conducts its own relations with non-members. In a union, member states usually cede to a central authority significant control over domestic affairs and the conduct of foreign and defense policy. Interests become defined in unitary rather than conjoint terms. A shared identity is gradually transformed into a common identity. The feu-

Type of Stable Peace	Benign Character	Agreement on Order	Interests	Identity	Legitimation
Rapprochement	Yes	No	Congruent	Compatible	No
Security Community	Yes	Yes	Conjoined	Shared	No
Union	Yes	Yes	Unitary	Common	Yes

FIGURE 2.2 Types of Stable Peace and Defining Characteristics

dal lords have merged their separate fiefdoms into a unitary state and direct their loyalty to a central government.

Rapprochement, security community, and union thus differ as to the formality and scope of the key bargains that lock in stable peace. Rapprochement rests on tacit understandings to preserve peace; practice, not principle, guides behavior. The participants in a security community go one step further, reaching agreement upon the group's ordering rules and often making them explicit in declarations and charters; practice and principle combine to guide behavior. A union generally entails codified agreement not just about ordering rules, but also about rules for making rules. The agreed-upon order is normally formalized through a constitution that specifies legally binding commitments; principle guides practice and behavior. These key attributes of the three types of stable peace are summarized in figure 2.2.

QUALIFICATIONS

Several qualifications help delimit and narrow the phenomenon under study. As mentioned previously, instances of militarized and "cold" peace, even if long-lasting, do not qualify as cases of stable peace. From the late 1940s until the early 1990s, a "long peace" may have characterized relations between the United States and Soviet Union, but both parties had war plans at the ready; the absence of conflict was the product primarily of deterrence. Brazil and Argentina last went to war in the 1820s, but not until the 1980s did mutual suspicion and hostility between them give way to reconciliation and programmatic cooperation. Stable peace is thus reserved for a class of events in which the absence of war is the product of comity rather than either competition or indifference.

Short-lived and threat-specific alliances also lie outside the scope of this study. States form such alliances to amass countervailing power against a common external threat. It may well be that the states joining forces for the purposes of collective defense do not contemplate war with each other. But these conditions are the temporary product of geopolitical circumstance, not of the emergence of a warm and durable peace. It is the case that some alliances eventually evolve into zones of peace—as did the Quadruple Alliance after 1815 and the Atlantic Alliance over the course of the Cold War. But such cases constitute a unique subset, with most alliances dissolving well before they develop into a zone of stable peace.

Also excluded are cases in which stable peace emerges as the direct product of war and occupation. Lasting reconciliation in the immediate aftermath of war certainly does qualify as a legitimate pathway to stable peace. But the defeat and surrender of one of the parties, the ensuing occupation of territory and purge of the vanquished regime, and the construction of a new regime by the victor render this form of stable peace somewhat "artificial." Examining such cases would shed light on how occupation and reconstruction can promote lasting political change, but not on how interstate comity can be built through measures other than war. For these reasons, America's post–World War II reconciliation with Germany and Japan, Franco-German rapprochement, and other similar cases are not included in this study.[29]

In similar fashion, zones of stable peace that emerge as the result of armed coercion are also outside the scope of this study. This qualification is particularly important in examining cases of union, many of which are forged through acts of war. For example, the union of England, Wales, Scotland, and Northern Ireland currently constitutes a zone of peace, with the units conjoined consensually through representative institutions (the obvious caveats about Northern Ireland notwithstanding). But the process of unification was long and bloody as England forcibly asserted its dominion over its neighbors. In contrast, the cases of union examined in this book involve peaceful change, historical episodes in which separate states willfully pool their sover-

---

[29] In chapter 5, I examine the onset of European integration, of necessity examining Franco-German rapprochement after World War II. However, I do so to study the pathway through which security community took shape in Western Europe, not to examine only reconciliation between France and Germany.

eignties and merge into a unitary polity. This distinction arises from the need to focus on instances of geopolitical transformation that occur consensually rather than as the result of force and coercion.[30]

A final qualification concerns the standards for determining when a zone of stable peace has emerged. Ideally, the standards should be high and consistent—unequivocal evidence that the states in question have no war plans against each other, have demilitarized their borders and interactions, and have come to see armed conflict as outside the realm of the possible. Many of the cases examined below meet these standards, but some fall short.[31] For example, the five members of the Concert of Europe did fashion a rules-based order and agreed to resolve any disputes among themselves through negotiation. But a hint of geopolitical rivalry remained, and war among the members of the Concert, though a remote prospect, was not entirely unthinkable. A similar assessment applies to a contemporary case of security community—ASEAN.

Such cases are nonetheless included in this study for two principal reasons. First, groupings that succeed only in muting rather than completely eliminating geopolitical competition are still part of the family of political formations defined by the notion of stable peace. Inasmuch as their members let down their guard, forego opportunities for individual gain, and agree to resolve disputes peacefully, they play by the rules of international society and defy the logic of anarchic competition. Furthermore, a certain degree of variation in outcomes affords analytic leverage, with exploration of nascent or more contingent zones of peace providing insight not only into how states succeed in escaping rivalry but also why the process of reconciliation may find a stable resting point short of the complete elimination of security competition.

Second, such groupings constitute a significant class of events in their own right. A grouping of states that agree to resolve disputes peacefully and fashion practices and conventions for doing so is a rare and important phenome-

---

[30] I treat Italian and German unification as successful and noncoercive instances of union even though violence occurred among the units that eventually formed the new states. In both cases, such violence occurred primarily amid wars against parties not included in the resulting union—Austria and France in the case of Italy, and Denmark, Austria, and France in the case of Germany. Moreover, the ultimate acts of union generally occurred through consensual negotiations and—in the Italian case—plebiscites rather than coercive annexation.

[31] Security communities often retain an undercurrent of geopolitical rivalry. In the introduction to chapter 5, I examine this anomaly, exploring why security communities, although they in principle represent a more evolved form of stable peace than rapprochement, may in some circumstances be more shallow and fragile than rapprochement.

non. Furthermore, in light of the dim prospects for abolishing geopolitical competition globally, thinking through how to encourage the proliferation of regionally based security communities—even ones that fall short of entirely eliminating rivalry—may offer one of the most realistic avenues for extending stable peace as widely as possible.

HOW STABLE PEACE BREAKS OUT

Stable peace emerges through a sequential process that cuts across long-standing theoretical divides. Realism adequately explains the outset. Strategic necessity induces a state faced with an unmanageable array of threats to seek to befriend an existing adversary; resource constraints make accommodation and cooptation preferable to balancing and confrontation. The process next moves into the realm of liberalism. Domestic attributes—regime type, coalitional alignments, and substate interest groups—come into play, with societal integration facilitating and deepening the process of reconciliation. A constructivist perspective best explains the final stage of the process. Changes in political discourse and identity erode the self/other distinctions that are at the foundation of geopolitical competition.

This sequential process consists of four distinct phases, differentiated by the behavioral activity driving transformation in interstate relations, the political attributes being evaluated by the partner states, and the resulting attitude or affect of the parties toward each other. Phase one consists of *unilateral accommodation*. One party makes an initial concession to the other as an opening gesture of good will. It is then up to the target state to reciprocate with its own act of accommodation. During these opening concessions, the parties seek to discern the *intent* behind such moves and begin to entertain *hope* that they are dealing with a potential partner rather than an implacable adversary. Phase two entails *reciprocal restraint*. Expectations of reciprocity promote successive rounds of mutual accommodation. The parties evaluate one another's broader *motivation*, not just their narrow intent with respect to specific concessions. Hope gives way to mutual *confidence* that rivalry can be averted and that repeated acts of mutual accommodation can lead to peace and, possibly, programmatic cooperation. Phase three consists of *societal integration*. As the polities in question interact with increasing frequency and intensity, they come to attribute benign qualities to one another's *political*

Phase	Activity	Attribute Assessed	Resulting Affect
I	Unilateral Accommodation	Intent	Hope
II	Reciprocal Restraint	Motivation	Confidence
III	Societal Integration	Character	Trust
IV	Narrative Generation	Identity	Solidarity

FIGURE 2.3 Stable Peace: Four Phases of Onset

character. Confidence builds, giving way to a sense of mutual *trust.* The final phase consists of the *generation of new political narratives.* Using the discourse of community as a vehicle, the polities in question embrace a compatible, shared, or common *identity* and expectations of peaceful relations come to have a taken-for-granted quality, producing a sense of social *solidarity.* Figure 2.3 summarizes the four-phase process that leads to stable peace.

In its ideal form, the evolution of stable peace from rapprochement to security community to union is itself a sequential process. After states have passed through the four phases of onset, they attain rapprochement— peaceful coexistence. As their relationship matures, peaceful coexistence evolves into a rules-based security community. The process culminates in the pooling of sovereignty and the act of union. In this sense, rapprochement, security community, and union represent three stages along a continuum. Rapprochement lays the groundwork, with a core grouping of states moving away from adversarial competition and embracing compatible identities. As the parties institutionalize cooperation and expand societal linkages, security community forms around this kernel, with its members agreeing on rules to govern their relations and embracing a shared identity. Over time, the deepening of societal integration and the generation of a narrative of common identity legitimate supra-state institutions of governance and pave the way for union.

In reality, this sequential model represents only an ideal type. Each instance of the onset of stable peace follows a historically contingent path. Some security communities form after a brief and fleeting period of rapprochement, while others come together only after years of reconciliation. Some unions take decades to mature, while others form more suddenly. The cases also vary

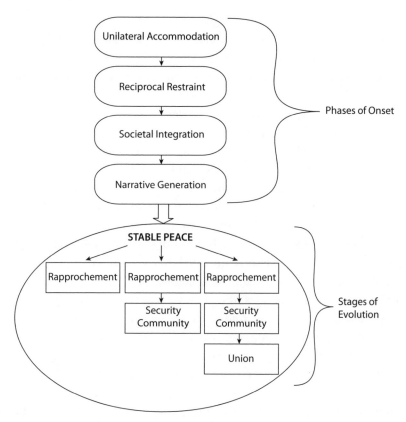

FIGURE 2.4 The Sequential Pathway to Stable Peace

widely in that some instances of stable peace proceed further along the continuum than others. Some states attain rapprochement but go no further, others stop at security community, while still others proceed all the way to formal union (see figure 2.4). The cases do shed some light on when and why different groupings of states reach different endpoints along this continuum —an issue taken up at the end of this chapter. First, the four-phase process of onset and the conditions leading to stable peace are examined in detail.

Phase One: Unilateral Accommodation

The road to stable peace begins amid peril. A state facing an array of threats against which it has insufficient resources attempts to improve its strategic environment by seeking to befriend one of its adversaries. It does so by send-

ing a signal of benign intent through the offer of an unambiguous concession on a matter of mutual interest. Through this opening gambit, the initiating state deliberately makes itself vulnerable to exploitation. Such demon-
strable vulnerability is important for two reasons. First, by undertaking an
unusual and costly action—such as backing down on a border dispute or
unilaterally withdrawing forces from a contested area—the initiator increases
the chances that its actions will be noticed and correctly interpreted by the
target state. Second, by deliberately seeking to make itself vulnerable, the initiating state is taking a calculated risk that it will not be taken advantage of
by the target state, revealing not only that it does not have predatory intent,
but also that it believes (or is at least willing to hold out hope) that the target
state does not have predatory intent. By indicating both that its own intentions are not predatory and that it believes that the intentions of the target
state may also be other than predatory, the initiator has sent a clear signal of
its desire to step away from geopolitical competition.

The target state then decides its first move. If it exploits the initiator's concession or fails to respond in kind, the opening gambit falls short of its objective and geopolitical rivalry continues. If the target state accurately inter-
prets the act of accommodation as a potential peace offering and reciprocates,
then the stage has been set for additional rounds of mutual concession. The
parties have taken the first critical step toward stable peace.

Edelstein and other scholars are skeptical that such acts of accommodation have the potential to lead to reconciliation, claiming that mutual uncertainty as to intent ultimately remains an insurmountable obstacle to moving
from isolated concessions to regularized reciprocity. Both parties would fear
they are being tricked, expect exploitation, and thus be unprepared to let
down their guard. But as Glaser, Kydd, and Schweller have observed, states
can and do go to considerable lengths to reveal the intentions behind their
actions. Glaser writes that "a state seeking security should be concerned
about whether its adversary understands that its motivations are benign."[32] A
state can enhance its ability to demonstrate benign intent by pursuing policy
initiatives that are both costly and unambiguous—those that it would be very
unlikely to pursue unless it is sincerely interested in befriending its adversary.
The clarity of such signaling is further enhanced if the policy measures taken
are difficult to reverse, ameliorating the target state's fear that the measure

---

[32] Glaser, "Realists as Optimists," p. 67.

could be a ruse. Demilitarizing contested areas, destroying fortifications, and making territorial concessions are examples. Such moves facilitate the target state's ability to read intent into behavior. As Kydd notes, a "security seeker . . . needs to go beyond tokens, and make concessions weighty enough so that a state contemplating attack or coercion would be unwilling to make them. Thus the concessions are inherently risky and would not carry conviction if they were not."[33] It is when both initiator and target state make such costly concessions— and as a result attribute benign intent to each other's actions— that the mutual suspicion that sustains rivalry gives way to guarded hope in reconciliation, thereby initiating the sequential process that has the potential to lead to stable peace.

The nature and import of this opening interaction are well captured in a scene from the film, *The Hunt for Red October*.[34] The film is about a Soviet submarine that is attempting to defect to the United States. It is being silently tracked by an American submarine, whose commander has been ordered to destroy the vessel; officials in Washington believe the renegade Soviet submarine to be intent on launching nuclear missiles against the United States. Meanwhile, an American intelligence officer aboard the U.S. submarine, who is aware of the Soviet commander's true intentions, is trying to convince the U.S. commander that the Soviet vessel is in fact attempting to defect.

Faced with the difficult task of probing the intentions of the Soviet boat without imperiling his own vessel, the U.S. commander decides to reverse his submarine's propeller, thereby disrupting the flow of water and causing noise audible to the adversary. In so doing, he makes his presence and position known to the Soviet commander—a cardinal sin of submarine warfare— running the risk of being fired upon. As the U.S. commander colloquially describes his vessel's sudden vulnerability, "We just unzipped our fly." It is precisely because the U.S. ship deliberately and unnecessarily makes itself vulnerable to attack that the Soviet commander has good reason to believe that the American submarine has benign intent. Why else would it have deliberately exposed its position? The Soviet submarine reciprocates by consciously avoiding the usual course of action in such circumstances— full preparation to fire upon the U.S. vessel—revealing that it too does not have hostile intent. The U.S. commander cannot but notice this extraordinary and

---

[33] Kydd, "Sheep in Sheep's Clothing," pp. 144–145.
[34] The film is based on Tom Clancy's novel, *The Hunt for Red October* (New York: Berkeley, 1984).

costly gesture, noting, "He's a very cool customer." Thereafter, the two commanders communicate directly—first through sonar "pings," next via periscope and Morse code, finally through a face-to-face meeting aboard the Soviet vessel—successfully arranging for the peaceful defection of the Soviet submarine to the United States. Enemies became friends.

It was the opening move of the U.S. commander that averted conflict and cleared the way for the two adversaries to back away from hostile engagement. By reversing its propeller, the U.S. boat was attempting to send a clear signal of its benign intent. The Soviet commander could not be certain of the objective behind this act. But the move was sufficiently unusual, costly, unambiguous, and irreversible that it made little sense except as a deliberate signal of benign intent. After the Soviet commander reciprocated the gesture of good will, diminishing uncertainty enabled both commanders to stand down their weapons systems, discuss directly the arrangements for defection, and secure the equivalent of stable peace. The onset of stable peace among nations begins with similar moves. Costly and unambiguous acts of accommodation send signals of benign intent, opening the door to a standing down of rivalry and the advance of reconciliation.

Although this section of the analysis is focused on how, not when, initial accommodation occurs, discussion of the conditions under which the opening gambit takes place helps clarify the logic at work. According to much of the existing literature, a strategy of accommodating the demands of an adversary is usually associated with the notion of bandwagoning; a weaker state capitulates to its stronger adversary because it does not have the resources to do otherwise. If it did have those resources, it would balance instead of bandwagon, affording it greater security and autonomy.[35]

The historical cases examined in the following chapters challenge this conventional account, revealing that it is usually the stronger of the parties that undertakes the opening gambit and makes the initial concession to its adversary. The initiator faces a sufficiently pressing threat environment to induce it to attempt to befriend one of its foes. But its relative strength also puts it in a better position to offer concessions since it is more confident than the weaker party that it will not suffer unacceptable costs should the target state fail to reciprocate. To return to *The Hunt for Red October*, the U.S. commander was willing to take the risk of making his presence known to his adversary in part

---

[35] See, for example, Walt, *The Origins of Alliances*.

because he was in firing range of the Soviet submarine and was ready to take hostile action if its commander failed to reciprocate his act of accommodation. A similar logic applies to relations between states. A concession coming from a stronger power is more likely to be seen by the target state as an optional act intended to reassure than a concession coming from a weaker state—which is likely to be seen by the stronger party as an act of self-interested necessity. Had the tracked and vulnerable Soviet submarine been the one to make the opening gambit, the U.S. commander may well have interpreted the concession as an act of submission or desperation rather than a signal of benign intent.

It is also the case that an initial assessment of the target state's motivations plays a role in determining if and when a country considering unilateral accommodation actually follows through and offers a major concession. The state contemplating an act of accommodation must have at least some indication that it is not dealing with a greedy state, one bent on predatory conquest. Otherwise, it would accurately perceive a concessionary strategy to be an invitation to aggression and consequently adopt a threatening or deterrent strategy rather than make an exploratory probe. In *The Hunt for Red October*, the U.S. commander had good reason to believe that the Soviet submarine was indeed attempting to defect; the U.S. intelligence officer making the case for defection had succeeded in establishing his credibility with the captain. Had the U.S. commander been convinced that the Soviet commander had hostile intent, he would not have run the risk of revealing his location to his adversary. In similar fashion, a state contemplating efforts to befriend an adversary will undertake a costly act of accommodation only if it has reason to believe that the target may have other than hostile intent. How states locked in geopolitical competition make such initial determinations of the nature of their adversary is discussed later in this chapter.

Phase Two: Reciprocal Restraint

During the second phase of the onset of stable peace, the trading of individual acts of accommodation gives way to the practice of reciprocal restraint. Concessions are no longer bolts from the blue—risky gambits aimed at sending benign signals and probing the other's intentions. Rather, both parties readily practice accommodation and expect reciprocity; cautious testing gives way to a purposeful effort to dampen rivalry and advance reconciliation.

In his book on stable peace, Kenneth Boulding recognizes the importance of iterative acts of mutual accommodation, labeling such behavior as Graduated and Reciprocated Initiative in Tension-Reduction (GRIT). Boulding writes, "The GRIT process begins by some rather specific, perhaps even dramatic, statement or act directed at a potential enemy (like Sadat's 1977 visit to Israel), intended to be reassuring. . . . If the potential enemy responds, then a third act by the first party, a fourth by the second party, and so on" provides the foundation for a "peace dynamic."[36]

As unilateral accommodation gives way to reciprocal restraint, the practice of reciprocity becomes normalized. Amid the onset of rapprochement, restraint takes the form of *self-binding*: the parties move beyond the exchange of individual acts of accommodation by regularizing the reciprocal withholding of power through measures such as demilitarization, territorial concession, and the removal of barriers to commerce. The exercise of strategic restraint becomes the rule, not the exception. Amid the onset of security community and union, reciprocal restraint also entails *co-binding*: the parties bind themselves to one another through informal pacts or codified agreements that institutionalize restraint and specify the terms of a rules-based order. Co-binding and the institutionalization of restraint involve the establishment of power-checking devices. These power-checking mechanisms take many different forms, including: rules for resolving disputes and reaching decisions through consensus; provisions to contain or set aside disagreements in order to prevent disputes from leading to conflict; and instruments for redistributing and de-concentrating political influence, military strength, and wealth in order to reduce the political consequences of power asymmetries.[37]

This account of how reciprocal restraint lays a foundation for reconciliation is, at least at first glance, entirely consistent with a liberal approach to the evolution of cooperation as articulated by scholars such as Robert Keohane, Robert Axelrod, and Kenneth Oye.[38] Entrenched competition gives way

[36] Boulding, *Stable Peace*, pp. 112–113.

[37] On the concepts of binding and co-binding, see Daniel Deudney, *Bounding Power: Republican Security Theory from the Polis to the Global Village* (Princeton, NJ: Princeton University Press, 2007); Ikenberry, *After Victory*; and Charles A. Kupchan, "After Pax Americana: Benign Power, Regional Integration, and the Sources of a Stable Multipolarity," *International Security* 23, no. 2 (Fall 1998): 42–79. For further discussion, see the introduction to chapter 5.

[38] Robert Keohane, *After Hegemony: Cooperation and Discord in the World Political Economy* (Princeton, NJ: Princeton University Press, 1984); Robert Axelrod, *The Evolution of Cooperation* (New York: Basic Books, 1984); Kenneth Oye, *Cooperation under Anarchy* (Princeton, NJ: Princeton University Press, 1986).

to regularized cooperation as international regimes increase transparency, create enforcement mechanisms to induce compliance, and give states incentives to develop a reputation for reciprocity. The parties remain self-regarding and utilitarian, but their interests are better furthered by cooperation than competition. As Keohane writes, institutionalized cooperation "is not the result of altruism but of the fact that joining a regime changes calculations of long-run self-interest."[39]

The second phase of the onset of stable peace does, however, go beyond a liberal account of international cooperation in important and consequential respects. The concessions exchanged by the parties engaging in reconciliation are unique in nature and scope. They involve instances of strategic self-restraint in which states demonstrate their willingness to risk high-value interests such as physical security and territorial integrity. Strategic restraint is a rare commodity in international politics—precisely why it stands out and serves as an exceptional signal of benign intent.[40] Self-restraint is especially rare when practiced by a preponderant state, which, as mentioned above, is often the party to initiate the opening gambit. The practice of strategic restraint need not overstep the bounds of a liberal perspective, as John Ikenberry has demonstrated by articulating a rationalist account of the benefits of such behavior. When preponderant states withhold their power and influence, they willingly give up the full advantages of primacy and forego immediate opportunities to capitalize on material advantage. They instead invest in stability over the long term by inducing smaller states to enter into a bargain based on the practice of mutual accommodation. Weaker states have a strong incentive to take up this bargain inasmuch as they have on offer a rare chance to minimize the disadvantages associated with material inferiority.[41]

Although Ikenberry offers a compelling account of the incentives inducing strong and weak states alike to engage in mutual accommodation, he fails to capture fully the transformative effects of reciprocal restraint on interstate relations. Amid reciprocal restraint, states are no longer just probing each

[39] Keohane, *After Hegemony*, p. 116.

[40] A standard realist critique of a liberal account of institutionalized cooperation is that most instances of cooperation entail economic transactions, where the stakes are lower than in the security realm. See John Mearsheimer, "The False Promise of International Institutions," *International Security* 19, no. 3 (Winter 1994/1995). The infrequency of unambiguous acts of restraint on the security front is one of the main reasons they serve as credible and visible signals of benign intent.

[41] Ikenberry, *After Victory*.

other's intent through isolated acts of accommodation. Rather, they begin to form assessments of each other's broader motivations, weaving iterated acts of accommodation into a stable evaluation of the other's long-term objectives. Perceptions of benign intent cumulate and intensify, gradually becoming perceptions of benign motivation. The parties come to see one another as having broadly congruent interests in the international arena, not just compatible intent with respect to the issues on which they have made concessions.

From this perspective, the practice of reciprocal restraint ultimately changes how the states engaging in reconciliation perceive the geopolitical implications of power asymmetries. When states exercise strategic restraint and explicitly reveal the benign motivations for doing so, they are able to endow their power with a magnetic ability to attract and reassure other countries instead of a propensity to threaten them and trigger balancing. Material power loses its coercive dimension, instead becoming an ingredient critical to bringing about cooperation and consensual outcomes.

This critical transformation in the structural effects of material power can be conceptualized from three different angles. From a functionalist perspective, power wedded to benign motivation emits centripetal rather than centrifugal force, "convening" or "grouping" states instead of prompting them to run for cover. A concentration of power thus exerts an anchoring or centering pull on the states around it, drawing them toward one another. In Deutsch's words, preponderant states come "to form the cores of strength around which in most cases the integrative process developed."[42] Economic power offers the prospect of mutual gain, military power the prospect of mutual security. The realist logic of power balancing under uncertainty thus ceases to operate when the states in question are confident in their assessment of the other's benign motivations.

From a constructivist perspective, practice alters social reality. As states regularize strategic restraint, they embrace, in the words of Adler and Barnett, "shared meanings and understandings" or "cognitive structures."[43] The normalization of cooperative practices informs a social reality that both parties deem to be noncompetitive, in turn enabling them to further let down

---

[42] Deutsch, *Political Community*, p. 38.

[43] Adler and Barnett, *Security Communities*, p. 40. See also Alastair Iain Johnston, *Social States: China in International Institutions, 1980–2000* (Princeton, NJ: Princeton University Press, 2008).

their guard. In this sense, a self-fulfilling prophecy is at work. If both parties come to conceive of their relationship as noncompetitive and behave accordingly, then the relationship becomes effectively noncompetitive. As the practice of reciprocal restraint becomes the norm, social reality is, as it were, pacified.[44] This interpretation follows directly from Alexander Wendt's now classic formulation: "Anarchy is what states make of it."[45]

From a psychological perspective, affect and emotion play an important role in transforming how partner states respond to one another's material power.[46] Through reciprocal restraint, the parties grow comfortable with each other's power as they come to see accommodating behavior as the product of benign motivation rather than just situational intent. The respective strength of each state and their combined ability to secure desired outcomes becomes a source of mutual reassurance. They let down their guard not because of a probabilistic calculation suggesting that exploitation is unlikely, but because a favorable emotive bias prevails as mutual perceptions of benign motivation solidify. Just as acts of generosity engender empathy among individuals, acts of strategic restraint engender affinity among states.

As the case studies will demonstrate, these three analytic perspectives are by no means incompatible; all three processes are often at work as stable peace advances. Indeed, it is these mechanisms and the insights they offer about the transformative effects of reciprocal restraint that explain how states succeed in going beyond neutrality to warm peace. Glaser and Kydd accept that the mutual perception of benign intent can arrest the operation of the security dilemma. Unintended spirals do not occur when both parties have concluded that the other has benign intentions. But their story stops there.

In contrast, the analysis presented here posits that the practice of reciprocal restraint succeeds not only in arresting the security dilemma, but also in enabling it to work in reverse. Each state takes actions to increase the other's security, in the first instance winding down rivalry and attaining neutrality,

---

[44] For a thorough discussion of the relationship between the practice of self-restraint and the formation of security community, see Emanuel Adler, "The Spread of Security Communities: Communities of Practice, Self-Restraint, and NATO's Post Cold War Transformation," *European Journal of International Relations* 14, no. 2 (2008).

[45] Alexander Wendt, "Anarchy Is What States Make of It: The Social Construction of Power Politics," *International Organization* 46, no. 2 (Spring 1992). See also Jeffrey Checkel, "International Institutions and Socialization in Europe," *International Organization* 59, no. 4 (October 2005).

[46] See John Mercer, "Emotion Adds Life," paper presented at the Annual Meeting of the International Studies Association, 18–21 February, 1999, Washington, DC.

but thereafter actively promoting amity and taking incremental steps toward warm peace. Put differently, the political momentum behind reconciliation gradually shifts from the negative to the positive. At its outset, the exercise of reciprocal restraint, the regularization of accommodation, and the institutionalization of power-checking devices are about dampening rivalry and avoiding competition. As these practices and institutions mature, they become about building up amity and producing friendship. As reassurance and comfort deepen, the relationship starts to become demilitarized or, to use Ole Waever's terminology, "desecuritized."[47] In the first phase of the onset of stable peace, each state is hopeful that the other has benign intent. In this second phase, each state becomes confident that the other has benign motivations.

Phase Three: Societal Integration

The third phase of the onset of stable peace is about societal integration. Reciprocal restraint, the gradual winding down of geopolitical competition, and the mutual attribution of benign motivation clear the way for the intensification of direct contact between the reconciling societies. In contrast to the first two phases, when governing elites are the primary agents driving forward the process of reconciliation, the third phase entails the involvement of bureaucracies, private firms, and mobilized citizens. The mechanisms at work track closely Deutsch's transactional approach and his focus on the broadening and deepening of social communication. Officials regularly come into direct contact, drawn together by improving political ties and the opportunities to coordinate policy. Interest groups in favor of reconciliation form within the bureaucracy and among political parties. Private firms take advantage of the opportunity to increase trade and investment. Societal integration also takes place among ordinary citizens through tourism, business ties, new communication links, and cultural and academic exchanges—especially since the advent of modern transportation and electronic communication systems.

Societal integration thus occurs at multiple levels. Regular face-to-face meetings between government officials foster ideational convergence on substantive policy issues. During the first and second phases of reconciliation,

---

[47] See Ole Waever, "Insecurity, Security, and Asecurity in the West European Non-War Community," in Adler and Barnett, *Security Communities*, pp. 69–118.

elite contact is sporadic and usually prompted by negotiations over specific issues. During this third phase, elite contact becomes routine.[48] At this point, the dialogue has fully advanced beyond modalities for avoiding rivalry, now focusing primarily on measures that will deepen cooperation and amity. The concept of an "epistemic community"—a grouping of policy makers who come to share common ideational and normative orientations—neatly captures one of the key consequences of intensifying elite contact.[49]

Governmental interest groups also play a prominent role in promoting societal integration—a development key to managing the domestic politics of accommodation. The initial steps toward stable peace are often opposed by hardliners and nationalists who portray concessions as a dangerous gesture of weakness likely to invite aggression. Even elites who support accommodation may remain silent, fearful of being labeled by hardliners as unpatriotic appeasers. Once the opening gambit has worked and the practice of reciprocal restraint has been sustained, however, factions favoring such strategies form and openly acknowledge their preferences, providing political cover for accommodation and building momentum behind reconciliation. There are usually three main sources of such support. First, policy makers and bureaucrats step forward, making clear that they back the new direction of policy. Second, the military throws its support behind reconciliation, recognizing that it offers the prospect of a major reduction in commitments. Finally, internationalist political parties that would reap benefits from reconciliation back accommodation, often working in unison with like-minded parties in the partner state. The strengthening of internationalist coalitions in one state tends to benefit the political fortunes of like-minded coalitions in the other.[50]

Private-sector firms benefiting from increasing flows of goods and services help strengthen societal linkages. Powerful constituencies on both sides come to have a vested interest in stable peace, lobbying within their countries for policies of reciprocal restraint and economic integration. Importantly, and

[48] Experimental research has made clear that face-to-face communication substantially increases trust and the likelihood of cooperative outcomes. See Elinor Ostrom, "A Behavioral Approach to the Rational Choice Theory of Collective Action," *American Political Science Review* 92, no. 1 (March 1998).

[49] See Peter Haas, "Introduction: Epistemic Communities and International Policy Coordination," *International Organization* 46, no. 1 (Winter 1992).

[50] See John Owen, "Pieces of Stable Peace: A Pessimistic Constructivism," unpublished paper, University of Virginia; and Etel Solingen, *Regional Orders at Century's Dawn: Global and Domestic Influences on Grand Strategy* (Princeton, NJ: Princeton University Press, 1998).

contra Deutsch, the positive political impact of economic integration usually follows from rather than precedes the dampening of strategic rivalry. Economic interdependence may intensify even while strategic competition ensues. But it plays a prominent role in the onset of stable peace only when it takes place within the context of strategic restraint and political reconciliation.

Societal integration also takes place among publics, with ordinary citizens in partner states exposed to more information about the other, in some cases through direct contact. Public engagement is frequently the product of explicit efforts to build political support for reconciliation through education campaigns, the media, and exchange programs sponsored by governments as well as the private sector. Societal integration at the popular level also follows from the greater opportunities for travel afforded by the expansion of land, sea, and air links. In line with the processes described in Deutsch's *Political Community*, increases in social communication—official delegations, cultural exchanges, trade, tourism, and migration—gradually give rise to "a matter of mutual sympathy and loyalties; of 'we feeling,' trust, and mutual consideration; of partial identification in terms of self-images and interests."[51]

As these forms of societal integration concurrently proceed, they advance reconciliation and the onset of stable peace on four key dimensions. First, interstate linkages become more fully institutionalized, starting at the official level, but often extending to the private sector and to citizen exchange programs. The benefits offered by institutionalization have been well articulated by liberals—increased transparency, lower transaction costs, and extended expectations of reciprocity. At least as important are the sociological effects of institutionalization, with a network of linkages developing between the societies in question. As Deutsch's work illuminated, these linkages over time foster a sense of community and we-ness. Émile Durkheim's notion of "organic solidarity" is useful here. As integration proceeds across different sectors of society, "the more individuals there are who are sufficiently in contact with one another to be able mutually to act and react upon one another."[52]

Second, at this stage in the process, elites explicitly seek to shape public attitudes. The first two phases of reconciliation—unilateral accommodation and reciprocal restraint—are primarily elite enterprises. Indeed, governing officials deliberately avoid public engagement in order to obtain the political

[51] Deutsch, *Political Community*, p. 36.
[52] Émile Durkheim, *The Division of Labor in Society* (New York: Free Press, 1984), p. 201.

room for maneuver necessary to orchestrate the initial acts of accommodation. In contrast, during the stage of societal integration, elites attempt to build broader domestic support for their conciliatory policies by explaining their benefits to the public. They also begin to reframe political discourse, starting to portray the partner state as an ally or friend rather than an enemy. These efforts at public outreach help disarm nationalist opposition to accommodation, and make it less likely that a popular backlash against reconciliation will interrupt if not scuttle the process. They also make reconciliation less dependent upon a specific set of leaders, giving the process deeper political and social roots. A change of government is then less likely to end or reverse efforts to promote stable peace.

Third, as societal integration advances, governments begin to form assessments not just of the partner state's motivations, but also of its political character. The parties have increasing knowledge of each other's society and governing institutions, enabling them to attribute to the other a benign political character. Each side begins to interpret its partner's behavior as dispositional—a product of its values and political system—rather than situational—a product of specific circumstance.[53] The mutual attribution of benign character represents a critical turning point. States are no longer basing their policies of accommodation on the discrete intentions or motivations of the other, feeling their way forward with each round of concessions. Rather, they are prepared to let down their guard as a matter of course; the prospect of armed conflict is becoming remote, if not unthinkable. Stable peace begins to enjoy a taken-for-granted quality.

The fourth dimension along which societal interaction promotes stable peace follows directly. The main affect that polities exhibit toward each other advances from confidence to trust. Amid reciprocal restraint, assessment of benign motivation enables states to be confident that partner states will not exploit their concessions. Amid societal integration, assessment of benign character leads each state to trust that its partner states will not defect from cooperative practices. Trust minimizes the effects of uncertainty, enabling each side to keep its guard down even in the face of incomplete information.

---

[53] Jonathan Mercer argues that states initially view desirable behavior by adversaries to be the result of situational pressures, not disposition. It follows that only after a significant period of mutual accommodation will they come to see concessions as the product of disposition rather than situation. See Mercer, *Reputation and International Politics* (Ithaca, NY: Cornell University Press, 1996).

In this respect—and directly countering the realist claim that uncertainty constitutes an inescapable obstacle to cooperation—states become willing to tolerate mutual vulnerability despite irreducible uncertainty about the other's motivations. In the words of Barbara Misztal, "What makes trust so puzzling is that to trust involves more than believing; in fact, to trust is to believe despite uncertainty."[54] Magnus Ericson agrees that trust enables states "to divine the true, non-malevolent, intentions behind each other's actions, *prior* to any particular reckoning of motives or rational cost/benefit calculation."[55]

Inasmuch as trust is a key ingredient of social capital, its presence extends the social character of the evolving relationship between the parties in question. Trust also heightens the emotive impact of societal interaction, deepening a mutual sense of affinity. By this stage in the transition from enemy to friend, the processes at work have become less rationalist and more sociological in character, marking the onset of international society.

Phase Four: Narrative Generation and Identity Change

The fourth and final phase of the onset of stable peace is about identity change. Through the generation of new narratives, the states engaged in reconciliation recast the identities they hold of each other.[56] In the case of rapprochement, identities remain separate, yet become compatible. In the case of security community, identities overlap and the states in question come to enjoy a shared identity or we-ness. In the case of union, partner states embrace a common identity. These changes in identity ultimately blur the self/other distinctions that animate geopolitical rivalry. Trust advances to solidarity, deepening the taken-for-granted quality of stable peace.

The generation of new narratives begins at the elite level, with officials altering the language they use to refer to the partner state. Adversarial or neutral references give way to language that connotes images of partnership and

---

[54] Barbara Misztal, *Trust in Modern Societies: The Search for the Bases of Social Order* (Cambridge: Polity Press, 1996), p. 18. See also Rikard Bengtsson, "The Cognitive Dimension of Stable Peace," in Kacowicz et al., *Stable Peace Among Nations.*

[55] Magnus Ericson, "The Liberal Peace Meets History: The Scandinavian Experience," unpublished paper, Lund University, p. 3. See also Rikard Bengtsson, "The Cognitive Dimension of Stable Peace," in Kacowicz et al., *Stable Peace Among Nations,* pp. 94–96.

[56] For discussion of the mechanisms through which collective identities form, see Alexander Wendt, "Collective Identity Formation and the International State," *American Political Science Review* 88, no. 2 (June 1994): 384–396.

friendship. The precise content of the narrative that informs compatible, shared, and common identities varies among the cases, but the discourse usually contains a standard set of concepts and markers. The parties in question regularly allude to bonds of kinship and family. The change in discourse often involves a new accounting of the past—one that downplays conflict and highlights historic ties and common values. In the Anglo-American case, for example, narratives focusing on adversarial competition gradually gave way to preoccupation with ancestral and racial bonds, common Anglo-Saxon values, and the proposition that war between the United States and Great Britain would constitute "fratricide." In security communities and unions, communal symbols such as flags and anthems often accompany these changes in discourse. The new language and symbols are also propagated by non-state agents, including the press, private firms that favor economic integration, and teachers, intellectuals, and writers who shape public opinion through education, literature, film, and theater.

If changes in practice inform the new understandings of social reality that open the door to stable peace, then changes in discourse inform the new identities that lock in stable peace. The post-modernist tradition, with its emphasis on "speech acts," provides a useful theoretical platform.[57] The work of Janice Bially Mattern is especially instructive, as her subject matter is the preservation of stable peace between the United States and Great Britain. In examining the durability of the Anglo-American security community amid the Suez Crisis, Mattern argues that both the United States and Great Britain relied on "representational force, a form of power exercised through language, to stabilize their collective identity."[58] She contends that U.S. and British elites alike used language to "fasten" or "cement" a shared conception of Anglo-American identity. This shared identity, which was the culmination of

---

[57] See J. L. Austin, J. O. Urmson, and Marina Sbisa, *How To Do Things With Words* (Oxford: Oxford University Press, 1976); Jacques Derrida, *Of Grammatology* (Baltimore: Johns Hopkins University Press, 1976); and John Searle, *Speech Acts: An Essay in the Philosophy of Language* (Cambridge: Cambridge University Press, 1969). For applications in the international relations literature, see Thomas Risse, "'Let's Argue!' Communicative Action in World Politics," *International Organization* 54, no. 1 (Winter 2000); Frank Schimmelfennig, "The Community Trap: Liberal Norms, Rhetorical Action, and the Eastern Enlargement of the European Union," *International Organization* 55, no. 1 (2001); Ronald Krebs and Patrick Jackson, "Twisting Tongues and Twisting Arms: The Power of Political Rhetoric," *European Journal of International Relations* 13, no. 1 (2007); and Patrick Thaddeus Jackson, *Civilizing the Enemy: German Reconstruction and the Invention of the West* (Ann Arbor: University of Michigan Press, 2006).

[58] Janice Bially Mattern, "The Power Politics of Identity," *European Journal of International Relations* 7, no. 3 (2001), p. 349.

the process of reconciliation that began in the nineteenth century, enabled a sense of community to endure even when short-term interests diverged—as they did during the Suez Crisis. "The 'reality' of we-ness," Mattern writes, "depends upon the persistence of a narrative . . . depicting an appropriately deep and trusting friendship among actors."[59]

The generation and consolidation of a narrative of communal identity bring the onset of stable peace to completion. It is through this four-phase sequence of unilateral accommodation, reciprocal restraint, societal integration, and narrative generation that states find their way to stable peace. The process starts in the realist world of suspicion and competition, with tentative signals of benign intent opening the door to the moderation of rivalry. It ends in the constructivist world of discourse and identity change, with partner states generating new narratives and identities which blur the self/other distinctions that fuel rivalry. Along the way, international anarchy is transformed into international society and enemies turn into friends.

WHY STABLE PEACE BREAKS OUT

This chapter has thus far addressed how peace breaks out—the sequential process through which geopolitical rivalry gives way to stable peace. The analysis now turns to the question of when and why peace breaks out—the causal conditions under which enemies are able to escape geopolitical rivalry and find their way to lasting friendship. This effort to build a theory of stable peace proceeds with due modesty. The phenomenon under study is a very complex one, and the relevant theoretical literature is still evolving. Although the cases examined in this book constitute a representative subset of the universe of cases, they are by no means exhaustive. Mining the many cases not considered in this study could shed new light on the causes of stable peace. Moreover, each of the historical cases in this study is open to competing historical interpretations, preventing the drawing of definitive conclusions as to why stable peace breaks out.

These qualifications notwithstanding, the cases reveal that the onset of stable peace depends on the presence of three main ingredients—*institutionalized restraint*, *compatible social orders*, and *cultural commonality*. Institu-

---

[59] Bially Mattern, "The Power Politics of Identity," p. 364.

tionalized restraint is a facilitating condition, whereas compatible social orders and cultural commonality are necessary conditions. The essential causal logic at work is as follows.

States that embrace institutionalized restraint possess domestic attributes that make them particularly well suited to pursue foreign policies of accommodation and partnership. Liberal democracies as well as non-democratic constitutional orders, because they institutionalize restraint and power-checking devices at home, are more likely than other regime types to practice strategic restraint in the conduct of their foreign policy. In addition, the transparency afforded by liberal order enables partner states to assess with confidence each other's intent, motivation, and political character. Institutionalized restraint is of particular importance during the first two phases of the onset of stable peace—unilateral accommodation and reciprocal restraint. It emerges as a facilitating rather than necessary condition because the cases will make clear that even states that do not embrace institutionalized restraint at home can nonetheless practice strategic restraint in the conduct of statecraft.

Compatibility of social orders is a permissive condition. When the political influence and economic interests of elite sectors in partner states are strengthened by reconciliation, they throw their support behind stable peace and advance its onset. In contrast, when partner states have incompatible social orders, reconciliation is usually blocked by political and economic constituencies threatened by integration. The compatibility of social orders is of particular importance during the third phase of the onset of stable peace—societal integration.

Cultural commonality plays an important role at both the outset and the completion of the process. At the outset, a preexisting sense of cultural affinity encourages potential partner states to contemplate the prospect of mutual accommodation and reconciliation. Such similarity prompts states to select each other as possible partners and to run the risks associated with accommodation. Cultural commonality plays a more prominent role in the final phase of the onset of stable peace—the embrace of a compatible, shared, or common identity. Public officials and opinion makers draw heavily on ethnic, racial, and religious ties in developing a narrative of friendship and kinship.

Figure 2.5 depicts these causal relationships. Institutionalized restraint, compatible social orders, and cultural commonality are now examined in greater depth.

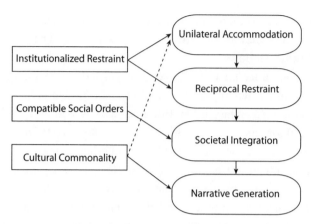

FIGURE 2.5 Causal Conditions for Stable Peace

Institutionalized Restraint

The democratic peace school offers one of the more robust findings in inter-national relations theory—that liberal democracies do not go to war with each other. It follows that liberal democracies may well be particularly suited to form zones of stable peace. Nonetheless, the relationship between regime type and stable peace is a complicated one. On the one hand, liberal democ-racies do appear to be better suited than other types of regimes to form inter-national societies. On the other, liberal democracy is neither a sufficient nor necessary condition for stable peace. It is not sufficient inasmuch as liberal democracy does not automatically lead to stable peace—as ongoing geopo-litical rivalry between Greece and Turkey makes clear. It is not necessary in-asmuch as stable peace can break out in the absence of liberal democracy; the Concert of Europe, ASEAN, the Iroquois Confederation, the United Arab Emirates, a unified German Kingdom—these are all instances of stable peace that evolved in the absence of liberal democracy.

The causal linkage between democracy and interstate peace does not stand up to empirical scrutiny because it is the exercise of strategic restraint, not regime type per se, that is a necessary condition for stable peace. As discussed above, strategic restraint and the withholding of power are essential to send-ing signals of benign intent to potential partners—a critical first step in ame-liorating geopolitical rivalry. To be sure, the practice of strategic restraint is regularly the product of the types of institutionalized restraint found among democracies—domestic checks on the executive associated with institutions that distribute power among multiple centers of authority. States whose power is checked at home are more likely to practice strategic restraint in the conduct of their foreign policy. The mechanisms—constitutions, parliaments, courts—that constrain the power of elites with respect to domestic governance also apply to decision making on matters of statecraft.

But liberal democracies have no monopoly on institutionalized restraint. Non-democratic regimes often contain elements of constitutional restraint, thereby endowing them with some of the key attributes needed to pursue reconciliation and the elimination of rivalry. Indeed, even states that do not embrace institutionalized restraint at home can nonetheless be willing to practice strategic restraint in the conduct of their foreign relations, making clear that regime type alone does not determine when stable peace can break out.[60]

This explication of the connection between institutionalized restraint and stable peace begins by examining why liberal democracies are better suited to build international society than other types of regimes. Thereafter, the analysis explores why non-democratic regimes are also able to fashion zones of stable peace.

Liberal democracy does not make states suited to stable peace simply by virtue of the fact that partner states identify each other as democratic. Rather, democracies exhibit regime attributes and types of behavior that give them a particular advantage in building stable peace. At work is not a sense of similarity or mutual identification as democracies, but specific capacities and behavioral characteristics that are the product of liberal institutions. Four key attributes, all aspects of institutionalized restraint, appear to be at work: the presence of power-checking political structures, transparency, the ability to make credible commitments, and policy adaptability.

First, a hallmark of liberal democracy is the presence of institutions that check and diffuse political power. States that possess such institutions are intrinsically more likely to practice strategic restraint than those that do not; in

---

[60] As some of the case studies will demonstrate, not only is liberal democracy not a necessary condition for stable peace, but the process of transition to liberal democracy can in fact pose threats to stable peace by encouraging nationalism and undermining the practice of strategic restraint. In this respect, states in the midst of regime change may be less suited to stable peace than either non-democratic regimes or mature democracies. See, in particular, the examination of the unraveling of the Concert of Europe in chapter 5. See also Jack Snyder, *From Voting to Violence: Democratization and Nationalist Conflict* (New York: Norton, 2000); and Edward Mansfield and Jack Snyder, *Electing to Fight: Why Emerging Democracies Go to War* (Cambridge, MA: MIT Press, 2007).

the conduct of all aspects of policy, leaders are constrained by power-checking devices. In addition, leaders that are accustomed to adhering to a rules-based order at home are more likely to favor the establishment of a rules-based order internationally. The habits of political restraint are the habits of strategic restraint; in important respects, zones of peace represent the replication of norms and institutions of domestic governance at the level of interstate relations.

Second, liberal democracies are open and transparent polities, affording other states the opportunity to observe carefully decision-making processes and assess, with a relatively high degree of confidence, the intentions and motivations that inform behavior. Elections, legislative processes, polls and plebiscites, debate in the media—all these activities put on public view the strategic and political considerations that shape policy. The transparency that accompanies liberal democracy plays an important role in enabling rivals to back away from geopolitical competition; only when partner states are able to attribute benign behavior to benign intentions and motivation are they willing to let down their guard and begin taking the sequential steps that lead to stable peace. As Andrew Kydd observes, "If a democracy is really a security seeker, the openness of its policy processes will reveal this to the world."[61]

Third, liberal democracies are well suited to make credible commitments, assuring potential partners that their declarations of benign intent are sincere. Elected leaders face "audience costs" if they fail to stand by their policies; electorates hold them accountable for fickle behavior.[62] These domestic constraints give elites in other states confidence that declared policies will in fact be sustained over time. In addition, liberal democracy can promote the durability of stable peace by engaging broader publics in the process of reconciliation and partnership. Public engagement lends stable peace more robustness and credibility by making it less dependent upon a specific group of elites; regimes may come and go, but international society will endure if it has deeper civic roots, both in terms of societal interdependence and mutual identification.

The credibility of commitments is particularly important as a means of

---

[61] Kydd, "Sheep in Sheep's Clothing," p. 119.

[62] See James Fearon, "Domestic Political Audiences and the Escalation of International Disputes," *American Political Science Review* 88, no. 3 (September 1994).

reducing the geopolitical consequence of power asymmetries.[63] The promise of institutionalized restraint reassures small states that they will not be taken advantage of as they let down their guard and pursue reconciliation with much larger partners. Small states are thereby less fearful that they will lose their autonomy as they cautiously adhere to the tacit understandings and explicit arrangements that accompany the onset of stable peace. Such reassurance is particularly important amid the formation of unions. Small states contemplating a political merger with a more powerful state as a matter of course fear absorption or annexation. The credible promise of strategic restraint by their preponderant partner reassures them that they will retain some measure of autonomy and voice even after the act of unification.

Fourth, the pluralism associated with liberal democracy enables states to handle more effectively the domestic political challenges that accompany the practice of strategic restraint. The onset of stable peace necessitates concessionary strategies and the toleration of vulnerability, posing considerable political risk to elites who pursue such policies. Especially in a geopolitical environment characterized by long-standing rivalry, hardliners usually stand at the ready to charge as weak and cowardly elites who adopt a strategy of accommodation.

The challenge for governing officials is to ensure that the *politics of accommodation* prevails over the *politics of humiliation*. Doing so requires that decision makers portray concessions as opportunities rather than necessities, making clear to domestic audiences that they are taking advantage of openings, not backing down under pressure. Effectively communicating the rationale and appropriateness of accommodation is easier to do in a liberal democracy for a number of reasons. Elites in democracies derive their legitimacy at least in part through representative government, making them less reliant on confrontational foreign policies to sustain their authority. Elite and public debate is more receptive and responsive to novel ideas and courses of action, increasing the likelihood that the arguments deployed in favor of concessions are able to challenge support for the status quo. Unlike in a unitary government, elites are also able to reach out to interest groups that benefit from reconciliation, enlisting their help in reorienting strategic debate. Finally, political pluralism makes it less likely that entrenched interests opposed to reconciliation will be able to serve as veto points, effectively blocking efforts to

---

[63] See Ikenberry, *After Victory*, pp. 50–79.

implement a strategy of accommodation. In sum, liberal democracies exhibit greater flexibility and adaptability than do unitary or fragmented policies, making democracies more conducive to strategic adjustment.[64]

The pluralism inherent in liberal democracy facilitates not just strategic adjustment within each partner state, but also ideational convergence between them. The congruent interests and compatible identities that form a foundation for rapprochement require a measure of ideational convergence across the states in question. In order for rapprochement to evolve into security community and union, such convergence must extend further, enabling elites in partner states to reach agreement on order-producing rules. Such agreement is facilitated by the exchange of ideas and the degree to which elites move toward each other's positions. As Karl Deutsch and John Owen have both pointed out, liberalizing coalitions often form within and across national boundaries, providing a ready vehicle for cooperation and flows of information.[65] In contrast, authoritarian rule often inhibits pluralism and makes ideational convergence more fragile, generally limiting partnerships among non-democratic states to temporary marriages of convenience.

Although power-checking structures, transparency, the ability to make credible commitments, and adaptability may be more fully developed among liberal democracies, non-democracies that embrace institutionalized restraint are able to fashion zones of peace in large part because they exhibit many of these same attributes. For example, Piedmont and Prussia, although neither was a liberal democracy, succeeded in guiding Italy and Germany, respectively, to unification. Both had adopted constitutional rule after the revolutions of 1848, a move that helped reassure their less powerful neighbors that unification would mean consensual merger, not coercive exploitation. The constituent communities of the Iroquois Confederation were not liberal democracies, but tribal traditions of restraint and consensual governance practiced at the local level were replicated in the institutions of the union, effectively providing the makings of a constitutional order. These cases suggest

---

[64] See Hendrik Spruyt, *Ending Empire: Contested Sovereignty and Territorial Partition* (Ithaca, NY: Cornell University Press, 2005). In his study of decolonization, Spruyt finds that pluralistic and less fragmented polities are better able to embrace the strategies of adjustment and adaptation needed to step back from imperial commitments. On the role that pluralism plays in enabling moderates to prevail against hardliners, see Joe Hagan, "Domestic Political Sources of Stable Peace: The Great Powers, 1815–1914," in Kacowicz et al., *Stable Peace Among Nations.*

[65] Deutsch, *Political Community,* pp. 176–178; and Owen, "Pieces of Stable Peace: A Pessimistic Constructivism."

that the key ingredient making stable peace possible is not popular control, but rather the willingness of governments to control themselves by embracing institutionalized restraint and the power-checking devices needed to reassure potential partners in peace.

The case studies also include a significant number of outliers—states that practice strategic restraint abroad despite the absence of institutionalized restraint at home. Russia, Prussia, and Austria during the Concert of Europe, the Soviet Union and China during the 1950s, Indonesia in 1966, Brazil in 1979—these are all instances in which absolutist regimes embarked down the path toward stable peace. As the case studies will reveal, when faced with strategic imperatives or compelling domestic incentives, even autocratic regimes that do not exercise political restraint at home are capable of practicing strategic restraint in the conduct of their foreign policy.

These findings are consistent with recent scholarship that challenges the supposition that only elected leaders are constrained by "audience costs"— the need to demonstrate credibility and competence to their citizens. Democratic accountability, the argument runs, strengthens the ability of elected officials to make credible commitments and demonstrate resolve.[66] Audience costs thus help states convey predictable intentions to others—as discussed above, a key asset when states seek to send signals of benign motivation and develop the practice of reciprocal restraint. But as Jessica Weeks argues— and as the cases in the following chapters demonstrate—it is not the case that "members of domestic audiences in democratic regimes are on average more likely to value credibility or competence than audiences in various types of autocratic regimes." On the contrary, Weeks contends, "most authoritarian leaders require the support of domestic elites who act as audiences in much the same way as voting publics in democracies."[67] Authoritarian and democratic leaders alike are thus subject to audience costs that enhance their capacity to make commitments and demonstrate resolve.

The literature on audience costs has tended to focus only on their relationship to the credibility of threats. But as Weeks appropriately points out, "Just as leaders may generate domestic costs by backing down from a threat, they can also incur costs by reneging on peaceful promises such as commitments not to invade neighboring states. Thus, higher audience costs may alleviate

---

[66] See Fearon, "Domestic Political Audiences and the Escalation of International Disputes."

[67] Jessica Weeks, "Autocratic Audience Costs: Regime Type and Signaling Resolve," *International Organization* 62, no. 1 (Winter 2008): 42, 36.

the security dilemma by reducing uncertainty about whether a promise to keep peace is genuine."[68] Indeed, cases such as rapprochement between Brazil and Argentina and the onset of ASEAN make clear that, even among military dictatorships, domestic audience costs can play an important role in advancing stable peace. Weeks's two important amendments to this literature thus help explain why autocracies, and not only liberal democracies, can be reliable members of a zone of peace. As discussed in the concluding chapter, these findings caution against overweighting the causal importance of regime type in explaining the onset of stable peace.

Compatible Social Orders

Compatible social orders constitute a second key ingredient of stable peace.[69] Such compatibility is a function of three main dimensions of social order: the distribution of political power among different classes; the distribution of political power among different ethnic, racial, and religious groups; and the organizing principles of economic production and commercial activity. When the onset of stable peace reaches the phase of societal integration, the dominant social sectors in the partner states begin to interact with each other. When social orders are similar, societal integration advances the political and economic interests of these dominant sectors—and the onset of stable peace proceeds apace. When social orders are incompatible, societal integration threatens and undermines the political and economic interests of these dominant sectors—and they consequently step in to arrest the advance of stable peace. The process of societal integration and reconciliation then begins again only if and when social convergence removes such domestic obstacles.

Integration between a state dominated by its aristocracy and one with an egalitarian society is likely to stall as the aristocracy's privileged position is threatened by a partner state in which power is not based on class. Increasing interaction between capitalist and socialist countries, agrarian and industrial polities, and open and closed economies similarly pits dominant social sectors against each other, creating powerful impediments to the onset of stable peace. In general terms, elites whose political power and economic privilege

---

[68] Weeks, "Autocratic Audience Costs," p. 60.
[69] See David Skidmore, ed., *Contested Social Orders and International Politics* (Nashville, TN: Vanderbilt University Press, 1997).

are based on a given social order will resist forms and levels of political and economic integration that threaten to overturn that order.

Incompatibilities in social order do not prevent states from embarking down the path of stable peace. Rather, the societal obstacles to stable peace intensify as political and economic integration proceeds. The Soviet Union and China fashioned a close partnership during the 1950s. But the conflicting social demands and ideological tensions that divided an industrializing Russia from an agrarian China would, by the end of the decade, contribute to its demise. Unions between Egypt and Syria and between Senegal and Gambia got off the ground, but both soon foundered over differences in social order and disputes over tariffs and trade. Union between Malaysia and Singapore similarly fell prey to differences in social order, with the predominantly Chinese population of Singapore upsetting the delicate ethnic balance in Malaysia. Even among democracies, divergences in social orders imperil stable peace. The United States, for example, suffered a bloody civil war as a result of the incompatible social orders of its north and south. Liberal democracy is no guarantor of political harmony in the face of potent social cleavages.

Changes in social order can have an important impact on the prospects for stable peace. The Concert of Europe functioned as a successful security community for over three decades—despite the fact that it consisted of two liberalizing countries (Britain and France) intent on consolidating constitutional monarchy, and three conservative regimes (Austria, Prussia, and Russia) determined to safeguard absolute rule. Differences in regime type were offset by the fact that all five countries were dominated by an aristocratic elite, each of which agreed not to interfere in the domestic affairs of other member states. The Concert, however, eventually became the victim of social divergence. Differential rates of commercialization and industrialization—and contrasting state responses to the rise of middle and working classes—led to a widening social and political gap between the Concert's liberalizing members and its absolutist ones. The revolutions of 1848 brought this divergence to the fore, overturning the political status quo and effectively bringing the Concert to an end. So too was it social change that eventually brought civil war to the United States. During the country's early decades, a rough political equilibrium between the North and South contained the divisive potential of the two region's differences over slavery and the desirability of urbanization and industrialization. As westward expansion and the North's faster growth in population and wealth upset the political balance, however, union proved no match for diverging social orders.

In similar fashion, social convergence can advance the prospects for stable peace. During the first half of the nineteenth century, efforts to promote political and economic integration among a multitude of Germanic states were stymied by the diverging interests of the more commercial north and the more agrarian south. As commercialization spread to southern states, however, the interests of their political and economic elite converged with those in the north, helping clear the way for the founding of the German Kingdom in 1871. Incompatibilities in social order were a potent obstacle to societal integration, whereas convergence in social order then facilitated the onset and consolidation of stable peace.

Cultural Commonality

Cultural commonality is the third key ingredient of stable peace. Culture refers to a repertoire of practices, significations, and symbols that arises primarily, although not exclusively, from ethnicity, race, and religion. The historical cases indicate that perceptions of cultural affinity guide states toward each other; cultural commonality conditions which polities seek each other out as they search for an enemy that could potentially become a friend. The role played by cultural commonality is akin to social selection. When geopolitical necessity prompts states to seek to befriend an adversary, that state usually targets a party with which it enjoys an overlapping network of cultural practices and symbols. A preexisting sense of commonality appears to act as a marker, giving both states an initial inkling that they may be able to step away from geopolitical rivalry.[70] Cultural affinity also plays an important role in the later phases of the onset of stable peace. As societal integration proceeds and elites in partner states seek to generate a new narrative that blurs self/other distinctions, cultural commonality provides ready ground for the fashioning of a compatible, shared, or common identity. These findings are very much consistent with Hedley Bull's conclusion that "a common feature of . . . international societies is that they were all founded upon a com-

[70] See Christopher Hemmer and Peter Katzenstein, "Why Is There No NATO in Asia? Collective Identity, Regionalism, and the Origins of Multilateralism," *International Organization* 56, no. 3 (Summer 2002).

mon culture or civilization."[71] Bruce Cronin agrees that transnational communities require a "shared characteristic," such as a common ethnicity, to help shape "social identities that transcend juridical boundaries."[72]

Instances of stable peace are most often found among states that enjoy cultural commonality. Rapprochement succeeded between Great Britain and the United States—in part due to the sense of affinity resulting from a common Anglo-Saxon heritage. In contrast, rapprochement between Great Britain and Japan failed—in part due to an estrangement stemming from racial differences. Successful security communities tend to be culturally homogenous. The Concert of Europe and the European Community both benefited from narratives of cultural and religious commonality. In contrast, Australia and New Zealand have been excluded from ASEAN—despite their strategic proximity to the grouping—primarily because their dominant populations are not of Asian extraction. In similar fashion, stable unions tend to run along cultural lines—the United States, Italy, the Iroquois Confederation, and the United Arab Emirates are cases in point. In contrast, the Swiss Confederation was repeatedly tested by conflict between its Catholics and Protestants. Switzerland found its way to stable peace only after the military defeat of Catholic cantons seeking secession in the 1840s and the arrival of a liberal variant of nationalism associated with the revolutions of 1848. Rivalry between ethnic Malays and ethnic Chinese contributed to the unraveling of union between Singapore and Malaysia. In general, unions that cut across cultural boundaries often face chronic instability, at times breaking up along cultural dividing lines, as made clear by the recent fates of the Soviet Union and Yugoslavia.

Notably, linguistic dividing lines appear to be much less important than ethnic, racial, and religious ones. Linguistic commonality does help facilitate the deepening of international society and the construction of national states, as examination of the unification of the United States, Germany, and the United Arab Emirates makes clear. But the cases of the Concert of Europe, ASEAN, and the EC, among others, also demonstrate that language differences do not stand in the way of stable peace. And in instances in which the deepening of peace falls prey to the return of geopolitical rivalry, such as the

[71] Bull, *The Anarchical Society*, p. 16.
[72] Cronin, *Community Under Anarchy*, pp. 31–32.

Sino-Soviet and Swiss cases, linguistic differences were not the cause of dissolution.

In exploring the mechanisms through which ethnic, racial, and religious linkages contribute to stable peace, Durkheim's notion of social solidarity sheds important light. Durkheim distinguishes between primitive types of communities and those that are more mature. Primitive communities are held together by mechanical solidarity, a uniformity stemming from similarity. Mature communities enjoy organic solidarity, which stems from different social units working together in a complementary fashion. Mechanical and organic solidarity are sequentially linked. In Durkheim's words, "For social units to be able to differentiate from one another, they must first be attracted or grouped together through the similarities they display. . . . We know in fact that higher societies are the result of the coming together of lower societies of the same type. . . . It is in this way that more complex organisms are formed by the replication of more simple organisms, similar to one another, which only differentiate after they have been associated together."[73] Economic interdependence, Durkheim adds, promotes social solidarity only when it operates in the presence of commonality and affinity.

Inasmuch as international society represents a nascent or primitive form of community, its solidarity tends to be mechanical rather than organic in nature. Cultural affinity is a background condition that helps make solidarity possible and ensures that growing interdependence enhances not just wealth but also social bonds. As zones of stable peace mature, the solidarity they enjoy matures in step, with more complex social bonds arising from differentiation rather than uniformity. But in its early phases, stable peace often relies on cultural commonality as a primary source of social affinity.

An important caveat must condition this theoretical claim about the direct link between cultural affinity and stable peace. What constitutes cultural commonality is admittedly open to political and social construction. Through political and social change as well as shifts in discourse, cultural others can become kin, and kin can become cultural others. For centuries, Europe's geopolitical fault lines paralleled religious cleavages. Today, Europe's Catholics and Protestants (with some notable exceptions) enjoy a stable social solidarity. During the 1800s, Sweden was Norway's primary other. Today, they both embrace a common Nordic identity. Over the course of the 1990s, the com-

---

[73] Durkheim, *The Division of Labor in Society*, p. 219.

munal identity once enjoyed by Yugoslavs was lost to the reawakening of ethnic rivalries.

Despite the malleability of the notion of cultural affinity, social construction does run up against what Ernest Gellner calls "entropy-resistant traits." "A classification is entropy-resistant," Gellner writes, "if it is based on an attribute which has a marked tendency *not* to become, even with the passage of time . . . evenly distributed throughout the entire society."[74] Conceptions of ethnicity, race, and religion may be malleable, but only to a certain degree. Convincing Frenchmen that they share a common heritage with Germans was difficult enough. Convincing Frenchmen of their cultural affinity with Turks is another matter altogether. Over the course of the twentieth century, a security community between the United States and Canada evolved more quickly and extensively than between the United States and Mexico. Ethnic differences and identity politics played a major role.[75]

The point here is not that ethnicity, race, and religion should be seen as indelible determinants of where stable peace has a chance of taking root. Today's cultural dividing lines could become tomorrow's historical artifacts. On the other hand, it would be illusory to dismiss the important role that cultural similarity plays in enabling states to back away from geopolitical competition and build international society. Although perceptions of cultural commonality and difference are often mediated by public discourse, which narratives of commonality are privileged over others is a function of their availability. Britain successfully pursued lasting rapprochement with the United States rather than with Japan in part because of the ready availability of a narrative of Anglo-Saxon unity. The Iroquois Confederation consisted only of Iroquois tribes partly due to their proximity, but also as a result of cultural affinity. Despite the malleability of perceptions of cultural affinity, ethnic, racial, and religious similarity remains a reliable predictor of where zones of stable peace are likely to form and endure.

Although this analysis places considerable weight on cultural factors, it is quite distinct from Samuel Huntington's work on the clash of civilizations.[76]

[74] Ernest Gellner, *Nations and Nationalism* (Ithaca, NY: Cornell University Press, 1983), p. 64.

[75] See Guadalupe Gonzalez and Stephan Haggard, "The United States and Mexico: A Pluralistic Security Community?" in Adler and Barnett, *Security Communities*, p. 326.

[76] Samuel Huntington, *The Clash of Civilizations and the Remaking of World Order* (New York: Touchstone, 1996).

In step with Huntington, this book recognizes the geopolitical import of civilizational dividing lines. But whereas Huntington stresses that different civilizations are destined to clash, the argument here is quite different—states that share cultural commonality are uniquely positioned to enjoy stable peace. This finding has important prescriptive implications, suggesting that attempts to construct and preserve zones of peace will be most successful when such zones parallel—as opposed to cut across—cultural groupings. If Turkey is to invest in building international society, its natural partners may be its neighbors in the Middle East rather than those in the European Union. If East Asia is ultimately to enjoy a security community similar to the one that has evolved in Europe, states of the region—China and Japan, for example—may well be a more suitable anchor than the United States.[77]

Triggering Conditions

Institutionalized restraint, compatible social orders, and cultural commonality lay a foundation for stable peace, but they are not sufficient conditions; stable peace does not automatically emerge whenever they are present. Accordingly, a final issue concerns the triggering conditions that induce the onset of stable peace. What factors activate the processes of reconciliation spelled out in the first half of this chapter?

Three conditions appear to help trigger the onset of stable peace. The first, alluded to throughout this chapter, is geopolitical necessity. The state that initiates the effort to back away from rivalry does not do so out of altruism. Rather, it faces a threatening environment and lacks the resources needed to

---

[77] The pathways through which institutionalized restraint, compatible social orders, and cultural commonality facilitate stable peace are often intertwined. In the case of rapprochement between Norway and Sweden, for example, political reform at once introduced institutionalized restraint and led to a convergence in social order by diminishing the power of Sweden's aristocracy. These changes in turn helped clear the way for a new narrative that stressed cultural bonds between the two countries. In the Anglo-American case, political reform enhanced institutionalized restraint in Britain by strengthening the power of Parliament. But it also led to a convergence in social order by weakening the influence of Britain's aristocracy—a stronghold of anti-American sentiment. Singapore's separation from Malaysia was on the surface the product of cultural difference—tension between ethnic Chinese and ethnic Malays. But the split was ultimately a question of social order—the balance of power between Chinese and Malays—not one of ethnic difference. Cultural difference played a more prominent role at the regional level, where ASEAN excluded Australia and New Zealand from membership primarily because much of their population was of European rather than Asian extraction.

deal adequately with those threats. Its effort to befriend an existing adversary is a product of necessity, not opportunity.

A second triggering condition, often but not always present, is the existence of a preponderant state that anchors the zone of peace. As Karl Deutsch hypothesized, security communities tend to take shape around cores of strength. The most powerful party in a region is not always the instigator of stable peace, but it must be willing to exercise strategic restraint and entertain the prospect of reconciliation if stable peace is to have a chance. If the dominant state remains confrontational, its weaker neighbors tend to band together in alliance, meaning that the logic of balancing amid international anarchy prevails over the logic of "grouping" amid international society. If the predominant power practices strategic restraint and gives up some of the advantages of its material superiority, its weaker neighbors have a compelling incentive to let down their guard and risk investing in stable peace.

A third triggering condition is policy entrepreneurship. Elites that pursue stable peace must "run the gauntlet," accepting the risks associated with accommodation and the strategic and political vulnerabilities that result. Often, such entrepreneurship comes about in the wake of regime change and the opportunities it affords for a marked change of course. It was a change of government in Sweden and its willingness to pursue political reform that paved the way for rapprochement with Norway. Indonesia ended its policy of *konfrontasi* only after the demise of the Sukarno regime and the rise to power of General Suharto. In other cases, seminal events, such as war and revolution, provided the impetus behind a new and risky brand of statecraft. The Concert of Europe emerged in the aftermath of the Napoleonic Wars. The Iran-Iraq War cleared the way for the founding of the Gulf Cooperation Council. The Revolutionary War that began in 1775 triggered union among the American colonies, while the revolutions of 1848 put both Italy and Germany on the pathway to unification. Although an intrinsic randomness governs the timing of the events that encourage entrepreneurship, regime change and policy innovation often occur amid the periods of reevaluation and realignment that follow political crisis or military conflict.[78]

---

[78] On the role that critical junctures can play in producing policy innovation, see Ruth Berins Collier and David Collier, *Shaping the Political Arena: Critical Junctures, the Labor Movement, and Regime Dynamics in Latin America* (Notre Dame, IN: University of Notre Dame Press, 2002); and G. John Ikenberry and Charles A. Kupchan, "Socialization and Hegemonic Power," *International Organization* 44, no. 3 (Summer 1990).

THEORIZING A CONTINUUM OF STABLE PEACE AND ITS BREAKDOWN

Rapprochement, security community, and union represent different stages along a continuum of stable peace. As partner states move along this continuum, their interests evolve from being congruent, to conjoined, to unitary, and their identities from being compatible, to shared, to common. In addition, practices of self-binding and co-binding become more regularized and institutionalized as zones of peace mature. Rapprochement is more about practice than institutions. The parties succeed in reaching a state of peaceful coexistence, but cooperation takes the form of self-binding rather than co-binding and is regularized but not institutionalized. Security communities advance beyond peaceful coexistence; they represent a more evolved type of international society that rests upon an articulated and institutionalized set of order-producing rules. A union goes one step further, establishing suprastate institutions to which constituent members cede their sovereignty as they seek to act as a single unit on the international stage.

This study does not advance a theory of when and why states advance along this continuum; this topic is left for future research. Rather, it offers a generalized account of the sequential process that leads to stable peace and the conditions that facilitate its onset. Nonetheless, the case studies do provide a number of leads as to the potential determinants of progression from rapprochement to security community to union. The following discussion of these leads consists of observations and reflections, not empirically confirmed findings.

Rapprochement is the result of a spontaneous reaction to strategic necessity. At the outset, it is first and foremost an effort to redress strategic deficiencies; the prospect of building stable peace materializes only as reconciliation proceeds. In this sense, rapprochement is the consequence of tentative efforts to use diplomacy to neutralize a threat, which, when successful, then open up the possibility of a more profound change in relations. When in 1896 London decided to accommodate Washington's demands in a dispute over the border between British Guiana and Venezuela, it was seeking only to reduce its commitments in the Western Hemisphere, not make a lasting partner of the United States. When Sweden chose not to invade Norway in 1905, it was responding to immediate strategic circumstances, not yet pursuing stable peace with its neighbor. Rapprochement is by no means accidental, but neither is it the result of a fully articulated strategic vision; it emerges incrementally as geopolitical rivalry wanes.

In contrast, security community and union are the products of foresight and strategic vision; elites from the outset have as their objective a rules-based order and the potential emergence of a zone of peace. It is for this reason that an initial episode of rapprochement usually precedes the onset of security community and union; a cooperative, rules-based order becomes imaginable only as rivals back away from geopolitical competition. Not until long after the consolidation of Anglo-American rapprochement in the early 1900s could elites in both the United States and Britain contemplate a transatlantic security community. That development arguably awaited the Atlantic Charter fashioned by Franklin Roosevelt and Winston Churchill in the summer of 1941. Rapprochement between Indonesia and Malaysia cleared the way for the founding of ASEAN, just as rapprochement between France and Germany and between Abu Dhabi and Dubai was a precondition for the establishment of the EC and the UAE, respectively.

Once rapprochement offers a foundation for imagining the establishment of a rules-based order, several conditions appear to play a role in determining whether rapprochement then advances only to security community or all the way to union. Security communities are more likely among groupings that cover a large territorial expanse and exhibit greater diversity as to culture, language, and regime type. The Concert of Europe and ASEAN are examples. The size of their member states, their diverse languages, and differences in regime type required the pluralism afforded by security community. Unions tend to form among groupings that are smaller in size and exhibit less diversity as to culture, language, and regime type. The UAE, the Iroquois Confederation, Germany, and Italy are examples. The United States is a notable exception due to the size of its territory, but it does exhibit homogeneity as to culture and regime type. It is also the case that unions that are culturally and linguistically diverse are more prone to instability than those that are more homogeneous. Yugoslavia, Czechoslovakia, Canada, and Belgium are cases in point.

Political culture and the intensity of attachments to sovereignty may also play a role in determining how far particular groupings of states advance along the continuum of stable peace. Despite the formal act of union in 1789, the United States took decades to evolve into a centralized federal state; amid a libertarian political culture, the separate states slowly and reluctantly devolved power to Washington. That same political culture ensures that the transatlantic community is unlikely to progress beyond a loose security community; the United States would be loath to accept the formal attenuation of sovereignty entailed, for example, in today's European Union. In contrast, a more communitarian political culture eased the process of state formation in Europe. Germany more readily cohered as a federal union than did the United States, and Italy formed as a unitary state from the outset. Less intense attachments to sovereignty help explain why the EU has been evolving gradually from a security community into a union.

As to what factors are responsible for movement along the continuum from security community to union, societal interaction and economic integration appear to be the dominant drivers. Societal interaction, new transportation and communication infrastructure, and growing social networks all help shared identities become a common identity. Economic integration advances economic interdependence, providing both public and private sectors new incentives for advancing from security community to union. From this perspective, although Deutsch appears to have erred in attributing the formation of zones of peace to societal interaction, his transactional account does appear to provide a compelling explanation of when and why security communities may evolve into unions.

An increase in external threat can play a role in inducing security communities to consolidate into unions.[79] But it can also have the opposite effect. Among security communities with sufficient capability to address external threats through internal mobilization, such threats appear to lead to consolidation. Among security communities that must rely on outside powers to meet external threats, such threats have the potential to weaken internal cohesion.

The unification of Italy and Germany occurred amid wars against foreign powers—wars that were orchestrated by Italian and German leaders in the name of national unity. The founding of the United States resulted from the Revolutionary War, and the consolidation of the federal government's size and authority then substantially advanced by America's rise as a major power during the nineteenth century and the geopolitical contests that followed. In

---

[79] On the relationship between international competition and the centralization of states, see Michael Mann, *The Sources of Social Power: The Rise of Classes and Nation-States, 1760–1914* (Cambridge: Cambridge University Press, 1993); and Deudney, *Bounding Power*, especially pp. 175–176.

these cases, the constituent states of Italy, Germany, and the United States were able to amass military strength sufficient to prevail against their respective external challengers. In contrast, the GCC was weakened by the rising threat from Iran and Iraq after 1990; rather than advancing to union, the GCC's prior progress toward security community was compromised as its members, unable to confront Iraq and Iran on their own, sought external protection from the United States. In similar fashion, the Iroquois Confederation, although at times strengthened by external threat, was ultimately split asunder by internal disagreements about whether to ally with the American colonies or the British during the Revolutionary War.

Theorizing about a continuum of stable peace necessitates consideration of backward as well as forward movement along the continuum. The GCC's backsliding, the demise of the Iroquois Confederation, the unraveling of Sino-Soviet rapprochement—these and other cases of failure broach the question of how and why zones of stable peace break down.[80] The theoretical framework developed in this chapter has focused exclusively on how and when stable peace breaks out. There is, however, no need for a separate theoretical discussion of instances of stable peace that either stall as they form or unravel soon after they materialize. Rather, the historical episodes of failure are used to elaborate and extend the basic theoretical model that explains the onset of stable peace. The unraveling of stable peace follows the same causal pathway spelled out above, but the process operates in reverse; narratives of opposition trigger societal separation, which in turn awakens the security dilemma, reciprocal strategies of competition, and the return of geopolitical rivalry. On the question of when stable peace unravels, it is the absence of the key ingredients identified above—institutionalized restraint, compatible social orders, and cultural commonality—that explains why.

Notably, social and cultural tensions, not geopolitical ones, instigate the

---

[80] This account of the relationship among the three stages of stable peace is far more contingent and complex than the relationship Alexander Wendt posits among analogous stages of anarchy (see note 4 above). Wendt suggests that the international system will not regress—for example, from a Lockean anarchy to a Hobbesian one. He also contends that due to the human need for recognition and the growing costs of war, primitive and more violent anarchies are less stable than mature and peaceful ones. Accordingly, the international system will tend to progress toward a peaceful world state. The empirical cases explored in this book cast doubt on such a teleological view of the prospects for global peace. History suggests that progression from early to more advanced stages of stable peace is by no means necessary and that regression from stable peace back to enmity is possible, if not common. See Wendt, *Social Theory of International Politics*, pp. 310–312; and Wendt, "Why a World State Is Inevitable."

unraveling of zones of peace. It is only after the awakening of political tensions stemming from cultural and social differences that geopolitical competition commences. The U.S. Civil War was initially prompted not by territorial disputes between North and South, but by differences over slavery and the desirability of agrarian versus industrial development. The succession of civil wars that plagued the Swiss Confederation was the result of social tensions between rural and urban cantons and religious disputes between Catholics and Protestants. The unraveling of Sino-Soviet partnership in the late 1950s originated from clashes over ideology, which only later awakened security competition. The United Arab Republic collapsed because Egypt succeeded in alienating all of Syria's elite sectors, prompting them to support a military-led coup against the union. The Concert of Europe unraveled as a result of the revolutions of 1848—a contagion of upheaval wrought by modernization and social change. In all of these cases, the geopolitical competition that marked the collapse of stable peace can be traced back to social and cultural separation.

The main exceptions to this generalization are cases of failure resulting from divergent perceptions of how best to respond to external threats. America's Revolutionary War broke apart the Iroquois Confederation as its members could not reach consensus on what side to take. The GCC was stymied by diverging perceptions of the necessity and desirability of reliance on U.S. power to check Iraq and Iran. Even in these cases, the breakdown of stable peace was not a direct function of geopolitical rivalry. Rather, different responses to external events awakened identities of opposition and divergence in policy, which in turn led to a return of geopolitical rivalry. ASEAN has had the potential to suffer a similar fate—but its members have not faced an external threat sufficiently acute to bring to the surface divergent threat perceptions or necessitate strategic dependence on outside powers.

These insights provide cautionary admonitions about the fragility of zones of peace. Even after geopolitical competition and territorial issues have been resolved, stable peace may nonetheless falter as the result of differences over social and cultural issues or divergent responses to external threats. As discussed in the concluding chapter, this finding warns against complacency about the durability of existing zones of peace and underscores the potential for disputes over social issues and divergent responses to external threats to escalate into conflicts of geopolitical consequence.

CHAPTER THREE

ANGLO-AMERICAN RAPPROCHEMENT

This chapter and the one that follows explore both successful and failed episodes of bilateral rapprochement. This chapter focuses exclusively on Anglo-American rapprochement at the turn of the twentieth century. This case has been carefully studied by historians; it therefore offers a wealth of material for examining both the sequential process leading to the onset of stable peace and the conditions making it possible.

The following account of Anglo-American rapprochement will reveal that strategic necessity prompted the initial opening between London and Washington. Britain sought to befriend the United States in order to scale back the scope of its commitments in the Western Hemisphere, thereby freeing up resources to address threats in other theaters. London's willingness to accommodate Washington on a number of different fronts ultimately gave way to reciprocal restraint, enabling both parties to back away from decades of adversarial competition. Once rivalry was mitigated, societal interaction provided new momentum behind rapprochement, with the private sector and engaged citizens on both sides working to build new linkages between the two countries. The process culminated with the generation of a narrative of cultural kinship between Britons and Americans, one that propagated the notion that armed conflict between Britain and the United States would be tantamount to civil war. The case highlights the importance of institutionalized restraint, the convergence of social orders, and cultural commonality in making possible the emergence of an Anglo-American zone of stable peace.

GREAT BRITAIN AND THE UNITED STATES, 1895–1906

The United States and Great Britain were implacable rivals for well over a century. In 1775, the American colonies went to war with Britain to achieve their independence. After successfully defeating colonial rule and thereafter fashioning a federal union in 1789, the young republic again found itself at war with Great Britain in 1812. The cause was British interference with America's maritime commerce as part of Britain's naval blockade against Napoleonic France. The war ended in an effective stalemate, but not before British troops marched on Washington and burned down the White House.

After the end of the War of 1812, the two countries remained watchful antagonists. The main issues of contention were the boundaries of Maine and Oregon, mutual harassment across the Canadian border, and fishing rights. During the U.S. Civil War, Great Britain supported the South's secession and came close to intervening on behalf of the Confederacy. Commercial interests played a role, but so did London's calculation that disunion would weaken America and thereby enable Britain to retain its dominant strategic position in the Western Hemisphere. Despite the North's resentment of British support for the South, Anglo-American animosity subsided somewhat after the Civil War, in part because Britain withdrew its land forces from Canada, and the United States gradually demilitarized its side of the Canadian border. Nonetheless, tensions remained over a host of territorial issues in North and South America as well as Britain's continuing naval dominance in the western Atlantic and Caribbean. Until the closing years of the nineteenth century, the two countries saw one another as adversaries and kept war plans against each other at the ready.

How Peace Broke Out
UNILATERAL ACCOMMODATION

After more than a century of open rivalry between the United States and Britain, Anglo-American relations began to improve markedly in the mid-1890s. The main impetus behind the change was Britain's realization that its global commitments outstripped its resources. Soon after the U.S. Civil War, London recognized that it did not have the wherewithal to compete with the United States as a land power. Accordingly, it withdrew ground troops from Canada and focused on maintaining naval superiority along the North American littoral. Even that objective became difficult to maintain by the 1890s, as the United States, which had long focused its naval policy on coastal protection, instead decided to build a blue-water battle fleet. In 1890, the U.S. fleet did not contain a single battleship. By 1905, the United States had twenty-five battleships, making it one of the world's premier naval powers. Britain's fleet remained second to none, but the construction of a U.S. battle fleet made it increasingly difficult for the Royal Navy to maintain naval supremacy in the western Atlantic.

It was not only in North America that the British found themselves facing a gap between their resources and their imperial commitments. Russia was extending its reach as a major land power, posing a threat to India, perhaps Britain's most prized imperial possession, and was expanding its presence in East Asia. Japan was building up its naval power, enabling it to prevail in the Sino-Japanese War of 1894–1895 and posing a growing threat to the security of British positions in the Far East. Concurrently, Boer opposition to British rule in South Africa was placing additional strain on imperial resources, especially within the context of Germany's newfound imperial ambition and its support for Boer resistance. Early in 1896, just as London was reconsidering its relations with the United States in the aftermath of a dispute that had broken out over the Venezuelan boundary, Kaiser Wilhelm sent his infamous Kruger Telegram to the president of the Transvaal, congratulating the Boers for successful attacks on British settlers. When Germany began to build a high seas fleet in 1898, Anglo-German rivalry mounted in the European theater as well as in the imperial periphery.

It was against the backdrop of London's increasing anxiety about this growing gap between resources and commitments that a new round of Anglo-American rivalry erupted in 1895. The crisis was triggered by Washington's decision to intervene in a dispute between Britain and Venezuela over the latter's border with British Guiana. On December 17, President Grover Cleveland submitted a blustery letter to Congress arguing in favor of U.S. involvement in the dispute and requesting the funds needed to support a boundary commission to settle the issue. The request was unanimously approved by both houses of Congress. Acting under instructions from President Cleveland, Secretary of State Richard Olney pressed Britain to settle the border dispute through arbitration with the United States. Olney justified U.S. involvement on the basis of the broad sway granted Washington by the Monroe Doctrine. His letter to the British was forceful and provocative, insisting that, "To-day the United States is practically sovereign on this continent, and its fiat is law upon the subjects to which it confines its interposition."[1] Talk of war animated Washington.

[1] Charles S. Campbell, *From Revolution to Rapprochement: The United States and Great Britain, 1783–1900* (New York: John Wiley & Sons, 1974), p. 177.

Lord Salisbury, Britain's prime minister, initially rejected Washington's request, dismissing Olney's claim that the Monroe Doctrine provided the United States a voice in the dispute. Over the course of 1896, however, London changed its position, entering negotiations with Washington and, by the end of the year, agreeing to submit its disagreement with Venezuela to a tribunal. Concurrently, London and Washington also sought to negotiate a broader agreement that would commit both parties to settle all future disputes through arbitration. That deal was codified in the Olney-Pauncefote Arbitration Treaty signed in January 1897 by Olney and the British ambassador to Washington, Lord Julian Pauncefote. It failed to win ratification by the U.S. Senate, however, falling short of approval by only three votes the following May. Although Anglophobia played a role in blocking ratification, "the truly significant thing," C. S. Campbell observes, "is not that the treaty was defeated but that it was signed and nearly approved. No one would have dreamed of general arbitration with Britain at an earlier date."[2]

The main impetus behind London's change of course was strategic necessity. With threats mounting in all theaters, Britain was increasingly pressed to look for ways of reducing at least some of its imperial commitments. Especially when the Venezuelan dispute raised the prospect of an Anglo-American war, the Admiralty made a strong case that it simply did not have the resources to cope effectively with hostilities against the United States. Naval officials stated emphatically that, "This contingency would produce entirely exceptional conditions for which no provision can be made even approximately beforehand."[3]

Scholars of Anglo-American rapprochement are in near-universal agreement about the paramount importance that concerns about strategic overcommitment played in motivating Britain's effort to back away from geopolitical rivalry with the United States. As A. E. Campbell notes, "the crisis in Anglo-American relations over Venezuela arose at a time when there was much to cause Great Britain anxiety in other parts of the world," leaving Britain "particularly hard pressed."[4] In the words of Stephen Rock, "Britain's cultivation of American friendship was part of a broader policy of im-

---

[2] Campbell, *From Revolution to Rapprochement*, p. 188.

[3] Kenneth Bourne, *Britain and the Balance of Power in North America, 1815–1908* (Berkeley: University of California Press, 1967), p. 343.

[4] A. E. Campbell, *Great Britain and the United States, 1895–1903* (London: Longman's, 1960), pp. 11, 30.

perial consolidation, a cautious retreat dictated by the exigencies of her strategic position." "Although their principal concern in both the short and long term was to avoid war with America," Rock writes, "they were also eager to secure the fiscal and strategic benefits associated with the elimination of the United States as a potential adversary."[5] Kenneth Bourne concludes that the "dominating factor" shaping British policy "was that Great Britain's resources were now stretched beyond their limit by the effects of increasing expansionist and naval activity among the European powers as well as in the United States."[6] Befriending the United States thus promised not only to reduce the chances of major conflict in the Western Hemisphere, but also to ease Britain's global strategic predicament.[7]

To ensure that Britain's act of unilateral accommodation sent a clear message of its broader intent, London cast its opening gambit in unambiguous terms. The British not only agreed to settle the Venezuelan dispute through arbitration, but they also stated their readiness to accept the Monroe Doctrine, thereby making explicit that they were deliberately seeking to oblige American demands. As Arthur Balfour, leader of the House of Commons, told his colleagues in Parliament in February 1896, "in the disputes between successive English Governments and Venezuela there never has been, and there is not now, the slightest intention on the part of this country to violate what is the substance and the essence of the Monroe doctrine . . . a principle of policy which both they [the United States] and we cherish."[8] In January 1896, James Bryce, an Oxford professor, parliamentarian, and future ambassador to the United States, wrote to Theodore Roosevelt:[9] "There is nothing but friendliness on this side. [As to] the notion that we want to interfere with American rights or with the balance of power in the New World. Nothing further from people's minds. Our hands are more than sufficiently full elsewhere." Bryce also communicated this message to the U.S. public in an article entitled, "British Feeling on the Venezuelan Question."[10]

[5] Rock, *Why Peace Breaks Out*, p. 36; and. Rock, *Appeasement in International Politics*, p. 30.

[6] Bourne, *Britain and the Balance of Power in North America*, p. 340.

[7] As it sought to redress its strategic deficiencies, Britain turned to diplomacy not only with the United States. After the turn of the century, London also pursued diplomatic accommodation with Japan, France, and Russia. The Anglo-Japanese case is addressed in the following chapter.

[8] Rock, *Appeasement in International Politics*, p. 27.

[9] At the time, Roosevelt was head of the New York City Police Board. He would become assistant secretary of the navy the following year.

[10] Campbell, *Great Britain and the United States, 1895–1903*, pp. 39–40.

By making explicit and public the rationale behind their policy, the British were attempting to do more than solve the dispute over Venezuela; they were seeking to send a clear signal of benign intent. It was important that Washington interpret London's behavior not as a product of weakness but as a peace offering, a deliberate effort to reduce geopolitical rivalry between the two countries. The British were hopeful that doing so would constitute an important first step in turning an implacable adversary into a potential friend.

RECIPROCAL RESTRAINT

When confronted with Britain's willingness to accommodate U.S. demands, Washington responded in kind. The United States did not take advantage of London's compliant stance by increasing its demands or pressing for a resolution that would have been disadvantageous to British interests. Indeed, Washington backed away from its initial insistence that Venezuela's entire claim be arbitrated, instead agreeing to Britain's request that certain districts be excluded from the jurisdiction of the tribunal. When the dispute over Venezuela's border was resolved in favor of the British claim, Washington readily accepted the decision. The United States also practiced reciprocity in its handling of a separate dispute that had arisen over the hunting of seals. At the same time that the two parties were seeking a resolution of the Venezuela question, Britain was pressing the United States for damages incurred by U.S. interference with British sealing vessels in the Bering Sea. Washington agreed to settle this disagreement by establishing a tribunal of arbitration.

Just as debate in Parliament made British intentions known to Washington, the transparent nature of U.S. democracy revealed American thinking to London. In his inaugural address in March 1897, President William McKinley insisted that arbitration of the sort practiced with Britain was not a temporary departure, but was becoming routine: "Arbitration is the true method of settlement of international as well as local or individual differences. . . . Its application was extended to our diplomatic relations by the unanimous concurrence of the Senate and House of the Fifty-first Congress in 1890." McKinley went on to note that arbitration was "the leading feature of our foreign policy throughout our entire national history—the adjustment of difficulties by judicial methods rather than force of arms."[11] In the same

[11] President William McKinley, March 4, 1897, available at: http://www.bartleby.com/124/pres40.html.

way that British elites sought to broaden the context of the concessions they made over Venezuela, McKinley was moving from the specific to the general to indicate that Washington's benign motivations extended beyond the dispute in question. This effort to regularize mutual accommodation set the stage for the successive acts of reciprocal restraint that would lay the groundwork for lasting rapprochement.

The next step forward in Anglo-American rapprochement came in 1898, when the United States went to war with Spain to oust its forces from Cuba. After accomplishing this task, Washington extended America's naval presence in the Caribbean and Pacific, establishing a number of formal colonies, including the Philippines and Hawaii. Britain was the only European power to side with the United States in its war with Spain. London also quietly backed America's arrival as a Pacific power and its colonization of the Philippines.[12] Amid this flexing of U.S. muscle, Joseph Chamberlain, the colonial secretary, told the House of Commons, "What is our next duty? . . . It is to establish and to maintain bonds of permanent amity with our kinsmen across the Atlantic." Parliamentary debate over Chamberlain's speech was decidedly positive. In a dispatch to Washington, the U.S. ambassador to London, John Hay, noted the "agreement of all the speakers, of every shade of opinion, as to the desirability of an intimate and cordial understanding between England and the United States."[13]

The policies and rhetoric emanating from London were strongly indicative of the benign motivations informing British strategy, winning the British a repository of good will among U.S. elites and the public. In a conversation with President McKinley, the U.S. ambassador to London explicitly endorsed a U.S. strategy of reciprocity: "What seems called for as [sic] reciprocation of so much friendliness. I think the present attitude of the British Government and people is most valuable to us, and may be still more so in the future."[14] That British behavior was having a tangible impact on American attitudes was amply evident to observers. In May 1898, a Canadian newspaper noted, "Our American neighbors now fully realize, as they never did before, that

[12] Robert G. Neale, *Great Britain and United States Expansion: 1898–1900* (East Lansing: Michigan State University Press, 1966), pp. 148–149. See also Merze Tate, "Hawaii: A Symbol of Anglo-American Rapprochement," *Political Science Quarterly* 79, no. 4 (December 1964).

[13] Charles S. Campbell, *Anglo-American Understanding, 1898–1903* (Baltimore: The Johns Hopkins University Press, 1957), p. 47.

[14] Lionel M. Gelber, *The Rise of Anglo-American Friendship: A Study in World Politics, 1898–1906* (London: Oxford University Press, 1938), p. 22.

Great Britain is practically the only friend they have in Europe. . . . In a very important sense the United States is holding out the olive branch of peace and good will to Great Britain."[15]

The United States did in fact hold out that olive branch when the Boer War broke out in October of the following year. Despite congressional and public support for the Boers, the McKinley administration quietly backed British efforts to put down the rebellion. Washington kept its distance from Boer requests for mediation and exported military supplies to Britain. American bankers floated loans that helped Britain cover the costs of the war. In a message to Lord Salisbury in early 1900, Pauncefote interpreted U.S. behavior as "evidently intended to show their desire to maintain & promote the entente cordiale."[16]

The next challenge to U.S.-British reconciliation came from Washington's interest in building a canal through the isthmus of Central America. The Clayton-Bulwer Treaty of 1850, concluded at a time of active Anglo-American rivalry in Central America, prohibited the United States from constructing a canal on its own or fortifying one should it be built. Nonetheless, Congress in 1899 began debating legislation to authorize a Central American canal, a move that would have constituted unilateral abrogation of the Clayton-Bulwer pact. London reacted by entering negotiations with Washington, leading in 1900 to the signing of an agreement between U.S. Secretary of State John Hay and Lord Pauncefote. The British agreed to let the United States build the canal as long as Washington agreed to forego fortification. The latter provision proved unacceptable to the U.S. Senate. London acquiesced again, leading in 1901 to a second Hay-Pauncefote agreement that permitted the United States to construct, operate, and fortify a Central American canal. Lord Salisbury was remarkably frank in admitting that Britain was sacrificing short-term interests to invest in rapprochement with the United States, noting that discarding Clayton-Bulwer "would be, if not actually harmful to Great Britain, a gesture of goodwill for which concessions might reasonably be expected elsewhere."[17]

As Salisbury intimated, concessions on one issue cleared the way for ac-

[15] "England's Sympathy for US," *The Halifax (Nova Scotia) Chronicle*, reprinted in *New York Times*, May 19, 1898.

[16] Stuart Anderson, *Race and Rapprochement: Anglo-Saxonism and Anglo-American Relations, 1894–1904* (East Brunswick, NJ: Associated University Presses, 1981), p. 131.

[17] Campbell, *Great Britain and the United States*, p. 49.

commodation on others. The practice of reciprocal restraint soon resolved one of the few remaining disputes between the United States and Britain— the border between Alaska and the Yukon Territory of Canada. Fueled by the discovery of gold in the Klondike region, Canada in the late 1890s sought to interpret existing boundary treaties so as to extend its territory across the Alaska panhandle to the coast. Washington resisted and, in a show of force, President Theodore Roosevelt sent several hundred cavalry troops to the region in 1902.

Once again, both parties backed away from confrontation. The following year, Britain and the United States concluded the Hay-Herbert Treaty, which established a commission to settle the dispute through arbitration. Roosevelt was unambiguous in revealing his motivation for submitting the issue to arbitration: "Nothing but my very earnest desire to get on well with England . . . and my reluctance to come to a break made me consent to this appointment of a Joint Commission in this case. . . . I wish to exhaust every effort to have the affair settled peacefully and with due regard to England's dignity."[18] The tribunal's findings disappointed both parties. Canada was denied access to the coast, while the United States was confronted with a narrowing of Alaska's panhandle. But reciprocal restraint prevailed. All parties accepted the ruling. President Roosevelt noted that the Alaska dispute was "the last serious trouble between the British Empire and ourselves as everything else could be arbitrated."[19]

At least at the outset, these successive acts of mutual accommodation were motivated by self-interest, not altruism. From Washington's perspective, Britain was the party making the most concessions. Meanwhile, the United States was able to pursue its newfound geopolitical ambition, effectively replacing Britain as the hegemon of the Western Hemisphere and extending U.S. naval power into the Pacific. Attaining these objectives with British acquiescence was far less risky and costly than doing so through direct confrontation. America's interest in rapprochement was thus directly related to its rising power and the opportunity it provided to extend the country's strategic reach.

Britain was also guided by geopolitical concerns, although its policies were determined more by necessity than opportunity. Despite growing alarm in

---

[18] Gelber, *The Rise of Anglo-American Friendship*, p. 150.
[19] Gelber, *The Rise of Anglo-American Friendship*, p. 166.

the War Office and other quarters about Britain's increasingly exposed position in North America, many British officials had by the late 1890s come to the realization that Britain simply could not keep pace with the growth of American naval power. In a review of the relative strength of Britain's North America and West Indies Squadron, the Admiralty notified the cabinet in December 1899 that, "Our squadron, which in 1889 was superior to that of the United States, is now in 1899 completely outclassed by them."[20] Furthermore, the construction of an Isthmian canal would leave London little choice but to cede to the United States naval superiority in the Western Hemisphere. As London's naval attaché in Washington wrote in 1900, "it needs little consideration to show how profoundly the balance of sea power, not only in the Gulf, but also upon the Atlantic and Pacific coasts of North America would be influenced in favour of any country which possessed an unfettered control of the canal in wartime."[21] In the words of one historian, the treaty permitting the United States to build the canal "committed Great Britain to naval inferiority in American waters and therefore to friendship with the United States."[22]

Although reciprocal restraint was initially the product of self-interest, successive acts of mutual accommodation gradually had a more profound effect on Anglo-American relations. Over time, both parties came to see that their interests were congruent and mutually reinforcing; one state's gain was not necessarily the other's loss. Furthermore, both the United States and Britain began to attribute to each other not just benign intent with respect to the specific disputes that had troubled their relations, but also benign motivation with respect to their overall objectives on the global stage. This mutual shift in assessments of each other's broader motivation constituted a critical turning point; geopolitical competition was not just abating, but it was giving way to a shared sense of confidence that the two countries had congruent interests and common goals.

Britain eventually agreed to arbitrate the Venezuelan dispute and embrace the Monroe Doctrine not only to avoid conflict, but also because London

[20] Campbell, *Great Britain and the United States*, p. 31.

[21] Aaron L. Friedberg, *The Weary Titan: Britain and the Experience of Relative Decline* (Princeton, NJ: Princeton University Press, 1988), p. 165. For a detailed discussion of the impact of naval assessments on British policy, see chapter 4.

[22] Bourne, *Britain and the Balance of Power in North America*, p. 350

calculated that British interests in South America could potentially be advanced by welcoming a more assertive U.S. role. British elites, according to A. E. Campbell, came to believe that the United States, by increasing its engagement in the region, would be assuming "some degree of responsibility for the behaviour of the South American republics, who had an evil reputation for maltreating foreign nationals and not paying debts. . . . From this it was a short step to the idea that American supervision of South American republics would actually be profitable to Britain."[23]

In similar fashion, Britain supported the Spanish-American War and America's consequent expansion into the Pacific not only as a means of befriending the United States, but also because London calculated that its own interests would be furthered by America's arrival in East Asia. Through its open-door policy in China, the United States was resisting the efforts of other European powers to set up preferential trading zones; Britain was a primary beneficiary. Moreover, as the scope of Britain's global naval mastery diminished, London preferred that the United States fill the resulting vacuum. Should Germany or other powers have done so instead, London would have perceived a direct threat to British interests.

The Times (London) viewed America's annexation of the Philippines "with equanimity and indeed with satisfaction. We can only say that while we would welcome the Americans in the Philippines as kinfolks and allies united with us in the Far East by the most powerful bonds of common interest, we should regard very differently the acquisition of the archipelago by any other power."[24] These views were widely shared among British officials.[25] Indeed, James Bryce informed Roosevelt that "nearly everyone here applauds your imperialistic new departure."[26] As Kenneth Bourne summarizes elite opinion, "the British cabinet, including Salisbury, preferred American acquisition to that of any other power."[27] A similar logic shaped British policy toward the Panama Canal. As Lionel Gelber writes, "Soon Great Britain would be increasingly absorbed elsewhere, in other political and defensive problems. In

---

[23] Campbell, *Great Britain and the United States*, p. 44.

[24] Neale, *Great Britain and United States Expansion*, p. 90.

[25] Neale, for example, writes that "Britain quite favoured an expansion of United States territories and hence of her naval power and her diplomatic weight in the Pacific." See *Great Britain and United States Expansion*, p. 114.

[26] Anderson, *Race and Rapprochement*, p. 125.

[27] Bourne, *Britain and the Balance of Power in North America*, p. 345.

such circumstances, it was in the hands of a friendly rather than hostile Power that the command of the projected canal might best repose."[28]

The British were thus coming to see America's broader motivations as benign, not just its intent with respect to the issue at hand. In the words of A. E. Campbell, the British "failed to see in the rise of the United States to the status and to the pretensions of a world Power any threat to their own position." From London's perspective, he writes, "the emergence of the United States as a great Power was in a large sense likely to be advantageous to Britain."[29] This benign perception of America's ascent is quite remarkable in light of the resources at its disposal, the scope of its naval buildup, and the speed with which the growing ambition of the United States was undermining Britain's dominant strategic position in the Western Hemisphere.

Similar changes took place in American perceptions of Britain's geopolitical motives. Especially in the wake of the accord over Venezuela and British support for the United States in the Spanish-American War, elite and public attitudes toward Britain improved dramatically. Charles Schurz, writing in the *Atlantic Monthly* in 1898, noted that "even the most inveterate Anglophobist was bound to admit" that Great Britain was "positively friendly."[30] Top-ranking American officials began to make generalized assessments of British motivations, extrapolating from successive acts of accommodation. The year 1898 was a key turning point in this respect, with important members of the executive branch and Congress coming to see Britain as a benign great power. Roosevelt expressed his contentment that "there seems to be so friendly a feeling between the two countries."[31] Senators well known for their Anglophobic views were lining up to express their change of mind and their new fondness for Great Britain.[32] In 1898, Pauncefote, the British ambassador to Washington, sent a dispatch to London reporting that Americans were exhibiting "the most exuberant affection for England & 'Britishers' in general."[33]

Although they certainly welcomed Britain's decision to scale back its imperial ambitions in the Western Hemisphere, American officials were coming to see Britain's reach in other parts of the world as an asset to the United States.

---

[28] Gelber, *The Rise of Anglo-American Friendship*, p. 54.

[29] Campbell, *Great Britain and the United States*, pp. 4, 36.

[30] Campbell, *Anglo-American Understanding*, p. 54.

[31] Gelber, *The Rise of Anglo-American Friendship*, p. 18.

[32] Gelber, *The Rise of Anglo-American Friendship*, p. 23.

[33] Campbell, *Anglo-American Understanding*, p. 49

Henry Cabot Lodge wrote to Roosevelt in 1900 that there was in Washington "a very general and solid sense of the fact that . . . the downfall of the British Empire is something which no rational American could regard as anything but a misfortune to the United States."[34] In 1899, Roosevelt admitted, "I have been one of the people who have experienced a change of heart [about Great Britain]. . . . Fundamentally I feel that all English speaking peoples come much nearer to one another in political and social ideals, in their systems of government and of civic and domestic morality, than any of them do to any other peoples. . . . I earnestly hope that there will not be the slightest rift come between the English speaking peoples themselves."[35] Two years later, Roosevelt had become even more confident of British motives, insisting that the United States had "not the least little particle of danger to fear in any way or shape" from Great Britain.[36] Looking back on the impact of Britain's support for America in 1898, C. S. Campbell writes, "Britain as the friend and champion of the United States—this was a new concept for Americans who habitually had thought of her as the deadly foe."[37]

This shift in American perceptions is to some extent understandable; Britain was steadily making concessions to the United States and effectively welcoming its arrival as a great power. But it is nonetheless remarkable how quickly such changes took place in light of the long decades of enmity that came before. With Britain and America now attributing benign motives to each other, tentative hope in potential reconciliation was giving way to confident investment in durable rapprochement.

SOCIETAL INTEGRATION

As the process of reconciliation between the United States and Britain advanced, it spread outward from the exclusive realm of politicians, diplomats, and military officials to engage a wider range of actors on both sides. In its early phases, rapprochement was primarily an elite phenomenon; reconciliation proceeded in step with changes in elite assessments of the other party's intentions and motivations. As the onset of rapprochement advanced, its social reach broadened, with bureaucracies, private economic interests, the

---

[34] Campbell, *Revolution to Rapprochement*, p. 203.

[35] Howard K. Beale, *Theodore Roosevelt and the Rise of America to World Power* (Baltimore: Johns Hopkins University Press, 1966), p. 89.

[36] Rock, *Appeasement in International Politics*, p. 45.

[37] Campbell, *Anglo-American Understanding*, p. 54.

media, and concerned citizens all coming to play an important role. Interaction between British and American societies also intensified and deepened. As a consequence, the two parties gradually embraced benign assessments of each other's political character, not just of each other's foreign policy intentions and motivations.

On the British side, the Admiralty was the most important bureaucratic player actively pressing for a diplomatic strategy of accommodating and befriending the United States. As mentioned above, its overriding concern was the growing gap between strategic commitments and naval resources, a gap made manifest by Britain's disappearing naval superiority in the Western Hemisphere. As Bourne writes, "it was the Admiralty who first saw in the late 1880s that . . . [Anglo-American] relations had better be improved as soon as possible."[38] This concern intensified markedly during the 1890s, due to America's own naval expansion as well as Germany's building program—a move that ultimately prompted Britain to begin concentrating its naval assets in the European theater. The War Office was the Admiralty's main opponent, pressing the Royal Navy to maintain sufficient capability to deploy and support ground forces along America's east coast. The Admiralty, however, would have none of it: "In a characteristically imperious display of bureaucratic independence, the navy simply refused, after March 1898, to respond to the army's requests for comments on its invasion schemes. Turning a deaf ear to War Office fretting and pleading, the Admiralty for its part was becoming less and less willing to contemplate the possibility of a naval clash with the United States."[39]

In the early 1900s, the Admiralty effectively dropped the United States from the list of potential adversaries used to calculate naval requirements and began to undertake a redistribution of the fleet that left British commitments in the Western Hemisphere virtually undefended. The Colonial Defence Committee (CDC) charged that these moves effectively meant that in wartime "the United States' naval forces would hold the sea command in the waters of the Western Atlantic and Caribbean Sea." The Admiralty retorted, "The consideration of the point raised by the CDC emphasizes the necessity for preserving amicable relations with the United States."[40] Within the British

---

[38] Bourne, *Britain and the Balance of Power in North America*, p. 405.

[39] Friedberg, *The Weary Titan*, p. 164.

[40] Friedberg, *The Weary Titan*, pp. 187–188. See also Gelber, *The Rise of Anglo-American Friendship*, p. 405, and Bourne, *Britain and the Balance of Power in North America*, p. 393.

government, the Admiralty was thus the driving force behind rapprochement with the United States. It played a key role in guiding the pursuit of this objective through the shoals of bureaucratic politics, ultimately prevailing over the objections of the War Office.

The U.S. Navy played a positive—although less prominent—role in advancing rapprochement on the other side of the Atlantic. The navy's officer corps was generally pro-British, influenced by Commander Alfred Thayer Mahan, Admiral George Dewey, and others within its ranks who looked to the Royal Navy as a model for the United States as it developed a blue-water fleet. Mahan himself was a very popular and influential figure in Britain as well as in the United States. His influence in Washington was enhanced by his close friendship with Theodore Roosevelt—an ardent proponent of America's naval expansion and, from 1898 onward, an enthusiastic supporter of U.S.-British rapprochement.[41] Mahan himself was "a firm believer in good Anglo-American relations." In a letter to an English friend in 1896, he stressed the importance of avoiding conflict between Britain and the United States, noting that "no greater evil can possibly happen to either nation or to the world than such a war."[42]

Whereas the Royal Navy's predilection for rapprochement was the product primarily of resource constraints, the U.S. Navy's support for reconciliation stemmed from its abundance of resources. Not only did rapprochement clear the way for America's unimpeded rise as a world-class naval power, but Great Britain actively welcomed its ascent, backing the United States during the Spanish-American War and supporting its expansion into the Pacific. The U.S. Navy therefore had a vested interest in making the case for rapprochement within the councils of Washington. Its civilian leaders and officers also became outspoken proponents of reconciliation among the broader American public, becoming a lobby group not only for naval expansion, but also for U.S.-British rapprochement.

The private sector played its own role in advancing reconciliation, primarily through the engagement of individuals and firms whose economic interests were furthered by Anglo-American rapprochement. The stakes were high. Britain was by far America's main export market, attracting more than

[41] See Margaret Tuttle Sprout, "Mahan: Evangelist of Sea Power," in Edward Mead Earle, ed., *Makers of Modern Strategy: Military Thought from Machiavelli to Hitler* (Princeton, NJ: Princeton University Press, 1971).

[42] Bourne, *Britain and the Balance of Power in North America*, p. 320.

40 percent of U.S. products shipped abroad between 1896 and 1905. Three-quarters of the raw cotton processed by British mills came from the United States. America provided almost two-thirds of Britain's imports of wheat and wheat flour. As an American commentator observed, "a quarrel with Great Britain would be disastrous. If her ports were closed to us . . . to the farmers of our prairie States and to the planters of our Southern States, such an obstruction to the export of their staples would mean catastrophe." British analysts agreed on the dire economic consequences of a disruption of U.S. imports, arguing that it could shut down the country's textile industry and lead to widespread starvation.[43] A large volume of goods also flowed in the opposite direction, with Britain's exports to the United States during the 1890s accounting for roughly 10 percent of its total exports.[44] As Bourne notes, "while security dictated Britain's decision to appease the United States . . . her trading interests confirmed the wisdom of the choice involved and . . . did play their part in promoting good relations."[45]

The investment community provided a further source of support for rapprochement. In the late nineteenth century, surplus capital was fast accumulating in Britain, leading to the emergence of a new class of financiers. The United States emerged as the top recipient of British investment; in the early 1900s, U.S. assets represented some 20 percent of Britain's overseas holdings.[46] In 1899, the value of U.S. stocks and bonds held by British investors stood at roughly $2.5 billion, representing about 75 percent of the value of U.S. securities held by foreigners.[47] Geopolitics had a direct impact on the investment climate, as made evident when the dispute over the Venezuelan boundary initially prompted British investors to withdraw their capital, triggering a crash in the American market. These developments encouraged the financial community to take a particular interest in U.S.-British reconciliation. As C. S. Campbell notes, "At the end of the century a large community of business men and financiers moved back and forth between the two coun-

[43] Rock, *Appeasement in International Politics*, pp. 45, 32.

[44] Campbell, *Revolution to Rapprochement*, pp. 201–202.

[45] Bourne, *Britain and the Balance of Power in North America*, pp. 410–411.

[46] See H. Feis, *Europe: The World's Bankers, 1870–1914* (New York: Norton, 1965), p. 23. See also Michael Edelstein, "The Determinants of U.K. Investment Abroad, 1870–1913," in *Journal of Economic History* 34, no. 4 (December 1974).

[47] Charles J. Bullock, John H. Williams, and S. Rufus, "The History of our Foreign Trade Balance from 1789 to 1914," *Review of Economic Statistics* 1, no. 3 (July 1919): 216–233.

tries, at home in both. Their fortunes depended on the Atlantic economic connection and therefore on good Anglo-American relations. Such men enjoyed public esteem; governments heeded their counsel. As economic ties deepened, so did British-American friendship."[48]

Economic interdependence between the United States and Great Britain was nothing new. Financial flows did increase toward the end of the nineteenth century, but commercial trade had been thriving for decades. Indeed, when measured as a percentage of their overall foreign trade, bilateral trade between Britain and the United States actually *declined* during the 1890s due to the diversifying trade relations of both countries. Between 1890 and 1898, British exports to the United States fell from 23.6 to 17.7 percent of total American imports. By 1905, they had fallen further to 16 percent of U.S. imports. Between 1890 and 1898, U.S. exports to Britain fell from 52.2 to 43.9 percent of total U.S. exports. By 1905, they had fallen further, to 34.4 percent of U.S. exports.[49] In this sense, it was not growing economic interdependence per se that was helping to promote rapprochement. Rather, private economic agents on both sides, taking advantage of the improvement in Anglo-American relations orchestrated by diplomats, became more active and vocal proponents of reconciliation and helped shape public discourse.

A dinner meeting of the New York Chamber of Commerce in November 1898—soon after the U.S. victory over Spain—put on display the remarkable change in attitudes that had taken place on both sides of the Atlantic. Against the backdrop of the British and American flags, the participants opened the evening by singing "God Save the Queen" as well as "The Star Spangled Banner." "The scene," the *New York Times* reported, "could have been enacted on the banks of the Thames almost as well as on the banks of the Hudson." Lord Herschell, one of the two British judges appointed to the panel established to arbitrate the Venezuelan border dispute, proclaimed, "All agree that there is a bond which unites Great Britain and the United States which does not unite other countries. . . . In that union I see the real safeguard for the maintenance of peace in the world and of the extended reign of liberty." "I

[48] Campbell, *Revolution to Rapprochement*, p. 202.

[49] Campbell, *Revolution to Rapprochement*, pp. 201–202; Susan B. Carter, Scott Sigmund Gartner, Michael R. Haines, Alan L. Olmstead, Richard Sutch, and Gavin Wright, eds., *Historical Statistics of the United States*, Millennial Edition On Line (Cambridge: Cambridge University Press, 2006), Table Ee551-568 Imports, by country of origin: 1790–2001; and Table Ee553-550 Exports, by country of destination: 1790–2001.

can assure you," Herschell continued, "that all my countrymen reciprocate
the feeling which has been expressed; that they desire as you do that the cordial relationship continue, and that they have toward the United States of
America nothing but feelings of good will and a desire for its welfare and
progress." Speaking soon thereafter, an American general, Nelson Miles, affirmed that "there is a cordial friendship and a profound respect between the
people of the United States and the people of Great Britain that I trust will
grow stronger and stronger."[50]

New organizations also formed to advance Anglo-American reconciliation. In July 1898, a group of prominent Britons formed the Anglo-American
Committee, with James Bryce as its chairman. The body adopted a charter
declaring that the United States and Great Britain should capitalize on their
common heritage and interests to cooperate in global affairs. Two weeks later,
an American branch of the Anglo-American Committee was established in
New York. It issued a founding letter calling for "an intimate and enduring
friendship between these two kindred peoples." The letter was eventually
signed by over one thousand of the country's leading opinion makers.[51]

The media and mobilized citizenry also played an increasingly important
role in broadening social support for rapprochement between the United
States and Britain. It is worth quoting at length Robert George Neale's description of the profound shift in public attitudes that took place in Britain:

> Public opinion in Great Britain outside court circles was almost unanimous
> in its support for the United States action against Spain in both the Carib-
> bean and the Pacific. That this was the case has been proven conclusively
> and repetitively on many occasions. Leaders and articles from all the major
> newspapers and journals practically without exception were in favour of
> America's actions. Addresses were received by the government from nu-
> merous political associations in support of Anglo-American friendship.
> The Fourth of July was widely celebrated in England and was made an oc-
> casion for political gestures in the interests of Anglo-Saxon unity. Both the
> non-conformist and established churches, leaders and laity alike, vied with
> one another in expressions of Anglo-Americanism. Prominent men in all
> walks of life and from all classes spoke so often and so favourably of this
> ideal that it seemed they were determined not to be outdone one by the

[50] "Commercial Leaders Dine," *New York Times*, November 16, 1898.
[51] Anderson, *Race and Rapprochement*, pp. 119–120.

other in expressions of the fashionable sentiment. Traditional functions in Britain, such as Lord Mayoral balls and banquets and military and naval reviews, were throughout 1898 made the occasion for highlighting the Stars and Stripes and for allegorical representations of a close Anglo-American association. Finally there was formed the Anglo-American League under the sponsorship of leading citizens throughout the United Kingdom and dedicated to securing cordial transatlantic co-operation.[52]

A similar shift took place in the United States. One diplomat in Washington noted that "unanimous, or almost unanimous friendliness to England is now manifested by the Press throughout the length and breadth of the country . . . pass[ing] the bound of moderation in as great degree as the dislike and distrust of yesterday."[53] According to Neale, America's "traditional Anglophobia seemed for the time being to be in abeyance."[54] Groups of mobilized citizens not only shaped public discourse, but in some instances actively intervened to shape policy. During the debate over a permanent arbitration treaty, for example, thousands of Americans signed a petition in favor of the pact, noting that "all English-speaking peoples united by race, language, and religion, should regard war as the one absolutely intolerable mode of settling the domestic differences of the Anglo-American family."[55]

As made clear by the profound changes taking place in elite and public attitudes, ties between the United States and Britain were taking on a deeper social character. Contact was increasing among officials, the business community, and the ordinary citizens who traveled on regular steamship service across the Atlantic.[56] According to Christopher Endy, "Most U.S. travelers felt a closer kinship with Britain than with any other host nation, and private travel to Europe was an important element in the 'great rapprochement' of the two nations around the turn of the century."[57] By the turn of the century, reconciliation was about much more than the diplomatic practice of reciprocal restraint; public sentiment was undergoing a transformation. The two countries were coming to see one another as benign in character, not just in

---

[52] Neale, *Great Britain and United States Expansion*, pp. 134–135.

[53] Rock, *Appeasement in International Politics*, p. 44.

[54] Neale, *Great Britain and United States Expansion*, p. 135.

[55] Campbell, *Revolution to Rapprochement*, p. 183.

[56] Campbell, *Anglo-American Understanding*, p. 10.

[57] Christopher Endy, "Travel and World Power: Americans in Europe, 1891–1917," *Diplomatic History* 22, no. 4 (Fall 1998): 584.

motivation. The British believed that the United States, despite its growing economic and naval strength, would not evolve into a predatory power whose rise would come at the expense of British interests.[58] As Lord Herschell proclaimed at the dinner meeting of the New York Chamber of Commerce, Britons "can rejoice as much as you rejoice to-day in the fact that you are one of the leading nations of the world."[59] Americans were simultaneously letting go of Anglophobia, coming to see Britain as a strategic partner. As the former secretary of state, Richard Olney, ventured at a speech at Harvard in 1898, Britain and America would soon be "standing together against any alien foe by whom either was menaced with destruction."[60] Geopolitical rivalry was giving way to a nascent sense of trust.

These changes in elite and public attitudes helped ensure that the politics of accommodation prevailed over the politics of humiliation in Britain and the United States. Backing away from confrontation entailed political risks for the governments on both sides, making them vulnerable to claims from the opposition that policies of accommodation were imperiling the country's security. London was more exposed than Washington in this respect, inasmuch as Britain was the party making most of the concessions and openly compromising its strategic position in the western Atlantic. When the dispute over Venezuela first emerged, public opinion in Britain ran strongly against accommodating Washington's demand for arbitration. The *New York Times* noted that "the line of British opinion . . . is unanimously against any arbitration" and that "it will be a surprise to every one if Lord Salisbury . . . has not firmly declined to admit the right of the United States to interfere in the dispute."[61] In response to London's eventual acquiesence to Washington, critics of accommodation sought to take advantage of the public's skepticism, complaining about the government's "overstrained eulogium" of U.S. statesmen and the "fatuous courting of their goodwill."[62] As mentioned above, the War Office was a vocal opponent of the government's readiness to cede naval supremacy in the western Atlantic to the United States.

Government ministers went out of their way to rebut such criticism, arguing that the benefits of good relations with the United States warranted broad

---

[58] Campbell, *Great Britain and the United States*, p. 207.
[59] "Commercial Leaders Dine," *New York Times*, November 16, 1898.
[60] Neale, *Great Britain and United States Expansion*, p. 2.
[61] "Britons Against Arbitration," *New York Times*, December 8, 1895.
[62] Rock, *Appeasement in International Politics*, p. 42.

political support for accommodation. While London and Washington were still in the midst of negotiations over Venezuela, Lord Salisbury explained to Parliament that, "We desire, *in a question which is certainly not one of Party*, that the best intellects that we have on both sides should apply themselves to a matter that affects the welfare of the human race in a singular degree, and especially the good relations of a State with which we so desire to be on good terms as the United States of America."[63] The Liberal opposition generally complied.[64] Henry Asquith, a Liberal member of Parliament, noted in a letter to William Harcourt, the leader of the Liberals, that "it is very important to avoid saying anything that can stiffen the backs of the American jingoes."[65] Harcourt not only avoided rhetoric that could provoke U.S. resentment, but also criticized Salisbury for moving too slowly to avert the crisis and encouraged him to agree to arbitration. In general terms, the Liberals were more disposed to cooperative foreign policies than the conservative government, easing Salisbury's task of building parliamentary support for rapprochement. Nonetheless, as reconciliation advanced, the government continued to stress its merits in Parliament. In a speech to the House of Commons in 1898, George Curzon, the undersecretary for foreign affairs, defended the government's pliant handling of disputes with the United States: "On all sides we see the temperate and courteous handling of these American disputes by Lord Salisbury three years ago bearing fruit, which we hope will produce peace in the future."[66]

At times worried about a domestic backlash, the British government did hide from public view certain changes in policy that it thought might provoke opposition to rapprochement—such as the decision to drop the U.S. fleet from consideration in calculating Britain's naval requirements.[67] It also cast the benefits of accommodation exclusively in terms of the opportunity it afforded for better relations, avoiding discussion of the reality that a growing gap between British resources and commitments was a main rationale for pursuing reconciliation with America. In combination with the broader shift

[63] Campbell, *Great Britain and the United States*, p. 38. Italics added.

[64] For discussion of the opposition's position on the Venezuela dispute, see Campbell, *Great Britain and the United States*, pp. 37–46.

[65] A. G. Gardiner, *The Life of Sir William Harcourt*, vol. 2 (London: Constable and Co., 1923), p. 400.

[66] Campbell, *Anglo-American Understanding*, p. 11.

[67] See Friedberg, *The Weary Titan*, pp. 179–180; see also Paul M. Kennedy, *The Rise and Fall of British Naval Mastery* (London: Macmillan, 1983), chap. 8.

in societal attitudes noted above, these efforts to manage the politics of accommodation successfully prevented the buildup of significant domestic opposition to rapprochement.

Managing the domestic politics of rapprochement in the United States was
even less challenging than in Britain. From the outset, Washington was making more demands than concessions. Secretary of State John Hay, who had
previously served as the ambassador in London, remarked, "All I have ever
done with England . . . is to have wrung great concessions out of her with no
compensation."[68] Washington's initial salvo—its request that London agree
to submit the Venezuelan border dispute to arbitration—was in large part an
attempt to placate nationalist opposition. The Democrats had lost both
houses of Congress in the mid-term elections of 1894. The Republican majority was intensifying its charge that President Cleveland's foreign policy in
Central America was weak and ineffective. The United States was also suffering from a sharp economic downturn, further hurting the Democrats. For
Cleveland, taking a firm stand on Venezuela offered an effective means of
shoring up domestic support for his presidency. From this perspective, Britain's eventual willingness to settle the dispute through arbitration constituted
a diplomatic victory for the White House.

After McKinley's victory in 1896, reconciliation with Britain continued to
occur against the backdrop of U.S. expansionism. The McKinley administration was thus able to wrap itself in the mantle of strength and nationalism—even as it backed away from confrontation with Britain. Furthermore,
in the elections of 1896, the Republicans took the White House and maintained control of both houses of Congress, giving them a relatively free hand
over matters of foreign policy. McKinley's political dominance, his administration's successful expansion of American power in the Caribbean and Pacific, the pro-British sentiment that captivated Congress and the public beginning in 1898—these developments all combined to close off the potential
for a sharp nationalist critique of Washington's decision to pursue rapprochement with Britain.

THE GENERATION OF A NEW NARRATIVE

The final phase in the onset of Anglo-American rapprochement entailed the
generation of a new narrative of the other—one that eliminated oppositional

---

[68] Gelber, *The Rise of Anglo-American Friendship*, p. 55

identities and blurred self/other distinctions. This change in narrative had three distinct elements. First, both British and American elites began to refer regularly to the friendship emerging between their countries. A discourse of hostility was giving way to one of amity. Second, officials and opinion makers on both sides referred with increasing frequency to the racial and cultural bonds between their two peoples. Third, Britons and Americans began to state plainly that war between their countries was becoming unthinkable. Such statements were more than mere rhetoric. British and American war plans were concurrently redrafted to reflect the fact that both sides were coming to see armed conflict between them as a very remote prospect.

On the British side, sporadic references to the United States as a potential friend and ally can be found well before the 1890s.[69] Nonetheless, 1896 appears to be a pivot point inasmuch as high-ranking officials with increasing frequency referred publicly to the United States as a possible partner rather than a geopolitical competitor. As Joseph Chamberlain, the colonial secretary, stated that year, "I should look forward with pleasure to the possibility of the Stars and Stripes and the Union Jack floating together in defence of a common cause sanctioned by humanity and justice."[70] The switch in narrative appears to track closely Britain's growing sense of the urgent need to reduce its commitments in the Western Hemisphere. London needed to convince Washington that Britain had benign intentions and that Americans could let down their guard. As Stephen Rock puts it, the British launched "what can best be described as a public relations campaign aimed at influencing American opinion."[71] British citizens themselves were an equally important audience. If London would be regularly making concessions to Washington, the British public had to be prepared accordingly.

On the other side of the Atlantic, 1898 appears to have been the pivotal year in terms of changes in public discourse. London's accommodating actions and rhetoric, coupled with British support for the United States in its war with Spain, provided both reason and justification for American elites to begin referring to Great Britain as a friend rather than foe. In March, Olney referred to Britain as America's "most natural friend."[72] The list of high-ranking officials who explicitly touted America's burgeoning friendship with

[69] See, for example, Campbell, *Revolution to Rapprochement* pp. 89–90.
[70] Campbell, *Revolution to Rapprochement*, p. 183.
[71] Rock, *Appeasement in International Politics*, p. 42.
[72] "Olney Talks at Harvard," *New York Times*, March 3, 1898.

the United States included Henry Cabot Lodge, John Hay, Alfred Thayer Mahan, and Theodore Roosevelt. As mentioned above, journalists and intellectuals picked up on the new discourse, with one foreign diplomat noting the "unanimous, or almost unanimous friendliness to England" in the U.S. press.

A second narrative that became prevalent in elite and public discourse was that of racial and cultural affinity. Most historians of the period agree on the important role played by the mutual recognition of cultural commonality. A. E. Campbell writes that among the British there was "an important irrational element in the *rapprochement*. The good understanding between the two countries was held to be not the result of good-will and good management, but something mystic and inevitable, a law of nature."[73] Kenneth Bourne agrees that many Britons, elites and the public alike, came to see the prospect of armed conflict with the United States as tantamount to civil war.[74]

Public allusions to cultural bonds between Britain and the United States were hardly new to the 1890s. In 1857, for example, the *Manchester Guardian* referred to Americans as "our transatlantic cousins," noting that, "their language, their race, their institutions should render them our natural allies."[75] This perspective, however, did not gain widespread popularity in Britain or the United States until the second half of the 1890s, becoming a mainstay of public discourse by the early 1900s. Indeed, a "cult of Anglo-Saxonism" took shape, one that sought to appropriate Darwinian conceptions of natural selection to argue not just for Anglo-American unity, but also for Anglo-Saxon dominance of global affairs.[76]

In 1896, Arthur Balfour, leader of the House of Commons, ventured that "the idea of war with the United States carries with it some of the unnatural horror of a civil war. . . . The time will come, the time must come, when someone, some statesman of authority . . . will lay down the doctrine that between English-speaking peoples war is impossible."[77] Joseph Chamberlain agreed, contending that war between Britain and the United States would constitute "fratricidal strife."[78] 1898 proved to be a banner year for British proclamations of kinship with America. As war between America and Spain looked

[73] Campbell, *Great Britain and the United States*, p. 155.
[74] Bourne, *Britain and the Balance of Power in North America*, p. 411.
[75] Campbell, *Revolution to Rapprochement*, pp. 89–90.
[76] Anderson, *Race and Rapprochement*, pp. 26–61.
[77] Rock, *Appeasement in International Politics*, p. 32.
[78] Campbell, *Revolution to Rapprochement*, p. 183.

likely, *The Times* wrote that the United States "is knitted to us yet more closely by the ties of blood."[79] When the United States soon thereafter colonized the Philippines, *The Times* endorsed the move and referred to Americans as "kinfolks."[80] In June, Lord Coleridge claimed that the United States and Britain "have a common kinship of race, we have one language, we have one literature, we have one law." He made this statement at an Anglo-American banquet in a London hotel; the backdrop was a flag in which the American and British designs had been merged, with "Stars and Stripes on the union jack, with the eagle and the lion at the corners, and clasped hands between."[81] Over the course of the year, public speeches by top officials, statements in the House of Commons, and newspaper columns made frequent references to Anglo-Saxon unity and the indelible racial bonds between Britons and Americans.

These sentiments were echoed by American officials and opinion makers from 1898 onward. Indeed, important public figures who had earlier espoused Anglophobic sentiments, Theodore Roosevelt and Henry Cabot Lodge among them, embraced and propagated the notion that racial affinity promised to ensure that Americans and Britons would become lasting partners. By the early 1900s, according to Stuart Anderson, Roosevelt had come to the conclusion that the "'English-speaking race' . . . was united by blood, culture, and world view, as well as by language."[82] In the wake of British support for the United States during the Spanish-American War, Lodge proclaimed that "race, blood, language, identity of beliefs & aspirations, all assert themselves."[83]

In the same speech at Harvard in which he referred to Britain as America's "best friend," Richard Olney noted "the close community . . . in origin, speech, thought, literature, institutions, ideals—in the kind and degree of civilization enjoyed by both."[84] He acknowledged that the United States and Britain "may have such quarrels as only relatives and intimate neighbors indulge in," affirming that "England, our most formidable rival, is our most natural friend. There is such a thing as patriotism for race as well as for

---

[79] Campbell, *Revolution to Rapprochement*, p. 192.
[80] Neale, *Great Britain and United States Expansion*, p. 90.
[81] "Anglo-American Banquet," *The London Mail*, reprinted in *New York Times*, June 19, 1898.
[82] Anderson, *Race and Rapprochement*, p. 75.
[83] Anderson, *Race and Rapprochement*, p. 118.
[84] Campbell, *Revolution to Rapprochement*, p. 201.

country."[85] The industrialist Andrew Carnegie labeled himself "a race patriot," and called for "the whole Anglo-Celtic race to get together."[86] Carnegie believed that a "race union" would preserve peace not just between the United States and Britain, but globally: "A reunion of the Anglo-Americans ... would dominate the world and banish from the earth its greatest stain— the murder of men by men."[87] Mahan similarly believed that Anglo-American commonalities were genetically determined, with their shared ideas and laws "inborn" and "inbred."[88]

Public groups joined in, with the petition circulated to garner support for the general arbitration treaty stating plainly that the "Anglo-American family" was "united by race, language, and religion."[89] Cecil Rhodes, a British-born South African business magnate, had "race unity" in mind when he founded the Rhodes scholarships. Initially designed to be open only to residents of British colonies, Rhodes extended eligibility to American students in his will of 1899, a step toward providing "a common education for potential leaders of all Anglo-Saxon countries."[90] Popular literature also served as a vehicle for propagating notions of racial affinity. As Anderson notes, "novelists and storytellers were both publicists of race theories and purveyors of the Anglo-Saxon creed in the 1890s and 1900s."[91] It is worth quoting at length Paul Kramer's assessment of the impact of intellectual and literary networks on societal integration and public discourse:

> The success of Anglo-Saxonism as a racial-exceptionalist bridge between the United States and the British Empire was due in part to the social, familial, intellectual, and literary networks that tied elite Americans and Britons together. Such complex and long-standing exchanges widened and deepened as accelerating travel and communication enabled greater contacts between the British and American upper classes; middle-class tourists; business, professional and academic elites; and abolitionist, temperance, civil service, and Progressive reformers. Anglo-American dialogue and Anglo-Saxonist racism were also given life by a publishing revolution

---

[85] "Olney Talks at Harvard," *New York Times*, March 3, 1898.
[86] Campbell, *Anglo-American Understanding*, p. 10.
[87] Anderson, *Race and Rapprochement*, pp. 53–54.
[88] Anderson, *Race and Rapprochement*, p. 19.
[89] Campbell, *Revolution to Rapprochement*, p. 183.
[90] Anderson, *Race and Rapprochement*, p. 51.
[91] Anderson, *Race and Rapprochement*, p. 57.

in the 1890s. Many of Anglo-Saxonism's chief literary exponents published through transatlantic houses with joint centers in New York and London: genteel Anglo-American literary-political magazines—*Atlantic Monthly*, the *North American Review*, the *Fortnightly Review*, *Scribner's*, *Century Magazine*, *Nineteenth Century*—burdened late-Victorian tabletops on both sides of the Atlantic. The new publishing circuits helped create an "imagined community" of literate, English-speaking Americans and Britons with common affiliations and reference points, even among the less traveled. The title of one short-lived publication, the *Anglo-Saxon Review*, suggests the role of journals in establishing self-consciously racist solidarities."[92]

As the first decade of the 1900s progressed, a third concept emerged alongside this discourse of friendship and common heritage—the notion that armed conflict between the United States and Britain was becoming unthinkable. Statements to this effect were appearing in Britain by 1904. According to Lord Selborne, the first lord of the Admiralty, war with the United States was "the greatest evil which could befall" Britain. A. H. Lee, the civil lord of the Admiralty, was even more direct: "I cannot for a moment contemplate the possibility of hostilities really taking place." An Anglo-American war, he continued, would be "the supreme limit of human folly, and I cannot conceive that any British statesman is willing to contemplate it under any circumstances."[93] Similar statements were common on the other side of the Atlantic. In 1905, President Roosevelt wrote to Lee: "You need not ever be troubled by the nightmare of a possible contest between the two great English-speaking peoples. I believe that is practically impossible now, and that it will grow entirely so as the years go by. In keeping ready for possible war I never even take into account a war with England. I treat it as out of the question."[94]

In Britain, such statements were in keeping with the concrete changes in war plans that had been taking place. By 1901, the U.S. Navy no longer figured in the Admiralty's calculation of the two-power standard—the fleet strength Britain needed to maintain superiority over the next two most powerful navies. In defending this redefinition of naval requirements, Lord Sel-

[92] Paul A. Kramer, "Empires, Exceptions, and Anglo-Saxons: Race and Rule between the British and United States Empires, 1880–1910," *Journal of American History*, 88, no. 4 (March 2002): 1326.

[93] Bourne, *Britain and the Balance of Power in North America*, pp. 380–381.

[94] Rock, *Appeasement in International Politics*, pp. 29–30.

borne argued that Britain should prepare only for contingencies that are "reasonably probable."[95] The Royal Navy proceeded to abandon plans to maintain sea control in the western Atlantic, instead concentrating on the defense of the eastern empire and missions in the European theater. For the Admiralty, war with the United States may not have been completely ruled out, but it was remote enough to warrant a dramatic shift in planning.

For the next several years, the War Office objected vociferously to the Navy's effective abandonment of the western Atlantic, arguing that it left Britain impotent in a conflict with the United States and exposed Canada to a ground invasion. The Admiralty did not deny this charge, instead responding that the shifting balance of power in the Atlantic necessitated that both Britain and Canada preserve amicable relations with the United States. The Admiralty and War Office continued to lock horns on this issue until the middle of the decade, at which time Britain's decision makers and bureaucrats had come to the collective conclusion that war with the United States was out of the question and that, in the words of the first sea lord, Admiral Sir John Fisher, "it seems an utter waste of time to prepare for it."[96] As Aaron Friedberg concludes, "For all practical purposes the British presence in the Western Hemisphere and the protracted squabbles over it had come to an end."[97] Bourne is in agreement, noting that, "By 1902 it was clear to British statesmen at large, and by 1906 even to the War Office, that Anglo-American relations had improved so much that war could virtually be discounted."[98] Indeed, the War Office acted on this assessment by withdrawing the last units of British regulars from Canada.

America's strategic plans underwent a similarly profound change at the turn of the century. Although it maintained war plans for a ground invasion of Canada well into the 1900s, the United States left its border with Canada largely undefended throughout the last quarter of the nineteenth century, indicating that it viewed a land war with Britain as a very remote prospect well before the onset of rapprochement. Prior to the 1890s, the U.S. Navy had focused primarily on coastal defense and commerce protection, effectively ceding naval supremacy to Britain. During the last decade of the century, however, America's battle fleet grew in step with its geopolitical aspirations. One

---

[95] Friedberg, *The Weary Titan*, p. 174.
[96] Friedberg, *The Weary Titan*, p. 197.
[97] Freidberg, *The Weary Titan*, p. 199.
[98] Bourne, *Britain and the Balance of Power in North America*, p. 405.

of the aims was to challenge Britain for sea control in the western Atlantic, an objective that certainly had potential to trigger conflict. But as rapprochement proceeded and the Admiralty effectively ceded to the United States naval supremacy in the Western Hemisphere, American expectations about the likelihood of conflict with Britain diminished accordingly.

By the early 1900s, American officials viewed the prospect of a naval clash with Britain as fast fading into the past. A study by the U.S. General Staff concluded that war with Britain was the "least of all possible conflicts."[99] Planning for a possible war against Canada continued until the 1930s, but was viewed largely as an academic exercise.[100] Instead, American strategists concentrated on the projection of the country's growing naval strength, broadcasting the arrival of the United States as a great power. Preparation for a potential engagement with Britain gave way to a new focus on addressing the challenges associated with both defending possessions in the Caribbean and Pacific and meeting the rising threats posed by expansion of the Japanese and German fleets.[101] Britain's overt welcoming of America's emergence as a major naval power only solidified sentiment on both sides of the Atlantic that an Anglo-American war was becoming unthinkable.

The new narrative of the other generated by elites on both sides of the Atlantic thus played an important role in consolidating the onset of stable peace. Through a discourse of friendship and common Anglo-Saxon heritage, Britain and the United States were fashioning compatible identities, blurring self/other distinctions, and forging a sense of solidarity. Both parties had come to believe that conflict between them would constitute fratricidal war. Over the course of the succeeding decades, the two countries grew even closer, eventually constituting a security community and, with other Western democracies, together erecting the liberal international order that took shape at the close of World War II. Arguably, it was not until that war and the military alliance it fostered between the two nations that the "special relationship" of today came into being. But the emergence of Anglo-American rapprochement be-

---

[99] N. F. Dreisziger, "The Role of War Planning in Canadian-American Relations, 1867–1939," *Canadian Review of American Studies* 10, no. 3 (Winter 1979): 343.

[100] Richard A. Preston, *The Defence of the Undefended Border: Planning for War in North America, 1867–1939* (Montreal: McGill-Queen's University Press, 1977).

[101] See Allan Millet and Peter Maslowski, *For the Common Defense: A Military History of the United States of America* (New York: Free Press, 1984), pp. 317–323; and Ute Mehnert, "German Weltpolitik and the American Two-Front Dilemma: The 'Japanese Peril' in German-American Relations, 1904–1917," *Journal of American History* 82, no. 4 (March 1996): 1452–1477.

tween 1895 and 1906 laid the groundwork for this security community. By World War I, stable peace between the Britain and the United States had already set in. It would only deepen as strategic alliance and societal interaction advanced and the two polities embraced a shared Western identity.

Why Peace Broke Out

Chapter 2 identified three main conditions that favor the onset of stable peace: institutionalized restraint, the compatibility of social orders, and cultural commonality. The trajectory of U.S.-British rapprochement makes clear that it was strategic necessity that initially drove the process. Britain faced a range of global commitments that it could no longer sustain, prompting London to accommodate the United States in order to befriend it. Washington responded in kind, not out of altruism, but to take advantage of an opportunity to extend its hegemony over the Western Hemisphere. Strategic necessity on its own, however, did not produce lasting reconciliation. Institutionalized restraint, social compatibility, and cultural commonality all helped channel strategic imperatives toward rapprochement rather than conflict.

INSTITUTIONALIZED RESTRAINT

Throughout the long decades of hostility between Britain and the United States, both countries practiced institutionalized restraint at home. Britain had long been a constitutional monarchy; it then embraced liberal democracy over the course of the nineteenth century through parliamentary reforms and the expansion of suffrage. The United States was a liberal democracy (albeit slave-owning) from inception. From this perspective, both countries possessed regime types that favorably disposed them to the practice of strategic restraint in their foreign policies. That rapprochement did not emerge until the 1890s suggests that the consolidation of democratization in Great Britain may have contributed to the onset of stable peace.

One strand of the democratic peace literature posits that it is liberal democracy per se—not the behavioral attributes that it produces—that is the primary cause of pacific relations between democratic states. Democratic states recognize one another as such, enabling them to enjoy a unique affinity and mutual respect. Other versions of the argument maintain that the power-checking mechanisms and ideological centrism that accompany liberal democracy better explain its peace-causing effects.

The trajectory of Anglo-American rapprochement suggests a complicated relationship between democratization and the onset of stable peace. To the degree that democratization advanced rapprochement, it did so through the behavioral attributes of democratic regimes—in particular the exercise of strategic restraint— not through the mutual identification fostered by shared regime type. During the balance of the nineteenth century, most Americans viewed Britain as a monarchy, not a republic—despite the fact that the 1832 Reform Act made the cabinet responsible to Parliament rather than the Crown, substantially expanding public leverage over the executive.[102] American perceptions of the nature of Britain's government appear to have been the product more of Britain's hostile behavior toward the United States than of dispassionate assessment of the character of the country's governing institutions.[103] The prevailing view that Britain was not a liberal democracy in turn contributed to American distrust of British intentions. As John Owen writes, in the eyes of Americans, "Britain remained a monarchy and therefore a despotism" that threatened liberty and republican values.[104]

The British Reform Act of 1884 significantly expanded the powers of Parliament and substantially enlarged the franchise. If democracies automatically accord one another mutual respect and enjoy mutual affinity, American elites should have thereafter recognized Britain as an emerging partner. But they did not. As Owen notes, "Many Americans in the 1890s still viewed Britain mainly as a monarchy and thus not democratic."[105] Moreover, this perception had significant political consequences. For example, opposition to monarchy played a role in preventing the ratification of the Anglo-American Arbitration Treaty that accompanied efforts to resolve the crisis over Venezuela. In giving King Oscar of Sweden and Norway a role in selecting the individuals to sit on the arbitration panel, the treaty invited the principled opposition of the Illinois Legislature, which claimed that the treaty "exalts monarchy and subordinates democracy. . . . The United States should be free

---

[102] For analysis of U.S. perceptions of British regime type and the implications for policy, see John M. Owen, "How Liberalism Produces Democratic Peace," in Michael Brown, Sean Lynn-Jones, and Steven Miller, eds., *Debating the Democratic Peace* (Cambridge, MA: MIT Press, 1996), pp. 133–148.

[103] For elaboration of the logic behind this interpretation, see Ido Oren, "The Subjectivity of the 'Democratic' Peace: Changing U.S. Perceptions of Imperial Germany," *International Security* 20, no. 2 (Fall 1995).

[104] Owen, "How Liberalism Produces Democratic Peace," p. 139.

[105] Owen, "How Liberalism Produces Democratic Peace," pp. 143–144.

from and untrammeled by any monarchical influence or intrigue in all matters pertaining to the American continent."[106]

The key changes in U.S. perceptions of Britain's system of government—and the readiness of Americans to attribute to the country benign character—resulted not from the institutional changes of 1884, but from the shift in British policy toward the United States that began in 1895. American Anglophobia ran strong until the second half of the 1890s, a full decade after the major reforms of 1884. What transformed U.S. attitudes toward Britain was London's strategy of accommodating the United States, not discrete reforms to Britain's domestic institutions. This finding is consistent with the work of Ido Oren and other scholars who argue that states make subjective judgments about the democratic character of other states, basing those judgments on the "peacefulness of their foreign policies" rather than the institutional design of their governments.[107]

It is also the case that although Britain perceived the United States as a liberal democracy, such recognition did not reassure London about the pacific nature of U.S. statecraft. Again, U.S. behavior played a far more important role in shaping British perceptions of U.S. intent than did the structure of the American government. Indeed, the democratic nature of American politics was on occasion a source of concern, not reassurance.

British officials worried that the boisterous and, at times, jingoistic nature of American democracy might do more to precipitate war than to avert it. With a potent and ambitious strain of American nationalism having emerged during the 1890s, the British General Staff privately expressed concern that public passions could induce aggressive behavior on the part of the United States.[108] Lord Salisbury "doubted the reliability of the American government and . . . distrusted the emotionalism that often found its way into American foreign policy."[109] Three days after President Cleveland delivered to Congress his fiery message concerning U.S. intervention in the Venezuelan boundary dispute, Pauncefote reported from Washington that "nothing is heard but the voice of the Jingo bellowing defiance to England."[110] In similar fashion, James Bryce in 1896 privately expressed anxiety to Theodore

[106] "Opposed to Arbitration," *New York Times*, January 27, 1897.
[107] Oren, "The Subjectivity of the 'Democratic' Peace," p. 148.
[108] See, for example, Bourne, *Britain and the Balance of Power in North America*, p. 403.
[109] Anderson, *Race and Rapprochement*, p. 87.
[110] Anderson, *Race and Rapprochement*, p. 97.

Roosevelt about "the apparent existence of ill-will towards Britain in a large part of your population."[111]

Such concerns were also voiced publicly. In response to Congress's support for U.S. intervention in the Venezuelan boundary dispute, *The Times* wrote: "We are afraid that the Americans will not be moved by arguments drawn from precedents and established principles of international law. They have always shown themselves a sentimental, excitable Nation. They have the haziest idea of what the Monroe doctrine really is, but nevertheless they are quite willing to enter upon a holy war to defend it."[112] In general, elite opinion in Britain held that "there is beyond doubt a very large and powerful party which does deliberately desire war with somebody, and by preference with the United Kingdom."[113] Such concerns about American jingoism were not unjustified, as made clear by the prominent role that public opinion played in precipitating the Spanish-American War.[114]

British anxieties about the volatile nature of American democracy notwithstanding, it is the case that specific attributes of liberal democracy and the behavior they produced did facilitate the onset of rapprochement. Liberal democracy advanced the process of reconciliation by regularizing the practice of strategic restraint. Both Britain and the United States were liberal polities. Their governing institutions were structured to check power, ensure the rule of law, and discourage the exploitation of political advantage. These domestic attributes manifested themselves in the conduct of foreign relations. Both parties readily embraced arbitration as a means of settling territorial disputes. Such commitments had particular credibility because they had to pass muster among legislators and the public. Both London and Washington generally let pass opportunities to capitalize on unilateral advantage, as made clear by the extended period of peace that endured along a Canadian border left largely undefended after the U.S. Civil War. The language of restraint and accommodation that helped shift popular opinion was familiar to publics in both countries. These liberal attributes helped make political space for mutual accommodation.

The transparency afforded by democratic debate also enabled both sides to

[111] Campbell, *Great Britain and the United States*, p. 39.
[112] "The 'Thunderer' Alarmed," *The Times* quoted in *New York Times*, December 20, 1895.
[113] *The Saturday Review*, in Campbell, *Great Britain and the United States*, p. 43.
[114] See George Kennan, *American Diplomacy, 1900–1950* (Chicago: University of Chicago Press, 1984), pp. 3–20.

assess with confidence the intentions and motives of the other. Speeches by high-ranking officials, congressional and parliamentary debate, the open deliberation afforded by a free press, the actions and statements of citizen groups—these all ensured that political processes in both Britain and the United States were in the public domain. When Lord Balfour declared in Parliament that Britain would honor the Monroe Doctrine, his words no doubt had a bigger impact in Washington than London. When both houses of Congress in 1895 "earnestly recommended" that Britain turn to arbitration to resolve its border dispute with Venezuela, London was on notice that Washington was prepared to take a hard line on the issue.[115] The two polities had open access to each other's societies and could form reliable assessments of the considerations driving policy. Transparency thus helped reassure both parties that the other did not have predatory intent, but could instead be trusted to reciprocate gestures of good will and strategic restraint.

Finally, the pluralism intrinsic to liberal democracy enabled governments on both sides of the Atlantic to adapt in a timely fashion to the rapidly changing strategic environment. This attribute was particularly important in Britain, where elites had to ensure that the politics of accommodation prevailed over the politics of humiliation. By making the case that British and American interests were compatible, that Americans represented Anglo-Saxon kin, and that British concessions were the result of negotiation rather than acquiescence, the British government was able to avoid a nationalist backlash. It is the case that elites at times hid from public view important strategic considerations—such as Britain's exposed position in the western Atlantic, the exclusion of the United States from the two-power standard, and the decision to prepare for the dispatch of ground forces to the continent in the event of war with Germany.[116] Such dissimulation did mean that democratic transparency was impaired to some extent, but it also makes clear how mindful elites were of the need to manage the domestic politics of strategic adjustment.

Although Anglophobia remained a potent political force in the United States through at least 1898, managing the domestic politics of rapproche-

---

[115] Campbell, *From Revolution to Rapprochement*, p. 176.

[116] See Friedberg, *The Weary Titan*, pp. 179–180. As Anglo-German rivalry mounted, the cabinet hid from public view its plans to send an expeditionary force to fight on the continent in the event of a German attack on France and the Low Countries. See Charles A. Kupchan, *The Vulnerability of Empire* (Ithaca, NY: Cornell University Press, 1994), p. 127.

ment was less challenging in America than in Britain. London was backing down more regularly than was Washington, and the McKinley administration had strong nationalist credentials, protecting it against charges that it was too accommodating in its handling of disputes with Britain. Nonetheless, the U.S. government did have to convince both Congress and the public to support reconciliation with Britain—no easy task, as the Senate's rejection of the general arbitration treaty made clear. With the help of British support during the Spanish-American War and a press that generally came to embrace Anglo-American reconciliation, American elites were able to deploy a set of strategic arguments and generate a new narrative of friendship that succeeded in creating political conditions conducive to rapprochement. As in Britain, pluralism and political flexibility played an important role in facilitating strategic adjustment and building the political support necessary to sustain it.

COMPATIBLE SOCIAL ORDERS

From the founding of the United States until the late nineteenth century, relations between the United States and Britain suffered from the political tensions resulting from contrasting social orders—both within the United States and across the Atlantic. Within the United States, the cleavage between the North and South had a direct and deleterious impact on Anglo-American relations. The North and its dominant Federalist Party envisaged a progressive and urbanized America. Northerners looked to the British economy as a model for the republic's development. The South and its dominant Republican Party were more populist and agrarian in orientation. Southerners looked toward France as a model for the United States. These contrasting social perspectives led to a deep regional divide over whether to side with Britain or France during the Napoleonic Wars. The ferocity of partisan disagreement over this issue—exacerbated by French raids against U.S. commercial vessels crossing the Atlantic—prompted the pro-British Federalists in Congress to pass the Alien and Sedition Acts of 1798, an effort to silence pro-French Republicans. The War of 1812 produced a similarly sharp divide. The South pushed for war, animated by anti-British sentiment and the Royal Navy's interference with transatlantic commerce. Prompted by a progressive pacifism and its greater affinity for Britain, the North opposed the war.

The North and South also parted company on economic relations with Britain, although commercial concerns ran counter to the alignments favored by social proclivities. The South depended heavily on Britain as an export market for its raw materials, defended its reliance on slavery to produce agricultural products, and was a strong proponent of free trade. Meanwhile, the North favored tariffs to protect its infant industries from imported goods and supported an economy based on wage labor. The diverging economic interests of the two regions combined with their contrasting social orders to hamper the formation of a political coalition in favor of reconciliation with Britain. Well into the second half of the nineteenth century, relations between Britain and the United States were enmeshed in the tempestuous political and economic confrontation between America's North and South.

Social impediments to Anglo-American rapprochement also existed on the other side of the Atlantic. During the first half of the nineteenth century, anti-American sentiment ran strong among Britain's "official class," still comprised primarily of aristocrats resentful of America's rejection of British rule. In return, Americans, as noted above, saw Britain as an anachronistic monarchy with a rigid social hierarchy—and thus a country that stood in the way of the spread of republican liberty. Britain's tilt toward the Confederacy during the U.S. Civil War then heightened transatlantic tensions by further embedding Anglo-American relations in the North-South divide. Economic as well as geopolitical considerations shaped Britain's support for the Confederacy. Britain's commercial class was heavily dependent on imports from the southern states, while its strategists believed that disunion would remove the threat that America's rise would otherwise pose to British hegemony in the Western Hemisphere.

By the late nineteenth century, these social impediments to rapprochement had dissipated considerably on both sides of the Atlantic. In the United States, the Civil War and ongoing industrialization brought an end to the most acute social and political differences between North and South. Slavery was abolished. The South's preference for an agrarian America gave way to a country that was headed toward urbanization and wage labor. The North's factories had developed into globally competitive enterprises, prompting industrialists to line up with agricultural exporters to support free trade. Managing America's relationship with Britain was no longer an issue that pitted North against South.

In Britain, political liberalization, the growth of the middle class, and the rise of a financial community heavily invested in the United States diluted the anti-American proclivities of the traditional political class. Constituencies whose sentiments and economic interests favored Anglo-American reconciliation were ascendant. In this respect, the advance of democratization led to a "social peace" more than a "democratic peace." Universal suffrage neutralized a social structure that privileged those who preferred to sustain a rivalry with the United States. Americans responded accordingly, coming to see Britain as a country that shared its social and political proclivities—a change in perception that helped replace a sense of social estrangement with one of affinity. C. S. Campbell summarizes these changes as follows:

> The widening of the franchise by electoral reform bills had greatly altered the British social structure. No longer in 1900 was Britain the aristocratic and somewhat arrogant nation that had so irritated republicans like Thomas Jefferson and James Madison one hundred years earlier. And if a more democratic Britain had greater appeal for the ordinary American, the United States no longer seemed a subversive rabble-rousing republic to upper-class Britons.[117]

These changes in the respective social orders of Britain and the United States were not driving forces behind rapprochement. Had it not been for Britain's perceived sense of strategic over-commitment, a policy of appeasing the United States likely would not have been forthcoming. But these social changes did mean that as the two countries headed down the path of reconciliation for strategic reasons, social differences did not stand in the way. On the contrary, compatible social orders provided additional political momentum behind rapprochement.[118] By the time the need for accommodation of the United States emerged in Britain, and American politicians were confronted with the prospect of reciprocity, the social landscape had changed sufficiently to neutralize the principal societal impediments to reconciliation.

CULTURAL COMMONALITY

The United States and Britain enjoyed cultural commonality on several critical dimensions: race, ethnicity, religion, and language. As made clear in the preceding discussion of societal integration and changes in political narra-

[117] Campbell, *From Revolution to Rapprochement*, p. 203.

[118] The case of Britain and Germany provides an interesting contrast. Although moving toward parliamentary democracy, Germany in the early 1900s was still a quasi-absolutist state, its politics dominated by the landed aristocracy. Social incompatibility with Britain factored into growing geopolitical rivalry between the two countries. See Rock, *Why Peace Breaks Out*, pp. 84–89.

tive, cultural commonality and Anglo-Saxon heritage figured prominently in the evolving discourse that accompanied the onset of rapprochement.[119] Officials and opinion makers on both sides of the Atlantic regularly made references to the racial and linguistic connection between Britons and Americans, using terms such as "kin," "family," "cousin," and "natural ally." It was this sense of common heritage that both prompted and enabled political leaders and commentators alike to contend that war between the United States and Britain would constitute "fratricide" and have the "unnatural horror of a civil war." That such statements were repeatedly made in private as well as public suggests that these claims about the pacifying effects of cultural commonality were sincere, and not just intended to sway popular opinion. As C. S. Campbell concludes, "Enormously important was the widely held conception of a shared Anglo-Saxon race. . . . Without it there would have been no such rapprochement as occurred around 1900."[120]

Cultural affinity appears to have mattered most during the early and late stages of rapprochement. At the outset of the process, as Britain searched for adversaries that it could potentially convert into friends, it singled out the United States at least in part due to cultural commonality and the familiarity and comfort that it bred. It was strategic necessity that prompted London to attempt reconciliation with Washington. But Britain's latent sense of kinship with America helps explain why London worked hardest to befriend the United States rather than other challengers. In Stephen Rock's words, "For reasons of geography, race, and ideology, the United States, despite its long tradition of anglo-phobia, seemed better suited to this role than any other power."[121] The British, for example, did form an alliance with Japan at the turn of the century. But as will become evident in the examination of this case in the next chapter, cultural differences played a role in preventing that alliance from developing into a zone of stable peace.

Cultural commonality also mattered in the later stages of reconciliation, as British and American publics became more involved and as elites sought to generate a communal Anglo-Saxon identity to help solidify the political foundations of rapprochement. A shared heritage alone was insufficient to ensure peace between Britain and the United States—as successive decades of hostility made clear. But when strategic considerations compelled Britain

---

[119] For a thorough treatment of the issue, see Anderson, *Race and Rapprochement*.

[120] Campbell, *From Revolution to Rapprochement*, p. 204.

[121] Rock, *Appeasement in International Politics*, p. 35.

to pursue reconciliation—and political and social conditions helped clear the way—cultural commonality certainly made it easier for elites to propagate the notion that the two peoples enjoyed a special kinship. The sense of solidarity arising from compatible identities in turn helped Americans and Britons embrace the notion that war between them was becoming unthinkable.

Institutionalized restraint, compatible social orders, and cultural commonality were the key causal conditions enabling stable peace to break out between Britain and the United States. Strategic necessity prompted Britain's initial attempt to befriend the United States through unilateral accommodation. The presence of these three conditions then enabled reciprocal restraint, societal integration, and the generation of new narratives to proceed, ultimately turning implacable adversaries into lasting friends.

CHAPTER FOUR

RAPPROCHEMENT: SUPPORTING CASES

This chapter examines four additional cases of bilateral rapprochement. Two successful cases are explored: Norway and Sweden between 1905 and 1935, and Brazil and Argentina between 1979 and 1998. Two failed cases follow: Great Britain and Japan from 1902 to 1923, and the Soviet Union and China from 1949 to 1960.

The case of Norway and Sweden sheds important light on the causal relationship between democratization, institutionalized restraint, and stable peace. The practice of strategic restraint in Sweden advanced in step with the deepening of parliamentary democracy and the end of aristocratic rule. The resulting changes in Swedish foreign policy opened the door to rapprochement with Norway. The case of Argentina and Brazil then provides an important counterfactual, calling into question the relationship between strategic restraint and regime type. Brazil and Argentina took the crucial first steps down the path of rapprochement when both were governed by military dictatorships. Although stable peace was not consolidated until democracy took root in both countries during the 1980s, the case demonstrates that autocratic regimes are capable of practicing strategic restraint and making peace with rivals. Both the Norway/Sweden and Brazil/Argentina cases also demonstrate that political reconciliation precedes and clears the way for economic interdependence, not vice versa.

The failure of lasting rapprochement between Britain and Japan is particularly instructive when juxtaposed with the Anglo-American case. At roughly the same time that Britain successfully appeased the United States to help balance its resources and commitments in the Atlantic, it sought a similar strategic understanding with Japan in order to address naval deficiencies in the Pacific. In contrast with the Anglo-American case, however, the relationship between Britain and Japan never advanced beyond instrumental alliance. The absence of cultural commonality appears to have been a key impediment to lasting rapprochement between the two parties. The rise and demise of Sino-Soviet rapprochement illustrates the potential for autocracies to form very close strategic partnerships, but also underscores the vulnerability of such partnerships to rapid collapse. In the absence of institutionalized restraint and as the result of divergent social orders, sharp ideological cleavages emerged between the Soviet Union and China, ultimately leading to the return of geopolitical rivalry.

RAPPROCHEMENT BETWEEN NORWAY AND SWEDEN, 1905–1935

From the Union of Kalmar in 1397 until the Treaty of Kiel in 1814, Norway was the junior partner in a union with Denmark. As part of the settlement reached at the end of the Napoleonic Wars, Denmark, which had allied with France, ceded Norway to Sweden, which had allied with the victors. The Norwegians promptly revolted against their new overseers, triggering a Swedish invasion. The Norwegians were no match for their more populous and better armed neighbor, acquiescing after several weeks of fighting.[1] The terms of union were then worked out during the second half of 1814, and the Act of Union won royal assent in August 1815. Norway retained considerable autonomy over its domestic affairs, but Sweden controlled the union's foreign and defense policy and the Swedish monarch also became the king of Norway.

Throughout nine decades of union, Norway bristled at Swedish rule, regularly seeking to expand the scope of Norwegian autonomy. Societal integration between the two populations was minimal; the borderlands were sparsely populated and mountainous and there was little cross-border flow of either people or goods. Norway traded primarily with Britain, and Sweden with Germany. Norway maintained its own institutions of domestic governance, although they were generally under the control of Sweden. Norwegians did not have their own diplomatic corps and although they maintained their own army and navy, both were under the command of the Swedish king. Sweden's political dominance, coupled with the condescending attitudes of its elites

---

[1] At the time of union, Norway's population was 885,000, while that of Sweden was 2.3 million. See Raymond Lindgren, *Norway-Sweden: Union, Disunion, and Scandinavian Integration* (Princeton, NJ: Center for Research on World Political Institutions, 1979), p. 18.

and media toward Norwegians, ensured that anti-Swedish sentiment generally prevailed among Norway's public and its press.[2]

The union came apart in 1905. Norway unilaterally declared its dissolution
following a dispute over Norway's right to maintain its own consular representation abroad. In response, the Swedish government prepared to invade
Norway. Sweden had a pronounced military advantage—its navy was twice
the size of Norway's and its army, four times larger. The ministers of marine
and war argued in favor of an immediate attack to restore the union. Dissolution, they contended, threatened Swedish security by exposing its west
coast and by offering Russia a potential invasion route through Norway.[3] Despite these threats, as well as indignation over Norway's affront to Sweden
and its monarch, the government ultimately decided against war, dissuaded
by both the prospective costs of sustaining the union by force and opposition
to a Swedish invasion from other European powers.[4] In light of mounting
Anglo-German rivalry and shifting alliances in Europe, the major powers did
not welcome the prospect of the outbreak of war in Scandinavia. Faced with
the material costs of conflict as well as strong outside opposition, the Swedes
chose to stand down and instead seek a consensual resolution of Norway's
secession from the union.

Over the course of the next three decades, stable peace broke out between
Norway and Sweden. Democratization in Sweden and the accompanying institutionalization of strategic restraint were the key factors enabling the two
adversaries to become lasting friends. Political reform also prompted a convergence in the social orders of the two states, clearing the way for their cultural commonality to help serve as a foundation for stable peace.

How Peace Broke Out

Sweden's decision to accept Norway's secession from the union was the opening gambit—the initial act of unilateral accommodation—that was to develop into the practice of reciprocal restraint and ultimately lead to the onset
of lasting rapprochement. Sweden made its acceptance of Norwegian independence contingent upon a number of provisions. Norway had to renounce

[2] Lindgren, *Norway-Sweden*, pp. 24–39.
[3] Rikard Bengtsson, *Trust, Threat, and Stable Peace: Swedish Great Power Perceptions 1905–1939* (Lund, Sweden: Lund University Department of Political Science, 2000), p. 70.
[4] Lindgren, *Norway-Sweden*, pp. 72, 132, 143.

its abrogation of the union and instead enter into negotiations and hold a plebiscite; both conditions were meant to ensure that dissolution be a product of mutual consent rather than unilateral action. Sweden also demanded that Norway dismantle the forts along their common border and agree to establish a neutral zone between the two countries.

Despite war scares and partial mobilization by both parties as the negotiations proceeded, Norway eventually accepted Sweden's terms.[5] An initial act of unilateral accommodation by Sweden was reciprocated with costly concessions by Norway. Sweden had indicated its benign intent by agreeing to Norway's secession. Norway sent an equally important signal of benign intent by agreeing to begin the demilitarization of its border with Sweden. The two parties had not only averted war, but also taken initial steps toward dampening geopolitical rivalry.

The ensuing decade is best characterized as a period of cold and wary peace rather than deepening reconciliation. Both countries adhered to the agreement on disunion. Several years later, they turned to arbitration to resolve peacefully a lingering territorial dispute over several small islands. Nonetheless, the benign intent demonstrated by these mutual concessions did not overcome residual suspicion of one another's broader motivation. Norway negotiated a great-power treaty in 1906–1907 to guarantee its territorial integrity, demonstrating a lack of confidence in peace with Sweden. Norway maintained war plans to defend itself against Sweden—and Sweden maintained war plans against Norway, including ones envisaging offensive scenarios. The Swedish military also continued to produce reconnaissance reports on Norwegian fortifications and military infrastructure.[6] Overt geopolitical competition was in abeyance, but mutual suspicion remained.

The onset of World War I was the triggering event that enabled Norway and Sweden to move beyond cold peace to lasting rapprochement. The outbreak of great-power war prompted the two countries to issue a joint declaration of neutrality in August 1914. In addition to proclaiming their neutral status, the agreement stated that "the two Governments have exchanged binding assurances, with a view to precluding the possibility that the condition of war in Europe might lead to hostile measures being taken by either

---

[5] For a detailed discussion of the negotiations, see Lindgren, *Norway-Sweden*, pp. 145–197.

[6] Magnus Ericson, *A Realist Stable Peace: Power, Threat, and the Development of a Shared Norwegian-Swedish Democratic Security Identity, 1905–1940* (Lund, Sweden: Lund University Department of Political Science, 2000), pp. 85–96; Lindgren, *Norway-Sweden*, pp. 214–227.

country against the other." Eight days after this agreement was greeted with approval in both parliaments, a memorial stone for Oscar I, king of the union in the middle of the 1800s, was placed on the Norwegian-Swedish border. The inscription quoted the monarch: "Hereafter is war between the Scandinavian brothers impossible."[7]

King Oscar's declaration had been premature when declared in the nineteenth century, but it became markedly less so over the course of World War I. During the war, regular meetings took place among Norwegian, Swedish, and Danish ministers to coordinate policies and protect neutrality. The three countries fashioned trade agreements to alleviate shortages of food and other goods. According to Eric Cyril Bellquist and Waldemar Westergaard, "Perhaps the most striking expression of Scandinavian solidarity during the war was given by the meetings held by the rulers of the three Northern countries and their ministers. Altogether, ten conferences were held under the auspices of the three foreign offices, two under the naval ministries, two under the ministries of finance, three under the portfolios of justice, over a dozen under the departments of public works and communications, and many others."[8] The Nordic Inter-Parliamentary Union, a body established in the late nineteenth century as a regional branch of the European Inter-Parliamentary Union, served as a forum for forging a common position on the postwar settlement—one that supported the establishment of the League of Nations.[9] And Norway and Sweden signed a joint arbitration treaty after the end of the war, committing to the settlement of all disputes through negotiation.

The concrete acts of reciprocal restraint and the advances in societal integration that took place during World War I played a key role in facilitating the onset of rapprochement. Regular contact between Norwegian and Swedish elites, and joint efforts to coordinate foreign policy and fashion trade agreements to address the shortages caused by the war, contributed to a growing sense of congruent interest. An assessment produced by the Norwegian military reveals the cumulative effects of wartime cooperation on relations with Sweden:

[7] Lindgren, *Norway-Sweden*, p. 238.

[8] Eric Cyril Bellquist and Waldemar Westergaard, "Inter-Scandinavian Cooperation," in "Supplement: Contemporary Problems of International Relations: Regional Groupings in Modern Europe," *Annals of the American Academy of Political and Social Science*, vol. 168, American Policy in the Pacific (July 1933), pp. 186–187.

[9] On the Nordic Inter-Parliamentary Union, see Bellquist and Westergaard, "Inter-Scandinavian Cooperation," pp. 183–184.

The outcome of the World War has changed our war-political situation in a number of important regards. Our relationship with Sweden is better than ever. Through friendly negotiations have conflictual matters . . . been removed. Any imminent causes for conflict cannot be discerned at present. . . . Concerning Sweden, the Norwegian policy will probably be geared towards further improving the present good relationship. There are reasons to believe this is also the Swedish intention.[10]

The experience of wartime cooperation and societal integration encouraged the two countries to begin attributing to each other benign character, enabling lingering suspicion to give way to a nascent sense of trust during the early 1920s. Norway cancelled its great-power integrity treaty in 1924, a bold and overt signal that it no longer feared Swedish aggression. During the second half of the 1920s, a consensus emerged among Norwegian elites that war with Sweden, although not out of the question, was of "very small likelihood."[11] By the end of the decade, prominent voices called for major reductions in defense spending. One influential individual justified such reductions on the grounds that Sweden no longer posed a threat to Norwegian territory: "Whatever the military may say . . . there is no denying that this is an extraordinarily favorable time for reduction of the defense budget. Our strategic situation has undergone a considerable change for the better, due to the favorable—and I will venture to say, permanently favorable—relations achieved with the nation that we formerly armed ourselves against."[12]

By the mid-1930s, the Norwegian military had effectively precluded the possibility of conflict with Sweden. Magnus Ericson's review of Norwegian planning documents from the period finds that "they do not refer to Sweden as a threat of any degree of probability" and that "Sweden does not figure as a potential aggressor."[13] On the Swedish side, the last offensive war plan against Norway was drafted in 1917. After 1924, military planners no longer entertained the prospect of conflict with Norway. Planning documents from the early 1930s treat Norway as "a state that poses no threat, neither presently nor in the foreseeable future."[14] In a letter concerning road construction

[10] Ericson, *A Realist Stable Peace*, p. 128.

[11] Ericson, *A Realist Stable Peace*, p. 91.

[12] David G. Thompson, *The Norwegian Armed Forces and Defense Policy, 1905–1955,* Scandinavian Studies, vol. 11 (Lewiston, NY: Edwin Mellen Press, 2004), p. 60

[13] Ericson, *A Realist Stable Peace*, pp. 95–96.

[14] Ericson, *A Realist Stable Peace*, p. 89.

and its impact on the movement of forces, a Swedish army captain wrote to his Norwegian counterpart in 1935, "I do not think I have to say that we are not considering the possibility of a Norwegian enemy."[15]

By the early 1930s, Norway and Sweden enjoyed stable peace. Elite and public discourse in both countries readily embraced the notion that war between them was "unthinkable."[16] So too did references to a distinct Nordic community, based on shared language, culture, and history become commonplace. As Europe's geopolitical environment deteriorated over the course of the decade, rapprochement between Norway and Sweden provided a foundation for significant advances in strategic cooperation. Regular talks between the military staffs of Norway and Sweden began in 1934. Although the two countries made no binding alliance commitments during the 1930s, military cooperation and the sharing of intelligence intensified as Nazi Germany grew more threatening. Stable peace between Norway and Sweden began to assume a taken-for-granted quality.

Societal integration—direct contact between Norwegians and Swedes as well as flows of trade—did increase over the period in question, helping to consolidate stable peace. However, growing personal and commercial ties were the product more than the cause of rapprochement; commercial interests took advantage of, rather than orchestrated, reconciliation and growing strategic cooperation. Mail, telegraphic correspondence, and trade between the two countries all rose from the late 1800s onward. Nonetheless, relative economic interdependence actually declined during the early 1900s because both Norway and Sweden were diversifying their external commerce and rapidly developing trade links to Europe's major powers. Furthermore, periods of intensifying economic integration—such as during World War I—were the product of wartime efforts to alleviate shortages, not secular growth in interdependence. As Magnus Ericson concludes, "If anything, economic interaction follows political reality and expediencies rather than the opposite."[17]

Why Peace Broke Out

The advance of rapprochement between Norway and Sweden correlates with the onset of liberal democracy in both countries. Throughout the 1800s and early 1900s, Norway's democratic development ran well ahead of Sweden's.

---

[15] Ericson, *A Realist Stable Peace*, p. 84.

[16] Ericson, *A Realist Stable Peace*, chapter 5.

[17] Ericson, *A Realist Stable Peace*, p. 125.

Norway effectively abolished its aristocracy in the early 1800s; thereafter, political power was shared among peasants, the growing middle class, and the bureaucracy. Political reforms in the late nineteenth century led to universal male suffrage and parliamentary control of the cabinet. Meanwhile, Sweden's political system remained dominated by the monarchy and the landed nobility throughout the nineteenth century and into the twentieth. As a consequence, Swedish elites felt directly threatened by Norway's liberal order. Several rounds of political reform did occur in Sweden in the late 1800s. But at the time of disunion, Sweden was one of Europe's least democratic countries. It was not until the reforms adopted between 1917 and 1921 that Sweden embraced universal suffrage and consolidated parliament's control of the cabinet and influence over foreign policy. From this perspective, the onset of stable peace coincides closely with the onset of liberal democracy in Sweden.

The causal connection between democracy and stable peace stemmed primarily from the changes in foreign policy and social order produced by democratization, not from the two parties' mutual recognition of each other's democratic character. Political reform institutionalized strategic restraint and the practice of self-binding; the new course in Swedish foreign policy stemmed in no small part from parliamentary checks on the power of the monarchy and the military. Political change also helped resolve the incompatibilities in social order that had long contributed to estrangement between Norway and Sweden. After the completion of democratization in Sweden and the dismantling of aristocratic rule, Norway no longer posed a threat to Sweden's social order. Finally, political reform cleared the way for societal integration, promoting transparency and increasing contact and trade, both of which facilitated the mutual attribution of benign character.

These causal connections between political reform and the onset of stable peace took the following discrete forms. Throughout the period of union, Norway's liberal proclivities and hostility toward nobility were at odds with Sweden's aristocratic preferences. In Sweden, the monarchy allied with the aristocracy and the clergy to resist the empowerment of farmers, the middle class, and professionals—the triumvirate that had come to dominate Norway's political system. From 1815 through the dissolution of the union, these social incompatibilities fueled political tensions, with Swedish elites viewing Norwegian resistance as a challenge to not just Swedish rule, but also the power and stability of the country's ruling class. There was very little societal contact between Norwegians and Swedes, due in part to Sweden's fear that the spread of landholding and political rights to its peasantry would imperil the country's conservative political order. In urging that Sweden put down with force Norway's unilateral declaration of independence in 1905, the nobility and military were seeking to preserve their political dominance, not just union with Norway.[18]

It was no accident that the Swedish government that decided against invasion was the country's first government to be controlled by the Liberal Party, which helped counter the pro-war inclinations of the aristocracy and military. To be sure, conservatives soon reasserted their control over the cabinet. But the advance of political reforms meant that they no longer had unchecked control over foreign policy. Although Sweden had a constitution and a parliament during the 1800s, the cabinet was selected by the king and not subject to parliamentary approval. The monarch was the commander-in-chief of the army and navy, and along with his military advisers and the nobility, exercised near absolute power, especially on matters of foreign policy.[19] As Rikard Bengtsson observes, King Oscar II, who assumed the throne in 1872, "considered the foreign policy of the union very much his own domain."[20]

Beginning in 1905, however, the cabinet became a parliamentary body, giving both the cabinet and parliament more control over foreign policy. As Raymond Lindgren notes, "1905 was a year of great moment for Sweden, for she lost the Union with Norway but gained for herself a parliamentary system of government."[21] When the Liberals again took power in 1911, the prime minister for the first time in Swedish history appointed a civilian as minister for defense, increasing institutional constraints on the military's control over security matters. Reforms adopted between 1919 and 1921 further strengthened parliamentary oversight of foreign and defense policy, effectively excluding the king and royal family from decision making.[22] Sweden's embrace of institutionalized restraint on foreign policy thus coincided with the first moves toward stable peace. Reconciliation and the advance of rap-

---

[18] Raymond Lindgren, "Nineteenth Century Norway and Sweden: A Contrast in Social Structures," in Karl Deutsch, unpublished manuscript, pp. 531–536

[19] Lindgren, *Norway-Sweden*, p. 21; Ericson, *A Realist Stable Peace*, pp. 107–108.

[20] Bengtsson, *Trust, Threat, and Stable Peace*, p. 80. See also pp. 68–69.

[21] Lindgren, "Nineteenth Century Norway and Sweden," pp. 543–544. Lindgren notes that parliamentary reforms in 1885 gave the parliament some say over foreign policy, but that the cabinet as a whole was not subject to parliamentary approval until 1905.

[22] Bengtsson, *Trust, Threat, and Stable Peace*, p. 73.

prochement then progressed in step with democratization and the extension of parliamentary control over security policy. The growing political strength of Liberals and Social Democrats in parliament also played an important role in ensuring that the politics of accommodation prevailed against conservative voices which continued to insist that reconciliation with Norway humiliated the monarchy and jeopardized Sweden's political stability.

Although World War I ultimately deepened Swedish ties to Norway, the legacy of social incompatibilities meant that the war temporarily opened up the prospect of a new geopolitical rift. Some in Sweden's traditional ruling class argued in favor of alliance with Germany, a country they saw as defending Europe's aristocratic heritage against liberal change.[23] Had they prevailed, a break with Norway would have been inevitable, especially in light of Norway's long-standing alignment with Britain. More centrist voices carried the day, however, enabling Sweden and Norway to pursue together a policy of neutrality. Furthermore, Germany's defeat was viewed from Stockholm as a victory for liberal democracy, providing impetus for the completion of Sweden's political reform and the convergence of its social order with that of Norway.[24] With their foreign policies and their social orders finally in alignment, Norway and Sweden were coming to see one another as benign polities; the process of reconciliation that had begun in 1905 finally culminated in stable peace.

Along with institutionalized restraint and social compatibility, the third condition making rapprochement possible was cultural commonality. Norwegians and Swedes shared the same Lutheran religion, their languages were closely related, and they had long seen themselves as part of a common Nordic/Scandinavian community. When Johan Caspar Herman Wedel-Jarlsberg, a prominent Norwegian politician, argued in favor of union with Sweden in 1814, he based his position on "grounds of propinquity" as well as on "common culture, common religion, common race . . . common old speech."[25] Although these commonalities were for many centuries not powerful enough to

---

[23] The prospect of Sweden's alignment with Germany was sufficiently credible to influence Britain's preference that Norway remain neutral instead of allying with the Triple Entente. The calculation in London was that should Sweden side with Germany and Norway with the Triple Entente, Norway might well find itself exposed to attack, and "not even the Royal Navy could protect Norway from invasion if Sweden sided with Germany." Thompson, *The Norwegian Armed Forces and Defense Policy*, p. 46.

[24] Bengtsson, *Trust, Threat, and Stable Peace*, pp. 93–96, 148.

[25] Lindgren, *Norway-Sweden*, pp. 17–18.

override geopolitical rivalry, they did facilitate the onset of rapprochement once reconciliation was under way. In 1919, the Norden Association was founded "for the promotion of common concepts of culture among the northern peoples."[26] During the 1930s and especially after World War II, references to Nordic kinship and brotherhood became a fixture of political discourse. The generation of this narrative and the salience given to cultural commonality helped lay the groundwork for the Nordic security community that emerged after 1945.

RAPPROCHEMENT BETWEEN BRAZIL AND ARGENTINA, 1979–1998

Rivalry and war between Argentina and Brazil date back to colonial-era contests over territory and trade. The last major war between the two countries occurred in the 1820s, but geopolitical competition continued long thereafter. Despite forming an alliance against Paraguay in a conflict that lasted from 1865 to 1870, Argentina and Brazil remained wary antagonists throughout the balance of the nineteenth and most of the twentieth centuries. They took opposite sides in the Chaco War—a conflict pitting Bolivia against Paraguay between 1932 and 1935—and in World War II. During the early decades of the Cold War, Brazil tended to cast itself as a first-world country in alignment with the United States, making it a proxy for U.S. imperialism in the eyes of Argentines. Tensions percolated over a host of issues, including influence in the buffer states of Bolivia, Paraguay, and Uruguay, use of the Parana River for hydroelectric generation, and the development of nuclear technology. As Joao Resende-Santos notes, "from World War II to the 1970s, Brazil and Argentina continually viewed each other as enemies."[27] They maintained war plans against each other. Brazil concentrated troops in its southern sector near the border, while Buenos Aires pursued a policy of "empty provinces" intended to deny Brazil military targets and transportation infrastructure in the north of Argentina. As David Pion-Berlin observes, "Mutual

---

[26] Paul Dolan, "The Nordic Council," *Western Political Quarterly* 12, no. 2 (June 1959): 512. See also Bellquist and Westergaard, "Inter-Scandinavian Cooperation."

[27] Joao Resende-Santos, "The Origins of Security Cooperation in the Southern Cone," *Latin American Politics and Society* 44, no. 4 (Winter 2002): 94. See also Jack Child, *Geopolitics and Conflict in South America: Quarrels Among Neighbors* (New York: Praeger, 1985), pp. 98–104.

distrust was aggravated by a lack of transparency in diplomatic relations, characterized by a complete absence of informational exchanges, reciprocal visitation, or controls."[28]

Beginning in the late 1970s, however, Argentina and Brazil launched a process of mutual accommodation and reconciliation that was to lead to rapprochement. By the early 1990s, the two countries had not only brought to an end their long-standing geopolitical rivalry, but also founded Mercosur, a body aimed at facilitating economic integration throughout their region. Notably, they embarked down the path toward stable peace when they were both ruled by military juntas, making clear that even states that do not embrace institutionalized restraint at home may nonetheless practice strategic restraint in the conduct of their foreign policy. The case of rapprochement between Argentina and Brazil also demonstrates clearly that political reconciliation clears the way for, rather than follows from, societal integration and economic interdependence.

How Peace Broke Out

The key breakthrough in relations between Argentina and Brazil occurred in 1979–1980. The two parties were motivated by somewhat different concerns. Argentina's effort to befriend Brazil was animated by its deteriorating strategic environment. Three concurrent developments during the second half of the 1970s had an adverse impact on Argentina's security. A dispute with Chile over the Beagle Channel came to a head, with both sides mobilizing for war late in 1978. Tensions with major Western powers were worsening. Relations with Britain grew increasingly strained over competing claims to the Falkland Islands, while ties to the United States were eroding due to Washington's reactions to the military government's violations of human rights. Finally, Buenos Aires was worried about Brazil's growing power and regional ambition, a concern heightened by the widening economic gap between the two countries as well as Brazil's purchase of a nuclear fuel cycle from Germany in 1975. Argentina's tensions with Chile further tested its already strained relations with Brazil, in part due to Buenos Aires' decision to block commercial traffic heading from Brazil to Chile.

---

[28] David Pion-Berlin, "Will Soldiers Follow? Economic Integration and Regional Security in the Southern Cone," *Journal of Interamerican Studies and World Affairs* 42, no. 1 (Spring 2000): 45.

Facing escalating tensions with Chile and Brazil and worsening relations with Britain and the United States, Argentina turned to reconciliation with Brazil as the best means of alleviating its strategic predicament. As Resende-Santos observes, "Argentina found itself encircled by its most powerful enemies. Accommodating Brazil was a strategic necessity, both because Argentina simply could not hope to confront both rivals simultaneously and because it could not be certain of Brazil's reaction if war broke out over the Beagle Channel."[29]

Brazil's readiness to respond in kind to Argentina's initial acts of accommodation was the product primarily of domestic circumstance, not external threat. Over the course of the 1970s, Brazil's internal security services had grown increasingly autonomous and repressive. The power of the intelligence and security apparatus not only weakened the relative influence of the military, but also divided it by triggering struggles between hardliners and moderates. According to Alfred Stepan, "the intelligence system became more autonomous than in any other modern authoritarian regime in Latin America."[30]

In order to reassert the military's control over the government and to weaken extremist factions within the officer corps, General Ernesto Geisel, who was president from 1974 to 1979, and General Golbery do Couto e Silva, one of his chief advisers, pursued a policy of *abertura* (opening) during the late 1970s. Liberalizing the political system and working with rather than suppressing civil society were intended to undermine the authority of the security apparatus and its backers in the military. As Resende-Santos observes, "Gradual political opening, including restoring press and civic freedoms, was intended to reduce domestic tensions, thereby making it easier both to expose the abuses of extremist organs and to undercut their *raison d'etre*."[31] *Abertura* would also help reclaim the support of the middle and upper classes, both of which had become reluctant to collaborate with the government as repression intensified.[32] To these ends, Geisel allowed civic associations, such as neighborhood and workers' organizations, to reenter the political arena, at-

---

[29] Resende-Santos, "The Origins of Security Cooperation," p. 99.

[30] Alfred Stepan, *Rethinking Military Politics: Brazil and the Southern Cone* (Princeton, NJ: Princeton University Press, 1988), p. 13. See also chapters 2 and 3.

[31] Resende-Santos, "The Origins of Security Cooperation," pp. 101–102

[32] Maria Helena Moreira Alves, *State and Opposition in Military Brazil* (Austin: University of Texas Press, 1985), pp. 168–173.

tempted to curb the use of torture against political prisoners, and repealed Institutional Act No. 5, which had eliminated many civil liberties.[33]

Brazil's pursuit of reconciliation with Argentina was a direct consequence of *abertura*; opening at home required an opening abroad. Protracted rivalry between Brazil and its neighbor stood in the way of domestic liberalization; a heightened sense of external threat strengthened hardliners and their case for repressive rule. In contrast, a more benign security environment would help give moderates the upper hand, providing them the breathing room to pursue domestic reform. According to Resende-Santos, "the moderates pursued a dual strategy of liberalization at home and détente abroad to limit the corrosive influence of extremist forces, specifically the internal security and intelligence apparatus lodged inside the military and the state."[34] To help implement his foreign policy of "responsible pragmatism," Geisel appointed moderates to key positions throughout the government. He also selected as foreign minister a former ambassador to Argentina (Antonio Azeredo da Silveira) who was known for his particularly good relations with decision makers in Buenos Aires.

The external threats facing Argentina and the internal threats facing Brazil—these were the conditions that prompted the mutual acts of accommodation that would culminate in rapprochement. Argentina made the first explicit move by approving—after years of refusing to do so—Brazil's plans to generate electricity by building the Itaipu Dam on the Parana River. A few months after the signing of the Corpus-Itaipu Agreement in October 1979, Brazil's new president, General João Baptista de Oliveira Figueiredo, reciprocated by visiting Argentina—the first visit by a Brazilian leader since 1935. That Figueiredo was continuing Geisel's policy of *abertura* made clear that reconciliation would outlast a change in leadership. A few months later, the Argentine president, General Jorge Rafael Videla, made a return visit to Brazil. Unilateral acts of accommodation were giving way to reciprocal restraint. Negotiations produced bilateral accords committing both sides to the peaceful use of nuclear energy, cooperation in developing nuclear technology, joint production of conventional armaments, and enhanced trade, cultural contacts, and scientific exchanges. According to Videla, "our agreement refutes forever the legend that Argentina and Brazil are engaged in a nuclear arms

[33] Scott Mainwaring, "The Transition to Democracy in Brazil," *Journal of Interamerican Studies and World Affairs* 28, no. 1 (Spring 1986): 155.
[34] Resende-Santos, "The Origins of Security Cooperation," p. 100.

race and opens perspectives for concrete steps in a vast area of common interest."[35]

Although off to a good start, reconciliation between Argentina and Brazil slowed during the first half of the 1980s as both countries focused on other issues—domestic political change, economic crisis, and the Falklands War. The Brazilian government was particularly mindful of the need to move slowly, fearful that extremists would take advantage of domestic reform and accommodation of Argentina to reassert their control. Right-wing efforts to destabilize the government mounted between 1979 and 1981, a direct response to *abertura* and the "fatal threat" it posed "to the position and interests of the hardliners and the internal security apparatus."[36] In this sense, the moderates maneuvered carefully to ensure that the politics of accommodation prevailed against the politics of humiliation. As Resende-Santos notes, "aside from the need to retain moderate support, the fear of provoking hardliner backlash was the major constraint on domestic and foreign policy. . . . Geisel always had to placate *duros* [hardliners] with each advance of *abertura*. . . . Opposition from hardliners determined the limits of opening domestically and externally."[37]

The 1982 Falklands War initially distracted Argentina from its effort to improve relations with Brazil. But the conflict ultimately furthered reconciliation between the two countries. Argentina's war with Britain and the strains it caused in its relations with the United States prompted Buenos Aires to pursue an even more accommodating stance with its neighbors, especially Brazil. Although Brasilia was not about to jeopardize its relations with Europe and the United States by allying with Argentina, Brazil was careful to take steps to keep alive the recent improvement in its ties with Argentina. Brazil supported Argentine sovereignty over the islands, represented Argentina's diplomatic interests in London, facilitated talks to resolve the conflict, granted short-term loans to Argentina during the crisis, and put restrictions on landing rights for British aircraft on their way to the Falklands. According to Wayne Selcher, "Brazil's position, both during the conflict and afterwards, was well-received by the Argentines despite Brazil's lack of official fervor and its desire to safeguard relations with Great Britain."[38]

Argentina and Brazil redoubled efforts to advance reconciliation during

[35] Juan de Onis, "Argentina and Brazil in New Ties," *New York Times*, May 18, 1980.
[36] Resende-Santos, "The Origins of Security Cooperation," p. 109.
[37] Resende-Santos, "The Origins of Security Cooperation," pp. 102–103, 108–109.
[38] Wayne A. Selcher, "Brazilian-Argentine Relations in the 1980s: From Wary Rivalry to

the second half of the 1980s, by which time both countries had made the transition to democratic rule (Argentina in 1983, Brazil in 1985). Whereas the presidents of Brazil and Argentina met only three times and signed four agreements between 1976 and 1982, during 1985–1986, they met eight times and signed thirty-one agreements.[39] In 1985, Brazilian president José Sarney and Argentine president Raul Alfonsin signed the "Declaration of Iguazu," which committed both sides to annual presidential visits and codified deepening cooperation on nuclear issues, including the mutual renunciation of nuclear programs with military applications. Of particular importance were working groups on nuclear technology and agreements to allow each party unfettered access to the other's nuclear sites. Argentina announced in 1988 that it had visited all Brazilian nuclear facilities not already under international supervision.[40]

Economic and societal integration remained limited through the 1980s, but cooperation among nuclear scientists and inspectors played a significant role in building confidence among elites and publics alike that discrete acts of accommodation were having a cumulative effect, opening up the prospect of lasting rapprochement. Disclosing information about nuclear facilities and sharing the same technology upon which geopolitical rivalry had previously been based helped Argentines and Brazilians attribute to each other benign motivations, not just benign intent with respect to individual concessions. Arie Kacowicz contends that nuclear cooperation was central to eliciting public support for rapprochement:

> The efforts that paved the way for government action in the nuclear regime were marked by a number of discussions and consultations between Argentine and Brazilian scientists under the aegis of the societies of physicists of both countries. These exchanges helped bring the subject to public attention through newspaper stories, and this increased attention facilitated later actions of the two governments, especially after the return of democracy.[41]

Friendly Competition," *Journal of Interamerican Studies and World Affairs* 27, no. 2 (Summer 1985): 30.

[39] Arturo C. Sotomayor Velazquez, "Civil-Military Affairs and Security Institutions in the Southern Cone: The Sources of Argentine-Brazilian Nuclear Cooperation," *Latin American Politics and Society* 46, no. 4 (Winter 2004): 35.

[40] Resende-Santos, "The Origins of Security Cooperation," pp. 116–118.

[41] Arie Kacowicz, "Stable Peace in South America: The ABC Triangle 1979–1999," in Arie Kacowicz, et al., eds., *Stable Peace Among Nations*, p. 213.

Over the course of the 1980s, reciprocal restraint thus enabled Brazil and Argentina to step away from geopolitical rivalry; the security dilemma was in suspension and the two countries enjoyed a newfound, albeit watchful, amity. Over the course of the 1990s, societal integration and the generation of new narratives then followed, substantially advancing the onset of rapprochement. By the end of the decade, the security dilemma was not just in suspension, but, as described below, was working in reverse, ultimately enabling Argentina and Brazil to enjoy the trust and solidarity that are the hallmarks of stable peace. "Trust," Kacowicz writes, "has been not only a condition for consolidating stable peace but also a consequence of its establishment."[42] Brazil was still the region's preponderant state, but Argentina and South America's smaller countries no longer sought to balance against it. Rather, changes in mutual perceptions or "cognitive structures" meant that Brazilian power had taken on a benign and magnetic quality, serving as the core of a broadening project of regional integration.[43]

In 1990, the two parties formalized their nuclear agreements, creating an organization to monitor all nuclear activities and signing a revised version of the Treaty of Tlatelolco, a pact banning nuclear weapons from Latin America and the Caribbean.[44] Mercosur was launched the following year, a trade pact committing Brazil, Argentina, Uruguay, and Paraguay to establish a common market by the end of 1994. Giving impetus to the push for economic integration in the Southern Cone were the advancing projects of regionalism elsewhere—NAFTA, the EU, and APEC. Mercosur would ensure that South America would enjoy the benefits of economic regionalism on offer in North America, Europe, and the Asia Pacific.

Deepening levels of military cooperation followed soon after the launching of Mercosur. As Etel Solingen notes, "the leap in economic liberalization was matched by a leap in bilateral cooperation."[45] In 1996, the Brazilian and Argentine armies held joint maneuvers, the first time that Brazilian troops had been on Argentine territory since the two countries were allies in a war against Paraguay in the 1860s. The following year, Brazil and Argentina signed a

---

[42] Kacowicz, "Stable Peace in South America," p. 216.

[43] Andrew Hurrell, "An Emerging Security Community in South America?" in Adler and Barnett, *Security Communities,* pp. 252–253.

[44] For an overview of the evolution of nuclear cooperation and establishment of the Brazilian-Argentine Agency for Accounting and Control of Nuclear Materials (ABACC), see http://www.abacc.org/engl/abacc/abacc_history.htm.

[45] Solingen, *Regional Orders at Century's Dawn,* p. 154.

memorandum of understanding on measures to enhance mutual security. Chiefs of staff agreed to meet twice a year as part of a broadening program of military-to-military contacts. Also in 1997, Operation Southern Cross brought together 2,300 troops from Argentina, Brazil, and Uruguay "to improve cooperation, trust, and friendship between the participants, and develop the capacity to plan and execute combined operations."[46] Andrew Hurrell observes that the dramatic increase in personal contacts played an important role in consolidating rapprochement: "the institutionalization of visits, exchanges by presidents and officials was leading to a broader 'habit of communication.'"[47]

Not only had Brazil and Argentina arrived at rapprochement, but nascent aspects of security community, such as the institutionalization of order-producing rules and peacetime military cooperation, were beginning to emerge. Political reconciliation cleared the way for societal integration, which in turn led to deeper levels of economic and strategic cooperation. The progress has continued more recently. In 2008, Brazil and Argentina exchanged presidential visits, and Brazil took the lead in founding a regional defense union—the South American Defense Council—an effort to formalize the security community that has gradually been evolving around the strategic core of Brazil and Argentina.[48]

Existing studies of rapprochement between Brazil and Argentina have yet to specify with documentary evidence the precise period during which the prospect of war between the two parties was effectively eliminated. Kacowicz contends that the possibility of armed conflict informed military plans on both sides "until the early 1980s," suggesting that the relationship began to be demilitarized soon after reconciliation began.[49] It was not until the end of the 1980s, however, that military spending began to decline markedly, with defense budgets in Argentina and Brazil falling off sharply during the early 1990s.[50] Hurrell contends that demilitarization awaited the more institutionalized forms of cooperation that emerged during the first half of the 1990s.

[46] Pion-Berlin, "Will Soldiers Follow?" p. 48.
[47] Hurrell, "An Emerging Security Community in South America?" p. 246.
[48] See "The South American Defense Council, UNASUR, the Latin American Military and the Region's Political Process," Council on Hemispheric Affairs, available at http://www.coha.org/2008/10/the-south-american-defense-council-unasur-the-latin-american-military-and-the-region%E2%80%99s-political-process/.
[49] Kacowicz, "Stable Peace in South America," p. 203.
[50] SIPRI Yearbook, 1995, p. 445; Sotomayor Velazquez, "Civil-Military Affairs and Security Institutions in the Southern Cone, p. 44.

By that time, he observes, the border was no longer fortified, Brazil had redeployed its troops away from the south, and Argentina had abandoned its "empty provinces" strategy, instead investing in the trans-border infrastructure that would help Mercosur thrive.[51] Pion-Berlin dates the onset of stable peace slightly later, writing that by the second half of the 1990s, "Brazil no longer considers its southern neighbor a military threat. The conflicts that may have pitted it against Argentina in the past have now been laid to rest."[52] This view is consistent with Mercosur's own—the grouping declared itself a zone of peace in 1998. A conservative assessment would thus identify the mid-1990s as the period during which stable peace was consolidated and relations between Argentina and Brazil conclusively demilitarized.

In parallel with the cases of rapprochement between Britain and the United States and between Norway and Sweden, societal interaction followed from, rather than preceded, the onset of rapprochement between Argentina and Brazil; political reconciliation cleared the way for the expansion of economic ties, not vice versa. Despite the joint commitments to regional integration secured in 1979–1980, interdependence between the two countries actually declined during the first half of the 1980s, due largely to the debt crises and deteriorating economic conditions that plagued the region.[53] Bilateral efforts to promote economic integration advanced during the second half of the 1980s, but the results were "meager, even insignificant."[54] Furthermore, apart from the scientific exchanges on nuclear issues, societal contact remained limited throughout the decade. The absence of more interaction between the two societies did not, however, stand in the way of rapprochement; the early steps toward reconciliation taken in 1979 began a process that was sustained throughout the 1980s. As Hurrell comments, "Deutsch's emphasis on social transactions in such fields as trade, migration, tourism, or cultural exchanges does not appear relevant in this case."[55]

Matters changed considerably during the 1990s, when the launching of Mercosur and other institutionalized forms of cooperation led to a sharp increase in interdependence and societal integration. At this point, private groups benefiting from growing trade did make their interests felt, becoming

[51] Hurrell, "An Emerging Security Community in South America?" p. 250.

[52] Pion-Berlin, "Will Soldiers Follow?" p. 52.

[53] See Luigi Manzetti, "Argentine-Brazilian Economic Integration: An Early Appraisal," *Latin American Research Review* 25, no. 3 (1990): 109–149.

[54] Kacowicz, "Stable Peace in South America," p. 205.

[55] Hurrell, "An Emerging Security Community in South America?" p. 252.

effective lobbies for lasting rapprochement and deepening social ties between the two countries. According to Hurrell, "this period sees a gradual but steady creation of interest-groups and networks within the state favouring integration." The advance of rapprochement, he contends, led to "an expansion in the range of actors involved—for example the greater organization of business interests and the creation of more formalized involvement of those regions and provinces most closely affected by integration."[56] Kacowicz agrees that "initial rapprochement . . . was motivated by security concerns," but that the "rapid improvement in bilateral relations" then led to "an increasing web of economic interdependence that has helped to maintain peaceful relations over the long run."[57] Pion-Berlin argues that "the initial thrust that generated cooperative ventures in the economic realm resulted from the political changes in the region."[58] Andrea Oelsner similarly observes that "increased exchange and interdependence brought the business communities of both countries closer together, which in turn resulted in increased communication and cooperative action among them. With exchange and fluid dialogue, business circles came to realize that cooperation could bring about greater advantages."[59]

This interpretation is clearly borne out by trade data. At the beginning of the 1970s, prior to the onset of rapprochement, less than 10 percent of Argentina's trade was with Brazil, and less than 6 percent of Brazilian trade was with Argentina.[60] By the end of the 1980s, Argentina's trade with Brazil still stood at 10 percent of its total trade, while Brazil's trade with Argentina had fallen to 3.7 percent of its trade. Trade flows increased dramatically in the early 1990s. By 1993, Argentina's trade with Brazil had risen to 20 percent of its trade, and Brazilian trade with Argentina had more than tripled to 13 percent of its total trade. Whereas in 1990, Argentina was Brazil's tenth most important market, by 1994 "Argentina had become Brazil's second largest trading partner, taking up half of Brazil's trade with South America."[61]

---

[56] Hurrell, "An Emerging Security Community in South America?" pp. 246, 252.

[57] Kacowicz, "Stable Peace in South America," p. 215.

[58] Pion-Berlin, "Will Soldiers Follow?" p. 46.

[59] Andrea Oelsner, *International Relations in Latin America: Peace and Security in the Southern Cone* (New York: Routledge, 2005), pp. 178–179. See also Monica Hirst, "Mercosur's Complex Political Agenda," in Riordan Roett, ed., *Mercosur: Regional Integration, World Markets* (Boulder, CO: Lynne Rienner, 1999), p. 43.

[60] Resende-Santos, "The Origins of Security Cooperation," p. 94.

[61] Oelsner, *International Relations in Latin America*, p. 179.

Between 1990 and 1994, trade among Mercosur members rose from $3.5 billion to $14 billion.[62]

Why Peace Broke Out

The trajectory of reconciliation between Argentina and Brazil makes clear that neither liberal democracy nor institutionalized restraint is a necessary condition for rapprochement—at least in its early phases. As Etel Solingen states, "The democratic nature of regimes thus has marginal utility for understanding peace and 'deep' cooperation in the Southern Cone."[63] The initial acts of unilateral accommodation and reciprocal restraint that set the process of reconciliation in motion occurred when both countries were governed by repressive military juntas that did not observe the rule of law at home. This finding challenges the proposition that mutual accommodation and the winding down of geopolitical rivalry occur only among regimes that embrace institutionalized restraint. In the case of Argentina and Brazil, governments that wielded unchecked power at home were nonetheless willing to practice strategic restraint in the conduct of their foreign relations.

Two observations, however, limit the extent to which the case completely calls into question the existence of a causal link between rapprochement and institutionalized restraint. First, the Brazilian military officers responsible for launching rapprochement were moderates who were explicitly using foreign policy as a tool of domestic reform. They were seeking to undermine the extremists in the security services and military who favored coercive repression of the regime's opponents and instead argued in favor of political liberalization and engagement with civil society. These moderates appreciated that an environment of geopolitical rivalry stymied domestic liberalization by strengthening hardliners. A policy of *abertura*—reform at home and détente abroad—was the result. In this sense, rapprochement was at least in part a product of elites who, albeit members of a military junta, understood the importance of institutionalized restraint at home and pursued strategic restraint abroad to further domestic reform and re-engage civil society.

Second, although reconciliation began under authoritarian regimes, it was consolidated only after both countries had gone through democratic transitions. Furthermore, the onset of democracy clearly advanced rapprochement,

---

[62] Solingen, *Regional Orders at Century's Dawn*, p. 151.
[63] Solingen, *Regional Orders at Century's Dawn*, p. 157.

deepening and broadening its scope, regularizing cooperation, and engaging a broader cross-section of society. From this perspective, democratization played a key role in bringing the onset of rapprochement to completion. As in the other cases, key attributes of democratic governance—transparency, adaptability, and institutionalized restraint—appear to have been important factors contributing to stable peace. As Pion-Berlin notes, one of the main obstacles to rapprochement had been that "Mutual distrust was aggravated by a lack of transparency in diplomatic relations, characterized by a complete absence of informational exchanges, reciprocal visitation, or controls."[64] Societal contact and democratization made both states far less opaque, enabling Argentines and Brazilians alike to see each other as benign polities.

As for social orders, Argentina's and Brazil's have been largely compatible since the colonial era. Both have had ethnically mixed populations, with families of European background gradually losing their privileged status in both political and economic terms. Both have long had an economic elite drawn primarily from the landed gentry and the commercial bourgeoisie. From the end of World War II until the 1980s, both Argentina and Brazil mixed centralized and protectionist economic policies with those favoring privatization and commercial openness—what Solingen calls "a coalitional equipoise between internationalizing and statist-nationalist strategies."[65] Their social orders then converged over the course of the 1980s, as civilian leaders in both countries saw nuclear cooperation, economic integration, and rapprochement as means of limiting the power of the military, winning the support of the business community, and broadening political participation. The liberalization of commerce occurred in step, with Mercosur advancing rapprochement not only by increasing economic interdependence but also by strengthening the commercial sector, the middle class, and liberalizing political coalitions in both countries.[66] By the 1990s, statist and protectionist coalitions in Buenos Aires and Brasilia had given way to liberal and internationalist ones.

Argentina and Brazil have long enjoyed a high degree of cultural commonality. Argentines speak Spanish while Brazilians speak Portuguese, but the two languages are closely related. Their post-colonial cultures have much in common. Both populations are predominantly Catholic and of mixed race

[64] Pion-Berlin, "Will Soldiers Follow?" p. 45.
[65] See Solingen, *Regional Orders at Century's Dawn*, p. 127. See also pp. 120–142.
[66] Solingen, *Regional Orders at Century's Dawn*, pp. 142–154.

and ethnicity. It is also the case that mutual perceptions of cultural commonality have increased dramatically since the 1970s. This convergence was fostered in part by Brazil's decision to forego its self-image as a first-world country allied with the United States, instead becoming part of an exclusive
regional community comprising the countries of South America. The emergence of compatible identities was also advanced by the project of integration that accompanied rapprochement, one that generated a new narrative of
regional solidarity. Especially as Mercosur developed during the 1990s, talk
of "friendship bridges" and kinship among the peoples of South America
helped Argentines and Brazilians fashion a stronger sense of communal identity.[67] According to Oelsner, "The formal process of integrating Mercosur has
very gradually awakened a perception of common or shared destiny not just
among political and economic elites, but also in wider circles of society."[68] As
of yet, the "we feeling" that exists between the populations of the two countries remains tentative, leaving open the question of whether a more mature
security community will emerge in the years ahead.

THE RISE AND DEMISE OF THE ANGLO-JAPANESE ALLIANCE, 1902–1923

The Anglo-Japanese Alliance lasted from 1902 until the ratification of the
Washington Naval Treaty in 1923. The pact was the result of concurrent developments in Japan and Great Britain. Japan had begun to pursue a more
ambitious and assertive foreign policy in the wake of the Meiji Restoration in
1868. Britain reacted with a measure of alarm, concerned that Japan's anti-
foreign sentiment and shipbuilding program might combine to compromise
British naval supremacy in the Far East. Japan's naval victories in the Sino-
Japanese War of 1894–1895 and the Russo-Japanese War of 1904–1905
heightened British anxieties about the potential threat posed by an expanding and improving Japanese fleet. As discussed in chapter 3, Britain in the
late nineteenth century faced a range of imperial commitments that it found
increasingly difficult to sustain. The enlargement of the Japanese fleet and
the heating up of great-power rivalry in the western Pacific meant that in the
Far East as well in other theaters, the Admiralty faced the prospect of an in-

[67] Hurrell, "An Emerging Security Community in South America?" p. 254.
[68] Oelsner, *International Relations in Latin America*, p. 184.

adequate naval presence. Just as Britain sought to befriend the United States to address deficiencies in the western Atlantic, Britain sought an alliance with Japan to redress a shortfall in the Pacific. Strategic necessity prompted London's efforts to befriend not only Washington, but also Tokyo.

Whereas Anglo-American rapprochement took the form of dispute resolution and informal strategic understandings, Anglo-Japanese cooperation was codified through a formal alliance, one that led to both peacetime and wartime naval cooperation. Nonetheless, Anglo-Japanese relations failed to advance beyond military collaboration, falling well short of the stable peace that developed between the United States and Britain. Why did lasting rapprochement between Japan and Great Britain fail to materialize? Why did peacetime and wartime cooperation not lead to societal integration and a growing sense of trust and affinity? The next section summarizes the history of the Anglo-Japanese alliance, followed by a discussion of why strategic cooperation did not lead to stable peace. The absence of both institutionalized restraint and cultural commonality best explain why rapprochement stalled and why the alliance ultimately eroded and gave way to geopolitical rivalry.

The Evolution of the Anglo-Japanese Alliance

Following Japan's victory in the Sino-Japanese War, Japan doubled the size of its army, significantly expanded its naval fleet, and sought to enlarge its political and economic influence in Korea, Manchuria, and China. Russia, meanwhile, was proceeding with the construction of the trans-Siberian railway and extending its reach eastward, fueling geopolitical competition with Japan. The intensification of European rivalry in Northeast Asia raised the prospect of greater French engagement in the region, posing an additional threat to British interests. Allocating new resources to the region proved difficult when Britain was already bogged down in the Boer War and confronted with the challenge of maintaining its two-power standard amid ambitious naval building programs in Europe and the United States. As Ian Nish notes, London had come to the realization that "one of the centres of international affairs had moved to the far east where Britain was isolated and vulnerable."[69]

In 1895, the Admiralty noted that keeping pace with the combined fleets of

[69] Ian Nish, *The Anglo-Japanese Alliance: The Diplomacy of Two Island Empires, 1894–1907* (London: Althone Press, 1966), p. 66.

Russia and France in the Far East "can only be done by weakening our Squadrons at home."[70] By 1901, the problem had only grown more acute, with Lord Selborne, the first lord of the Admiralty, informing the cabinet that reinforcing the China squadron would leave "little or nothing more than bare equality in the Channel and Mediterranean, and bare equality at the heart of the Empire is a dangerous risk."[71] Lacking the resources needed to maintain naval superiority in the Pacific, the British responded diplomatically. By allying with Japan, London could not only sidestep potential rivalry with a rising power, but also combine its naval assets with Japan's expanding fleet to offset Britain's strategic shortfall in the eastern reaches of the empire. Helping to solidify support in London for a formal alliance was the fact that Tokyo had in 1900 agreed to Britain's request to send ground troops to China to help put down the Boxer Rebellion.[72]

Britain made the initial overtures during the second half of 1901, sounding out Tokyo about its interest in a mutual defense pact.[73] Japan was initially reluctant, wondering whether it made more sense to reach an accommodation with the Russians, offering them a sphere of influence in Manchuria in return for Japan's effective control of Korea. Tokyo soon calculated that its long-term interests were in closer alignment with those of London than St. Petersburg, and after compromises by both parties, a formal alliance was signed in 1902.[74] Tokyo was attracted by the prospect of British protection as well as London's backing for Japan's continental ambition. In return, Britain was able to retain effective naval supremacy in the region. Russia and France became allies during the first half of the 1890s; together they had seven first-class battleships, two second-class battleships, and twenty cruisers in the theater. An Anglo-Japanese combination produced eleven battleships as well as a preponderance of cruisers.[75] The two parties made arrangements for joint fleet operations and exchanged information on signals and intelligence. Again

[70] Hamish Ion, "Towards a Naval Alliance: Some Naval Antecedents to the Anglo-Japanese Alliance, 1854–1902," in Phillips Payson O'Brien, ed., *The Anglo-Japanese Alliance, 1902–1922*, (London: RoutledgeCurzon, 2004) p. 35.

[71] Cited in David Steeds, "Anglo-Japanese Relations, 1902–23: A Marriage of Convenience," in Ian Nish and Yoichi Kibata, eds., *The History of Anglo-Japanese Relations, Vol. 1: The Political-Diplomatic Dimension, 1600–1930* (New York: St. Martin's Press, 2000), p. 202.

[72] Nish, *The Anglo-Japanese Alliance*, pp. 80–95.

[73] For a detailed summary of the negotiations, see Nish, *The Anglo-Japanese Alliance*, pp. 143–228.

[74] The main disagreements concerned the geographic scope of the pact, the extent of Japan's ambitions in Korea, and the number of naval vessels that Britain intended to maintain in the theater. See Nish, *The Anglo-Japanese Alliance*, pp. 211–218.

[75] Nish, *The Anglo-Japanese Alliance*, p. 174.

looking to ease strategic requirements in the imperial periphery, the British also pressed Tokyo to extend the alliance to the Malay peninsula and the Indian Ocean, but Japanese leaders declined the request in favor of focusing the pact exclusively on their own strategic theater.

Emboldened by its alliance with Britain, Japan tightened its grip on Korea and sought to limit Russia's presence in Manchuria, contributing to the outbreak of war between Japan and Russia in 1904.[76] Britain was not bound by the Anglo-Japanese Alliance to enter the conflict. The pact stipulated that each party would remain neutral if the other found itself at war with one enemy, and that commitments to collective defense would be triggered only when one of the signatories was at war with two or more powers. The British did, however, take steps to aid their ally, buying two Chilean battleships to prevent their transfer to Russia and concluding an accord with France to keep its fleet out of the war. Although the British government refrained from providing economic assistance to Japan, loans from private British banks did help finance the war.

Amid Japan's victory over Russia in 1905, its alliance with Britain was extended and upgraded; reciprocal accommodation was leading to more extensive forms of cooperation. The revisions stipulated that alliance commitments would be triggered should either country find itself at war with even a single power. Japan in principle agreed to extend the scope of the alliance to include India, indicating its readiness to dispatch ground troops to help defend the British possession if so requested. In return, London acquiesced to Japan's de facto occupation of Korea, recognizing Tokyo's right "to take such measures of guidance, control and protection ... as she may deem proper and necessary."[77] The peninsula had effectively become a Japanese protectorate. The two parties also elevated their respective diplomatic delegations to embassy status.

The alliance was revised and extended in 1911 for a ten-year term. It was soon put to the test by the onset of World War I—with impressive results. Japan undertook naval operations against German positions in the Far East, capitalizing on the opportunity to increase its presence in China and seize a number of German-controlled islands in the Pacific. Although it refused re-

---

[76] Nish argues that the Anglo-Japanese Alliance did encourage Japan to take a harder line in negotiations with Russia, but that Japan's war with Russia would likely have occurred even had its alliance with Britain not materialized. See Nish, *The Anglo-Japanese Alliance*, pp. 262–282.

[77] Steeds, "Anglo-Japanese Relations, 1902–23," p. 208.

quests to send ground troops to fight in the European theater, Japan did send naval vessels to help patrol and escort convoys in the Indian Ocean and the Mediterranean.

Despite the close cooperation that emerged during World War I, however, the Anglo-Japanese Alliance came to an end soon after the close of the war. In contrast to Norway and Sweden, for whom cooperation during World War I consolidated stable peace, wartime collaboration had no such effect on relations between Britain and Japan. Instead, Britain negotiated a multilateral naval pact, agreeing with the United States, France, and Japan to a ceiling on the respective fleet strength of each party. The signing of the Washington Naval Treaty in 1921 marked the effective end of the Anglo-Japanese Alliance, although it did not formally lapse until the treaty was ratified in 1923. During the 1920s, relations between Britain and Japan remained generally stable and cooperative. But early in the next decade, Japan invaded Manchuria and unilaterally abrogated the agreement on naval limitations, putting it on a collision course with Britain and other Western powers.

The Limits of the Anglo-Japanese Alliance: How Rapprochement Failed

Britain and Japan enjoyed two decades of formal alliance. They exchanged technology and naval intelligence, and coordinated their naval operations, even engaging in joint naval warfare during World War I. In concrete terms, their level of strategic cooperation far surpassed that of Britain and the United States between 1895 and 1906—the period during which Anglo-American rapprochement took root. Moreover, just as Britain appeased the United States to shore up its eroding strategic predicament, so too did Britain accommodate Tokyo's growing ambition as a means of befriending Japan, thereby redressing naval deficiencies in the Pacific. The United States and Japan were both rising powers and therefore ready to reciprocate Britain's overtures and enjoy the enlarged sway over their respective regions.

Despite these similarities, the two cases followed quite different trajectories. By the early 1900s, after only a few years of active reconciliation, Britain and the United States had effectively ended over a century of enmity and were coming to enjoy stable peace. In contrast, Britain and Japan, despite over two decades of formal alliance, fell far short of a lasting partnership and the consolidation of rapprochement; they were unable to attain the sense of mutual affinity and trust that ultimately tamed relations between Britain and the United States. What explains this stark difference? In terms of both the process through which rapprochement emerges and the conditions making it possible, what barriers stood in the way, preventing Britain and Japan from transforming alliance into stable peace?

The main impediment to rapprochement was the inability of Britain and Japan to advance from mutual accommodation to the regularization of reciprocal restraint and the onset of societal integration. Despite its longevity and the concrete naval cooperation it produced, the strategic partnership between Britain and Japan remained politically limited and socially shallow. The two parties were quite adept at fashioning strategic bargains and trading concessions in order to meet their respective strategic goals. Britain and Japan were unable, however, to move beyond specific reciprocity to broad reciprocity; they attributed benign intent to each other with respect to discrete policy initiatives, but did not impute from those policies either benign motivation or character. In this respect, the alliance was persistently seen by each party as only an instrumental vehicle for pursuing its individual strategic objectives; their respective interests temporarily intersected, but they were not congruent. Moreover, Britain and Japan never even reached the stage of societal integration—indeed, they mutually shunned it. The alliance received little public attention in either country and had minimal impact on commercial relations. As a result, there were very few public or private agents pressing for rapprochement and generating the changes in narrative and discourse that produce shifts in identity. As one historian of the alliance concludes, the Anglo-Japanese Alliance was "a marriage not of love, but of mutual convenience."[78]

ASSESSING INTENTIONS

In the years leading up to the conclusion of their alliance, Britain and Japan arrived at somewhat asymmetric assessments of each other's intentions. Japanese elites viewed the British Empire as having reached its apex. From Tokyo's perspective, Britain's primary objective would be to defend the status quo. In contrast, British elites saw Japan as a rising power with expansionist aims. From London's perspective, Japan's primary objective would be to enhance its geopolitical influence in the Far East by enlarging its maritime strength and its position on the Asian mainland.

[78] Steeds, "Anglo-Japanese Relations, 1902–23," p. 197.

By 1900, Japanese elites were well aware that Britain was bogged down in South Africa and facing rising threats in the European theater. In the middle of 1901, the prime minister, General Katsura Tarō, saw a stark contrast between Russian and British intentions. Russia, he believed, would seek to expand into Manchuria and Korea, "until there is no room left for us." He saw Britain in a quite different light:

Britain can by its interests remain on good terms with us: it is not a country with territorial ambitions and, with its power extending almost all over the world, it can unquestionably be assumed that its territorial ambitions are not likely to lead to a conflict with us. The essence of Britain's policy is to get us to resist Russian expansion into the far east. This is especially so at a time when she has her hands full with the disturbances in South Africa.

The head of the Political Affairs Department in the Foreign Ministry agreed that London "wants to preserve the *status quo*," noting that "Britain has already passed her zenith and will to some extent tend to decline." An Anglo-Japanese alliance, he contended, would "keep peace in the east on a relatively permanent basis." [79] Japan's minister in London, Katō Takaaki, agreed with such assessments and emphasized Britain's practice of strategic restraint toward Japan, pointing to London's willingness to revise the "unequal treaties" in 1894 as well as the fact that "she held aloof from interference after the Sino-Japanese war."[80] That some of Japan's top diplomats had served in London and that Japan relied heavily on Britain for naval training and shipbuilding may have contributed to Tokyo's evaluation that British policy was shaped by benign intentions.

London was from the outset more wary of Japan's intentions, sensing that Japan's rising economic and military capability would translate into mounting geopolitical ambition. In the mid-1890s, the British minister in Tokyo wrote that the Japanese "would not readily enter into an alliance in which they would have to play second fiddle."[81] In 1898, the colonial secretary, Joseph Chamberlain, wrote to the prime minister, Lord Salisbury, that the Japanese "are rapidly increasing their means of offence and defence. . . . They

[79] Quotations from Nish, *The Anglo-Japanese Alliance,* pp. 382–385.
[80] Ian Nish, "Origins of the Anglo-Japanese Alliance: In the Shadow of the Dreibund," in O'Brien, *The Anglo-Japanese Alliance*, p. 13.
[81] Nish, *The Anglo-Japanese Alliance*, p. 40.

are worth looking after as it is clear that they do not mean to be a *quantité négligeable* in the East."[82] Especially after Japan's defeat of China, London worried about the potential threat to shipping posed by the growing Japanese navy as well as Tokyo's designs on the Asian mainland. One of the main arguments that British officials made against the proposal to fashion an alliance with Japan was that it would embolden Tokyo to extend its sway over Korea. Well aware of such concerns, Tokyo assured London during negotiations over the pact that it did not have designs on Korea and was looking only to contain Russian ambition.[83]

Even when not attributing expansionist aims to Japanese behavior, British officials in London as well as those serving in Japan were frustrated by the difficulties encountered in attempting to discern Japanese intentions. For example, Vice-admiral Cyprian Bridge, one of the most influential officers helping to coordinate naval operations in the Far East, expressed uneasiness with his Japanese counterparts, noting that they retained "the innate suspiciousness of the Oriental," and were watching the British "very closely."[84] Politicians and officials in London echoed this view; a member of Parliament noted, "In making a treaty with the Japanese we were making a treaty with a people who were more or less an enigma to us."[85] Such uncertainty about Japanese intentions was ultimately offset by strategic imperatives; to redress its naval deficiencies, Britain needed an ally in the Far East, and Japan was the obvious choice. Nonetheless, such declarations of unease about Japanese intentions stand in stark contrast to the relative confidence of British elites in the benign intentions of the rising power that was meanwhile challenging Britain's naval supremacy in the Atlantic—the United States.

Britain's misgivings about Japan's objectives did not stand in the way of the conclusion of the alliance, making clear that the two countries had overlapping interests in the Far East, particularly with respect to containing Russian expansion. Nonetheless, diverging expectations soon heightened concern in both London and Tokyo about the other's intentions. Japan presumed that the pact would induce London to maintain its naval presence in the Pacific in order to honor its alliance commitments. Indeed, Tokyo exacted a written commitment from London that it would maintain, "so far as possible," ade-

---

[82] Nish, *The Anglo-Japanese Alliance*, p. 64.

[83] Nish, *The Anglo-Japanese Alliance*, pp. 212–213.

[84] John Chapman, "The Secret Dimensions of the Anglo-Japanese Alliance, 1900–1905," in O'Brien, *The Anglo-Japanese Alliance*, p. 87.

[85] Nish, *The Anglo-Japanese Alliance*, p. 343

quate fleet strength in the region.[86] Instead, London was busy planning how best to take advantage of the alliance to reduce the number of vessels it maintained in the Pacific—and proceeded to withdraw two cruisers from the China Station in 1902. The following year, Tokyo complained to London about the Royal Navy's declining tonnage in the Far East.

British expectations went similarly unfulfilled. London hoped that the alliance would help satisfy Japan's security needs, thereby limiting its continental ambitions. Instead, Tokyo's expansionist urge intensified, fueling a confrontation with Russia. Furthermore, the British felt the alliance to be imbalanced, with the Japanese securing a primary strategic objective—effective dominance of Korea—but refusing to reciprocate by extending the pact to cover areas of primary British concern, namely, the Malay peninsula and the Indian Ocean. From early on, each party saw the other as capitalizing on the alliance to pursue individual advantage rather than mutual interests and joint gains.

THE FIRST RENEWAL

The revision of the alliance in 1905 ostensibly elevated its strategic importance to both parties. Commitments to collective defense would be triggered should either party find itself at war with a single power, and the revision broadened the scope of the strategic partnership to the Indian Ocean. But in the wake of Russia's defeat by Japan, the pact had to some extent lost its original raison d'être; Japan and Britain no longer needed each other to balance against Russian power. Consequently, London and Tokyo both looked for ways to make the pact more relevant to their respective security needs. Japan wanted British backing of its growing presence on the Asian mainland, as well as a deterrent against a Russian war of revenge. In return, Britain wanted Japan's assistance in South Asia. Despite deep reservations about its legality and strategic implications, Britain agreed to recognize Japan's effective occupation of Korea. In return, Japan agreed, at least in principle, to send troops to India should the British possession face a Russian attack. Mutual accommodation prevailed. But again, each side saw the other as pursuing individual advantage, not joint gains.[87]

---

[86] Keith Neilson, "The Anglo-Japanese Alliance and British Strategic Foreign Policy, 1902–1914," in O'Brien, *The Anglo-Japanese Alliance*, p. 52.

[87] On British and Japanese motivations during the negotiations over revision, see Nish, *The Anglo-Japanese Alliance*, pp. 304–312.

Tokyo may have finally acquiesced to London's long-standing request to extend the alliance to the Indian Ocean, but it did so primarily in the service of furthering Japan's expansionist aims on the Asian mainland. Indeed, in the wake of Russia's defeat, influential Japanese voices argued against renewal of the alliance, contending that it was no longer needed and would only constrain Japan's continental ambitions. Lieutenant Colonel Tanaka Giichi asked, "Should we resign ourselves to the constraints of a lengthy continuation of the bilateral (Anglo-Japanese) alliance in the future? We should determine our policy exclusively on our own national interests." Others argued for forgoing renewal in favor of alliance with Germany or Russia, countries with which Japan enjoyed greater social and political affinity due to their conservative social orders and governments.[88] Ultimately, London's willingness to accept Japan's establishment of a protectorate in Korea, coupled with the view that the alliance helped insure against the formation of a broad European coalition against Japan, convinced Tokyo to support renewal.

From London's perspective, the alliance still served to alleviate strategic deficiencies in the Eastern Empire—its original objective. As evidence, London took advantage of the defeat of Russia and the renewal of the alliance to withdraw five battleships and six first-class cruisers from the Pacific. But especially after Russia's defeat, London increasingly viewed the alliance as an instrument for restraining Japanese ambition rather than redressing its own naval deficiencies, reflecting its growing discomfort with Japanese intentions.[89] As Lord Lansdowne, one of the primary architects of the alliance, commented after the outbreak of war between Japan and Russia, "the alliance had, and was sure to have, the effect of making Japan feel that she might try conclusions with her great rival in the Far East, free from all risk of a European coalition."[90]

Although both parties were exchanging mutual concessions and giving ground on issues of strategic concern to each other, the nature of the concessions and the context in which the bargains were struck limited the degree to which they fostered a mutual perception of benign motivation and a sense of common purpose. Britain was making itself vulnerable to Japan by drawing down its naval presence in the Pacific. However, Japan saw British behavior

[88] Frederick R. Dickinson, "Japan Debates the Anglo-Japanese Alliance: The Second Revision of 1911," in O'Brien, *The Anglo-Japanese Alliance*, pp. 101, 113–115.

[89] Nish, *The Anglo-Japanese Alliance*, pp. 372–377.

[90] Nish, "Origins of the Anglo-Japanese Alliance," p. 23.

as a breach of Britain's pledge to maintain adequate force levels in the region, not as a signal of benign intent. Japan did agree to help defend British interests outside Northeast Asia, but London saw this primarily as a quid pro quo for Britain's grudging recognition of Japan's occupation of Korea. Each country appeared to the other as continuing to take advantage of the alliance for individual gain. London and Tokyo consequently attributed to each other narrow, self-interested motivations, assessments that served as a critical barrier to transforming an instrumental alliance into lasting rapprochement.[91]

THE SECOND RENEWAL

Although the alliance as revised in 1905 had a ten-year duration, Tokyo pressed for revision and renewal in 1911, primarily to secure British recognition of its annexation of Korea the previous year. From Tokyo's perspective, the alliance no longer filled pressing strategic needs. Japan had bested Russia and secured its position in Korea. The threat posed by Russia having receded, Japan was coming to see the United States as its main strategic rival. The alliance with Britain did little to alleviate Japanese concerns about the United States. Rapprochement between Britain and the United States meant that London had insisted on revisions to the alliance to ensure that a conflict between America and Japan would not obligate Britain to join the conflict on Japan's behalf. Negotiations over renewal were also strained by Tokyo's pique over London's persistent admonitions against Japan's growing sphere of influence on the Asian mainland. Nonetheless, Tokyo saw little choice but to renew the Anglo-Japanese Alliance. Other allies simply were not available; letting the alliance lapse therefore risked strategic isolation.[92] Moreover, Japanese elites, as during the debate over renewal in 1905, were worried that mounting concern in Europe, the United States, and the dominions about the "yellow peril" raised the possibility that an anti-Japanese coalition might form among the major powers. As Nish observes, "the treaty was their only link with the outside world, the only thing which saved Japan from isolationism in a world which was afflicted by suspicions based on fear of the Yellow Peril."[93]

Tokyo's push for revision of the alliance reinforced London's perception

---

[91] For details of the negotiations over revision, see Nish, *The Anglo-Japanese Alliance*, pp. 301–331.

[92] See Dickinson, "Japan Debates the Anglo-Japanese Alliance," pp. 109–111; and Ian Nish, *The Alliance in Decline: A Study in Anglo-Japanese Relations, 1908–1923* (London: Athlone Press, 1972), p. 73.

[93] Nish, *The Anglo-Japanese Alliance*, p. 377.

that Japan was taking advantage of the pact to pursue self-interested objectives. London attributed expansionist intent, not legitimate security needs, to Japan's insistence that Britain accede to Tokyo's demands for a *droit de regard* not only in Korea, but also in Manchuria and North China. As a result, Britain insisted that the renewed treaty affirm "the independence and integrity of the Chinese Empire."[94] From London's perspective, the alliance was changing in character, increasingly becoming an instrument for containing Japanese expansionism rather than addressing British naval deficiencies. Moreover, as Japan's fleet strength continued to grow, London was concerned about not only Japanese expansion on the Asian mainland, but also the potential threats Japan posed to the British dominions. In reflecting on the circumstances at the time of renewal, Sir Conyngham Greene, London's ambassador in Tokyo, commented that British policy was aimed at arriving at an understanding with Japan "with a view to safeguarding our interests against her insidious encroachment upon the accepted policy of equal opportunity for all."[95]

The level of British concern about the importance of restraining Japanese expansion was made clear by the tenor of the arguments marshaled in favor of revising and extending the alliance. As the Committee of Imperial Defense maintained in making the case for renewal, the alliance renders "the risk of attack by Japan excluded from the category of reasonable possibilities to be provided against."[96] In contrast, if London allows the alliance to lapse, "Japan will have her hands free to act in the Far East without restraint or control by us."[97] Sir Edward Grey, the foreign secretary, pointed out that Britain would not only have "to count the Japanese fleet as it now exists as possible enemies," but it would also confront the larger fleet Japan would likely build should it no longer be a British ally.[98]

Japan's willingness to send its navy to the Indian Ocean and the Mediterranean during World War I—although much appreciated by Britain and its European allies—did not fundamentally alter the strategic calculus that prevailed during the negotiations over renewal. Tokyo struck a hard bargain in responding to London's request that Japan not only help hunt and destroy German ships in the Pacific, but also assume naval responsibilities in the In-

[94] Nish, *Alliance in Decline*, p. 68.

[95] Murashima Shigeru, "The Opening of the Twentieth Century and the Anglo-Japanese Alliance, 1895–1923," in Nish and Kibata, *The History of Anglo-Japanese Relations*, p. 181.

[96] Nish, *Alliance in Decline*, p. 61.

[97] Nish, *Alliance in Decline*, p. 51.

[98] Neilson, "The Anglo-Japanese Alliance," p. 58.

dian Ocean and Mediterranean. In return for agreeing to take on these expanded missions, Tokyo demanded the right to take control of Germany's
concessions in China as well as its Micronesian islands. British officials objected to Japan's quid pro quo, with Foreign Secretary Grey welcoming Japanese help in attacking German vessels, but repeatedly warning Tokyo against
seizing control of German territories. Anxious to ensure Japan's help outside
East Asia, however, London ultimately acquiesced to Japan's demands.[99]

Tokyo's insistence on taking over German concessions in China prompted
London's ambassador to call Japan "a frankly opportunist, not to say selfish,
country, of very moderate importance compared with the giants of the Great
War, but with a very exaggerated opinion of her own role in the universe."[100]
According to Nish, many British officials "felt that her action in China was
imperialistic and was synonymous with territorial aggrandizement."[101] The
predominant view from London was that Japan was taking advantage of
Britain's misfortunes in Europe to pursue its imperial ambitions in the Far
East. Ambassador Greene made this attitude clear in a memo to the foreign
minister in 1916: "As long as Great Britain was able to maintain her prestige
in the Far East, Japan was enthusiastic for the Anglo-Japanese Alliance, but
when the hour of our distress arrived and we began to pay the penalty for
our national unpreparedness, she wavered. We now see our Ally as she is, and
not as some of us were inclined to visualise her."[102] Another British official,
looking back on the period, commented, "Close cooperation was supposed
to exist between Great Britain and Japan in virtue of the Alliance Agreement. This, however, had been misused by Japan to further her own interests
with little or no regard to those of her partner."[103]

Even the intentions behind Japan's willingness to send vessels to the Indian
Ocean were questioned, with some officials positing that Tokyo's ultimate
objective was to foment anti-British sentiment in the service of driving the
European powers from Asia and undermining British rule in India.[104] As

[99] Neilson, "The Anglo-Japanese Alliance," p. 59.

[100] Cited in Antony Best, "India, pan-Asianism and the Anglo-Japanese Alliance," in O'Brien,
The Anglo-Japanese Alliance, p. 242.

[101] Nish, *Alliance in Decline*, p. 260.

[102] Nish, *Alliance in Decline*, p. 193.

[103] Ian Nish, "Echoes of Alliance, 1920–30," in Nish and Kibata, *The History of Anglo-Japanese Relations*, p. 257.

[104] Nish, *Alliance in Decline*, pp. 186–187.

Antony Best summarizes Nish's conclusions, "by the end of the Great War many British policy-makers had come to distrust the Japanese, and suspicion of the latter's activities in India played an important part in influencing the sense of alienation."[105] In analyzing the problems plaguing the alliance, Ambassador Greene pointed to: "1. The arrogance, opportunism and selfishness of Japan's foreign policy. 2. Japan's aspiration to the hegemony of the Far East. 3. Japan's philandering with India."[106] British officials also expressed doubts about Japan's ultimate loyalties, suspecting that Tokyo might side with Germany if it thought its aims would be better served.[107] As a sign of the growing distrust, Britain by 1917 was no longer willing to share its best military technology with Japan.[108] As Nish summarizes the consensus in London, "There was a great deal of distrust of Japan in Britain during the war period. There are minutes galore which testified to British officials' suspicions that Japan was either inactive or self-interested in any actions she took."[109]

Upon the close of World War I and the impending expiration of the ten-year extension negotiated in 1911, the alliance was again renewed in 1921. Despite its reservations, London decided not to allow the pact to lapse, calculating that its continuation would give Britain at least a measure of leverage over Japanese behavior and prevent Tokyo from pursuing military or diplomatic actions that might threaten British interests. In Nish's words, "Britain, by keeping the alliance going despite the distrust involved, hoped to exercise some control over Japan's policy."[110] According to a Foreign Office memo from 1920, the case for extension rested on "the conviction that it affords us the only means of exercising a restraining and moderating influence on Japanese ambitions."[111] The foreign secretary, Lord Curzon, agreed, noting that "a hostile and suspicious Japan may be a great nuisance—in China, in India, in the Far East generally. As it is we can keep a watch on her intrigues, mitigate her aggressions and from time to time obtain useful support."[112] Curzon

---

[105] Best, "India, pan-Asianism and the Anglo-Japanese Alliance," p. 242.
[106] Nish, *Alliance in Decline,* p. 220.
[107] Nish, *Alliance in Decline,* p. 256.
[108] John Ferris, "Armaments and Allies: The Anglo-Japanese Strategic Relationship, 1911–1921," in O'Brien, *The Anglo-Japanese Alliance,* p. 258.
[109] Nish, *Alliance in Decline,* p. 256.
[110] Nish, *Alliance in Decline,* p. 395.
[111] Shigeru, "The Opening of the Twentieth Century," p. 190.
[112] Cited in Best, "India, pan-Asianism and the Anglo-Japanese Alliance," p. 245.

also noted that Japan "kept her word to us faithfully [during World War I], giving us all the help she was bound by Treaty to give and, at a price, going beyond her obligations. Her statesmen are sensitive upon points of honor and though they drive hard bargains at times, it must be admitted that they have attempted to play the game."[113]

Japan's calculations were not dissimilar. The benefits of extension outweighed the costs. Britain might continue to constrain Japan's room for maneuver, but extension would preserve the post-war status quo and consolidate Japanese gains in the Pacific. Despite the renewal of the alliance, however, Japanese elites resented what they saw as the racially biased and unequal "pax Anglo-Americana" that emerged from Versailles, London's lack of consultation with Tokyo as it negotiated the Washington Naval Treaty, and the clear signals from Britain and the United States that they were alarmed by Japan's growing ambition.

The alliance technically remained in effect until the Washington Naval Treaty, which was signed in December 1921, was ratified in 1923. But it was in practice defunct well before its formal end. Britain had come to see the alliance almost exclusively as a tool for containing Japan's growing appetite for expansion. Indeed, by the early 1920s, the Admiralty was already drafting war plans for a conflict with Japan, calculating the number of capital ships it would need to dispatch to Singapore.[114] The United States and the dominions were also pressing Britain to cancel the alliance, disgruntled with the extended reach of Japan's power resulting from its seizure of German islands in the Pacific. To alleviate such concerns, Japan was prohibited by the League of Nations from fortifying the islands. It was precisely such restrictions that engendered Japanese resentment and heightened doubts about the value of alliance with Britain. When the Anglo-Japanese Alliance formally lapsed with the ratification of the Washington Naval Treaty in 1923, both sides were well aware that the pact had already lost much of its political and strategic consequence.

THE ABSENCE OF SOCIETAL INTEGRATION

The absence of societal integration between Britain and Japan was a reflection—and perhaps also a cause—of the failure of the two countries to move

---

[113] Nish, *Alliance in Decline,* p. 298.
[114] Nish, *Alliance in Decline,* pp. 319–320.

from discrete acts of mutual accommodation and cooperation to an enduring rapprochement. Throughout the two decades of alliance, societal links
between the two countries remained quite limited. From the initial conclusion of the alliance through three renewals, the alliance resided primarily in
the realm of high politics. When the pact was first concluded, a limited number of pro-alliance rallies took place in Japan, with commentators noting the
elevated status resulting from Japan's alignment with the world's leading
power.[115] In Britain, however, there was virtually no public reaction. The British government deliberately played down the conclusion of the pact, fearful
that publicity would only invite opposition from parties that regarded the alliance as "a sacrifice of Britain's independence in the far east and a blank
cheque for Japan there."[116] Despite some coverage in the media, opinion makers and ordinary citizens remained largely uninterested. The parliamentary
reaction was muted. A few members of the Liberal opposition voiced mild
reservations, but the party as a whole tended to support the opening to Japan.[117] In these respects, Britain's improving relationship with Japan shared
none of the public visibility—and eventual societal support—enjoyed by its
rapprochement with Washington. The Anglo-Japanese pact remained, in
Nish's words, a "secretariat alliance."[118]

Not only was public and parliamentary engagement missing, but even
those societal groups with vested interests in rapprochement had only a
minor impact on the alliance. The Japanese navy and army did press for the
alliance, especially in its early years, viewing it as a source of prestige as well
as a device that would facilitate the extension of Japan's geopolitical reach.
But enthusiasm waned as Japanese officers later began to see Britain as standing in the way of Japanese ambition. Their British counterparts were on balance supporters of the alliance for strategic reasons, but British officers regularly expressed a measure of discomfort with strategic cooperation, seemingly
arising from racial attitudes as well as concern that British reliance on Japan
would be seen as a source of weakness among Britain's European rivals. Furthermore, direct contact between British and Japanese officers remained limited, even during the coordinated operations that took place amid World
War I.

[115] Shigeru, "The Opening of the Twentieth Century," p. 169.
[116] Nish, *The Anglo-Japanese Alliance*, p. 219.
[117] Shigeru, "The Opening of the Twentieth Century, p. 169.
[118] Nish, *The Anglo-Japanese Alliance*, p. 366.

Economic ties between the two countries also remained limited. British shipyards building vessels for the Japanese navy did emerge as a pro-alliance lobby, but strategic cooperation did not otherwise lead to major new profits for private firms in either country. Financial flows were similarly constrained. Japan's credit rating did improve as a result of the alliance, inviting new flows of private capital from London. But as Janet Hunter notes, British investment in Japan "was a very small part of the overall flow of capital out of Britain in the early twentieth century."[119] During the negotiations over renewal in 1911 and thereafter, Japan proposed expanding the alliance into a broader commercial partnership, but was rebuffed by London. Foreign Minister Grey was advised by his staff that Britain's relationship with Japan was "a political alliance and we want no industrial partnerships."[120] And during World War I, after Japan pronounced its "twenty-one demands" for special privileges in China, British firms denounced Tokyo's efforts to impair their access to Chinese markets; the business community was coming to see the alliance as a hindrance, not an opportunity.[121] During the first decade of the alliance, British trade with China remained static while Sino-Japanese trade increased markedly, reinforcing the sense that Japanese enterprises were expanding at the expense of British firms.[122] Over the course of the alliance, strategic ties had little appreciable impact on commerce, leaving partnership between the two countries with quite shallow societal roots.

Why Rapprochement Failed

The history of the rise and demise of the Anglo-Japanese Alliance makes clear that Britain and Japan, despite two decades of strategic cooperation, failed to capitalize on their pact to move down the path of stable peace. Why did the two countries remain mutually suspicious and not come to attribute to one another benign motivations? Why did the alliance stall at mutual accommodation, remaining merely an instrument of statecraft instead of ad-

[119] Janet Hunter, "Bankers, Investors and Risk: British Capital and Japan during the Years of the Anglo-Japanese Alliance," in O'Brien, *The Anglo-Japanese Alliance*, p. 176.

[120] Nish, *Alliance in Decline,* pp. 108–109.

[121] On the generally negative attitudes of the British business community toward the alliance, see Steeds, "Anglo-Japanese Relations, 1902–23," p. 211. See also Nish, *The Anglo-Japanese Alliance*, pp. 254–255.

[122] Nish, *Alliance in Decline,* pp. 10–11.

vancing toward societal integration and the onset of rapprochement? A realist response to this puzzle would focus on the basic incompatibility of interests. Japan was intent on continental expansion; Britain was therefore right to question Tokyo's long-term objectives. Britain was intent on maintaining its imperial commitments and subordinating all challengers, including Japan; Tokyo was right to see the alliance as a self-serving instrument of British imperialism.

But this explanation is too simplistic and fails to capture the contingent nature of how behavior is assessed and motivation imputed. American behavior at the turn of the century was considerably more aggressive than that of Japan. Japan helped preserve Britain's strategic presence in the Far East, where London was intent on protecting its imperial outposts. In addition, Japan's expansionist ambitions focused primarily on Korea, which lay outside Britain's sphere of influence. In contrast, the United States was working to rid Britain—albeit with London's acquiescence—from the western Atlantic. Moreover, a lasting partnership with Japan was arguably more important than one with the United States because Britain intended to retain its empire in India and the Far East even as it withdrew from the Western Hemisphere. America also built a battle fleet far larger than Japan's, and established colonial outposts in the Pacific, potentially posing a threat to Britain's naval supremacy in the Far East as well as in the western Atlantic. Nonetheless, Britain ultimately saw American power as benign, going so far as to welcome America's colonial presence in the Pacific.

Anglo-Japanese relations followed a quite different trajectory, best explained by the fact that, unlike Britain and the United States, Britain and Japan shared none of the three key conditions that provide a foundation for stable peace: institutionalized restraint, compatible social orders, and cultural commonality. The absence of social compatibility appears to be the least consequential; since societal integration never advanced, the obstacles that would have been presented by different social orders did not weigh heavily in blocking the onset of stable peace. The historical record does, however, indicate that the absence of institutionalized restraint in Japan and the lack of cultural commonality between the two countries did play a key role in arresting rapprochement.

Japan adopted the Meiji Constitution and established the Diet in 1889. But it was a constitutional monarchy only in name. The constitution established the emperor as "the head of the Empire, combining in Himself the rights of sovereignty."[123] The emperor effectively wielded unchecked power, and could appoint and dismiss all government officials, including the cabinet. He had sole authority over matters of war and peace and was the commander of the army and navy. The Diet's powers paled in comparison with those of the emperor and his cabinet. Moreover, during the late 1800s, only about 1 percent of the population had the right to vote. Furthermore, the *genro*—a privy council of elder statesmen that advised the emperor—exerted considerable influence on most major policy issues.

The absence of institutionalized restraint in Japan posed fundamental obstacles to rapprochement. The character and behavior of the Japanese government left British elites wary of Japanese intentions throughout the period of alliance. The untrammeled power of the emperor and the absence of checks and balances among the emperor, cabinet, and military establishment encouraged the British to see Japan as "opportunistic" and "selfish," seeking unilateral advantage, not mutual gains. Japan did on occasion limit the scope of its territorial ambition to accommodate British concerns. But offensive wars versus China and Russia, territorial aggrandizement on the Asian mainland, and the seizure of German positions in the Pacific during World War I colored British perceptions of Japan as an expansionist as opposed to a benign power.

Contributing to British wariness was the opaque nature of decision making in Tokyo. The deliberations that informed Japan's statecraft lacked transparency, leaving London uncertain about Japanese motivations and forced to impute intentions from behavior. As mentioned above, the British tended to see the Japanese as "an enigma," meaning that there was an essential asymmetry in assessment during the early stages of alliance: Tokyo expressed confidence in the benign nature of London's intentions, but London was unable to reciprocate. The transparency of British democracy made an important difference, affording Japanese elites a much richer account of British politics and strategy than their British counterparts could attain in Tokyo. The uncertainty stemming from Britain's inability to discern Japanese motives prevented them from letting down their guard, limiting the nature and scope of strategic restraint. Japan, in turn, sensed British distrust of its motives, en-

---

[123] Stephen S. Large, *Emperor Hirohito and Shōwa Japan: A Political Biography* (New York: Routledge, 1992), p. 7.

suring that the security dilemma, even if moderated, continued to operate. Each party saw the other as pursuing only its own interests. Accordingly, neither ultimately had the confidence to move from discrete episodes of restraint and cooperation to the practice of broad reciprocity necessary to advance to lasting rapprochement.

Reinforcing British suspicion of Japanese intentions was the chronic instability of its governments. The unpredictable nature of Japanese politics induced caution in London. Japanese cabinets tended to be short-lived; between 1894 and 1898, for example, Japan had five different cabinets. The resulting uncertainty left London skittish about Tokyo's reliability and its capacity to make credible commitments. Indeed, some British officials argued against the conclusion of the alliance—and its successive renewals—on the grounds that Japan lacked the necessary political maturity.[124] Inconstancy also stemmed from the unpredictable nature of decision making, with the rising and falling power of the *genro* and frequent changes in ministers at times producing unexpected changes in statecraft.[125]

Finally, as in the cases of rapprochement between Britain and the United States and Norway and Sweden, differences in regime type were connected to differences in social order. Britain's brand of governance was too liberal and democratic for Japan, one of the reasons that it looked to Germany as a political model. Britain, meanwhile, saw Japan's illiberal political order and hierarchical social order as anachronistic. Such differences led to regular divergence over policy. Amid the political turmoil that engulfed China in 1911, for example, Britain favored the establishment of a republic while Japan argued for a constitutional monarchy. During World War I, British fears that Tokyo might defect from the alliance and side with Germany stemmed in part from Japan's affinity for Germany's aristocratic social order. These differences in perspective reinforced the sense among both parties that the alliance represented little more than a temporary intersection of interests.

The absence of cultural commonality also played an important role in arresting rapprochement. Racial considerations figured prominently in official and public debate about the alliance, particularly in Britain. One prominent British opponent of the alliance wrote, "Close, wise and binding friendships are not discreetly given to strangers, whom we have seen and know but little,

---

[124] Nish, *The Anglo-Japanese Alliance*, p. 9.
[125] See, for example, Nish, *The Anglo-Japanese Alliance*, pp. 46–49, 165.

and whose traditions, customs and habits are so different from our own. The ties of alliance are safest, and most useful, when entered into between two neighbours, or with one's own kin."[126] Sensitivity to racial difference was evident even among supporters of the alliance. As Nish observes, the British singled out Japan as the most economically and politically advanced country in the Far East, but London approached Tokyo with a strong measure of "patronizing admiration."[127]

Policy documents and parliamentary debate make clear that Japan, in the minds of British elites, represented a foreign and inferior "other." Policy deliberations contain none of the references to kinship and common heritage that imbued thinking about strategic partnership with the United States. After the Russo-Japanese War broke out, Admiral Bridge complimented the Japanese on their naval successes, noting, "I admire them greatly." "But," he continued, "I feel no social or moral affinity with them and I would rather live with any branch of the Caucasian race, even the Russian, than I would with them."[128] Some British newspapers lamented Japan's military prowess, with the *Daily Chronicle* commenting that "the defeat of a white race by a yellow race must injuriously affect the prestige of the whiter races in general eyes of the Asiatic."[129] John Sommerville, Britain's military attaché in Tokyo, wrote just before the outbreak of World War I, that the Japanese army was "formidable," but lacked originality and adaptability, features "almost entirely due to racial characteristics and the exclusiveness common to insular peoples." He also complained about corruption within the Japanese navy, noting "the complete untrustworthiness, where money is concerned, of the whole Japanese race—lock, stock, and barrel. . . . Is it that they are still too low on the evolutionary ladder?"[130]

For many British elites, strategic reliance on Japan came grudgingly and not without a sense of discomfort. It was one matter to align with Japan in its own neighborhood, giving Britain greater influence over developments on the Asian mainland. But turning to Japan to help defend other quarters of the empire was another matter altogether. Although London from early on pressed Tokyo to extend the scope of the alliance to India, the prospect of

[126] Akira Iikura, "The Anglo-Japanese Alliance and the Question of Race," in O'Brien, *The Anglo-Japanese Alliance*, p. 233.
[127] Nish, *The Anglo-Japanese Alliance*, p. 11.
[128] Chapman, *The Secret Dimensions*, p. 88.
[129] Iikura, "The Anglo-Japanese Alliance and the Question of Race," p. 227.
[130] Ferris, "Armaments and Allies," p. 250.

deploying Japanese troops on imperial territory was accompanied by a certain revulsion. In commenting on the issue after Japan in principle agreed to assume defense commitments in India, the Committee on Imperial Defence argued that bringing Japanese troops to India would be "clear proof of our national decadence" and jeopardize "our prestige throughout the Asiatic continent."[131]

During World War I, Britain was reluctant to ask Japan to contribute ground troops to the effort, with Lord Milner, a member of the war cabinet, noting, "I know there is a very strong prejudice against Japan among the Entente Powers."[132] The British maintained similar attitudes toward Chinese laborers brought to work in Europe during wartime. According to Xu Guoqi, the Chinese workers faced "widespread British racism," and the War Office expressed "the greatest apprehension" about the labor scheme.[133] Racial considerations continued to loom large after the war, as the dominions and the United States pressed Britain to drop the alliance with Japan in favor of closer links to them. London's ambassador to Tokyo was unequivocal, preferring alignment with "our great White Outposts in the Pacific" and "our great White Neighbour," the United States.[134] The Admiralty argued against renewed alignment with Japan in a way that would alienate the United States, "the country which is allied to us in blood, in language, and in literature, and with whom we share the mutual aspiration of maintaining the peace and progress of the world."[135] A Foreign Office memo from 1921 called Japan "the only non-white first-class Power," and then went on to state, "In every respect, except the racial one, Japan stands on a par with the great governing nations of the world. But however powerful Japan may eventually become, the white races will never be able to admit her equality."[136]

Racial overtones similarly informed debate over Japanese emigration, with the dominions and the United States pressing Tokyo, often with the help of Britain, to stem the outflow of its citizens. Australia was the first to pass legislation that effectively prohibited the immigration of non-whites, doing so in 1902. Canada and the United States soon thereafter adopted their own mea-

---

[131] Nish, *The Anglo-Japanese Alliance*, pp. 354–355.

[132] Nish, *Alliance in Decline*, p. 235.

[133] Xu Guoqi, *China and the Great War: China's Pursuit of a New National Identity and Internationalization* (Cambridge: Cambridge University Press, 2005), pp. 134, 123.

[134] Nish, *Alliance in Decline*, p. 220.

[135] Ferris, "Armaments and Allies," p. 257.

[136] Iikura, "The Anglo-Japanese Alliance and the Question of Race," p. 232.

sures to limit the settlement of Japanese. Ambassador Greene made reference to this issue in an analysis of the problems facing the alliance, pointing to the importance of "the colour bar, which baffles agreement between Japan and our Over-Seas Brethren, and finds implacable opposition in Australia, New Zealand, South Africa and Canada."[137]

For the Japanese, who were by the early 1900s looking to confirm their arrival as a major power, alliance with Britain came with a certain sense of pride. Nonetheless, Tokyo was hardly oblivious to the patronizing nature of British policy, frequently expressing concerns over its racial overtones. Throughout the period of alliance, Japanese elites were worried that fear of the "yellow peril" would jeopardize its link with Britain, especially after anti-Japanese sentiment began to mount in the dominions and the United States. As Foreign Minister Komura Jutarō acknowledged in 1904, "Yellow Peril feelings lie concealed in the thinking of Europeans and Americans."[138] Japan's demand prior to the conclusion of formal alliance that Britain revoke the "unequal treaties" that governed bilateral trade, its desire to upgrade the status of diplomatic ties in 1905, its insistence that London consult Tokyo as an equal ally during World War I, its futile request that the founding documents of the League of Nations include a clause on racial equality, its chagrin over its ancillary role in negotiating the Washington Naval Treaty—these were all manifestations of Japan's awareness of its inferior status in the eyes of its British ally and its struggle to put itself on an equal footing with Britain.[139] It is also the case that anti-Japanese sentiment in Britain, the dominions, and the United States triggered a powerful anti-white sentiment among the Japanese public.[140]

Britain and Japan were separated by a profound sense of cultural and racial difference that persisted throughout the two decades of alliance. Indeed, it seems to have intensified, not abated, during the second half of their strategic partnership, with mounting British concern about Japanese expansionism perhaps being translated into discomfort with dispositional attributes such as culture and race. As Nish concludes, "Racial equality had been an unspoken problem of the Anglo-Japanese alliance since its beginning."[141] It is impossi-

---

[137] Nish, *Alliance in Decline*, p. 220.

[138] Nish, *The Anglo-Japanese Alliance*, p. 389.

[139] See Naoko Shimazu, *Japan, Race and Equality: The Racial Equality Proposal of 1919* (New York: Routledge, 1998).

[140] Iikura, "The Anglo-Japanese Alliance and the Question of Race," p. 222.

[141] Nish, *Alliance in Decline*, p. 269.

ble to specify whether the perception of cultural difference fueled, or was fueled by, substantive disagreements about strategy and policy. But the empirical evidence makes clear that mutual recognition of racial and cultural difference served as an obstacle to forging the sense of communal identity and common purpose central to advancing reconciliation and consolidating stable peace.

As Akira Iikura concludes in his study of the impact of race on the alliance, "It can be said the Alliance couldn't make the two island empires 'true' friends. Yet, it may be inappropriate to conclude that it failed to overcome the racial difference between the two because it did not intend to do so from the beginning."[142] Had such cultural differences not existed—or had they been overcome—it is at least conceivable that Britain and Japan might have been able to consolidate rapprochement and that Japan's confrontation with the Western powers in the 1930s would have never materialized, changing quite radically the history of the twentieth century. As several historians have suggested, had the alliance deepened and endured, it "might have saved Japan (and the world) from future calamity."[143] David Steeds goes further, contending that Britain's decision to walk away from the alliance "was one of the main causes of the breakdown of the 1930s and the sequence of events leading to Pearl Harbor."[144]

THE RISE AND DEMISE OF SINO-SOVIET RAPPROCHEMENT, 1949–1960

During the first half of the 1950s, Sino-Soviet rapprochement advanced swiftly, producing extensive economic and strategic cooperation. By the middle of the decade, thousands of Russian scientists and engineers were living in China. They transferred to their communist ally the Soviet Union's best industrial and military technology, and even helped the Chinese develop a nuclear weapons program. The demise of Sino-Soviet rapprochement, however, occurred with equally remarkable speed. After sharp disagreements over domestic and foreign policy emerged in 1958, the Soviets in 1960 withdrew their experts and broke off cooperation. Mutual accusation and insult read-

---

[142] Iikura, "The Anglo-Japanese Alliance and the Question of Race," pp. 233–234.
[143] Dickinson, "Japan Debates the Anglo-Japanese Alliance," p. 100.
[144] Steeds, "Anglo-Japanese Relations, 1902–23," p. 221.

ily replaced talk of brotherly friendship and socialist solidarity. Within a few short years, both countries had militarized their common border, and stable peace gave way to open geopolitical rivalry.

The trajectory of the Sino-Soviet Alliance is notable not just for the rapidity of its rise and fall. The two parties that succeeded in carving out a zone of peace—even if only a short-lived one—were both authoritarian states, raising important questions about the relationship between institutionalized restraint and stable peace. Furthermore, the Soviet Union and China did not share a common ethnicity, race, or religion and thus did not enjoy cultural affinity. From this perspective, the Sino-Soviet case raises important questions about the role that regime type and cultural commonality play in the onset of stable peace.

How did two authoritarian countries that lacked cultural commonality succeed in building one of the closest strategic partnerships of modern times? Why did that partnership unravel even more quickly than it emerged? The historical record points to the critical role played by ideology in both the rise of stable peace and its demise. It was communist ideology that brought the Soviet Union and China into close alignment. Indeed, the ideological unity made possible by the absence of domestic pluralism in part explains the remarkable depth of the strategic partnership that emerged and why cultural differences did not serve as obstacles to the demilitarization of Sino-Soviet relations.

At the same time, the dependence of stable peace on ideological solidarity also explains the rapid demise of the Sino-Soviet Alliance. Both countries lacked the moderating and stabilizing influence of institutionalized restraint and pluralism, leaving the relationship vulnerable to the diverging ideological proclivities of Nikita Khrushchev and Mao Zedong. Moreover, ideological differences were rooted in the fundamentally incompatible social orders of the two countries; an industrializing economy in the Soviet Union and an agrarian one in China put the two parties on divergent ideological paths. Just as ideological convergence was the foundation of the alliance, ideological rivalry readily translated into the onset of geopolitical rivalry.

The Rise of the Sino-Soviet Alliance: How Peace Broke Out

Following the Russian Revolution in 1917, the Bolshevik regime pledged to end the tsarist government's long-standing imperial confrontation with

China. Soon thereafter, however, Russian expansionism returned. During the 1920s, the Soviet army occupied Outer Mongolia and intervened in Manchuria. In the 1930s, armed incursions consolidated Xinjiang as part of the Soviet Union's sphere of influence, but Japanese advances in Manchuria and North China began to focus the Chinese and Soviets alike on Tokyo's ambitions. Japan's occupation of China and the outbreak of World War II followed soon thereafter.

Toward the end of World War II, China and the Soviet Union allied against Japan. The Soviet Union signed a treaty of alliance with the Chinese Nationalists in 1945, coordinating operations against Japan and restoring Soviet influence in Manchuria and North China. Amid the Chinese civil war that ensued after the defeat of Japan, Moscow continued to lean toward the Nationalists despite its ideological ties to the Chinese Communist Party (CCP), calculating that in the aftermath of the war the Nationalists would be able to provide a more effective counterweight against Japan and the Western powers. The Soviets also feared that a communist victory in China might invite a U.S. invasion, ultimately confronting Moscow with the prospect of a war with the United States.[145] Soviet policy was guided more by considerations of realpolitik than ideology.

The CCP's military successes against the Nationalists cleared the way for much closer political and military ties between Moscow and the Chinese communists. The first major advance came in January 1949, when Anastas Mikoyan, a member of the Soviet Politburo, traveled to China to meet with Mao. Soon thereafter, Moscow expanded Soviet assistance to China, transferring heavy weaponry, helping with railway repairs, and increasing economic assistance. That summer, a Chinese delegation led by Liu Shaoqi, Mao's second in command, traveled to Moscow to meet with Stalin and other top officials. They succeeded in securing additional military and economic aid. Mao followed in December, clearing the way for the conclusion of a formal alliance in February 1950.

Strategic imperatives compelled both parties toward alliance. The Soviets were keen on preserving their territorial and political gains in East Asia in order to maintain a buffer against Japan and the United States. The Chinese communists were vulnerable on multiple fronts, facing threats from abroad as

---

[145] Niu Jun, "The Origins of the Sino-Soviet Alliance," in Odd Arne Westad, ed., *Brothers in Arms: The Rise and Fall of the Sino-Soviet Alliance, 1945–1963* (Washington, DC: Woodrow Wilson Center Press, 1998), pp. 55–61.

well as political instability and economic duress at home. As Odd Arne Westad notes, "Only an alliance with Moscow would provide the new revolutionary regime with the protection it needed from attacks by the United States, its ally Japan, and anti-Communist forces in China."[146] John Gittings agrees, arguing that the main impetus behind China's enthusiasm for alliance was "the military and political backing which it provided at a time when the new government was at its most vulnerable."[147] Two Chinese historians, Chen Jian and Yang Kuisong, offer a similar interpretation, noting that "it was the possibility of military intervention from imperialist countries that decided the necessity of China allying itself with socialist countries."[148]

The Sino-Soviet Treaty of 1950 was much more than a mutual commitment to collective defense against common enemies. From the outset, both parties demonstrated a remarkable degree of confidence in the other's intentions, readily engaging in acts of reciprocal restraint and accepting mutual vulnerability. Even before the signing of the treaty, the Soviets were sending technical experts to China to assist with industrial and military projects, including the development of a modern air force and navy. Moscow approved a $300 million loan to China at 1 percent interest, half the rate set for other members of the socialist bloc. China reciprocated by assenting to the continuation and expansion of Soviet influence in the region. Beijing approved Moscow's privileges in Xinjiang and North China, its continued access to naval bases in Lushan and Dalian, and joint Soviet-Chinese ownership of industrial enterprises in China. In discussing with Stalin the option of Soviet withdrawal from Chinese naval bases, Mao insisted that "this question worries us only because it may have undesirable consequences for the USSR."[149] In effect, the security dilemma was working in reverse from the early days of the Sino-Soviet Alliance; the parties shared congruent interests and pursued joint gains.

The burgeoning strategic partnership between China and the Soviet Union was strengthened considerably by the Korean War, which began in June 1950.

[146] Odd Arne Westad, "Introduction," in Westad, *Brothers in Arms*, p. 9.
[147] John Gittings, *Survey of the Sino-Soviet Dispute: Commentary and Extracts from the Recent Polemics, 1963–1967* (London: Oxford University Press, 1968), p. 17.
[148] Chen Jian and Yang Kuisong, "Chinese Politics and the Collapse of the Sino-Soviet Alliance," in Westad, *Brothers in Arms*, p. 247.
[149] Record of Conversation, Stalin and Mao Zedong, January 22, 1950, in Westad, *Brothers in Arms*, p. 325.

China entered the war in October, encouraged to do so by the Soviet Union. From Moscow's perspective, China demonstrated not only its military prowess, but also its willingness to bear the costs of communist solidarity—some 900,000 Chinese were killed or wounded in the war. From Beijing's perspective, the Soviets proved to be steady allies, offering air transport and air cover, military supplies, and advisers. Close contact during the war helped build institutional and personal ties between the Chinese and Soviet leadership and military establishments.[150]

Although Sino-Soviet rapprochement proceeded with remarkable speed and scope, its early years were not without their difficulties. The Soviets rejected Chinese requests for effective control over Mongolia, political and material support for conquering Taiwan, and joint efforts to foment revolutionary change throughout East Asia. Furthermore, although Mao and his colleagues recognized the Soviet Union's political and ideological leadership, they resented its domineering attitude toward China. As Westad comments, "the Soviet side consistently forced the Chinese into the role of supplicants, and Stalin, especially, missed no opportunity to lord over his visitors."[151]

In part due to Mao's discomfort with Stalin, the Soviet leader's death in 1953 and the subsequent ascent of Nikita Khrushchev cleared the way for a further deepening of relations between China and the Soviet Union. Indeed, Sino-Soviet relations reached their peak during the mid-1950s, with strategic and economic cooperation as well as societal linkages growing steadily until the alliance began to stumble in 1958.

Khrushchev visited Beijing in the fall of 1954—his first foreign trip as premier and the first-ever visit of a Soviet leader to China—significantly elevating the Sino-Soviet Alliance in both symbolic and concrete terms. Under his leadership, the Soviet Union substantially increased its economic, technical, and military assistance to China. Moscow approved a sizable new loan, sent legions of experts and advisers, and opened the way for China to receive the Soviet Union's best industrial and military technology. Sergei Goncharenko reveals that "enterprises built with Soviet assistance were sometimes equipped with state-of-the-art machinery not yet available at Soviet enterprises."[152] The

[150] Westad, "Introduction," pp. 12–15.
[151] Westad, "Introduction," p. 12.
[152] Sergei Goncharenko, "Sino-Soviet Military Cooperation," in Westad, *Brothers in Arms*, p. 155.

Soviets transferred MIG-17's, short-range missiles, and nuclear technology and fuel, enabling China to open a nuclear reactor in 1958. The Soviet Union even promised to help China develop its nuclear weapons program.[153] Although that pledge appears not to have come to fruition, the Soviets nonetheless helped China's weapons program advance through the transfer of technology and the training of scientists. In addition, Moscow exported to China ballistic missiles—though without warheads.[154] In 1958, the Soviets wanted to deepen further strategic cooperation, proposing a unified submarine fleet under shared command and a joint military communications center to coordinate maritime operations.

Moscow not only undertook these significant efforts to strengthen China's economy and its military capability, but also overtly practiced strategic restraint. The Soviets no longer insisted upon maintaining political dominance in Manchuria and Xinjiang, returned to Chinese control the naval bases at Lushan and Dalian, transferred to China ownership of jointly held enterprises, and gave up their stake in the Changchun Railway, one of China's primary transportation networks. Along with Khrushchev's support for greater equality among members of the socialist bloc—which he unveiled at the Twentieth Congress of the CPSU in 1956—these moves helped alleviate Chinese concerns about Moscow's domineering ways, leading Mao to conclude that he could "place himself as a theoreticist [sic] and political leader at least on par with the Soviet leader himself."[155] These policies reinforced the perception among Chinese officials that they had succeeded in building an "indestructible friendship" with the Soviet Union.[156]

A document drafted by the Soviet Foreign Ministry later in the decade noted these important changes in Chinese attitudes toward the Soviet Union. It admitted that Moscow had initially kept Beijing in a "subordinate position," but that Khrushchev's more pliant leadership had "played an important role in the establishment of closer and more trusting relations." The memo concluded that "an analysis of Soviet-Chinese relations over the past

---

[153] Aleksandr Fursenko and Timothy Naftali, *Khrushchev's Cold War: The Inside Story of an American Adversary* (New York: Norton, 2006), p. 328.

[154] On the transfer of nuclear technology, see Shu Guang Zhang, "Sino-Soviet Cooperation," p. 207, and Constantine Pleshakov, "Nikita Khrushchev and Sino-Soviet Relations," pp. 232–233, both in Westad, *Brothers in Arms*.

[155] Odd Arne Westad, "The Sino-Soviet Alliance and the United States," in Westad, *Brothers in Arms*, p. 174.

[156] First National People's Congress, in Gittings, *Survey of the Sino-Soviet Dispute*, p. 57.

decade confirms that relations of fraternal amity and fruitful cooperation have been established on a lasting basis and are growing wider and stronger every passing year."[157]

By the mid-1950s, China and the Soviet Union enjoyed a level of strategic partnership that is quite rare among peacetime allies. Indeed, during the second half of the decade rapprochement appears to have evolved into security community. The prospect of war between the two countries was out of the question, the Soviets were sharing with the Chinese their best industrial and military technology, and the two countries had embraced a common set of principles for guiding their relationship and the conduct of their foreign policies. As a joint declaration published in late 1954 stated, the two parties "note the full coincidence of their views both on the all-round cooperation developing between their two countries and on international affairs. . . . [The alliance] is founded on the sincere desire of the Chinese and Soviet peoples to assist one another, to promote the economic and cultural progress of their two countries, to continually strengthen and broaden their brotherly friendship, and thereby contribute to peace and security in the Far East and throughout the world."[158]

As this account of the evolution of the Sino-Soviet Alliance makes clear, societal integration and narratives of friendship and common purpose began even as the partnership was still taking shape. Soviet experts and technicians began flowing into China in the early 1950s, with equal numbers of Chinese heading to the Soviet Union for education and technical training. By the end of the decade, some 10,000 Soviet experts had worked in China, and some 11,000 Chinese had trained in the Soviet Union.[159] Bilateral trade mounted quickly over the course of the decade, fueled by the industrial enterprises launched in China with Soviet aid and technology. Chinese trade with the Soviet Union represented almost 50 percent of its foreign commerce by the late 1950s, by which time China was the Soviet Union's top trading partner.[160]

---

[157] Report from Mikhail Zimyanin, Head of the Soviet Foreign Ministry's Far Eastern Department, September 1959, in Westad, *Brothers in Arms*, pp. 357–360.

[158] Joint Declaration of the Government of the USSR and the Government of the Chinese People's Republic, in Gittings, *Survey of the Sino-Soviet Dispute*, p. 289.

[159] Gittings, *Survey of the Sino-Soviet Dispute*, p. 135. The sources vary as to the precise number of people who participated in these technical and educational exchanges.

[160] Oleg Hoeffding, "Sino-Soviet Economic Relations, 1959–1962," *Annals of the American Academy of Political and Social Science*, "Communist China and the Soviet Bloc," 349, no. 1 (September 1963), p. 97.

Alexander Eckstein estimates that "in the absence of these [Soviet] imports, Communist China's economic growth might possibly have fallen from an average annual rate of 6–7 per cent to 3–5 per cent."[161] Cultural exchanges, friendship societies, and other elite-led efforts to promote amity emerged in step. Importantly, and in a manner consistent with the other cases, economic integration followed from rather than preceded the conclusion of a strategic partnership. Interdependence and societal contact then helped turn what had begun as an instrumental alliance into a deeper bond.

From early on, both private and public declarations of amity and friendship accompanied the onset of Sino-Soviet cooperation. During their meeting in the summer of 1949, Liu Shaoqi presented to Stalin a report on Sino-Soviet relations. With Mao's approval, Liu informed Stalin that

> the strong friendship between the great peoples of the USSR and China is of paramount importance for our two countries and the entire world. . . . The CCP shall stint no effort in the cause of strengthening the friendship between our two peoples. . . . We would like to settle as soon as possible matters related to establishing postal, telegraph, railway, and air services with the USSR and, also, we would like to set up a joint Soviet-Chinese air company. . . . We believe it is necessary to establish the closest mutual ties between the two parties."[162]

During 1949, Mao himself asserted that "the relationship between China and the Soviet Union is a close and brotherly relationship."[163] The Chinese press frequently referred to relations between the Soviet Union and China as similar to that between "big elder brother" and "little brother" or "father and son." Soviet leaders and the media similarly attributed familial attributes to the relationship, often using terminology such as "ties of brotherly friendship" and "fraternal amity" to refer to the alliance.[164]

Although strategic necessity was initially the driving force behind the Sino-Soviet Alliance, ideological solidarity contributed to the rapid onset of not only reciprocal restraint and strategic cooperation but also societal integra-

---

[161] Bernhard Grossman, "International Economic Relations of the People's Republic of China," *Asian Survey* 10, no. 9 (September 1970), p. 790.

[162] Translated report available in Westad, *Brothers in Arms*, pp. 301–313.

[163] Niu Jun, "The Origins of the Sino-Soviet Alliance," in Westad, *Brothers in Arms*, p. 67.

[164] Lowell Dittmer, *Sino-Soviet Normalization and Its International Implications, 1945–1990* (Seattle: University of Washington Press, 1992), p. 17; Gittings, *Survey of the Sino-Soviet Dispute*, p. 289; Foreign Ministry document of September 15, 1959, in Westad, *Brothers in Arms*, p. 360.

tion and narratives of amity—stages in the onset of rapprochement that usually take much longer to develop. For the Soviet Union, alliance with China
meant extending and strengthening the international socialist movement. As
Nikita Khrushchev stated soon after coming to power, "After the Great October Socialist Revolution, the victory of the Chinese people's revolution is
the most outstanding event in world history."[165] For China, the Soviets provided not just ideological guidance and a role model, but an advanced polity
ready and willing to provide concrete help to China in building a socialist
society. In Mao's own words, "The Communist Party of the Soviet Union . . .
is the most advanced, the most experienced, and the most theoretically culti-
vated Party in the world. This Party has been our model in the past, is our
model at present, and will be our model in the future."[166] Even after disagreements had begun to emerge during the second half of the 1950s, Mao reassured the Soviet ambassador that "We trust your people, because you are
from a socialist country, and you are sons and daughters of Lenin."[167]

As Donald Zagoria observes, "One cannot stress too much that the partners to the Sino-Soviet alliance are dedicated to a common purpose and
bound together by a common ideology."[168] John Gittings agrees: "No doubt
the common bond of ideology accentuated the degree of [China's] inclina-
tion to the Soviet side."[169] Scholars may disagree about whether ideology or
strategic interest played a more important role in consolidating the partnership, but few, if any, question that ideological commonality was a key source
of strategic cooperation and a shared sense of affinity.[170]

The Demise of the Sino-Soviet Alliance: How Rapprochement Failed

Rapprochement between China and the Soviet Union peaked between 1955
and 1958. After substantial disagreements began to emerge in 1958, the relationship deteriorated quickly. In 1959, the Soviets ended nuclear cooperation
with China. The following year, Moscow withdrew its experts, the parties
broke off economic and military cooperation, and Khrushchev and Mao became open rivals for dominance within the socialist bloc.

Ideological divergence was the chief cause of the breakdown of stable

---

[165] Gittings, *Survey of the Sino-Soviet Dispute*, p. 56.

[166] Dittmer, *Sino-Soviet Normalization*, p. 17.

[167] Westad, *Brothers in Arms*, p. 350.

[168] Donald Zagoria, *The Sino-Soviet Conflict, 1956–1961* (New York: Atheneum, 1964), p. 8.

[169] Gittings, *Survey of the Sino-Soviet Dispute*, p. 16.

[170] On this debate, see Dittmer, *Sino-Soviet Normalization*, pp. 2–13.

peace between China and the Soviet Union. According to Zagoria, "what began as a dispute over alternative revolutionary strategies . . . developed into an incipient struggle for power in the international Communist movement."[171] Doctrinal disagreements over both domestic and foreign affairs led to not only differing policy preferences, but also competition between Moscow and Beijing over questions of status and hierarchy. The shared sense of affinity and trust that had built up began to deteriorate. Mutual perceptions of benign character and communal identity eroded and were gradually replaced by mutual suspicion and narratives of opposition. Societal separation followed; scientific and cultural exchanges ended and bilateral trade plummeted. Geopolitical rivalry came soon thereafter. By 1963, border disputes prompted both China and the Soviet Union to start remilitarizing their common border. The causal mechanisms that had led to rapprochement were working in reverse; doctrinal differences and narratives of opposition led to societal separation, in turn reawakening the security dilemma and geopolitical rivalry.

IDEOLOGICAL DIVERGENCE

In the aftermath of Stalin's domineering rule, the CCP initially reacted enthusiastically to Khrushchev's more pliant leadership. Khrushchev's speech at the Twentieth Congress of the CPSU in 1956 marked an ideological high point for the alliance. Mao welcomed Khrushchev's criticism of Stalin's cult of personality and the notion of a more polycentric socialist bloc in which individual countries would enjoy more equality and autonomy. The common ground, however, did not last long. During the second half of the 1950s, Khrushchev pursued ideological moderation and centrism, seeking to promote social and political stability. In contrast, Mao moved fast to the left, by 1958 embracing more radical stances on a number of key issues.

The most visible manifestation of Mao's shift to the left was the Great Leap Forward, his effort to stimulate rapid economic growth through mass mobilization of the peasantry. The proliferation of small industrial enterprises in the countryside, the establishment of agricultural communes, and the formation of a people's militia—these initiatives would at once invigorate the economy and unleash the revolutionary potential of the peasantry. This turn in Chinese doctrine and policy challenged not only the Soviet model of

---

[171] Zagoria, *The Sino-Soviet Conflict*, p. 385.

centralized industrialization, but the Marxist-Leninist emphasis on the urban working class as the political base of the socialist revolution. Furthermore, while Khrushchev was looking to consolidate his rule and neutralize domestic opposition by normalizing political and economic life in the Soviet Union, Mao was doing the opposite—consolidating his power and neutralizing the opposition by stoking revolutionary fires and insisting upon social upheaval as a necessary element in the transition to communism.

Sharp ideological differences also emerged over matters of foreign policy. Although Mao looked favorably on Khrushchev's call for greater pluralism within the socialist bloc, he ultimately concluded that Moscow had become too tolerant of dissent, risking the dissolution of the bloc by accommodating Yugoslavia's drift toward neutrality. Mao believed that political solidarity could and must accompany a polycentric bloc. The Central Committee of the CPSU responded, "It would be wrong to 'excommunicate' Yugoslavia from socialism . . . to cut her off from the socialist countries and to push her into the camp of imperialism, as the CPC leaders are doing."[172]

Beijing and Moscow also parted company on how to deal with nations outside the bloc. While Khrushchev pursued "peaceful coexistence" with the United States, Mao insisted that war between socialist and capitalist countries was an inevitable stage along the path to communism. And while Moscow embraced a doctrine of peaceful transition to socialism in the developing world, Beijing favored a more aggressive effort to foment revolutionary upheaval.[173]

POLICY DIFFERENCES

Ideological divergence readily translated into sharp differences over policy, compromising the degree to which China and the Soviet Union attributed benign motivation to each other's statecraft. At the height of the Sino-Soviet partnership, Beijing would likely have responded with enthusiasm to the Soviet proposal in 1958 for a joint submarine fleet and naval communications center. But in the context of growing ideological estrangement, the Chinese responded quite differently. Mao reacted to the proposal by telling Pavel Iudin, Moscow's ambassador in Beijing, "Well, if [you] want joint ownership and operation, how about having them all—let us turn into joint ownership

---

[172] Gittings, *Survey of the Sino-Soviet Dispute*, p. 87.

[173] For extensive discussion of the ideological split between the Soviet Union and China, see Zagoria, *The Sino-Soviet Conflict*.

and operation our army, navy, air force, industry, agriculture, education. . . .
With a few atomic bombs, you think you are in a position to control us
through asking for the right of rent and lease." "These remarks of mine,"
Mao continued, "may not sound so pleasing to your ear. You may accuse me
of being a nationalist or another Tito. My counter argument is that you have
extended Russian nationalism to China's coast."[174]

China and the Soviet Union also parted company on foreign policy. From
Moscow's perspective, China was growing dangerously aggressive in its external relations, needlessly risking international conflict. In the summer of 1958,
China shelled Jinmen and Mazu, Nationalist-held islands off the coast of
Taiwan. The following summer, Chinese and Indian troops exchanged fire
across the Sino-Indian border. Khrushchev vehemently criticized both developments, commenting that China was "craving for war like a cock for a
fight."[175] He later warned a gathering of delegations from the socialist bloc,
"When there are two world systems, it is imperative to build mutual relations
between them in such a way as to preclude the possibility of war breaking
out. . . . One cannot mechanically repeat what Lenin said many decades ago
on imperialism, and go on asserting that imperialist wars are inevitable until
socialism triumphs throughout the world."[176] No longer was China pursuing
the common interests of the bloc, but was instead acting on "narrowly nationalist interests."[177] Moscow interpreted the border skirmishes with India,
which came on the eve of Khrushchev's 1959 visit to the United States, as
aimed at "torpedoing the relaxation of international tension."[178] The Soviet
response to Chinese behavior only intensified Beijing's increasing skepticism
of Moscow's intentions, viewing Soviet policy as a betrayal of the socialist
cause.

By the middle of 1959, reciprocal restraint had given way to reciprocal
confrontation. The Soviets announced that they were breaking off all nuclear
cooperation with China, setting back Beijing's quest for nuclear weapons.
Soon thereafter, the rift spilled into the public domain, with both China and
the Soviet Union seeking to woo other members of the socialist bloc to their
side. As Mao commented, Khrushchev "is afraid that the Communist parties
in Eastern Europe and other countries of the world will not believe in them,

[174] Record of Conversation between Mao Zedong and Pavel Iudin, July 22, 1958, in Westad,
Brothers in Arms, pp. 347–356.
[175] Gittings, *Survey of the Sino-Soviet Dispute*, p. 118.
[176] Westad, *Brothers in Arms*, p. 25.
[177] Westad, *Brothers in Arms*, p. 380.
[178] Gittings, *Survey of the Sino-Soviet Dispute*, p. 112.

but in us." At a bloc congress in Bucharest in June 1960, the Soviets circulated to all delegations a letter clarifying their position on key doctrinal and policy issues and chastising the Chinese for factionalism. At a meeting of party heads, Khrushchev called Mao "an ultra-leftist, an ultra-dogmatist, indeed, a left revisionist."[179]

The following month, Moscow informed Beijing that it had recalled all Soviet experts from China, ordering them home by the end of August. The Soviets also canceled ongoing scientific and industrial projects and put an end to any new collaborative initiatives. The Central Committee of the CCP responded by dispatching a letter to its counterpart in Moscow, informing the CPSU that "you violate the principle of mutual assistance between socialist countries and use the sending of experts as an instrument for exerting political pressure on fraternal countries, butting into their internal affairs and impeding and sabotaging their socialist construction."[180]

A Warsaw Treaty conference in Moscow in November marked the de facto end of Sino-Soviet rapprochement. The declaration adopted at the meeting rejected virtually all of China's main doctrinal positions. Exchanges between the Soviet and Chinese delegations were not just devoid of references to "brotherly friendship," but also infused with hostile and accusatory language. Mutual perceptions of benign intent had given way to a mutual narrative of hostility.

From Beijing's perspective, Moscow was asserting its dominance over the socialist bloc, "demanding that fraternal parties should obey its baton, liquidating the principles of independence and equality in relations among fraternal parties, and replacing the principle of reaching unanimity through consultation by the practice of subduing the minority by the majority."[181] The Soviets were no longer seeking to defeat capitalism, but had instead turned "the spearhead of struggle against us and not against US imperialism."[182] From Moscow's perspective, Beijing was seeking to divide the socialist bloc: "Ever since the world communist movement came into being the reactionaries all over the world have been making frantic efforts to split its ranks. Today the Chinese leaders are trying to achieve what the imperialist reactionary forces have been unable to bring about."[183]

[179] Westad, *Brothers in Arms*, p. 25.
[180] Gittings, *Survey of the Sino-Soviet Dispute*, p. 140.
[181] Gittings, *Survey of the Sino-Soviet Dispute*, p. 149.
[182] Gittings, *Survey of the Sino-Soviet Dispute*, p. 126.
[183] Mikhail Suslov, Secretary of the CPSU CC, reflecting on the Moscow conference in remarks from February 1964, in Gittings, *Survey of the Sino-Soviet Dispute*, p. 150.

Societal separation followed from, rather than precipitated, the growing gap over ideology and policy. The withdrawal of Soviet experts and growing estrangement among high-level elites compromised the extensive network of contacts that had developed over the previous decade. Institutionalized efforts to promote societal integration ceased. In the summer of 1960, for example, Moscow suspended the distribution of *Druzhba* (Friendship), a Russian-language magazine published by China's Sino-Soviet Friendship Society.[184] Bilateral trade, which had grown at a healthy pace in the late 1950s, began to plummet after the open break between Moscow and Beijing. In 1959, the value of Sino-Soviet trade was $2.09 billion, representing about one-half of China's foreign trade. By 1962, bilateral commerce had dropped by 40 percent. In 1970, the total value of bilateral trade was $4.72 million, roughly 0.2 percent of its value a decade earlier.[185]

Political acrimony and societal separation soon translated into geopolitical rivalry. In 1962, the Soviets responded to the heating up of the Sino-Indian border controversy by providing India increased economic and military assistance, including MIG fighters and 1.5 million tons of refined petroleum. China vehemently opposed the U.S.-Soviet nuclear test ban treaty, arguing that Moscow was trying "to bind China by the hands and feet through an agreement with the USA."[186] From China's perspective, the Soviets not only abrogated their promise to help China acquire nuclear weapons, but were now seeking to impede China's program. In 1963, disputes emerged between Beijing and Moscow over the Sino-Soviet boundary. Both sides proceeded to remilitarize the border areas, ensuring that the former allies had, by the mid-1960s, become outright geopolitical rivals.

A commentary published in *People's Daily* in February 1967 makes clear the extent to which rapprochement between China and the Soviet Union had collapsed:

Is openly supporting the Indian aggressors and opposing China in collusion with India on the Sino-Indian border question to be counted as a manifestation of "friendship"? Is swinging cudgels to attack the Chinese Communist Party and the Chinese people at a series of international conferences to be counted as a manifestation of "friendship"? The unilateral

---

[184] Zagoria, *The Sino-Soviet Conflict*, p. 328.
[185] Dittmer, *Sino-Soviet Normalization,* p. 26.
[186] Deng Xiaoping, quoted in Westad, *Brothers in Arms*, p. 381.

scrapping of several hundred agreements and contracts at a time when China was suffering hardships, the withdrawal of all Soviet experts from China and the instigation of Sino-Soviet border disputes—are these also to be counted as manifestations of "friendship"? ... You new Tzars in the Kremlin listen: "The great Soviet people will one day rebel against you, and overthrow you—you handful of arch criminals who are trying to undermine the friendship between the people of China and the Soviet Union!"[187]

Looking back on the period, Khrushchev used equally caustic language in describing the rift: "We took great care never to offend China until the Chinese actually started to crucify us. And when they did start to crucify us—well, I'm no Jesus Christ, and I didn't have to turn the other cheek."[188]

Why Rapprochement Failed

The strategic necessities of the postwar landscape provided the initial impetus behind the Sino-Soviet Alliance. Ideological convergence then played a central role in deepening the strategic partnership, leading to levels of economic and military cooperation rare even for long-standing democratic partners. In similar fashion, ideological divergence during the late 1950s explains why the alliance came apart so rapidly. In examining the background conditions that so elevated the role of ideology in the demise of Sino-Soviet rapprochement, regime type—the absence of institutionalized restraint—and contrasting social orders emerge as key factors.

THE ABSENCE OF INSTITUTIONALIZED RESTRAINT

The Soviet Union and China were both ruled by autocratic regimes. The absence of institutionalized restraint contributed to the demise of stable peace in three important respects. First, both countries were ruled by dictatorial individuals. The overweening political power wielded by Stalin, Khrushchev, and Mao opened the door to major and unpredictable swings in ideology and policy. When Soviet and Chinese leaders agreed on the issues of the day, cooperation followed. But when they did not share common ideological ground,

---

[187] Shi Niexu, "What 'Friendship'!" *People's Daily*, February 14, 1967, in Gittings, *Survey of the Sino-Soviet Dispute*, pp. 51–52.
[188] Fursenko and Naftali, *Khrushchev's Cold War*, p. 328.

the relationship readily foundered. Missing were the continuity, moderation, and political restraint provided by institutionalized checks on autocratic power.

Both the Soviet and Chinese leaderships regularly complained about the personality-driven and unpredictable nature of the other's government. One member of the Central Committee of the CPSU, for example, blamed the rift with China on Mao's cult of personality, arguing that "the subjectivism and personal whims of one person are turned into the official political course; favourable soil is created for unjustified experiments, lack of controls and excessive ambitions; veerings from side to side, instability, adventurism and nationalism are created."[189] The Chinese leveled similar charges at the Soviets. According to *People's Daily*, "Stalin erroneously exaggerated his own role and counterposed his individual authority to the collective leadership. . . . The cult of the individual was accepted and fostered, and the arbitrariness of a single person prevailed." Stalin, the article continued, placed himself "over and above the Party and the masses instead of in their midst."[190]

Second, precisely because they were autocratic states whose legitimacy depended upon ideological purpose rather than deliberation and consent, ideology became a crucial battleground for influence and leadership within the socialist bloc. As Zagoria observes, "ideologically oriented powers such as Russia and China have much greater difficulty in harmonizing differences of view and interest than do the more pragmatic non-communist powers which are accustomed to having and to adjusting conflicting interests."[191] In a political arena defined primarily by ideological objectives, the struggle over ideas was inseparable from the struggle over power. The Chinese leadership accepted the dominant position of the Soviet Union in both ideational and material terms; after all, Russia was at the forefront of the socialist revolution and was far ahead of China in terms of economic development and military power. At the same time, China had long been the victim of Japanese and European imperialism, and was not about to accept permanent subjugation by another major power.

In the late 1940s and early 1950s, the drive to assert ideological independence manifested itself in terms of Mao's effort to "sinify" Marxism-Lenin-

---

[189] Leonid Ilyichev in Gittings, *Survey of the Sino-Soviet Dispute*, p. 215.

[190] *People's Daily*, April 5, 1956, in Gittings, *Survey of the Sino-Soviet Dispute*, p. 291.

[191] Zagoria, *The Sino-Soviet Conflict*, p. xix.

ism.[192] Mao was effectively adapting orthodox Marxism to Chinese conditions. During the early 1950s, the Chinese leadership certainly resented Stalin's blustery leadership style, but basic convergence on ideology and policy provided a foundation for partnership. After the ideological parting of ways that took place in the late 1950s, however, Chinese concern about Soviet domination mounted steadily.[193] Beijing did not question Moscow's right to leadership, but it did object to the absolute form that leadership was taking. In reflecting on the increasing strains that emerged after 1957, the editorial departments of *People's Daily* and *Red Flag* observed:

> Fraternal Parties should be independent and completely equal, and at the same time they should be united. . . . It is a flagrant violation of these principles . . . for the leaders of the CPSU to consider themselves the leaders of the international communist movement and to treat all fraternal Parties as their subordinates. . . . We hold that the existence of the position of head does not contradict the principle of equality among fraternal Parties. It does not mean that the CPSU has any right to control other Parties; what it means is that the CPSU carries greater responsibility and duties on its shoulders.[194]

From 1958 onward, Mao and his colleagues complained regularly about the Soviet Union's "big-power chauvinism."[195] Beijing's perception of Soviet intentions changed markedly. Initiatives such as the 1958 proposal to form a joint submarine fleet were in fact Moscow's response to Chinese requests for naval cooperation.[196] But they were seen in Beijing as overt attempts to subjugate China, not to deepen the Sino-Soviet partnership. As Deng Xiaoping told the CPSU in the early 1960s, Moscow was trying "to bring China under its military control. But we guessed your intentions and you were not able to attain your goals."[197] Mao not only rejected the proposal, but went on to tell the Soviet ambassador, "You [Russians] have never had faith in the Chinese people, and Stalin was among the worst. The Chinese [Communists] were re-

---

[192] See Gittings, *Survey of the Sino-Soviet Dispute*, pp. 8–9.

[193] See Zagoria, *The Sino-Soviet Conflict*, p. 14.

[194] "The Leaders of the CPSU are the greatest splitters of our times," February 4, 1964, in Gittings, *Survey of the Sino-Soviet Dispute*, p. 78.

[195] Mao speech on January 27, 1957, in Westad, *Brothers in Arms*, p. 345.

[196] Westad, *Brothers in Arms*, p. 347.

[197] Westad, *Brothers in Arms*, p. 379

garded as Tito the Second; [the Chinese people] were considered a backward nation. You [Russians] have often stated that the Europeans looked down upon the Russians. I believe that some Russians look down upon the Chinese people."[198]

Not surprisingly, the Soviets responded to such charges in kind, accusing China of "not only groundless criticism but also malicious slander." Its intentions were clear; Beijing was seeking "to defame the policies of the CPSU and thereby further worsen the relations between our two parties and countries."[199] In the absence of pluralism and political restraint, ideological disputes were more than disagreements about ideas; they had become contests for power and prestige.

Third, the challenge of legitimating autocratic rule led the Soviet and Chinese governments to use ideology as an instrument of domestic policy, orchestrating doctrinal shifts to mobilize the public and neutralize domestic opponents. Khrushchev's ideological detour in the mid-1950s and his embrace of a doctrine of peaceful coexistence with the West—which ultimately contributed to the breach with Mao—emerged in part from the succession struggle that followed Stalin's death and Khrushchev's use of doctrinal change to consolidate his rule and undercut his main political challengers.[200] Similarly, Mao's radical turn to the left in the late 1950s was in part an effort to neutralize a more conservative faction within the CCP that had begun to call for the partial restoration of capitalism.[201] Concern about domestic legitimacy also informed Mao's opposition to the notion of peaceful coexistence; continuous struggle and the inevitability of war were key components of his strategy of popular mobilization.[202]

This interpretation is not meant to suggest that ideological innovation played a purely instrumental role for either the Soviet or Chinese leadership. But the timing and content of doctrinal shifts were clearly affected by domestic calculations. As Westad observes, "Instability in foreign policy priorities is common for revolutionary regimes and probably is connected to the leaders' perceptual changes, which occur when the needs of the state surmount those

[198] Record of Conversation between Mao Zedong and Pavel Iudin, July 22, 1958, in Westad, *Brothers in Arms*, pp. 347–356.
[199] Boris Ponomarev, head of the International Department of the CPSU CC Secretariat, in Westad, *Brothers in Arms*, p. 386.
[200] Goncharenko, "Sino-Soviet Military Cooperation," p. 146.
[201] See Zagoria, *The Sino-Soviet Conflict*, pp. 68–69.
[202] Pleshakov, "Nikita Khrushchev and Sino-Soviet Relations," p. 233.

of a movement with international lineages or linkages as its main points of reference."[203]

THE INCOMPATIBILITY OF SOCIAL ORDERS

The connection between doctrinal change and domestic politics leads directly to the other main source of ideological divergence between China and the Soviet Union—their different social orders. The political and social demands of the Soviet Union's industrializing economy conflicted with those of China's primarily agrarian economy; this contrast served as a primary source of the ideological rupture that led to the demise of Sino-Soviet rapprochement.

In the Soviet Union, the power of the Communist Party was based in urban areas. Amid economic modernization and industrialization, the urban proletariat was to provide the foot soldiers for the socialist revolution. Between 1939 and 1959, almost 2,000 new cities and towns were established in the Soviet Union.[204] The rural population, which constituted over 85 percent of the workforce in the 1920s, was less than 50 percent of the workforce by the late 1950s.[205] Moreover, the Soviet leadership had long distrusted the peasantry and sought to extract from collective farms as many resources as they could to support urbanization and industrialization. In contrast, the CCP came to power in the countryside. China's population was largely agrarian; the country's vast peasantry, which represented over 80 percent of the population, was to provide the foot soldiers for China's revolution.

This fundamental difference in social structure was one of the main reasons for Mao's ideological departure from Soviet doctrine; the Great Leap Forward and the establishment of people's militias and agricultural communes were explicit efforts to mobilize the peasantry behind the party and the demands of building a communist society. As Zagoria observes, the leftward shift in Chinese doctrine that took place in the late 1950s emerged from "a number of conditioning social and economic factors never or no longer relevant in the Soviet Union." The left wing of the party, he continues, "had an almost mythical faith in the power of the masses if properly mobilized."[206]

Chinese and Soviet officials openly acknowledged that contrasting social

[203] Westad, "The Sino-Soviet Alliance and the United States," p. 182.

[204] Victor P. Petrov, "Some Observations on the 1959 Soviet Census," *Russian Review* 18, no. 4 (October 1959): 337.

[205] Jan S. Prybyla, "Problems of Soviet Agriculture," *Journal of Farm Economics* 44, no. 3 (August 1962): 820.

[206] Zagoria, *The Sino-Soviet Conflict*, pp. 78, 68.

orders were indeed contributing to ideological disagreement. As Lin Biao wrote in *People's Daily*:

> The peasantry constituted more than 80 percent of the entire population of semi-colonial and semi-feudal China. . . . It was essential to rely mainly on the peasants if the people's war was to be won. . . . As far back as the period of the First Revolutionary Civil War, Comrade Mao Tse-tung had pointed out that the peasant question occupied an extremely important position in the Chinese revolution, that the bourgeois-democratic revolution against imperialism and feudalism was in essence a peasant revolution and that the basic task of the Chinese proletariat in the bourgeois-democratic revolution was to give leadership to the peasants' struggle.[207]

L. Ilyichev, in a report to the Academy of Social Sciences and the Institute of Marxism-Leninism, offered a remarkably similar analysis:

> What is the explanation for the Chinese leadership's departure from the general line of the world Communist movement, its effort to break away from it? . . . The *social structure* of China's society is linked to its economic backwardness. China is the largest peasant country in the world. . . . The industrial proletariat, which by virtue of its position is the leading force of the socialist revolution, at the time of the revolution in China did not amount to even 1% of the country's population. . . . The activity of the CPC developed largely in remote rural places, divorced from the main working-class base, away from the large cities and industrial centers.[208]

The timing of the ideological break between China and the Soviet Union also correlates well with the different economic trajectories of the two countries over the course of 1950s. By the second half of the decade, the Soviet Union was enjoying a steady expansion in industrialization, healthy rates of economic growth, and impressive technological successes.[209] Khrushchev was less interested in ideological mobilization than in boosting production and consumption in order to leave behind the deprivations of World War II and the Stalinist era. Russian advances in the space race—long-range ballistic

---

[207] Lin Biao, "Long Live the Victory of People's War!" *People's Daily*, September 2, 1965, in Gittings, *Survey*, pp. 32–33.

[208] Gittings, *Survey of the Sino-Soviet Dispute*, pp. 33–35.

[209] Estimates of annual growth vary, but the Soviets appear to have sustained growth rates of roughly 7 percent per year during the second half of the 1950s. See Robert W. Campbell, "The Post-War Growth of the Soviet Economy," *Soviet Studies* 16, no. 1 (July 1964): 1–16.

missiles were successfully tested and *Sputnik* was launched into orbit in 1957—confirmed the country's accomplishments; having attained technological parity with the West, the Soviet Union could focus on consolidating its gains. This attitude was reflected in the bureaucratization of the Soviet leadership. Particularly on matters of foreign policy, stability and pragmatism could take precedence over mobilization and ideological fervor.[210]

In China, the revolution was still in its early stages. The Communist Party was struggling to consolidate its rule and to implement an economic program that would bring sustained growth. Power was concentrated in the hands of Mao and his inner circle rather than in a vast party bureaucracy; the leadership still needed to rely on revolutionary fervor to maintain its authority and legitimacy. The empowerment of the peasantry, the inevitability of conflict with the capitalist bloc, the need for continuous struggle in the service of socialism—these were all ideological markers of a regime that, unlike that of the Soviet Union, continued to see mass mobilization and social upheaval as key ingredients of the transition to communism. As Constantine Pleshakov notes, "Mao and Khrushchev were dealing with two societies at different stages of revolution. Mao's was still to undergo the highest point of revolutionary tide with the Great Leap Forward and the Cultural Revolution, whereas many of Khrushchev's backers were already tired of the physical effects of revolution and longed for domestic stability."[211]

The concentration of power in the hands of individual leaders combined with these underlying differences in Soviet and Chinese social orders to undermine the Sino-Soviet Alliance. The temporary alignment of Soviet and Chinese ideology helped produce a remarkably close strategic partnership between 1949 and 1958. But contrasting social orders ultimately put Mao and Khrushchev on divergent ideological trajectories, rapidly undermining rapprochement and triggering the onset of geopolitical rivalry.

TWO ANOMALIES

Fully capitalizing on the analytic leverage afforded by this case study warrants taking note of two anomalies that distinguish the Sino-Soviet case from many of the others. First, the absence of institutionalized restraint, although it contributed to the demise of rapprochement, did not stand in the way of

---

[210] Zagoria, *The Sino-Soviet Conflict*, pp. 154–158.

[211] Pleshakov, "Nikita Khrushchev and Sino-Soviet Relations," p. 232. See also Zagoria, *The Sino-Soviet Conflict*, pp. xii–xiv, 18, 154–158, 244.

the initial onset of stable peace. Second, unlike in the other cases, cultural differences did not play a prominent role in affecting either the rise or demise of Sino-Soviet rapprochement. How can these two anomalies be understood? Again, the dominant role of ideology provides the best explanation; ideological convergence appears to have compensated for the absence of both institutionalized restraint and cultural commonality.

The Sino-Soviet case makes clear that the practice of strategic restraint is not the exclusive provenance of democracies or states subject to constitutional checks on power. Although autocratic states, China and the Soviet Union readily engaged in reciprocal restraint during the 1950s, exposing themselves to unusual levels of mutual vulnerability. The Soviets held joint control of China's strategic industries, infringed upon China's territorial sovereignty, and had direct access to China's military establishment. China was receiving state-of-the-art technology from the Soviet Union (including nuclear technology), capabilities that could potentially be turned against the Soviets—and indeed eventually were. From the early days of the alliance, the security dilemma was not just in abeyance, it was working in reverse.

This anomaly is best explained as the product of ideological affinity. Despite the sporadic nature of cooperation between the CPSU and the CCP before the communist victory in 1949, soon thereafter both parties were prepared to let down their guard and treat one another as benign polities. Especially after the Korean War and the sense of solidarity and common cause it engendered, the Soviet Union and China engaged in extraordinary levels of economic and military cooperation, motivated by common ideological objectives and the shared geopolitical interests that followed.

In similar fashion, the absence of the transparency usually associated with pluralist regimes does not appear to have constrained Sino-Soviet relations during either the rise or the collapse of rapprochement. On the contrary, despite the autocratic nature of both regimes, information was freely shared and neither side expressed chronic uncertainty about the intentions of the other party. Indeed, it would not be an exaggeration to suggest that the ready availability of information may well have expedited the demise of the partnership. The charged and public confrontations at party congresses, the steady flow of economic, scientific, and military data resulting from expert exchanges, the publication of polemical attacks by both sides—these vehicles for the free flow of information made both governments well aware of each other's ideological proclivities. As Mao made clear to the Soviet ambassador amid a harangue about Soviet policy, "We have held no secrets from you. Because more than one thousand of your experts are working in our country, you are fully aware of the state of our military, political, economic, and cultural affairs."[212]

This finding does challenge the notion that the transparency unique to liberal politics is a key ingredient of stable peace. To be sure, the Sino-Soviet case is an outlier; rarely do two countries, be they democratic or not, engage in such close cooperation so readily. The network of elite contacts and exchanges that grew soon after the alliance was concluded more than offset the constraints on information associated with the closed nature of the two regimes. That these ties took root so quickly and in such wide scope is a testament to the degree to which ideological commonality provided a ready sense of trust and affinity. That sense of comfort enabled both parties to bypass the normal sequence of steps in which signaling, testing, and the cautious assessment of intentions precede the onset of stable peace and the unfettered exchange of information.

Finally, there is very little evidence to suggest that the absence of cultural commonality either stood in the way of Sino-Soviet rapprochement or expedited its demise. To be sure, Mao and his comrades frequently complained about Soviet "great-power chauvinism" or Moscow's tendency to look down on the Chinese as backward. But the available literature provides no reason to believe that cultural differences figured prominently in the relationship. This finding is particularly striking in light of the important role that cultural commonality plays in the other cases.

Ideology again emerges as the most plausible explanation for this anomaly. In its Soviet variant, Marxism-Leninism was intended to transcend national culture. According to communist doctrine, ideology and class were to replace nationalism, ethnicity, and religion as the key sources of identity. If the peoples of China and the Soviet Union were united by bonds of socialism, then their cultural differences would be of no consequence. Mao may have sought to sinify Marxism-Leninism to adapt it to China's social conditions, but not to its culture. Indeed, the Chinese variant remained committed to the notion of a socialist solidarity that transcended nation, ethnic group, and language. Inasmuch as such cultural issues are curiously absent from discourse about Sino-Soviet rapprochement and its demise, this tenet of socialist doctrine appears to have been faithfully implemented.

[212] Record of Conversation, in Westad, *Brothers in Arms*, p. 350.

CONCLUSION

In probing how and when stable peace emerges, the five cases of rapprochement examined in chapters 3 and 4 provide quite consistent answers. As to process, there is striking similarity across the cases. Strategic necessity prompts one state to seek to befriend a potential partner through the practice of accommodation. The next step entails reciprocal restraint, with both states trading concessions and attributing to the other benign intent and motivation. Societal integration follows from rather than paves the way for political reconciliation; through growing interaction and interdependence, a sense of mutual trust sets in. The capstone of the process is the onset of compatible identities through the generation of a new narrative of friendship and kinship.

In those cases in which the initial advance of reconciliation did not lead to stable peace, this process either stalled or operated in reverse. In the Anglo-Japanese case, both parties initially practiced accommodation; Britain and Japan did attribute benign intent to one another's specific acts of cooperation. But the onset of rapprochement then stalled, failing to reach the stages of broad reciprocity and societal integration. London and Tokyo ultimately saw the alliance as no more than an instrumental partnership in which the other party was seeking only individual gain. Accordingly, Britain and Japan did not attribute to each other benign motivations, and they failed to develop the sense of trust and solidarity needed to lock in rapprochement. In the case of China and the Soviet Union, the parties rapidly advanced from reciprocal restraint to societal integration and mutual generation of a narrative of friendship. But a sharp ideological rift then sent the process into reverse. Chinese and Soviet leaders began to trade accusations of betrayal, undermining the narrative of common purpose. Societal separation came next, followed by the end of strategic accommodation and the return of geopolitical rivalry.

As for the conditions favoring the onset of rapprochement, figure 4.1 summarizes the main findings. Institutionalized restraint, compatible social orders, and cultural commonality were the causal conditions leading to rapprochement. At the same time, the cases reveal quite interesting deviations and exceptions. Institutionalized restraint is not a necessary condition for rapprochement to begin. Indeed, the initial acts of strategic restraint were regularly taken by autocratic regimes—Japan in the early 1900s, China and

	Case	Institutionalized Restraint	Compatible Social Orders	Cultural Commonality
Successes	United States and Great Britain (1895–1906)	Y	Y	Y
	Norway and Sweden (1905–1935)	Y	Y	Y
	Brazil and Argentina (1979–1998)	N at outset Y at completion	Y	Y
Failures	Great Britain and Japan (1902–1923)	N	N	N
	Soviet Union and China (1949–1960)	N	N	N

FIGURE 4.1   Rapprochement: Summary of Findings

the Soviet Union in the early 1950s, and Brazil and Argentina in 1979. It is
also the case that China and the Soviet Union, despite the autocratic nature
of both regimes, built a remarkably close and cohesive relationship that lasted
almost a decade. During the high point of Sino-Soviet rapprochement, the
two states did come to see one another as benign polities, underscoring the
extent to which benignity is in the eye of the beholder—in the Sino-Soviet
case the result of common ideological purpose.

Although institutionalized restraint was not necessary for rapprochement
to begin, it was a key factor enabling it to advance and endure. Only after
transitions to democracy were complete was stable peace consolidated between Great Britain and the United States, Norway and Sweden, and Argentina and Brazil. Democratic transitions facilitated the convergence of social
orders, bringing to an end aristocratic privilege in Britain and Sweden,
thereby facilitating rapprochement with the United States and Norway, respectively. Democratization also advanced the prospects for stable peace in
South America by leading to the ascendance of liberalizing and internationalist coalitions in Brazil and Argentina. In the Anglo-Japanese and Sino-Soviet cases, rapprochement did not last due in part to the absence of liberal
restraint. Incompatible social orders also played a key role, particularly in the
failure of Sino-Soviet rapprochement.

The Sino-Soviet case also stands out in terms of the insignificant role
played by cultural factors. Differences in language, religion, and ethnicity did
not block rapprochement during the first half of the 1950s, nor were these
differences responsible for the unraveling of the relationship after 1958. In
contrast, cultural factors figured prominently in all the other cases. In the

Anglo-Japanese case, racial tensions played a particularly pronounced role in constraining strategic partnership. As mentioned above, the adherence of China and the Soviet Union to communist ideology offers a compelling explanation of the insignificance of cultural variables to both the rise and demise of rapprochement.

CHAPTER FIVE

SECURITY COMMUNITY

Rapprochement entails the winding down of interstate rivalry and the muting, if not elimination, of geopolitical competition; peaceful coexistence results. Security community represents a more evolved form of stable peace, one in which the states in question go beyond mutual expectations of peaceful relations and consensually arrive at a set of rules and norms to guide their interactions. Rivalry gives way to not just peaceful coexistence, but an international society pacified and ordered by institutionalized codes of conduct. The interests of the member states become conjoined rather than merely congruent. And the members come to embrace a shared identity instead of possessing separate identities that are compatible. For these reasons, a security community is a more advanced or "thicker" form of international society than is rapprochement.

Security community and rapprochement also differ as to the nature of the power-checking mechanisms through which they take shape. The practice of strategic restraint is a critical ingredient for both. But whereas rapprochement is fostered primarily by self-restraint or self-binding, security community also entails co-binding.[1] The parties engaging in rapprochement regularize strategic restraint, with both sides demonstrating their willingness to withhold their power and accommodate the interests of the other. In contrast, the members of a security community also bind themselves to one another, using pacts and other types of informal and formal instruments to tether themselves together. Co-binding both arises from and contributes to the order-producing norms, conjoined interests, and shared identity that are the defining features of security community. To return to the historical analogy used in chapter 2, feudal lords have not only stopped plundering each other and learned to coexist peacefully, but they have forged a league of fiefdoms, promoting their collective welfare and working together to safeguard their common interests.

Security communities vary widely as to the scope and formality of the rules

---

[1] See Deudney, *Bounding Power*; and Ikenberry, *After Victory*.

that they embrace to promote cooperation. Their effects also vary, with some security communities significantly muting geopolitical rivalry and others eliminating it altogether. Adler and Barnett usefully distinguish between three types of security community: nascent, ascendant, and mature.[2] In a nascent security community, the member states agree to settle disputes peacefully and identify rudimentary mechanisms for doing so, but mutual suspicions remain. An example would be ASEAN during its early years. In an ascendant security community, the member states agree on a more extensive set of guiding rules and norms, institutionalize and often codify those rules and norms, and broaden their political and societal contacts. Nonetheless, an undercurrent of wariness remains. An example would be the Concert of Europe. In a mature security community, the member states enjoy a constitutional order in which armed conflict becomes unthinkable. An example would be the European Union today.

The power-checking practices and institutions that provide the foundation for security community take three primary forms: self-binding and co-binding, the fencing off of disputes, and the establishment of mechanisms to deconcentrate power. The starting point for the formation of a security community is the fashioning of consensual norms and procedures for resolving disputes. Especially in its early phases, dispute resolution tends to occur in an ad hoc manner rather than through established mechanisms. Just as during the initial phases of rapprochement, acts of unilateral accommodation or self-binding serve as concessions that signal benign intent. As the parties respond in kind, unilateral accommodation evolves into reciprocal restraint. States regularize the trading of concessions and deliberately refrain from taking advantage of opportunities for individual gain. Examples of such measures include arms control, the settlement of territorial disputes, and the demilitarization of boundaries.

The practice of reciprocal restraint gradually evolves into the practice of co-binding. Members of a security community fashion informal pacts or codified agreements to govern their mutual relations. Such agreements usually permit change to the territorial status quo only through consensus. The fashioning of a consensus can emerge through informal mechanisms; a majority of states seeks to "group" dissident members through persuasion. During the Concert of Europe, for example, members convened congresses only

---

[2] Adler and Barnett, *Security Communities*, pp. 49–57.

as needed to resolve disputes. In other instances, security communities establish standing secretariats and regularized summits with formalized voting procedures, as in the case of the European Community and the Gulf Cooperation Council. In addition, states may take additional steps to bind themselves to each other, forming joint military units and coordinating efforts to provide collective defense. Member states may also extend co-binding to other policy areas, seeking to deepen economic interdependence and broaden societal linkages.

Security communities also take steps to fence off disputes, seeking to isolate or contain particularly controversial issues and ensure that they do not block the maintenance of group cohesion. Individual members may be granted spheres of influence which acknowledge that state's special interests and recognize its *droit de regard*. Buffer zones, neutral zones, and demilitarized zones may be established to diffuse conflicts of interest over disputed areas. Mechanisms for "opting out" of specific initiatives are common; states that oppose a policy supported by a majority of members may simply absent themselves from that policy rather than attempt to block it. Also, states often identify issues as lying outside the ambit of the security community—such as the domestic affairs of the members—again seeking to isolate such matters and prevent them from threatening group cohesion.

Finally, the members of a security community adopt mechanisms to deconcentrate power and thereby minimize the strategic consequences of material asymmetries. Power differentials and prospective changes in the balance of power are primary causes of international rivalry. Accordingly, embarking down the path of stable peace often entails the adoption of instruments designed to dampen the strategic consequences of power inequalities and forestall the tendency for countervailing coalitions to form against concentrations of economic and military might.

Instruments for de-concentrating power take several different forms. In some cases, states take steps to amplify the power and influence of smaller members. Britain and Russia, the two dominant members of the Concert, enlarged the borders of Prussia and gave Austria a relatively free hand in the Italian peninsula in order to alleviate Prussian and Austrian fears of being overshadowed by their larger partners. In other cases, larger powers implement measures to discount the strategic advantages associated with their material superiority. France and Germany, the two dominant members of the EC, used a co-binding pact—the European Coal and Steel Community—to restrain, individually and collectively, their industrial might and war-making potential. They also used institutional mechanisms to enhance the political influence and prosperity of their smaller neighbors. Both measures reassured smaller states that the material advantages of France and Germany would no longer be used in the service of exploitation and territorial expansion.

The rotation of capitals and leadership posts is another vehicle for diffusing power. The Concert of Europe had no capital; its congresses met in different sites on an ad hoc basis. The EC deliberately chose to establish its governing institutions in multiple locations. Its main offices were placed in Brussels, the capital of a small European country, while others were located in Luxembourg, hardly a geopolitical titan. It also established an institutional presence in Strasbourg, a city that abuts the Franco-German boundary. The EC decided that its presidency would rotate every six months, providing reassurance that no single country would exercise inordinate influence. ASEAN initially avoided a fixed headquarters and standing secretariat for similar reasons. In contrast, the GCC from the outset established its headquarters in the capital of its dominant member, Saudi Arabia, contributing to persistent concerns about Saudi domination of the group.

This "anatomy" of security community warrants several qualifications. According to this book's typology of stable peace, security community represents a more advanced form of international society than rapprochement. Security community entails agreement on ordering rules and norms, while rapprochement entails only mutual expectations of peaceful coexistence. Nonetheless, the case studies do not readily conform to this deductive framework; security community can often be more fragile than rapprochement and retain more pronounced elements of geopolitical competition. For example, rapprochement between Great Britain and the United States and between Norway and Sweden constituted deeper and more enduring instances of stable peace than did the onset of security community among the members of the Concert of Europe.

This observed deviation from the model can be explained as follows. Security communities usually include more than two states. Compared with bilateral rapprochement, multilateral reconciliation and cooperation in important respects constitute less demanding tasks with more shallow political and societal consequences. The presence of multiple parties dilutes the strategic setting; former rivals may proceed to fashion agreement on ordering rules of the road without fully settling their differences. Residual suspicions and undercurrents of balancing are more easily masked in this broader context. Furthermore, agreement on norms and rules for managing order can often be attained without the societal integration that helps consolidate rapprochement.

Seen from another perspective, states interested in investing in stable peace may "skip over" specific types of interactions that may threaten their domestic orders—such as societal integration—instead moving directly from reciprocal restraint to the fashioning of a rules-based order. Societal integration, for example, can threaten illiberal states by empowering coalitions that favor political and economic openness, giving such states incentives to prefer more shallow forms of stable peace. This preference may also result from the fact that illiberal states, inasmuch as they are more prone to rely on external confrontation for domestic legitimation, may be less well suited than liberal states to managing the domestic politics of accommodation. Accordingly, rapprochement is more likely to take place among liberal states or at least among states sharing similar regime type, whereas security community is better able to accommodate illiberal states and groupings that include different regime types.

The pluralism and diversity that ready security communities to include different regime types can also make them fragile. Absent the full settling of scores and the elimination of competitive jockeying, security communities are prone to the return of geopolitical rivalry. Moving to agreement on ordering rules and norms without first locking in durable peace may leave unattended residual historical tensions and disputes. By accommodating different regime types, security communities exhibit the benefits of inclusiveness. But inclusiveness can be a liability when domestic differences lead to diverging interests and foreign policies. In addition, without the extensive societal integration that often accompanies rapprochement and union, security communities may erode as the result of changes of government. If ordering norms and cooperative practices have been embraced exclusively at the elite level, then a security community may lack the deeper societal foundations necessary to weather regime change.

This chapter examines three examples of successful security community: the Concert of Europe from 1815 to 1848, the European Community from its inception in 1949 through 1963, and ASEAN from its founding in 1967 through the present. The Concert of Europe makes clear that even if states do not share similar regime types, they can nonetheless join together to form a zone of stable peace. The evolution of the EC sheds important light on the central role that self-binding and co-binding institutions play in giving rise to security community. Contrary to conventional interpretations of the development of the EC, the case also reinforces this book's claim that political reconciliation opens the door to economic integration, not vice versa. The trajectory of ASEAN confirms one of the insights gleaned from rapprochement between Brazil and Argentina—that military dictatorships with unchecked power at home are nonetheless capable of practicing strategic restraint in the conduct of foreign policy. ASEAN also highlights the degree to which village traditions of deliberation and consensus formation can inform governance at the interstate level.

Two cases of failed security community are examined: the Concert of Europe after 1848, and the Gulf Cooperation Council from inception in 1981 through the present. The unraveling of the Concert was the product of the revolutions of 1848. The case demonstrates the potential for social upheaval and incompatible social orders to scuttle stable peace. The faltering of the GCC occurred for different reasons. Despite an impressive first decade for the community of Gulf sheikhdoms, the GCC stalled after Iraq's invasion of Kuwait in 1990. Unlike most security communities, which become more cohesive when faced with a rising external threat, the mounting threat posed by Iraq and Iran had the opposite effect on the GCC. Unable to marshal the collective capability needed to counter these threats, individual members tended to respond by increasing their strategic reliance on U.S. power, a trend that provoked political controversy within the GCC and ultimately came at the expense of multilateral cooperation within the grouping. The case also demonstrates the degree to which the reluctance of member states to attenuate their sovereignty proved to be a potent obstacle to the consolidation of security community.

THE EVOLUTION OF THE CONCERT
OF EUROPE, 1815–1848

The Concert of Europe preserved peace in Europe from the end of the Napoleonic Wars in 1815 until the revolutions of 1848. The Concert operated as a directorate of Europe's major powers, providing a forum in which they forged a set of rules and norms for regulating their relations and peacefully resolving disputes. War among the members of the Concert did not become unthinkable; an undercurrent of strategic rivalry continued to animate their relations. But the Concert did constitute a security community inasmuch as strategic rivalry was significantly muted and armed force effectively eliminated as a legitimate tool of statecraft among its members.

The onset of stable peace among Concert members demonstrates the powerful pacifying effects of self-binding and co-binding. The formation and successful operation of the Concert for over thirty years are particularly interesting in light of the political divide that existed between its two liberalizing members (Britain and France) and its three absolute monarchies (Russia, Prussia, and Austria). The case thus reveals that stable peace can break out among states with different regime types and reaffirms that even states that do not embrace institutionalized restraint at home can nonetheless practice strategic restraint in the conduct of their foreign relations.

How Peace Broke Out

The motivation behind joint efforts to forge a cooperative security order among Europe's great powers was provided primarily by Napoleon's bid for continental hegemony. Starting soon after the French Revolution, Napoleonic France coupled economic warfare against Britain with efforts to impose direct military control over its neighbors. By the early 1800s, Britain, France's chief challenger for naval and economic dominance, was already contemplating not only a countervailing alliance capable of defeating Napoleon, but also a postwar order that would inoculate Europe against future great-power conflicts.

In response to a vague Russian proposal dealing with possible postwar arrangements, Prime Minister William Pitt in 1805 drafted a memo that effectively laid the groundwork for the concert system that was to emerge a decade later. Pitt envisaged "a general agreement and Guarantee for the mutual protection and security of different powers, and for re-establishing a general system of public law in Europe." He went on to call for "a Treaty to which all the principal Powers of Europe should be parties . . . and they should all bind themselves mutually to protect and support each other . . . and provide, as far as possible, for repressing future attempts to disturb the general tranquility, and above all, for restraining any projects of Aggrandizement and Ambition similar to those which have produced all the Calamities inflicted on Europe since the disastrous era of the French Revolution."[3]

This plan remained little more than a distant vision until strategic necessity began to generate a new level of great-power cooperation. Napoleon invaded Russia in 1812, pushing Russia into alliance with Britain. Soon thereafter, Prussia and Austria joined, giving rise to the Quadruple Alliance. During the course of 1813 and 1814, Britain took the lead in directing military operations, subsidizing its allies, and negotiating the terms of peace. The rules and norms that would govern the postwar order were first spelled out in the Treaty of Chaumont in 1814. These rules and norms were then put into practice and refined through a series of congresses, the most important of which was the Congress of Vienna, which concluded in 1815. In Vienna, the Quadruple Alliance began to function as a peacetime concert of the victorious powers. At the Congress of Aix-la-Chapelle in 1818, France was integrated into the grouping, creating the five-power directorate that was to bring Europe more than three decades of stable peace.

STRATEGIC RESTRAINT AND POWER-CHECKING DEVICES

What sequence of steps led to the taming of Europe's strategic landscape, suspending balance-of-power rivalry among its great powers? British self-restraint was the critical ingredient, providing assurance to the other major powers—including a defeated France—that Europe's dominant state had no intention of exploiting its position for individual gain. The spirit if not the letter of Pitt's 1805 memo remained valid, informing Britain's effort to construct a postwar order based on strategic restraint, cooperation, and shared notions of public law. As Lord Castlereagh, Britain's foreign minister and one of the chief architects of the Concert, wrote, "Rather than put herself at the head of any combinations of Courts to keep others in check, it is the province of Great Britain to turn the confidence she has inspired to the account of peace, by exercising a conciliatory influence between the Powers."[4] Castlereagh explicitly reached out to Russia, by far Europe's strongest power in terms of men under arms.[5] In a letter to Tsar Alexander, he argued that

---

[3] Ikenberry, *After Victory*, pp. 99–100.

[4] Robert Steward Castlereagh, *Correspondence, Dispatches, and Other Papers of Viscount Castlereagh*, 3rd series, vol. 11 (London: H. Colburn, 1850), p. 105.

[5] In 1816, Russia had 800,000 men under arms (although a good number were not well-

"forebearance, moderation, and generosity" could "secure to Europe the repose" to which they were both committed.[6] Britain found in Alexander a willing partner.

The self-binding practiced by Britain and Russia took two main forms. First, they passed up on opportunities for individual gain, each making clear that it did not intend to take advantage of France's defeat for the purposes of territorial aggrandizement. Britain could easily have made a satellite of an independent Dutch state, but instead insisted that the Netherlands enjoy autonomy, even if it came at the expense of Britain's short-term economic and strategic interests. Russia refrained from using its dominant manpower to assert its influence westward into Central Europe or southward into the Ottoman Empire, similarly forestalling the rivalries that might have otherwise ensued.

Second, Britain and Russia refrained from constructing a bipolar order, instead elevating the status of Prussia, Austria, and France in order to put all of Europe's major states on a more level playing field. The boundaries of Prussia were extended to augment its territory, population, and political clout. Austria was accorded special sway over southeastern Europe, and its foreign minister, Clemens von Metternich, became a key player in designing how the Concert would function. Rather than imposing a punitive peace on France, the four founding members integrated their defeated adversary into the Concert in 1818.

Through these practices, Britain and Russia indicated benign intent to each other and to their emerging partners. The stage was set for the onset of Concert diplomacy—even if Pitt's preference for formal security guarantees had fallen by the wayside. The House of Commons, still committed to the notion of "splendid isolation," had little appetite for assuming peacetime obligations on the continent. And Tsar Alexander, although he shared Castlereagh's desire for a stable postwar order, was nonetheless an autocratic (and erratic) ruler predisposed against taking up the legal commitments that would accompany formal guarantees.[7] Britain and Russia preferred to exercise self-binding through practice rather than codified commitment.

The second stage in the formation of the Concert entailed moving from

trained). By comparison, Britain had 255,000 men under arms and the Habsburg Empire, the second ranking continental power, 220,000.

[6] Ikenberry, *After Victory*, p. 97.
[7] See Ikenberry, *After Victory*, pp. 75, 81–83, 109.

individual and reciprocal acts of restraint to institutionalized restraint and co-binding. Paul Schroeder calls the Concert a *pacta de controhendo*—a compact of restraint. If the Concert was guided by a core strategic concept, it was that the five powers would bind themselves to one another, sublimating their individual interests to the preservation of group cohesion. As a joint protocol signed in 1818 reaffirmed, "the five powers . . . are firmly resolved never to depart, neither in their mutual Relations, nor in those which bind them to other states, from principles of intimate union."[8]

Changes to the postwar territorial settlement would occur only through consensus. Congresses were held to resolve disputes as they arose. Individual states contemplating unilateral action were grouped by the other powers; moral suasion, not coercion, was the currency of diplomacy. Despite initially divergent views over a host of issues—such as the borders of Poland and Saxony and how to respond to uprisings in Italy, Greece, and Belgium— great-power cohesion consistently took precedence over the individual interests of each member. The premium placed on great-power cooperation was to endure for more than three decades. In 1841, King Louis Philippe explained why he was backing away from pursuing policies toward Egypt that had strained Concert cohesion: "She [France] wishes to maintain the European equilibrium, the care of which is the responsibility of all the Great Powers. Its preservation must be their glory and their main ambition."[9]

The maintenance of great-power peace was not left entirely to the good will and diplomatic talents of Europe's leaders. As a military alliance matured into a peacetime security community, the Concert's practices evolved and its members adopted a number of mechanisms to de-concentrate power and fence off disputes, thereby forestalling the potential return of geopolitical competition. For starters, power was diffused by rotating the congresses among different locations; there was neither a fixed headquarters nor a designated leader of the Concert system. The resulting equality in diplomacy helped mute balancing by offsetting asymmetries in material power.

Each of the members of the Concert was effectively granted a sphere of influence. The power in question did not have a free hand in these spheres, but other members tended to defer to its preferences. Britain oversaw the low

---

[8] Cronin, *Community Under Anarchy*, p. 60.
[9] René Albrecht-Carrié, *The Concert of Europe* (New York: Walker, 1968), p. 60. The crisis was precipitated by the efforts of Egyptian leader Mehemet Ali Pasha to challenge Ottoman rule and European influence in the region by asserting Egypt's autonomy and its sway over Syria.

countries, Iberian peninsula, and North America, while Russia's sphere extended to parts of eastern Europe, Persia, and Ottoman territory. Austria held sway in northern Italy and jointly managed the German confederation with Prussia. France's reach was initially curtailed after its defeat, but it gradually came to enjoy special influence in the southern and eastern Mediterranean. By recognizing that individual members had particularly salient interests in specific areas, the designation of spheres of influence preempted disputes that might have otherwise jeopardized group cohesion. Such spheres helped manage and contain crises in the periphery by effectively apportioning regional responsibilities among Concert members. In addition, granting the great powers special prerogatives in areas to which they attached historical importance helped facilitate the domestic politics of accommodation—an important move inasmuch as the practice of strategic restraint had the potential to awaken a sense of national humiliation and the political opposition it would provoke. As Bruce Cronin notes, a guiding norm of the Concert was "that great powers must not be humiliated and that they must not be challenged either in their vital interests or in their prestige and honor."[10]

Again motivated by efforts to obviate or at least circumscribe conflicts of interest, Concert members also fenced off certain issues and areas. Each agreed not to interfere in the domestic affairs of other members. As discussed below, this norm was particularly important inasmuch as autocratic monarchies in Russia, Austria, and Prussia were intent on resisting the more liberal brand of monarchic rule that had taken root in Britain and France. The Concert also established buffer zones and demilitarized areas to forestall potential territorial disputes.[11] And it embraced a norm of "opting out," enabling an individual member that disagreed with a particular initiative to refrain from participating in joint action. In so doing, a member could register its disapproval without destroying group cohesion. Britain, for example, opposed Austria's proposed intervention to suppress a liberal uprising in Italy

[10] Cronin, *Community Under Anarchy*, p. 63.

[11] For example, the Kingdom of the United Netherlands, although initially established as a defensive barrier against France, was also to serve as an intermediary body— a polity over which the great powers shared joint influence, thus forestalling explicit competition over its status and strategic alignment. Scandinavia and Switzerland were granted similar status as means of containing great-power competition for influence. See Paul Schroeder, "The 19th-Century International System: Changes in the Structure," *World Politics* 39, no. 1 (October 1986): 18–20. See also Charles A. Kupchan and Clifford A. Kupchan, "Concerts, Collective Security, and the Future of Europe," *International Security* 16, no. 1 (Summer 1991), pp. 140–144.

in 1820–1821. But instead of blocking the operation, Castlereagh chose to watch from the sidelines while allowing Austria, which enjoyed the support of Prussia and Russia, to proceed. Castlereagh conditioned his assent only on the readiness of the powers "to give every reasonable assurance that their views were not directed to purposes of aggrandisement subversive of the Territorial System of Europe."[12]

SOCIETAL INTEGRATION AND COMMUNAL IDENTITY

The final stage in the maturation of the Concert involved societal integration and the generation of a communal discourse and identity. During the early 1800s, societal integration occurred almost exclusively among elites. Prior to the strengthening of elected legislatures and the extension of political rights beyond the aristocracy, the conduct of foreign policy and interstate diplomacy engaged only the top echelon of society. The onset of security community had little impact on economic ties among Concert members. The Concert appears to have had limited effect on trade flows in part because it took years for continental Europe to recover from the damage done by the Napoleonic Wars. British trade with Concert members grew in value between the 1820s and the 1840s, but this trend was the result of growth in the British economy, not a Concert-based agenda of regional integration. French and Russian trade with Concert members remained generally static during the 1830s and 1840s.[13] Furthermore, overland transportation was slow and difficult, meaning that ordinary citizens, apart from shippers and traders, had little contact with or knowledge of residents of other Concert members.

In contrast, the leaders of Europe's major powers were in frequent contact with each other. Indeed, the gatherings that took place under the auspices of the Quadruple Alliance and then the Concert offered a unique forum in which personal bonds formed and deepened. As Metternich remarked in reflecting on the coalition that formed to defeat France, "the chief personages in the great drama found themselves together in the very same place. The Emperors of Austria and Russia, the King of Prussia, and their three cabinets, were really never separated. The leader of the English cabinets had also generally been with his colleagues of Austria, Russia and Prussia."[14] During

---

[12] Albrecht-Carrié, *The Concert of Europe,* p. 50.

[13] B. R. Mitchell, *International Historical Statistics, Europe, 1750–1993* (London: Palgrave Macmillan, 1998), pp. 607, 644, 661.

[14] Cronin, *Community Under Anarchy,* p. 58.

the war and after the Concert had been formed, Castlereagh repeatedly acknowledged the importance of regular and direct contact, on one occasion stressing the vital role of "face to face" deliberations among "the authorised Ministers of the respective Powers."[15]

The substantive agreements and personal ties that emerged from the Quadruple Alliance and the Concert system to which it gave rise contributed to an unprecedented sense of pan-European community and solidarity. At one of their gatherings in 1814, the members of the Quadruple Alliance declared that they were seeking to negotiate a peace with France "in the name of Europe, which is but a single entity."[16] Concert members made frequent reference to the "intimate union" that they had formed.[17] Metternich noted that Europe "has acquired for me the quality of one's own country."[18] For Castlereagh, Europe had developed a "unity and persistence of purpose such as it had never before possessed."[19] The congress system, he wrote on another occasion, gives "the counsels of the Great Powers the efficiency and almost the simplicity of a single State."[20] Even France's foreign minister, Charles Maurice de Talleyrand-Perigord, began to appreciate the evolving sense of solidarity, calling Europe "a society . . . a family . . . a republic of Princes and peoples." The sense of commonality was strengthened by religious bonds, with a Concert protocol from 1818 noting that the union of the five powers was "more strong and indissoluble from the bonds of Christian brotherhood which join them."[21]

The sense of transnational commonality and solidarity encouraged by the Concert did run up against a formidable obstacle: the divide that existed between Britain and France, which had embraced constitutional rule and institutionalized political restraint at home, and Russia, Prussia, and Austria, which were staunch defenders of absolute monarchy. This divide was formalized in Paris in 1815, when Russia, Prussia, and Austria formed the Holy Alliance, a pact pledging mutual assistance to preserve monarchic rule and resist liberal change at home and abroad. With the French parliament regularly dominated by ultraroyalist deputies, France on occasion sympathized with

---

[15] Ikenberry, *After Victory*, p. 103.
[16] Cronin, *Community Under Anarchy*, p. 50.
[17] See Cronin, *Community Under Anarchy*, pp. 60–61.
[18] Cronin, *Community Under Anarchy*, p. 50.
[19] Cronin, *Community Under Anarchy*, p. 50.
[20] Ikenberry, *After Victory*, p. 105.
[21] Cronin, *Community Under Anarchy*, pp. 50, 60–61.

the Holy Alliance's anti-liberal inclinations, even if it was not formally a member.

Emblematic of this political divide within the Concert was the consistent divergence between Britain and the Holy Alliance over how to respond to liberal change. Russia, Prussia, and Austria wanted to put down all liberal revolts, fearful of contagion if they failed to do so. In contrast, Britain tended to welcome liberal change and believed that joint military intervention, instead of serving as an instrument for repressing the spread of constitutional rule, should be directed at regimes that had expansionist ambitions and threatened to overturn the territorial status quo. The Holy Alliance more often prevailed, with the British opting out—a model that carried the day in the early 1820s in both Italy and Spain. In other instances—such as Belgium in 1830—Britain succeeded in securing independence against the wishes of Russia and Prussia, an outcome facilitated by French objections to intervention by the Holy Alliance.

Throughout these and other disputes, the congress system and the power-checking devices embraced by Concert members succeeded in preserving great-power harmony even when a formal consensus could not be attained. The norms and practices of the Concert enabled solidarity to endure amid strategic differences that otherwise would have likely led to armed conflict. That the Concert functioned successfully even in the presence of a fundamental political cleavage among its members is a testament to the degree to which it tamed Europe's landscape and muted geopolitical competition. War had not become unthinkable.[22] But it had been de-legitimated as a tool of statecraft among great powers that had succeeded in making the preservation of peace their top priority and equating their separate national interests with the collective welfare of their "intimate union."

Why Peace Broke Out

The conditions that gave rise to the formation and maturation of the Concert confound easy categorization. As in the other cases, strategic necessity provided the initial impetus; the Quadruple Alliance emerged in response to the threat posed by Napoleonic France. But as to the importance of institution-

---

[22] As John Ikenberry points out, the failure of the Concert to embrace more formal security guarantees was both a reflection and a cause of the undercurrent of suspicion that informed great-power relations even at the Concert's height. Ikenberry, *After Victory*, pp. 106–109.

alized restraint, compatible social orders, and cultural commonality, the case of the Concert yields complicated findings.

The Concert functioned effectively for over three decades despite considerable diversity as to regime type. Britain was a constitutional monarchy. Suffrage was quite limited, as was the political power of the House of Commons, but the crown did not wield unchecked power.[23] As for France, Louis XVIII, Napoleon's successor, granted a written constitution which guaranteed a bicameral legislature, but the franchise was limited to men with considerable property holdings. Russia, Prussia, and Austria were absolute monarchies—and determined to remain so. Such differences in regime type represented the greatest challenge to Concert diplomacy, regularly setting Britain, and sometimes France, against its illiberal partners in responding to the armed revolts against monarchic rule that frequently occurred in Europe during the first half of the nineteenth century.

The five members of the Concert also had relatively diverse social orders. Britain and France were predominantly agrarian societies, with power still held mainly by a landed aristocracy. But the growth of trade and industry in Britain and the popular mobilization resulting from the French Revolution were gradually empowering other social sectors—in particular the rising commercial class. Indeed, these underlying social changes helped fuel the liberalization of political institutions in both countries. Meanwhile, Russia, Prussia, and Austria formed the Holy Alliance to protect their traditional social orders against just those types of changes that were occurring in Britain and France. For them, the Concert was not just about preserving great-power peace; it was also about arresting social change and suppressing the threat to monarchy and aristocratic privilege represented by developments in Britain and France.

Finally, there was not a high degree of cultural commonality among Concert members. The religious cleavages that had long fueled bloody conflicts across Europe had by no means disappeared. It is true that Europe was no longer wracked by religious conflicts that pitted one form of Christianity against another. But church and state had not yet been formally detached. And the French Revolution had helped awaken a new political force—nationalism—that was making more salient cultural and linguistic dividing lines

---

[23] Prior to the reform acts that were implemented over the course of the 1800s, seats in the House of Commons were often attained by appointment or purchase, not open election. Moreover, the cabinet was responsible to the king, not the parliament.

and fueling a new and powerful source of ideological tension. So too were the works of the founding fathers of German nationalism, such as Johann Gottlieb Fichte and Johann Gottfried Herder, becoming increasingly influential. Furthermore, even if Castlereagh dismissed the Holy Alliance as "a piece of sublime mysticism and nonsense," it nonetheless formalized the separation of the great powers into two distinct groupings, risking that a political and social divide intensify identities of opposition.[24]

How, then, can the onset of the Concert be understood? Is this case an outlier, with stable peace taking shape despite the absence of the three conditions that normally facilitate its emergence? A more nuanced interpretation of the period suggests that the Concert is less of an aberration than it initially appears to be.

Although none of the Concert's members was a liberal democracy, its primary architect and benefactor, Britain, was a constitutional monarchy whose leaders understood the critical importance of political self-restraint and institutionalized checks on power. The British were intent on replicating among Europe's powers the liberal order that had succeeded in pacifying Britain's own politics. Especially because Britain was Europe's most powerful state and had guided and helped pay for the war effort against France, its leadership in shaping the postwar order was decisive. Although the leaders of Russia, Prussia, and Austria insisted on having unchecked power within their borders, they understood that a European order based on the institutionalization of consensus and restraint offered the most promise for peace. As long as their power at home remained uncontested, even autocratic states were prepared to embrace liberal norms in the conduct of foreign policy. France's inclusion in the Concert was similarly predicated upon adherence to these norms. From this perspective, the most important factor making the Concert possible was Britain's commitment to institutionalized restraint and its success in convincing the other great powers to adhere to the practices of self-binding and co-binding in constructing a postwar order.

It is also the case that Concert members enjoyed a high level of transparency despite the absence of liberal institutions. Such transparency was afforded by the congresses and consultations that frequently took place. As Castlereagh observed during one of the Concert's congresses in 1818, "these reunions . . . [are] a new discovery in the European government, at once extinguishing the cobwebs with which diplomacy obscures the horizon, bring-

---

[24] Cronin, *Community Under Anarchy*, p. 65.

ing the whole bearing of the system into its true light."[25] In addition, although security commitments were not codified through treaty as Pitt had originally suggested, the personal bonds and sense of solidarity formed among European ministers created a mutual confidence that all the parties would uphold their commitments to Concert norms. Despite the absence of legal procedures for ratification and implementation, the parties saw one another as making credible and binding commitments.

The architects of the Concert were quite realistic in recognizing that informality and flexibility were vital to the Concert's effective operation. British leaders understood the value of institutionalized restraint—as Pitt's original memo made clear—but they also understood Parliament's discomfort with codified international commitments. The leaders of Russia, Prussia, and Austria were even more averse to taking on formal international commitments. In this sense, the codification and further institutionalization of the Concert would have done more harm than good, probably discouraging its prospective members from participating in the security community. If the Concert's leaders were not prepared to take up the formal constraints that would have accompanied legal guarantees, then more informal and innovative instruments would have to do. A British memorandum from 1818 captured this pragmatic spirit:

> There is no doubt that a breach of the covenant [of the territorial system of Europe] by any one State is an injury which all the other States may, if they shall think fit, either separately or collectively resent, but the treaties do not impose, by express stipulation, the doing so as matter of positive obligation. . . . The execution of this duty seems to have been deliberately left to arise out of the circumstances of the time and of the case, and the offending State to be brought to reason by such of the injured States as might at the moment think fit to charge themselves with the task of defending their own rights thus invaded.[26]

As for the impact of differences in social order among members, the Concert appears to have benefited from the fact that societal integration among member states was very limited. The Concert was an elite phenomenon with very shallow roots in broader society. Its agenda for strategic cooperation was not accompanied by a plan for economic integration and growing inter-

---

[25] Ikenberry, *After Victory*, p. 105.
[26] Albrecht-Carrié, *The Concert of Europe*, p. 37.

dependence. The elite, intergovernmental character of the Concert insulated it from social tensions that might have otherwise emerged. The monarchies of the Holy Alliance would hardly have tolerated the Concert if it meant increasing cross-border social linkages and risked the export of the revolutionary political movements that had swept France in the late eighteenth century and occurred sporadically across Europe during the Concert era.[27] In addition, Britain and France may have been constitutional monarchies, but they were still aristocratic societies with the franchise generally limited to the landed gentry and the wealthy. The advancing liberalization in Britain and France was in large part aimed at coopting the emerging commercial elites and bringing them into the old order, not doing away with the power of the traditional aristocratic elite. The Concert was thus an exclusive club of nobility, not a socially diverse institution.

On the question of cultural compatibility, the architects of the Concert again appear to have deliberately steered around potential obstacles, downplaying differences and deliberately developing a political discourse that emphasized commonalities. The sense of solidarity that emerged from the allied effort to defeat Napoleon certainly helped them in this task. Anglicans, Lutherans, Catholics, and Orthodox were now part of a "Christian brotherhood." Despite the differences in regime type and culture, Concert leaders regularly stressed their common commitment to European values. A marriage between language and nation may have been coming into vogue, but elites and intellectuals in Russia and German territories often preferred French to their mother tongues. At least for the political class, Europe was taking on the characteristics of a "family." Wartime alliance and peacetime concert thus helped inculcate a sense of commonality that transcended previous cultural cleavages. Political and social construction was at work. The practices of the Concert not only shaped the institutions that served to preserve peace, but also encouraged the generation of a political discourse that stressed cultural commonality.

The Concert thus sheds important light on how and when states that do not practice institutionalized restraint at home are nonetheless able to practice strategic restraint in their external relations. It demonstrates that zones of peace can form even among states that do not share similar regime type.

---

[27] As discussed below in the section dealing with the demise of the Concert, concern about cross-border societal linkages and political contagion rose dramatically after the revolutions of 1848.

The history of the Concert also points to other important factors that made stable peace possible: the strength of personal networks as compensation for shallow societal integration; collective institutions that of necessity remained flexible and informal to ensure that each member retained autonomy over domestic affairs; and a discourse of community and cultural commonality that helped propagate a shared European identity.

THE EVOLUTION OF THE EUROPEAN COMMUNITY, 1949–1963

Scholars and policy makers alike regularly look to the European Community (EC) as an archetypal security community. After centuries of bloodshed, the states of Western Europe finally escaped geopolitical rivalry through the steady process of political and economic integration that began in the late 1940s. According to much of the substantial literature on the topic, the onset of stable peace has been the product primarily of economic interdependence, with joint production of coal and steel, a common market, and a common currency gradually knitting together Europe's national states. The function-alist, institutionalist, and liberal accounts that dominate the literature on the EC may disagree about the precise causes and implications of economic inte-gration, but they all agree on its pivotal role in bringing peace to Europe.[28] As Andrew Moravcsik writes, European integration was pursued "for largely economic reasons."[29]

If accurate, this traditional account of the onset of stable peace in Western Europe would refute one of this book's core arguments—that societal and economic integration follows from, rather than clears the way for, political reconciliation and the elimination of strategic rivalry. However, the interpre-tation of European integration presented in this case study challenges this consensus about the economic roots of the evolution of security community

---

[28] Prominent examples of functionalist, institutionalist, and liberal studies of European inte-gration are, respectively: Ernst Haas, *The Uniting of Europe: Political, Social and Economic Forces, 1950–1957* (Stanford, CA: Stanford University Press, 1958); Paul Pierson, "The Path to European Integration: A Historical Institutionalist Analysis," Center for German and European Studies, University of California at Berkeley, November 1996; and Andrew Moravcsik, *The Choice for Europe: Social Purpose and State Power from Messina to Maastricht* (Ithaca, NY: Cornell University Press, 1998).

[29] Moravcsik, *The Choice for Europe*, p. 5.

in postwar Europe. To be sure, economic integration has played a critical role in the construction of the EC and its graduation to the European Union (EU). Nonetheless, taking place beneath the surface of institutionalized economic cooperation has been a process of political reconciliation that both provided a foundation for stable peace and cleared the way for economic integration. Economic interdependence and societal integration have proceeded apace and had geopolitical consequence, but only after unilateral accommodation, reciprocal restraint, and the initial onset of rapprochement created a political environment conducive to the pursuit of joint gains.

Especially during the early postwar years, when antagonism and suspicion were still fresh, it was the practice of self-binding and co-binding that at once secured Franco-German rapprochement and reassured Europe's smaller powers that participation in the project of European integration would not entail political domination by France and Germany. The decisive move toward economic integration came thereafter—as both a product of advancing reconciliation and a response to the stalled effort to build supranational institutions in the political and defense realms. Although the private sector initially resisted economic integration, once its commercial benefits became apparent, societal groups began to support the formation of a common market, helping turn a nascent security community into a more durable zone of stable peace.

The European Coal and Steel Community: How Peace Broke Out

In the immediate aftermath of World War II, the victims of Nazi aggression sought to impose a punitive peace on Germany. The country was divided into four independent zones of occupation. In March 1948, France, Great Britain, and the Benelux countries concluded the Treaty of Brussels, committing the signatories to mutual assistance against renewed German aggression. France's Monnet Plan called for a Germany that would remain permanently decentralized and demilitarized, with its ample natural resources under international control.[30] The Ruhr's coal and industrial potential would be used to make France Europe's primary steel producer, at once stimulating France's economic recovery and denying Germany the capacity to rebuild its manu-

---

[30] Jean Monnet, a French diplomat, was a founding father of European integration and would later become the first president of the High Authority of the ECSC.

facturing and military base.[31] According to Alan Milward, "France's aims in European reconstruction were concentrated on a partition and permanent weakening of Germany and on acquiring a guaranteed access to German coal and coke resources."[32]

By 1949, strategic imperatives necessitated a change of course. Economic recovery across Europe was slow and halting, raising concern about political instability. As William Clayton, U.S. assistant secretary of state, wrote after a visit to Europe in 1947, "Europe is steadily deteriorating. The political position reflects the economic. One political crisis after another merely denotes the existence of grave economic distress."[33] As postwar cooperation between the United States and the Soviet Union gave way to the Cold War, American and European officials worried that the Soviets would take advantage of these economic and political uncertainties to build support for communist movements in Western Europe. So too was Moscow likely to capitalize on Germany's decentralization and economic disarray to pull the country into its sphere of influence, as it was doing with Berlin and its zone of occupation in eastern Germany.

America's Marshall Plan was a direct response to these challenges. American assistance was to promote the economic recovery and political self-confidence needed to stabilize postwar Europe. The Federal Republic of Germany was established in September 1949, and its inclusion in the Marshall Plan made it clear that Washington saw Germany's economic recovery as a priority. The outbreak of the Korean War in 1950 compelled the United States to put an additional premium on European rearmament, making it likely that Germany would rebuild not only its industrial base, but also its military establishment.

The deteriorating conditions in Europe not only compelled U.S. action, but also effectively forced France's hand. As Milward comments, "French political and public opinion on the German question evolved in the way it did because it had to come to terms after June 1947 with harsh international political and economic realities."[34] France wound up with little choice but to find an alternative to the Monnet Plan—which it did over the course of 1949.

---

[31] *See Alan S. Milward,* The Reconstruction of Western Europe, 1945–1951 *(Berkeley: University of California Press, 1984), pp. 128–129.*

[32] Milward, The Reconstruction of Western Europe, 1945–1951, *p. 467.*

[33] Milward, The Reconstruction of Western Europe, 1945–1951, *p. 2.*

[34] Milward, The Reconstruction of Western Europe, 1945–1951, *p. 142.*

Instead of taking advantage of Germany's defeat to exploit its resources and block the restoration of its sovereignty, the Schuman Plan was designed to permit Germany's recovery—an American priority—without again risking the return of German aggression—a French imperative. As Milward notes, "the Schuman Plan was called into existence to save the Monnet Plan."[35]

The Schuman Plan, which was announced in May 1950, called for the practice of both self-binding and co-binding.[36] Unilateral accommodation was to open the door to rapprochement between France and Germany, in turn making possible German recovery and rearmament. France would pursue self-binding by backing away from its plans for a punitive peace and accepting that Germany would both rebuild its industrial economy and reemerge as a unitary (albeit divided) state. Paris would pursue co-binding by merging its coal and steel industry with Germany's, establishing the European Coal and Steel Community (ECSC) and ceding control of this vital sector to a supra-national authority.[37] As Jean Monnet described the initiative, "If . . . the victors and vanquished agreed to exercise joint sovereignty over part of their resources . . . then a solid link would be forged between them."[38]

The Schuman Plan had a telling impact on Germany by sending a clear signal of France's benign intent; Paris was not only prepared to accommodate German concerns, but also to fuse its war-making industry to that of its former adversary. Chancellor Konrad Adenauer readily reciprocated, making concessions on a number of fronts. Most importantly, he agreed to put off the question of when military occupation would end and he proceeded to dismantle the powerful cartels that had long controlled the Ruhr's coal and steel industry. The successful negotiations over the implementation of the Schuman Plan cleared the way for the regularization of reciprocal restraint; the ECSC was the opening gambit that set Europe on the path toward stable peace.

Although the purview of the ECSC was limited to matters of commerce and industry, its establishment was driven primarily by geopolitical, not economic, considerations. Indeed, the private sector in both France and Ger-

[35] Milward, The Reconstruction of Western Europe, 1945–1951, *p. 475.*

[36] Robert Schuman was France's foreign minister from 1948 to 1952.

[37] Belgium, the Netherlands, Luxembourg, and Italy were also founding members of the ECSC.

[38] *Desmond Dinan,* Ever Closer Union: An Introduction to European Integration *(Boulder, CO: Lynne Rienner, 2005), p. 24.*

many opposed the initiative. France's steel industry resisted cooperation with the government and even refused to provide it production statistics. In Germany, breaking up the country's industrial cartels proved one of Adenauer's greatest domestic challenges.[39] As Milward notes, "The major political actors have first to make the decisive political step and build the arena in which the neo-functionalist interplay of vested interests can push the process of integration further, if, indeed, they do. Many of those vested interests were firmly opposed to the building of that arena."[40]

The key participants themselves were quite explicit about the geopolitical objectives of the bargain they were striking. For Schuman, "This proposal will create the first concrete foundation for a European federation which is so indispensable for the preservation of peace."[41] "The solidarity in production thus established [by the ECSC] will make it plain that any war between France and Germany becomes not merely unthinkable, but materially impossible."[42] Adenauer acknowledged that European integration "protects Germany from itself," and went on to assert in his memoirs that "the significance of the Schuman proposal was first and foremost political and not economic. This Plan was to be the beginning of a federal structure of Europe."[43] According to Desmond Dinan, "the Coal and Steel Community had a narrow economic focus but an ambitious political goal: to achieve a peace settlement primarily between France and Germany."[44] John Gillingham agrees that the ECSC stands as "the diplomatic breakthrough without which the subsequent integration of Europe . . . might never have occurred."[45]

If this initial act of co-binding was to lead to the "federation" envisaged by the ECSC's founders, they would have to address directly how to establish a rules-based order on the foundation of the emerging Franco-German cou-

---

[39] *On the position of French industry, see John Gillingham,* Coal, Steel, and the Rebirth of Europe, 1945–1955: The Germans and French from Ruhr Conflict to Economic Community *(Cambridge: Cambridge University Press, 1991), p. 237. On German cartels, see pp. 229–231, 257–258, 301.*

[40] *Milward,* The Reconstruction of Western Europe, 1945–1951, *p. 496.*

[41] Cited in Gregory F. Treverton, *America, Germany, and the Future of Europe* (Princeton, NJ: Princeton University Press, 1992), p. 104.

[42] Schuman, "Declaration of 10 May 1950." Available at: http://europa.eu.int/comm/dg10/publications/brochures/docu/50ans/decl_en.html#DECLARATION.

[43] *Cited in Moravcsik,* The Choice for Europe, *p. 94, and in Wim F. V. Vanthoor,* A Chronological History of the European Union, 1946–2001 *(Northhampton, MA: Edward Elgar, 2002), p. 8.*

[44] *Dinan,* Ever Closer Union, *p. 2.*

[45] Gillingham, *Coal, Steel, and the Rebirth of Europe,* p. 3.

pling. On this front, Europeans enjoyed a paradoxical mix of institutional failure but substantive success. The founding fathers of European integration looked to the Concert of Europe as a prototype, but they were not content with the informality of its rules and the absence of governing institutions, characteristics which they believed contributed to its demise. They therefore envisaged a more formal order, one with legally binding commitments and more authoritative mechanisms of governance. Accordingly, they fashioned standing bodies to guide the ECSC, and thereafter sought to codify and institutionalize defense cooperation and coordination of foreign policy by establishing the European Defense Community (EDC) and the European Political Community (EPC).

Both EDC and EPC were ultimately stillborn, largely due to France's unwillingness to pool sovereignty and transfer political authority to supranational institutions. America's strategic presence in Europe also played a role in undercutting enthusiasm for EDC. Although Washington backed the formation of a European defense community as a means of speeding German rearmament, reliance on NATO (which was formed in 1949) and America's security umbrella offered an alternative that ultimately prevailed over the option of forging a European defense union.[46] Indeed, throughout the late 1940s and early 1950s, U.S. economic assistance, U.S. security guarantees, and the integrative and stabilizing framework of the Atlantic Alliance all played a critical role in facilitating Franco-German rapprochement and the evolution of the EC.

Despite the failure of EDC and EPC, Germany and its former enemies succeeded over the course of the 1950s in not only eliminating geopolitical rivalry, but also laying the groundwork for a maturing security community. Although negotiations over the Schuman Plan sidestepped the question of the military occupation of Germany—a key issue for the German government—all parties generally recognized by the time the plan was implemented in 1951 that arrangements had to be made for terminating the occupation statutes.[47] Even though the consequent efforts to establish EDC and EPC did not come to fruition, the accompanying negotiations did lead to a series of contractual agreements that by the middle of 1952 ended the occupation in all but name. Germany would become a member of NATO and the Western

[46] Gillingham, *Coal, Steel, and the Rebirth of Europe*, pp. 349–352.
[47] *Vanthoor,* A Chronological History, *pp. 8–9.*

European Union (which came into existence in 1954 to institutionalize the Treaty of Brussels). The end of occupation and the commencement of rearmament would then occur within the framework of co-binding institutions. In exchange for regaining its territorial sovereignty, Germany committed itself to reasserting its geopolitical weight only within the constraining context of multilateral bodies. In Adenauer's words, "The question [is] not whether Germany should be brought into the general defensive plan but rather how this could be done without disrupting anything else that we [are] doing and without putting Germany in a position to act as the balance of power in Europe. . . . [We are] thinking along the lines of the possible creation of a European army or a North Atlantic Army."[48]

The Paris Agreements of 1954 formally ended the military occupation of Germany. The Bundeswehr was created the following year and Bonn agreed to raise twelve divisions to contribute to collective defense. France and Germany even forged a plan for joint production of nuclear weapons, though Charles de Gaulle cancelled the initiative after assuming the presidency.[49] The consolidation of Franco-German rapprochement was also furthered by France's acceptance of the Saarland referendum in 1955, a plebiscite that returned the region to Germany. As a diplomat at the time put it, France's concession of the Saar to Germany was "very, very important . . . in creating trust."[50] The capstone of this building process of reconciliation was the Elysée Treaty of 1963, a pact that formalized the Franco-German coalition and institutionalized coordination of policy between the two governments. This treaty symbolized the degree to which France and Germany had come to attribute to one another benign character, making war between them unthinkable and giving stable peace a taken-for-granted quality. The treaty proclaimed that "the reconciliation of the German people and the French people, ending a centuries-old rivalry, constitutes an historic event which profoundly transforms the relations between the two peoples." It also noted that "cooperation between the two countries constitutes an indispensable stage on the way to a united Europe."[51]

---

[48] Gillingham, *Coal, Steel, and the Rebirth of Europe*, p. 253.

[49] Moravcsik, *The Choice for Europe*, p. 149.

[50] Moravcsik, *The Choice for Europe*, p. 144.

[51] Text of the treaty available at http://www.info-france-usa.org/news/statmnts/1997/germany/coop.asp.

SOCIETAL INTEGRATION AND THE GENERATION
OF A EUROPEAN IDENTITY

The economic integration of Europe followed from, and did not precede, the political reconciliation produced by reciprocal restraint and the evolution of co-binding institutions. The settling of geopolitical scores cleared the way for growing interdependence, enabling Europe's states to see their economic interests as conjoined. Even Moravcsik, a stalwart proponent of the view that economic interest drove European integration, accepts that, "in every country, potential opponents were mollified not by a conversion to European geopolitical ideas but by the realization that geopolitical issues were no longer at stake."[52] Thus, the initial onset of stable peace set the stage for economic integration, not vice versa.

Moreover, the decision by European leaders to switch their focus from geopolitical issues to economic integration was in part a matter of necessity, not choice. The champions of supranational governance were rebuffed in their attempts to establish the EDC and EPC during the mid-1950s. Thereafter, they turned back to the economic realm because they assumed that it offered the most promising arena for advancing their federalist ambitions.[53] Monnet teamed up with Paul-Henri Spaak, Belgium's foreign minister, to devise the next steps. Their plan was to expand economic integration and supranational governance beyond coal and steel, extending both to other sectors and ultimately fashioning a single market guided by European institutions.

Planning and negotiations, which began immediately after the French National Assembly rejected the EDC in August 1954, moved quickly. These efforts culminated in the signing of the Treaty of Rome in March 1957. The agreement served as the founding document of the European Economic Community (EC), laid out plans for a common market to be implemented in three stages over the ensuing twelve years, and cleared the way for the High Authority and Common Assembly of the ECSC to develop into the Commission and Parliament of the EC. Regular meetings of heads of state and government began in 1961, soon evolving into the European Council, the EC's main decision-making body.

As with the ECSC, reciprocal restraint between France and Germany lay

---

[52] Moravcsik, *The Choice for Europe*, p. 136.

[53] Moravcsik, *The Choice for Europe*, p. 139; *Vanthoor,* A Chronological History, *p. 11; and Dinan,* Ever Closer Union, *pp. 10–11.*

at the heart of the deal. France secured price supports for its large agricultural sector, while German industry benefited from the gradual elimination of interstate tariffs. Again tracking the experience of the ECSC, economic integration was driven by political leaders, not by the private sector—which was generally opposed to trade liberalization. Sectoral interests gradually became strong backers of integration only after they began to benefit from it—which they readily did. Between 1958 and 1960, trade among the six founding members of the EC grew by 50 percent.[54] Although political and geopolitical concerns fueled the effort to advance economic integration, the process then succeeded in coopting different sectors of society, enlisting their support for the European project. Exporters and farmers were not the only beneficiaries. Left-wing parties and the laborers they represented also came to embrace the advance of economic union "because they see in supranational rules and organs the means to establish a regulated large-scale industrial economy permitting the development of permanent worker influence over industry."[55]

From its outset, then, geopolitical intent drove the European project. But especially after the failure of EDC and EPC, its architects enlisted economic integration as the leading edge of their efforts to consolidate stable peace. By tapping into the vested interests of the many firms and sectors that benefited from the common market, this move brought a self-reinforcing momentum to the enterprise. Growing prosperity also gave the EC a magnetic attraction, with the allure of market access gradually inducing most of Europe's democracies to clamor for membership. In addition, if France was to dash the hopes of federalists on matters of security, then they had little choice but to turn to trade and monetary matters to enhance supranational governance. De Gaulle made clear his preferences on these questions, calling a united Europe a "myth" and making clear that France preferred "l'Europe des États."[56]

Especially for the many elites who harbored federal aspirations, growing economic integration and societal contact would serve to enlarge the scope of supranational governance by fostering a European identity that would take its place alongside national identities and loyalties. In Schuman's words, "that fusion of interest which is indispensable to the establishment of a common economic system" would be "the leaven from which may grow a wider

---

[54] Dinan, *Ever Closer Union*, p. 47.
[55] Haas, *The Uniting of Europe*, p. 292.
[56] Vanthoor, A Chronological History, p. 24.

and deeper community between countries long opposed to one another by sanguinary divisions."[57] Once Franco-German rapprochement was secure and economic integration moving ahead, the EC set its sights on this new goal, undertaking a host of initiatives to facilitate changes in national narratives and identities. At ceremonies marking the twentieth anniversary of the Rome Treaties in 1977, President G. Leone of Italy eloquently expressed the long-term objective: "We must now prepare to take a new step which, once internal solidarity becomes reality, means that we really concentrate on creating conditions for the advent of the 'European,' a person who will find his spiritual, cultural, and social equilibrium in a new society. We hope that if that can be achieved, then just as people once proudly said '*Civis romanus sum*,' so they will be able to say 'I am European."[58]

The chosen instruments of social engineering took numerous forms. In 1987, the EC launched Erasmus, a program aimed at promoting the mobility and exchange of university students and staff. One of the main goals was "educating future generations of citizens in a European context."[59] In 1985, Europe adopted a common flag, in 1986 a common passport, and in 1998 a single currency, along the way (1993) graduating from EC to European Union (EU). In addition, the Schengen Convention, which came into effect in 1995, enabled citizens to cross from one member state to another without encountering border controls. Public opinion surveys reveal that integration has in fact been successful in nurturing a pan-European identity that complements individual national identities.[60]

This intensifying sense of belonging to a European polity has in part achieved its objectives; Europe's collective institutions of governance have gradually increased their authority and legitimacy. At the same time, as they did during the 1950s, member states have continued to guard important aspects of their sovereignty, especially on matters of defense. Even after more than six decades of integration, EU members remain reluctant to accept the substantial extension of supranational forms of governance into the realm of foreign and security policy. Europe has become a stable zone of peace, but

---

[57] Schuman, "Declaration of 10 May 1950."

[58] Vanthoor, A Chronological History, p. 82; italics in original.

[59] See http://ec.europa.eu/education/programmes/llp/erasmus/what_en.html.

[60] According to a Eurobarometer survey from 2005, six in ten EU citizens feel very or fairly attached to Europe. More than 50 percent of EU citizens identify as Europeans as well as members of their nation-state. See http://ec.europa.eu/publications/booklets/eu_documentation/05/txt_en_2.pdf.

continues to fall well short of amalgamating into a federation capable of acting as a unitary state, especially on geopolitical issues.

SMALL STATES AND POWER-CHECKING DEVICES

This account of European integration has thus far focused largely on the Franco-German coalition, an analytic bias that is primarily a function of the centrality of this coupling to the onset of stable peace. As Milward observes, "The nexus of economic and political ties between France and the Federal Republic was what held the second peace settlement together, just as the absence of these ties was a main cause of the ineffectiveness of the first. The various attachments which bound the other European countries into the settlement could not have been completed without those ties and would not survive their breaking."[61] Security community in postwar Europe thus took shape around the kernel of Franco-German rapprochement.

Nonetheless, this emphasis on France and Germany leaves out vital elements of the story, both as to the role that the four other founding members of the ECSC/EC played in the early years and as to the mechanisms that the EC employed to mitigate the consequences of power asymmetries between its larger and smaller members. Of the many dimensions of the European project affected by the objective of turning Franco-German rapprochement into a broader political community, this treatment deals with the one most critical to consolidating the EC as a zone of peace—the role of devices for checking and de-concentrating power in making integration safe for Europe's smaller states.

If bilateral rapprochement between the continent's two preponderant rivals was to turn into a security community open to all of Europe's democracies, the smaller states had to be reassured that they would not be dominated by the combined power and influence of the Franco-German coalition. The strategic restraint that naturally accompanied co-binding arrangements provided part of that reassurance; if the war-making capacities of France and Germany were indelibly linked, then each state would check the ability of the other to use its power in the service of coercion or predation. That prospect was incentive enough for smaller states to welcome the ECSC. But the question of political influence still weighed heavily. Would small states lose their autonomy and voice if integrated into a security community designed and

---

[61] *Milward,* The Reconstruction of Western Europe, *p. 491.*

managed primarily by its two main powers? It was to address these concerns that the EC adopted a host of additional devices for managing power asymmetries.

Monnet had wanted to establish a federal district along the lines of Washington, DC to ensure that a collective Europe's headquarters would be independent of any of its national states—especially its larger ones. Although his wishes never materialized, the High Authority of the ECSC was located in Luxembourg, one of Europe's smallest countries. As the ECSC evolved into the EC, its primary institutions were co-located in Brussels and Strasbourg, again avoiding the capitals of major powers. The symbolism was also important, with Strasbourg sitting astride the geopolitical fault line between France and Germany.

Amid the tortuous negotiations about decision-making procedures that took place throughout the 1950s, France and Germany regularly accommodated the concerns of smaller countries. As during the Concert of Europe, the two preponderant states deliberately elevated the voice and status of lesser powers. Furthermore, they did so in a codified and institutionalized manner, locking in devices for de-concentrating power through legally binding commitments. The negotiations leading to the Treaty of Rome, although they did lay out a specific plan for forming a common market, focused more on making rules than on making policy. As Moravcsik notes, the treaty "was a 'framework' document, describing institutional procedures through which rules would be elaborated rather than specific rules themselves."[62] In this sense, the EC represented a nascent constitutional order, a security community that established not just guiding norms, but also rules about making rules—guaranteeing smaller states that decisions would be the product of established voting procedures rather than the will of preponderant members.

In addition, the rules themselves enhanced the influence of the EC's smaller states. As the institutions of the common market were taking shape, the Commission was granted considerable authority over commercial matters, its agenda-setting power blocked only by a unanimous vote of the member states. This delegation of power to a supranational body offset the ability of Paris and Bonn to exercise unchecked influence. Italy and the Benelux countries proposed that decisions be taken by simple majority, giving them the same decision-making power as France and Germany. Although Paris and

---

[62] See Moravcsik, *The Choice for Europe*, p. 152.

Bonn rejected this suggestion, they were willing to accept qualified majority voting (QMV)—a system that weighted a nation's voting power to its population size. They also agreed that the assent of at least four countries was needed to approve policy initiatives, again strengthening the influence of the EC's smaller members. In instances in which the smaller countries opposed specific proposals that they thought would compromise their influence, they regularly succeeded in blocking the proposals—as they did with the Fouchet Plan for defense integration proposed by France in the early 1960s.[63] Especially under de Gaulle, France at times sought to break out of some of these restrictions, insisting, for example, that unanimous voting replace QMV on certain issues. Even amid these challenges, however, France adhered to the basic norms of decision making that evolved during the 1950s, preserving the integrity of a rules-based order.

France and Germany also agreed to make side payments to the smaller powers to induce their willingness to buy into the evolving project of integration. As negotiations over the ECSC proceeded, Paris and Bonn approved subsidies for Belgium and Italy to ensure that their steel industries remained competitive.[64] Later, the EC created a budget for what it called "structural funds"—direct payments to member states to spur economic growth and close the income gap between the richer and poorer members. This redistribution of wealth acted as yet another incentive for Europe's lesser powers to enter a political formation that would be subject to the preponderant power of the Franco-German coalition.

The EC, with the Franco-German coalition at its core, thus acted as a constitutionalized *pacta de controhendo*—a pact of restraint that immunized Europe against the geopolitical consequences of power asymmetries. But the European project was more than a zone of peace based on mutual restraint; it evolved into a security community, a new political formation resting on a rules-based order. With economic integration and growing interdependence leading the way, Europe's national states erected supranational institutions of governance to oversee trade and monetary affairs. The pooling of sovereignty was to have gradually extended to matters of foreign policy and defense—EPC and EDC were the initial attempts—but it has yet to do so. At least for now, the EU's member states are still jealously guarding this last re-

[63] See Moravcsik, *The Choice for Europe*, pp. 152–157; and Dinan, *Ever Closer Union*, pp. 45–46.

[64] Gillingham, *Coal, Steel, and the Rebirth of Europe*, pp. 248–250.

doubt of sovereignty. That stable peace has nonetheless deepened and broadened eastward is a testament to the durability of both the initial bargains struck between France and Germany and the security community that evolved thereafter.

Why Peace Broke Out

Strategic necessity, not altruism, motivated the reciprocal acts of restraint that set Europe on the path toward stable peace. France initially planned to exploit the resources of Germany, permanently leaving its defeated adversary without a sovereign government or a military or industrial base. Severe economic distress, the onset of the Cold War, and the outbreak of the Korean War then made Germany's economic recovery and rearmament an imperative, effectively forcing France to pursue rapprochement rather than exploitation. America's security guarantees provided a critical backdrop, enabling France and its wartime allies to run the risk of German rearmament.

Strategic necessity may have induced France to contemplate reconciliation with Germany, but other conditions made possible Franco-German rapprochement and the onset of security community. The three main ingredients of stable peace—institutionalized restraint, compatible social orders, and cultural commonality—were all present as postwar Europe embarked down the path of political and economic integration.

There is scant evidence to suggest that France and Germany identified one another as democracies and therefore pursued reconciliation; Germany's democratic transition alone was not sufficient to convince the French government to let down its guard and make itself again vulnerable to German power. Rather, key attributes of democratic governance and constitutional rule encouraged both parties to take tentative steps toward reconciliation. Norms of constitutional restraint and the rule of law facilitated the practice of self-binding and co-binding, increasing confidence among France, Germany, and their smaller neighbors that all parties would uphold their commitments. Even if domestic interests opposed certain measures—for example, the sacrifices associated with collective control over steel production—they "were compelled by national legislative action to accept the ECSC rules."[65] Establishing authoritative institutions at the supranational level was also

---

[65] Haas, *The Uniting of Europe*, p. 294.

about locking in agreements and "bolstering the credibility of interstate commitments."[66]

The transparency afforded by democratic institutions also played an important role in enabling rapprochement and economic integration to proceed apace. Continuous negotiations and consultations, coupled with public debate in the media and national legislatures, enabled Europe's founding members to assess with confidence the intent and motives of their partners. Especially during the early postwar years, when mutual suspicion continued to run high, military occupation further enhanced transparency by affording the allies direct access to German elites. Thereafter, the presence of NATO troops in West Germany and the allied military presence in West Berlin helped sustain the ready availability and exchange of information.[67]

The social orders of Western Europe's major states were broadly compatible by the 1940s. According to Ernest Haas, "There can be little doubt that broad similarities in the social values entertained by the dominant elites of the ECSC countries explain in large part why the Treaty was accepted and successfully implemented."[68] World War I was in many respects the last gasp of the traditional order, undermining the aristocracy's residual control of political and economic life in Germany. Notably, France and the United States ensured that this social transition was completed after World War II, making a priority of eliminating what remained of the coalition between "iron and rye" that had emerged during the second half of the nineteenth century. Amid the negotiations over economic recovery and the formation of the ECSC, Washington and Paris insisted that Germany dismantle the powerful cartels that controlled the Ruhr's industry. As Gillingham writes, "The decartelization of the Ruhr . . . was the indispensable precondition of the Schuman Plan."[69] Promoting market competition was part of the motivation, but this policy was also an instrument of social engineering aimed at removing

---

[66] Moravcsik, *The Choice for Europe*, p. 18.

[67] Beginning in the 1980s, the flowering of German democracy was accompanied by an open accounting of the past. German willingness to address the crimes of the Nazi regime and accept responsibility for World War II and the Holocaust helped deepen reconciliation between Germany and the victims of its aggression. Interestingly, security community and the advance of reconciliation proceeded apace from 1949 even though Germans did not systematically address the past until decades later. See Ann Phillips, "The Politics of Reconciliation Revisited: Germany and East-Central Europe," *World Affairs* 163, no. 4 (Spring 2001); and Ian Buruma, *The Wages of Guilt: Memories of War in Germany and Japan* (New York: Meridian, 1994).

[68] Haas, *The Uniting of Europe*, p. 286.

[69] Gillingham, *Coal, Steel, and the Rebirth of Europe*, p. 301.

domestic obstacles to integration and the onset of security community. Thereafter, growing interdependence enriched and empowered a broad cross-section of societal interest groups in ECSC members, enlisting their support in furthering the European project.

As during the Concert of Europe, elites engaged in the construction of the ECSC and EC stressed Europe's cultural homogeneity, not its dividing lines, drawing on the multiple dimensions of religious and ethnic similarity. The members of the ECSC and EC were all predominantly Christian and Caucasian—even if divided by nation, language, and branch of Christianity. As Anthony Smith describes this mottled picture, "there are shared traditions, legal and political, and shared heritages, religious and cultural. Not all Europeans share in all of them; some share in particular traditions and heritages only minimally. But at one time or another all Europe's communities have participated in at least some of these traditions and heritages."[70] Europe thus enjoyed the building blocks of a strong sense of cultural commonality.

That Europeans have not always appreciated their commonalities illustrates both the malleable nature of perceptions of cultural affinity and the susceptibility of these perceptions to political construction. At times, Europe's major powers have been implacable enemies; identities of opposition have prevailed, with elites magnifying cultural, linguistic, and religious differences. At other times, elites have invoked an alternative narrative, one that stresses a common heritage and culture. Especially since the Peace of Westphalia and the rise of the secular, sovereign state, intellectuals and statesmen alike have made frequent reference to Europe's cultural and political homogeneity and the opportunities it has afforded for building a peaceful league of states.[71] Indeed, these aspirations were fully realized during the Concert of Europe, only to be replaced by narratives of opposition during the first half of the twentieth century.

From this perspective, European elites had a ready historical narrative on which to draw when, as they started work on building a political and economic union, they sought to reclaim the sense of commonality and solidarity that prevailed after the Napoleonic Wars. They were helped along by the presence of the Soviet Union, which represented not only an external threat, but also an ideological "other." So too was a sense of commonality ultimately

[70] Anthony Smith, "National Identities and the Idea of European Unity," in Michael O'Neill, *The Politics of European Integration* (New York: Routledge, 1996), p. 318.
[71] O'Neill, *The Politics of European Integration*, p. 7.

strengthened by the educational exchanges, community-wide flag and passport, a single currency, and other policy initiatives aimed at fostering a European identity. It remains to be seen whether this shared identity ultimately becomes a common identity, laying the foundation for Europe to mature into a federal union.

THE EVOLUTION OF ASEAN FROM 1967

In the aftermath of World War II, the countries of Southeast Asia struggled to emerge from decades of domination by imperial powers. Conditions were hardly ripe for the emergence of a zone of peace. War raged in Indochina, first over decolonization, then as an extension of the Cold War. Indonesia objected to the formation of Malaysia in 1963 and resorted to armed intervention to stymie the success of the new federation. The end of confrontation between Indonesia and Malaysia then cleared the way for the formation of the Association of Southeast Asian States (ASEAN) in 1967. But numerous obstacles stood in the way of stable peace. ASEAN's five members did not have similar regime types; Indonesia and Thailand were governed by military regimes, while the Philippines, Malaysia, and Singapore were, to varying degrees, experimenting with democratic institutions. Trade and other forms of societal interaction among ASEAN members were at relatively low levels. And their populations were ethnically and religiously diverse, denying the grouping a preexisting sense of communal identity.

Despite Southeast Asia's different regime types, its ethnic diversity, and its multiple sources of intra-regional rivalry, ASEAN evolved into an effective forum for resolving political and territorial disputes among its members and for addressing common security threats. By the 1980s, the group had succeeded in becoming a nascent zone of peace; the armed rivalries of the 1960s had given way to a regional community within which the prospect of war had been all but eliminated. Amitav Acharya notes the apparent anomaly, pointing out that ASEAN "evolved toward a security community without sharing liberal-democratic values or a substantial degree of intra-regional economic interdependence."[72] Furthermore, ASEAN, especially in its early years, lacked the institutions and codified rules and norms that accompanied the onset of

[72] Amitav Acharya, "Collective Identity and Conflict Management in Southeast Asia," in Adler and Barnett, *Security Communities*, p. 200.

stable peace in Europe after World War II. Indeed, the absence of European-style integration in Southeast Asia has led many analysts to discount the relevance of ASEAN and question whether it has indeed contributed significantly to the region's stability.[73]

To compare ASEAN and the EC, however, is misleading; the more appropriate historical comparison is between ASEAN and the Concert of Europe. Like the Concert, ASEAN has focused on preserving regime stability and countering domestic, not external, threats to regional peace. Its members have relied on implicit norms and practices rather than a codified and institutionalized order. Disputes are contained and a consensus maintained through informal practices of grouping and the fencing off, rather than the resolution, of contentious issues. In addition, ASEAN, like the Concert did, tolerates political diversity and relies almost exclusively on elite socialization rather than broader societal integration.

As in the case of the nineteenth-century Concert, these features do leave the security community that has evolved in Southeast Asia with distinct vulnerabilities; even though war is a very remote prospect, undercurrents of political instability and geopolitical uncertainty stand in the way of a stable peace that enjoys a durable, taken-for-granted quality. Changes in regime also have the potential to compromise intra-regional cooperation. These vulnerabilities have intensified of late due to ASEAN's enlargement as well as its effort to serve as a vehicle for security cooperation throughout East Asia. Political instability in Thailand and a border dispute between Thailand and Cambodia recently complicated matters.[74] Nonetheless, ASEAN's success in establishing a security community in Southeast Asia constitutes an important instance of the onset of stable peace in a region of considerable political and ethnic diversity.

How Peace Broke Out

The push toward regional cooperation in Southeast Asia began in the early 1960s. The countries of the region, some of which had only recently attained independence, were looking not only to counter threats from communist in-

---

[73] See, for example, Shaun Narine, *Explaining ASEAN: Regionalism in Southeast Asia* (Boulder, CO: Lynne Rienner, 2002).

[74] The long-standing border dispute between Thailand and Cambodia that broke out in 2008 was over land surrounding the 11th-century Preah Vihear temple.

surgents, but also to promote a secure strategic environment that would enable young, weak states to build stable economies and robust institutions of governance. In 1961, Thailand, the Philippines, and Malaya founded the Association of Southeast Asia (ASA). It was effectively stillborn, however, due to a territorial dispute between the Philippines and Malaya over Sabah, formerly a British crown colony in North Borneo. A second attempt at regional integration took place in 1963, when the three nations that were populated primarily by ethnic Malays—Malaya, the Philippines, and Indonesia—teamed up to form Maphilindo. But Maphilindo too swiftly ran aground due to the formation of the federation of Malaysia, which both the Philippines and Indonesia refused to recognize. Under the leadership of General Sukarno, Indonesia reacted to the establishment of Malaysia by pursuing a policy of *konfrontasi*, subjecting the struggling federation to a combination of economic isolation and sporadic military incursion. With the help of British forces, Malaysia turned back Indonesia's efforts to spoil the federation, which continued until Sukarno fell from power in the spring of 1966. Thereafter, Sukarno's successor, General Suharto, ended *konfrontasi*, clearing the way for rapprochement between Jakarta and Kuala Lumpur and reviving the prospects for regional cooperation.

As the area's dominant power, Indonesia was the most important player in shaping the regional security environment. Jakarta's embrace of *konfrontasi* made regional cooperation impossible by encouraging its neighbors to balance against, rather than align with, Indonesian power. Indonesia's decision to end *konfrontasi* and instead pursue rapprochement with Malaysia was accordingly a key turning point. It signaled a switch from predatory to benign intent, in turn enabling Indonesia to serve as the dominant core around which ASEAN was to cohere. Reconciliation between Indonesia and Malaysia set the stage for the founding and development of ASEAN—just as rapprochement between Germany and France did during the founding of the EC. Examining the beginnings of stable peace in Southeast Asia thus requires exploring the trajectory of Indonesian foreign policy between 1963 and 1966.

The formation of Malaysia was prompted by the concerns of Tunku Abdul Rahman, the prime minister of Malaya, that Singapore was headed toward a communist takeover.[75] Singapore's growing economy also made it an attrac-

---

[75] For further discussion of the founding of Malaysia, see the discussion of the separation of Singapore from Malaysia in the following chapter.

tive candidate for inclusion in a broader union. In light of Singapore's pre-dominantly Chinese population, however, its incorporation into a federal Malaysia would tilt the overall ethnic balance of the union against Malays. To offset the addition of Singapore's Chinese population, Tunku sought to include in Malaysia the North Borneo territories of Sabah and Sarawak (see map 5.1).[76] General Sukarno promptly opposed the formation of the federa-tion, arguing that its extension into North Borneo posed a direct threat to Indonesia's security. He also complained that Jakarta was not appropriately consulted in the matter and asserted that the new federation constituted a neocolonial outpost of the British.[77] Sukarno broke off diplomatic relations with Kuala Lumpur, stopped all trade with the federation (even though it ac-counted for 50 percent of Indonesian exports), and launched a "Crush Ma-laysia" military campaign.

Sukarno's policies were to a considerable degree shaped by domestic pres-sures. The military establishment and the communist party (PKI), arguably the country's only two national institutions, both favored *konfrontasi*. Armed rivalry with Malaysia augmented the military's political strength and its bud-gets. For the PKI, opposition to Malaysia constituted a principled stand against neocolonialism and a means of aligning Indonesia with the commu-nist bloc. Sukarno was therefore able to strengthen his hand at home by chal-lenging Malaysia's legitimacy and portraying the federation as an "unrepre-sentative alien-inspired polity designed to perpetuate colonial economic and military interests in South-East Asia which, by their nature, posed a threat to the viability and regional role of Indonesia."[78]

Even if politically savvy in the short term, Sukarno's gambit ultimately backfired by strangling the Indonesian economy. As Michael Leifer notes, "politics took priority over economics."[79] The country not only gave up half of its exports by breaking off relations with Malaysia, but it also triggered international sanctions, inducing the United States and the IMF to end eco-nomic assistance. The consequences for the Indonesian economy were disas-

---

[76] According to Kuala Lumpur's initial plan, the federation was to incorporate Brunei as well as Sabah and Sarawak. The small sultanate ultimately decided against inclusion in the federation.

[77] On Sukarno's objections to the formation of Malaysia, see J.A.C. Mackie, *Konfrontasi: The Indonesia-Malaysia Dispute 1963–1966* (London: Oxford University Press, 1974), p. 201.

[78] Michael Leifer, *Indonesia's Foreign Policy* (London: George Allen & Unwin, 1983), p. 75.

[79] Leifer, *Indonesia's Foreign Policy*, p. 92.

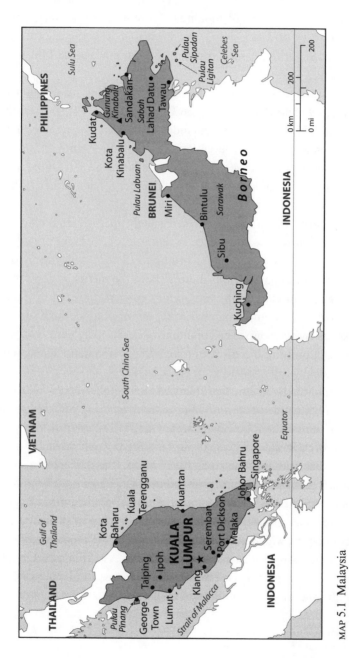

MAP 5.1 Malaysia

Source: http://www.lib.utexas.edu/MAPS/cia08/malaysia_sm_2008.gif.

trous. In 1965, the inflation rate was 500 percent and the cost of rice rose 900 percent.[80] Domestic discontent mounted. Moreover, the military, although initially supportive of *konfrontasi*, was displeased with the Jakarta-Beijing alignment that Sukarno pursued as part of his crusade against Malaysia and neocolonialism.

Economic crisis combined with the military's growing disaffection to set the stage for the coup that occurred on October 1, 1965. It was readily put down by General Suharto, the commander of the strategic reserve, enabling Sukarno to remain in power—even if only nominally—until the spring of 1966. But the events of October ultimately undermined Sukarno's rule and cleared the way for a radical switch in Indonesian foreign policy from *konfrontasi* to rapprochement and regional cooperation.

The officer corps, which had grown increasingly uneasy with the tilt toward China, had started to lose confidence in Sukarno's belligerent brand of foreign policy even before the coup. According to Leifer, "senior army officers had already begun to have serious doubts about the merits of confrontation and had engaged in clandestine exploratory conversations with Malaysian representatives."[81] The other main backer of confrontation, the PKI, was fatally weakened by the coup. The communists were widely perceived to have played a role in plotting the effort to topple the government. Thereafter, the PKI was politically isolated and soon declared illegal.

Amid the political vacuum that followed the October coup, General Suharto gradually assumed control of the government, and Sukarno formally ceded power to him the following March. Once in full control, the Suharto government orchestrated an about-face in foreign policy. Stabilizing the economy was its primary objective. Adam Malik, the new foreign minister, "made explicit that the first priority of Indonesia's foreign policy was to serve its developmental needs."[82] Getting inflation under control meant regaining access to foreign assistance. Doing so necessitated a repair of relations with the Western powers, which in turn depended upon an end to *konfrontasi*. The change of course was seen as a strategic necessity. As Leifer notes, "Indonesia did not possess the capacity in material resources and political will to sustain confrontation as a serious undertaking."[83]

[80] Leifer, *Indonesia's Foreign Policy*, p. 113.
[81] Leifer, *Indonesia's Foreign Policy*, p. 104.
[82] Leifer, *Indonesia's Foreign Policy*, p. 136.
[83] Leifer, *Indonesia's Foreign Policy*, p. 110.

Suharto moved slowly and cautiously, well aware that a bold and rapid opening to Malaysia would likely provoke the politics of humiliation and an accompanying domestic backlash from quarters still wedded to Sukarno's combative brand of leadership. Indeed, he deliberately prolonged Indonesia's confrontational stance toward Malaysia "because that policy served an important domestic political function during the internal transfer of power." When ready to make an opening to Kuala Lumpur, he chose to dispatch a group of officers from the Crush Malaysia Command to negotiate with Tunku, calculating that the direct involvement of military hardliners would "avoid an agreement which might appear to be a capitulation by Indonesia."[84] After securing Tunku's assent to hold a referendum in Malaysia's North Borneo territories to ensure that their citizens wished to be part of the federation, formal relations were reestablished between Jakarta and Kuala Lumpur. The vote provided Suharto a face-saving rationale for his sudden willingness to recognize Malaysia.

Indonesia's decision to end its geopolitical rivalry with Malaysia was the seminal act of unilateral accommodation that precipitated new efforts to advance regional security cooperation. Once Sukarno was no longer a political force, Suharto made unequivocal that *konfrontasi* was gone for good, on one occasion offering a remarkably open critique of his predecessor: "The arrogant attitude, Indonesian conspicuous leadership, the role of posing as the pioneer, champion and the like we have dropped and replaced by more proper ways of approach based on an equal footing and respect."[85] Through such clarity about Indonesia's new intentions, Suharto helped ensure that unilateral accommodation led to reciprocal restraint. In return for Indonesia's new stance, Kuala Lumpur willingly ceded to Jakarta the ostensible lead in shaping ASEAN—an important concession to Suharto, especially since Malaysians tended to view the new body as an extension of ASA, which they had played a key role in launching and which had not even included Indonesia. But "the need for Indonesia to avoid giving the impression of capitulation" took precedence.[86] By allowing Indonesia to claim authorship of the new regional organization, Indonesia's neighbors enabled Suharto to further inoculate himself against nationalist critics of his foreign policy of accommodation.

[84] Leifer, *Indonesia's Foreign Policy*, pp. 108–109.
[85] Leifer, *Indonesia's Foreign Policy*, p. 117.
[86] Leifer, *Indonesia's Foreign Policy*, p. 119.

Reciprocal restraint also prevailed on the question of relations with extra-regional powers—a critical issue inasmuch as it revealed differing views of the ultimate purposes of regional cooperation. For Indonesia, ASEAN was about facilitating regional stability through security cooperation, thereby ending the need for reliance on external powers. With the benefit of Indonesia's leadership, cooperation and integration would advance the cause of regional autonomy. For ASEAN's smaller members, the organization was also a vehicle for ensuring regional stability, but one of the key mechanisms for doing so was the containment of Indonesian power through the regularization of strategic restraint.[87] Moreover, they tended to see the continued role of the Western powers in the region as contributing to, not threatening, regional stability.

These differences manifested themselves during negotiations over the founding terms of ASEAN, with Indonesia and other prospective members taking opposing positions on the status of foreign bases in the region. Jakarta envisaged a region free from external interference, while the other ASEAN members maintained defense links to either Britain or the United States. Indonesia wanted to minimize if not eliminate such links, urging that ASEAN warn all outside states that their involvement in the region "should not be used to serve the particular interest of any of the big powers." In the end, ASEAN members fenced off the issue, effectively agreeing to disagree and compromising on the language contained in ASEAN's founding declaration. The document noted that "all foreign bases are temporary and remain only with the expressed concurrence of the countries concerned and are not intended to be used directly or indirectly to subvert the national independence and freedom of States in the area."[88]

As they designed ASEAN and fashioned its agenda, the five founding states set as their top priorities bolstering regime stability, resolving peacefully regional disputes, and countering communist insurgents. Inasmuch as ASEAN was comprised of weak states, mutual respect for the sovereignty and territorial integrity of members, as well as non-interference in each other's domestic affairs, emerged as guiding norms.[89] In this respect, ASEAN members were intent on strengthening their borders, not making them more

[87] Narine, *Explaining ASEAN*, p. 15.

[88] Arnfinn Jorgensen-Dahl, *Regional Organization and Order in South-East Asia* (New York: St. Martin's Press, 1982), pp. 38–39.

[89] Acharya, "Collective Identity and Conflict Management in Southeast Asia," p. 209.

porous; regional cooperation was meant to enhance rather than erode individual sovereignty. Intra-regional conflicts and cross-border communist movements constituted the primary threats to security. Although both Vietnam and China were identified as potential adversaries, ASEAN was not meant to be a defense pact against outside aggression, especially since the threat posed by these states was deemed to be more ideological than military in nature. Furthermore, ASEAN identified regime stability ("national resilience") and solidarity among member states ("regional resilience") as the best antidotes to outside interference. At ASEAN's first formal summit in 1976, Philippine president Ferdinand Marcos summed up the group's consensus on threat assessment: "Insurgency is the cause of insecurity and it probably will be the cause of insecurity within our region for the next five to ten years. I cannot foresee any threat of outright external aggression from any country."[90]

DECISION MAKING AND POWER-CHECKING MECHANISMS

In contrast to the EC's legalized and institutionalized mechanisms for decision making and dispute resolution, ASEAN has maintained a low level of codification and institutionalization. During its early years, the main forum for decision making was an annual meeting of foreign ministers. Routine business was handled by national bureaucracies and the ASEAN Standing Committee, the chairmanship of which rotated annually. Participants were the ambassadors serving in the member state that held the chair. A secretariat was not established until 1976, the same year as the first formal ASEAN summit. Although Manila initially lobbied to host the secretariat, the Philippines deferred to Indonesia's insistence that it be located in Jakarta, announcing that, "In deference to President Suharto's wishes and in the interest of regional unity and harmony, the Philippines hereby withdraws its offer in favor of Indonesia."[91] In addition to official ASEAN meetings, there was a proliferation of governmental and nongovernmental gatherings under ASEAN's umbrella. In 1982, for example, over four hundred meetings took place under ASEAN auspices according to the Thai foreign ministry.

ASEAN members have also relied on informal approaches to put into practice their commitments to the renunciation of force and the settlement

---

[90] Amitav Acharya, *Regionalism and Multilateralism: Essays on Cooperative Security in the Asia-Pacific* (Singapore: Eastern Universities Press, 2003), p. 56.

[91] Jorgensen-Dahl, *Regional Organization and Order in South-East Asia*, p. 185.

of disputes through peaceful means. The group borrowed two concepts from Indonesian village culture. *Musjawarah*, consultation and deliberation among kin, was to lead to *mufakat*, a communal consensus that reflected the interests of all parties. Preferably, disputes would be solved through consultation among members and the gradual emergence of a consensus. When necessary—that is, when a consensus was unattainable—the dispute in question would be set aside and fenced off to ensure that it did not disrupt communal solidarity.[92]

ASEAN's approach to dispute resolution and cooperative action—often labeled the "ASEAN Way"—has thus resembled the practice of grouping frequently employed during the Concert of Europe. The collective pursuit of regional peace woud take precedence over individual opportunities for self-interested gain. However, the fashioning of a consensus did not mean unanimity, but instead the toleration of differences in the service of unity. To fashion consensus in the absence of unanimity, ASEAN would permit members to opt out of specific initiatives and then take steps to contain the potential fallout. Lee Kuan Yew offered the following description of how this process would work: "So long as members who are not yet ready to participate are not damaged by non-participation, nor excluded from future participation, the power of veto need not be exercised . . . when four agree and one does not object, this can still be considered a consensus, and the four should proceed with a new regional scheme."[93]

This informal approach to the practice of self-binding and co-binding enabled ASEAN members to resolve or set aside a host of simmering disputes. In 1968, the year following ASEAN's formation, its future was called into question by the continuing controversy over Sabah, with Malaysia accusing the Philippines of using the island of Corregidor to train insurgents intended to infiltrate the disputed territory. The confrontation escalated to the point that the two nations effectively broke off diplomatic relations. By 1969, however, relations were normalized and the dispute effectively over. The Philippines had not dropped its claim to Sabah, but had simply shelved it in the name of regional harmony.[94] The Philippines, to draw on the terminology of Concert diplomacy, had been grouped.

[92] Narine, *Explaining ASEAN*, p. 31. For other examples of the important role that cultural practices at the local level play in promoting regional peace, see the case studies on the Iroquois Confederation and the United Arab Emirates in the following chapter.
[93] Acharya, *Regionalism and Multilateralism*, p. 257.
[94] Jorgensen-Dahl, *Regional Organization and Order in South-East Asia*, pp. 205–211.

During the late 1960s and early 1970s, informal practices of strategic restraint and consensus-building resolved a host of other disputes. Indonesia and Malaysia not only settled their territorial differences, but cooperated on controlling their common border in North Borneo and teamed up to fashion a new regime to manage shipping through the Malacca Strait. In 1968, regional conflict came close to breaking out after Singapore executed two Indonesian marines that had been convicted of murder. Anti-Chinese riots occurred in Indonesia and the government was pressed by popular outrage to retaliate, risking a confrontation with Singapore. A crisis was averted only by Jakarta's willingness to practice strategic restraint and avoid a provocative response while allowing popular passions to dissipate. As Leifer comments, "Within ASEAN, Indonesia assumed a cautious role, conscious of the sensitivity of the smaller regional partners to any revival of grandiloquent design at their expense."[95]

In a manner similar to other nascent security communities, ASEAN provided a forum for concrete military cooperation as well as for the resolution of regional disagreements. Unlike in the Concert of Europe and the EC, however, military cooperation among ASEAN members has been primarily bilateral rather than multilateral in form. Especially during ASEAN's early years, the most frequent type of military cooperation entailed joint border patrol and counterinsurgency operations. Members regularly exchanged intelligence information, carried out bilateral exercises and maneuvers, and shared facilities for training and weapons testing. One source reported that forty-five bilateral exercises took place between 1972 and 1980, thirty-eight of which involved Indonesian forces. According to a high-ranking Indonesian army officer, ASEAN turned into a "defense spider web."[96]

For skeptics of ASEAN, its reliance on bilateral initiatives constitutes evidence of its telling limitations.[97] The member states, critics contend, have yet to develop sufficient trust or congruence of interest to enable them to commit to multilateral engagement. Absent a thick network of multilateral linkages, ASEAN is destined to fall short of constituting a security community.

Such skepticism is misplaced. The regularity of joint military exercises demonstrated a high level of mutual confidence; sharing information about command structures, operations, and intelligence required a reciprocal willingness to tolerate considerable transparency on security matters. The prefer-

---

[95] Leifer, *Indonesia's Foreign Policy*, p. 124.
[96] Acharya, *Regionalism and Multilateralism*, pp. 86, 79.
[97] See, for example, Narine, *Explaining ASEAN*.

ence of ASEAN members for bilateral ties has been a product of the group's objectives and the strategic environment in which it functions, not a reflection of its shortcomings. From its formation through the 1980s, communist insurgents posed the principal threat to regional stability as well as the security of individual ASEAN members. To the degree this threat could be addressed at the interstate level, cooperation on border control and counterinsurgency operations was the main means of doing so. These tasks required bilateral, not multilateral, undertakings along the interstate boundaries in question.

Bilateral initiative also predominated because ASEAN explicitly avoided becoming a defense pact. Member states agreed that there was only a remote prospect of external threat, they held differing views about how to define that threat, and they calculated that the formation of a formal alliance was more likely to trigger external intervention than to provide an effective deterrent.[98] Moreover, should ASEAN members at some point confront a major external aggressor, they presumed that they would ultimately require the help of an outside power to defend themselves. As Malaysia's chief of staff put it, "In terms of deterrence value, it is very doubtful if an ASEAN alliance would really deter any would-be aggressor . . . To achieve deterrence ASEAN will have to form an alliance with one of the superpowers."[99]

ASEAN's focus on regional security rather than collective defense does not mean that its members have been indifferent to the policies and intentions of neighboring states or extra-regional powers. On the contrary, developments in Indochina and the trajectory of great-power involvement in Southeast Asia had important effects on the evolution of ASEAN, encouraging member states to turn to regional cooperation to meet their security needs. Paradoxically, however, ASEAN was primarily the beneficiary of the threat of great-power withdrawal, not the prospect of outside intervention.

The year after ASEAN's formation, Great Britain announced that it was withdrawing from all strategic outposts to the east of the Suez Canal. Southeast Asia was losing its primary external arbiter; Singapore and Malaysia would no longer be able to count on Britain to help provide for their security needs. The prospect of British retrenchment provided an impetus for the resolution of the Sabah dispute and gave Singapore and Malaysia new incentives to settle their outstanding disagreements.[100] America's withdrawal from

[98] Acharya, *Regionalism and Multilateralism*, p. 88.
[99] Acharya, *Regionalism and Multilateralism*, pp. 91–92.
[100] Narine, *Explaining ASEAN*, pp. 15, 19.

Vietnam in the early 1970s had a similar effect. Washington not only retreated from Southeast Asia, but also adopted the Nixon Doctrine, letting it be known that the United States would look to regional actors to provide for their own security.[101]

Especially in the wake of America's new posture, Vietnam's invasion of Cambodia in 1978 did heighten fears of the possibility of external aggression against ASEAN territory. This threat led to an unprecedented effort among ASEAN members to develop a common policy toward Vietnam. Member states did not formally assume commitments to collective defense, but they did fashion a consensus on a diplomatic strategy to prevent spillover onto Thailand's territory.[102] ASEAN's successful handling of its first external crisis helped build member-state confidence in the effectiveness of the institution.

SOCIETAL INTEGRATION

Despite the gradual increase in ASEAN's institutionalization and the frequency of its meetings, economic interdependence among member states has remained quite limited. ASEAN gatherings have regularly debated policy initiatives aimed at speeding economic integration—reducing tariff barriers, establishing joint industrial initiatives, launching a regional airline and shipping line, to name a few—but most of these plans have failed to materialize. For most of its history, intraregional trade has hovered around 20 percent of total ASEAN trade. The comparative figure for the EC/EU is over 70 percent. Moreover, Singapore's exports have accounted for much of ASEAN's internal commerce, with intraregional trade among the other four members representing only 5 percent of total trade. More recently, intraregional trade has enjoyed a minor increase due to European-style efforts at market integration. But Northeast Asia, North America, and Europe remain the main export markets for ASEAN members.[103]

Societal integration has been similarly stunted. ASEAN began life as, and has remained, a largely elite undertaking. As during the Concert of Europe, the forging of personal bonds among officials and the socialization of a regional elite promoted mutual trust and facilitated the onset of security community. Even skeptics of ASEAN's impact note its important role in building

---

[101] Jorgensen-Dahl, *Regional Organization and Order in South-East Asia*, p. 75.

[102] Narine, *Explaining ASEAN*, pp. 41–47; and Acharya, "Collective Identity and Conflict Management in Southeast Asia,", pp. 209–210.

[103] Narine, *Explaining ASEAN*, pp. 27–30.

contacts "between the governmental and social elites of its member states," and creating "ties of personal obligation and familiarity among national leaders."[104] But socialization has not spread widely beyond the policy-making community. The low level of economic integration has meant that the private sector has had limited interest in regional cooperation. As Arnfinn Jorgensen-Dahl notes, "the leaders have no extensive or influential elite groups which support or, indeed, oppose them on regional cooperation."[105] Nor has there been much public engagement in building regional community: "Cooperation and conflict management among the ASEAN states rested on a narrow consensus among its elite and leaders without support and sustenance from their civil societies."[106]

In light of the fact that regional integration in Southeast Asia has shallow societal roots, ASEAN's progress toward becoming a mature security community is particularly impressive. Nonetheless, absent the deeper engagement of the private sector or civil society, the zone of peace that has taken root among ASEAN members does remain vulnerable to regime change and other unforeseen challenges. Just as the Concert of Europe lacked durability due to its heavy reliance on personal bonds among an exclusive club of elites, so too does ASEAN risk falling prey to changes in government and personnel. Indeed, a change of government in Thailand in 1988 did severely strain the organization's integrity. Not only were personal bonds lost, but Thailand, without consulting its ASEAN partners, switched from a policy of isolating Vietnam to one of engagement. As Shaun Narine comments, "a change in governing elites within Thailand was all that was necessary to undermine ASEAN's coherence. The intraregional commitment to ASEAN may be dependent upon far too few people within the member states."[107] ASEAN weathered this storm, in part because Vietnam withdrew from Cambodia soon thereafter. Nonetheless, a worrisome precedent was set.

The challenges of maintaining cohesion and consensus within ASEAN have grown more acute as a consequence of several rounds of enlargement. Brunei joined in 1984, followed by Vietnam in 1995, Burma (Myanmar) and Laos in 1997, and Cambodia in 1999. The serial expansion of membership in

[104] Narine, *Explaining ASEAN*, p. 31.
[105]   Jorgensen-Dahl, *Regional Organization and Order in South-East Asia*, p. 187.
[106] Acharya, *Regionalism and Multilateralism*, p. 297.
[107] Narine, *Explaining ASEAN*, p. 60.

the 1990s has both broadened diversity as to regime type and imported new sources of political instability. Meanwhile, ASEAN has also sought to provide a foundation for broader regional cooperation by establishing the ASEAN Regional Forum (ARF). The ARF includes all parties that have an impact on security in Southeast Asia, Northeast Asia, and Oceania, including the United States, Russia, and the EU. Neither enlargement nor ASEAN's broader regional ambition has shaken stable peace among its founding members. But its ability to export such stability to its new members and beyond remains in question. As one observer notes, "the ASEAN Way was founded upon strong interpersonal ties among its founders, which have been diluted by its own expansion."[108]

Whether ASEAN today constitutes a mature security community and, if so, when its members began to enjoy a state of stable peace remain questions of lively debate among regional experts. Primary sources indicating whether and when the founding members stopped maintaining war plans against each other are unavailable. Officials involved in ASEAN tend to point to the first half of the 1980s as the period when stable peace was consolidated.[109] Singapore may represent the one exception to this assessment due to its small size and its self-perception as a Chinese island in a "Malay sea."[110] But its sense of insecurity is existential in nature and does not arise from the perception that its neighbors have hostile intent and contemplate armed aggression.

Despite the ambiguity about exactly when stable peace set in, a consensus does exist among scholars that ASEAN constitutes a security community. Acharya writes that "it can be safely asserted that no ASEAN country seriously envisages war against another" and that there exists "a sturdy structure of trust, confidence and goodwill between the member states."[111] Leifer agrees that "one can claim quite categorically that ASEAN has become an institutionalized vehicle for intramural conflict avoidance and management."[112] Noordin Sopiee joins the consensus, observing that "Most certainly, when it comes to producing security, stability and sub-regional order, it has been a

---

[108] Acharya, *Regionalism and Multilateralism*, p. 339.

[109] Acharya, *Regionalism and Multilateralism*, p. 92.

[110] Jorgensen-Dahl, *Regional Organization and Order in South-East Asia*, p. 41.

[111] Acharya, "Collective Identity and Conflict Management in Southeast Asia," p. 214; Acharya, *Regionalism and Multilateralism*, p. 164.

[112] Leifer in Acharya, "Collective Identity and Conflict Management in Southeast Asia," p. 214.

resounding success, whose record is possibly unmatched in the contemporary experience of the Third World."[113]

Why Peace Broke Out

Previous case studies in this book have already demonstrated that neither liberal democracy nor institutionalized restraint is a necessary condition for the onset of stable peace. ASEAN's success in building a security community in Southeast Asia reinforces this finding. During the formative years of ASEAN, its member states varied as to regime type. Singapore, Malaysia, and the Philippines were evolving as illiberal democracies. Indonesia and Thailand were effectively military dictatorships. Tellingly, neither regime diversity nor autocratic rule in the region's dominant state stood in the way of the practice of strategic restraint and the onset of security community.

As in other cases explored above—Argentina-Brazil, Soviet Union-China, the Concert of Europe—even autocratic rulers are able to practice self-restraint when faced with powerful incentives to do so. At home, Suharto ruled with a heavy hand, regularly resorting to violence to suppress opposition. Soon after he took power, campaigns against alleged communists, many of whom were ethnic Chinese, took the lives of between 500,000 and one million people, and many more were jailed for years without trial. But repression at home did not stand in the way of restraint abroad. Once Suharto had succeeded in wresting control from Sukarno, he readily switched from *konfrontasi* to a policy of accommodation—the key turning point that led to rapprochement with Malaysia and set the stage for the formation of ASEAN. A *New York Times* obituary noted the paradox: Suharto's "32-year dictatorship was one of the most brutal and corrupt of the 20th century," but he also "ended Sukarno's policy of confrontation with Malaysia and became a force for regional stability by helping to establish the Association of Southeast Asian Nations."[114]

Like the Concert, ASEAN not only contained regimes that were repressive at home, but also encompassed states of varying regime type. Nonetheless, they were all interested in preserving intraregional peace, in no small part to

---

[113] Noordin Sopiee, "ASEAN and Regional Security," in Mohammed Ayoob, ed., *Regional Security in the Third World* (Boulder, CO: Westview Press, 1986), p. 221.

[114] "Suharto Dies at 86; Indonesian Dictator Brought Order and Bloodshed," *New York Times*, January 28, 2008.

enable fragile governments to build effective state institutions. As was the case for the Concert in nineteenth-century Europe, a key objective of ASEAN was to strengthen sovereignty, not erode it in the name of regional or supra-national integration. Both bodies valued regional stability as means of fur-thering their domestic political objectives.

Again in a manner similar to the Concert, ASEAN compensated for the lack of institutionalized restraint by providing public goods often associated with more liberal regimes. These public goods helped enable its members to let down their guard and back away from geopolitical rivalry. The organiza-tion substantially enhanced transparency on security issues through regular sharing of intelligence and routine contact among high-level elites. The mem-bers had easy access to one another's military establishments through exer-cises, joint border patrols, and integrated staff colleges. ASEAN also made commitments to the peaceful resolution of disputes more credible. Unlike in the EC, it did not do so through codified agreements and parliamentary rati-fication. Instead, the credibility of commitments was strengthened by virtue of the trust and sense of personal obligation that emerged among leaders. Sustaining regional consensus might not have been a matter of legal obliga-tion, but it was a matter of personal honor.

ASEAN's founding members enjoyed similar social orders. With the excep-tion of Thailand, they were all emerging from decades of colonial rule. They were unified in their opposition to communism, instead seeking to build capi-talist economies resting on industrial development and urbanization. In ad-dition, they faced the same set of essential trade-offs: growth versus equity, national integration versus ethnic pluralism, and political stability versus participation.[115] With the exception of Singapore, ASEAN members had pri-marily agrarian economies and were seeking to develop manufacturing sec-tors that would promote export-led growth. The similarities of their eco-nomic programs actually stood in the way of regional economic integration, with member states protecting their own markets as they focused on produc-ing manufactures for the industrialized world. Due to Singapore's more ad-vanced manufacturing base, it expressed frustration with such protection. Indeed, even during Singapore's temporary inclusion in Malaysia, Kuala Lumpur refused to grant it unfettered market access, contributing to the po-litical tensions that led to Singapore's eventual separation from the union.

---

[115] Acharya, *Regionalism and Multilateralism*, p. 56.

Otherwise, the slow pace of economic integration had few negative consequences for ASEAN's political evolution, allowing countries with similar social orders to pursue similar growth strategies.

To the degree that issues of social order have impaired ASEAN's political
evolution, the primary stumbling block has been the privileged economic position enjoyed by ethnic Chinese throughout the region. Resentment against
ethnic Chinese led not only to regional tensions, but also to domestic violence and political instability. After the execution of two Indonesian marines
in Singapore, angry mobs attacked Chinese homes and shops in Indonesia.
Rivalry along ethnic lines was the main reason that Singapore was ultimately
excluded from Malaysia. Singapore was expelled from the federation after
only two years primarily because the size of its Chinese population compromised the political power of ethnic Malays.[116] The problem was not racial
discrimination per se, but concern among Malays that Chinese could become
the majority ethnic group within the federation.

The Chinese minority aside, ASEAN members have quite diverse populations in both religious and ethnic terms. Indonesia and Malaysia are predominantly Muslim, Thailand and Singapore predominantly Buddhist, and the
Philippines mostly Catholic. Singapore and Malaysia are home to a significant number of Hindus. ASEAN member states also contain a multitude of
ethno-linguistic groups, with numerical estimates varying with the system of
classification used.[117] As Acharya observes, "The members of ASEAN were,
and remain to date, remarkably divergent in terms of their . . . ethnic composition, and linguistic/cultural make-up."[118]

Paradoxically, the cultural diversity of individual member states has
worked to ASEAN's advantage. Due to their diverse populations, member
states were compelled to embrace inclusive national identities, making it
easier for them to embrace inclusive regional identities. Put differently, the
cultural heterogeneity of individual ASEAN members was a source of commonality for the group as a whole. This dynamic became apparent as proposals for regional integration evolved during the 1960s. One of the first was

[116] For further discussion of Singapore's expulsion from Malaysia, see chapter 6.
[117] Sukhumbhand Paribatra and Chai-Anan Samudavanija write that some thirty-two ethno-
linguistic groups populate ASEAN member states. See "Internal Dimensions of Regional Security in Southeast Asia," in Ayoob, *Regional Security in the Third World*, p. 62. According to the
New York Times, Indonesia alone is home to "300 ethnic groups speaking 250 languages." See
Berger, "Suharto Dies at 86."
[118] Acharya, "Collective Identity and Conflict Management in Southeast Asia," p. 206.

based on ethnic commonality among Malaysia, Indonesia, and the Philippines. The proposal to create Maphilindo arose from the fact that elites "regarded the ethnic and cultural affinities between the three nations as powerful bonds of association."[119] But sizable minority groups in all three countries served as obstacles to the notion of a Malay-only grouping, pushing governments in the region toward a more inclusive notion of regional identity—one that included Thais, Chinese, South Asians, and after enlargement, other Southeast Asian nations.

There was, however, a clear limit to how far cultural inclusiveness would go. Australia and New Zealand, despite their strategic proximity, were excluded from ASEAN—primarily for racial reasons.[120] Simply put, ASEAN members saw neither country as "Asian," and thus not eligible for participation in a regional community that was defined, at least in part, by a shared sense of "Asianness." By excluding Australia and New Zealand, ASEAN was also identifying an "other" that helped give its own diversity a greater aura of homogeneity. ASEAN leaders have frequently evoked the terminology of familial linkages to reinforce this sense of homogeneity, regularly referring to the bonds of "kinship" and "brotherhood" that unite its members.[121] The "ASEAN Way," a concept that incorporated the group's reliance on traditional village culture, was propagated to help nurture regional solidarity and help cut across linguistic and ethnic dividing lines. ASEAN also adopted a flag, a hymn, and other symbols aimed at inculcating a common regional identity.

Scholars agree that cultural commonality has played an important role in consolidating regional peace. Sopiee argues that ASEAN's activities and symbols have helped extend throughout the region the "sense of community" previously limited to Malays.[122] Jorgensen-Dahl compares the sense of cultural commonality among ASEAN members with that enjoyed by other regional groupings, noting that "similar or identical sentiments have been manifest in the relations between the countries of the Anglo-Saxon world, between the white Commonwealth countries . . . and they have been prominently present within such groups of countries as the Be-Ne-Lux and the

---

[119] Mackie, *Konfrontasi*, p. 167.

[120] Richard Higgot and Kim Richard Nossal, "Australia and the Search for a Security Community in the 1990s," in Adler and Barnett, *Security Communities*, pp. 282–283.

[121] Acharya, "Collective Identity and Conflict Management in Southeast Asia," p. 212. See also the ASEAN website, "The Founding of ASEAN," http://www.aseansec.org/11835.htm.

[122] Sopiee, "ASEAN and Regional Security," p. 226.

Scandinavian."[123] As in the cases of the Concert of Europe and the EC, cultural commonality provided an initial sense of affinity important to ASEAN's successful launch as well as a communal identity and shared normative framework important to the onset and deepening of stable peace.

THE DEMISE OF THE CONCERT OF EUROPE, 1848–1853

The Concert of Europe functioned successfully as a security community from the close of the Napoleonic Wars in 1815 through the middle of the nineteenth century. During the intervening years, there were numerous challenges to stable peace. Cooperation among Concert members was repeatedly tested by diverging responses to the liberal uprisings that sporadically occurred in Europe's smaller states and by jockeying for influence in the Balkans, Black Sea region, and Middle East as the Ottoman Empire began to falter. Nonetheless, the exercise of strategic restraint and adherence to Concert norms of consensual decision making and, when necessary, grouping succeeded in preventing the reawakening of great-power rivalry. Concert members continued to see the preservation of peace as their top priority, regularly backing away from the temptation to return to balance-of-power strategies that would have compromised solidarity and stability.

The Concert's demise began in 1848, when revolution swept across Europe. As Peter Stearns writes, "the collective impact of the Revolutions shattered the diplomatic framework of Europe that had been created by the Congress of Vienna."[124] Although the uprisings were readily put down and the clamor for political reform generally suppressed, the revolutionary contagion undermined the foundations of the Concert. The popular demand for change led to the departure from government of some of the key individuals who had shaped the Concert and forged the bonds of familiarity and trust that sustained it. In Austria, Metternich was forced to step down. In France, King Louis Philippe abdicated and Napoleon Bonaparte's nephew, Louis Napoleon Bonaparte, was elected president. He vowed to overturn the territorial settlement of 1815 and soon declared himself emperor. Prussia embraced constitutional monarchy as well as a new enthusiasm for leading the unification of German lands, awakening nationalist rivalry with Austria. Britain was spared a popular uprising, but the prospect of revolutionary upheaval

---

[123] Jorgensen-Dahl, *Regional Organization and Order in South-East Asia*, p. 167.
[124] Peter Stearns, *1848: The Revolutionary Tide in Europe* (New York: Norton, 1974), p. 6.

nonetheless induced British elites to pursue a confrontational foreign policy; the turmoil convinced them that domestic quiescence and political legitimacy now depended upon foreign ambition. Russia too was spared domestic instability, but it was soon forced to respond to the more nationalistic foreign policies adopted by its Concert partners.

The demise of the Concert of Europe occurred gradually; there was no sudden return to balance-of-power logic, unilateral action, and geopolitical rivalry. Rather, stable peace eroded from the inside out: political and social pressures at the domestic level induced elites to back away from the Concert's norms and practices. Foreign policy was no longer the exclusive preserve of a rarified group of aristocrats, but was becoming the fare of popular politics—especially in Britain and France. Mounting nationalist sentiment made it difficult for leaders to put great-power solidarity above a more self-regarding notion of national interest. The practice of strategic restraint, so crucial to building and sustaining trust, was becoming a source of national discontent. Strategies of reciprocal restraint aimed at demonstrating benign intent gave way to strategies of coercion and confrontation aimed at satisfying domestic audiences; growing concern about national prestige translated into preoccupation with the assertion of national power. These shifts in policy in turn awakened the security dilemma, transforming the differences that the Concert had so effectively neutralized into insurmountable conflicts of national interest.

The disputes that triggered the Crimean War in 1853 were hardly more intractable than those that Europe's great powers had readily resolved during the preceding four decades. They arose from a disagreement between France and Russia over control of religious sites in Jerusalem, which then broadened into a quarrel over which power had more sway over the Ottoman court. Nonetheless, the Concert's mechanisms for dispute resolution and its power-checking devices had been severely weakened by the upheaval of 1848. As a consequence, this dispute not only went unresolved, but gradually escalated until it triggered the outbreak of war.

The unraveling of the Concert thus followed a sequential process that represents the reverse of that which led to its formation. The Concert's demise began with political and social change. Domestic developments induced elites to generate narratives of opposition about their great-power allies and to abandon the practice of strategic restraint in favor of confrontational foreign policies. The mutual attribution of benign character gave way to the mutual attribution of aggressive intent, turning trust into reciprocal suspicion. Stable peace then fell prey to the return of geopolitical rivalry, with Europe's great powers again prepared to resort to arms rather than diplomacy to settle disputes over hierarchy and influence.

Notably, Britain and France, the Concert's most liberal and democratic members, were the two powers primarily responsible for undermining it. The political and social changes associated with urbanization and industrialization were most advanced in these two countries. Nationalism and foreign ambition proved to be particularly attractive tools for managing class cleavages and preserving the power of the aristocracy and the growing middle class amid the rising clamor for universal suffrage. Meanwhile, Russia, Austria, and Prussia, despite the upheaval of 1848, were prepared to defend the status quo and uphold the Concert. As great-power competition for influence over the Ottoman Empire mounted, the Tsar was ready to compromise and Austria's leaders to mediate. But France and Britain instead chose war, bringing to an end the decades of stable peace that had ensued since the close of the Napoleonic Wars.

The Revolutions of 1848: How the Concert Failed

The Crimean War was a symptom, not a cause, of the Concert's collapse. Even historians who maintain that the Concert system continued to function until the actual outbreak of war in 1853 admit that it failed to avert conflict because "its basic principles [were] repudiated and its fundamental rules broken."[125] It was the revolutions of 1848 and their political consequences that had so discredited and undermined the Concert's practices and power-checking institutions. As Gordon Craig observes, absent from Europe after the turmoil of 1848 were "national self-restraint, respect for the public law as defined in treaties, and willingness to enforce its observance by concerted action."[126] Indeed, the Concert system was deemed obsolete by many of Europe's leaders, reflecting "an impatience with the old conservative restraints that preserved peace but also seemed to throttle all progress."[127] From this perspective, the demise of the Concert was not accidental or the product of an unforeseen crisis. Rather, it was willfully dismantled by the great powers that had built it and benefited from its peace-causing effects.

[125] Paul Schroeder, *Austria, Great Britain, and the Crimean War* (Ithaca, NY: Cornell University Press, 1972), pp. 407–408.

[126] Schroeder, *Austria, Great Britain, and the Crimean War*, p. xi.

[127] Schroeder, *Austria, Great Britain, and the Crimean War*, p. 22.

Why did Europe's great powers deliberately undermine the Concert? What was the causal link between the revolutions of 1848 and the erosion of the norms and practices that had succeeded in preserving peace since 1815? The most immediate impact of the revolutionary upheaval was that Europe's leaders could no longer insulate foreign policy from domestic politics. All European governments were threatened by the instability, calls for liberal reform, and growing nationalist sentiment. It is true that Britain and Russia were spared the turmoil and that the revolutions in France, Austria, and Prussia were put down. But the widespread suppression of domestic reform served to divert the pressure for change to matters of foreign policy. Nationalism and foreign ambition were release valves, domestic tools used to arrest the expansion of political freedoms and ease class cleavages.[128] Moreover, the social base of the revolutions of 1848 was the professional middle class, not the working class. As a result, an ideological agenda of liberal reform abroad—as opposed to social reform at home—was sufficient to satisfy the revolutionary fervor. Indeed, the middle class, eager to increase its wealth and political power, was none too enthusiastic about the demands for labor reform and the broadening of suffrage demanded by Europe's expanding urban proletariat. As Stearns comments, "Middle-class liberals were incapable of consenting to the kind of unemployment relief that the lower classes so desperately needed and demanded."[129]

In the context of such political ferment, it became increasingly difficult for governments in Britain and France to justify strategic cooperation with autocratic regimes in Austria, Prussia, and Russia. Before 1848, the divide between constitutional monarchy and autocracy may have led to significant policy differences over how to react to nationalist uprisings in the European periphery, but it did not stand in the way of political solidarity and the maintenance of a communal identity. The revolutions put differences in regime type into much sharper relief. In the face of a mobilized public and media, the government in Britain found it perilous to talk of partnership with autocratic monarchs: "Austria represented the odious antithesis to Whig ideals as much as Russia did."[130] In France as well, the government was under domes-

---

[128] Nationalism was a double-edged sword for Austria due to the multiethnic composition of the Habsburg Empire and the push for Hungarian rights awakened by the events of 1848. Vienna's insistence on preserving the multiethnic character of its empire played an important role in enabling Prussia to assume leadership of the drive for German unification (see chapter 6).

[129] Stearns, *1848: The Revolutionary Tide in Europe*, p. 227. See also pp. 41–45.

[130] Schroeder, *Austria, Great Britain, and the Crimean War*, p. 416.

tic pressure to distance itself from the illiberal regimes to its east. Alphonse de Lamartine, the first foreign minister of the new republic that was declared in 1848, accepted that, "Monarchy and republicanism are not, in the eyes of wise statesmen, absolute principles, arrayed in deadly conflict against each other." But he did warn against efforts to suppress liberal uprisings and nationalist movements, noting that in the face of such repression, "the French republic would think itself entitled to take up arms in defence of these legitimate movements towards the improvement and nationhood of states."[131]

British leaders embraced similar rhetoric. Such pronouncements undercut the Concert, indicating that France and Britain were prepared to opt out of the norm that military action take place only in the context of great-power consensus. Should the two countries cease exercising strategic restraint, then others would follow, if only out of justifiable caution. Rather than presuming that their Concert partners would continue to forego opportunities for individual gain, Europe's great powers once again raised their guard.

The events of 1848 and the changes in regime they produced also led to the erosion of communal solidarity. The personal relationships and resulting trust built up through decades of consultation were lost to the turnover precipitated by domestic unrest. The Concert had shallow societal roots; as the elites that perpetuated it left office, there were few individuals or social groups left to sustain societal linkages. Moreover, the growing participation of the body politic in matters of foreign policy did more to weaken than to consolidate the Concert's social foundations. Inasmuch as the popular clamor for broader political participation challenged the exclusive and aristocratic nature of the elite club that managed European security, it weakened the legitimacy of the Concert system. And the allure of catering to popular pressure gave elites new incentives to abandon strategic restraint in favor of foreign ambition. The following summary of the events of 1848 and their consequences for the conduct of foreign policy flesh out these core arguments.

REVOLUTION, NATIONALISM, AND THE ABANDONMENT OF STRATEGIC RESTRAINT

The upheaval of 1848 began in France. In February, violent demonstrations broke out in Paris—close to four hundred people lost their lives—ultimately precipitating the abdication of King Louis Philippe. A sharp economic down-

---

[131] Frank Eyck, *The Revolutions of 1848–49* (New York: Barnes & Noble, 1972), pp. 40, 43.

turn during 1846–1847 played a role in fueling the discontent, but so did foreign policy, with the regime's opponents criticizing its retreat during the Eastern Crisis of 1839–1841 and its generally compliant approach to great-power relations.[132] During his transition from romantic poet to nationalist leader, Lamartine complained that "France is bored" and asserted that "France is revolutionary or it is nothing."[133] Jules Michelet and other nationalists of the era echoed the call for a return to the revolutionary and progressive spirit of 1789.

Following Louis Philippe's abdication in February, the provisional government soon introduced universal manhood suffrage and held elections for a constituent assembly. At the end of 1848, Louis Napoleon Bonaparte was elected president and quickly set about strengthening his grip on power. Late in 1851, he effectively assumed dictatorial power and dramatically curtailed the role of the National Assembly. A year thereafter, he took the title of Emperor Napoleon III, turning the Second Republic into the Second Empire. As he gradually centralized power, Napoleon kept a close watch on popular sentiment—one of the main reasons his government vowed to reassert France's ambitions abroad. Foreign Minister Lamartine declared that "the treaties of 1815 have no longer any lawful existence in the eyes of the French republic," and vowed "to make this emancipation of the republic from the treaties of 1815, understood and honestly admitted." Lamartine did qualify his declaration by noting that revision of the Vienna settlement would be done "pacifically" and was "in no way irreconcilable with the repose of Europe." Nonetheless, France's former rivals feared that the country would again seek to export revolution and return to the path of territorial aggression.[134] It was becoming increasingly difficult for them to maintain that French foreign policy was still based on benign motivations. According to one scholar of the period, "the advent of Napoleon III brought to power a government in France which not only lacked any commitment to the Concert, but sought in the long run to undermine the 1815 settlement and the Concert norms and mechanisms."[135]

The events of 1848 similarly produced a more nationalistic foreign policy

[132] James L. Richardson, *Crisis Diplomacy: The Great Powers since the Mid-Nineteenth Century* (Cambridge: Cambridge University Press, 1994), p. 100.

[133] Stearns, *1848: The Revolutionary Tide in Europe*, pp. 49–50.

[134] Eyck, *The Revolutions of 1848–49*, p. 7. Lamartine quotes on pp. 42–43.

[135] Richardson, *Crisis Diplomacy*, p. 105.

in Britain, albeit in a less direct fashion. Britain experienced neither domestic unrest nor major political change. The Chartists, a working-class movement which called for universal male suffrage and opposed the requirement that members of parliament be property owners, staged a demonstration in April. But the protesters were confronted by police and soon dispersed.[136] Britain's relative quiescence was not serendipitous. As noted above, the revolutions of 1848 were driven primarily by Europe's middle classes—in Britain, a social sector whose influence had already been enhanced through parliamentary reforms.[137] Accordingly, the British bourgeoisie had a vested interest in defending the domestic status quo even while demands for liberalization were sweeping the continent.

Nonetheless, Britain was not entirely insulated from the progressive and nationalist forces stirred up by the turmoil of 1848. Indeed, Lord Palmerston and the cabinet of which he was arguably the most influential member feared that unrest could cross the Channel and fuel the causes of Irish independence and mass democracy.[138] Palmerston and his colleagues responded by seeking to inoculate the government against popular demands for reform. They did so by diverting pressure for liberalization to matters of foreign policy, effectively exporting the public's progressive enthusiasm. For Palmerston, social imperialism—the use of nationalism and foreign ambition to strengthen popular support for the government—was the strategy of choice for ensuring domestic stability at home. Responding to and shaping public opinion was far preferable to repressing it; leaders ignoring the popular will, Palmerston warned, "will find their weapon snap short in their hand."[139]

With the help of the media, Palmerston stoked public fervor for confronting autocracy on the continent. In contrast to the situation in 1815, foreign policy was no longer insulated from public debate. Accordingly, the popularity of Palmerston's foreign policy helped him prevail against more moderate voices in the cabinet. Amid the blustery public mood of the late 1840s and

---

[136] J.P.T. Bury, "Great Britain and the Revolution of 1848," in Francois Fejto, ed., *The Opening of an Era: 1848* (New York: Howard Fertig, 1966), pp. 183–186.

[137] The reforms of 1832 increased the representation of the industrializing cities at the expense of less populated rural areas and expanded voter eligibility to about 20 percent of adult males.

[138] Palmerston was foreign secretary at the time of the 1848 revolutions, home secretary when war broke out in 1853, and he then became prime minister in the midst of the war in 1855.

[139] See Jack Snyder, *Myths of Empire: Domestic Politics and International Ambition* (Ithaca, NY: Cornell University Press, 1991), pp. 180–181; and Bury, "Great Britain and the Revolution of 1848," pp. 188–189.

early 1850s, the policies of strategic restraint preferred by the moderates would, according to Palmerston and his allies, humiliate the country, damage its prestige, and lead to domestic instability.[140] His hawkish views won out despite the fact that Lord Aberdeen, who became prime minister in 1852, was openly pro-Russian and sought to avert the confrontation that was building between Britain and Russia. But, according to John Shelton Curtis, "the jingoistic movement swept all before it, so that Aberdeen, deserted by the other ministers and in despair, could do little but fight a forlorn delaying action."[141]

Unlike the French government, the British government was not initially intent on overturning the Concert system. Palmerston, after all, had been present at the creation and played a key role in shaping British foreign policy throughout much of the Concert period. But the new turn in policy did exacerbate the growing divide between Britain and the Concert's autocratic troika. Relations with Russia suffered the most, in part due to Palmerston's deliberate effort to "raise public opinion against her. . . . I am all for making a clatter against her."[142] Potent strains of anti-Russian sentiment among the public helped put Britain on a collision course with Russia once great-power tensions began to heat up over influence in Constantinople.[143] According to James Richardson, "It was Britain's inflexibility, due to internal political instability and the strength of anti-Russian sentiment, which negated any prospect of a settlement."[144]

Among the Concert's three conservative members, the revolutions of 1848 had the most significant impact in Austria. Francis Joseph replaced Ferdinand as the Habsburg emperor. Of more consequence, Metternich was forced to resign and was replaced by Prince Schwarzenberg. The Concert was thereafter absent one of its founding and guiding personalities, denying its councils of a figure who had played a central role in promoting a shared sense of trust and solidarity.[145] Austria also faced nationalist uprisings in Hungary

[140] Schroeder, *Austria, Great Britain, and the Crimean War*, pp. 385–386.

[141] John Shelton Curtis, *Russia's Crimean War* (Durham, NC: Duke University Press, 1979), p. 114.

[142] Snyder, *Myths of Empire*, p. 175.

[143] See John Howes Gleason, *The Genesis of Russophobia in Great Britain: A Study of the Interaction of Policy and Opinion* (Cambridge, MA: Harvard University Press, 1950).

[144] Richardson, *Crisis Diplomacy*, p. 104.

[145] It is notable that even after leaving office, Metternich cautioned Austria to remain neutral and to serve as a mediator as great-power tensions mounted. Schroeder comments that Metternich's ideas had become obsolete in post-1848 Europe: "His program presupposed a solidarity

and Italy, threatening the integrity of the empire as well as Vienna's influence on the Italian peninsula. Although Britain ultimately backed suppression of both uprisings in order to protect the territorial status quo, doing so put increasing pressure on the British government to stand behind its rhetorical support for liberal change. In addition, Austria eventually turned to Russia to help preserve the empire; the Tsar sent some 360,000 Russian troops to Hungary to put down the rebellion. Despite Vienna's short-term gratitude, these developments intensified concern in Austria, France, and Britain about Russia's growing influence in southeast Europe. These worries helped strengthen the resolve of France and Britain to stand firm against Russia as the competition for influence in Constantinople mounted. They also figured into Austria's decision to side with the western powers, a move that particularly irked the Russians in the wake of the military help given to Vienna in suppressing the Hungarian uprising.[146] By aligning with Britain and France, Austria ensured that the Crimean War would confirm the demise not just of the Concert, but the Holy Alliance as well.

In Russia and Prussia, the main impact of the events of 1848 was growing nationalist pressure. There was no consequential change of government in Russia. But confronted with foreign policies in France and Britain that had grown more ideological and nationalistic, Russia felt compelled to respond in kind as the standoff over influence in Constantinople intensified. In Prussia, both liberal reforms and a new surge in German nationalism followed the upheaval of 1848. Despite the push for constitutional and parliamentary reform, the Prussian government accepted only limited constitutional constraints and proceeded to undermine the assembly established in Frankfurt. Mounting nationalist sentiment proved of more immediate consequence, manifesting itself in terms of a new Prussian effort to unify the German states.[147] The result was building tension with Austria, the other contender to lead Germany to unification, creating yet another threat to the integrity of the Holy Alliance.

In the aftermath of 1848, then, France and Britain both embraced a more

---

of interest and principle among the great powers and reserves of good sense and caution that no longer existed." Schroeder, *Austria, Great Britain, and the Crimean War*, p. 395.

[146] Schroeder, *Austria, Great Britain, and the Crimean War*, p. 42. See also Charles W. Hallberg, *Franz Joseph and Napoleon III, 1852–1864: A Study of Austro-French Relations* (New York: Octagon Books, 1973), p. 67.

[147] Stearns, *1848: The Revolutionary Tide in Europe*, pp. 4–6.

ambitious and nationalistic brand of foreign policy that had the potential to overturn the territorial status quo and undermine the Concert. Meanwhile, although the Concert's three autocracies sought to preserve the status quo, nationalism and the return of geopolitical competition were also creating fissures within the Holy Alliance.

THE CRIMEAN WAR: THE CONSEQUENCES OF THE CONCERT'S DEMISE

Napoleon III bears primary responsibility for setting in motion the sequence of events that led to the outbreak of the Crimean War. The political dispute that culminated in the return of great-power war to Europe started in 1850 when Greek Orthodox and Roman Catholic clergy in Jerusalem quarreled over control of the city's Christian holy sites. Palestine's Ottoman overseers preferred to play down the disagreement, but the French government proceeded to intervene on behalf of its Catholic brethren. Napoleon was currying favor with the French Church and following through on his populist pledge to pursue a more assertive foreign policy.[148] Once Tsar Nicholas responded by supporting the Orthodox clergy, Napoleon's move readily escalated into a broader dispute over which country had greater influence in Constantinople. Since Russia was the continent's premier power, curtailing its sway would further Napoleon's aim of breaking out of the constraints of the Concert system. It was also likely to divide the Holy Alliance by inflaming latent competition between Austria and Russia over their spheres of influence in southeastern Europe. Prompted by France's expanding geopolitical aims, the Tsar too perceived more than a religious issue at stake, viewing the dispute as a threat not just to the rights of the Orthodox community, but also to Russia's influence over the Ottoman Empire.[149]

What began in 1850 as a peripheral dispute over control of religious sites in Jerusalem by 1853 escalated into major war. In March of that year, France dispatched a fleet to the Black Sea, successfully encouraging Constantinople to resist Russian pressure and accept the Roman Catholic Church as the supreme authority over Holy Sites in Jerusalem. The Tsar responded in July by dispatching his army to the Danubian provinces. British and French fleets promptly headed to the Dardanelles. In October and November, Russian and

---

[148] Norman Rich, *Why the Crimean War? A Cautionary Tale* (Hanover: University Press of New England, 1985), p. 20.

[149] Schroeder, *Austria, Great Britain, and the Crimean War*, pp. 23–24; and Rich, *Why the Crimean War?* pp. 20–21.

Ottoman forces clashed along the Danube, followed by a Russian attack on an Ottoman fleet anchored at the Black Sea port of Sinope in November. The attack on Sinope triggered a widening of the conflict by prompting France and Britain to declare war in March 1854.

During the era of the Concert, a quarrel of such minor magnitude would never have escalated in this manner; it would have been readily resolved, or at least fenced off and set aside. Indeed, disputes of far more geopolitical consequence were regularly settled well before they reached the point at which armed conflict would have been contemplated. But the revolutions of 1848 had dramatically altered the political landscape, awakening a strategic logic altogether different than the one that had prevailed since 1815. As Schroeder observed, "The first and great commandment of the Concert was, 'Thou shalt not threaten or humiliate another great power'."[150] By the early 1850s, however, France was deliberately violating this dictum, instead seeking to humble Russia and use foreign ambition as a tool of domestic politics. According to Richardson, "France under a second Emperor Napoleon could not but aspire to revising the territorial settlement . . . by diplomatic initiatives calculated to enhance French prestige with little regard for the system as a whole or for the Concert mechanisms which sustained it."[151]

The statements of French leaders themselves substantiate this interpretation. Drouyn de Lhuys, who became foreign minister in 1852, described his government's intentions as follows: "The question of the Holy Places and everything affecting them was of no importance whatever to France. . . . All this Eastern Question which provoked so much noise was nothing more for the imperial government than a means of dislocating the continental alliance which had tended to paralyze France for almost half a century. When finally an opportunity presented itself to provoke discord within this powerful coalition, the Emperor Napoleon immediately seized it." Napoleon himself admitted that his primary goal in confronting Russia was to break apart the Holy Alliance: "That was the great objective of the war; to separate the two powers [Russia and Austria] and to regain for France . . . its liberty of action abroad."[152]

Even if unintended at the outset, Britain's role in sidelining the Concert and rekindling geopolitical rivalry was at least as important as that of France.

[150] Schroeder, *Austria, Great Britain, and the Crimean War*, p. 405.
[151] Richardson, *Crisis Diplomacy*, p. 80.
[152] Rich, *Why the Crimean War?* pp. 20–21.

Palmerston and his allies capitalized on the growing tension between Russia and the western powers to whip up anti-Russian sentiment among the public, isolate Aberdeen and other moderates, and win the cabinet's support for a more muscular brand of foreign policy. During the heyday of the Concert, Britain would have taken the lead in seeking to group Russia—as it did with France during the Eastern Crisis of 1839–1841. But during the early 1850s, Britain did just the opposite, steadily seeking to maneuver itself into a confrontation with Russia. As Schroeder writes, British leaders "frustrated every hopeful effort at a diplomatic solution. . . . [They] were willing to accept war over a quarrel they knew was inherently soluble."[153]

In Britain, as in France, a strategic discourse of accommodation gave way to one of confrontation, undermining the normative guideposts of the Concert era. Instead of referencing familial ties and brotherhood among Europe's great powers, Britain and France portrayed Russia as a despotic and expansionist state. Suspicion replaced the mutual trust that emerged after 1815; London was loath to accept a negotiated settlement in part "as a result of British mistrust of Russia; except for Aberdeen, no one any longer considered Nicholas an honest man."[154] In the eyes of British policy makers, Russia had lost not only its benign character, but also its benign intentions. Even though Russia continued to practice strategic restraint and was at several stages of the crisis prepared to accept a diplomatic solution, Palmerston portrayed Russia as bent on expansion and determined to consolidate its sphere of influence over the Ottoman Empire. He interpreted Russian ambitions not as specific to the brewing crisis but as reflective of its broader expansionist disposition: "The policy and practice of the Russian Government has always been to push forward its encroachments as fast and as far as the apathy or want of firmness of other Governments would allow it to go, but always to stop and retire when it was met with decided resistance, and then to wait for the next favourable opportunity to make another spring on its intended victim."[155]

In the context of these revised assessments of Russian intentions, Britain took it upon itself not just to deny the Tsar his immediate goal of wielding decisive influence over the Ottoman court, but also to deal Russia a material

---

[153] Schroeder, *Austria, Great Britain, and the Crimean War*, pp. xii, 393. See also pp. 408–409.

[154] Schroeder, *Austria, Great Britain, and the Crimean War*, p. 77. Lord Aberdeen was prime minister from 1852–1855.

[155] Richardson, *Crisis Diplomacy*, p. 97.

and psychological blow that would extinguish its expansionist ambitions. As Palmerston explained, "Until [Russia's] pride is really humbled, the contest must be carried on."[156] In stark contrast to British diplomacy during the Concert, London was now explicitly seeking to humiliate the Russian government. Moreover, this logic laid the foundation for Britain's embrace of its own expansionist aims. Once the war had started, Palmerston insisted that the goals go well beyond halting Russian expansion. "The best & most effectual security for the future peace of Europe," he wrote in May 1854, "would be the severance from Russia of some of the frontier territories acquired by her in later times, Georgia, Circassia, the Crimea, Bessarabia, Poland & Finland." As part of his "beau ideal" for the war, he also envisaged the end of Austrian rule in Lombardy and Venice and the advance of constitutional reform throughout Europe.[157] British war aims were more extensive than those of the French and Austrians, focused on not just expelling Russian troops from Ottoman territory, but occupying Sebastopol, diminishing Russia's naval strength, and forcing the Tsar to embrace liberal reforms. Palmerston agreed to a peace that fell short of these aims only under considerable pressure from his coalition partners.[158] Britain had in effect become a revisionist power, seeking to extend its geopolitical influence and export its liberal ideology.

As France and Britain backed away from the practices and policies of the Concert era, the initial reaction of Russia, Austria, and Prussia was to protect the status quo. Russia certainly stood its ground on matters pertaining to Orthodox Christians in Ottoman lands, and at times resorted to blustery ultimatums in dealing with Constantinople. It also took provocative actions that moved the great powers closer to a military confrontation, such as sending its troops to occupy the Danubian provinces in 1853. But on successive occasions, Russia was prepared to make concessions and accept a negotiated settlement, only to have Constantinople reject such settlements under direct pressure from France and Britain. As Richardson notes, "the most striking feature of the Russian situation . . . is the extent to which the Tsar was willing and able to make concessions."[159] Although Schroeder acknowledges the

---

[156] Snyder, *Myths of Empire*, p. 172.

[157] Rich, *Why the Crimean War?* pp. 108–109.

[158] On war aims and negotiations over ending the fighting, see Rich, *Why the Crimean War?* pp. 140–198.

[159] Richardson, *Crisis Diplomacy*, p. 101.

Tsar's hubris and unpredictability, he agrees that the diplomatic record makes clear that Nicholas "did not intend to wreck the European Concert or defy the other powers." "Whatever else Russia can be blamed for," Schroeder continues, "she did not cause Concert diplomacy to fail. The last thing she wanted was a confrontation with the West, especially Britain, and the moment she saw she might be caught in such a confrontation, she began backing down."[160]

Unlike Prussia, which succeeded in staying on the sidelines, Austria sought to play the role of diplomatic arbiter, invoking Concert norms to facilitate a peaceful solution. Vienna faced a difficult choice. On the one hand, Austria did not welcome growing Russian influence over its Ottoman neighbor. But on the other, it was threatened by the liberalizing fervor that had taken hold in France and Britain and fearful that alignment with the western powers would weaken Austria's hold on Hungary as well as its dominating position in Italy.[161] In the end, Britain and France succeeded in drawing Austria into their camp, in so doing deliberately dismantling the Holy Alliance by setting Vienna against the Russian government.[162] After Austria formally joined the Franco-British coalition in December 1854, the French chargé in Constantinople informed Paris that, "You have mortally wounded the Holy Alliance and given it a first-class funeral." According to a British historian, "The result was the disappearance of the last relics of the system of 1815. . . . No longer were there three powers in favour of the maintenance of the *status quo*; no longer was there any European Concert, even in embryo."[163]

In sum, the revolutions of 1848 set in motion political changes in France and Britain that prompted both of them to break out of the security community that had formed after 1815. Although France was more explicit in making clear its desire to escape the strictures of the Vienna settlement, it was Britain that repeatedly sabotaged all efforts to arrive at a peaceful settlement. As Schroeder concludes, "The only power that consistently violated

---

[160] Schroeder, *Austria, Great Britain, and the Crimean War*, pp. 29, 408. For further discussion of Russia's willingness to compromise, see Rich, *Why the Crimean War?* pp. 28, 50–57, 73–78.

[161] For example, Austria resented Britain's insistence that the Ottoman government neither intern nor extradite the Hungarian rebels that had fled to Ottoman territory. Such actions convinced many Austrians that Britain was intent on exporting liberal change to Austria and fomenting nationalist uprisings that would undermine its imperial reach. See Schroeder, *Austria, Great Britain, and the Crimean War*, pp. 9–11.

[162] Schroeder, *Austria, Great Britain, and the Crimean War*, p. 418.

[163] Rich, *Why the Crimean War?* p. 145. The quoted historian is Gavin Henderson.

Concert rules, rejected or frustrated Concert solutions, and insisted on turning the crisis into a head-to-head confrontation between great powers was Britain."[164] It was British leadership that brought the Concert into being— and British intransigence that played a primary role in its demise.

Why the Concert Failed

The sources of the Concert's demise challenge conventional thinking about the moderating effects of democratic governance and institutionalized restraint on the conduct of statecraft. The two countries that had made the furthest advances toward liberal democracy—Britain and France—were the powers that were primarily responsible for defecting from Concert norms and abandoning strategic restraint in favor of revisionist aims. The introduction of universal male suffrage in France did little to curtail the nationalist ambitions of Napoleon III. Indeed, his popularity stemmed in no small part from his imperial heritage and his avowed commitment to free France from the geopolitical constraints of the Concert.

In similar fashion, the empowerment of Britain's middle class and the rise of its working class, far from serving as sources of popular constraint, abetted Palmerston's resort to social imperialism as a means of securing the political status quo. His belief that domestic stability depended upon exporting liberal change and stoking anti-Russian sentiment played a decisive role in convincing the cabinet to abandon strategic restraint.[165] Meanwhile, Russia, Austria, and Prussia were keen on preserving the Concert and its cooperative practices despite—indeed, because of—the upheaval caused by the revolutions of 1848. From this perspective, the two members of the Concert that embraced institutionalized restraint at home—Britain and France—were those most ready to abandon strategic restraint in the conduct of foreign policy. The manner in which the Concert unraveled thus supports the proposition that states in the midst of transitions to democracy are more likely to embrace revisionist aims than either autocracies or mature democracies.[166] This insight adds further support to one of this book's main findings—that regime type alone is an inadequate predictor of a state's readiness and ability to practice strategic restraint in its statecraft.

[164] Schroeder, *Austria, Great Britain, and the Crimean War*, p. 409.
[165] Schroeder, *Austria, Great Britain, and the Crimean War*, pp. 413–420.
[166] See Mansfield and Snyder, *Electing to Fight: Why Emerging Democracies Go to War*.

The return of geopolitical rivalry after 1848 also illustrates the complicated role that societal engagement plays in sustaining security community. The Concert functioned effectively for over three decades in part because it was an elite club. Its leaders were able to conduct the affairs of state with little domestic interference. In addition, the exclusive, aristocratic nature of the grouping facilitated the forging of a shared identity. Although an advantage in these respects, the Concert's shallow societal roots did leave it particularly vulnerable to the upheaval of 1848. As power changed hands, a political order that lacked backing by the private sector or the public at large was denied its domestic foundations. Moreover, the increasing impact of domestic politics on foreign policy did more to undermine than to advance the cause of stable peace. The challenges of responding to the growing power of the middle class and adjusting to the rise of the working class played a central role in inducing elites to embrace the expansionist policies that undercut the rules-based European order. Not until the consolidation of liberal democracy a century later did European leaders successfully return to the task of rebuilding security community. These observations lend further credence to the proposition that both autocracies and mature democracies may be better suited to fashioning stable peace than states in the midst of democratic transitions.

Economic development in Britain and France also meant that the differences in social order separating the powers in Europe's west from those in the east were widening. Between 1815 and the middle of the century, social orders in France and Britain changed far more than they did in Prussia, Austria, and Russia. Britain had a thriving middle class, and industrialization was rapidly expanding its urban working class. The same social trends were taking place in France, although industrialization was occurring more slowly. Nonetheless, it had a far more advanced class structure and a more powerful middle class than any other state on the continent.[167]

The revolutions of 1848 brought these differences in social order to the fore, underscoring the incompatibilities existing between urbanizing and industrializing societies in Britain and France and the largely agrarian societies to their east. Confronted with domestic unrest, France substantially broadened political participation. Soon thereafter, Napoleon may have emasculated the parliament, but his nationalist rhetoric and pledges to overturn the Vienna settlement were an outgrowth of the rising importance of public

[167] Stearns, *1848: The Revolutionary Tide in Europe*, pp. 1–68.

opinion. In Britain as well, Palmerston's new foreign policy and the anti-Russian sentiment that accompanied it were by-products of a domestic strategy for arresting the political pressures arising from rapid social change. As Edward Mansfield and Jack Snyder note, the "old elites" and the "urban middle-class" were incompatible political allies. Accordingly, "Lord Palmerston's pseudo-liberal imperialism turned out to be the only successful formula for creating a durable ruling coalition during this transitional period of democratization."[168] In both Britain and France, the middle classes were being incorporated into power structures still dominated by the aristocracy. British and French leaders were therefore seeking to satisfy the liberalizing instincts of the bourgeoisie, creating a political alliance that would prevail against the more ambitious social and economic aspirations of the rising working class.[169]

The contagion of 1848 did trigger domestic unrest in Austria and Prussia, prompting a change in leadership in both countries and the beginnings of constitutional rule in Prussia. But the tectonic shifts in social order that were reshaping politics in Europe's west were yet to take place farther east. The rise of a commercial class in Germany's north was fueling calls for political reform in Prussia and its neighboring states. But the more agrarian south resisted the push for constitutional rule. Meanwhile, Russia still practiced institutionalized serfdom and its middle class had yet to develop. Had it been up to Austria, Prussia, and Russia, monarchic solidarity and the Concert system would have long outlasted the upheaval of 1848.

The widening political and social gap among Europe's great powers—and the different domestic pressures that were at play—made it increasingly difficult for the Concert's members to maintain the sense of cultural commonality and shared identity forged by its founders. Close personal relationships and the familiarity they bred were casualties of changes in personnel. As public opinion grew in importance in Britain and France, elites faced political incentives to abandon the rhetoric of "intimate union" and "family" in favor of more confrontational and oppositional discourse. In the west, autocracy became the despotic "other" against which the nation had to rally its

---

[168] Edward Mansfield and Jack Snyder, "Democratization and War," *Foreign Affairs* 74, no. 3 (May/June 1995): 89.

[169] Jonathan Sperber, *The European Revolutions, 1848–1851* (Cambridge: Cambridge University Press, 1984), pp. 246–247; see also Reinhart Koselleck, "How European Was the Revolution of 1848/49?" in Axel Körner, ed., *1848—A European Revolution? International Ideas and National Memories of 1848* (New York: St. Martin's Press, 2000), p. 211.

resources and discipline its politics. In Russia, Britain and France became rivals that posed a threat not just to the territorial status quo but to the founding principles of monarchism. "Christian brotherhood," which had been regularly referenced as a source of shared identity and solidarity after 1815, succumbed to religious divisions. Indeed, the initial dispute that culminated in the Crimean War was over the relative power of Catholics and Orthodox in Ottoman lands.

The history of the unraveling of the Concert of Europe thus demonstrates the malleability of perceptions of communal identity. In the context of political and social changes that confronted elites with a new domestic landscape, welcome diversity became intolerable difference and a narrative of competition and division replaced one of restraint and community. Notably, the main agents of change were the more liberal powers, Britain and France. In insisting on exporting liberal reform and supporting movements of national liberation, they overturned the status quo and defected from the Concert. Absent the Concert's moderating practices and institutions, minor differences over the status of holy sites in Jerusalem gradually escalated into major clashes over prestige and interest. The breakdown of security community and the onset of the Crimean War were the result.

THE EVOLUTION AND FALTERING OF THE GULF COOPERATION COUNCIL FROM 1981

Long subject to tribal rivalries and imperial conquest, the Arabian Peninsula had had little experience with regional integration at the time of Britain's announcement in 1968 that it would soon withdraw from the region.[170] Nonetheless, the Gulf Cooperation Council (GCC), which was launched in 1981, enjoyed notable success in advancing regional cooperation during its first decade. The GCC was able to capitalize on several factors working in its favor. Its founding members—Oman, Saudi Arabia, the United Arab Emirates (UAE), Qatar, Bahrain, and Kuwait—were predominantly Sunni and they shared a common language, religion, and tribal social order.[171] In a region

---

[170] Saudi Arabia represents a notable exception. The Kingdom of Saudi Arabia was formed in 1932 through the unification of the principal regions of Al-Hasa, Qatif, Nejd, and Hejaz.

[171] Ibadi Muslims make up over 50 percent of Oman's population, and most of the rest are Sunni. Bahrain is ruled by a Sunni royal family, but a majority of its population is Shiite.

divided by competing notions of the relationship between ethnicity, religion, and nationhood, GCC states also agreed on a particular conception of *ummah* (Islamic community) that departed from both the revolutionary Islam of Iran and the secular Arab nationalism of Iraq. The strategic setting also favored regional cooperation. The potential export of the Islamic revolution in Iran, coupled with extremist attacks in Kuwait, Bahrain, and Saudi Arabia, posed a domestic threat to the GCC's monarchical regimes. Meanwhile, the outbreak of the Iran-Iraq war in 1980 and the possibility of its southward spread posed an external threat to the territory of the peninsular states and to their economic lifeline—shipping in the Persian Gulf.

After its launch, the GCC made rapid and substantial progress toward the establishment of a security community. Its members either resolved or set aside a host of territorial disputes. They cooperated closely on border control, intelligence, and visa regimes in order to counter the domestic threats posed by Islamic insurgents. They took ambitious steps to respond to the external threat posed by the Iran-Iraq war, including establishing a joint military force and seeking to build an integrated air defense network. They also advanced an extensive agenda of economic and societal integration. Following the GCC's first joint military exercise in 1983, Sultan Qabus of Oman summarized the progress as follows: "Now that the six Gulf countries have organized themselves in the Gulf Cooperation Council, the chances of a stable Gulf are better than at any time before. We are thinking together; we are talking together; we are planning together; and we are seeing things together instead of individually."[172]

Despite the auspicious start, the GCC was unable to sustain the progress that it made toward stable peace during the 1980s.[173] Indeed, the organization began to falter in 1990, a trend that only deepened over time, prompting Michael Barnett and Gregory Gause to label the organization a "stalled" security community.[174] This backsliding is especially puzzling in light of the ele-

---

[172] Interview on November 7, 1983, in R. K. Ramazani, *The Gulf Cooperation Council: Record and Analysis* (Charlottesville: University of Virginia Press, 1988), p. 155.

[173] In keeping with the definition in chapter 1 that a successful case entails at least ten years of stable peace, I code the GCC as a failure due to the fact that its reversal began in 1990 with the invasion of Kuwait. Although armed conflict did not return among GCC members, multilateral defense cooperation began to stall and territorial disputes reemerged. Moreover, this reversal was not merely episodic. Since 1990, security cooperation among GCC members has been eroding, not advancing.

[174] Michael Barnett and F. Gregory Gause III, "Caravans in Opposite Directions: Society,

vated external threat that GCC members faced as a consequence of Iraq's invasion of Kuwait in 1990. The Iraqi invasion constituted a direct attack on the territory of a member state. In principle, the GCC should have consolidated the gains of the 1980s, banding together more tightly in response to the demands of collective defense. Instead, the advances of the 1980s were reversed during the early 1990s, with the GCC experiencing the re-nationalization of security policy and the return of territorial disputes among member states. The Iraqi threat should have helped consolidate security community, but it had the opposite effect.

Explaining why the GCC faltered is the central puzzle of this case study. Ultimately, the GCC's backsliding was the result of dependence on U.S. power; member states invested in bilateral defense ties to the United States at the expense of their defense ties to each other. In contrast to ASEAN, which was able to fence off diverging opinions about reliance on outside powers due to a low level of external threat, the GCC was unable to avoid deep divisions over the U.S. role in the region due to the urgent threat posed to Gulf stability by both Iran and Iraq. Fear that regional security cooperation would expose smaller GCC states to the unchecked power of Saudi Arabia and the reluctance of member states to countenance the infringements on sovereignty needed to aggregate their defense capabilities also served as obstacles to stable peace. The Concert of Europe failed from the inside out; political and social changes within member states induced them to defect from the security community. The GCC failed from the outside in; external threats induced member states to look to the United States for protection, inducing them to back away from the cooperative practices of security community.

How Peace Broke Out

After decades of imperial rule and armed rivalry in the Persian Gulf littoral, proposals for establishing a regional security regime began to circulate in the mid-1970s, pushed primarily by Sultan Qabus of Oman. The main impetus came from concern that the Gulf was losing its external guardians. Not only had the British withdrawn from positions east of Suez, but the United States, in the aftermath of its retreat from Vietnam, had unfurled the Nixon Doc-

---

State, and the Development of Community in the Gulf Cooperation Council," in Adler and Barnett, *Security Communities,* p. 162.

trine, stipulating that Washington would look to local states to provide security in the Persian Gulf. Fears heightened that the return of age-old regional rivalries would accompany the end of great-power oversight; even during the colonial era, tribal competition not infrequently led to bloodshed. Oman's initial efforts to prepare for regional self-sufficiency by promoting security cooperation did not yield tangible results. Nonetheless, the Emir of Kuwait embraced the cause in 1978 and became its most active proponent. The regionwide consultations that he initiated laid the foundation for the launch of the GCC in 1981.[175]

Two major developments made defense cooperation among the states of the Arabian Peninsula a strategic necessity. First, the overthrow of the Shah of Iran in 1979 heightened worries among Gulf monarchs that domestic unrest and militant Islamist movements could topple their own regimes. Coupled with sporadic Shiite uprisings and extremist attacks throughout the region, the Iranian revolution provided the Gulf states a compelling reason to advance regional cooperation. Second, the outbreak of the Iran-Iraq war and its potential spillover posed a direct threat to the territory and shipping lanes of the Gulf sheikdoms (see map 5.2). Equally important, it enabled the peninsular states to pursue regional initiatives without having to fear Iraqi domination of the effort. In light of its military superiority and its secular and anti-monarchical orientation, Iraq's inclusion in a regional body would have threatened its weaker neighbors. Iraq therefore had to be removed from the equation if the Gulf's Arab states were to be comfortable with the prospect of regional integration. Iraq's war with Iran provided a rationale and justification for excluding Iraq from the GCC.[176]

A final key ingredient was Saudi Arabia's willingness to exercise strategic restraint. In terms of its territory, population, and economy, Saudi Arabia was larger than the other GCC states combined.[177] Concern about domina-

---

[175] On early proposals for regional cooperation in the Gulf, see John Christie, "History and Development of the Gulf Cooperation Council: A Brief Overview," in John A. Sandwick, ed., *The Gulf Cooperation Council: Moderation and Stability in an Interdependent World* (Boulder, CO: Westview Press, 1987), pp. 7–20; Emile Nakleh, *The Gulf Cooperation Council: Policies, Problems, Prospects* (New York: Praeger, 1986), p. 2; and Ramazani, *The Gulf Cooperation Council*, pp. 1–10.

[176] See Barnett and Gause, "Caravans in Opposite Directions," pp. 165–166; and Ramazani, *The Gulf Cooperation Council*, pp. 6–7.

[177] Saudi Arabia covers some 830,000 square miles, while Oman, the second largest GCC member, covers 120,000 square miles. The other members are much smaller. In the early 1980s Saudi Arabia had a population of roughly 11 million, while all other members had a population

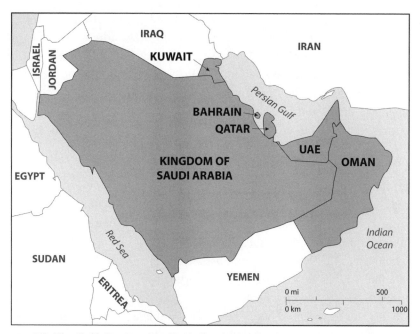

MAP 5.2 The Gulf Cooperation Council
Source: http://www.kingfahdbinabdulaziz.com/jpghi/f140.htm.

tion by Baghdad had been alleviated by Iraq's war with Iran, but fear of subjugation to Saudi power remained an obstacle to regional integration. The Saudi government deliberately sought to alleviate such concerns. It backed away from a host of territorial disputes with its neighbors, including its long-standing confrontation with Abu Dhabi and Oman over the Buraimi Oasis. It provided economic assistance to Oman and Bahrain. And the Saudis agreed to equality of decision-making power within the evolving regional body. As Erik Peterson notes, "From the standpoint of organizational influence, the dominant regional position of Saudi Arabia was not translated into an equally dominant position within the consensus-based GCC framework."[178]

The charter of the GCC was signed by its six founding members on May 25, 1981. The charter stressed "their mutual bonds of special relations, com-

---

under 2 million, with Qatar's the smallest, at 290,000. Erik R. Peterson, *The Gulf Cooperation Council: Search for Unity in a Dynamic Region* (Boulder, CO: Westview Press, 1988), p. 15.

[178] Peterson, *The Gulf Cooperation Council*, p. 95.

mon characteristics and similar systems founded on the Creed of Islam."[179] The GCC's founding charter made no mention of security affairs, focusing instead on less controversial political, social, and economic issues. But behind the scenes, matters of national security figured prominently. As John Christie observes, "If the press releases were about economic cooperation, the urgent discussions within the GCC were about defense and internal security."[180] In addition, a commission was established to settle disputes among members through negotiation and mediation.[181]

Concrete cooperation on security followed soon after the GCC's launch. During its first two years, GCC members focused primarily on matters of internal security. The Iran-Iraq war showed few signs of spilling over, but the Islamic revolution in Iran made member states particularly worried about extremist threats to regime stability—as did a series of attacks throughout the peninsula. In 1979, fundamentalists seized the Grand Mosque in Mecca and Saudi Arabia grew increasingly concerned about the potential mobilization of its Shiite minority. Shiite uprisings occurred in Bahrain in 1979 and 1980. Kuwait experienced domestic unrest. And late in 1981, a plot to assassinate the Sunni leadership of Bahrain was uncovered. In this strategic environment, member states looked to the GCC to serve as a "counterrevolutionary alliance." "What they feared most," according to R. K. Ramazani, "was the tremors of the Islamic revolution among their own people and within their own societies, particularly because of the presumed susceptibility of their own Shia inhabitants to an Islamic revolutionary movement."[182]

These concerns prompted GCC members to focus strategic cooperation on patrolling borders, integrating their visa and extradition regimes, coordinating counterinsurgency operations, and exchanging intelligence information. The first joint meeting of GCC chiefs of staff took place in September 1981.[183] As in the case of ASEAN, formalized security pacts were concluded on a bilateral basis, with Saudi Arabia negotiating agreements with all GCC members except Kuwait. Kuwait's reluctance to follow suit appears to have stemmed from its concerns about Saudi dominance and interference in its

[179] Ramazani, *The Gulf Cooperation Council*, p. 15.

[180] Christie, "History and Development of the Gulf Cooperation Council," p. 11.

[181] Barnett and Gause, "Caravans in Opposite Directions," p. 169.

[182] Ramazani, *The Gulf Cooperation Council*, pp. 8, 192.

[183] John Duke Anthony, "The Gulf Cooperation Council," in Robert Darius, John Amos II, and Ralph Magnus, eds., *Gulf Security into the 1980s: Perceptual and Strategic Dimensions* (Stanford, CA: Hoover Institution Press, 1984), p. 83.

omestic affairs, a harbinger of the dynamic that was to compromise the GCC's evolution during the 1990s.[184]

The GCC also served as a valuable forum for regularizing self-binding and co-binding. Reciprocal restraint led to the resolution of remaining territorial disputes. Under the GCC's auspices, Bahrain and Qatar tackled two such disputes, one involving Subarah, a piece of land on the north coast of Qatar, and the other concerning Hawar Island, which was ruled by Bahrain but located close to Qatar. The latter quarrel was not settled, but the two parties agreed to set it aside so that it would not impair regional cooperation.[185] As occurred often among Concert and ASEAN members, GCC members fenced off the dispute. The GCC also helped mediate a conflict between Oman and South Yemen and, in the mid-1980s, a third territorial conflict between Bahrain and Qatar. Norms of reciprocal restraint and the informal practice of grouping were maturing and yielding tangible results. As the GCC evolved, it was succeeding in not only addressing the domestic threats posed by extremist uprisings, but also advancing the cause of stable peace among its members.

Over the course of 1982, the strategic focus of the GCC began to shift from domestic security and multilateral rapprochement to collective defense. The impetus behind this strategic reorientation was a series of successful Iranian offensives against Iraq, raising concerns that Iran might soon pose a direct threat to the territory of member states. This fear intensified in 1984 in step with Iranian air attacks on foreign shipping in the Persian Gulf. The GCC did not codify formal commitments to collective defense, but ministers began to affirm publicly that the GCC would "view any aggression against any GCC member as an aggression against all GCC members" and that "the region's security and stability is a collective responsibility that falls on all GCC countries."[186]

The foiled assassination plot in Bahrain and the succession of terrorist attacks that later took place in Kuwait ensured that the GCC continued to focus on internal security; counterinsurgency remained a priority. But during the second half of 1983, the GCC also began to make concrete plans for territorial defense. In October, all six members participated in a joint military

[184] Ramazani, *The Gulf Cooperation Council*, pp. 35–38.
[185] Ramazani, *The Gulf Cooperation Council*, p. 126.
[186] GCC Ministerial Council, February 7, 1982, in Ramazani, *The Gulf Cooperation Council*, p. 45.

exercise in the UAE called Peninsula Shield I. The exercise lasted three weeks and involved some 6,500 troops. At a summit in November, GCC leaders laid the groundwork for a standing rapid deployment force. The following October, a second major exercise took place, Peninsula Shield II. At a summit in November 1984, the GCC took a formal decision to establish the standing military unit, which would be called the Peninsula Shield force. It was assembled in 1985, commanded by a Saudi officer, and located at Hafr al-Batin, a Saudi base near the Kuwait border.[187]

Concurrently, in response to Iranian and Iraqi attacks on shipping, efforts proceeded apace to erect an integrated air defense network. The stark advantages of the Saudi air force—the Reagan administration had transferred F-15's and AWACs aircraft to the kingdom—made the other GCC states heavily reliant on Saudi capabilities. As Ramazani observes, "it was the strength of Saudi Arabia that was pivotal to the whole idea of creating an integrated regional defense system."[188] Work on the air defense network proceeded slowly, but in 1984 Saudi Arabia did succeed in shooting down an Iranian fighter that was over Saudi territorial waters.

By the second half of the 1980s, the GCC had thus achieved remarkable progress in advancing security cooperation; its members had succeeded in replacing mutual suspicion with mutual confidence, coordinated efforts to defeat domestic threats to stability, and begun integrating their ground and air forces in order to provide collective defense. At a summit in 1985, GCC members affirmed that an attack on one country would be "a threat to all the GCC countries because the security of the GCC countries is indivisible."[189]

GCC officials and observers alike noted the impressive pace and scope of progress, with results running substantially ahead of expectations. According to Barnett and Gause, "the Gulf states were progressing toward military inte-

---

[187] The initial proposal was that the force would consist of two brigades. The force that materialized eventually consisted of roughly 4,000 personnel from all six members. Plans to increase its size, form a "semi-unified" command to oversee the separate national armies, rationalize procurement policy, and establish an integrated training academy did not come to fruition. There was also a lack of clarity as to whether Peninsula Shield would focus on territorial defense or counterinsurgency, stemming from ambiguity about whether the GCC was meant to address domestic security, collective defense, or both. See Barnett and Gause, "Caravans in Opposite Directions," p. 174; Ramazani, *The Gulf Cooperation Council*, pp. 61–67; and Serge Herzog, "Arms, Oil and Security in the Gulf: A Tenuous Balance," in Abbas Abdelkarim, ed., *Change and Development in the Gulf* (New York: St. Martin's Press, 1999), pp. 240–241.

[188] Ramazani, *The Gulf Cooperation Council*, p. 66.

[189] Ramazani, *The Gulf Cooperation Council*, p. 65.

gration that far outpaced anything they had initially envisioned. . . . The general impression is that the GCC states were taken by surprise by what they had accomplished."[190] At the close of the GCC's fifth summit in 1984, King Fahd of Saudi Arabia made clear his satisfaction with the group's achievements: "The fifth session of the Supreme Council was one of the important stages of cooperation and coordination consolidating the GCC march toward wider horizons of integration and cohesion. . . . The methodical nature of the march . . . during the short period of our existence . . . has led to achievements which are a source of pride. We have made a great step in the various spheres of cooperation, something which makes us feel confident about the march of this council."[191]

THE GCC AND U.S. POWER: MANAGING CONTROVERSY

During its first five years, the GCC succeeded in becoming a nascent security community, helped along by both internal and external threats. However, the effort to add to its initial focus on domestic threats the new burdens of collective defense did expose a key vulnerability—the absence of consensus among members about the GCC's relationship to outside powers, the United States in particular. ASEAN had the same quandary over how to deal with its members' different views on the appropriate role of the great powers in Southeast Asia. But in the absence of a pressing external threat that required outside help, ASEAN was able to sidestep the issue. The Iran-Iraq war meant that the GCC did not have that luxury.

From the GCC's outset, its members held quite different views on whether to rely on U.S. power to safeguard their territorial security as well as shipping lanes in the Gulf. The issue not only touched sensitive chords related to the region's recent colonial past, but also risked provoking Islamist threats to domestic stability, especially in light of U.S. policy toward the Arab-Israeli conflict. Judging by its public pronouncements, the GCC's goals were quite similar to those of ASEAN: to promote stable peace throughout the region, thereby forestalling the intervention of outside powers. As noted in a GCC working paper drafted in 1981, "International designs will not be able to find a foothold in a merged region which has one voice, opinion and strength. However, they will be able to find a thousand footholds if this region . . . re-

---

[190] Barnett and Gause, "Caravans in Opposite Directions," p. 175.
[191] Transcript from November 29, 1984, in Ramazani, *The Gulf Cooperation Council*, p. 164.

mains made up of small entities that can be victimized."[192] Following a summit in 1983, the Emir of Qatar described the GCC's guiding philosophy as follows: "the GCC member countries are agreed that the best way to achieve our goals is to rely primarily on ourselves and to lay down sound foundations for building our own strength, because, more than any other strength, it safeguards our ability to avert all interference in our affairs and to keep our area free of superpower conflict."[193] Others, including the secretary general of the GCC, stated this position more forcefully. According to an official summary of a news conference with Abdullah Bishara in 1981, "The secretary general strongly reiterated that the member-states object to foreign intervention, the establishment of bases and the presence of fleets and foreign influence, adding that the purpose of this [council] is to keep the region free of and removed from any foreign intervention."[194] This sentiment was widely shared among publics; a survey in Kuwait revealed that almost three-fourths of respondents saw the GCC as a means of protecting the region from the designs of the great powers.[195]

This apparent consensus on keeping the Gulf free from great-power interference masked the diversity of opinion that existed on the question of the GCC's links to the United States. Oman, which had long maintained close ties to the British Navy, was developing an extensive relationship with the U.S. Navy, offering it access to its facilities to help provide security in and around the Strait of Hormuz. As the GCC was taking shape, Oman circulated a working paper arguing that the GCC did not have sufficient capabilities to provide for its own security, and therefore had to pursue close cooperation with the United States. The paper proved quite controversial and was readily shelved.[196]

At the other end of the spectrum was Kuwait, which took a strong stand against reliance on U.S. military power and in favor of strategic independence for the GCC. Kuwait also maintained good diplomatic relations with the Soviet Union, in part to counterbalance U.S. influence. Saudi Arabia took a position in between that of Oman and Kuwait. For reasons of strategic necessity, the Saudis maintained that the GCC had to buy U.S. arms and,

[192] "GCC Working Paper," May 26, 1981, in Ramazani, *The Gulf Cooperation Council*, p. 29.
[193] Transcript from November 7, 1983, in Ramazani, *The Gulf Cooperation Council*, p. 157.
[194] Summary from press conference on May 27, 1981, in Ramazani, *The Gulf Cooperation Council*, p. 31.
[195] Nakleh, *The Gulf Cooperation Council*, p. 89.
[196] Christie, "History and Development of the Gulf Cooperation Council," p. 11.

even if not overtly, look to the United States to help deter and, if necessary, defend against external threats. But strategic cooperation with the United States had to be quiet and unobtrusive. The GCC should rely more on U.S. technology than on America's own military. The purchase of AWACs and F-15s, the mainstay of the GCC's air defense system, was a case in point. Although these systems required the stationing of U.S. support personnel in the kingdom, the Saudis were ostensibly acquiring the capability to defend themselves.

Saudi Arabia's position ultimately prevailed, helped along by the kingdom's material preponderance as well as the spillover from the Iran-Iraq war. Attacks on neutral shipping in the Gulf undercut opposition to strategic cooperation with the United States. GCC states did initially turn down America's offer of air cover in return for basing rights. But soon after air attacks on neutral shipping began, U.S. warships started to escort tankers in the Gulf that were supplying U.S. ships, eventually leading to the re-flagging and escort of Kuwaiti tankers that began in 1987. Although America's strategic presence in the Gulf grew, much of it remained offshore and out of sight. In 1984, for example, the United States had 11,500 sailors and soldiers in the region, but more than 10,000 of them were based at sea. The Saudis also hosted several thousand American civilians on Pentagon contracts, many of whom were providing technological support for weapons systems purchased from the United States.[197] In addition, Saudi Arabia overbuilt its facilities and pre-positioned stocks of weapons and materiel in case more demanding missions necessitated a U.S. base of operations in the region.[198]

Despite the relatively unobtrusive nature of America's military presence, the GCC's growing reliance on U.S. power nonetheless triggered opposition. As Secretary General Bishara noted in 1986, "although the United States may have understood the GCC trend, may have gotten acquainted with it, and supported it, it failed to realize the strength of the GCC's links with Arab problems. . . . The United States failed to realize the degree of seriousness about self-reliance and rejecting fleets in Gulf waters."[199] Divisions within the GCC over the U.S. role in the Gulf never came to a head, however,

---

[197] J. E. Peterson, "The GCC and Regional Security," in Sandwick, *The Gulf Cooperation Council*, pp. 201–202.

[198] See Charles A. Kupchan, *The Persian Gulf and the West: The Dilemmas of Security* (London: Allen & Unwin, 1987), chap. 6.

[199] Transcript from January 24, 1986 in Ramazani, *The Gulf Cooperation Council*, p. 183.

as threats to shipping moderated and the military balance in the Iran-Iraq war swung to Iraq's advantage. Military stalemate gave way to successful Iraqi counteroffensives, followed by a UN-brokered cease-fire in August 1988. The issue of strategic ties to the United States receded in step with the diminishing threat, enabling the GCC to set aside the divisive question of its dependence on American power and to consolidate the substantial gains it had made since 1981.

DECISION MAKING AND SOCIETAL INTEGRATION

In terms of its decision-making procedures and agenda for societal integration, the GCC followed the European model more closely than it did that of Southeast Asia. ASEAN avoided summits and a formal secretariat throughout its early years. In contrast, the GCC from its outset planned a full schedule of summits, ministerial gatherings, and other lower-level meetings. During a sample three-month period in 1985, for example, the GCC held nineteen meetings.[200] The organization established a secretariat in Riyadh, and appointed Bishara, an experienced and high-profile Kuwaiti diplomat, as its first secretary general. In the top decision-making body, the Supreme Council, substantive decisions were taken by unanimity while procedural matters were decided by majority. Chairmanship of the GCC rotated on an annual basis. Unanimity and the rotating chairmanship were adopted as power-checking mechanisms; "the structure of the GCC deemphasized as much as possible any disproportionality [sic] of power among its member states."[201]

The GCC's founding documents, as well as its founding leaders, left unspecified the ultimate aims of the undertaking. Although the architects of the GCC explicitly used the European experience as a model, member states did not harbor aspirations of federation and were not self-consciously embarking on a project that envisaged the political unification of the peninsula. At the first summit in 1981, Bishara stated that the organization "is neither a confederal nor a federal one, but a cooperation council."[202] By the following year, however, the secretary general had begun to embrace a different perspective, presumably as a result of the GCC's successes and gathering momentum. Early in 1982, he stated that the GCC is "not [like] the United Na-

---

[200] Nakleh, *The Gulf Cooperation Council*, p. 3.

[201] Peterson, *The Gulf Cooperation Council*, p. 95.

[202] Ramazani writes that Bishara "reportedly" made this statement at the first summit in May 1981. See Ramazani, *The Gulf Cooperation Council*, p. 195.

tions, which is an organization of sovereign states, [or] the Arab League, which is an association of states. We are ahead of that. We are a confederate structure with dynamics toward unity." By the organization's second anniversary in May 1983, he was even more explicit: "Despite the fact that the GCC Charter does not contain a clear-cut political theory, there is consensus on some form of confederacy between its six member states. . . . There is common agreement that, acting under the umbrella of the Council, they will be able to pool their political, economic and other efforts in a confederal manner."[203]

Bishara's vision, however, seems to have prevailed primarily in the secretariat and not in the governments of member states. Public discussion about the ultimate political character of the GCC was scarce, indicating the decided preference of national leaders to focus on concrete cooperation, not on institutional mechanisms that entailed a formal compromise of sovereignty—the prospect of which elicited little enthusiasm in Kuwait and the smaller members of the GCC. In the early 1970s, Britain had pressed Qatar and Bahrain to join the federation of sheikdoms that became the UAE, but both preferred to guard their autonomy. Kuwait's continuing refusal to sign a security pact with Saudi Arabia made clear that it had little appetite for participation in schemes that would formally limit its sovereignty.

The GCC drew on the European model on matters of economic integration as well as political design.[204] Efforts to promote an integrated trade bloc stumbled, however, as some of the main initiatives aimed at liberalizing markets were not implemented; concerns over sovereignty again played a role. Furthermore, the economies of the GCC members were quite similar, with oil exports representing a significant share of national product. As a result, intraregional trade as a share of total trade remained in the single digits even as some progress was made toward reducing tariff and nontariff barriers.[205]

Despite the low levels of intraregional trade, the GCC did have an appreciable impact on societal integration. GCC citizens were allowed to work and open businesses in any GCC country, leading to an increase in labor mobility. Funding for intraregional joint ventures encouraged new business contacts,

[203] Peterson, *The Gulf Cooperation Council*, pp. 104, 102.

[204] Anthony Cordesman, *The Gulf and the Search for Strategic Stability* (Boulder, CO: Westview Press, 1984), pp. 625–629.

[205] Peterson, *The Gulf Cooperation Council*, pp. 114, 145–164. See also Abdullah Ibrahim El-Kuwaiz, "Economic Integration of the Cooperation Council of the Arab States of the Gulf: Challenges, Achievements and Future Outlook," in Sandwick, *The Gulf Cooperation Council*.

and a Gulf Chamber of Commerce was established in 1981. Visa requirements for travel within the GCC were dropped. And the GCC invested in
transportation infrastructure, facilitating intraregional travel.[206]

Elite discourse about Gulf solidarity supplemented increasing societal contact to contribute to the generation of a communal Gulf identity. GCC com-
muniqués and leaders frequently drew on a narrative of community, noting
the GCC's "common destiny and unity of objectives," as well as the "natural
solidarity" and "fraternal spirit" of member states.[207] And in contrast to
ASEAN, the evolution of a regional spirit was not just an elite phenomenon.
Political leaders sought—and received—a great deal of media attention. As
one observer noted in 1986, "it would not be an exaggeration to say that the
GCC has been the premier media event of the past five years."[208] A public
opinion poll in Kuwait revealed that 78 percent of respondents followed
GCC news regularly. A similar percentage also believed that the GCC was
founded upon political commonalities among its member states.[209] As Barnett and Gause observe, the citizens of the GCC "see themselves as having
common interests and a common identity as 'khalijiin' (literally, 'residents of
the Gulf'). . . . It is undeniable that 'Gulf' discourse is much more common
now than before and that increasing numbers of citizens identify their material interests and political identity as (at least partially) tied up with the
GCC."[210]

The GCC thus enjoyed remarkable success during its first decade, advancing the cause of regional peace and integration more substantially than either
participants or observers had expected. Soon after its founding, its members
coordinated efforts to combat extremist threats to regime stability and
launched an ambitious program of economic integration. By 1983, the GCC
turned its attention to the Iran-Iraq war, organizing a unified diplomatic
stance and, with the help of the United States, countering threats to commercial shipping in the Gulf. All the while, its members set aside long-standing
territorial disputes, instead integrating their defense policies, launching a
GCC rapid deployment force and the beginnings of a regionwide air defense
network. Its institutionalization of strategic restraint and its success in ad-

---

[206] Barnett and Gause, "Caravans in Opposite Directions," p. 178.
[207] Ramazani, *The Gulf Cooperation Council*, pp. 13, 28, 29.
[208] Nakleh, *The Gulf Cooperation Council*, p. 82.
[209] Nakleh, *The Gulf Cooperation Council*, pp. 88–89.
[210] Barnett and Gause, "Caravans in Opposite Directions," pp. 162–163.

dressing both internal and external threats to security consolidated a sense of solidarity and trust among its members.[211] As the deputy prime minister of Kuwait put it, "What exists among the GCC countries is greater than an alliance. Alliances are between dissimilar countries, but we are states that trust each other."[212] In short, the GCC over the course of the 1980s evolved into a nascent security community.

Iraq's Invasion of Kuwait and the Faltering of the GCC

The advance of the GCC toward stable peace during the 1980s stands in stark contrast to the setbacks it suffered during the 1990s. In theory, the Iraqi invasion of Kuwait in 1990 should have strengthened regional solidarity; a direct attack on the territory of a member state should have compelled GCC members to broaden and deepen strategic cooperation. Indeed, it did—at least at the outset of the conflict. The GCC acted on its tacit commitment to collective defense, readily joining the military coalition put together by the United States to coerce Iraqi forces to quit Kuwait. The organization's joint force, Peninsula Shield, participated in the war, as did the individual national forces of member states. In addition, the region's integrated air defense system was upgraded. As Barnett and Gause note, "The speed and unanimity with which the Gulf states came together to support Kuwait and accept the American and other international forces that would expel Iraq from Kuwait were remarkable. . . . The GCC navigated the Gulf crisis with an impressive showing of solidarity and commitment."[213]

Nonetheless, Iraq's invasion of Kuwait soon did more to impede than to advance the deepening of security community among GCC members. Rather than coordinating their security policies, most member states went their separate directions. Oman argued that Peninsula Shield should be expanded to 100,000 troops, but the proposal was stillborn. Instead of working to consolidate intraregional multilateralism, each member state invested in bilateral ties with extra-regional powers—primarily the United States.[214] All but Saudi Arabia concluded formal security pacts with Britain, France, or the United

---

[211] Barnett and Gause, "Caravans in Opposite Directions," p. 177.

[212] Ramazani, *The Gulf Cooperation Council*, p. 162.

[213] Barnett and Gause, "Caravans in Opposite Directions," p. 180.

[214] See Abbas Abdelkarim, "Change and Development in the Gulf: An Overview of Major Issues," and Herzog, "Arms, Oil and Security in the Gulf," in Abdelkarim, *Change and Development in the Gulf*.

States. Meanwhile, the Saudis quietly tightened defense cooperation with Washington, substantially upgrading the kingdom's arsenal of high-tech weaponry. Defense spending among GCC states rapidly increased—by over 50 percent between 1992 and 1993—but each member purchased its capabilities separately, diversifying suppliers and technology rather than coordinating their efforts. According to Barnett and Gause, the Gulf War triggered "not the promotion of regionalism but rather the retreat to statism."[215]

The re-nationalization of the security policies of GCC members manifested itself in the return of territorial disputes. In 1992, Qatar and Saudi Arabia quarreled over their border. Egypt, not the GCC, took the lead in mediating the disagreement. Territorial disputes also emerged between Qatar and Bahrain, and Oman objected to a demarcation agreement between Saudi Arabia and the UAE, claiming that it encroached on Omani territory. More recently, the UAE and Saudi Arabia again engaged in disputes over their boundary, with the Emirates claiming rights to an oilfield under Saudi control.[216] Moreover, these disputes over territory were more than friendly spats. The 1992 clash between Qatar and Saudi Arabia produced three fatalities. Barnett and Gause maintain that "the residents of the region could easily imagine border disputes igniting into border wars." The nascent security community of the 1980s "stalled," they argue, and growing solidarity gave way to "mistrust and suspicion."[217] Serge Herzog agrees that "lingering territorial disputes" have played an important role in "preventing the organization from taking decisive steps toward a unified posture" on security policy.[218] According to an Oxford Analytica report from 2003, "Intra-GCC clashes involving threatened or actual use of force cannot be ruled out."[219]

The pattern established during the first half of the 1990s set the stage for the rest of the decade; GCC members continued to invest in their bilateral ties to the United States at the expense of multilateral ties to each other. Bahrain, which had long hosted a small U.S. flotilla in the Gulf, expanded the facility into a major U.S. naval base. By 1993, the base was home to over 18,000 U.S. sailors. During the 1980s, the UAE had been a staunch opponent

[215] Barnett and Gause, "Caravans in Opposite Directions," p. 181

[216] Oxford Analytica Daily Brief, Monday, January 8, 2001, "Gulf States: Boundary Disputes Strain Regional Ties," and Oxford Analytica Daily Brief, Friday, April 7, 2006, "Gulf States: Iran Threat Exposes GCC Defence Rifts," p. 1.

[217] Barnett and Gause, "Caravans in Opposite Directions," pp. 183–184, 162–163.

[218] Herzog, "Arms, Oil and Security in the Gulf," pp. 240–241.

[219] Oxford Analytica Daily Brief, Monday, November 17, 2003, "Gulf States: Military Balance Shifts to Small States."

of a major U.S. presence in the Gulf. After the Gulf War, it served as the largest liberty port in the world for U.S. sailors. Having regained its sovereignty thanks to the U.S.-led coalition, Kuwait no longer opposed America's presence in the region and hosted U.S. assets needed to monitor and contain an Iraqi government that, albeit defeated in Kuwait, maintained its belligerent posture.

To be sure, not all parties welcomed the decided shift from intraregional cooperation to bilateral relationships with the United States. At the GCC Summit in 2001, Crown Prince Abdullah, then heir apparent to the Saudi throne, was quite frank in lamenting the state of affairs: "The GCC has not yet accomplished its projected aspirations. . . . We have not yet created a military force capable of confronting enemies and supporting friends; we have not yet achieved a unified common market; we have not yet been able to forge a unified political position with which to face political crises."[220]

Saudi concerns were not, however, sufficient to reverse the re-nationalization triggered by the Gulf War. Indeed, the strategic trends that emerged during the 1990s only strengthened after the events of September 11, 2001 and the consequent U.S. invasion of Iraq in 2003. GCC states opposed the invasion, but they nonetheless intensified strategic cooperation with the United States. Qatar hosted a major U.S. air base at al Udeid, which became the main U.S. headquarters for air operations in the Gulf following Washington's decision to remove most of its military personnel from Saudi Arabia. The U.S. withdrawal from the kingdom was prompted by security threats as well as growing political tension over the U.S. presence. Naval operations at the base in Bahrain, the headquarters for the U.S. Fifth Fleet, expanded considerably, as did U.S. operations at the UAE's al Dhafra airfield and its Jebel Ali and Fujaira ports. Kuwait became a major staging area for operations in Iraq, hosting thousands of U.S. military and civilian personnel.

Once again, strategic ties to the United States came at the expense of, rather than complemented, intraregional cooperation. In 2005, Oman and Qatar announced that they were withdrawing their forces from Peninsula Shield. Saudi Arabia revealed that those troops still assigned to the collective force would no longer be posted to Hafr al-Batin, but would be billeted in their own countries.[221] According to the International Institute for Strategic Stud-

---

[220] Address to GCC Summit, December 30, 2001, in *Middle East Policy* 9, no. 1 (March 2002).

[221] Oxford Analytica Daily Brief, Friday, April 7, 2006, "Gulf States: Iran Threat Exposes GCC Defence Rifts," p. 1.

ies, "Kuwait, Qatar, UAE, Bahrain and Oman all maintain bilateral ties to the United States and privilege that relationship in contrast to their own multilateral GCC obligations. . . . Each country proceeded to seek the security of an external security guarantor in the form of the United States, rather than in the enhancement of the collective capabilities of the GCC itself."[222] Oxford Analytica pronounced that "the GCC is collapsing as a collective defense mechanism."[223] In reflecting on the GCC's loss of momentum, Prince Saud al-Faisal commented that "separate arrangements are not compatible with the spirit and character of the Gulf Cooperation Council . . . [and] weaken not only the solidarity of the GCC . . . but also each of its members."[224]

Paradoxically, the backsliding of the GCC on matters of defense and security coincided with substantial advances on the economic and social fronts. In effect, regional cooperation on security has been inversely related to societal integration. Sharp increases in energy prices helped the GCC states diversify their economies, advancing the region's economic integration. Intraregional trade and investment picked up and business groups became more outspoken in pressuring governments to pursue structural reforms. A customs union was implemented on January 1, 2003, a common market achieved at the beginning of 2008, and GCC members have agreed in principle to adopt a single currency.[225] Intra-regional political contacts also increased. In 1994, members of the consultative councils and parliaments of GCC states met for the first time. In addition, awareness of a Gulf identity has intensified, especially among intellectuals, but also among ordinary citizens.[226] In short, economic interdependence and societal contact have advanced despite the trend of re-nationalization on matters of security.[227] This deepening of societal integration makes the GCC's concurrent unraveling as a security community all the more puzzling.

---

[222] International Institute for Strategic Studies, "The GCC and Gulf Security: Still Looking to America," *Strategic Comments* 11, no. 9 (November 2005): 2. Available at: http://www.iiss.org/index.asp?pgid=8431.

[223] Oxford Analytica Daily Brief, November 17, 2003, "Gulf States: Military Balance Shifts to Small States."

[224] International Institute for Strategic Studies, "The GCC and Gulf Security," p. 3.

[225] "A Brief Overview of the Achievements of the GCC," Secretariat-General of the GCC, document prepared for the 25th Anniversary of the GCC, December 18–19, 2005. Available at: http://library.gcc-sg.org/English/Books/sessions/cs026.html.

[226] Barnett and Gause, "Caravans in Opposite Directions," pp. 186–189.

[227] For data on increasing economic interdependence, see http://library.gcc-sg.org/English/Books/ArabicPublish-142.html.

Why the GCC Faltered

Of the three causal conditions associated with the onset of stable peace, institutionalized restraint is the one that is glaringly absent from the GCC. Kuwait was the only member to have had a parliament at the time of the GCC's inception—and it powers were quite limited compared to those of the ruling family. The other five monarchies did not have representative institutions. To the limited degree that monarchical power was checked, such restraint came exclusively from appointed consultative councils and tribal elders.

The absence of institutionalized restraint did not stand in the way of the onset of stable peace during the 1980s. Saudi Arabia as well as the peninsula's smaller states all proved able and willing to exercise strategic restraint and back away from long-standing territorial disputes. They were prepared to undertake codified commitments to self-binding and co-binding, signing the GCC charter and assuming other obligations that constrained their autonomy. The lack of transparency associated with liberal institutions was to some extent offset by the openness afforded by regular GCC meetings, the sharing of intelligence, collaboration on borders and internal security, and cooperation on collective defense—including the fielding of a joint ground force and the initial construction of an integrated air defense network.

It is also the case that the absence of institutionalized restraint does not appear to have played a major role in undermining stable peace after the Iraqi invasion of Kuwait. The re-nationalization of security policy since 1990 has occurred while most GCC states have been taking incremental steps toward, not away from, political liberalization. Bahrain decided in 2001 to establish a parliament and Qatar followed suit in 2003. The establishment of Al-Jazeera and other news channels has widened public debate. In this respect, a more pluralist politics has coincided with less security cooperation. If anything, political liberalization and the GCC's fortunes as a security community are inversely related. According to one assessment, "As democratic civil society develops in the GCC, nationalistic tensions, posturing and inter-state clashes are likely to accompany the nation-state building process."[228]

The social orders of GCC states were not just compatible, but virtually identical. Ruling families, along with powerful tribal and familial networks, controlled most of the region's energy resources and the accompanying

[228] Oxford Analytica, Daily Brief, November 17, 2003, "Gulf States: Military Balance Shifts to Small States."

wealth. In the GCC states with small populations, foreign laborers represented a major portion of the workforce. But guest workers have been granted neither citizenship nor political rights, and thus have had virtually no impact on matters of regional security. Had local populations been larger, GCC members might have sustained more sizable military establishments, providing additional bureaucratic momentum behind regional integration. Some analysts contend that ruling families deliberately limited the size of national militaries to circumvent the institutional threat that they might have otherwise posed to the traditional social hierarchy and monarchical rule.[229]

GCC members also enjoyed a high level of cultural commonality. The citizenry of all six states is almost exclusively Arab, Arabic-speaking, and predominantly Sunni.[230] Tribes and families often have branches in several member states. Populations in all states have had a conservative social orientation, preferring traditional Arab dress and social customs to the more westernized mores of most other Arab countries. The Gulf states have also enjoyed a self-identified political homogeneity, with their traditional monarchism contrasting with many other Arab states. The one peninsular state that did not adhere to conservative monarchism—Yemen—was excluded from the GCC on those grounds.

Political leaders, intellectuals, and the media have made frequent reference to the cultural, religious, and social similarity of GCC members. A working paper drafted in preparation for the GCC's launch noted the grouping's "natural solidarity" and argued that, "if challenges are enough to create effective cooperation in any part of the world, the circumstances of the Gulf region are even more opportune for such cooperation. We constitute part of an ethnicity which has one religion, a joint civilization and joint values and customs."[231] Sheik Sabah al-Ahmad al-Jabir Al-Sabah, then deputy prime minister and foreign minister of Kuwait, noted in 1984 that "the alliance is a family alliance, it is the heritage and history of the GCC countries."[232] Other leaders noted that the GCC states enjoyed more commonality than the states of Western Europe, which had already accomplished a substantial degree of

[229] Herzog, "Arms, Oil and Security in the Gulf," p. 245.
[230] Bahrain has a Shiite majority but Sunnis dominate the government.
[231] "GCC Working Paper," May 26, 1981, p. 29.
[232] Transcript of press conference on November 26, 1984, in Ramazani, *The Gulf Cooperation Council*, p. 162.

regional integration: "These Arabs have a great deal in common among themselves. Certainly they are by far more homogeneous than the nations of Europe, members of the EEC."[233]

The absence of institutionalized restraint did not prevent the onset of security community during the 1980s, and political liberalization only advanced thereafter. From the outset, the members of the GCC enjoyed compatible social orders and high levels of cultural commonality. Why, then, did the re-nationalization of security policy occur during the 1990s?

The turning point for the GCC came with the Iraqi invasion of Kuwait. Saddam Hussein's bold attack on a member state should have strengthened the GCC's unity and rallied its members to new levels of political and military integration. But it had the opposite effect, encouraging member states to invest in bilateral alliances with the United States rather than to strengthen multilateral security cooperation. The initial decision to seek U.S. help is hardly puzzling; GCC members simply did not have the aggregate military capability needed to protect themselves from Iraq or drive Iraqi forces from Kuwait. In the late 1980s, the GCC states together had roughly 190,000 men under arms, while Iraq's armed forces had more than 600,000 personnel. To make good on their pledges of collective defense, the GCC had little choice but to turn to America's military power to drive Iraqi forces from GCC territory and provide a security umbrella.

The strategic necessities of collective defense, however, do not fully explain why growing dependence on the United States should come at the expense of regional integration. Why did the focus on collective defense arrest the GCC's progress on matters of regional cooperation? Why did the GCC not follow in the footsteps of the EC, which took advantage of America's protective umbrella to pursue a regional agenda that resulted in the consolidation of a European security community?

Having settled their own geopolitical rivalries in the 1980s—as Europe did in the 1950s—the GCC was well situated to take advantage of the luxury of external protection to pursue its own agenda of regional integration. The case for doing so was even stronger after the U.S. invasion of Iraq in 2003, when the threat environment in the Gulf was particularly conducive to regional cooperation on defense. Rising anti-American sentiment in the Arab

---

[233] Sultan Bin Mohamed Al-Qasimi, Ruler of Sharjah, in Ramazani, *The Gulf Cooperation Council*, p. xi.

world raised the domestic costs of strategic cooperation with the United States. Iraq no longer posed a ground threat, leaving GCC members facing two main challenges: domestic threats in the form of extremist attacks or Shiite unrest, and Iranian threats—primarily airborne—to energy infrastructure. In other words, the strategic environment closely resembled that of the 1980s—the GCC's heyday. According to an assessment by the International Institute for Strategic Studies, "Under these circumstances, GCC states might be expected to band together more tightly than they did in the past."[234]

They did not do so for two main reasons— the political fragmentation induced by strategic dependence on the United States and the reluctance of member states to countenance the further loss of autonomy that would accompany deeper integration on matters of security. As mentioned above, the scope and nature of America's presence in the Gulf was perhaps the most divisive issue facing the GCC during its evolution. The strategic environment of the 1980s effectively allowed member states to sidestep the issue; the demands of security necessitated only limited reliance on U.S. power, much of which was over-the-horizon. After the Iraqi invasion of Kuwait, however, the scope and imminence of the threat to Gulf security necessitated a far more overt and substantial U.S. presence in the region. Herzog nicely summarizes the essence of the consequent dilemma: "Individually, they all lack the capability and resources to muster sufficient military strength to defend themselves against Iran or Iraq; collectively as members of the Gulf Cooperation Council (GCC) they fail to foster the requisite unity to turn the organization into a preferred vehicle for regional defence. Instead, they depend on Western, primarily US, power projection capabilities to deter and, if necessary, fight an outside aggressor, even though doing so invites domestic political pressure and criticism from other Arab and Muslim states."[235]

America's presence was essential to the security of GCC states, but that same presence, for political reasons, could not be the basis for a new consensus within the GCC. In Europe, strategic cooperation with the United States was not only necessary, but also legitimate. In the Gulf, it was necessary, but could not provide a legitimating foundation for regional integration. The dilemmas of strategic dependence upon the United States—and hence the disagreements within the GCC—became especially pronounced after the events

[234] International Institute for Strategic Studies, "The GCC and Gulf Security," p. 2.
[235] Herzog, "Arms, Oil and Security in the Gulf," pp. 238–239.

of September 11, which caused an acute strain in U.S.-Saudi relations and the withdrawal of U.S. forces from the kingdom. Concurrently, as it geared up for the war against Iraq, the United States dramatically deepened strategic cooperation with the Gulf's smaller states. In this respect, Saudi Arabia's relationship with the United States was rapidly deteriorating at the same time that America's ties to other GCC members were rapidly expanding.[236]

The impact of this divergence in strategic orientation was magnified by lingering discomfort among the GCC's smaller states about Saudi hegemony. According to the International Institute for Strategic Studies, "the desire to dilute Riyadh's predominant presence within the confines of the GCC" was a major impetus behind "the impulse to cultivate foreign protectors rather than build a joint defence capability, especially one that would entail burden-sharing and rational allocation of security responsibilities."[237] Oxford Analytica took note of "the growing resentment of the smaller GCC states towards Saudi dominance of GCC bodies."[238] Barnett and Gause agree that "there remains a real if muted fear of Saudi domination all along the Gulf littoral."[239] For the Saudis, a GCC overtly dependent upon America's military power was unacceptable. But for the smaller Gulf states, a GCC dependent upon Saudi Arabia's military power was equally unattractive. The divergence in strategic orientation between Saudi Arabia and its smaller neighbors was a primary cause of the re-nationalization of security policy and the key development that dealt regional multilateralism a decisive blow. Had Saudi Arabia, as other dominant regional powers examined in this study, been willing to alleviate such concerns through a deeper commitment to consensus-building and the practice of strategic restraint, the GCC may have been able to advance regional integration even as its members depended more heavily on the United States to counter external threats.

---

[236] It is difficult to discern whether U.S. policy was deliberately designed to discourage regional security cooperation. In the case of Europe, the United States actively encouraged regional integration. In the case of Northeast Asia, the United States actively discouraged regional integration, instead preferring a hub-spoke pattern of security relations with Washington as the hub. In the Persian Gulf, the focus on bilateral ties between GCC members and the United States appears to have been more the product of the preferences of GCC states than Washington's deliberate effort to forestall regional security cooperation.

[237] International Institute for Strategic Studies, "The GCC and Gulf Security," p. 2.

[238] Oxford Analytica Daily Brief, April 7, 2006, "Gulf States: Iran Threat Exposes GCC Defence Rifts."

[239] Barnett and Gause, "Caravans in Opposite Directions," pp. 182, 164.

The other principal constraint, also a political consequence of the strategic environment that emerged after the first Gulf War, was the reluctance of member states to further attenuate their sovereignty by substantially upgrading their integration on matters of defense. Had the GCC taken collective steps to address more effectively its common defense needs, the result would have been much deeper and broader integration of national militaries. As Oman proposed, the Peninsula Shield force could have been usefully enlarged to 100,000 men under unified command. Member states would have had to rationalize and coordinate weapons procurement to ensure the interoperability of forces. And they would have had to reach a common position on the nature and scope of strategic cooperation with the United States.

These measures entailed sacrifices in sovereignty that GCC states were simply unwilling to countenance. The less demanding integration of the 1980s was tolerable, but not the more ambitious brand of security cooperation that was now required to ensure collective defense. As Crown Prince Abdullah put it, "our adherence to an exaggerated concept of sovereignty is the main obstacle to our endeavors for unity."[240] Conservative monarchies, not unlike the liberal democracies of Europe, proved unwilling to give up the ultimate prerogatives of sovereignty on matters of national defense. The attack on Kuwait itself reawakened political sensitivity to the sanctity of territory and borders. According to Barnett and Gause, "their insistence on the sanctity of borders and the centrality of state sovereignty during the Gulf crisis imprinted intra-GCC relations after the war."[241]

As a consequence of sovereignty concerns, fear of Saudi dominance, and diverging perceptions of strategic dependence upon the United States, the GCC's status as a security community will remain in limbo for the foreseeable future. Whether the organization returns to the path of stable peace depends upon developments in Iraq and Iran, as well as the ability and willingness of its members to pursue regional integration even as they continue to rely on U.S. power to counter external threats. Should Iraq stabilize and Iran tame its quest for regional dominance, it is at least conceivable that the GCC might pursue a strategy of enlargement similar to that of the EU and ASEAN, ultimately evolving into a broader regional security organization, if not a Gulf-wide security community.

[240] Address to GCC Summit, December 30, 2001.
[241] Barnett and Gause, "Caravans in Opposite Directions," p. 182.

CONCLUSION

These historical case studies confirm that the process through which security communities rise and fall follows closely the ideal-type sequential path presented in chapter 2. In all the cases, the initial drive to create a cooperative security order was born of strategic necessity; external threat usually combined with fear of domestic instability to prompt the search for stable peace. The states that forged the Concert of Europe had just experienced the cost and destruction of the Napoleonic Wars and were also mindful of domestic threats to regime stability; the Concert was intended to preserve the status quo territorially and politically. For the members of the EC, the devastation of World War II and the Soviet threat combined with fear of communism at home to ensure the advance of regional integration. The states that formed ASEAN and the GCC faced domestic and transnational insurgents as well as potential external threats, driving forward their search for security community.

Unilateral accommodation and reciprocal restraint were essential first steps in all of the cases. The exercise of strategic restraint enabled the parties to back away from long-standing rivalries. As mutual fears subsided, they then institutionalized power-checking devices and engaged in security cooperation to address both external and internal threats. In all of the cases, the onset of stable peace depended upon the willingness of dominant powers to at once practice strategic restraint and provide regional leadership. It was the readiness of Britain and Russia to self-bind and elevate the influence of less powerful neighbors that cleared the way for the Concert and its co-binding institutions. ASEAN emerged only after Indonesia abandoned *konfrontasi* in favor of regional cooperation. The foundation of the EC was the Franco-German coalition and the co-binding and power-checking mechanisms inherent in the ECSC. It was Saudi Arabia's willingness to forego the advantages of its regional dominance—and the opportunity to exclude Iraq due to its war with Iran—that set the stage for the formation of the GCC. Consistent with this logic, security community was imperiled when these dominant players abandoned restraint. The Concert unraveled when Britain and France defected from norms of reciprocal restraint, and the GCC experienced backsliding when fear of Saudi domination returned during the 1990s.

The final stages in the onset of security community were more sociological in nature, although the contribution of societal integration to the onset of security community was notably limited. The one exception was the EC, where economic integration played a substantial role in consolidating stable peace and promoting supranational institutions. Nonetheless, economic integration followed from, and did not precede, the key strategic and political bargains enabling France, Germany, and their smaller neighbors to back away from geopolitical rivalry. Moreover, greater public engagement in matters of integration, although it can deepen the foundations of security community, can also have the opposite effect. Public input has of late not been advantageous to the European project. The effort in 2005 to adopt a European Constitution foundered on referenda in France and the Netherlands; public engagement did more to impede than facilitate the further deepening of the union. It was no accident that European elites tried to ensure that the Reform Treaty that replaced the Constitution did not require public approval in most member states.

In the other cases, the building of security community was primarily an elite phenomenon. During the Concert, interstate trade and societal contact remained quite limited, and matters of foreign policy were handled by a rarified and largely aristocratic group. When publics became more engaged in such matters, as they did by mid-century, the result was the unraveling of the Concert, not its consolidation. ASEAN has prospered despite the absence of significant levels of public engagement or intraregional trade. The GCC fared best during its first decade—when societal engagement and regional trade were lowest. Security cooperation has eroded in step with increases in societal contact and intraregional trade. These findings suggest that security communities may prosper when there is less public engagement rather than more; at a minimum, public engagement is not a necessary condition for stable peace. These findings also reinforce the conclusion that transactional accounts of the onset of stable peace assign unwarranted causal importance to economic and societal integration.

Despite the relatively shallow scope of societal integration in all of the cases except the EC, the generation of a narrative of cultural commonality and kinship played a prominent role in all the cases. Elites were deliberately fashioning a shared identity that would encompass all members of the security community. The leaders of the Concert readily embraced a discourse of community, referring to Europe as an "intimate union," "a single entity," and a "family." In Southeast Asia, the leaders of regional integration popularized the notion of the "ASEAN Way." The GCC inculcated a Gulf identity among the citizens of its member states, and the EU has similarly succeeded in endowing its citizens with a European identity that complements national loyalties. In contrast, the Concert of Europe started to erode when France and Britain began verbal attacks against their "despotic" partners. A narrative of opposition preceded, rather than followed from, the concrete conflicts of interest that resulted in the Crimean War. In this respect, the unraveling of the Concert represented a reversal of the process that leads to stable peace; narratives of opposition at the domestic level led to strategies of confrontation rather than restraint, ultimately reawakening geopolitical rivalry.

The faltering of the GCC occurred for altogether different reasons. Its backsliding on security cooperation was prompted by a sharp increase in external threat stemming from Iraq's invasion of Kuwait and, later, Iran's more muscular regional stance after the U.S. invasion of Iraq in 2003. In the other cases of rapprochement and security community, a mounting external threat was generally associated with the deepening of stable peace. The opposite has been true for the GCC primarily because most members turned to the United States for protection from Iran and Iraq. Not only is the question of military ties to the United States a sensitive issue throughout the Middle East, but the small Gulf states ultimately chose to deepen their dependence on American power at the same time that the U.S. military was effectively withdrawing from the GCC's dominant power, Saudi Arabia. This divergence between Saudi Arabia and its smaller partners ensured that America's increasing role as the security guarantor of the Gulf weakened rather than strengthened security cooperation within the GCC.

The question of strategic reliance on the United States led to similar controversy within ASEAN, but the absence of a pressing external threat mitigated the implications of diverging approaches to the issue. Should China one day pose a military threat to Southeast Asia, it is conceivable that ASEAN could, like the GCC, be unable to reach a consensus on the appropriate scope of its reliance on U.S. power. In the European context, France's discomfort with dependence on American power, manifested in de Gaulle's decision to withdraw from NATO's integrated military structure, did complicate the advance of European integration. But strong support for America's strategic umbrella in most other European countries ultimately ensured that America's presence facilitated, rather than posed an obstacle to, the deepening of stable peace across Western Europe.

As for the conditions that made security community possible, the picture is

	Case	Institutionalized Restraint	Compatible Social Orders	Cultural Commonality
Successes	Concert of Europe (1815–1848)	N	Y	Y
	EC (1949–1963)	Y	Y	Y
	ASEAN (from 1967)	N	Y	Y
Failures	Concert of Europe (1848–1853)	N	N	Y
	GCC (from 1981)	N	Y	Y

FIGURE 5.1 Security Community: Summary of Findings

a mixed and complicated one, as reflected in figure 5.1. Of the cases examined, the EC was the only one comprised of liberal democracies. The contributions of democratic governance and institutionalized restraint to the onset of stable peace were amply evident. The transparency afforded by democratic debate enabled France, Germany, and the other founding members of the ECSC to assess with confidence the intentions of their emerging partners. The legalized and institutionalized character of integration dampened mutual fears of defection; the credibility of commitments to self-binding and co-binding strengthened confidence in the durability of the emerging security community. The attributes of democratic governance thus contributed to the EC's ability to lock in stable peace.

At the same time, the democratic character of the EC's member states ensured that the onset of security community met with substantial resistance; on a regular basis, the process was hostage to potent domestic constraints. In particular, France's persistent efforts to block supranational decision making and its veto of EDC were to a significant extent the consequence of domestic political pressures. Critics of the EU today regularly charge that the union is an elite construction, lacking democratic legitimacy.[242] Such criticisms may well be on target. But the history of the EC/EU suggests that greater democratic participation need not advance the community's fortunes. With the rejection of the EU Constitution in 2005 and the increasingly populist tenor of politics within member states—stoked by economic and social dislocations

[242] For a prescient critique of the proposition that the EU would benefit from greater democratic input at the supranational level, see Ezra Suleiman, "Is Democratic Supranationalism a Danger?" in Charles A. Kupchan, ed., *Nationalism and Nationalities in the New Europe* (Ithaca, NY: Cornell University Press, 1995), pp. 66–84.

and the influx of Muslim immigrants—more extensive democratic participation within the EU may well constrain, rather than advance, the further deepening of stable peace.

The Concert of Europe, ASEAN, and the GCC all challenge the notion that institutionalized restraint is a necessary condition for stable peace, demonstrating that autocratic polities can be well-equipped to form security communities. In these three cases, elites were checked by neither public accountability nor liberal institutions, but they nonetheless embraced the norms of accommodation and reciprocal restraint that made possible the onset of security community. The practice of strategic restraint *is* necessary for stable peace to cohere, but such practice can and does occur even in the absence of domestic institutions of restraint. In addition, the pathway through which the Concert of Europe unraveled raises troubling questions about the impact of liberalizing reforms on the prospects for stable peace. Inasmuch as democratization in Britain and France undermined the international bargains that led to the onset of security community, the expansion of political freedoms played an important role in eroding stable peace by stoking aggressive brands of nationalism. Again, states in the midst of democratic transitions may be particularly ill-suited to be partners in peace.

Compatible social orders, unlike institutionalized restraint, appear to be a necessary condition for security community. When the Concert first emerged, Britain and France were at the forefront of political liberalization in Europe, having embraced institutionalized constraints on the authority of the monarchy. But political and economic power still resided primarily in the hands of the aristocracy and landed nobility—as it did in Austria, Prussia, and Russia. It was not until the middle of the nineteenth century, after Britain and France both experienced the empowerment of the middle class and the stirrings of the working class, that social upheaval and diverging social orders put the western powers on a collision course with the Concert's eastern autocracies. As for ASEAN, the GCC, and the EC, their members all enjoyed similar and compatible social orders. As a result, regional integration and the onset of stable peace strengthened rather than undermined key domestic constituencies.

Finally, all of the security communities examined in this chapter were comprised of states that enjoyed cultural commonality—even if the historical record makes clear that the concept is an elusive and malleable one. The founders and supporters of the Concert and the EC alike made much of Europe's common heritage and history in seeking to buttress their regional projects with a shared identity. They were not the first to do so; since Roman times, leaders and intellectuals had frequently referenced Europe's common religious and cultural roots. Needless to say, such commonality often did little to prevent geopolitical rivalry, and religion was regularly a cause of bloodshed, not community. Nonetheless, the leaders of the Concert and the EC did have a long tradition on which to draw when they sought to create a narrative of cultural commonality, religious brotherhood, and familial ties to help foster a sense of solidarity. To be sure, perceptions of cultural commonality in Europe are malleable and open to political construction—as the collapse of the Concert and the ensuing century of European war made clear. But the ready availability of a narrative of shared history, culture, and religion gave those interested in building stable peace much with which to work.

GCC members enjoyed a shared ethnicity, language, religion, and social conservatism. Its founders made much of this shared heritage in official documents and pronouncements. At the core of ASEAN were the three Malay nations of Southeast Asia—Malaysia, the Philippines, and Indonesia. Maphalindo, a precursor to ASEAN, attempted to institutionalize regionalism along ethnic lines. Singapore and Thailand were then added to the mix. Although not Malay, they were sufficiently "Asian" to be part of the "ASEAN Way." That ethnicity and race mattered in ASEAN's self-selected membership was made clear by the exclusion of Australia and New Zealand, which have remained ineligible for membership even as ASEAN has expanded.

It is interesting to note that despite facing the same conditions (no institutionalized restraint, compatibility of social orders, and cultural commonality), the GCC represents a failed case, while the Concert of Europe and ASEAN succeeded in consolidating stable peace. Yet several considerations limit the degree to which the GCC should be interpreted as an anomalous case. The GCC did make substantial strides toward security community during its first decade, suffering a significant setback only after Iraq invaded Kuwait. Although the backsliding that followed did undercut multilateral cooperation on security, its members did not return to armed rivalry with each other. In this respect, the cohesion afforded by compatible social orders and cultural commonality appear to have helped forestall the renewal of more serious forms of geopolitical competition. In addition, the GCC's backsliding was the product of two idiosyncratic factors—acute external threats from Iraq and Iran prompting reliance on U.S. protection, and fears of Saudi domination stemming from the stark power asymmetries existing between the kingdom and the other GCC members. Moreover, it is quite possible that the GCC will reemerge as a security community should Iraq stabilize and the Iranian threat moderate, enabling Gulf states to focus more on regional integration than their individual defense ties to the United States.

In sum, as in the cases of rapprochement, compatible social orders and cultural commonality are necessary conditions for security community. The practice of strategic restraint is equally important, but the cases of security community confirm that even states that do not embrace institutionalized restraint at home are able to exercise restraint in the conduct of their foreign policy.

CHAPTER SIX

UNION

Union is the most advanced form of stable peace. The constituent states not only escape geopolitical rivalry and embrace rules and institutions to regulate their relations, but they go on to pool their sovereignty and merge into a new political entity. In so sacrificing their individual autonomy, these states advance, in Deutsch's words, from a "pluralistic" into an "amalgamated" security community. Unions differ from security communities in several important respects. In a security community, interests are conjoined and identity shared. In a union, interests are unitary and identity is common. Security communities rely primarily on intergovernmental cooperation; member states send delegates to a decision-making council, but retain their individual sovereignty. Unions are governed by collective institutions which supersede the sovereignty of member states and have authority over a broader range of policy issues. A security community regulates security and, in some instances, economic relations among its members, but those members are normally free to conduct their own diplomacy and commerce with outside states. A union usually exercises control not only over relations among its constituent states, but also over their collective diplomatic and commercial relations with other states; unions act as a single entity in the international arena.

The sequential steps that lead to the onset of union represent an extension and deepening of those that lead to rapprochement and security community. Strategic necessity triggers the search for efforts to escape rivalry, and then the onset of stable peace proceeds through four key phases: unilateral accommodation, reciprocal restraint, societal integration, and the generation of a communal identity. The power-checking practices that provide the foundation for security community—self-binding and co-binding, the fencing off of disputes, and the establishment of mechanisms to de-concentrate power—mature and become more fully institutionalized. So too are the same causal conditions at work: institutionalized restraint, compatible social orders, and cultural commonality. When states successfully form a union, they "run to completion"—albeit at varying speeds—the evolution of stable peace from rapprochement to security community to union. Accordingly, the later phases of the process—societal integration and the convergence of identity—play a more pronounced role. Indeed, it is the emergence of a common identity that legitimates a supra-national realm of governance and helps convince the constituent states to merge their individual sovereignties. Since unions entail high levels of political and economic integration, compatible social orders and cultural commonality weigh heavily as necessary causal conditions.

This chapter explores three successful cases of union: the Swiss Confederation from 1291 to 1848, the Iroquois Confederation from 1450 to 1777, and the United Arab Emirates from 1971 through the present.[1] The evolution of the Swiss Confederation makes clear the potential for social and religious differences to impede the onset of union. Although the grouping of three forest cantons formalized by the pact of 1291 has endured as a zone of peace to this day, the expansion of the confederation led to its repeated division along social (rural versus urban) and religious (Catholic versus Protestant) lines. Its final consolidation awaited the liberal constitution of 1848, which codified social, religious, and linguistic diversity. The evolution of the Iroquois Confederation and the United Arab Emirates both reveal the key role that tribal traditions can play in forming unions. The Iroquois case underscores the importance of village traditions of reciprocity, restraint, and deliberation in securing peace among the individual tribes. The UAE illustrates the role that economic incentive and the redistribution of material wealth can play in consolidating union.

This chapter then explores two cases of failed union: the United Arab Republic from 1958 to 1961, and the Senegambian Confederation from 1982 to 1989. The relatively rapid demise of the UAR was due primarily to Egypt's preponderant power and Cairo's unwillingness to practice strategic restraint

[1] Some instances of stable peace straddle the line between security community and union. The Swiss and Iroquois cases, for example, could be coded as security communities rather than unions. They are included in the chapter on unions primarily due to the substantial powers of the Swiss diets and the Iroquois Grand Council. Although the separate cantons and individual Iroquois tribes were in theory free to fashion their own diplomatic relations with third parties, in practice the diets and Grand Council did regularly seek to coordinate the external policies of the individual members. In the Swiss Confederation, the separate Catholic and Protestant diets often coordinated relations between the two communities and with third parties. In the Iroquois Confederation, especially during its later decades, the Grand Council regularly provided oversight of relations with European settlers. Indeed, the inability of the council to reach a consensus on whether to back the British or the American rebels during the Revolutionary War was the main cause of the confederation's demise. Moreover, the councils that oversaw both unions dealt not just with security affairs, but a host of other matters, including resource allocation and legal and social issues.

in its dealings with Damascus. The incompatibility of social orders also played an important role. Syria's more open and unregulated market meant that its economic elites staunchly opposed Egypt's effort to centralize the Syrian economy, ultimately inducing Syria's landowners and merchants to press for secession. The Senegambian Confederation similarly fell prey to power asymmetries and incompatible social orders. The union foundered as a result of Gambia's fear of Senegalese hegemony and incompatibility between Senegal's centralized, high-tariff economy and Gambia's more decentralized and open economy. With their power directly threatened by societal integration, Gambia's political and economic elites blocked the advance of union, ultimately prompting its demise.

   The conclusion to this chapter presents a summary of a number of additional cases of successful union—the United States (1789), Italy (1861), and Germany (1871)—and failed union—the U.S. Civil War (1861) and Singapore's expulsion from Malaysia (1965). These supplementary cases add historical diversity to the exploration of unions while providing additional empirical support for this study's central findings.

THE EVOLUTION OF THE SWISS CONFEDERATION, 1291–1848

The cantons that eventually joined together to form a unitary Switzerland followed a long and circuitous route to stable peace. From one perspective, Switzerland represents a successful case of union. The three forest cantons that formed the nucleus of the Swiss Confederation in 1291 have been at peace with each other ever since. The gradual expansion and maturation of this initial confederation led to the unitary Swiss state that emerged with the federal pact of 1848. From another perspective, Switzerland's emergence as a zone of peace has been more about repeated failure than unqualified success. As the initial union of the forest cantons expanded into a larger confederation, it took over 500 years to consolidate into a zone of stable peace, experiencing five civil wars along the way. Furthermore, from the Reformation in the early sixteenth century until the French invasion in 1798, the confederation was weak and fragmented, suffering from a fundamental political divide between its Catholic and Protestant cantons. This religious cleavage produced intra-union bloodshed as recently as 1847, when the defeat of the Catholic *Sonderbund* finally cleared the way for a stable federation.

Examining the evolution and consolidation of the Swiss Confederation thus offers a valuable opportunity to study periods of advance as well as setbacks, shedding important analytic light on the conditions that facilitate the onset of stable peace as well as those that impede it. The following account of the checkered history of the Swiss Confederation yields three chief insights. First, the union's power-checking devices and the de facto and de jure autonomy of the individual cantons helped make the confederation acceptable to its members, but they were also a persistent source of political weakness. Cantons willingly joined the union because they could preserve significant elements of sovereignty even after doing so, but their residual autonomy left the union vulnerable to division and war. Second, institutionalized mechanisms for checking power and resolving disputes, although they at times weakened the union, also played a critical role in preventing conflict. Even though civil war did break out on successive occasions, communal norms limited the scope and duration of the conflicts and encouraged the victors to forego punitive settlements that might have sustained ongoing grievances. The warring parties were readily persuaded by partner cantons to end the fighting and resolve their differences, ensuring that conflict did not fatally wound the union. Third, the Swiss case underscores the critical role that social order and religion play in making—and breaking—zones of stable peace. The cleavage between the rural cantons, which were predominantly Catholic, and the urban ones, which were predominantly Protestant, plagued the confederation for centuries. It gave way to social solidarity and a common Swiss identity only after the spread of liberal nationalism during the middle of the nineteenth century.

How Peace Broke Out

As a strategic crossroads between southern and northern Europe, the territory of contemporary Switzerland was long a target of the Roman Empire, which completed its occupation of the area by 15 BCE.[2] The Romans brought Christianity and Latin to the predominantly Celtic, French-speaking population that had settled the territory bounded by the Alps and Jura to the south and north and the Rhone and Rhine to the west and east. As the Roman Empire weakened in the third and fourth centuries, German tribes moved in,

---

[2] James Murray Luck, *A History of Switzerland—The First 100,000 Years: Before the Beginnings to the Days of the Present* (Palo Alto, CA: Society for the Promotion of Science and Scholarship, 1985), p. 4.

coming to dominate the area during the fifth and sixth centuries. The Alle-
manians were the strongest tribe, eventually Germanizing the areas they in-
habited. To the west, Burgundians were more isolated from Germany; they
ended up being assimilated into the French-speaking Celtic population. The
pattern of Allemanian and Burgundian settlement was to lead to the linguistic divide that exists in contemporary Switzerland.[3] Romansh—debased Latin—survived only among a small portion of the population.

Two developments during the thirteenth century led to the formation of
the initial confederation among the three forest cantons of Schwyz, Uri, and
Unterwalden (see map 6.1).[4] First, the opening of the St. Gotthard pass connected the forest cantons to northern Italy, turning the alpine area into an
important strategic and economic corridor. The court of the Holy Roman
Empire and feudal authorities were both interested in controlling the pass,
prompting the cantons to band together to resist external interference. As E.
Bonjour, H. S. Offler, and G. R. Potter comment, "the desire of powerful dy-
nasties to control and exploit the new artery impelled the communities
through which it ran to co-operate in defence of their independence."[5]

Second, in 1273 Rudolph I, head of the House of Habsburg, became Holy
Roman Emperor, fusing feudal and imperial power. The Holy Roman Empire had been weakening since the ninth century, enabling the peasants of the
forest cantons to secure a significant degree of autonomy as they played feudal lords against imperial authority. Moreover, many peasants in the rugged
alpine regions had originally been induced to settle there by promises of economic and political liberty, making the residents of the forest cantons
particularly sensitive to questions of autonomy.[6] King Rudolph encroached
upon these liberties, asserting tight political control over the cantons and im-

[3] E. Bonjour, H. S. Offler, and G. R. Potter, *A Short History of Switzerland* (Oxford: Oxford
University Press, 1952), p. 17.

[4] Historians offer several explanations for why the three forest cantons were at the forefront of
efforts to form a confederation. The difficult soil and weather of high alpine regions attracted
rugged individuals who were intent on resisting feudal and imperial authority. Mountainous se-
clusion also long offered these cantons political autonomy, enabling them to develop traditions
of liberty not enjoyed by inhabitants of lower lying plains who were earlier subjected to feudal
jurisdiction. The contacts and trading traditions afforded by Lake Lucerne may have also played
a role. See Luck, *A History of Switzerland*, p. 25; and Oliver Zimmer, *A Contested Nation: History, Memory and Nationalism in Switzerland, 1761–1891* (Cambridge: Cambridge University
Press, 2003), pp. 21–22. Unterwalden is on occasion referred to by its two component parts—
Nidwalden and Obwalden— as in map 6.1.

[5] Bonjour, Offler, and Potter, *A Short History of Switzerland*, p. 12.

[6] Unidentified author, "The Complicated Case of Switzerland," in Deutsch, *Backgrounds for
Community*, p. 21-4.

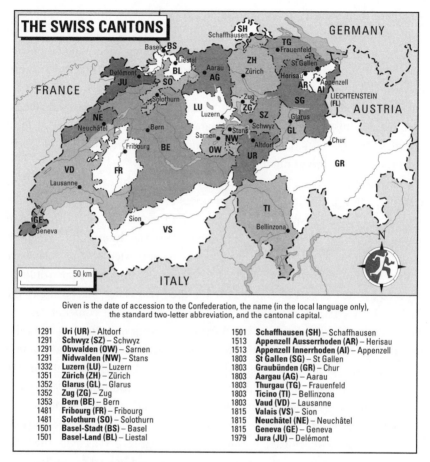

THE SWISS CANTONS

Given is the date of accession to the Confederation, the name (in the local language only),
the standard two-letter abbreviation, and the cantonal capital.

1291	**Uri (UR)** – Altdorf	1501	**Schaffhausen (SH)** – Schaffhausen
1291	**Schwyz (SZ)** – Schwyz	1513	**Appenzell Ausserrhoden (AR)** – Herisau
1291	**Obwalden (OW)** – Sarnen	1513	**Appenzell Innerrhoden (AI)** – Appenzell
1291	**Nidwalden (NW)** – Stans	1803	**St Gallen (SG)** – St Gallen
1332	**Luzern (LU)** – Luzern	1803	**Graubünden (GR)** – Chur
1351	**Zürich (ZH)** – Zürich	1803	**Aargau (AG)** – Aarau
1352	**Glarus (GL)** – Glarus	1803	**Thurgau (TG)** – Frauenfeld
1352	**Zug (ZG)** – Zug	1803	**Ticino (TI)** – Bellinzona
1353	**Bern (BE)** – Bern	1803	**Vaud (VD)** – Lausanne
1481	**Fribourg (FR)** – Fribourg	1815	**Valais (VS)** – Sion
1481	**Solothurn (SO)** – Solothurn	1815	**Neuchâtel (NE)** – Neuchâtel
1501	**Basel-Stadt (BS)** – Basel	1815	**Geneva (GE)** – Geneva
1501	**Basel-Land (BL)** – Liestal	1979	**Jura (JU)** – Delémont

MAP 6.1 The Swiss Confederation

Source: http://images.switzerland.isyours.com/images/rg.MAPS.cantons.pdf.

posing high taxes—including a toll on passage through the St. Gotthard artery. According to Bonjour, Offler, and Potter, "Old freedoms were threatened by submersion beneath the uniformity of a Habsburg 'state.' In reaction
to this danger of various communities with traditions of independence are to
be found the origins of the Swiss confederation."[7]

Rudolph died in 1291, and Schwyz, Uri, and Unterwalden immediately
took advantage of the interregnum to assert their autonomy. Within two
weeks, they concluded a pact of mutual defense, pledging joint efforts to

[7] Bonjour, Offler, and Potter, *A Short History of Switzerland*, pp. 70–71.

safeguard their security and territorial integrity. Notably, the agreement went well beyond collective defense, committing the three cantons to preserving peace among themselves. The forest cantons had long been plagued by violence stemming from territorial disputes and family feuds. Imperial authorities and Habsburg nobility regularly capitalized on such discord to justify intervention and enhance their influence. Resisting imperial and feudal domination thus required not only alliance, but also the settlement of local disputes through mutual acts of accommodation and the adoption of mechanisms to preserve communal solidarity.

To achieve these ends, the three cantons turned to the exercise of strategic restraint. They institutionalized the practices of self-binding and co-binding, agreeing to submit disputes to arbitration and mediation and to take joint action against any member that threatened the peace by rejecting a negotiated settlement. Recalcitrant parties would be subjected to the persuasive powers of the majority—in effect, the practice of grouping that would be adopted by the Concert of Europe five hundred years later. According to the pact of 1291, "If any dissension should arise among the confederates, the wisest among them should, by whatever means seem expedient to them, intervene to settle the dispute, and the other confederates should take action against the party that rejects their decision."[8] The confederation also established institutions for the administration of justice, requiring that judges be local residents rather than imperial or feudal emissaries. In addition, the cantons developed a set of rules for making rules, convening joint meetings as the need arose—gatherings that were to become regularized as diets, the main decision-making forum of the confederation. James Luck sums up the functions of the pact as follows: "crime, punishment, justice, the maintenance of internal peace, and a common defense against enemies: an attack on one of the cantons to be judged as an attack on all three."[9]

The nascent confederation advanced its fortunes on the battlefield when its forces defeated Austrian troops at Morgarten in 1315. Military success led to the deepening of the collective character of the pact. The three cantons agreed that they would not form alliances or conclude peace agreements

[8] William Bross Lloyd Jr., *Waging Peace: The Swiss Experience* (Washington, DC: Public Affairs Press, 1958), p. 6. The pact of 1291 appears to have been a renewal of a similar agreement signed several decades earlier, perhaps in 1273. Historians have been unable to locate a copy of the text of that earlier pact. See Luck, *A History of Switzerland*, pp. 38–40.
[9] Luck, *A History of Switzerland*, p. 57.

without the consent of their partners. Military success against the Habsburgs also cleared the way for the expansion of the confederation. Buoyed by the confidence of military victory, the forest cantons were looking to enhance their wealth and security by expanding the confederation to surrounding areas. And their success in resisting Habsburg hegemony meant that neighboring communities looked to membership in the confederation as a means of securing their own political independence.

Lucerne was the first addition to the original confederation, joining in 1332. As the main trading town located astride the forest cantons, Lucerne was a logical addition to the confederation. But Lucerne's inclusion, even if unwittingly, also imported into the union a social divide between town and countryside that would prove to be one of its most telling vulnerabilities. At this early stage, social cleavages were offset by the fact that urban and rural areas were united in the struggle against imperial and feudal authority. The town's artisans were seeking to overturn the political and economic dominance of the nobility, and aligned themselves with the free peasants of the forest cantons in order to further their aims. Nonetheless, the confederation's inclusion of urban communities set the stage for sustained challenges to its integrity and viability stemming from the social tensions that were to arise between the rural peasantry and the emerging bourgeoisie in the towns.

This first round of enlargement helped institutionalize three defining features of the confederation. First, as was the case for the original members, Lucerne retained effective autonomy over all matters not explicitly covered by the pact. Lucerne was joining a confederation of largely independent cantons, not being absorbed into a new polity with its own attributes of statehood. Forging a union that was loose enough to grant its members considerable autonomy but centralized enough to provide both internal security and collective defense was to prove one of the key challenges for the confederation over the next five centuries. As William Lloyd comments, the confederates struggled to find "a maximum of autonomy with a maximum of security against armed conflict."[10]

Second, Lucerne was designated as a mediator and specifically tasked with acting as a neutral arbiter should disputes emerge among confederation members. Lucerne's special status was to be the first of repeated efforts by the confederation to appoint specific cantons as peace brokers.[11] Third, all can-

[10] Lloyd, *Waging Peace*, p. 69.
[11] Lloyd, *Waging Peace*, pp. 10, 69.

tons, regardless of size and population, would have an equal vote in collective decisions. This device for de-concentrating power had a leveling and constraining effect, ensuring that more populous and affluent cantons would not dominate the confederation when they joined. Equality in political power would pave the way for enlargement to urban centers such as Zurich and Berne in the years ahead. It would also, however, prove to be a source of internal discord as larger and more affluent cantons became discontented with a level of political influence that was incommensurate with their population and wealth.

The confederation continued its expansion during the 1350s, with Zurich (1351), Zug (1352), and Glarus (1352) forming pacts with the forest cantons in order to secure their assistance in winning political and economic freedoms.[12] In some instances, the expansion of the confederation entailed the use of force, but the forest cantons were resorting to armed conflict to support the independence of their neighboring communities, not to conquer and hold their territory. In the urban setting of Zurich, increasingly powerful artisan guilds turned to the confederation to help resist imperial and feudal authority. In rural areas, the peasantry regularly relied on military assistance from the forest cantons to defeat the nobility and resist Austrian power. Berne's motives for joining the confederation had less to do with throwing off the yoke of aristocratic rule—prominent families were firmly in control of the city—than with geopolitical concerns. After Zurich entered the union, Berne feared that its isolation might invite Austrian adventurism. In addition, Berne had an ongoing territorial dispute with Unterwalden, meaning that it could face the combined forces of the confederation if conflict were to break out. Berne therefore joined the confederation in 1353, effectively turning potential adversaries into strategic partners.[13]

The union's governing institutions expanded their authority as the fourteenth century progressed, especially after the confederates defeated Austria at Sempach in 1386.[14] Even if nominally part of the Empire until the Peace

[12] The confederation consisted of a network of overlapping pacts, not a single pact to which all cantons adhered. Moreover, not all cantons had the same status. Glarus, for example, effectively entered the confederation as an "associate" member, with limitations on its status and only conditional commitments to its defense.

[13] William Martin, with additional chapters by Pierre Beguin, translated from French by Jocasta Innes, *Switzerland: From Roman Times to Present* (New York: Praeger, 1971), p. 40.

[14] See Roger Sablonier, "The Swiss Confederation," in Christopher Allmand, ed., *The New Cambridge Medieval History*, vol. 7, c. 1415–c. 1500 (Cambridge: Cambridge University Press, 1998), pp. 649–650.

of Westphalia in 1648, the confederation and its separate members were largely self-governing by the late fourteenth century. Diets began to meet regularly. Oliver Zimmer reports that between 1401 and 1420, there were 126 meetings of the diet.[15] There was no seat of government; in the service of de-concentrating power, diet meetings rotated among the cantons. Although there was no sense of common "citizenship," the residents of individual cantons were subject to the jurisdiction of communal courts. In 1393, legislation was adopted governing the behavior of troops in the field and committing each canton to consult with its partners before using force against third parties.

Nonetheless, the cantons retained significant measures of autonomy, controlling all economic issues including taxation, tariffs, and currency. As Luck observes, "Despite their growing association as a federation of their own, they existed as distinctly separate autonomous States. Each had its own coinage and each was fenced in by customs barriers that impaired the intercantonal flow of agricultural and industrial products."[16] Despite the effort to manage collectively matters of peace and war, there was no joint force or unified command; each canton maintained its own militia.[17] Furthermore, the attempt to assert collective control over security policy proved futile, with cantons often failing to honor their commitments to consult within the confederation before forming alliances with or using force against outside parties.

The practices of self-binding, co-binding, grouping, and mediation evolved as the confederation enlarged and matured. When disputes arose, cantons not party to the disagreement would intervene. The confederates would first attempt friendly mediation (*in Minne*); if that failed, they would turn to formal arbitration (*in Recht*).[18] Examples of the peaceful settlement of disputes abound during the second half of the 1300s and throughout the 1400s. In 1357, Zurich, Unterwalden, and Schwyz successfully mediated a dispute between Uri and Lucerne over toll charges. In 1371 and again in 1374, the confederates defused a potential conflict between Berne and the forest cantons over the alleged efforts of the peasantry to foment popular uprisings among

---

[15] Zimmer, *A Contested Nation*, p. 24.

[16] Luck, *A History of Switzerland*, p. 97.

[17] Martin, *Switzerland*, pp. 43–44; Bonjour, Offler, and Potter, *A Short History of Switzerland*, p. 102; Lloyd, *Waging Peace*, p. 74.

[18] Lloyd, *Waging Peace*, pp. 11, 69.

the town's residents. Schwyz besieged Zug in 1404, backing Zug's peasants in a struggle against its bourgeoisie. Arbitration resolved the dispute by granting equal power to both classes.[19] In examining a sample twenty-year period in the 1400s, Lloyd identified forty cases of successful mediation and arbitration.[20]

The confederation also continued the practice of designating specific cantons as peacemakers. For example, when Appenzell first affiliated with the union in 1411, it did not have a vote in the diet but was instead assigned the role of neutral arbiter; full membership came only in 1513. According to the pact concluding Appenzell's association with the confederation, "We, the above-named people of Appenzell, must take no part whatever in the dispute nor be helpful or allied to either side, unless by sending our ambassadors we might unite the contestants with friendship." In the early 1500s, Basel and Schaffhausen entered the confederation on similar terms, pledging to act as peacemakers and to remain neutral parties should mediation fail.[21] A related mechanism for preventing conflict entailed the designation of specific territories as common lands or bailliages. To avoid having to sort out competing territorial claims among the cantons, the confederation chose instead to assign certain areas common ownership.

The practices of grouping and opting out proved to be particularly effective in preventing the expansionist aims of individual cantons from sowing internal dissension. Cantons at times contemplated unilateral acts of aggression against third parties, even though such moves were not supported by other members of the union. In some instances, the practice of grouping was used to dissuade a canton from pursuing such aims—as when its confederate partners convinced Berne not to attempt conquest of the Black Forest. As Lloyd comments, "confederate ties often acted as a restraint upon belligerent members."[22] In other instances, the confederation as a whole opted out of specific conflicts, preventing the ambitions of individual cantons from dividing the union.[23] Uri, for example, wanted to incorporate territories to the south of the St. Gotthard pass into the union, a goal that put it into direct conflict with the powerful families of Milan. Other members of the confed-

---

[19] Lloyd, *Waging Peace*, pp. 11–15.
[20] Lloyd, *Waging Peace*, pp. 91–93.
[21] Lloyd, *Waging Peace*, pp. 17, 37.
[22] Lloyd, *Waging Peace*, p. 24.
[23] Martin, *Switzerland*, p. 53; and Lloyd, *Waging Peace*, pp. 22–24.

eration opposed such a provocative move. But in order to preserve solidarity, they chose not to stand in the way of the operation—even though they refused participation. Uri successfully carried out the expansion, extending the confederation's reach to Italian-speaking populations.

The Fragmentation of the Confederation: Social and Religious Divides

Over the course of the fourteenth century, the Swiss Confederation emerged as one of Europe's leading military powers; the cantons were no longer rivals of each other, instead amassing and coordinating their collective capabilities against outside challengers. Through a combination of armed uprisings against local nobility and wars beyond its borders, the union had by the fifteenth century effectively brought to an end centuries of domination by the Holy Roman Empire and the House of Habsburg. The confederation's success in resisting imperial and feudal authority was the primary reason for its appeal to current and prospective members. But success also had its costs. The absence of an external threat weakened the bonds of union, bringing to the surface tensions among the individual cantons that had been suppressed by the struggle against a common enemy.[24]

The most formidable impediment to political cooperation and the consolidation of stable peace was the social divide that existed between rural and urban cantons. The forest cantons had a long history of participatory democracy and political equality. They constructed a "public discourse" of confederation that "had been condensed into a simple ideological dualism: peasant versus nobleman."[25] In contrast, town life was far more stratified and hierarchical. Although artisans and traders welcomed the help of peasants in ending dynastic rule, the new bourgeoisie then replaced the nobility as the town's power brokers, often allying with aristocratic families. Military success only widened the political and economic gap between peasants and the bourgeoisie; the peasantry did the fighting while townsmen reaped the benefits of booty and increased trade.[26]

Tensions between town and countryside were to lead to the confederation's first civil war. Although a territorial dispute that emerged in the late 1430s was the ostensible cause of the conflict, the outbreak of violence between

[24] Martin, *Switzerland*, p. 49.
[25] Zimmer, *A Contested Nation*, p. 32.
[26] Martin, *Switzerland*, p. 58.

Schwyz and Zurich was rooted in competition between peasants and bourgeoisie over their relative power in the confederation and their competing visions of the union. After the two cantons negotiated unsuccessfully over the status of the estate of the deceased Count Toggenburg, Zurich imposed an economic embargo on Schwyz. In keeping with established procedures, other cantons then intervened to mediate and arbitrate, but without success. In 1440, Schwyz led a coalition of confederate militias against Zurich. Sporadic fighting continued until an armistice was negotiated in 1446. Arbitration by five cantons then led to consensual settlement of the dispute. Territory that Zurich had lost during the fighting was returned to it, a clear demonstration of the norm and practice of strategic restraint.[27]

The confederation ably recovered from its first civil war. During the second half of the fifteenth century, it grew in membership and its mediation and arbitration mechanisms were frequently deployed to defuse conflicts. But the split between town and countryside had broken into the open with the war between Schwyz and Zurich. As Luck observes, "class solidarity was stronger than federal solidarity."[28] The forest cantons were reluctant to admit new towns into the confederation, fearful that their addition would tilt the political balance in the diet in favor of the bourgeoisie. The peasantry acquiesced only when the town cantons agreed not to form an exclusive alliance among themselves. This commitment was codified in 1481 through the Pact of Stans, clearing the way for the entry of Fribourg (which brought French speakers into the confederation for the first time) and Solothurn. The confederation thereafter had ten members, equally balanced between rural and urban cantons. Diets continued to meet on a rotating basis, often convening in neutral areas to avoid putting new strain on the divide between town and countryside.[29]

The presence of common external threats helped keep in abeyance the growing divide between town and countryside. At the end of the fifteenth century, the confederation fought its last war of independence—the Swabian War. The Empire had imposed a new tax on the cantons and sought to reassert the jurisdiction of imperial courts. German cities and nobles were fearful that the Swiss example would bring social upheaval their way; the Swabian

---

[27] Luck, *A History of Switzerland*, pp. 88–91.
[28] Luck, *A History of Switzerland*, p. 105.
[29] Lloyd, *Waging Peace*, p. 30.

War was "a preventive social war against the spread of masterlessness."[30] The confederate victory against the Germans cleared the way for the entry of three new cantons—Basel, Schaffhausen, and Appenzell—bringing the membership to thirteen. All three cantons entered the confederation as designated neutrals—a step aimed at preserving the confederation's balance between town and countryside.

The uneasy peace that had been maintained between urban and rural cantons since the war between Schwyz and Zurich was to be shattered by the Reformation. Huldrych Zwingli, a resident of Zurich, was the leading voice of the Swiss Reformation as it unfolded over the course of the 1520s. The reform movement spread rapidly from Zurich to most of the other urban cantons, while finding few adherents in rural areas. The towns were home to the intellectuals and bourgeoisie for whom a progressive message of religious reform was appealing. Town dwellers were also resentful of the political power of ecclesiastical overlords, whose influence and status they were happy to see diminished by the Reformation. The rural cantons remained conservative and predominantly Catholic; the social and political conditions that enabled the Reformation to take root in urban areas were absent.[31] Not only were intellectuals and bourgeoisie few in number, but the residents of the alpine regions, due to their traditions of autonomy, had already successfully challenged the political power of the clergy.[32] The rural cantons also relied heavily on mercenary soldiering for income, a practice that Zwingli sought to abolish.[33]

The confederation's religious divide thus largely tracked its social divide, widening the political gap between town and countryside.[34] As disputes mounted over both religion and political influence, Zurich in 1531 again resorted to economic coercion, imposing a blockade on the forest cantons. Five Catholic cantons promptly declared war, readily gaining the upper hand. The other Protestant cantons stayed out of the conflict, instead seeking to medi-

[30] Thomas Brady cited in Zimmer, *A Contested Nation*, p. 27.

[31] Martin, *Switzerland*, p. 81.

[32] Unidentified author, "The Complicated Case of Switzerland," pp. 21-5, 21-18.

[33] On the economic importance of mercenary service, see Sablonier, "The Swiss Confederation," pp. 665–667.

[34] Lucerne, along with the smaller towns of Fribourg and Solothurn, remained Catholic. Lucerne's aristocracy reaped substantial profits from the traffic in mercenaries. See Robert Varickayil, "Social Origins of Protestant Reformation," *Social Scientist* 8, no. 11 (June 1980): 14–31; and Andrew Pettegree, *The Reformation World* (London: Routledge, 2000), pp. 176–177.

ate. The Peace of Kappel ended the fighting within a matter of weeks, and all parties agreed that henceforth each canton would have exclusive provenance over its own religious affairs.

The Peace of Kappel seemingly resolved the union's confessional divide by confirming cantonal autonomy over matters of religion. But the religious rift that emerged with the Reformation was to compromise the confederation's unity for the next three hundred years. Beginning in the 1530s, the Protestant and Catholic cantons began to hold separate diets, which soon met more frequently than the federal diet. The Catholic diet often convened in Lucerne, while the Protestant cantons regularly gathered in Aarau. Cantons with mixed populations, such as Glarus and Appenzell, were divided along denominational lines into half-cantons. Forced transfers of minority populations were carried out to preserve the homogeneity of the half-cantons and forestall potential conflict.[35] The Protestant and Catholic cantons started to pursue separate foreign policies, forming alliances and conducting diplomacy without consulting or coordinating with each other. In 1586, the Catholic cantons created the Borromean League, formalizing their separate status within the confederation. As William Martin comments, "Far from restoring unity to the Confederation, the Peace of Kappel ruptured it . . . . The evolutionary process which had been eroding the sovereignty of individual cantons in favour of the solidarity of the nation as a whole was permanently checked and overthrown."[36]

With social and religious divides now reinforcing each other, the confederation's solidarity was to remain compromised until the nineteenth century. Between the Peace of Kappel and France's invasion of Switzerland in 1798, two more civil wars occurred, both along religious lines. In 1655, war broke out between the Catholic and Protestant cantons after Schwyz expelled its Protestant residents. Catholic and Protestant cantons again faced off in 1712. Tension had been mounting since France expelled its Protestants in 1685. Several developments then precipitated conflict. The Protestant cantons, which had more than double the population of their Catholic counterparts, resented their minority status within the federal diet, where they were outnumbered seven to six. Meanwhile, the confederation's peasantry was growing restive due to the mounting economic and political power of the bourgeoisie as well as family oligarchies, both of which were benefiting from

[35] Lloyd, *Waging Peace*, pp. 46–47.
[36] Martin, *Switzerland*, pp. 89, 120–121.

Europe's commercial and industrial advance.[37] The wars of 1655 and 1712 were relatively short in duration and ended with negotiated settlements. But the bloodshed made clear that the religious divide continued to deny the confederation any meaningful sense of political solidarity.

Although social and religious differences were to cleave the union into two antagonistic blocs, the resulting political stalemate in certain respects worked to the confederation's advantage. The two camps effectively checked each other, preventing the confederation from acting on a host of issues that would have been uniquely divisive. The further enlargement of the confederation, for example, would have tilted the delicate political balance between Catholic and Protestant cantons. As a result, membership in the union was effectively closed; the confederation consisted of thirteen cantons from the time of the Reformation until after the French invasion in 1798.

In similar fashion, the confederation's internal divide accidentally gave rise to the practice of Swiss neutrality; absent consensus within the diet, the union kept its distance from the religious and geopolitical struggles raging around it. Effectively paralyzed by the confrontation between Catholic and Protestant cantons, the confederation stayed out of the Thirty Years' War (1618–1648)—one of Europe's bloodiest religious conflicts. Germany was ravaged by the war, while Swiss territory was untouched. The concept of neutrality had played an important role in preserving peace within the confederation; now it was helping to keep the union from entanglement in wars outside its borders. Neutrality was less of a conceptual innovation than a strategy born of political stalemate. As Martin observes, "Internal strife forced the Swiss into a policy of neutrality. . . [which] evolved from the Confederates' inability in the sixteenth century to act in unison. It is not an idea but a fact, not a principle so much as negation."[38]

Through the balance of the eighteenth century the confederation was beset by social and religious divides. The Catholic and Protestant camps remained in an uneasy peace. Social tensions also mounted in step with the consolidation of patrician rule, which predominated even in the rural cantons.[39] Trade and the development of a commercial economy widened political and economic inequalities, on occasion prompting peasant revolts against what ap-

[37] Martin, *Switzerland*, pp. 111–126; Lloyd, *Waging Peace*, pp. 54–58; and Hans Kohn, *Nationalism and Liberty: The Swiss Example* (London: George Allen & Unwin, 1956), p. 22.

[38] Martin, *Switzerland*, pp. 90, 101. See also Kohn, *Nationalism and Liberty*, pp. 20–21.

[39] Lloyd, *Waging Peace*, p. 58.

peared to be the return of hereditary oligarchies. Amid these challenges to the confederation, the individual cantons continued to be the focal points of political power, loyalty, and identity.

Not until the French Revolution and the invasion of Napoleon's troops in 1798 did the confederation enjoy at least the semblance of unity. Paris imposed a liberal constitution which stipulated, "The Helvetic Republic is one and indivisible," designated Zurich as the republic's capital, established a bicameral assembly (one chamber represented the cantons and the other the citizenry), and attempted to introduce a single currency and to reduce barriers to trade among the cantons. Recognizing that residents "looked upon the other inhabitants of the canton, outside his home community, as step-brothers, and upon the inhabitants of other cantons as strangers," efforts were made to nurture loyalty to the new republic: a common citizenship was created, religious freedom declared, and universal suffrage instituted.[40] French authorities ended German's privileged status as the union's official language, instead establishing the Helvetic Republic as a trilingual community.

The Swiss cantons, however, were not ready for such formalized amalgamation—especially if imposed by a foreign power. In 1803, six additional cantons joined the confederation and the federal character of the republic was scaled back; the cantons reasserted their power over the center through a new "Mediation Constitution."[41] The effort to locate a permanent capital in Zurich—or any other canton, for that matter—was abandoned. Thereafter, meetings of the diet rotated among three Catholic and three Protestant cantons. Following France's defeat in 1815, the pretense of unity was cast aside, with a new pact effectively restoring the weak and decentralized confederation that had existed prior to the French invasion. The national assembly was disbanded and the cantonal diet reinstated as the only federal body; Uri, a canton of 12,000 residents, was back on an equal footing with Berne, a canton of 300,000. The efforts to remove barriers to trade and introduce a single currency were abandoned. After 1815, the confederation maintained some four hundred taxes at the communal, cantonal, and union levels; almost sixty different authorities issued currency.[42] As Hans Kohn observes, "The new pact was an alliance of sovereign states; it did not constitute a nation."[43]

[40] Clause from constitution and quotation from a parliamentary committee in 1789 are in Kohn, *Nationalism and Liberty*, pp. 40, 46.

[41] Luck, *A History of Switzerland*, p. 312.

[42] Luck, *A History of Switzerland*, pp. 345–346.

[43] Kohn, *Nationalism and Liberty*, p. 55.

From Divided Union to Stable Peace

The Swiss Confederation finally set itself on the path to stable peace during the 1830s, largely as the result of the building currents of liberalism and nationalism that were sweeping Europe. Individual cantons began adopting liberal constitutions at the same time that a movement was developing behind the notion of a common nationhood that would complement, if not supersede, the loyalty of the citizenry to their separate cantons. Intellectuals and politicians alike began to embrace a liberal nationalism that would transcend not only cantonal boundaries, but also social, religious, and linguistic ones.[44] For the first time in the confederation's history, public associations joined hands with political leaders and activists to promote a common identity and unitary sense of nationhood. As Count Pellegrino Rossi, a member of the diet, wrote in the early 1830s, "Yes, the idea of a common fatherland is not alien to us; the sentiment of nationality exists in our hearts. . . . The remedy to the evils which beset the fatherland must be found in a new Pact, in a strong Confederation." Another liberal nationalist, Heinrich Zschokke, made a similar appeal: "Not from Germany, not from abroad comes the enemy before whom the Swiss heart should quail. The most formidable adversary of our freedom and independence, when he comes, will appear in our midst. . . . It is he who prefers the honour of his own canton to the everlasting glory of the whole Confederacy, his own personal or family advantage to the public good."[45]

Over the course of the 1830s and 1840s, the confederation moved incrementally toward greater centralization. A general staff was established to coordinate military policy for the union, even though the troops it would oversee were still raised at the cantonal level. A flag—an important symbol of common nationhood—was adopted by the diet. The supporters of liberal nationalism also made progress in reducing barriers to commerce and promoting inter-cantonal trade.

As during previous periods in the confederation's history, these progressive and centralizing trends were staunchly resisted by the conservative Catholic cantons. To enhance the allure of deepening the union's federal character, a parliamentary commission proposed that the permanent capital be located in

[44] For a thorough study of the evolution of nationalist discourse during the late eighteenth and nineteenth centuries, see Zimmer, *A Contested Nation*.

[45] Quotes in Kohn, *Nationalism and Liberty*, pp. 71, 73.

Lucerne—in the heart of Catholic Switzerland. But the Catholic cantons remained fearful that liberal reform would undermine their political as well as religious traditions.[46] Prompted in part by the persecution of convents and Jesuits in the Protestant cantons, the Catholic cantons in 1847 formed the *Sonderbund*, withdrawing from the diet and effectively seceding from the confederation. In what was to be the union's last civil war, confederate troops put down the rebellion in a matter of weeks, with total fatalities on both sides amounting to just over one hundred soldiers. Notably, the traditional lines of cleavage had already begun to break down. A good number of Catholics fought in the confederate army and one of the leading commanders of the *Sonderbund* forces was a Protestant.[47]

The defeat of the *Sonderbund* cleared the way for the constitution of 1848, which laid the groundwork for the governing institutions of modern Switzerland. Berne was chosen as the permanent capital; it was located astride the confederation's main religious and linguistic divides. A bicameral legislature was established, with one house (the Federal Assembly) representing the citizenry and the other (the Council of States) the cantons. The Federal Assembly elected the Federal Council, a new body with executive authority. The constitution established freedom of religion and recognized German, French, and Italian as national languages. Major progress was made on the economic front, with the union successfully adopting a single currency and free trade among the cantons.

Despite these significant advances toward federalism, the cantons clung to important aspects of autonomy. Although a universal law for military service was adopted, the cantons continued to raise their individual military units. Even as the confederation became a free trade zone, the cantons fought to retain control over key aspects of commerce—such as the development of railroads.[48] Due to the German and Italian wars of unification during the 1860s and 1870s, political tensions emerged along linguistic lines. But the rise in nationalism did not threaten the integrity of the pact forged in 1848. Having overcome its social and religious divides, the confederation was able to withstand the greater political salience of linguistic differences. By the second half of the nineteenth century, the Swiss Confederation had finally become a zone of stable peace, embracing a federal structure and a common

[46] Kohn, *Nationalism and Liberty*, pp. 72, 85.
[47] Kohn, *Nationalism and Liberty*, p. 106.
[48] Martin, *Switzerland*, p. 233.

identity sufficiently durable to weather the potential threat posed by its religious and linguistic diversity.

Notably, as in most of the other cases examined in this book, societal and economic integration followed from, rather than preceded, the initial onset of stable peace. Trade among the cantons did increase as the commercial revolution unfolded. But it was not until after the federal pact of 1848 that barriers to trade were eliminated, monetary union achieved, and a national railway system gradually developed.[49] To be sure, the benefits of economic integration helped advocates of a unitary state make their case for a federal union.[50] But the major advances in societal integration that occurred during the nineteenth century were the product, not the cause, of the act of political unification embodied in the federal pact of 1848.

Why Peace Broke Out

The mutuality of interest in resisting imperial and feudal rule provided the primary impetus behind confederation among the Swiss cantons. A common external threat gave rise to the initial union of forest cantons and fueled the successive waves of enlargement that followed. As the German and Habsburg threat subsided, the solidarity of the confederation suffered accordingly; social and then religious divides compromised its integrity until the arrival of liberal nationalism in the nineteenth century. If strategic necessity provided the cause for the confederation's launch, institutionalized restraint, the evolution and gradual convergence of social orders, and the construction of cultural commonality were the key variables shaping its long and circuitous trajectory toward stable peace. As Hans Kohn points out, Switzerland represents an archetypal case of union—one in which social, religious, and linguistic cleavages were gradually overcome through a process of integration and federation.[51] The practice and institutionalization of strategic restraint kept the confederation alive from the late thirteenth century onward—even as it remained divided along social and religious lines. But it was not until the arrival of liberal nationalism in the nineteenth century—and the constitutional order it afforded and common identity it nurtured—that these internal divi-

---

[49] Bonjour, Offler, and Potter, *A Short History of Switzerland*, pp. 289–296. See also Luck, *A History of Switzerland*, pp. 345–346.

[50] Martin, *Switzerland*, p. 226.

[51] Kohn, *Nationalism and Liberty*, p. 9.

sions could be transcended, finally turning a weak confederation into a durable zone of stable peace.

The rule of law and participatory forms of government—even if in only nascent form—played central roles in the development of the Swiss Confederation from its outset. The three forest cantons that founded the confederation in 1291 practiced an early form of participatory democracy and had embraced legal traditions imported from the Holy Roman Empire. Geography played a role in the development of consensual politics; in communities located in isolated valleys, self-government was protected from outside interference by surrounding mountains.[52] The preservation of the political and economic liberties enjoyed by the free peasantry was the principal motivation for the alliance of the cantons against imperial and feudal authority. As the confederation expanded, mutual defense against the German Empire and Austria certainly facilitated the broadening and deepening of a cooperative security order. But at least as important was the effort of a rising class of traders and artisans to expand their political voice, introduce self-administration, and check aristocratic rule.

The practice of political restraint at the cantonal level was replicated at the confederal level—even as it was repeatedly tested, at times past the breaking point, by social and religious disputes. Decisions in the diet were generally taken by majority vote; each canton, regardless of population, had equal weight. The wealthier and more populous cantons such as Zurich and Berne accepted the leveling effect of the diet, even if it proved to be a persistent source of tension within the confederation. The cantons routinely subjected themselves to grouping, mediation, and arbitration, as well as the jurisdiction of communal courts. Although these mechanisms did not always succeed in averting conflict, they worked far more often than not. And even when violence was not averted, restraint prevailed amid conflict. Intra-union wars were generally of short duration and claimed relatively few lives. The victor was not interested in destroying the vanquished, only in settling the dispute in its favor, an outcome facilitated through the mediation of cantons not involved in the conflict.

The practice of neutrality constituted yet another form of strategic restraint. Initially used to facilitate enlargement and ensure that the confederation would have peacemakers at the ready, neutrality later became a valuable

---

[52] Unidentified author, "The Complicated Case of Switzerland," p. 21–8.

instrument of statecraft. The confederation came upon neutrality in its foreign policy unintentionally; it was so divided along religious lines that taking sides in external conflicts risked its dissolution. Nonetheless, this form of withholding power may have been the key brake on the union's entry into the Thirty Years' War and other European conflicts that could well have led to its demise through foreign occupation or irreparable division resulting from engagement in Europe's wars over religion.

To be sure, liberal restraint and participatory democracy operated in a truncated fashion until well after the federal pact of 1848. Nonetheless, from the thirteenth century on, the individual cantons and the confederation as a collective were certainly ahead of their political time in comparison with most of the rest of Europe. Furthermore, the progressive cantons were at the forefront of the liberalizing trends that gained momentum across Europe in the 1830s and 1840s. The uprisings in Paris in 1848 are commonly viewed as the trigger of the revolutionary contagion that would soon sweep across Europe. But events in the Swiss Confederation in 1847, including the defeat of the *Sonderbund*, also played a prominent role in precipitating the upheaval. Thereafter, the deepening of liberal democracy cleared the way for a loose and divided confederation to emerge as a stable and unitary federation.

The checkered history of the Swiss Confederation demonstrates the powerful centripetal force exercised on the union by contrasting social orders. The impact of social differences was magnified by the nature of the enterprise; the confederation was not just an alliance, but also an emerging union striving to embrace a common set of ordering principles. Accordingly, at stake was not only security against external threats, but also livelihoods, the character of society, and the distribution of power across different classes.

During the early decades of the confederation, the divisive effects of competing social orders were muted by the common struggle of peasants and artisans alike against empire and feudalism. Moreover, the deliberate maintenance of a roughly equal balance of power between rural and urban cantons helped forestall rivalry along social lines. But as imperial and aristocratic rule crumbled and the confederation expanded, social incompatibilities could not be contained. The peasantry and its agrarian way of life were pitted against an urbanized bourgeoisie which ultimately aligned itself with the nobility. Social conflict emerged as a contest for political power, with the rural and urban cantons each congealing as a voting bloc within the diet—or forming their separate diets. The Reformation then turned a social conflict into a reli-

gious one, pitting the conservative Catholic cantons against the progressive
Protestant ones. The resulting cleavage was to put on hold the consolidation
of the confederation for over three hundred years.

The onset of stable peace did not await the disappearance of this social
divide. In the middle of the nineteenth century, Switzerland still had a sizable population of rural and rugged farmers living a life quite different from
that of urban residents.[53] But the country was becoming more urbanized; in
1850, about 54 percent of the active Swiss population worked in agriculture,
compared with 63 percent in 1798.[54] In addition, liberal constitutions at the
cantonal and federal levels had come to minimize the political consequences
of social differences. With their political voice, religious practice, and language protected by law, the conservative Catholic cantons no longer saw
their progressive Protestant counterparts as threats to their political status
or way of life. So too had the mixing of population and the growth of towns
in the rural cantons diluted the homogeneity of the union's two main blocs.
Commercialization and the rise of a middle class were proceeding across the
confederation.

A sense of cultural commonality among the residents of the Swiss cantons
was from the outset attenuated by the autonomous nature of cantonal life.
Indeed, diversity and autonomy were key elements of the ethic of the union.
But the sense of separateness that typified cantonal life was as much the
product of localism as it was social, religious, or linguistic difference. Throughout its early decades, the confederation was relatively homogeneous; as a
product of occupation by the Romans and then the influx of Germanic tribes,
it was populated predominantly by Catholic German speakers. Nonetheless,
local communities and cantons were the focal points of political identities
and loyalties. The Reformation and successive waves of enlargement later
brought greater religious and linguistic diversity to the confederation. The
sharp divide between Catholic and Protestant cantons then stood in the
way of a union-wide sense of cultural commonality. A common Swiss identity did not cohere until the spread of liberal nationalism in the nineteenth
century.

Notably, while religious differences had enormous political consequences,

[53] For estimates on urban and rural population, see Bonjour, Offler, and Potter, *A Short History of Switzerland*, pp. 316–321; and Luck, *A History of Switzerland*, pp. 432–434.
[54] By 1900, the percent of the population in agriculture had dropped to 30 percent. See Zimmer, *A Contested Nation*, p. 166.

effectively segregating the confederation into hostile camps, linguistic divisions were far less consequential. The religious split tended to follow the social divide between forest and urban cantons, thereby reinforcing a preexisting cleavage. In contrast, linguistic boundaries cut across social and religious lines, one of the reasons they did not produce political instability. As Kenneth McRae observes, "It is one of the fortunate accidents of Swiss history that the linguistic and religious boundaries do not coincide."[55]

Several other factors militated against the evolution of political divisions along linguistic lines. Although a sizable majority of the confederation's populace has always spoken German, different communities had long spoken quite distinct dialects. As speakers of Italian and French entered the union, they therefore populated a confederation that was already linguistically diverse.[56] It is also the case that the wealthier and more aristocratic families in German-speaking cantons regularly spoke French during the seventeenth and eighteenth centuries, a trend that helped prevent linguistic barriers from becoming political ones.[57] Finally, by the time that German and Italian unification helped turn language into a key marker of nationhood, the Swiss had already taken constitutional steps to prevent potential divisions arising from linguistic diversity. Napoleon had introduced trilingual equality in the constitution of 1798. It was one of the few innovations to outlast the Helvetic Republic and then be renewed in the federal pact of 1848. A linguistic brand of nationalist sentiment was mobilized in Switzerland during the second half of the nineteenth century. But the Swiss were well aware of the dangers of internal division and external interference that could potentially follow, choosing instead to adhere to their developing tradition of liberal nationalism and neutrality.

By 1848, over five centuries had elapsed since the initial founding of a confederation among the three forest cantons of Schwyz, Unterwalden, and Uri. In the interim, the confederation markedly expanded its territorial scope and succeeded in defeating its feudal and imperial competitors. But it also experienced repeated fracture along social and religious lines. Only with the embrace of the liberal institutions and inclusive nationalism embodied in the constitution of 1848 were these social and religious cleavages overcome,

---

[55] Kenneth McRae, *Switzerland: Example of Cultural Coexistence* (Toronto: Canadian Institute of International Affairs, 1964), p. 3.

[56] McRae, *Switzerland*, p. 15.

[57] Martin, *Switzerland*, p. 132.

tamed by both institutionalized restraint and the onset of a common Swiss identity. The cantons of the Swiss Confederation had finally arrived at stable peace.

THE IROQUOIS CONFEDERATION, 1450–1777

The Iroquois nations that populated what is today upstate New York were some of North America's most ferocious warriors, regularly engaging in battle with each other and with neighboring Native American tribes. Beginning in the second half of the fifteenth century, five Iroquois nations—the Mohawk, Oneida, Onondaga, Cayuga, and Seneca—formed the Iroquois Confederation, which ended the violence and established a zone of stable peace that lasted until the late eighteenth century (see map 6.2). These five nations frequently waged war against other tribes and with the Europeans immigrants that began settling in the area in the early 1600s. But the Iroquois Confederation, guided by principles contained in an oral text, proved remarkably durable, maintaining peace among the Iroquois for over three hundred years.

Strategic necessity provided the initial impetus behind the formation of the Iroquois Confederation.[58] "Violent conflict was both common and costly among the original five nations," with losses particularly heavy because of the practice of "mourning wars."[59] After suffering deaths in battle, Iroquois tribes would embark on military campaigns intended to compensate communities for their warriors lost in battle. The prisoners were either adopted and

[58] Two authoritative scholars of the league, Daniel Richter and William Fenton, distinguish between the Iroquois "League" and the "Confederacy." They reserve the term "League" for the early period of Iroquois peace, when representation on the Grand Council was hereditary and the body was focused primarily on relations among member nations. They use the term "Confederacy" to refer to the period beginning in the second half of the 1600s, when positions on the council could no longer be filled by hereditary succession due to population decline and when the Iroquois nations were focused primarily on conducting diplomacy and war with outside tribes and with European settlers rather than with each other. I use the term "Confederation" throughout. See Daniel Richter, *The Ordeal of the Longhouse: The Peoples of the Iroquois League in the Era of European Colonization* (Chapel Hill: University of North Carolina Press, 1992), p. 7; and William N. Fenton, *The Great Law and the Longhouse: A Political History of the Iroquois Confederacy* (Norman: University of Oklahoma Press, 1998), p. 710.

[59] Neta Crawford, "A Security Regime among Democracies: Cooperation among Iroquois Nations," *International Organization* 48, no. 3 (Summer 1994): 345.

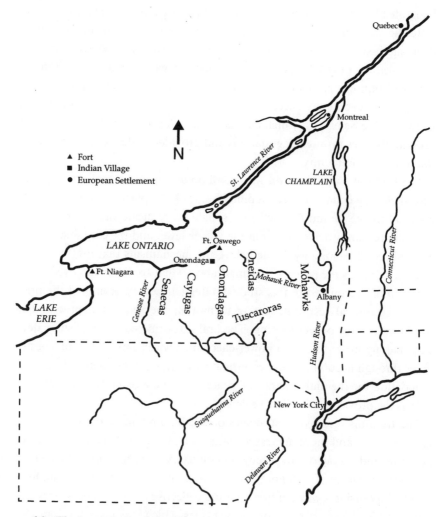

MAP 6.2   The Iroquois Confederation, c. 1750

Source: Reprinted with permission from Timothy J. Shannon, *Indians and Colonists at the Cross-roads of Empire: The Albany Congress of 1754* (Ithaca, NY: Cornell University Press, 2002), p. 19.

integrated into the community, or killed as part of a ceremony meant to alleviate the suffering of grieving families. Distressed by the deaths stemming from successive rounds of mourning wars, a warrior named Hiawatha, accompanied by a mystical peacemaker named Deganawidah, traveled among the five Iroquois nations to spread a message of peace and reconciliation.[60] The mission eventually succeeded, leading to the formation of the Grand Council, an assembly in which emissaries from each of the five nations addressed disputes through negotiations and provided collective governance of the Iroquois community.

The Iroquois Confederation was based on unique aspects of Iroquois culture, including condolence ceremonies that took the place of mourning wars, protocol in the Grand Council that sought to replicate the institutions of governance that provided order at the village level, and the exchange of gifts as symbols of reciprocity. Nonetheless, the mechanisms that the confederation used to preserve peace were remarkably similar to those employed by the other unions examined in this study. Strategic necessity prompted the practice of reciprocal restraint, setting in motion the sequential process that would lead to the onset of union. The oral text came next, establishing decision-making procedures and power-checking devices aimed at resolving disputes through negotiation and coordinating foreign policy, thereby laying the foundation for the maintenance of peace among confederation members as well as the provision of collective defense.

The Iroquois resorted to strategies of self-binding and co-binding to rein in their larger and more aggressive nations, and they embraced practices of grouping and opting out to sustain unanimity. At the same time, each nation retained a measure of autonomy by reserving the right to wage war and form pacts with outsiders without first securing collective consent. The five nations also developed a set of rules for making rules, which included procedures for adopting members of non-Iroquois tribes and for enlarging the union—the Tuscarora, an Iroquois tribe migrating from North Carolina, joined in the early 1700s. These practices and institutions successfully preserved peace

[60] Historical accounts differ as to whether Hiawatha was originally from the Onondaga or the Mohawk. Fenton maintains that Hiawatha was from the Onondaga, left the community to mourn the loss of family members, was then adopted by the Mohawk, and thereafter began his peace mission. Accounts of the establishment of the confederation also differ as to whether Deganawidah, to whom the founding myth ascribes supernatural powers, actually accompanied Hiawatha on his peace mission or was a mythical figure who appeared to him in a vision. See Fenton, *The Great Law and the Longhouse*, pp. 90–95.

among the Iroquois until 1777, when the American Revolutionary War pitted the Oneida and Tuscarora, who backed the colonies, against the confederation's other four nations, which elected to support the British. Stable peace among the Iroquois eventually succumbed to the challenges posed by the growing power of European immigrants to North America.

How Peace Broke Out

Warfare was long a way of life for the five nations that were to establish the Iroquois Confederation. According to one version of its oral constitution, "Feuds with outer nations and feuds with brother nations, feuds of sister towns and feuds of families and clans made every warrior a stealthy man who liked to kill."[61] The turn toward stable peace appears to have taken place around 1450.[62] Forlorn as a result of the continuing bloodshed produced by successive mourning wars, a warrior named Hiawatha quit the village in which he lived to take refuge in the forest. There he met Deganawidah, who convinced him of the need to spread a message of peace. Hiawatha and Deganawidah together traveled among the five Iroquois nations, eventually convincing each to join a league of peace. The resulting confederation preserved peace among its member nations even as they remained regular combatants with adjacent tribes and, in due course, with European immigrants. One French observer noted the stark contrast: "The Iroquois are the fiercest and the most redoubtable nation in North America; at the same time the most political nation and the most judicious that can be known."[63]

The confederation's founding entailed the fashioning of a decision-making system that reflected power and status differentials among the member nations. The Mohawks were regarded as the most accomplished warriors as well as the nation that initiated the diplomacy leading to the formation of the confederation. They would therefore be the first to deliberate on an issue of common concern, thereafter expressing their opinion to the other nations, which would then initiate their own deliberations. In return for the readiness

[61] Donald Lutz, "The Iroquois Confederation Constitution: An Analysis," *Publius* 28, no. 2 (Spring 1998): 124.

[62] Historians and anthropologists disagree about when the Iroquois Confederation took shape, although a tentative consensus has formed around the view that it emerged in the middle of the fifteenth century. For a summary of different positions, see Fenton, *The Great Law and the Longhouse*, pp. 66–73.

[63] Bacqueville de La Potherie cited in Fenton, *The Great Law and the Longhouse*, p. 330.

of the Mohawk to bind themselves to their weaker neighbors, the other Iroquois nations granted the Mohawk a leading position in the confederation. As Donald Lutz argues, "It is possible . . . to view the constitution as intended to ratify and formalize Mohawk preeminence within a structure that provides means for the other tribes to protect their vital interests, one of which was to tie the aggressive Mohawk to a broader community."[64]

Joining the Mohawk as the "elder brothers" or the more senior "moiety" were the Seneca, whose elevated status appears to have resulted from their population, which accounted for about 50 percent of the confederation's total. The Cayuga and Oneida were the "younger brothers," while the Onondaga were the hosts of the Grand Council, the confederation's main decision-making forum. The Onondaga initially refused the offer to form a league of peace. The peacemakers then proposed that they host the Grand Council, effectively making their main village a capital of sorts, an offer that succeeded in inducing their participation.[65] In addition, the Onondaga resided in the geographic center of the five nations, perhaps another reason they were selected to host the Grand Council.

The practices of strategic restraint relied upon to fashion consensus and preserve peace within the confederation were modeled on village-level traditions for providing social cohesion and communal governance. As William Fenton writes, "Local patterns for gaining consensus were projected to higher levels of integration."[66] The primary unit of village life was the longhouse, a long and narrow dwelling containing three to five central fires. Each fire was shared by two families which lived on opposite sides of the longhouse. The families collectively ran the dwellings, sharing not just the fires needed for heat and cooking, but also provisions and storage space. Village councils met regularly to provide governance, operating according to the same principles of reciprocity and consensus that prevailed in the longhouses.

The Grand Council of the confederation replicated the structure of the longhouses. The elder nations sat on one side, the younger nations on the other, and the Onondaga kept the fire in the middle. Each nation sent a speci-

---

[64] Lutz, "The Iroquois Confederation Constitution," p. 109.

[65] As with the timing of the confederation's founding, scholars differ over the details of the sequence of events that led to its formation, with the oral tradition offering competing accounts. The account in this study is based primarily on Fenton, *The Great Law and the Longhouse*, pp. 99, 247–248, 493; Richter, *The Ordeal of the Longhouse*, p. 39; and Lutz, "The Iroquois Confederation Constitution," pp. 101, 105–109.

[66] Fenton, *The Great Law and the Longhouse*, p. 715.

fied number of *sachems*—tribal leaders initially selected through matrilineal descent—to the Grand Council, which was comprised of fifty representatives.[67] The council operated according to a constitution transmitted orally, which came to be called the "Great Binding Law" or "the Great Law of Peace." Recitation of the law encompassed the founding myth as well as the traditions of governance that secured and preserved peace. The council maintained a strict separation between civil and military leadership; warriors were excluded from membership, although they regularly attended the meetings in an advisory capacity. It adopted regularized procedures for replacing sachems when they died and for removing them from office if they were incompetent or engaged in dishonest behavior.[68] The Grand Council met at least once a year, and often more frequently when the confederation needed to deal with pressing issues.

From its founding in the fifteenth century until its demise in the eighteenth, the confederation focused much more on collective solidarity than collective defense. As Lutz comments, "its primary purpose was to maintain peace among its members, not to coordinate outward action."[69] Each nation retained its autonomy when it came to relations with outsiders, preserving the right to fashion pacts and make war and peace on an individual basis.[70] Member nations were under no obligation to come to each other's defense. Accordingly, individual nations regularly waged their own wars against neighboring tribes and the French. Violence remained an integral part of Iroquois society throughout the period of confederation: "Participation in a war party was a benchmark episode in an Iroquois youth's development." Moreover, the customs of warfare were quite brutal; captives taken in battle were often killed in cruel fashion, scalped, and then eaten in a village feast.[71] Despite

[67] The number of sachems that each nation sent to the Grand Council ranged from fourteen for the Onondaga to eight for the Seneca. Nonetheless, the number of sachems had no impact on voting weight as each nation had one vote in the council. During the early decades of the confederation, the sachems were replaced by those in the same family line. When hereditary succession no longer became possible due to population decline, others were selected to serve on the Grand Council, but they did not retain the hereditary titles of the original sachems. See Lutz, "The Iroquois Confederation Constitution," p. 103.

[68] For a summary of the confederation's rules and regulations, see Fenton, *The Great Law and the Longhouse*, pp. 215–223.

[69] Lutz, "The Iroquois Confederation Constitution," p. 101.

[70] Crawford, "A Security Regime among Democracies," p. 356; and Fenton, *The Great Law and the Longhouse*, p, 275.

[71] Some captives were adopted while others were killed and eaten. For a description of this practice, see Richter, *The Ordeal of the Longhouse*, pp. 35–36. Quotation from p. 36.

this environment of bloodshed and cannibalism, however, the five nations did not fight each other. After the confederation's founding, there are no known episodes of war among any of the five nations. Isolated incidents in which individuals from different tribes engaged in deadly violence did occur, but the confederation effectively prevented these events from sparking broader conflicts.[72]

The main practices through which the confederation preserved stable peace entailed both self-binding and co-binding. As the name of the oral text indicated, the "Great Binding Law" was intended to tether each of the five nations to each other, committing them to engage in deliberation until they arrived at a common position. According to Fenton, the "Great Law . . . follows the tactics of surround and concert"—a form of grouping similar to that practiced by the members of the Swiss Confederation and the Concert of Europe.[73] As formulated by the oral tradition, "We bind ourselves together by taking hold of each others' hand so firmly and forming a circle so strong that if a tree should fall upon it, it could not shake or break it, so that our people and our grandchildren shall remain in security, peace, and happiness."[74]

Enabling that circle to form and endure was a commitment to practice accommodation and reciprocity in order to reach consensus—to deliberate until the five nations were in accord. As Fenton observes, the confederation "achieved unity through the principles of unanimity and reciprocity."[75] Neta Crawford maintains that, "In Iroquois policy, no one ordered anyone else around. Issues were agreed to consensus."[76] Daniel Richter agrees: "What kept the universe of political parties generally in orbit around a common nucleus was a shared belief in the ideal of consensus and in the spiritual power that comes from alliance with others."[77] Accordingly, the most revered sachems were those who developed reputations not for unwavering determination, but for "generosity, responsibility, imperturbability, and an ability to compromise."[78]

The communal solidarity of the longhouse was replicated not only in terms

---

[72] In 1656, for example, two Seneca ambassadors were killed by Mohawk warriors. The Grand Council interceded to prevent escalation. Fenton, *The Great Law and the Longhouse*, p. 252. For other examples of deadly conflict, see Richter, *The Ordeal of the Longhouse*, p. 65.

[73] Fenton, *The Great Law and the Longhouse*, p. 95.

[74] Cited in Crawford, "A Security Regime among Democracies," p. 355.

[75] Fenton, *The Great Law and the Longhouse*, p. 101.

[76] Crawford, "A Security Regime among Democracies," p. 357.

[77] Richter, *The Ordeal of the Longhouse*, p. 45.

[78] Richter, *The Ordeal of the Longhouse*, p. 46.

of the layout of the Grand Council. The confederation sought to function as an extended family, with the bonds of kinship serving as a social and spiritual source of unity: "Confederation was a long process of compromise, reformulating relationships, and providing for the extension of the Longhouse—the symbol of a polity based on kinship. . . . Its formation and successful operation depended on shared kinship usages that reached down to the local level."[79] Labeling the two sides of the Council fire "elder" and "younger" was only one of numerous instances of the use of familial terms. In the Grand Council, "equals called each other 'brothers,' and those in relationships traditionally characterized by more deference used 'father' and 'son' or 'uncle' and 'nephew,' in accordance with the respectively greater degrees of obligation those kinship connections entailed."[80] When population decline meant that sachems could no longer be replaced through matrilineal descent, a ceremony of "requickening" would induct a worthy individual into the position, transferring to the successor the responsibilities and spiritual potency of the deceased, and integrating him into the community of kinship represented by the Grand Council.

This emphasis on kinship, reciprocity, and restraint did not always succeed in producing unanimity. When a consensus could not be reached, the Grand Council simply put the issue aside: "unanimity does not mean that the minority subsides; it simply withdraws."[81] Informal discussions would then ensue in order "to bring dissenters gently around to the viewpoint of the majority."[82] In instances in which "surround and concert" failed to resolve differences, the minority faction would usually accede to the majority view. In extreme cases, the confederation resorted to various forms of opt-outs. In some cases, dissenting factions would leave the confederation and resettle elsewhere "rather than perpetuate a disruption of community peace."[83] In other instances, individual nations would forego attendance at meetings of the Grand Council.[84] Such abstentions denied the body unanimity, but nonetheless allowed the Grand Council to reach a consensus. Peace was main-

---

[79] Fenton, *The Great Law and the Longhouse*, pp. 95, 102.

[80] Richter, *The Ordeal of the Longhouse*, p. 41.

[81] Fenton, *The Great Law and the Longhouse*, p. 507.

[82] Richter, *The Ordeal of the Longhouse*, p. 46.

[83] Richter, *The Ordeal of the Longhouse*, p. 46.

[84] During the late 1600s, for example, the Onondaga and Mohawk competed for leadership of the confederation and control over foreign policy. During these disputes, the Mohawk delegation, as well as that of the neighboring Oneida, on occasion failed to attend meetings of the Grand Council. See Fenton, *The Great Law and the Longhouse*, p. 248.

tained throughout, and the boycotts of the Grand Council always proved to be only temporary departures from the norm of unanimity.

Concrete acts of altruism played a central role in preserving consensus; member nations regularly resorted to the "condolence ceremony" and the giving of gifts to symbolize empathy and solidarity. Absent regular mourning wars against each other to replace the dead with captives, the Iroquois developed the condolence ceremony to soothe families grieving lost members. The practice of requickening was meant to fill not only empty leadership positions, but also the spiritual void left by the dead: "Condolence rituals, ceremonial gifts, and Requickening rites symbolically addressed the same demographic, social, and psychological needs served by the mourning-war, restoring the deficit of spiritual power caused by death."[85] Council meetings regularly involved the exchange of valuable gifts—most often belts or strings of wampum (shells). In some instances, such gifts were a form of bribery intended to group outliers and induce compliance or compromise.[86] But the exchange of gifts was more often intended only to symbolize reciprocity and good will. According to Richter, "Words of peace and gifts of peace . . . were inseparable; together they demonstrated and symbolized the shared climate of good thoughts upon which good relations and powerful alliances depended."[87]

SOCIETAL INTERACTION AND THE GENERATION OF A COMMON IDENTITY

Increasing commerce among the Iroquois nations was neither a cause nor a product of the formation of the confederation. There were virtually no commercial linkages among the five nations. Each controlled its own economy, none of which operated as a commercial market. Warriors on occasion accumulated items of value—skins or wampum—that were the spoils of war. Otherwise, Iroquois economies operated according to principles of reciprocity and economic equality, with food surpluses distributed according to need.[88] This system of redistribution "gave very little opportunity for the development of any system of internal trade."[89] After the arrival of Europeans, the Iroquois began to participate in the lucrative fur trade. But fur markets

---

[85] Richter, *The Ordeal of the Longhouse*, p. 39.

[86] For an example of the confederation grouping the Mohawk through the giving of gifts, see Fenton, *The Great Law and the Longhouse*, p. 250.

[87] Richter, *The Ordeal of the Longhouse*, p. 48.

[88] Richter, *The Ordeal of the Longhouse*, p. 22.

[89] Sara Henry Stites, *Economics of the Iroquois* (Lancaster, PA: New Era Printing, 1905), p. 79.

developed primarily between the Iroquois and European settlers, not among the Iroquois themselves.

Regular meetings of the Grand Council did help forge societal ties among the five nations. The sachems serving on the council built personal relationships with each other, which contributed to the mutual trust critical to maintaining consensus and unanimity. Condolence rituals, requickening, and the exchange of gifts played an important role in nurturing a sense of communal and spiritual solidarity. Nonetheless, this form of societal integration was restricted to elites—sachems and warriors that participated in the meetings. Otherwise, there was little contact among the separate populations of the member nations. Through local councils that reached down to the village level, individual communities were well integrated into the confederation's political hierarchy. But societal interaction across the nations was infrequent—and not an important factor in the onset or longevity of the union.

In contrast, the generation and propagation of a shared historical narrative and communal identity were critical to the confederation's cohesion and durability. The founding myth, the centerpiece of which was the peacemaking mission of Hiawatha and Deganawidah, and the oral text, which was recited regularly and passed from one generation to the next, were the core elements of the confederation's efforts to propagate a common identity. The regular use of terms of kinship to denote political hierarchy and define relationships among the nations and their sachems contributed to a shared sense of community. The longhouse was a metaphor for the confederation and the Grand Council was organized to replicate its physical structure, underscoring the degree to which the Iroquois sought to portray their community as an extended household.

The Arrival of Europeans and the Ultimate Demise of the Confederation

The fifteenth and sixteenth centuries were the heyday of the confederation. The five nations successfully fashioned and maintained a zone of stable peace and enjoyed the stability and growth in population that accompanied the cessation of tribal rivalries. The arrival of European settlers during the early 1600s, however, began to reverse the confederation's good fortunes. With Europeans came new microbes, which devastated the population of the Iroquois tribes. In addition, interaction with French, Dutch, and English settlers con-

fronted the confederation with a challenge for which it was singularly ill prepared—forging a common foreign policy and providing for common defense.
Indeed, it was differences over diplomacy with North America's new settlers
that ultimately split the confederation and brought to an end three hundred
years of peaceful relations among its members.

The first major impact of the arrival of Europeans was the spread of new
diseases, smallpox in particular. Estimates vary, but the new microbes appear
to have killed at least 50 percent of the population of the Iroquois Confederation. In response, the Iroquois returned to mourning wars to replace their
losses, taking captives from the numerous tribes residing in neighboring
areas: "The main targets in the midcentury campaigns were native peoples
who could satisfy an insatiable demand for captives to replace the mounting
numbers of dead in the Five Nations."[90] Although the integration of captives
to some extent offset the losses due to disease, the new arrivals diluted the
homogeneity of the community and were not schooled in Iroquois tradition.
In some villages, two-thirds of the population was adopted from outside
tribes. The ongoing cycles of mourning wars also strengthened the political
influence of Iroquois warriors, giving them greater weight in the deliberations of the Grand Council and focusing the confederation more on external
relations than internal peace.[91]

The more belligerent orientation of the confederation combined with the
growing ambition of New France to trigger a succession of wars in the late
1600s. Although renowned fighters, the Iroquois did not fare well against the
new technologies of warfare imported from Europe. During the late seventeenth century, battles against the French killed almost one-half of the confederation's warrior population.[92] With mourning wars unable to keep up
with the pace of losses, the Grand Council for the first time began to focus
on coordinating Iroquois diplomacy and forging a common foreign policy
that would provide for collective defense. The inclusion in the confederation
of the Tuscarora, who had been expelled from North Carolina by European
settlers, helped stabilize the population and end the dependency on mourning wars, thus reinforcing the new turn toward diplomacy.[93]

[90] Richter, *The Ordeal of the Longhouse*, pp. 57–58, 64–65.

[91] Fenton, *The Great Law and the Longhouse*, pp. 10–11; Richter, *The Ordeal of the Longhouse*,
pp. 65–66.

[92] Fenton, *The Great Law and the Longhouse*, p. 329.

[93] Accounts differ as to the timing of the entry of the Tuscarora into the confederation. Richter argues that the wars driving the tribe from North Carolina occurred between 1711 and 1713.

As it sought to fashion a common approach to outsiders, the confederation's initial strategy was one of accommodation: it would seek peace with its Native American neighbors and remain neutral in the building rivalry between the French and British. The competing allegiances of the member nations complicated the challenge of balancing between the growing communities of European immigrants. In broad terms, the nations occupying the northwest—Seneca, Cayuga, and Onondaga—tilted toward the French. They had more political and economic contact with French settlers and some of their members had emigrated northward and taken up residence in areas primarily populated by the French.[94] Meanwhile, geographic proximity tilted the Oneida—and, at times, the Mohawk—toward the English, an orientation strengthened by growing commerce and the frequent dispatch of diplomatic missions to Albany.

Beginning in the 1670s, the confederation fashioned the "Covenant Chain," a series of alliances with traders along the Hudson River, which over time developed into a broader political pact with the English.[95] The tilt toward the English strengthened the confederation's hand in balancing against the French. As one New York official characterized this strategy, "To preserve the Ballance between us and the French is the great ruling Principle of the Modern Indian Politics."[96] This strategy paid off by the first half of the 1700s; neutrality brought the five nations a period of peace and stability, enabling them to replenish their population through the incorporation of the Tuscarora and other refugees. During a ceremony marking the conclusion of a treaty between the Iroquois and the English in 1744, an emissary from Onondaga shared with his European counterparts the ample benefits of union:

> We have one Thing further to say, and this is, We heartily recommend Union and a good Agreement between you our Brethren. Never disagree, but preserve a strict Friendship for one another, and thereby you, as well as we, will become the stronger.
>
> Our wise Forefathers established Union and Amity between the *Five Na-*

The Tuscarora appear to have been admitted to the confederation by 1720. See Richter, *The Ordeal of the Longhouse*, p. 239; and Crawford, "A Security Regime among Democracies," p. 345.

[94] Fenton, *The Great Law and the Longhouse*, p. 452.

[95] Fenton, *The Great Law and the Longhouse*, pp. 330–349.

[96] Peter Wraxall, New York's secretary for Indian affairs, quoted in Richter, *The Ordeal of the Longhouse*, p. 206.

tions; this has made us formidable; this has given us great Weight and Authority with our neighbouring Nations.

We are a powerfull Confederacy; and, by observing the same Methods our wise Forefathers have taken, you will acquire fresh Strength and Power; therefore whatever befals you, never fall out one with another.[97]

During the second half of the 1700s, the Grand Council's efforts to sustain a common foreign policy were less successful. The confederation's ability to conduct a unified foreign policy proved temporary. The individual nations reasserted autonomy over matters of external relations, in part due to the separate interests that stemmed from geographic location. The outbreak of the American Revolution then brought to a head divergent perspectives on whether the confederation should align with the American settlers or their British overseers. The Continental Congress sought to ensure that the Iroquois Confederation would abide by its tradition of neutrality. Meanwhile, the English sought Iroquois assistance in putting down the rebellion. The Seneca, Cayuga, Onondaga, and Mohawk sided with the British, assuming that the continuation of colonial rule would preserve the Iroquois' territorial rights and extend the duration of the Covenant Chain. The Oneida and Tuscarora backed the revolutionaries, with whom they had built closer ties.[98] Unable to reach unanimity at the Grand Council, the six nations agreed to dissolve the confederation, extinguish the council fire, and go their separate ways. Ensnared in the Revolutionary War by their competing allegiances, the Iroquois nations on August 8, 1777, in Orinskany, New York, faced each other in battle for the first time since the founding of the confederation in the fifteenth century.

Why Peace Broke Out

All three of the key ingredients of stable peace—institutionalized restraint, compatible social orders, and cultural commonality—were present in the Iroquois Confederation. The nations that comprised the confederation as well as the Grand Council that governed it practiced a truncated form of participatory democracy that included the exercise of institutionalized restraint. At the village level, local councils met regularly to deal with day-to-day matters

---

[97] Canasatego, quoted in Fenton, *The Great Law and the Longhouse*, p. 432.
[98] Lewis Henry Morgan, *League of the Iroquois* (New York: Corinth Books, 1962), pp. 27–29.

and each nation "shared similar political institutions."[99] Gatherings of all adults were called as needed to debate important policy issues and provide advice to village elders.[100] In addition, all the communities that comprised the nations in the confederation gathered their residents once every five years to approve collectively the extension of the confederation and its Great Binding Law. Sachems, although selected according to matrilineal descent, had to be approved at the village, national, and confederal levels. They were held accountable for their performance and could be removed from office on grounds of dishonesty or incompetence. Until population decline made the practice impossible to sustain, sachems were selected only from families that held the status of *royenah*, an effective aristocracy. Women played an important role at the village level, wielding considerable influence over the selection of sachems and deciding whether to adopt or kill captives. Women did not, however, serve on the Grand Council.

A similar form of truncated democracy operated in the Grand Council. As detailed above, each nation had one vote in the council and decisions required unanimity. At the same time, the status of different nations and sachems also played an implicit role in decision making and the fashioning of a consensus. As Lutz summarizes this mix of democracy and tribalism, "The Confederation Council . . . was essentially a hereditary oligarchy whose members were identified and selected by means of a process that was somewhere between traditional tribalism and institutionalized democracy."[101]

In similar fashion, institutionalized restraint was practiced at the village level and replicated within the Grand Council. The procedures for reaching unanimity embodied in the Great Binding Law entailed checking the power of individual nations and inducing their representatives to put the welfare of the confederation above the interest of its separate members. Tribal traditions such as grouping, opting out, and the institutionalization of reciprocity through the longhouse structure of the Grand Council, the condolence ceremony, and the ritual exchange of gifts all represent power-checking mechanisms transferred from the village to the confederation. Warriors were excluded from full membership in the council precisely to prevent it from succumbing to predatory ambitions—an early form of civilian control of the military. Although only an oral text, the Great Binding Law was remarkably

[99] Fenton, *The Great Law and the Longhouse*, p. 72.
[100] Stites, *Economics of the Iroquois*, p. 105.
[101] Lutz, "The Iroquois Confederation Constitution," p. 114.

similar to republican constitutions of the present day. Indeed, some historians argue that the drafters of the U.S. Constitution drew on the oral law of the Iroquois Confederation.[102]

The five nations that formed the confederation had identical social orders. Each nation was organized by clan and village, and had local, clan, and tribal patterns of authority in common. The males generally hunted and fished while the females tended to horticulture. The members of the confederation also enjoyed cultural commonality. The languages spoken by the five nations were all Iroquois in origin. As Bruce Trigger observes, the confederation "embraced groups of people who were culturally and linguistically related." Lutz too emphasizes the key role played by "a shared religion and culture, linked by language and intermarriage."[103]

The importance of cultural commonality was underscored by the fact that only Iroquois tribes were allowed to join—as demonstrated by the entry of the Tuscarora in the 1700s. As one sachem proclaimed after a meeting of the Grand Council, "The Tuscarore Indians are come to shelter themselves among the five nations. They were of us and went from us long ago and are now returned."[104] Individuals from non-Iroquois nations could be adopted and assimilated, but the confederation was not open to other tribes. Affinity among the Iroquois was not, however, a sufficient condition for stable peace. Despite the absence of conflict within the confederation, its members did at times find themselves at war with other Iroquois tribes residing to their north, primarily in the context of the repeated conflicts with the French during the late 1600s.[105] That only Iroquois were eligible for membership, however, makes clear that cultural commonality was an important source of affinity and common identity. Drawn together by their heritage, the Iroquois fashioned a zone of stable peace that withstood successive challenges to its integrity. The confederation proved remarkably resilient, breaking down only after being subjected to the potent political divides that accompanied the American revolt against British rule.

[102] Lutz and other experts challenge this view. See Lutz, "The Iroquois Confederation Constitution," p. 99, note 1.
[103] Trigger quoted in Fenton, *The Great Law and the Longhouse*, p. 72; Lutz, "The Iroquois Confederation Constitution," p. 126.
[104] Fenton, *The Great Law and the Longhouse*, p. 389.
[105] Richter, *The Ordeal of the Longhouse*, p. 169.

THE EVOLUTION OF THE UNITED
ARAB EMIRATES FROM 1971

Numerous obstacles to political unification confronted the seven emirates that joined together in 1971 to form the United Arab Emirates (UAE). The individual emirates had only rudimentary political institutions. Indeed, the concept of a territorial state with fixed borders was a recent innovation, having been imported by the British during colonial rule to help apportion strategic responsibilities among ruling families. The drawing of boundary lines, coupled with the discovery of oil, led to competing territorial claims and armed conflict among ruling families. External threat further unsettled and divided the region; the small sheikhdoms in the lower Gulf differed about how best to counter the hegemonic ambitions of Saudi Arabia, Iran, and Iraq. Moreover, the emirates' economies were relatively undeveloped and there was minimal intraregional commerce.

Despite these obstacles, the seven emirates looked to a federal union as the best way to provide for their security when confronted in the 1960s with the end of colonial rule and the prospect of a British withdrawal. Most observers were initially dismissive, viewing the federalist ambitions of the emirates with decided skepticism.[106] As one respected observer of the region wrote in 1966, "there is no realistic possibility of the present Gulf rulers coming together of their own accord in any political grouping worth mentioning."[107] British and American policy makers were equally guarded about the prospects for a durable political union.[108]

The UAE defied the skeptics. Not only did the federation launched as the British withdrew bring an end to decades of armed strife, but territorial disputes and tribal rivalries readily subsided—in marked contrast to the instabilities that accompanied decolonization in many other areas. The union admittedly matured slowly; plans for revising its provisional constitution were repeatedly postponed, as were efforts to extend the powers of the federal government. Nonetheless, the UAE has thrived, not only locking in a zone of

---

[106] Frauke Heard-Bey, "The United Arab Emirates: Statehood and Nation-Building in a Traditional Society," *The Middle East Journal*, 59, no. 3 (Summer 2005): 358.

[107] Quote from David Holden, *Farewell to Arabia*, cited in Malcolm Peck, *The United Arab Emirates: A Venture in Unity* (Boulder, CO: Westview Press, 1986), p. 49.

[108] Christopher Davidson, *The United Arab Emirates: A Study in Survival* (Boulder: Lynne Rienner, 2005), pp. 48–49.

stable peace, but also capitalizing on its ample income from the export of oil and gas to build a modern state and a diversified economy.

Despite the lack of formal institutions of restraint within the individual emirates, tribal traditions of consultation and power-sharing played a prominent role in the onset of union. As in the case of the Iroquois Confederation, tribal forms of governance that operated at the local level were replicated in fashioning the bargains that led to stable peace. The ample profits afforded by its energy reserves also enabled Abu Dhabi to redistribute wealth among its partner emirates, providing a powerful incentive for them to join the union. The exercise of strategic restraint and the practice of a tribal form of constitutionalism thus cleared the way for stable peace. As in the other cases, compatible social orders and cultural commonality facilitated the onset of union.

How Peace Broke Out

In the early 1800s, pirates operating from the southeastern reaches of the Arabian Peninsula began attacking British shipping heading to and from India. Britain responded by concluding strategic accords with the tribal leaders of the region, who exercised power through a combination of patriarchal authority and economic leverage; they provided resources to those in need and collected taxes on income derived primarily from pearling, fishing, and date cultivation. Britain offered these leaders protection in return for their willingness to help eradicate piracy. As a consequence of the resulting compacts, the British came to call the grouping of sheikhdoms the Trucial Emirates. Although the tribes in question had been primarily nomadic, exercising authority over people rather than land, Britain's efforts to establish an effective division of labor prompted colonial officials to affiliate the most powerful family lines with specific territories. Because some communities professed loyalty to a ruling family that resided in a non-contiguous location, the seven emirates and the union they eventually formed emerged with an unusual patchwork of enclaves (see map 6.3).

Although successful in countering piracy, Britain's strategic alliances in the lower Gulf did not bring an end to the region's long-standing tribal rivalries. Internecine warfare and armed competition for the allegiance of subtribe groupings living in the hinterland were common well into the 1900s. In 1940, the two dominant sheikhdoms, Dubai and Abu Dhabi, went to war over ter-

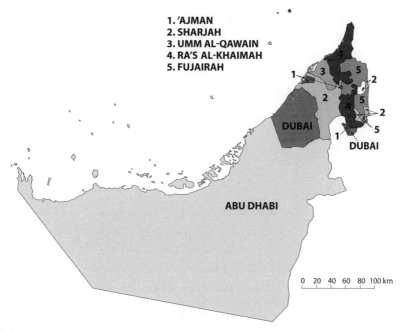

1. 'AJMAN
2. SHARJAH
3. UMM AL-QAWAIN
4. RA'S AL-KHAIMAH
5. FUJAIRAH

DUBAI

DUBAI

ABU DHABI

0 20 40 60 80 100 km

MAP 6.3 The United Arab Emirates
Source: http://commons.wikimedia.org/wiki/Image:UAE_en-MAP.png.

ritory as well as authority over Bedouins living in the interior. The discovery
of oil—exploration and the granting of concessions began in the 1920s, with
significant exports flowing by the 1960s—dramatically increased the economic significance of territorial claims, providing a new source of tribal competition. In response, the British assumed a more prominent role in oversee-
ing relations among the emirates, dispatching envoys to help draw borders,
establishing the Trucial Oman Scouts as a local military force under British
control, and regularly convening a council of the ruling sheikhs to facilitate
cooperation on political and strategic matters. The sheikhs looked to the
British for external protection as well as help in containing rivalries among
competing family lines.

Although British diplomacy and protection facilitated cooperation among
the emirates, it was the prospect of Britain's withdrawal from the region that
triggered efforts to fashion a political union among the sheikhdoms. Following London's announcement in 1968 that it intended to end its military presence in the Gulf, the emirates feared the intensification of local rivalries and

the potential threats posed by Iran and Saudi Arabia, both of which maintained territorial claims to lands that had been under British protection. The sheikhs initially tried to convince the British to reverse their decision, offering to compensate Britain for the costs of maintaining its presence in the Gulf.[109] When it became clear that London intended to proceed with withdrawal, mounting concern about external threats and the return of tribal conflict hastened attempts to replace the security provided by British protection with the stability potentially afforded by political union.[110]

The formal process of building and institutionalizing a federal union took shape around a nucleus of Abu Dhabi and Dubai. Sheikh Zayed bin Sultan Al-Nuhayyan of Abu Dhabi, and his counterpart in Dubai, Sheikh Rashid bin Sa'id Al-Maktum, met in February 1968. Abu Dhabi, by far the largest and wealthiest emirate, made the opening gambit. In an initial act of unilateral accommodation, it agreed to grant Dubai complete control over the disputed Fath oilfield.[111] The two leaders also agreed to forge a union whose main area of competence would be diplomacy and defense—a reflection of the strategic motivations behind the merger. Immediately thereafter, the leaders of the five smaller Trucial Emirates and of Qatar and Bahrain—both of which were also under British protection—gathered in Dubai with the aim of forming a nine-member federation. The ruling families of Dubai and Qatar were linked through marriage; Sheikh Rashid's son-in-law was the ruler of Qatar. Abu Dhabi had particularly close relations with Bahrain and had begun to use its currency in 1966.[112]

Power asymmetries were a potent obstacle from the outset. In order to offset disparities in population and wealth, an initial proposal called for the five smaller emirates—Sharjah, Ra's al-Khaimah, Fujairah, 'Ajman, and Umm al-Qawain—to forge a unitary polity which would be called the United Arab Coastal Emirates. This new state was to then enter into a five-member federation with Abu Dhabi, Dubai, Qatar, and Bahrain. The smaller emirates re-

---

[109] Davidson, *The United Arab Emirates*, p. 45.

[110] On the paramount role played by strategic necessity in motivating the push for union, see Ali Mohammed Khalifa, *The United Arab Emirates: Unity in Fragmentation* (Boulder, CO: Westview Press, 1979), pp. 14, 178; and Davidson, *The United Arab Emirates*, p. 44.

[111] Abdullah Omran Taryam, *The Establishment of the United Arab Emirates 1950–85* (London: Croom Helm, 1987), p. 90; and Frauke Heard-Bey, *From Trucial States to United Arab Emirates* (London: Longman, 1982), p. 341.

[112] Heard-Bey, *From Trucial States to United Arab Emirates*, p. 342.

jected the proposed merger mainly because it entailed the diminution of their influence and autonomy; they instead insisted on a federation of nine.

Although the nine leaders in principle reached agreement on the basic terms of union, the federation never got off the ground. Two main obstacles were at play. First, Iran maintained a territorial claim to Bahrain and insisted that it would not tolerate the island's inclusion in the federation. The Iranian Foreign Ministry pronounced that, "so long as the future status of Bahrain has not been legally clarified the Federation will under no circumstances be acceptable to Iran." Thereafter, the emirates of the lower Gulf were loath to launch a federation that would antagonize the region's predominant power. Second, the nine emirates ultimately failed to reach a consensus on the allocation of decision-making authority and how best to distribute power between the federal government and the individual members. Key sticking points included the location of the federal capital, voting weights in decision-making bodies, contributions to the federal budget, and the pace and scope of integration among the defense forces of the separate members.[113]

A UN survey released in the spring of 1970 revealed the preference of Bahrain's citizenry for independence, prompting Iran to drop its territorial claim. Rather than advancing the fortunes of the emerging federation, however, the settlement had the opposite effect. No longer needing the protective umbrella of union—and willing to insist on more favorable terms for participation in the federation—Bahrain backed out of the proposed federation and, in the middle of 1971, declared its independence. Qatar soon followed suit. Bahrain had been the center of British administration in the Gulf; its more developed political institutions eased its transition to independence. Qatar did not have the same institutional advantages. But it did have growing oil revenue and political support from Saudi Arabia, factors that encouraged it to follow Bahrain's lead.

Absent the political complications of including Bahrain and Qatar in the federation, Abu Dhabi and Dubai moved rapidly to establish the United Arab Emirates, which was formally proclaimed on December 2, 1971.[114] Ra's

[113] Heard-Bey, *From Trucial States to United Arab Emirates*, pp. 351–360 (quote from Iranian Foreign Ministry on p. 352); Davidson, *The United Arab Emirates*, pp. 47–48.

[114] Bahrain's prospective inclusion in the federation had been problematic not only because of Iranian objections. Bahrain had also argued that political influence in the federation should be proportional to population, a proposal that would have increased its voice at the expense of that of the smaller emirates. See Heard-Bey, *From Trucial States to United Arab Emirates*, p. 351.

al-Khaimah initially refused to join. The emirate expected to discover oil and was therefore unsatisfied with the political weight it would carry within the union. Ra's al-Khaimah was also disappointed that its prospective partners did not offer the emirate firmer backing in its standoff with Iran over the status of two offshore islands, the Greater and Less Tunbs. Its decision to forego union was, however, soon reversed. After several months of isolation, its ruler realized that the emirate would not fare well on its own, and Ra's al-Khaimah joined the UAE in February 1972.

The UAE got off to a slow start. Territorial disputes lingered, including one in 1972 between Sharjah and Fujairah that led to conflict and the loss of twenty lives. A quarrel between Dubai and Sharjah in 1975 proved to be the last major disagreement over territory; the active involvement of the federal government and the practice of mutual accommodation settled other outstanding disputes.[115] Even as strategic rivalry gave way to reciprocal restraint, centralization occurred haltingly. The provisional constitution adopted in 1971 was to have been revised and made permanent after five years, but the process was repeatedly delayed; a permanent constitution was not adopted until 1996. In similar fashion, the federal government was to have sole control over matters of defense, but it took more than two decades for the separate emirates to merge their forces into a federal army. Nonetheless, the exercise of strategic restraint and the institutionalization of a number of power-checking devices enabled the UAE to cohere as a zone of stable peace.

POWER-CHECKING DEVICES

The UAE rested on a political compact that had several core elements: wealth redistribution, a system of power-sharing that mixed constitutionalism and tribal patterns of governance, and defense integration. The self-binding and co-binding bargains struck on these issues were sufficiently credible to induce compliance and engender reciprocity among the individual emirates. But they were also sufficiently flexible to sustain union in the face of significant power asymmetries and the strong desire of the individual emirates to preserve a substantial degree of autonomy. Despite the autocratic nature of the union and the material preponderance of Abu Dhabi, the smaller emirates were able to impose significant brakes on the centralization of power. Indeed, the UAE survived in no small part because of its political weakness. Had the

---

[115] Khalifa, *The United Arab Emirates*, p. 102; Peck, *The United Arab Emirates*, p. 129.

founding president of the UAE, Sheikh Zayed of Abu Dhabi, insisted on greater federal control from the outset, the union would likely have foundered during its early years.[116]

The success of the UAE has to a significant degree been a product of a single core bargain: Abu Dhabi's willingness to trade money for power. To be sure, Abu Dhabi did practice unilateral accommodation on territorial and security issues. But its success in communicating benign intent to its smaller neighbors depended more heavily on economic largess than territorial concessions. As by far the largest and wealthiest emirate, Abu Dhabi not only assumed most of the costs of union, but also redistributed its oil income to enhance the prosperity of the other emirates. In return, the smaller emirates agreed to cede significant powers to Abu Dhabi—and, to a lesser extent, Dubai—effectively trading autonomy for prosperity. As Ali Mohammed Khalifa aptly observes, the UAE pursued "integration by dependence. . . . The flow of material rewards across state boundaries in generally one direction is probably the strongest and most obvious incentive in keeping the emirates together."[117]

Abu Dhabi constitutes roughly 85 percent of the territory of the UAE; it covers some 26,000 square miles, while the second largest emirate, Dubai, covers only 1,500.[118] When the union was founded in 1971, Abu Dhabi's annual oil income was roughly $450 million, Dubai's was $40 million, and the other emirates had no oil or gas. Well over 50 percent of the population lived in the two largest emirates; of 180,000 in total population, 46,000 citizens lived in Abu Dhabi and 59,000 in Dubai.[119] During the union's early years, Abu Dhabi covered over 90 percent of the union's budget, which represented roughly 25 percent of the emirate's expenditures.[120] As Dubai's economy has

---

[116] See Heard-Bey, *From Trucial States to United Arab Emirates*, p. 403; Heard-Bey, "The United Arab Emirates," p. 359; Taryam, *The Establishment of the United Arab Emirates*, p. 197. As discussed later in this chapter, the United Arab Republic represents an illustrative counter-example. This union of Egypt and Syria failed in large part because Egypt insisted on the prompt amalgamation of the two states' political and military institutions, readily leading to Syria's secession.

[117] Khalifa, *The United Arab Emirates*, p. 179.

[118] The size of the other emirates in square miles is: Sharjah—1000; Ra's al Khaimah—650; Fujairah—450; Umm al Qaiwain—300; 'Ajman—100. See Heard-Bey, *From Trucial States to United Arab Emirates*, p. 407.

[119] Heard-Bey, "The United Arab Emirates," p. 359.

[120] Khalifa, *The United Arab Emirates*, pp. 62–65.

grown, it has assumed a greater share of the federal budget, but Abu Dhabi has remained the UAE's primary benefactor.

Abu Dhabi not only assumed most of the costs of union, but also provided direct subsidies to the citizens of the new federation. A massive transfer of wealth from Abu Dhabi to the poorer emirates supported the construction of a modern infrastructure of urban centers, highways, and electricity and telecommunications grids. The federal government provided land, houses, and jobs to those in need. It even provided marriage funds to cover the cost of weddings among Emirati nationals. In some cases, such subventions came directly from Abu Dhabi to the recipients. In others, the funds were channeled through local elites so as not to threaten existing patronage systems. The result has been an effective scheme that engenders political allegiance through economic inducement: Abu Dhabi has provided affluence to the citizens of the UAE in return for their acceptance of the union and Abu Dhabi's political dominance of it. In the words of Christopher Davidson, "a material pact has emerged throughout the UAE, an unwritten and unspoken contract in which almost all of the population accept the legitimacy of the polity in exchange for the constancy and rewards of their well-paid employment."[121]

TRIBAL CONSTITUTIONALISM

The UAE's system of governance has rested on a unique mix of formalized constitutional restraint and informal networks of patronage emerging from a long history of tribal rule. Especially for a society with no liberal or democratic traditions and only rudimentary political institutions, that the seven emirates would embrace the principle and practice of codified political restraint was by no means a foregone conclusion. The founding constitution—the main text of which had been drafted in Qatar when it still expected to join the union—established federal institutions, specified their respective functions, and assigned the federal government responsibility for diplomacy and defense while leaving most other matters to the individual emirates. The constitution was provisional and was to be revised and made permanent after five years; prospective revisions were to address a number of issues, including contributions to the federal budget and defense integration. The location of the capital in Abu Dhabi was also temporary. Within seven years, a new capital was to be constructed on the border of Abu Dhabi and Dubai, symboliz-

---

[121] Davidson, *The United Arab Emirates*, p. 90.

ing the de-concentration of power and advancing integration between the two dominant emirates.[122]

The constitution established the Supreme Council as the top decision-making body, with each of the seven sheikhs having one vote. Substantive decisions required assent from five of the seven emirates, including Abu Dhabi and Dubai, granting them effective veto power. Cabinet positions were apportioned according to wealth and population. Abu Dhabi held the presidency plus six cabinet posts, Dubai held the vice presidency plus four cabinet posts (including prime minister), and the other emirates received portfolios ranging from one to three cabinet positions. A legislative body of sorts was also created—the Federal National Council—although its members were appointed and its function only advisory.

Despite the establishment of this formalized structure of power sharing, the UAE's seven leaders regularly relied on informal consultation and bargaining to govern. During the union's early years, the Supreme Council rarely met. Instead, Sheikh Zayed would consult with Dubai's leader, Sheikh Rashid, and the other heads of the ruling families to forge a consensus on policy. In many respects, tribal political culture trumped the constitutional order, replicating at the union level the patrimonial patterns of authority and patronage that operated within each emirate. As Davidson observes, the UAE's system of governance has been notable for "the continuing relevance of kinship loyalties both inside and outside of the immediate ruling family, the ongoing need for powerful tribal support."[123]

Governing through consultation and compromise has long been a hallmark of tribal leadership in the Gulf. The position of tribal head has not been hereditary; instead, influential figures from prominent families select the leader on the basis of personal charisma and his ability to command respect and authority. The individual chosen does not wield absolute power, but is instead an arbiter who is responsible for fashioning a governing consensus. As one member of the cabinet commented in 1999, "[Zayed's] leadership is based on consensus among the seven emirates. In keeping with Islamic tradition, he

[122] Ra's al Khaimah had argued that the new capital be constructed on the border between Sharjah and Dubai, checking Abu Dhabi's power and strengthening the influence of the smaller northern emirates. That plan was rejected and a decision was ultimately made to make Abu Dhabi the permanent capital. See Taryam, *The Establishment of the United Arab Emirates*, p. 131.

[123] Christopher M. Davidson, "After Shaikh Zayed: The Politics of Succession in Abu Dhabi and the UAE," *Middle East Policy* 8, no. 1 (Spring 2006): 55.

is seen as first among equals, continuing to serve as president because he commands the respect of the nation's other leaders and the reverence of the people."[124]

Just as material incentive played an important role in sustaining the union's core political compact, the power wielded by the UAE's leaders depended not just on tribal patterns of authority, but also on the astute allocation of political rewards. Sheikh Zayed and his counterparts regularly appointed influential individuals to federal and emirate-level positions as a means of political cooptation. As Khalifa describes the composition of the first cabinet, "Notably, most of the cabinet members appointed were either members of the ruling families of the member emirates or citizens aligned with such families in the configuration of tribal politics in the area."[125] The ruling families as well as influential figures in other important family lines have regularly filled sub-cabinet posts and staffed the bureaucracy. Davidson labels such postings "consolation prizes"—incentives for those not part of the inner circle to nonetheless buy into the system.[126] Marriages have also been used frequently to consolidate networks of loyalty and to fashion alliances among powerful families. In general, ruling families have dealt with rivals by coopting them, not excluding them from power, one of the main reasons that the federation has been able to avoid paralyzing disputes among rival patrimonial factions.[127]

Despite the influence that came with this potent combination of material inducement and political patronage, Sheikh Zayed enjoyed only limited success in strengthening federal institutions during the union's first two decades. The other emirates—Dubai in particular—staunchly resisted his efforts to regularize their contributions to the federal budget. In 1976, Zayed threatened to resign—and offered to move the capital—in a futile effort to convince the Supreme Council that each emirate should contribute 75 percent of its oil income to the union budget. A solution emerged five years later when Sheikh Rashid, who was already vice president, was also granted the post of prime minister. In return, he agreed to contribute 50 percent of Dubai's oil revenue to the federal budget.[128]

---

[124] Quote in Davidson, *The United Arab Emirates*, p. 72.

[125] Khalifa, *The United Arab Emirates*, p. 60.

[126] Davidson, *The United Arab Emirates*, p. 73.

[127] For examples of such cooptation, see Davidson, *The United Arab Emirates*, pp. 99–100.

[128] Davidson, *The United Arab Emirates*, pp. 201–204; and Heard-Bey, "The United Arab Emirates," pp. 362–366.

Centralized control over foreign and security policy was similarly elusive. As detailed below, it was not until 1996 that the emirates' separate militias were integrated into a union defense force. And even on matters of diplomacy, the UAE did not always operate as a unitary state. During the Iran-Iraq war, Abu Dhabi tilted toward Iraq, while Dubai, primarily for commercial reasons, tilted toward Iran. Abu Dhabi joined OPEC while Dubai did not, saddling Abu Dhabi with the task of adjusting its output to meet the UAE's overall quotas. For these reasons, some scholars of the UAE contend that the union functioned as a looser confederation, not a unitary polity, until the consolidation of the 1990s. From this perspective, it was only after more than two decades of de jure federation that the separate emirates were prepared to sacrifice their de facto autonomy in the name of union.

DEFENSE INTEGRATION

The provisional constitution gave the federal government unequivocal and undivided authority over matters of national defense. Nonetheless, the centralization of control over defense forces proceeded quite slowly. During the UAE's early years, the Ministry of Defense controlled only the Union Defense Force—the new name of the Trucial Oman Scouts that had been established by the British. Abu Dhabi, Dubai, Sharjah, and Ra's al-Khaimah all maintained independent militias, as permitted under Article 142 of the constitution. Abu Dhabi had by far the largest and most capable military, one of the main reasons the other emirates feared that a merger effectively meant absorption into Abu Dhabi's military establishment rather than the creation of a joint force that represented the union as a collective whole.[129] In 1976, a de jure merger did occur, but it was primarily cosmetic in nature. Even though all forces began to wear the same uniform and regional commands under the Ministry of Defense replaced the separate militias, the boundaries of the new commands fell along political lines, effectively leaving the emirates in control of their own militias.[130] It was not until 1997, following the adoption of a permanent constitution, that Dubai finally disbanded its own force and integrated it into a federal military fully controlled by the Ministry of Defense in Abu Dhabi.

It thus took more than twenty years for the Ministry of Defense to establish effective control over the military forces maintained by the individual

[129] Khalifa, *The United Arab Emirates*, pp. 81–82.
[130] Heard-Bey, *From Trucial States to United Arab Emirates*, p. 394.

emirates. Despite the authority granted the federal government by the constitution and the repeated efforts of Abu Dhabi to centralize defense policy, the smaller emirates remained unwilling to cede control of their independent militias. Sheikh Zayed's patience on this issue was a reflection of his consensus-oriented approach to governance and of his awareness that moving slowly on the question of defense integration was essential to ensuring the viability of the union.

SOCIETAL INTEGRATION AND GENERATION OF A NATIONAL IDENTITY

The UAE's emergence did not result from growing economic and societal interdependence. Prior to the 1970s, there was very little commerce among the seven emirates. After the decline of the pearling industry in the 1930s, the region's middle class dwindled, weakening the one constituency with a vested interest in intraregional economic integration. Trade among the emirates was also stymied by the absence of a transportation infrastructure. At the time of the union's founding in 1971, there was not even an asphalt road connecting Abu Dhabi and Dubai. The road network from the coast to the interior—and especially across the Hajjar Mountains to the UAE's territory on the Gulf of Oman—was even more rudimentary.

Funded by Abu Dhabi's oil revenues, the UAE's road network expanded markedly after the founding of the union. Modern highways soon linked the major urban areas along the northern coast, and a paved road crossing the Hajjar Mountains opened in 1976. This transportation network made possible the ambitious infrastructure projects and development programs launched by Sheikh Zayed to consolidate his political power and secure the allegiance of the poorer emirates. Even after the emirates were linked by modern highways and telecommunications networks, however, inter-emirate commerce remained low, with each emirate focused principally on developing foreign trade. In this respect, the prospect of largess and redistribution, not of commercial integration, remained the primary inducement making possible the deepening of the union.

The low levels of intra-union trade are partly due to the emirates' similar economies; they export energy and import commodities and tourists. But continuing rivalry among the emirates also played a role, as made clear by the development of the UAE's airline industry. Despite their proximity, Dubai, Sharjah, and Abu Dhabi have all built major international airports. Gulf Air, a joint venture with Bahrain, was originally meant to be the UAE's main carrier. But Dubai then decided to launch Emirates Airways. Not to be outdone, Abu Dhabi in 2003 established Etihad Airways, calling it the UAE's "national carrier." That a country of roughly 4.3 million people has established three major airlines is a testament to the tenacity of the political dividing lines that still shape the commercial strategies of the individual emirates.[131]

The persistence of local loyalties was also an impediment to the propagation of a union-wide identity. Despite their common religion, language, and culture, the communities that came together to form the UAE embraced identities defined primarily by tribal loyalties. Allegiance to a territorially defined emirate, not to mention to a federal union, was both novel and alien. There was a weak sense of shared identity even within individual emirates, especially in the interior, where communities were smaller, more isolated, and more distant from centers of political authority.

After the launch of the UAE, federal authorities were well aware of the need to pursue initiatives that would help build an inclusive, union-wide political identity. Investment in transportation and communications infrastructure was intended not just to improve economic conditions, but also to provide a psychological link among separate communities. Channeling financial largess through local leaders represented a means of "lifting" patronage systems to the union level; if a family or tribal leader directed his allegiance to Abu Dhabi, those who directed their allegiance to him would follow suit. Federal authorities also sought to strengthen a sense of communal identity through the usual symbols and practices of sovereignty: a flag, anthem, national holidays, and national education system. So too did they seek to expropriate from the past a defining set of cultural practices that would help shape a national identity. Camel racing, traditional dress, and conservative Islamic social codes played an important role in this respect.[132]

The UAE has faced a unique challenge in building an inclusive sense of community: a population in which citizens represent a distinct minority. At the time of the federation's founding, expatriates already represented some 60 percent of the workforce. That number has since risen steadily. Today, expatriates constitute over 90 percent of the workforce, representing about 85 percent of the UAE's resident population.[133] The presence of so many for-

[131] Davidson, *The United Arab Emirates*, p. 166.
[132] Davidson, *The United Arab Emirates*, pp. 77–82.
[133] These figures represent estimates; reliable census data are unavailable. See U.S. State De-

eigners has on balance made it easier for Emirati nationals to self-identify as a national grouping; the out-group is the large foreign population, not clans or tribes among Emiratis themselves. As Frauke Heard-Bey comments, the population imbalance "has helped to build a nation state out of the individual tribally-based emirates."[134] At the same time, dependence on expatriate workers has created a very diverse society, one that risks diluting a strong national identity and the social cohesion that accompanies it. Reliance on expatriate professionals in ministries and other influential institutions has also elicited resentment among nationals unqualified for positions requiring advanced education.

During the union's early years, the persistence of political loyalties to individual tribes and their ruling families contributed to the tenacious resistance of efforts to centralize power in federal institutions. As loyalties and identities have gradually been transferred to the union level, such resistance has diminished, one of the reasons that the federation has gradually been able to tighten its control over most policy areas, including the budget and the military. An informal survey conducted in 2002 revealed that almost 80 percent of UAE citizens feel greater loyalty to the union than to the emirate in which they live. Only in Dubai did a majority of those polled express a greater sense of loyalty to their emirate.[135]

Why Peace Broke Out

As in almost all the other cases in this book, the UAE was born of strategic necessity. Confronted with Britain's imminent withdrawal from the Persian Gulf, the emirates looked to political union to provide collective defense (Iran and Saudi Arabia posed pressing external threats) and regional peace (the tribes of the lower Gulf had a long history of conflict with each other). Britain used its leverage as an imperial power to help lay the groundwork by facilitating cooperation among the Trucial Emirates and by encouraging federation as it prepared for withdrawal.

If strategic necessity precipitated the search for union, what factors made it possible? Of the three conditions that usually contribute to the onset of sta-

partment, Bureau of Near Eastern Affairs, October 2006, "Background Note: United Arab Emirates," p. 1; Davidson, *The United Arab Emirates*, pp. 145–146.

[134] Heard-Bey, "The United Arab Emirates," p. 361.
[135] Davidson, *The United Arab Emirates*, p. 84.

ble peace, the individual emirates that joined together in union lacked institutionalized restraint, but enjoyed compatible social orders and cultural commonality. Neither the emirates that formed the UAE nor the union itself were democratic or liberal. Studies that rank countries according to their levels of freedom and democracy regularly put the UAE near the bottom of the list. Furthermore, the consolidation of the union has neither been facilitated by nor produced a process of political liberalization. If anything, domestic governance has become more illiberal over time, largely in response to the influx of expatriates, the intensification of Islamic extremism and Iranian ambition, and the unsettled regional environment stemming from the Iran-Iraq war, Iraq's invasion of Kuwait, and the U.S.-led invasion of Iraq in 2003.

Two factors have helped compensate for the absence of liberal restraint among the emirates. First, the combination of Abu Dhabi's substantial oil revenues and the UAE's relatively small population meant that wealth redistribution provided the smaller emirates a powerful incentive to enter the union and acquiesce to the loss of autonomy that federation entailed. The allure of settling festering territorial disputes and banding together against external threats provided a motivation for cooperation. But the prospect of substantial economic reward was the primary incentive behind the smaller emirates' readiness to accept the political hegemony of Abu Dhabi.

Second, although the individual emirates lacked formal institutions of political restraint, the power-checking devices adopted by the UAE in important respects replicated the tribal forms of constitutionalism that operated at the local level. As in the Iroquois Confederation, the traditions of communal deliberation and consensual decision making that characterized tribal politics were imported into the governing practices of the union.[136] To be sure, the authority of the Supreme Council has been checked by neither democratic accountability nor a separation of powers among independent institutions of government. Nonetheless, decision making within the Supreme Council has abided by the rules of the constitution. Sheikh Zayed's powers were hardly absolute, as made clear by his succession of failed attempts to revise the constitution and centralize the union. Tribal traditions of consultation and consensus meant that power was diffused and authority shared despite the absence of formal checks and balances. These traditions, more than

---

[136] Although both the UAE and the Iroquois Confederation benefited from tribal traditions of power sharing, the Iroquois nations embraced institutionalized restraint (such as village councils and procedures for selecting and approving sachems) while the tribes of the lower Gulf did not.

formal constitutional constraints, were the main source of the practices of self-binding and co-binding that made union possible.

All seven emirates enjoyed the same social order; wealth, as well as power, has generally fallen along family lines. Especially after the demise of the middle class following the decline of the pearl trade, families that wielded power also tended to be those that amassed wealth. The discovery of oil only strengthened the linkage between power and affluence. Ruling families not only prospered, but they were able to consolidate their power by redistributing wealth to less advantaged citizens. In this respect, the onset of union strengthened rather than undermined the traditional social order.

The rise of the UAE as a commercial hub as well as an energy exporter, even though it has meant greater wealth, has threatened this traditional social order by empowering and enriching the country's large expatriate community. Steps have been taken to ensure that nationals benefit from the dramatic expansion of commercial enterprises; by law, Emiratis have had to own at least 51 percent of all firms.[137] The effective subsidization of the national population might leave citizens prosperous, but it also provides them little upward mobility—especially in light of the influx of educated and highly skilled foreigners. According to Davidson, "citizenship in the UAE has become a financial asset, thus removing any need for meaningful and productive service."[138] Over time, such conditions could instill resentment among nationals and create a sense that they are being disenfranchised in their own country. The prospect of this destabilizing outcome is one of the reasons that the leadership has been pushing to diversify the economy and ensure that a larger percentage of the citizenry pursue advanced education, thereby opening up opportunities for higher-level employment.

Finally, the emirates that came together to form the UAE enjoyed a common culture. The peoples of the Trucial Emirates were Arab, Arabic-speakers, and predominantly Sunni Muslims. Furthermore, there were strong ties of consanguinity that cut across political boundaries. Indeed, the ruling families of Abu Dhabi and Dubai both trace their roots to the Bani Yas tribe. Rivalry between the two emirates began only in the nineteenth century when Dubai's ruling family seceded from the tribal hierarchy. Virtually all scholars

---

[137] In June 2007, the UAE announced that it intended to allow majority foreign ownership in some sectors. See Simon Kerr, "UAE Aims to Open up to Foreign Ownership," *Financial Times*, June 12, 2007.

[138] Davidson, *The United Arab Emirates*, p. 187.

of the UAE view this common culture as central to explaining the UAE's success. As Malcom Peck observes, "A common political culture, rooted in traditional Arab and Islamic values and a broadly shared history, linked all seven emirates."[139] Khalifa writes, "The existence of a common culture seems to have molded the political culture of . . . elites in a certain way. Their political ideology and outlook are more or less identical."[140] Cultural commonality, along with compatible social orders and tribal constitutionalism, thus served as the main ingredients of the UAE's successful emergence as a zone of stable peace.

THE RISE AND DEMISE OF THE UNITED
ARAB REPUBLIC, 1958–1961

The territory of present-day Syria was for centuries one of the primary targets of Egypt's geopolitical ambitions. Egypt's last military occupation of the area ended in 1840. The eastern Mediterranean was then the object of British and French imperialism until World War II. Thereafter, the relationship between Syria and Egypt evolved within a regional setting defined by the Cold War, the Arab-Israeli conflict, and pan-Arab nationalism.

After Egypt's Free Officers movement overthrew the country's constitutional monarchy in 1952, Gamal Abdul Nasser gradually asserted control over the government and sought to establish Egypt as the region's dominant player and the leader of pan-Arabism. Meanwhile, the stability of the Syrian government was compromised by factional rivalries, which also produced an erratic foreign policy. Relations between Syria and Egypt were not openly hostile, but Nasser persistently feared that entente between Iraq and Syria would jeopardize Cairo's bid for regional hegemony.[141]

The conclusion of the Baghdad Pact in 1955 proved to be a turning point in relations between Cairo and Damascus. Turkey and Iraq were the initial members of the U.S.-inspired alliance to contain Soviet expansionism. Iran, Pakistan, and Britain joined soon thereafter. Nasser opposed the Baghdad Pact as an instrument of Western imperialism, a view that won many adher-

---

[139] Peck, *The United Arab Emirates*, p. 120.

[140] Khalifa, *The United Arab Emirates*, pp. 128–129.

[141] Elie Podeh, *The Decline of Arab Unity: The Rise and Fall of the United Arab Republic* (Brighton: Sussex Academic Press, 1999), p. 30.

ents in Damascus. Egypt and Syria responded by forging a mutual defense pact in 1955, a move that led to building levels of strategic cooperation, culminating in the sudden and unexpected formation of the United Arab Republic (UAR) early in 1958. The UAR was founded as a unitary state, not a looser federation. The governments as well as the militaries of the two countries were merged. Syria and Egypt were to abandon their separate institutions and identities; Syria became the "Northern Region" and Egypt the "Southern Region" of the UAR. The new state was to advance the cause of Arab unity while serving as a bulwark against superpower influence in the Middle East.

This radical experiment in Arab unity did not last long. Following a military coup in Damascus in September 1961, Syria seceded from the UAR. Nasser promptly dispatched troops to preserve the union, but then aborted the mission when he realized that the Syrian army supported the rebels. Salvaging the union would have required Egypt's military occupation of Syria, a step that would hardly have furthered the cause of Arab unity. How did the UAR rise and fall in such short order? What enabled the union to form so suddenly, but also to unravel so quickly?

Paradoxically, the principal ingredient of the union's formation—Nasser's uncompromising leadership—was also the main cause of its demise. From the outset, Nasser insisted on maintaining tight control over the union, enabling two states with little history of cooperation and no common border to cohere into a unitary state. But it was also Egypt's unchecked domination of the UAR that alienated each of the social groupings in Syria, including the military, that had initially backed the merger. As Cairo's insistence on unitary control disempowered and disaffected Syria's old and new elite alike, Nasser effectively sowed the seeds of the UAR's demise. Absent the practice of strategic restraint by the union's dominant state—Egypt's population was over 25 million, compared with roughly 4 million in Syria, and its territory about five times that of Syria—Damascus came to see the UAR as little more than an instrument of Egyptian hegemony.

Exacerbating the tension between the two regions of the union was their incompatible social orders. Whereas Egypt had a centralized and socialized economy, Syria's was open and decentralized, with large landholders and a merchant class together representing the economic elite. When Nasser tried to export Egypt's political economy to Syria, he ran up against fierce resistance from both landholders and the business community. Rather than having the intended effect of undermining the old elite, the imposition of agrarian reform, the nationalization of banks, and state control of exchange rates and prices only ensured that Syria's economic elites teamed up with its disaffected military to break away from the UAR.

How Peace Broke Out

Beginning in 1956, prominent members of the Syrian Ba'ath Party and their allies in the Syrian officer corps together took the lead in advancing the idea of forming a federal union with Egypt. Their main motivation was to undercut the growing power of Syria's communists and forestall the country's descent into domestic chaos. The Ba'ath, due to their socialist orientation, and the younger officer corps, due to their affinity for Nasser's military background, assumed that federation with Egypt would further their political fortunes. Other influential sectors of Syrian society soon rallied behind the idea of union with Egypt. In an effort to outflank the Ba'ath Party's endorsement of federation and its appeal to Arab solidarity, the communists called for Syria and Egypt to merge into a unitary state. Even traditional elites—landowners, the middle class, and that segment of the officer corps hailing from privileged families—backed union with Egypt as the safest way to prevent domestic upheaval and the challenge it would pose to their economic and political power.[142]

By 1957, all of Syria's elite groupings, albeit for their own self-interested reasons, had come to back a political merger with Egypt. Such widespread support for union also made clear that Syrians had generally embraced a benign image of Egyptian leadership. By opposing the Baghdad Pact and confronting Israel and European "imperialism" during the Suez Crisis, Nasser had advanced his goal of putting himself at the forefront of the pan-Arab movement. Amid rising enthusiasm for pan-Arab nationalism throughout the region, Syrian elites saw close ties with Nasser as a means of strengthening their own domestic legitimacy. They feared the potential loss of autonomy that would accompany union, but believed the sacrifice was necessary to prevent the country's political fragmentation.

With a consensus in favor of union having formed in Damascus, the Syrian

[142] See Podeh, *The Decline of Arab Unity*, pp. 31–38; and James Jankowski, *Nasser's Egypt, Arab Nationalism, and the United Arab Republic* (Boulder, CO: Lynne Rienner, 2002), pp. 101–105.

parliament sent an exploratory mission to Cairo in December 1957. Nasser, however, rebuffed the overture, maintaining his previous position that any formal institutional linkage between Syria and Egypt was at least five years off and that he "was not thinking in terms of federation or confederation for the present.[143] Damascus persisted. In January 1958, a delegation of army officers, with the backing of the Ba'ath Party, went to Cairo to press Nasser. As a result of this mission, the Egyptian leader unexpectedly assented to union on January 20.

Nasser's initial motivations for forging close political and military ties with Syria were primarily geopolitical in nature. After the conclusion of the Baghdad Pact, Cairo was intent on ensuring that Iraq did not succeed in luring Syria into a Western orbit. Nasser was equally committed to preempting Syria's drift toward the Soviet Union. In 1957, he deployed 2,000 Egyptian troops to Syria to preserve domestic calm and prevent the communists from aligning Damascus with Moscow. Initially, Nasser calculated that such moves, along with the defense pact concluded in 1955, would be sufficient to keep Syria on a more neutral, pan-Arabist path; Egypt therefore did not need to accept the risks and burdens of formal union. Eventually, however, Nasser came to the conclusion that he would compromise his credentials as the leader of pan-Arab nationalism if he continued to reject Syria's repeated requests for a merger. Having consolidated his power by establishing himself as the Middle East's leading proponent of pan-Arab unity, he ultimately felt compelled to accede to Damascus's overtures. Nasser also remained worried about domestic instability in Syria and its potential alignment with Moscow.[144]

Nasser was well aware that Syria's internal divides would pose major challenges to a merger with Egypt; he admitted in private that union would be a "big headache."[145] Accordingly, Nasser made his offer contingent on four conditions: the resulting polity would be a unitary state, not a federation, assuring Cairo of adequate control; the Syrian army would withdraw from politics; all of Syria's political parties would disband; and referenda would be held in both countries to approve the union. The Syrians accepted all the conditions except one. Uneasy that Egypt would dominate a unitary state,

[143] Jankowski, *Nasser's Egypt*, p. 103.
[144] Jankowski, *Nasser's Egypt*, pp. 109–111.
[145] Jankowski, *Nasser's Egypt*, p. 114.

they asked Nasser to accept instead a federal structure. Nasser refused, Damascus acquiesced, and the UAR was proclaimed on February 1, 1958.

Parliamentary ratification and popular referenda followed. In a speech laying out the rationale for union before the Egyptian parliament on February 5, Nasser stressed two main themes: that Arab unity was a strategic necessity if the region was to resist domination by outside powers, and that Egypt and Syria shared a common history and culture. The crusaders, the Ottomans, Europe's colonial empires, the Cold War superpowers—the past and present made it amply clear that only if the "whole region was united for reasons of mutual security" would it be able to turn back external threats. A union between Egypt and Syria was a logical starting point, according to Nasser, because "the history of Cairo, in its main lines, is the history also of Damascus. The details may differ, but the essential factors are the same: the same states, the same invaders, the same kings, the same hearts and the same martyrs." Nasser went on to say that, "The road to this union between Egypt and Syria was paved through by a number of far-reaching factors. These were identity of nature, history, race, language, religions, beliefs, as well as common security and independence."[146] Such arguments received positive responses from legislators and citizens alike. By the end of February, lawmakers as well as publics in both Syria and Egypt approved the union by wide margins. The UAR was off to an impressive start.

The Demise of Union

Nasser's intransigence readily settled the initial disagreement between Syria and Egypt as to whether union should take the form of a unitary state or a federation. Nonetheless, discord over this issue was an early indication of the looming power struggle between Cairo and Damascus that would ultimately lead to the demise of the UAR. At the outset, Syria—which was called the "Northern Region" after the formation of the UAR—did have at least a semblance of autonomy. A central cabinet in Cairo would manage union-wide issues, such as diplomacy and defense. Meanwhile, each of the UAR's two regions would have its own cabinet to handle local policy matters such as domestic security, finance, and justice. In reality, however, Syria's ostensible

---

[146] Gamal Abdel Nasser, "A United Arab Republic," *Vital Speeches of the Day* 24, Issue 11 (March 15, 1958): 327.

autonomy failed to materialize. The central cabinet, which was comprised of one Syrian and eight Egyptians, took effective control of all major policy areas. As Elie Podeh notes, "The composition of the central cabinet assured that Egypt would dominate not only federal issues (i.e., military and foreign affairs) but also regional (such as economy and education)."[147]

The power of Syria's political elites had already been weakened by Nasser's insistence that the army remove itself from politics and that the country's parties be dissolved. Nasser then went one step further by appointing to positions in Cairo prominent Ba'ath Party members and Syrian army officers, detaching them from their bases of power in Damascus. Ostensibly a promotion, these transfers proved to be just the opposite; the new posts in the UAR government were devoid of significant responsibility. To further weaken the political influence of the Syrian military—which after union was called the UAR's First Army—the officer corps was purged and hundreds of Egyptian officers were sent to serve in Syria to keep watch over its armed forces. Meanwhile, Nasser sought to establish effective control of public debate in Syria. Eight of nineteen newspapers were closed and Syria's broadcasting system was integrated with Egypt's.[148] Domestic repression also increased, with Nasser ordering the arrest of hundreds of communists late in 1958.

It was not enough for Cairo to dominate the union's political institutions; for Nasser, integrating Syria into the UAR also meant restructuring its economy in Egypt's image. By the late 1950s, Egypt had already embraced agrarian reform—decisively breaking the power of the landed elite—and nationalized many companies, establishing a centralized, state-led economy. As Podeh notes, "The old elite was economically dispossessed, socially displaced, and politically overthrown." In contrast, Syria's economy was dominated by large landholders—over 80 percent of Syria's rural population owned either no land or only a small plot—and by a middle class whose commercial success depended upon private ownership, open trade, and a convertible currency.[149]

Late in 1958, Nasser set about replicating in Syria the transformation that had occurred in Egypt. Agrarian reform dramatically limited the size of landholdings, opening up vast tracts to be distributed among the peasantry. Import tariffs were also imposed on luxury goods. The immediate result was the

[147] Podeh, *The Decline of Arab Unity*, p. 52.
[148] J.S.F. Parker, "The United Arab Republic," *International Affairs* 38, no. 1 (January, 1962): 21; Podeh, *The Decline of Arab Unity*, pp. 53–55; and Jankowski, *Nasser's Egypt*, pp. 115–118.
[149] Podeh, *The Decline of Arab Unity*, pp. 19, 75.

disaffection of both the landed elite and the middle class. Moreover, these two sectors of the economy did not capitulate, but instead mounted an effort to block the reform program. According to Podeh, "the law failed to achieve its main aim: to crush the power of the traditional landowning and commercial élites. On the contrary, it succeeded in alienating these powerful groups."[150]

By the end of the UAR's first year, discontent with the union was mounting across Syrian society. The Ba'ath Party and its allies in the officer corps had presumed that they would be the primary beneficiaries of union, but they ended up as functionaries, assigned to prestigious, but hollow, posts. The communists had backed Nasser's call for an amalgamation of Syria and Egypt, but many of them ended up in jail. The landed elites and the middle class had supported union as the best way to prevent domestic chaos. Their calculation turned out to be accurate, but domestic order was coming at the expense of their own economic interests. Nasser had done an impressive job of alienating all the main social sectors that had initially supported union.

Cairo's initial reaction to the growing disaffection was to devolve more autonomy to Syria, but only on the surface. Nasser expanded the size of the regional and central cabinets and increased the number of ministers from Syria. But he also enhanced the power of the central cabinet—which was still in the firm control of Egyptians—ensuring that the regional cabinets were only subordinate, administrative bodies. When it became clear that Syrian resistance to Cairo's domination of the union was not abating, Nasser dispatched Field Marshall Abdul Hakim Amer to Damascus, effectively appointing the Egyptian officer as a "viceroy" and investing him with virtually unchecked executive power. Many Syrians saw Amer's appointment as a move that eliminated the last vestiges of their political influence within the union.[151]

Soon thereafter, prominent Ba'athists began to resign from the UAR government, complaining that their roles in shaping policy were "a mere formality."[152] Once again, Nasser responded to Syrian discontent by tightening his grip. More Egyptians were dispatched to Damascus to staff the bureaucracy. Worried about the loyalty of the First Army, Nasser sent additional Egyptian officers to fill its ranks. At the time, he told the U.S. ambassador in Cairo that he had succeeded in "destroying the political char-

[150] Podeh, *The Decline of Arab Unity*, p. 79.
[151] Jankowski, *Nasser's Egypt*, pp. 119–125.
[152] Podeh, *The Decline of Arab Unity*, p. 102.

acter of the Army through transfers and retirements and the stationing of
Egyptian officers in the Northern Region."[153] Cairo also stepped up efforts to
centralize Syria's economy, ending the currency's free convertibility, introduc-
ing price controls, and mandating that all banks be Arab-owned. These measures only intensified Syrian disaffection with the UAR, especially within the
business community.

Nasser's final effort to crush Syrian resistance to Cairo's domination of the
union came during the second half of 1961. He mandated the nationalization
of all banks and insurance companies. Nasser abolished both regional cabinets, formalizing the reality that they had no meaningful role. To the degree
that any Syrian wielded significant influence in Damascus, it was Abdul
Hamid Sarraj, who had been running the Ministry of the Interior. Sarraj had
a strong base of local support, in large part due to the repressive security apparatus that he oversaw. Precisely because of Sarraj's independent influence
in Damascus, however, Nasser in August appointed him as one of the UAR's
vice presidents, necessitating that he move to Cairo. After realizing that he
too had been given a hollow post, Sarraj resigned in September and returned
to Damascus.

Soon after Sarraj's resignation, a small group of officers from the First Army—with the political and financial backing of the business community—
carried out a coup. They seized the airport, communications centers, and
other strategic points in Damascus while detaining officers who might be
loyal to Cairo. Initially, the rebels sought to preserve the UAR, but insisted
on major changes to the union: the economic program of agrarian reform
and nationalization had to be dismantled, and the UAR had to be transformed into a federal union, with Syria and Egypt enjoying equal political
status. Nasser immediately rejected these terms and ordered the dispatch of
Egyptian forces to join loyal units of the First Army in putting down the rebellion. Syria promptly seceded from the UAR. When Nasser soon thereafter
realized that most units of the First Army backed secession, he recalled his
troops and accepted Syria's withdrawal from the union.[154]

The main cause of the UAR's demise was the pronounced political imbalance between Syria and Egypt and Nasser's ultimate emasculation—and
consequent alienation—of all influential sectors of Syrian society. From the
outset, Nasser's dominating and domineering brand of politics led to disaf-

[153] Podeh, *The Decline of Arab Unity*, p. 114.
[154] Podeh, *The Decline of Arab Unity*, pp. 148–151.

fection among Ba'athists, communists, and army officers, while his economic reforms did the same among the economic elite. Rather than exercising strategic restraint and giving the Northern Region a level of autonomy commensurate with Syrian expectations, Cairo did just the opposite, progressively tightening centralized control over the union and provoking only stiffer opposition. As J.S.F. Parker observes, "it is Egyptian institutions, methods, organizations, and planning that have spread to Syria, and not vice versa; it would be hard to think of any specifically Syrian element that has been worked into the overall running of the country."[155] Moshe Ma'oz agrees that "Egypt was guided by a hegemonic concept that led it to dominate the union politically and economically."[156]

By failing to appreciate the importance of strategic restraint and the institutionalization of the power-checking devices that would have enabled Syrians to retain at least some control over their own affairs, Nasser did the impossible: he united Syria's fractious political system. Syrians turned to union with Egypt in part because the country was deeply divided and headed for chaos; each of its powerful political groupings looked to the UAR to strengthen its position against the other. But by trying to disempower all of them, Nasser brought them together in opposition to the UAR. In 1958, Syrian elites and the public alike looked to Egypt to provide the benign leadership that would ensure stability, freedom from superpower coercion, and Arab unity. By 1961, they saw Egyptian leadership as synonymous with domination and oppression.

SOCIETAL INTEGRATION AND THE GENERATION OF A COMMON IDENTITY

Societal integration did more to undermine than to consolidate the UAR. Trade between the two regions of the union did increase substantially due to both the dropping of internal tariffs and political efforts to encourage commerce. Nonetheless, bilateral trade remained a marginal share of total trade for both Syria and Egypt. The absence of a land border meant that all goods had to be shipped by either sea or air. And Syria, with its privatized economy and open borders, had already developed thriving commercial links with its immediate neighbors.[157] Moreover, the benefits of a marginal increase in bilateral trade were more than offset by the fact that union had an adverse im-

[155] Parker, "The United Arab Republic," p. 19.
[156] Podeh, *The Decline of Arab Unity*, p. x.
[157] Jankowski, *Nasser's Egypt*, pp. 132–134. See also Amitai Etzioni, *Political Unification: A*

pact on Syria's economic elite. Not only were agrarian reform and the nationalization of the private sector resisted and resented, but new tariffs, price controls, and currency regulation led to capital flight and distorted trade with Syria's traditional markets, Lebanon in particular. As a result, opposition to the union among landed elites and merchants alike intensified as these economic reforms advanced.[158]

Societal contact between Syrians and Egyptians also did more to weaken than to strengthen the union. Most of the prominent Syrians posted to Cairo had little, if any, meaningful influence on policy, having been appointed by Nasser primarily to separate them from their power bases in Damascus. They came to resent the union and their Egyptian "overlords." Thousands of Egyptians relocated to Syria to govern the Northern Region, serve in the army, and staff the bureaucracy. Within the context of Syria's supplicant role within the union, however, Syrians readily begrudged their presence. Especially within the ranks of the First Army, Syrians saw Egyptian officers as intruders and, in some cases, spies. When the officers who carried out the coup announced Syria's secession over Radio Damascus, they complained that Egypt had "humiliated Syria and degraded her army."[159] Amid a drought that struck Syria during the UAR's short existence, a common joke revealed prevailing Syrian attitudes toward their guests: "There's been no rain since the Egyptians came and there'll be none till they go!" Also revealing was the reaction of Syrians to Nasser's proposal to rotate the UAR's seat of government between Damascus and Cairo. As a last ditch effort to sustain the UAR through the symbolic de-concentration of power, Nasser suggested late in 1961 that the central government annually relocate to Damascus from February through May. Rather than interpreting the move as a concession meant to share power more equally, Syrians complained that Nasser was assigning their capital "the status of a provincial town."[160]

Nasser's efforts to develop a common national identity for the UAR's two component states did little to offset Syrian resentment of the union. Soon after its launch, the UAR adopted a flag, a national anthem, and common holidays. The UAR logo appeared on all postal stamps, and textbooks were

---

Comparative Study of Leaders and Forces (New York: Holt, Rinehart and Winston, 1965), pp. 115–116.

[158] Podeh, *The Decline of Arab Unity*, pp. 188–190.

[159] Adeed Dawisha, *Arab Nationalism in the Twentieth Century: From Triumph to Despair* (Princeton, NJ: Princeton University Press, 2003), pp. 230–231.

[160] Jankowski, *Nasser's Egypt*, pp. 134, 164.

revised to stress Arab unity and the shared historical experiences of Syria and Egypt. The government put pressure on print and broadcast media as well as authors and intellectuals to shed positive light on the UAR's formation and the advances it would bring to the cause of Arab unity. Nasser's speeches regularly served as occasions for propagating a new national identity.

These efforts to generate a common identity failed to achieve their intended objective. In the context of Nasser's tightening grip over Syria, Cairo's attempt to develop a narrative of commonality backfired; it was seen as part of a strategy of domination, not unity. For Syrian elites and the public alike, their nation was being annexed and "Egyptianized" rather than contributing independently to the identity of a new union. Officials may have referred to the UAR's two territories as the Northern Region and Southern Region. But throughout Syria—and even in Egypt—the new terminology failed to enter common parlance.[161] The emerging communal identity that helped launch the union in 1958 had turned into a pervasive Syrian resentment of Egyptian hegemony that helped scuttle the UAR in 1961.

Why Union Failed

Although the UAR benefited from the linguistic, ethnic, and religious similarities of Egypt and Syria, it suffered from the absence of institutionalized constraints on Cairo's power as well as the contrasting social orders of its two constituent states. In Egypt and within the context of the UAR, Nasser's power was virtually unchecked. To be sure, Nasser turned to parliamentary ratification and popular referenda to legitimate the union, established a union-wide party (the National Union), founded a union parliament (which did not meet until two years after the union's founding), and adopted a union constitution (which was an abridged form of Egypt's constitution). But these initiatives were of little political consequence; institutionalized constraints on Nasser's power were effectively nonexistent. When confronted with resistance from Damascus, Nasser simply strengthened the powers of the central cabinet, turning the Northern Region's cabinet into an irrelevant body. When the resistance continued, Nasser abolished the regional cabinet and moved its most powerful member—Sarraj—to Cairo to undermine his influence. Ac-

---

[161] For a summary of efforts to generate a new national identity, see Podeh, *The Decline of Arab Unity*, pp. 56, 120–123, 181.

cording to the Library of Congress, "The UAR was completely run by Nasser."[162] In the absence of either institutionalized checks on Nasser or his personal willingness to exercise strategic restraint, Syria was exposed to Cairo's unfettered power. Its consequent disaffection was the main source of the UAR's collapse.

The UAR also lacked a second key ingredient of successful unions: compatible social orders. As Parker observes, "The social structures of the two countries are markedly different."[163] Karl Wittfogel identifies geography and climate as important determinants of social structure.[164] The Egyptian economy depended primarily upon irrigation and was therefore state-centric, while Syrian agriculture depended upon rain and was therefore more decentralized and open. Moreover, Nasser and the Free Officers movement had effectively broken the power of Egypt's landholders, while the Syrian elite was still dominated by "the landed-commercial oligarchy."[165] Nasser's effort to recast Syria's traditional social structure, especially because it was being imposed from outside, not only failed, but also set the country's landed and commercial elite against the UAR. Powerful families and wealthy merchants thus allied with the army and the Ba'athists to scuttle the union.

The UAR did enjoy the cultural commonality that facilitates the onset of stable peace. As Amitai Etzioni observes, among the factors working in the union's favor, "Syria and Egypt seemed quite similar; both populations were Arabic-speaking, predominantly Moslem, and identified with Arab nationalism."[166] During its founding era, the UAR's supporters, Syrian and Egyptian alike, made much of these commonalities, with Nasser arguing, "The affinity, nay the sameness and harmony, was absolute."[167] Cultural commonality, however, could not overcome the centrifugal forces produced by Cairo's hegemonic control or the differences in social order between the UAR's two regions. Cultural commonality played an important role in the union's establishment, but the affinity it engendered was not sufficiently

---

[162] Library of Congress Country Studies, "Syria," available at http://lcweb2.loc.gov/cgi-bin/query/r?frd/cstudy:@field(DOCID+sy0023).

[163] Parker, "The United Arab Republic," p. 16.

[164] See Karl Wittfogel, *Oriental Despotism: A Comparative Study of Total Power* (New York: Vintage, 1981).

[165] Podeh, *The Decline of Arab Unity*, p. 4.

[166] Etzioni, *Political Unification*, p. 97.

[167] Nasser, "A United Arab Republic," p. 327.

strong to sustain the UAR once all of Syria's once-competing factions had united in opposition to the union's continuation.

THE RISE AND DEMISE OF THE SENEGAMBIAN CONFEDERATION, 1982–1989

The formation of the Senegambian Confederation in early 1982 followed decades of discussion about the potential for political union among the states of West Africa. While Gambia was still a British colony, London had considered federating the small territory with Sierra Leone or Senegal. As Senegal in 1960 emerged from decades of French rule, an aborted attempt was made to fashion a union between Senegal and Mali. Upon Gambia's independence in 1965, association with Senegal was again under consideration; Gambia's small size, the fact that it was surrounded by Senegal, and cultural and historical ties between the two countries strengthened the case for union. According to one observer, Senegal and Gambia were long seen as "an area that begs for federation."[168] A UN commission charged with examining a potential association between the two states recommended confederation. Rather than acting on these exhortations, however, Senegal and Gambia decided to forego union in 1965 and instead opted to conclude a defense pact.

When the Senegambian Confederation eventually came into being some fifteen years later, it was virtually by accident. During a trip abroad by Gambia's president, Dawda Jawara, leftist militants attempted a coup. Gambia did not have its own defense force, prompting Jawara to call upon Senegal's army to put down the rebellion.[169] Thereafter, Senegalese troops remained in Gambia to serve as a presidential guard and protect other governmental sites. Gambia and Senegal promptly concluded an agreement founding the Senegambian Confederation, legitimating and providing political cover for Gambia's sudden strategic dependence on its larger neighbor. A confederal cabinet and assembly were established, an integrated military force created, and plans set forth for economic and monetary union.

---

[168] Jibrin Ibrahim, *Democratic Transition in Anglophone West Africa* (Dakar: Council for the Development of Social Science, 2003), p. 53.

[169] The absence of an army stemmed in part from Gambia's calculation that its best defense was no defense; without it own forces, the country would stay out of potential regional conflicts and effectively enjoy neutrality.

The Senegambian Confederation lasted only until 1989. While Senegal was keen to consolidate the union, Gambia was far more hesitant. Gambia was fearful that full implementation of the confederal pact would ultimately mean annexation; Senegal's population was eight times that of Gambia, and its aggregate wealth was twelve times larger. Gambia was particularly concerned about the impact of union on its economy. The country maintained much lower tariffs and taxes on imports than did Senegal. As a consequence, a substantial portion of government revenue as well as the prosperity of many private citizens depended upon the illicit re-export to Senegal of goods imported into Gambia. The formation of a customs union—a key objective of Senegal—thus threatened a mainstay of the Gambian economy. Civil servants and other elites also feared that the privileges afforded by their British education would be undermined through integration into a union dominated by their Francophone neighbor. In short, the two countries had incompatible social orders, prompting social sectors in Gambia threatened by union to block the full implementation and consolidation of the confederation. Unlike most failed unions, the Senegambian Confederation did not collapse in acrimony or mutual recrimination, it simply atrophied.

How Peace Broke Out

The territory of present-day Senegal and Gambia was long divided into "rival indigenous states," with wars frequently breaking out along ethnic and religious lines.[170] French and English ships began arriving in the mid-1500s, with imperial competition over the area mounting during the eighteenth and nineteenth centuries. The British focused their attention on the River Gambia, occupying Banjul (the future capital of Gambia) in 1816, while the French dominated the River Senegal and penetrated more deeply into the interior. In 1889, London and Paris agreed to establish an international boundary between Gambia and Senegal (see map 6.4).[171]

Senegal became independent in 1960, with Gambia following suit five years later. During the era of decolonization in the 1950s and 1960s, European and

---

[170] Arnold Hughes, "The Collapse of the Senegambian Confederation," *Journal of Commonwealth & Comparative Politics* 30, no. 2 (July 1992): 201.

[171] For a concise history of the colonial era, see Edmun B. Richmond, "Senegambia and the Confederation: History, Expectations, and Disillusions," *Journal of Third World Studies* 10, no. 2 (1993): 176–177.

MAP 6.4 Senegal and Gambia

Source: Map No. 4174 Rev. 3 United Nations, Department of Peacekeeping Operations, Cartographic Section, January 2004; http://www.un.org/Depts/Cartographic/map/profile/senegal.pdf.

African officials alike regularly explored the idea of political affiliation between Senegal and Gambia. Amid the pan-African sentiment that intensified during this period, Dakar proposed that Gambia, while retaining regional autonomy, should be annexed and made Senegal's eighth province.[172] Other plans favored looser forms of affiliation. Gambia rejected these proposals, fearing that Senegal, due to its much larger population and economy, would as a matter of course dominate a union of the two countries. Gambia did conclude the 1965 defense pact with Senegal, but felt it had little choice; upon independence, the small country chose not to field its own military force.

[172] Arnold Hughes and David Perfect, *A Political History of the Gambia, 1816–1994* (Rochester: University of Rochester Press, 2006), p. 255.

Banjul accordingly looked to Senegal to replace Britain as its external guardian. Senegal and Gambia proceeded to conclude some thirty collaborative treaties between 1965 and 1982.[173]

Despite the growing linkages between Senegal and Gambia, relations between the two countries took a turn for the worse in the late 1960s and early 1970s. Senegalese efforts to stop the illicit re-export of goods from Gambia led to temporary closings of the border as well as sporadic raids into Gambian territory by the Senegalese military. Relations between Dakar and Banjul were further strained by competing claims to villages that straddled their common border. These tensions provoked violent protests when the Senegalese president, Leopold Senghor, visited Banjul in 1969.[174] They also heightened concerns in Dakar that Gambia would ally itself with an Anglophone bloc in West Africa in order to balance against the threat of Senegalese domination.

A leftist coup in Banjul in 1981 served as the triggering event for union, suddenly making a reality of the proposal that had been circulating for decades. While President Jawara was in London, paramilitary forces took control of Banjul. Jawara requested help from Senegal, and President Abdou Diouf, who had succeeded Senghor earlier that year, promptly dispatched some 2,000 troops to Gambia to overturn the coup. Strategic necessity induced both parties to react to this unexpected turn of events by rapidly concluding a pact of confederation. Absent his own military force, Jawara was dependent upon Senegal to restore and protect his government; confederation provided at least a measure of legitimacy to strategic dependence. Gambia's vice president, Assan Camara, noted that the coup left Banjul with little choice but to accede to Dakar's wishes: "We were bargaining with these people sitting on our stomachs . . . it was an opportunity, an opening for the Senegalese."[175] Scholars of the period share this assessment. Tijan Sallah writes, "President Jawara was so anxious to restore and consolidate his authority under Senegalese protection . . . that the Confederation was not based on shared interests."[176] Arnold Hughes and Janet Lewis observe that "the

---

[173] Hughes, "The Collapse of the Senegambian Confederation," pp. 211–212, 204, 202.

[174] Hughes and Perfect, *A Political History of the Gambia,* p. 259.

[175] Michael Phillips, "Senegambia: The Limits of Pan-Africanism," *Christian Science Monitor,* May 5, 1988.

[176] Tijan Sallah, "Economics and Politics in the Gambia," *Journal of Modern African Studies* 28, no. 4 (December 1990): 642.

Gambian government ... was prepared to accept such military subordina-
tion in return for domestic stability."[177]

Senegal was more than ready to take advantage of this opening; by the
early 1980s, its interest in political union with Gambia had mounted. Strategic considerations were paramount. As Hughes and Lewis observe, "Un-
doubtedly, *security* was the most important factor, and explains the timing as
well as the priorities of the treaty."[178] Senegal's political stability, and that of
the region, would be compromised by a radical, left-leaning government in
Gambia; military intervention to keep Jawara in office was therefore a strategic priority. Dakar also wanted ready access through Gambia to Casamance,
its southern province where a rebellion among ethnic Jola was brewing. The
Jola had ethnic kin in Gambia and Guinea Bissau, raising the specter of an
anti-Senegalese alliance. In addition, Dakar was concerned that political dis-
sidents from Senegal were taking refuge in Gambia. Finally, Senegal saw the
union as a co-binding pact needed to ensure that Gambia did not ally itself
with Nigeria or fall prey to the revolutionary designs of Libya.[179] Added to
these strategic objectives was Dakar's long-standing goal of forming an economic union as a means of shutting down Gambia's re-export trade to
Senegal.

The coup in Banjul occurred at the end of July. By November, the pact
forming the Senegambian Confederation had been signed, and it took effect
in February 1982, following parliamentary ratification in both countries. The
president of Senegal served as the confederation's president and the president
of Gambia its vice president. The governing institutions of the union were
structured to de-concentrate power by offsetting the stark asymmetries
in wealth and population between the two countries—a clear indication of
Senegal's willingness to practice strategic restraint. Although Gambia's population was only one-eighth that of Senegal, Gambians were to fill four of
the nine seats on the Council of Ministers. Of sixty seats in the Confederal
Assembly, twenty went to Gambians. Furthermore, approval of legislation

[177] Arnold Hughes and Janet Lewis, "Beyond Francophonie? The Senegambia Confederation
in Retrospect," in Anthony Kirk-Greene and Daniel Bach, eds., *State and Society in Francophone Africa since Independence* (New York: St. Martin's Press, 1995), p. 231.

[178] Hughes and Lewis, "Beyond Francophonie?" p. 230.

[179] Hughes, "The Collapse of the Senegambian Confederation," pp. 203–205; Hughes and Perfect, *A Political History of the Gambia,* p. 256; and Hughes and Lewis, "The Senegambia Confederation in Retrospect," p. 231.

required a three-quarters majority, meaning that at least five Gambians had to vote with the majority to secure passage.[180]

The terms of the confederation committed both parties to work toward economic and monetary union and laid out an ambitious agenda on matters of foreign and security policy. Although Dakar and Banjul maintained separate representation in international institutions, they agreed to harmonize their external relations. The president would oversee security policy "in agreement" with the vice president, setting up a norm of consensual governance. Efforts to build an integrated military force started promptly, and an operational battalion was deployed in 1985. Gambia supplied one-third of the recruits and one-third of the funding for this joint unit. An integrated gendarmerie was also created. Whereas unions often move slowly and reluctantly to centralize control over foreign and security policy, the Senegambian Confederation proceeded with remarkable alacrity toward supranational decision making on matters of diplomacy and defense. The absence of a defense force in Gambia as well as Jawara's reliance on Senegalese forces for protection clearly contributed to the unusual pace of defense integration.[181]

The Demise of the Confederation

The political bargains and governing institutions of the Senegambian Confederation, inasmuch as they helped meet the security needs of both parties while effectively checking Senegal's dominant power, should have put the union on a solid foundation. Unlike Egypt, which denied Syria any meaningful role in governing the UAR, Senegal did the opposite, granting Gambians a level of political influence disproportional to their population in order to secure satisfaction with the union. Nonetheless, the Senegambian Confederation faltered. Throughout the 1980s, Senegal pressed for a deepening of the union, especially on the economic front. Gambia did not seek to exit the confederation, but Banjul exhibited little enthusiasm for consolidating it, instead blocking Dakar's efforts to advance economic integration. In 1989, Banjul and Dakar finally reached agreement on the terms of economic and monetary union, and were in the midst of negotiating a level of compensation that

---

[180] Hughes, "The Collapse of the Senegambian Confederation," pp. 210–211.

[181] Interestingly, unions that move slowly on defense integration, such as the Swiss Confederation, the Iroquois Confederation, and the UAE, appear to be more durable than those that move move rapidly, such as the UAR and the Senegambian Confederation.

Senegal would pay Gambia for the accompanying loss of income. But before the terms of this deal had been agreed upon, both parties suddenly withdrew from the union.

The Senegambian Confederation collapsed as it began—unexpectedly and accidentally. According to Hughes and Lewis, "the rapid dissolution of the Senegambia Confederation . . . came as a surprise to political commentators. Its speed and ease surprised Gambians and Senegalese as well."[182] In the midst of deteriorating relations with both Mauritania and Guinea Bissau, Senegal withdrew its forces from Gambia and redeployed them in response to these emerging threats. A few days later, Diouf proposed in a televised speech that the confederation be put "on ice."[183] Jawara did not resist; indeed, he had only a few weeks earlier made clear his growing dissatisfaction with the power imbalance within the confederation by demanding that the presidency of the confederation rotate between the Senegalese and Gambian heads of state. Diouf seemed equally discontented with the union, noting that it was like a "car which ran out of gas."[184] Within a matter of weeks after Diouf's public call for shelving the confederation, it was formally dissolved. In this respect, the confederation expired more from neglect than from a deliberate and planned exit by either party. When the opportunity for dissolution arose, both sides capitalized on it. As Diouf noted, "I am convinced that as of now, there is no serious perspective towards the integration of Senegambia. . . . All the institutional organs of the Confederation are just purposelessly, turning round."[185]

The Senegambian Confederation atrophied primarily because its two members had incompatible objectives and expectations. The Gambian government turned to Senegal to ensure regime survival in the wake of the 1981 coup; President Jawara had no choice but to call upon his neighbor's army for protection. But apart from the president, Gambia's elite and its public were generally opposed to union with Senegal. Political and economic integration threatened the privileges of government officials and the prosperity of the business community; the confederation had virtually no base of political support beyond the office of the presidency. By the end of the 1980s,

[182] Hughes and Lewis, "Beyond Francophonie?" p. 239.
[183] Hughes, "The Collapse of the Senegambian Confederation," p. 215.
[184] Sallah, "Economics and Politics in the Gambia," p. 642.
[185] Tale Omole, "The End of a Dream: The Collapse of the Senegambian Confederation, 1982–1989," *Contemporary Review* 257, no. 1496 (September 1990): 133.

Gambia had its own military units and gendarmerie, leaving Jawara free to back away from the confederation when the opportunity presented itself: "The Gambia felt that its changed security needs no longer warranted closer ties with Senegal."[186]

Senegal's elite and public alike were initially more enthusiastic about union than their counterparts in Gambia. But their support of the confederation waned as its key objectives proved elusive. On the security front, union did succeed in reinstalling and stabilizing a government aligned with Dakar. But Senegal's plans to use its military presence in Gambia to suppress the rebellion in Casamance did not come to fruition. Banjul rejected Dakar's proposal to improve strategic access to the south by building a bridge across the River Gambia to replace the antiquated ferry service. In addition, the rebellion in Casamance worsened over the course of the 1980s, making clear that the confederation was of little utility in neutralizing it. On the economic front, Senegal was unable to stop the continuing influx of re-exported goods from Gambia due to Banjul's staunch resistance to economic and monetary union. By the end of the decade, such unmet expectations had drained the confederation of most of the political support it initially enjoyed in Senegal. As Hughes comments, "Neither in Senegal nor The Gambia were there influential pressure groups within key elite groups in commerce or the public sector or powerful and more popularly based organizations committed to the survival of the Confederation."[187]

THE SOURCES OF SOCIETAL OPPOSITION

The opposition of Gambia's elite to economic union was the paramount obstacle to the deepening—and ultimately the survival—of the confederation. According to Tale Omole, "the failure to arrive at an acceptable harmonisation of the economic and financial systems of the two states" was a principal cause of the union's collapse.[188] Gambia's business community, which was heavily reliant on the re-export trade, worked hard to block Banjul from implementing its promise to proceed with economic union. At stake was not only the prosperity of the private sector, but also a major proportion of government revenue. A customs union would have eliminated up to one-third of Gambia's revenue by dramatically reducing the demand for re-exports and

[186] Hughes and Lewis, "Beyond Francophonie?" p. 239.
[187] Hughes, "The Collapse of the Senegambian Confederation," p. 217.
[188] Omole, "The End of a Dream," p. 135.

hence the income produced by import tariffs and taxes. It would also have increased the cost of living in Gambia by at least 20 percent. In Gambia, trade flowed with few regulatory restrictions, and taxes and tariffs accounted for only 18 percent of the value of imports. In Senegal, the flow of trade was heavily regulated and bureaucratized, and taxes and tariffs represented 86 percent of the value of imports. Accordingly, prices for staple goods were often 50 percent higher in Senegal than in Gambia—the main reason that the re-export trade was so profitable.[189] Not only did the confederation fail to shut down the flow of re-exports, but illicit trade across the border actually increased during the 1980s.

Gambian elites were concerned not only about the loss of government revenues that would result from full political and economic union. Civil servants, lawyers, and other professionals who worked in English and were trained in a British education system feared losing their positions of privilege were Gambia to be integrated into Francophone Senegal. The issue was not language per se; most Gambian professionals spoke French. Rather, the elite feared that their British-based skills would be less valuable as bureaucratic and legal systems were altered through union with Senegal.[190] As the *New York Times* observed on February 1, 1982, the day the union took effect, "the urban elite of Banjul . . . have consistently opposed a confederation."[191]

The absence of support among the Gambian electorate was a final obstacle to the survival of the Senegambian Confederation. From the outset, the Gambian public reacted cautiously to the merger—despite the institutional arrangements adopted to elevate Gambia's political influence in the confederation's cabinet and assembly. For many Gambians, "The Confederal Pact was clearly the imposition of Senegalese hegemony over the Gambia."[192] Gambians frequently criticized the contingent of Senegalese troops based in Banjul, viewing it as an army of occupation and suspecting that Dakar was ultimately intent on annexation. This perception was particularly widespread after an incident in 1985, during which Senegalese troops, without first consulting Gambian authorities, deployed at a football stadium to protect Sene-

[189] Lucie Colvin Phillips, "The Senegambia Confederation," in Christopher Delgado and Sidi Jammeh, eds., *The Political Economy of Senegal under Structural Adjustment* (New York: Praeger, 1991), p. 179; and Hughes and Lewis, "Beyond Francophonie?" p. 237.

[190] Hughes and Perfect, *A Political History of the Gambia,* p. 257.

[191] "Gambia Enters Union with Senegal on Wary Note," *New York Times,* February 1, 1982.

[192] Jibrin Ibrahim, *Democratic Transition in Anglophone West Africa* (Dakar: Council for the Development of Social Science, 2003), p. 54.

galese spectators from the allegedly aggressive behavior of Gambian fans.[193] Dakar's persistent efforts to implement economic union and to build a bridge across the River Gambia heightened worries among Gambian citizens that union effectively meant political subjugation to Senegal. Jawara's proposal in 1989 that the confederation's presidency rotate between Gambia and Senegal was in part a response to these concerns.

Gambia's main opposition parties capitalized on increasing public discontent with the confederation by playing the nationalist card against the government. The People's Democratic Organization for Independence and Socialism, for example, issued pamphlets criticizing the government's "dependence on, and subservience to, Senegal; confederation was portrayed as politically demeaning and economically disadvantageous to the Gambian people."[194] By the late 1980s, popular opposition to the union had broadened and deepened. According to Lucie Colvin Phillips, "Most Gambian citizens . . . were bitterly opposed to a confederation. It was the only real issue in the Gambian presidential and parliamentary elections held in March 1987, and the opposition parties have continued to play on the anti-Senegalese sentiment that has developed."[195] Even the ruling party lost its initial enthusiasm for union; as Hughes and Lewis comment, "No Gambian party unequivocally advocated total political integration with Senegal."[196]

In Senegal, public attitudes toward the confederation were more positive, especially at the outset. However, many Senegalese believed that Gambia should be incorporated into Senegal, and that confederation was a preparatory step toward annexation. As Mamadou Dia, a former prime minister of Senegal, stated at the founding of the Senegambian Confederation, "It is a veritable annexation. It has been called a confederation, but it is in fact an annexation. You must call a cat a cat."[197] Such statements from prominent Senegalese served only to intensify the concerns of Gambians that their country was being swallowed by its larger neighbor. Over the course of the 1980s, Senegalese enthusiasm for union waned as elites and the public alike grew frustrated with Gambia's reluctance to move forward with economic integra-

---

[193] Sallah, "Economics and Politics in the Gambia," p. 641; and Omole, "The End of a Dream," p. 137.

[194] Hughes and Perfect, *A Political History of the Gambia,* p. 265.

[195] Lucie Colvin Phillips, "The Senegambia Confederation," p. 177.

[196] Hughes and Lewis, "Beyond Francophonie?" p. 237.

[197] Quoted in "Gambia Enters Union with Senegal on Wary Note," *New York Times*, February 1, 1982.

tion. According to one account, the Senegalese increasingly questioned the "Gambian commitment to union and chafed at the delay in signing the economic agreements."[198] By the late 1980s, in Senegal as well as Gambia, support for confederation among elites and the public alike was at low ebb.

A unique aspect of the Senegambian Confederation was that it threatened to impede, not facilitate, cross-border trade. The flow of goods (mostly illicit) from Gambia to Senegal thrived before and after the formation of the confederation—but to the chagrin of Dakar. Although Senegalese and Gambians alike participated in the smuggling, Dakar pressed for a customs union that would equalize prices and thus undermine the re-export trade. In this sense, the confederation threatened to disrupt the main source of economic integration between the two populations. Indeed, Senegal in the mid-1980s effectively closed the border due to its frustration over the lack of progress on economic union. Especially in Gambia, the populace saw economic union as disrupting, not facilitating, societal integration.

The same holds for the presence of Senegalese troops in Gambia. Ostensibly, the integrated military battalion could have served to promote a communal identity. But the presence of Senegalese troops in Banjul—protecting prominent sites such as government offices, the airport, and the main radio station—did more to fuel resentment than a sense of solidarity. In this respect, perhaps the most visible sign of societal integration between Senegal and Gambia served as more of a liability than an asset in terms of its impact on Gambian attitudes toward the confederation.

Contributing to the atrophy of the union was the fact that neither elites nor the media generated significant public engagement in the affairs of the confederation.[199] In Senegal, the formation of the union attracted almost no attention in the media. Nor did President Diouf or other prominent leaders invest considerable time or energy in seeking to generate popular engagement. More public discussion ensued in Gambia, but much of it was critical of the new venture.[200] As Hughes notes, "there was certainly little enthusiasm for the confederation, or even much interest in it; it was noticeable how little public attention was paid to the deliberations of the confederal assembly, even though attempts were made to create interest through official publica-

---

[198] Colin Legum, ed., *Africa Contemporary Record: Annual Survey and Documents*, vol. 18, 1985–1986 (New York: Africana Publishing, 1987), p. B27.

[199] Hughes, "The Collapse of the Senegambian Confederation," p. 211.

[200] "Gambia Enters Union with Senegal on Wary Note," *New York Times*, February 1, 1982.

tions and newspaper reporting."[201] The lack of enthusiasm among the public and among Gambia's opposition parties dissuaded Jawara from making the confederation a centerpiece of his presidency. The result was that the union remained primarily a bureaucratic affair in both Senegal and Gambia. As the *Gambia Weekly* commented in 1989, "the ease with which the confederation was dismantled shows how superficial indeed it was. . . . It did not extend . . . beyond the two governments and did not affect Senegambians at all. . . . For the ordinary Senegambian . . . it did not essentially change anything. Instead, what it brought about in its wake was a mountain of paperwork."[202]

The confederation thus had very shallow roots in Senegalese and Gambian society. As a consequence, it had no source of support after Jawara and Diouf no longer found it politically expedient. Gambia had its own defense force, meaning that Jawara no longer needed to rely on Senegalese forces. Dakar tired of Banjul's reluctance to move forward on economic union. When Diouf withdrew Senegal's forces from Gambia to address mounting tensions with Mauritania and Guinea Bissau, both Dakar and Banjul had a good excuse to let the confederation lapse. Senegal promptly shut down trade with Gambia. Diouf argued that "Senegal will not accept to serve as a dumping ground for Gambian contraband. During the Confederation, because we wanted to play by the rules of integration, we were a bit lax, perhaps we let things go. We can no longer afford to do this."[203] Banjul retaliated, eventually increasing tolls on Senegalese vehicles by 1,000 percent.[204] Gambia also pursued a new strategic alignment with Mauritania as a means of balancing against Senegal. Union gave way to the beginnings of strategic rivalry.

Why Union Failed

The Senegambian Confederation benefited from institutionalized restraint and from cultural commonality, but the incompatibility of Senegal's and Gambia's social orders proved to be an insurmountable impediment to the onset of stable peace. During the period of union, Gambia was one of Africa's most successful liberal democracies. Jawara was popularly elected and

[201] Hughes and Perfect, *A Political History of the Gambia,* p. 263.

[202] *African Research Bulletin,* vol. 26, 1989–1990 (Crediton, UK: Africa Research Limited, 1991), pp. 9402–9403.

[203] "Gambia Weathers Senegal Split," *Christian Science Monitor,* July 19, 1990.

[204] John Wiseman, "Gambia," in Iain Frame, ed., *South of the Sahara—2006,* 35th ed. (New York: Routledge, 2005), p. 506.

the rule of law prevailed until democratic governance was ended by a coup in 1994. Senegal also became a republic after independence, but the country operated as an illiberal democracy under both Senghor and Diouf. Opposition parties and outside observers alike regularly accused the dominant Socialist Party of excessive concentration of power in the presidency and of manipulating electoral outcomes. Nonetheless, Banjul and Dakar both embraced the co-binding bargains and power-checking institutions embodied in the confederal pact. A stark asymmetry in material power persistently fueled Gambian fears of annexation, but Senegal did practice strategic restraint and abide by its commitment to overweight Gambia's representation in the union's institutions of governance.

The incompatible social orders of Gambia and Senegal were the main obstacle to the survival of the confederation. Gambia's territory and population were too small to support an economy that was primarily agrarian or industrial. Gambia therefore developed an "entrepot" economy heavily reliant on the relatively free flow of imports and exports—a development encouraged by Britain's laissez-faire legacy.[205] The country's bureaucracy and social order were structured accordingly. In contrast, Senegal inherited the French preference for a state-centric economy and society and sought tariff protection for its young industrial base. High taxes and tariffs, coupled with comprehensive regulatory and licensing controls, did not mesh with Gambia's more market-oriented economy. As in the case of Egypt and Syria, economic integration threatened and alienated, rather than empowered, Gambia's ruling elites. It was for this reason that Banjul was ultimately unwilling to implement economic and monetary union, denying Senegal one of its main objectives in pursuing confederation and eroding Dakar's interest in continuing the union.

Senegal and Gambia enjoyed high levels of cultural commonality, one of the main reasons that the confederation was launched to begin with. The population of both countries was over 90 percent Muslim and consisted of a mix of overlapping, linguistically related ethnic groups. The confederation's founding pact noted that the citizens of Gambia and Senegal "constitute a single people divided into two States by the vicissitudes of History."[206] Schol-

---

[205] Ebrima Sall and Halifa Sallah, "Senegal and the Gambia: The Politics of Integration," in Momar-Coumba Diop, ed., *Sénégal et ses Voisins* (Dakar: Societes-Espaces-Temps, 1994), p. 128.

[206] "Agreement between the Republic of the Gambia and the Republic of Senegal," preamble. Available at http://untreaty.un.org/unts/60001_120000/8/40/00016000.pdf.

ars of the region regularly reference the important role that cultural commonality played in bringing the two countries together. Tijan Sallah observes that Senegal and Gambia enjoy a "common ethnic, religious, and cultural heritage," while Richmond notes that "the two nations are culturally, linguistically, and historically homologous."[207] Jibrin Ibrahim agrees that, "The cultures and societies of Senegal and the Gambia dove-tail into each other and they otherwise have much in common. There is a Senegambian social space defined by geography and history."[208]

Despite these cultural linkages, differences in the ethnic composition of the Senegalese and Gambian populations were a potential source of political cleavage. Wolof made up over 40 percent of Senegal's population and dominated the political system. Meanwhile, Gambia was dominated by Mandika, and only about 15 percent of its population was Wolof. The different ethnic makeup of the two countries did not, however, significantly impair the functioning of the confederation or contribute to its dissolution; ethnic balance simply did not emerge as a significant source of political cleavage. Gambia's Wolof party, although it briefly supported the confederation at the outset, ended up opposing it in order to further its electoral fortunes.[209] Goran Hyden and Michael Bratton note that even during election time, there was a "virtually complete absence of ethnic tension." They go on to attribute the "low valence of ethnicity" to "long-standing close historical interactions of Senegambian populations, crosscutting ties of common religious affiliation, and the role of Wolof as lingua franca."[210] Incompatibilities in social order, not ethnic cleavages, ultimately led to the demise of the Senegambian Confederation.

CONCLUSION

The historical cases examined in this chapter provide a wide range of variation as to outcomes and explanatory variables. Among the successful unions, the Swiss case underscores the political cleavages produced by social and reli

[207] Sallah, "Economics and Politics in the Gambia," p. 640; Richmond, "Senegambia and the Confederation," p. 173.

[208] Ibrahim, *Democratic Transition in Anglophone West Africa*, p. 53.

[209] Hughes and Perfect, *A Political History of the Gambia*, p. 257.

[210] Goran Hyden and Michael Bratton, *Governance and Politics in Africa* (Boulder, CO: Lynne Rienner, 1992), p. 71.

gious dividing lines—and the ability of converging social orders, constitutional restraint, and liberal nationalism to overcome them. Warfare was a way of life for the Iroquois tribes. Nonetheless, the Iroquois Confederation, guided by the practices of reciprocity and restraint articulated in its oral law, endured for over three centuries. The UAE lacked any semblance of liberal democracy. But wealth redistribution and a unique brand of tribal constitutionalism functioned effectively to fashion and sustain a stable union. All three cases illustrate the importance of strategic necessity in initially prompting the formation of union, and the critical roles that the practice of strategic restraint (but not the presence of institutionalized restraint), compatible social orders, and cultural commonality play in the onset and maintenance of stable peace. They also confirm that economic integration generally follows from, rather than paves the way for, political integration. And they make clear that a common national identity evolves in step with, and is not a precursor to, the consolidation of union.

The failure of the UAR and the Senegambian Confederation confirm these findings. Both unions had strong prospects. Syria and Egypt enjoyed a common religion, culture, and language, and Senegal and Gambia also had strong ethnic, religious, and linguistic ties. Moreover, in the early years of the postcolonial era, the UAR and Senegambian Confederation benefited from pan-Arabism and pan-Africanism, respectively. Nonetheless, both foundered on the shoals of incompatible social orders. In Syria, landed elites and the commercial middle class rejected the agrarian reforms and nationalization scheme imposed by Egypt. In Gambia, both the government and private sector resisted Senegal's efforts to eliminate the lucrative re-export market. Moreover, the power asymmetries that existed between Egypt and Syria, and between Senegal and Gambia, made both Syria and Gambia wary of losing their autonomy through political amalgamation with a preponderant partner. In this respect, Egypt's unwillingness to practice strategic restraint played an important role in expediting the UAR's demise.

All of these five main cases are somewhat off the beaten path. They were chosen precisely for this reason: to enhance the diversity of the cases, broaden the temporal and geographic range of the unions examined, and maximize variation as to regime type, social order, and cultural milieu. Lest this approach appear to introduce its own bias by neglecting other cases—including more mainstream ones—this chapter ends with brief summaries of a number of additional historical instances of successful as well as failed unions. Three cases of successful unions are first examined: the United States (1789), Italy (1861), and Germany (1871). All three cases illustrate the centrality of strategic necessity, institutionalized restraint, and cultural commonality in the onset of stable peace. They also illuminate the obstacles posed by incompatible social orders to the successful conclusion of unions. Two cases of failed union are examined: the U.S. Civil War (1861) and Singapore's expulsion from Malaysia (1965). These cases underscore the degree to which incompatible social orders and ethnic cleavages stand in the way of stable peace.

Successful Unions: The United States, Italy, and Germany
THE UNITED STATES

The strategic challenge of defeating British rule precipitated the onset of union among the American colonies, each of which "felt itself to be autonomous and independent, a world of its own."[211] Only if they aggregated their resources and coordinated their political and military strategies would the thirteen colonies have the wherewithal to attain independence. That strategic necessity was the chief source of solidarity was made clear by the limited competence of the collective institutions that took shape following the end of the Revolutionary War. The main powers of the confederation formed in 1782 were restricted principally to matters of war and peace. Absent control over trade, taxation, and budgets, central institutions proved too weak to provide effective governance.

The strengthened union that took effect in 1789 gave the federal government authority over not just matters of alliance and war, but also commerce, currency, and taxation. The objective was to strike a balance between a system that was too decentralized—and therefore subject to balance-of-power rivalries among its members—and one in which the center wielded too much power—potentially subjecting the individual states to tyranny.[212] As the terms of the confederation forged in 1782 had made clear, the states were loath to sacrifice their autonomy in the service of union. Indeed, for many Americans, especially those hailing from the more libertarian south, the threat

[211] Felix Gilbert, *To the Farewell Address: Ideas of Early American Foreign Policy* (Princeton, NJ: Princeton University Press, 1961), p. 7.

[212] David Hendrikson, *Peace Pact: The Lost World of the American Founding* (Lawrence: University Press of Kansas, 2003), p. 259.

posed by foreign enemies was of less concern than that posed by domestic tyranny.[213]

Nonetheless, strategic considerations—the prospect of foreign intervention as well as fear of geopolitical rivalry among the constituent members of the union—prevailed in compelling the states to countenance more significant encroachments on their autonomy. The *Federalist Papers* repeatedly warned against the dangers that would accompany the absence of stable union. John Jay foresaw external perils, arguing "that weakness and divisions at home would invite dangers from abroad; and that nothing would tend more to secure us from them than union, strength, and good government within ourselves." Alexander Hamilton agreed that the alternative would be for the separate states to "become a prey to the artifices and machinations" of foreign powers guided by the logic of "divide and impera."[214]

Should such external threats materialize, Jay surmised, the separate states would likely be left to fend for themselves: each would "decline hazarding their tranquility and present safety for the sake of neighbors, of whom perhaps they have been jealous, and whose importance they are content to see diminished. Although such conduct would not be wise, it would, nevertheless, be natural." Jay was concerned not only about the potential for *sauve qui peut* attitudes, but also about the dangers of rivalry among the separate states, warning that without union they would "always be either involved in disputes and war, or live in the constant apprehension of them," ending up "formidable only to each other." Hamilton similarly foresaw a good chance of conflict over territory, warning that "to reason from the past to the future, we shall have good ground to apprehend, that the sword would sometimes be appealed to as the arbiter."[215]

The founding fathers translated strategic necessity into stable union through the practice of political restraint and its codification in the Constitution. The larger states, such as New York and Pennsylvania, engaged in uni-

[213] See Daniel Deudney, "The Philadelphian System: Sovereignty, Arms Control, and Balance of Power in the American States-Union, Circa 1787–1861," *International Organization* 49, no. 2 (Spring 1995).

[214] John Jay, *Federalist 5*, in James Madison, Alexander Hamilton, and John Jay, *The Federalist Papers* (London: Penguin Books, 1987), p. 101; Hamilton, *Federalist 7*, in Madison, Hamilton, and Jay, *The Federalist Papers*, p. 113.

[215] Jay, *Federalist 4*, in Madison, Hamilton, and Jay, *The Federalist Papers*, p. 100, Jay, *Federalist 5*, in Madison, Hamilton, and Jay, *The Federalist Papers*, p. 103; Hamilton, *Federalist 7*, in Madison, Hamilton, and Jay, *The Federalist Papers*, p. 111.

lateral accommodation by negating the advantages of their greater resources and population. They accepted an upper house in which all states, regardless of size, had equal representation. They compromised their economic autonomy and abolished interstate tariffs, giving up, in Hamilton's words, "opportunities which some States would have of rendering others tributary to them by commercial regulations." Such acts of accommodation by large states, Hamilton noted, were needed to ensure that the smaller states did not see "with an unfriendly eye the perspective of our growing greatness."[216] Although the Constitution endowed federal institutions with considerable powers, it also checked those institutions by vesting power in the states and the citizenry. A compound republic, the separation of powers, institutional checks and balances—these were all devices meant to ensure that "the states were circumscribed and embedded in a constitution of the negative—a cross-checking architecture of binded and bound authorities."[217] As James Madison put it, "You must first enable the government to control the governed; and next place oblige it to control itself."[218]

The center had to be strong enough to sustain the union, but not so strong that individual states refused participation. The co-binding bargains and power-checking devices that resulted took myriad forms. The federal government had the right to raise an army and navy, but state militias remained the main repository of military force. Americans feared that a large military force under the control of the federal government would lead to excessive centralization and come at the expense of state rights and individual liberties. Although the federal government had the right to coin money, a single currency did not emerge until the financial exigencies of the Civil War; states preferred to handle their own monetary affairs. The highest court in the land was a federal institution, but each state maintained its own judicial system and retained responsibility for law enforcement.

The location of the capital, although a particularly divisive issue, ultimately furthered the goal of de-concentrating power. Many southerners argued that Philadelphia, the initial location of Congress, would expose the government to the corrupting influences of urban life, advantage the North, and unduly magnify the political clout of Pennsylvania. Influential voices from New

[216] Hamilton, *Federalist 7*, in Madison, Hamilton, and Jay, *The Federalist Papers*, p. 111.
[217] Deudney, "The Philadelphian System," p. 195.
[218] James Madison, *Federalist 51*, in Madison, Hamilton, and Jay, *The Federalist Papers*, p. 320.

England proposed an "ambulatory Congress" that would rotate among different locations, thereby sidestepping rancorous debate about a permanent center of power. During the 1780s, many different locations were under consideration, including New York, Princeton, Trenton, Annapolis, and a site on the Potomac that would encompass the settlement at Georgetown and the harbor at Anacostia. The Potomac site emerged as a compromise solution, offering a location that sat astride North and South and that would serve agricultural and commercial interests alike. An independent District of Columbia was carved out from the existing territory of Maryland and Virginia to avoid the jealousies that would have emerged had the capital been located within a single state.[219]

Commercial integration and the generation of a common identity followed from, rather than paved the way for, the onset of stable union. As Murray Forsyth notes, "a primarily defensive union became a commercial union too."[220] During the union's early decades, the states traded primarily with Europe, not with each other. Although Americans enjoyed a substantial level of cultural commonality—shared ethnicity, language, and religion—it took decades for societal integration to foster a unitary identity. As David Hendrickson observes, "the sense of common nationality was more a consequence of mutual entanglement and exiguous necessity than of a sense of common peoplehood."[221] Not until the second half of the nineteenth century did the citizenry feel stronger bonds of loyalty and identity to the union than to their states. Only after the Civil War was it common to follow references to the United States with a singular rather than a plural verb. Prior to the centralizing effects of war, the defeat of the Confederacy, and southern reconstruction, the union was widely viewed as a pluralistic states-union, not a unitary federation.[222]

The incompatible social orders of the North and South proved to be the most significant obstacle to the durability of the federation. The North was developing an urbanized and industrialized economy, relied on wage labor,

[219] On the location of the capital, see Lawrence Delbert Cress, "Whither Columbia? Congressional Residence and the Politics of the New Nation, 1776 to 1787," *William and Mary Quarterly*, 3rd Ser., 32, no. 4 (October 1975): 581–600; Joseph Ellis, *Founding Brothers: The Revolutionary Generation* (New York: Vintage Books, 2002); John C. Miller, *The Federalist Era: 1789–1801* (New York: Harper and Brothers, 1960).

[220] Murray Forsyth, *Unions of States: The Theory and Practice of Confederation* (New York: Leicester University Press and Holmes and Meier, 1981), p. 68.

[221] Hendrikson, *Peace Pact*, p. ix.

[222] See Deudney, "The Philadelphian System."

and sought protectionism for its emergent industrial base. The South was agrarian, dependent on slavery, and backed free trade to maximize its agricultural exports. During the union's early decades, these differences were managed through political bargains; the Missouri Compromise of 1820, for example, stipulated that westward enlargement proceed by admitting one slave state for each free state. As discussed below, however, the union was eventually split asunder as a result of the irreparable political divide that stemmed from these contrasting social orders. Despite the practice of institutionalized restraint and the cultural commonality of the individual states, divergent social orders would violently interrupt the evolution of the United States as a zone of stable peace.

ITALY

The multiple Italian states that emerged from the fragmentation and eventual collapse of the Roman Empire were for centuries subject to foreign domination and war. By the nineteenth century, most of these states were under the rule of royal families from outside Italy. During the decades prior to unification, for example, Lombardy and Venetia were under Austrian rule, the royal families in Modena and Tuscany had ties to the Habsburgs, and the Kingdom of the Two Sicilies (Sicily and Naples) was governed by Bourbons. The Papal States were protected by France, and Piedmont, although governed by Italian aristocracy, was effectively an Austrian protectorate.[223]

The revolutions of 1848 were a turning point for Italy in two critical respects. First, the surge in nationalist sentiment that swept across Europe fueled calls within Italy for unity and resistance to outside domination. Italian states that still saw each other as geopolitical rivals found common cause in opposing foreign rule. In addition, the Pope's reliance on foreign protection pitted Catholicism against nationalism, isolating clerics and conservative aristocrats who called for preservation of the status quo. Second, the events of 1848 provided new momentum behind political liberalization, further discrediting dynastic rule and enabling Piedmont to emerge as the champion of both Italian unity and political reform. Only in Piedmont did constitutional monarchy and parliamentary government survive the repressive backlash against the upheaval of 1848. As Daniel Ziblatt observes, "Piedmont was the

[223] Cronin, *Community Under Anarchy*, pp. 78–79.

only Italian state to enter its last decade of independence in the 1850s with a constitution and parliament intact."[224]

The strategic restraint that emerged from constitutional checks on absolute power helped ameliorate previous concerns among Italy's smaller states that the call for unification was simply a disguise for Piedmont's expansionism. Elites in Lombardy and Venetia had feared that union would encourage Piedmont to "treat these provinces as conquered territories." Instead, "What Italy truly needs . . . is that Piedmont should act generously" and seek "not to absorb Italy into herself but to make herself more Italian."[225] Piedmont's embrace of constitutional rule served as a welcome act of unilateral accommodation; its smaller neighbors began to see it as a champion of liberty and independence, not a dominant state bent on hegemony. By resisting Austria's dominating role in northern Italy, Piedmont was able to tap into nationalist as well as liberal impulses in leading the push toward unification. Austria had, after all, played a prominent role in suppressing the liberalizing forces unleashed in 1848 and remained a staunch defender of dynastic rule.[226]

The amalgamation of the Italian peninsula occurred in two main stages, with the strategic challenge of resisting foreign domination providing the main rallying cry for union. Piedmont effectively manufactured a confrontation with Austria as a means of engendering solidarity among the Italian states. In 1848–1849, Piedmont took advantage of a succession of uprisings to maneuver itself and its northern neighbors into a war with Austria. Although Austria handily put down these liberal rebellions and maintained effective control over northern Italy, Piedmont succeeded in capitalizing on the alliance against Austria to establish itself as an agent of liberal change and national independence. Camillo Benso, Count of Cavour, who would soon become Piedmont's premier and a key figure in guiding Italy to unification, relied on a set of strategic arguments quite similar to those of America's founding fathers. Only if Italy rid itself of internal rivalries, he argued, would it be able to end domination by outside powers.[227]

---

[224] Daniel Ziblatt, *Structuring the State: The Formation of Italy and Germany and the Puzzle of Federalism* (Princeton, NJ: Princeton University Press, 2006), p. 112.

[225] Denis Mack Smith, *The Making of Italy, 1796–1870* (New York: Walker, 1968), pp. 152–155.

[226] Lucy Riall, *The Italian Risorgimento: State, Society and National Unification* (New York: Routledge, 1994), pp. 73–74.

[227] Mack Smith, *The Making of Italy*, p. 104.

In 1859, Piedmont again turned to war to orchestrate the advance of unification. Under Cavour's guidance, Piedmont conspired with France to provoke war with Austria. Although the war was inconclusive, Piedmont's alliance with Lombardy served as the initial core of an Italian union. Revolutionaries in Tuscany, Parma, and Modena overthrew their monarchic regimes, clearing the way for the union to expand to central Italy. Meanwhile, General Giuseppe Garibaldi, in the name of Italian independence and unity, led his forces against the dynastic regimes in Sicily and Naples.[228] Absent the "commercialized aristocracy" and the growing middle class that embraced liberal nationalism in the north, the south was poised to retain dynastic and foreign rule had it not been for the intervention of Garibaldi's forces.[229]

After Garibaldi's victory, Cavour promptly called for plebiscites in the south to legitimate unification, and the Italian Kingdom was established in 1861.[230] Its capital was relocated from Turin to Florence, in part to alleviate fears about Piedmont's hegemonic ambitions. Venetia joined the union in 1866, when Piedmont took advantage of Austria's war with Prussia to drive Vienna from its last stronghold in Italy. French troops left Rome in 1870, their recall prompted by the outbreak of the Franco-Prussian War. Following a siege of the city by Italian troops, papal forces capitulated, the city was annexed by the Kingdom of Italy, and it became the capital of a unified nation in 1871.

As in the American case, Italian unification was driven by geopolitical considerations; a defensive union later became an economic union. As Bruce Cronin notes, "political integration *preceded* economic integration."[231] Not until after unification did a railway network and other commercial infrastructure make possible economic integration among Italy's formerly independent states. In similar fashion, a national identity took root only gradually. Prior to unification, Italians did enjoy a sense of cultural, ethnic, and religious commonality. In justifying Piedmont's alliance with Lombardy and Venetia in 1849, for example, King Carlo Alberto referred to "our common race" and

---

[228] As mentioned in chapter 2, I code the unification of Italy as a case of peaceful amalgamation even though Garibaldi's forces fought against fellow Italians in Sicily and Naples. The fighting was in the service of liberating Italy from foreign domination, not a product of Piedmont's effort to annex territory by force.

[229] On the contrasting social orders in the north and south, see Ziblatt, *Structuring the State*, pp. 60–71.

[230] See Charles Delzell, *Unification of Italy, 1859–1961: Cavour, Mazzini, or Garibaldi?* (New York: Holt Rinehart, 1965), pp. 63–65.

[231] Cronin, *Community Under Anarchy*, p. 76.

pledged that "we are now coming to offer you . . . the help which a brother expects from a brother."[232] Nonetheless, residents of the new Italy spoke a plethora of different languages and dialects and maintained strong regional identities. As in the United States, it took decades of societal integration for a strong national identity to complement enduring regional and local loyalties. A common national identity was the result, not the cause, of political union.

Also paralleling the United States, the different social orders that existed in Italy's north and south proved to be a major obstacle to unification. Absent the liberalizing effects of commercialization that sped political reform in the north, it took military intervention to overthrow dynastic rule in the south. The contrasting social orders of north and south, although they converged as commercialization and industrialization proceeded throughout the new nation, have continued to foster political tensions between northern and southern Italy to this day.[233]

GERMANY

The idea of a shared German nationhood dates back to the era of the Holy Roman Empire. Nonetheless, it was not until the nineteenth century that Napoleon's bid for continental hegemony set in motion the concrete process of integration that led to a unified Germany. The series of incremental steps that culminated in the founding of the German Kingdom in 1871 began at the close of the Napoleonic Wars in 1815 with the formation of the German Bund, effectively an extension of the confederation of German principalities that had been organized by Napoleon. The Bund, which included Prussia, Austria, and over thirty smaller Germanic states, was a nascent security community. Like the Concert of Europe, it was a by-product of the strategic pacts formed to defeat Napoleonic France. Although its members could independently conclude alliances and declare war, they assumed commitments to collective defense and to the peaceful resolution of disputes among confederation members.[234] And, as did the Holy Alliance of Prussia, Austria, and Russia, the Bund entailed a common commitment not only to preserve

---

[232] Cronin, *Community Under Anarchy*, p. 88.

[233] See Robert Putnam, *Making Democracy Work: Civil Traditions in Modern Italy* (Princeton, NJ: Princeton University Press, 1984).

[234] Mark Hallerberg and Katja Weber, "German Unification 1815–1871 and Its Relevance for Integration Theory," *Journal of European Integration* 24, no. 1 (March 2002): 12–13.

peace among its members but also to resist liberal reform and defend monarchic rule.

The next major step toward unification occurred in 1834, when the German states established a customs union, the Zollverein. The Zollverein succeeded in substantially increasing trade among its members.[235] In contrast to most of the other instances of stable peace examined in this book, in the German case economic integration preceded and helped pave the way for political integration. Notably, however, the original objectives of the Zollverein were political as well as economic. The expansion of trade was meant to win the favor of the growing commercial class, thereby aligning it with—and preserving the power of—the Junkers, the landed aristocracy. Prussia and its smaller neighbors in the north, which had more commercialized economies, enthusiastically supported the Zollverein, while Austria, Bavaria, and other states of the south, whose economies were still primarily agrarian, were far less receptive.[236] Indeed, Austria chose not to join the Zollverein due to the threat it posed to its traditional social order. In addition, Austria and its neighbors in the south were predominantly Catholic, while Prussia and its neighbors were mainly Protestant. These differences in social order and religion contributed to rivalry between Prussia and Austria for leadership among the German states.

As in the case of Italian unification, the revolutions of 1848 proved to be a turning point for Germany. Nationalist sentiment and calls for liberal reform swept across the German states. Prussia became a constitutional monarchy, and most other German states embraced constitutional rule.[237] A German assembly began meeting in Frankfurt. The confederal diet served as a coordinating council, with the delegates in attendance representing states that still retained effective sovereignty. Although an advance from the early days of the Bund, the more centralized German confederation was still a nascent security community among autonomous states.

Otto von Bismarck, who became chancellor in 1862, provided the leadership necessary to fashion a federal union from a loose confederation of independent states. He pursued the same strategy as Cavour, resorting to war and strategic alliance with ethnic kin as a means of advancing political integra-

---

[235] Ziblatt, *Structuring the State*, pp. 35–37; and Theordore A. Hamerow, *The Social Foundations of German Unification* (Princeton, NJ: Princeton University Press, 1972), pp. 375–377.

[236] Ziblatt, *Structuring the State*, pp. 35–42.

[237] Ziblatt, *Structuring the State*, p. 113; Cronin, *Community Under Anarchy*, p. 111.

tion. Bismarck guided Prussia into conflicts with Denmark (1864), Austria (1866), and France (1870), each time capitalizing on the resulting alliances and the surge in German nationalism to advance toward a unified Germany under Prussian leadership. These successive conflicts and the nationalism they generated were important tools of domestic as well as foreign policy, wielded to preserve the political compact between the rising commercial class and the Junkers—the alliance between "Iron and Rye."[238]

The war against Denmark brought the territories of Schleswig and Holstein, both of which had German majorities, under joint Austrian and Prussian control. Although Austro-Prussian cooperation in this instance advanced the goal of national unification, it also heightened tension over which of the two states would hold sway over German lands. Prussia and Austria not only competed for primacy, but also clashed on matters of governance. In contrast to Prussia, Austria opposed commercial integration among the German states, resisted the establishment of the Frankfurt assembly, and remained a staunch defender of absolute monarchy.[239]

Prussia's victory against Austria in 1866 settled their struggle for primacy and represented a defeat for the forces of conservative monarchism. It also enabled Bismarck to take the next step toward union—annexing territory to unite the eastern and western halves of Prussia and joining with neighboring states to establish the North German Confederation. Although Prussia resorted to unilateral annexation and coercive diplomacy to form the confederation, Bismarck simultaneously practiced strategic restraint by institutionalizing a series of power-checking devices. As Ziblatt notes, Bismarck, like Cavour, was well aware of "the dangers of excessive centralization."[240] He introduced universal manhood suffrage, established a national parliament (the Bundestag), and an upper house (the Bundesrat) in which delegates represented the individual states. Due to Prussia's preponderant economic and military resources, Bismarck was keen to demonstrate his benign intentions, encouraging smaller states to conceive of unification as the collective fashioning of a new national polity rather than absorption into an expansionist Prussian state.[241]

[238] Erich Eyck, *Bismarck and the German Empire* (London: Unwin University Books, 1968), pp. 62–63.

[239] Eyck, *Bismarck and the German Empire*, pp. 62–63.

[240] Ziblatt, *Structuring the State*, p. 7.

[241] Eyck, *Bismarck and the German Empire*, p. 145; and Cronin, *Community Under Anarchy*, pp. 117–118. It should be noted that some historians see Bismarck as having constructed only a

Although the confederation established in 1866 was confined to German states north of the Main River, Bismarck also exercised strategic restraint with the southern states that had long aligned themselves with Austria. He refrained from imposing a punitive peace after the defeat of Austria, instead fashioning military pacts with Austria's former allies. Bismarck would have preferred to advance the cause of political integration, but the southern states still equated German unification with "Prussianization." Although they participated in the customs parliament and struck new deals on tariffs and trade, they were unwilling to accept the loss of autonomy that would have accompanied the southward enlargement of the North German Confederation.[242] Indeed, elections to the customs parliament in 1868 produced a resounding victory for anti-Prussian, Catholic, and conservative candidates.[243]

Faced with such resistance, Bismarck again turned to war, this time with France, to complete the project of German unification. As Otto Pflanze remarks, "Hatred of a foreign foe, rather than spontaneous devotion to Germany, had proved to be the force most capable of defeating the sentiment of separatism."[244] Bismarck calculated that the unifying effect of war offered the only way to bring the south into the confederation without making political concessions that he deemed unacceptable.[245] And even amid military victory and the nationalism it produced, Bismarck had to relax the terms of admission in order to finalize the union. The treaties founding the German Kingdom were signed with the confederation, not with Prussia. The powers of the Bundesrat were strengthened. Baden, Wurttemberg, and especially Bavaria were granted special privileges and powers. The Bavarian military, for example, remained an independent militia, and came under the command of the Kaiser only during wartime. Delegates to the Bundesrat were granted diplomatic rather than parliamentary immunity—an emblem of the continued rights and status of the individual states.[246]

---

façade of pluralism, offering face-saving measures to less powerful German states that had little option but to acquiesce to Prussian demands. See, for example, Gordon Craig, *Germany 1866– 1945* (New York: Oxford University Press, 1978).

[242] Otto Pflanze, *Bismarck and the Development of Germany: The Period of Unification, 1815– 1871* (Princeton, NJ: Princeton University Press, 1962), pp. 398–399.

[243] Jonathan Sperber, *A Short Oxford History of Germany* (Oxford: Oxford University Press, 2004), p. 87.

[244] Pflanze, *Bismarck and the Development of Germany*, p. 437.

[245] Eyck, *Bismarck and the German Empire*, p. 173.

[246] Ziblatt, *Structuring the State*, pp. 129–130; Pflanze, *Bismarck and the Development of Germany*, pp. 487–489.

It is worth quoting at length Pflanze's description of the compromises and power-checking devices that finally made possible a stable union among Germany's disparate states:

> [Bismarck] united the forces of German nationalism and particularism, and solved the problem of uniting states of disproportionate size. . . . Its national features were intended to attract southern peoples and its federal ones to reassure their governments. . . . Here then was Bismarck's mechanism of the balance. The institutions and powers of the confederation were to be in equilibrium with those of Prussia and the states. The former would receive more legislative, the latter more administrative authority. Within the central government a second division was to take place between two organs, one of which had only legislative, the other both legislative and executive functions. Pressure would be met by counterpressure: the nation against the dynasties, the confederation against Prussia, Reichstag against Bundesrat, parliament against parliament, centralism against particularism, the centripetal against the centrifugal.[247]

As made clear by this summary of the onset of federation, German unification was facilitated by the presence of institutionalized restraint. Beginning in 1848, Prussia adopted and supported the spread of constitutional rule. The practice of strategic restraint and the power-checking mechanisms built into federal institutions played a critical role in encouraging Germany's weaker states to follow Prussia's lead rather than balance against it. The formation of the union also benefited from a widespread sense of cultural commonality. Especially after the nationalist fervor unleashed by the revolutions of 1848, German unification was advanced by ethnic and linguistic homogeneity.

The main impediments to union were the differences in social order and religion that divided the northern from the southern states. The commercializing and Protestant north repeatedly ran into resistance from a predominantly agrarian and Catholic south as it pursued unification. Bismarck was quite explicit about his views of Catholicism, writing in 1854, "It is not a Christian creed, but a hypocritical, idolatrous papism full of hate and cunning, which conducts an unrelenting struggle with the most infamous weapons against the Protestant governments, and especially against Prussia. . . .

---

[247] Pflanze, *Bismarck and the Development of Germany*, pp. 338, 344.

'Catholic' and 'enemy of Prussia' are identical in meaning."[248] Differences in social order and religion had the potential to lead to two German states—a progressive, Protestant one centered on Prussia, and a conservative Catholic one around Austria. At a minimum, a German confederation might have suffered from the same internal divide as did the Swiss Confederation.

That these outcomes were eventually averted is a testament to the importance of liberal restraint and cultural commonality in explaining the onset of stable peace. Despite their differences in social order and religion, the states of southern Germany ultimately aligned with Prussia rather than Austria for two main reasons. First, as commercialization advanced in the south, so did its embrace of a more liberal and progressive politics. Pflanze observes that "German national feeling in the south was chiefly the property of middle-class liberals."[249] Austria, due to its staunch defense of conservative monarchy, thus became a less attractive candidate to lead the push toward German unity. The evolution of the south's social and political order brought it into closer political alignment with Berlin than Vienna. Second, Austria insisted on remaining a multiethnic empire. Indeed, only 8 million of the 36 million residents of the Austro-Hungarian Empire were German. If Germany was to cohere as a union of common ethnicity and language, it would therefore be under Prussian rather than Austrian leadership. As Cronin notes, "Austria's unwillingness to undergo the changes necessary to evolve from a multinational empire to a national state made it ultimately impossible for it to lead the German nation."[250]

Failed Unions: The U.S. Civil War and Singapore's Expulsion from Malaysia

THE U.S. CIVIL WAR

The founding of the United States constitutes an archetypal instance of the formation of a zone of stable peace. The initial impetus emerged from strategic necessity; the American colonies banded together in order to amass the capabilities needed to throw off British rule. Thereafter, the practice and institutionalization of strategic restraint enabled the union to cohere, aided by a common language, religion, and ethnicity. After its founding, the new re-

---

[248] Pflanze, *Bismarck and the Development of Germany*, p. 368.
[249] Pflanze, *Bismarck and the Development of Germany*, p. 384.
[250] Cronin, *Community Under Anarchy*, pp. 115–121; quote on p. 121.

public thrived; its establishment was followed by successive decades of political stability, economic growth, and territorial expansion.

The auspicious beginnings of the United States make its demise in the 1860s all the more puzzling. In 1789 and for decades thereafter, the conditions needed to sustain the union were amply present. The young republic not only proved durable, but also succeeded in keeping European powers at bay and extending westward its territorial reach. During the 1860s, however, the zone of peace established by the American colonies faltered; the South seceded and the United States survived only because the Union Army prevailed over the forces of the Confederacy. What caused the unraveling of stable peace? Why did the union, after successive years of progress, collapse at the beginning of its seventh decade?

The underlying cause of the Civil War was the incompatible social orders of the North and South. As Charles and Mary Beard write, "at bottom the so-called Civil War . . . was a social war," pitting the agrarian and slave-holding society of the South against the industrializing and free labor society of the North.[251] This sectional divide did not suddenly appear in the 1860s. Rather, the confrontation between North and South had been building since the union's founding. But America's political system initially provided for the effective management of sectional differences over tariffs, slavery, and the nature of the union's political economy, producing bargains that enabled North and South to pursue their diverging visions of development. As mentioned, the Missouri Compromise was a prime example.

Early America was able to accommodate the social incompatibilities of North and South for three main reasons. First, during the union's early decades, the economies of the two sections were both primarily agrarian. Northerners aspired to build a more urbanized and industrialized society, but that vision had not yet materialized. In 1800, roughly 70 percent of the North's workforce was in agriculture, slightly below the 80 percent of southerners who worked the land.[252] The economies of North and South were on different trajectories, but they had not yet diverged, holding in abeyance the political break that would ultimately result from competing social orders. Second, North and South were in effective political equilibrium. During the

---

[251] Charles and Mary Beard, *The Rise of American Civilization*, in Michael Perlman, ed., *The Coming of the American Civil War*, 3rd ed. (Lexington, MA: D.C. Heath and Co., 1993), p. 33.

[252] James McPherson, "Southern Exceptionalism: A New Look at an Old Question," in Perlman, ed., *The Coming of the American Civil War*, pp. 194–195.

late 1700s and early 1800s, "the two sections were evenly balanced in population and in the number of states, so that at the time there was no danger of either section's encroaching upon the interests of the other."[253] Sectional differences emerged over domestic issues as well as foreign policy, but the existence of a political balance encouraged North and South alike to seek pragmatic compromise.

Third, sectional compromise was facilitated by the structure of the party system; during the years prior to the realignment of the mid-1850s, partisan cleavages did not run neatly along sectional lines. Instead, the main parties had footholds in both North and South, and the delegations that the two regions sent to Congress contained a healthy mix of representatives from the union's main parties. During the 1840s, for example, "The Democrats and Whigs were national parties drawing their leaders and followers from both sections. . . . Congressmen voted not by region as Northerners or Southerners but primarily as Whigs and Democrats. Party rather than sectional interest prevailed in the roll calls on most issues reaching the national political agenda."[254] With the union's mainstream parties seeking to appeal to voters in North and South alike, the party system produced centrist policies as well as political bargains that cut across sectional lines.

The political equilibrium between North and South was not to last. Diverging economic trajectories both magnified sectional differences in social order and decidedly tilted the balance of political power in the North's favor. As the Beards note, "Had the economic systems of the North and the South remained static or changed slowly without effecting immense dislocations in the social structure, the balance of power might have been maintained indefinitely . . . keeping in this manner the inherent antagonisms within the bounds of diplomacy. But nothing was stable in the economy of the United States or in the moral sentiments associated with its diversities."[255] Over time, stark differences emerged between the economic and social profiles of the two regions. By 1860, the percentage of the North's workforce in agriculture had dropped to 40 percent. Only 1 percent of its population was black. In contrast, almost 85 percent of the southern labor force was in agriculture. One-third of the

[253] Frank Owsley, "The Irrepressible Conflict," in Perlman, ed., *The Coming of the American Civil War,* p. 35.
[254] Edward Pessen, "How Different from Each Other Were the Antebellum North and South," *American Historical Review* 85, no. 5 (December 1980): 1139.
[255] Charles and Mary Beard, *The Rise of American Civilization,* p. 24.

South's population was black, and 95 percent of them were slaves. The over-all population of the North, once roughly equal to that of the South, had by 1860 become 50 percent larger due to the arrival of immigrants from abroad and migrants from the South in search of jobs in manufacturing.[256]

Westward expansion further tilted the economic and political balance in the North's favor. The expanding railway network linked the western territories to the North, adding to the pace and scope of industrialization. Whether slavery would continue to move westward in step with territorial expansion proved to be a singularly divisive issue. Emboldened by the growing power of the North, the Republican government that came into office in 1860 insisted that slavery cease its westward spread, setting the stage for a further diminution of the electoral strength of slave states. Although the South was not then threatened with the abolition of slavery where it already existed, the southern states were well aware that the balance of political power was shifting decidedly against them. As the Beards describe this realization, "the South was fighting against the census returns—census returns that told of accumulating industrial capital, multiplying captains of industry, expanding railway systems, widening acres tilled by free farmers. Once the planting and the commercial states . . . had been evenly balanced; by 1860 the balance was gone."[257]

The consequences of the growing political imbalance between North and South were magnified by the demise of cross-sectional parties. The Republican Party formed in the mid-1850s in response to the South's successful bid to repeal the Missouri Compromise. The Republicans became the North's main party and the principal vehicle for pursuing the region's economic and political interests, which included stopping the westward spread of slavery: "As for the Republicans, by the late 1850s they had succeeded in developing a coherent ideology which . . . rested on a commitment to the northern social order."[258]

Meanwhile, Democratic voters in the North dwindled in number, making the Democrats the party of the South. The party system was no longer a vehicle for cross-sectional compromise, but instead helped ensure a sectional

---

[256] Pessen, "How Different from Each Other Were the Antebellum North and South," p. 1121; McPherson, "Southern Exceptionalism" pp. 194–196.

[257] Charles and Mary Beard, *The Rise of American Civilization*, p. 34.

[258] Eric Foner, "Politics, Ideology, and the Origins of the Civil War," in Perlman, ed., *The Coming of the American Civil War*, p. 182.

confrontation over slavery. As Eric Foner observes, "On the level of politics, the coming of the Civil War is the story of the intrusion of sectional ideology into the political system. . . . It is no accident that the breakup of the last major inter-sectional party preceded by less than a year the breakup of the Union or that the final crisis was precipitated not by any 'overt act,' but by a presidential election."[259] Michael Holt agrees that the union experienced a decisive "shift from a nationally balanced party system where both major parties competed on fairly even terms in all parts of the nation to a sectionally polarized one with the Republicans dominant in the North and Democrats in the South."[260]

In the same way that unions deepen as political and economic integration promotes a common identity, they come apart as political and economic segregation promotes diverging identities. As Brian Holden Reid writes, "A sense of social and cultural distinctiveness followed the political and economic imperative, not the other way around."[261] In the North, a narrative developed that critiqued the South not just for its commitment to "Slave Power," but also for its broader attachment to an antiquated and aristocratic social order.[262] A southern "nationalism" developed in parallel, one that stressed the region's distinct culture and way of life. As the *Charleston Mercury* wrote in 1856, "The North and the South are two nations, made by their institutions, customs, and habits of thought, as distinct as the English and French."[263]

To symbolize their political and cultural separation from the union, southern states began to adopt state flags. Many of them had single stars, a signal of states' rights and their separation from the collective community of the union: "The adoption of these single star flags during the secession crisis ran this process [of union] in reverse, as states 'plucked' their stars, to use the language of Jefferson Davis, rather than face future consolidation into a single mass."[264] As the seceding states formed their own government and army, they

[259] Foner, "Politics, Ideology, and the Origins of the Civil War," p. 171.

[260] Michael Holt, "Party Breakdown and the Coming of the Civil War," in Perlman, ed., *The Coming of the American Civil War,* p. 92.

[261] Brian Holden Reid, *The Origins of the American Civil War* (New York: Longman, 1996), p. 97.

[262] See Eric Foner, *Politics and Ideology in the Age of the Civil War* (New York: Oxford University Press, 1980), p. 48.

[263] Avery Craven, *The Repressible Conflict, 1830–1861* (Baton Rouge: Louisiana State University Press, 1939), p. 28. See also McPherson, "Southern Exceptionalism."

[264] Robert Bonner, *Colors and Blood: Flag Passions of the Confederate South* (Princeton, NJ: Princeton University Press, 2002), p. 28.

adopted a common flag for the Confederacy, symbolizing their consolidation as a separate union. As Foner observes, even as war broke out, "It is true that in terms of ethnicity, language, religion . . . Americans, North and South, were still quite close."[265] Nonetheless, these commonalities proved no match for the diverging social orders of North and South and the sectional confrontation this divergence spawned.

By the 1850s, the sequential process that led to the onset of stable peace had been thrown into reverse. In the late eighteenth century, geopolitical necessity combined with institutionalized restraint to lay the foundation for a federal union. Societal integration and the generation of a national identity then helped consolidate the union, while a political balance sustained compromise between the diverging social orders of the North and South. As the union matured, however, economic development led to a growing political imbalance between the North and South and a widening gap between their social orders. Societal separation followed, narratives of opposition triumphed over a common national identity, and political restraint gave way to brinkmanship and ultimatum. Geopolitical rivalry and the outbreak of war soon followed, violently interrupting the consolidation of the United States as a zone of stable peace.

THE EXPULSION OF SINGAPORE FROM MALAYSIA

The 1963 union between Malaya, Singapore, Sabah, and Sarawak was the culmination of roughly two decades of diplomatic efforts to prepare for the end of Britain's imperial presence in Southeast Asia.[266] Malaya became independent in 1957 and, as the Crown Colony of Singapore prepared to follow suit in the early 1960s, London believed that Singapore's security and economic viability would best be served through a merger with Malaya.

The main impediment to union was its prospective impact on the demographic balance between ethnic Malays and ethnic Chinese. The formation of Malaya was based on a political compact between its Malay majority and Chinese minority. The Malays would retain political dominance and benefit from affirmative action programs in education and employment. In return, the Chinese would continue to enjoy a decided economic advantage. As Mary Fletcher observes, "provisions were written into the constitutional documents insuring the special position of the Malays and granting them certain special

[265] Foner, "Politics, Ideology, and the Origins of the Civil War," p. 188.
[266] See map 5.1.

privileges . . . the Malays were to be insured political ascendancy to balance the economic dominance of the non-Malays."[267] This compact would be threatened by the merger of Malaya and Singapore; roughly 75 percent of Singapore's population was Chinese, making ethnic Chinese a plurality of the union's population should the merger proceed. For Malaya's prime minister, Tunku Abdul Rahman, this demographic shift posed an unacceptable challenge to the political dominance of Malays and the Malay character of the country.[268]

Tunku nonetheless proceeded with the incorporation of Singapore into the Malaysian Federation in 1963. His eventual decision to do so was the product primarily of strategic necessity.[269] The governments of Singapore and Malaya alike saw communist insurgency as the main threat to regional stability. Kuala Lumpur gradually came to support union out of fear that Singapore might serve as a base for communist activists intending to infiltrate Malaya. Singapore's government was itself more leftist in its orientation than that of Malaya, but elections there in the early 1960s shook the political establishment by favoring the far left, prompting the prime minister, Lee Kuan Yew, and his People's Action Party (PAP) to follow Tunku's lead in embracing union as a check against the communist threat. Lee was particularly interested in furthering his country's political stability by improving its economic fortunes; the free trade regime that was to accompany union would ensure a lucrative market for Singapore's manufactured goods and solidify its position as a hub for seaborne shipping.[270]

Confronted with the strategic imperatives of union, Tunku took steps to counterbalance the demographic implications of bringing Singapore into the federation. He secured the entry into the union of Sabah and Sarawak, former British possessions on the island of Borneo, to offset the growing number of ethnic Chinese in the federation. Indeed, Kuala Lumpur was so eager to lure these territories into the union that it offered them 25 percent of the seats in the parliament even though they were home to only 12 percent of the

[267] Nancy McHenry Fletcher, *The Separation of Singapore from Malaysia* (Ithaca, NY: Department of Asian Studies, Cornell University, 1969) , p. 56.

[268] Fletcher, *The Separation of Singapore from Malaysia* p. 7; John Oh, "The Federation of Malaysia: An Experiment in Nation-Building," *American Journal of Economics and Sociology* 26, no. 4 (October 1976): 426.

[269] Mohamed Noordin Sopiee, *From Malayan Union to Singapore Separation* (Kuala Lumpur: University of Malaysia Press, 1974), p. 142; Oh, "The Federation of Malaysia," pp. 425–437; and Fletcher, *The Separation of Singapore from Malaysia*, p. 72.

[270] Fletcher, *The Separation of Singapore from Malaysia*, p. 5.

federation's population. Tunku did the opposite with Singapore, offering Singaporeans only fifteen out of 159 parliamentary seats even though they deserved twenty-five seats based on their population. In addition, there was a tacit agreement between Lee and Tunku that the PAP would limit its political activities to Singapore, alleviating the threat that it potentially posed to the alliance between Tunku's party, the United Malays National Organization (UMNO), and the mainland's principal Chinese party, the Malayan Chinese Association (MCA). This deal was essential inasmuch as even with the entry of Sabah and Sarawak, the union's population would be roughly 42 percent Chinese and 39 percent Malay.[271] These mechanisms for protecting the political dominance of ethnic Malays succeeded in clearing the way for union. In August 1963, Malaya became Malaysia through a merger with Sabah, Sarawak, and Singapore.

The union, however, proved fleeting; despite the political bargain struck to clear the way for federation, Malaysia remained bedeviled by the shifting balance of power between ethnic Malays and ethnic Chinese. Tunku envisaged a "Malay Malaysia" in which Malays would retain political dominance despite the new demographic balance, while Lee foresaw a "Malaysian Malaysia" in which political power would be openly contested. The tension between these two visions began to mount after Lee decided in 1964 to extend the PAP's reach to the mainland and turn it into a union-wide party.

This decision constituted a critical turning point in the viability of the union; by threatening the UMNO-MCA alliance and opening up the prospect of a united front of ethnic Chinese, Lee directly challenged the political dominance of ethnic Malays. As Mohammed Noordin Sopiee observes, "What had been a political contest had started to become a dangerous communal one."[272] Indeed, violence broke out between Chinese and Malays in Singapore. But more worrisome than racial tension was the prospect that ethnic Chinese, through the extension of the PAP to the mainland, could come to dominate the union. "To the Tunku," Fletcher observes, "this participation was not only contrary to an earlier pledge which the Tunku felt Lee had made, but it was also, in the Tunku's eyes, an attempt to go back on the constitutional arrangements by which Singapore was accepted into the federation." Moreover, "Lee, by reporting population figures and historical data, made frighteningly clear to the Malays the fact that they were outnum-

---

[271] Fletcher, *The Separation of Singapore from Malaysia*, pp. 56–57.
[272] Sopiee, *From Malayan Union to Singapore Separation*, p. 193.

bered by the Chinese, and openly challenged the basis of the Malay claim to special status and special privileges. . . . The resultant fear of a Chinese take-over was shattering."[273]

In August 1965, Tunku decided to expel Singapore from Malaysia. Lee had little choice but to accept Singapore's eviction.[274] In the end, it was the ethnic divide and the prospect of a shift in the distribution of power between Malays and Chinese that sank the union. As Fletcher notes, "virtually every aspect of the Singapore-Malaya dispute became entangled in the racial embroilment."[275] A multiethnic Malaysia was itself not the problem; diversity thrived within the union. Rather, the union collapsed as a result of the demographic implications of Singapore's inclusion and the threat its sizable Chinese population posed to a political order predicated upon Malay dominance. The federation benefited from institutionalized restraint and from an inclusive Malaysian identity that embraced ethnic diversity. But it could not survive the threat to a Malay-dominated political order posed by Singapore's Chinese majority.

The separation of Singapore from Malaysia occurred peacefully. But the border between the two countries did soon become a geopolitical dividing line, with Singapore investing in an impressive defense establishment to protect itself against potential threats from a rump Malaysia as well as Indonesia. In the aftermath of disunion, not until the maturation of ASEAN did Singapore, Malaysia, and the wider region come to enjoy the onset of stable peace.[276]

―――――――――――

These concluding cases provide further evidence in support of the book's core arguments, as summarized in figure 6.1. To be sure, the ten cases of union examined in this chapter do not demonstrate uniformity as to the conditions that bring about stable peace. Although cultural commonality was present in all the instances of successful union, the cases reveal less consis-

―――――――――――

[273] Fletcher, *The Separation of Singapore from Malaysia*, pp. 36–37, 62, 57.

[274] R. S. Milne, "Singapore's Exit from Malaysia: The Consequences of Ambiguity," *Asian Survey* 6, no. 3 (March 1966): 182.

[275] Fletcher, *The Separation of Singapore from Malaysia*, p. 56. See also Stanley Bedlington, *Malaysia and Singapore: The Building of New States* (Ithaca, NY: Cornell University Press, 1978), p. 208; and Oh, "The Federation of Malaysia," p. 428.

[276] On the evolution of Singapore's defense policy after disunion, see Tim Huxley, *Defending the Lion: The Armed Forces of Singapore* (St. Leonards, New South Wales: Allen & Unwin, 2000).

	Case	Institutionalized Restraint	Compatible Social Orders	Cultural Commonality
Successes	Swiss Confederation *(1291–1848)*	Y	N*	Y
	Iroquois Confederation *(1450–1777)*	Y	Y	Y
	United Arab Emirates *(from 1971)*	N	Y	Y
	United States *(1789–1861)*	Y	N*	Y
	Italy *(from 1861)*	Y	Y	Y
	Germany *(from 1871)*	Y	Y	Y
Failures	United Arab Republic *(1958–1961)*	N	N	Y
	Senegambian Confederation *(1982–1989)*	Y	N	Y
	U.S. Civil War *(1861)*	Y	N	Y
	Singapore and Malaysia *(1965)*	Y	N	Y

FIGURE 6.1 Union: Summary of Findings
*See qualifications on pages 387–388.

tency as to the causal importance of institutionalized restraint. The UAE formed and endured in the absence of institutionalized restraint—even if it did, similarly to the Iroquois Confederation, benefit from tribal traditions of consensual decision making. The experience of the UAE reaffirms a key conclusion of the last chapter: although a favoring condition, institutionalized restraint is not a necessary condition for stable peace; states that do not embrace institutionalized restraint at home can nonetheless exercise strategic restraint in the conduct of statecraft.

On the surface, the cases of Switzerland and the United States call into question the hypothesis that compatible social orders are a necessary condition for stable peace. To draw this conclusion would, however, be to misinterpret these historical cases. To be sure, the Swiss Confederation and the United States did survive for more than a decade—the standard this book uses to code a case as a success—despite facing deep social divides among their constituent states. However, such social incompatibilities did in fact eventually split both unions asunder, exposing each to civil war before their eventual consolidation. Moreover, the dynamic through which social orders affected outcomes is quite similar in the two cases. Both unions held together when a rough political balance existed between their rural and urban sections. Civil war and disunion resulted from shifts in the political balance between these competing sections due to enlargement and differential rates of population and economic growth. Union was ultimately sustained by the military defeat of the minority social group as it attempted secession (the *Sonderbund* in the Swiss Confederation and the Confederacy in the United States). The eventual consolidation of both unions was then furthered by the social convergence afforded by commercialization and industrialization. From this perspective, the Swiss and U.S. cases ultimately confirm the hypothesis that compatibility in social order is a necessary condition for stable peace.

CHAPTER SEVEN

MAKING FRIENDS AND CHOOSING FRIENDS

This book has focused on two principal questions. First, through what pathway do states succeed in setting aside their grievances, escape geopolitical competition, and construct a relationship that precludes the prospect of armed conflict? In short, how do enemies become friends? Second, under what circumstances do zones of stable peace form and under what circumstances do they fail? In short, when and why do enemies become friends?

The case studies have provided straightforward answers to these questions. As to the pathway to stable peace, its onset is triggered by strategic necessity and subsequently unfolds through four phases. At the outset, a state faced with insufficient resources to deal with existing threats resorts to unilateral accommodation to befriend an adversary. Reciprocal restraint then regularizes cooperation and dampens rivalry. Societal integration follows, building personal and institutional linkages between the partner states. The final phase entails the generation of new narratives of amity and the consolidation of compatible, shared, or common identities. The mechanisms at work move from the rationalist to the sociological; strategic bargaining initiates the process of reconciliation, societal integration advances the onset of international society, and changes in political discourse and the construction of new identities complete the establishment of stable peace.

As to the causes of stable peace, there are three critical ingredients: institutionalized restraint, compatible social orders, and cultural commonality. Institutionalized restraint favors—although is not necessary for—the practice of strategic restraint, which is crucial to securing the initial rounds of accommodation that set adversaries on the path to peace. Compatible social orders facilitate societal integration by ensuring that political and economic elites seek to advance rather than block reconciliation and deepening ties. Cultural commonality helps adversaries select each other as potential partners and facilitates the generation of the communal identity that consolidates stable peace.

Rather than merely summarizing these conclusions, the purpose of this final chapter is to reflect on the more surprising and counterintuitive aspects of this book's findings—those that challenge conventional wisdom and run counter to prevailing thinking among scholars and policy makers about the causes of peace. Matters of process will be examined first, followed by consideration of the conditions under which stable peace breaks out. The chapter also explores the policy implications of these theoretical conclusions.

MAKING FRIENDS

One of the main goals of this book is to generate a road map to help states navigate the journey from enmity to friendship. Exploration of the sequential process through which peace breaks out provides the following insights about how states might go about escaping geopolitical rivalry and finding their way to international society.

Accommodation and Reciprocal Restraint

The practice of strategic restraint is an essential ingredient of stable peace. When states engage in self-binding and co-binding, even major asymmetries in territory, wealth, and military capability do not stand in the way of reconciliation and the formation of international society. Sweden overshadowed Norway in material terms, but peace broke out after 1905 in step with Sweden's embrace of liberal democracy and strategic restraint. Abu Dhabi was by far the largest and wealthiest emirate, but its willingness to withhold its power, redistribute its wealth, and cede political influence to the smaller emirates cleared the way for stable union. Peace broke out between the United States and Great Britain after London's appeasement of Washington led to mutual accommodation on a host of outstanding disputes. In contrast, the absence of strategic restraint correlates with the demise of zones of peace. Syria defected from the UAR after Nasser made clear that he intended to grant its elite little, if any, political power. The GCC continues to be plagued by power asymmetries and fear of Saudi hegemony among its smaller members. The Concert of Europe collapsed after the revolutions of 1848 stirred up nationalist passions, prompting Britain and France to capitalize on, rather than studiously avoid, opportunities to pursue unilateral advantage.

The political impact of accommodation and reciprocal restraint goes well beyond traditional accounts of the cumulative advantages of cooperation. In the early stages of the onset of stable peace, a liberal framework does adequately capture the degree to which discrete acts of bargaining and signaling alter strategic calculations and increase transparency. But thereafter, the process becomes more transformative. Through the exchange of costly concessions and unambiguous acts of accommodation, the parties come to attribute to one another benign motivations, clearing the way for the mutual attribution of benign character. This is a crucial turning point in several respects. States are no longer bargaining with each other under conditions of suspicion and competition; indeed, each party comes to presume that the other means it no harm. International society, even if "thin," begins to take shape. The uncertainty presumed by realists and liberals alike to impede cooperation is still present, but mutual confidence and trust minimize the hindrances that uncertainty poses to deepening partnership. Strategic uncertainty may be irreducible, but it becomes irrelevant when stable peace begins to enjoy a taken-for-granted quality.

The establishment of mechanisms for resolving disputes and checking power helps institutionalize the practices of self-binding and co-binding. Partners in peace embrace diverse procedures for containing disagreements and preventing them from reawakening geopolitical competition. The Concert of Europe grouped dissident members, restoring consensus through persuasion coupled with the threat of isolation. When a consensus was not forthcoming, dissenters opted out of joint action, but did not seek to block it. In the Iroquois Confederation, nations that disagreed with the majority refrained from sending sachems to the Grand Council, thereby avoiding the disputes that would have otherwise ensued. In the Swiss Confederation, specific cantons were designated as arbitrators, and cantons not involved in a given dispute would seek to group the estranged parties in order to guide them back to consensus. ASEAN, the UAE, and the Iroquois institutionalized the practice of deferral, putting off controversial issues until a consensus emerged—or simply dropping the matter altogether.

Despite the geographic and temporal diversity of the cases, they exhibit a remarkable similarity as to the nature of the power-checking mechanisms that enable zones of stable peace to take shape. The parties embrace decision-making rules and other instruments designed to de-concentrate power, all of which mitigate the consequences of material asymmetries. In some cases, the influence of smaller states is over-weighted to ameliorate concerns about domination by their larger partners. During the Concert of Europe, Britain and Russia elevated the political influence of Austria and Prussia, and welcomed into the club a defeated France. Gambia was given more seats in the Senegambian assembly than warranted by its population. In other cases, inequities in power and population are offset by codifying equality in decision making. The U.S. Senate ensured equal representation for all states prepared to enter the federal union—regardless of their size. During the long evolution of the Swiss Confederation, sparsely populated rural cantons had the same vote in the confederation's diet as densely populated urban ones. The five Iroquois nations, despite their varying populations and inequalities in the size of the delegations sent to Onondaga, all had one vote each in the Grand Council.

The location of the seat of governance is often selected—or rotated among different sites—so as to mitigate concern about the excessive concentration of power in a single member state. The EC established its governing institutions in multiple locations, avoiding the capitals of its most powerful members. The seat of the federal government in the United States was located in the District of Columbia in order to temper sectional rivalries and cater to both commercial and agrarian interests. The Swiss Confederation had multiple capitals and they changed over time, rotating to respond to the challenges posed by the urban/rural and Protestant/Catholic divides. As Italian unification proceeded, the capital moved from Turin to Florence to Rome, ameliorating fear of Piedmont's hegemony and drawing on the emotive appeal of Rome's imperial pedigree to help promote national unity. Nasser offered to move the UAR's capital from Cairo to Damascus on a seasonal basis—but the proposal came after the Syrian elite had already lost patience with Egypt's political domination of the union. Nasser was too late in recognizing the potential benefits of an ambulatory capital.

At the same time that self-binding and co-binding are practices critical to the onset of stable peace, so too is the exercise of power. Indeed, zones of stable peace usually form around cores of strength. From this perspective, international society evolves as the preponderant state (or supra-state authority) succeeds in finding a balance between the exercise of power and its negation.

The onset of stable peace in Southeast Asia and South America depended upon the leadership of Indonesia and Brazil; these dominant states had to guide their respective regions toward cooperative practices and shared norms. Nonetheless, the seminal turning points involved the willingness of both states to back away from confrontational foreign policies and withhold their power in order to appease their neighbors. Leadership combined with the practice of strategic restraint to encourage regional peace. The unification of Italy and Germany depended upon the preponderant power and leadership of Piedmont and Prussia, respectively. But constitutional restraint was equally important in shielding their smaller partners from the coercive potential of Piedmontese and Prussian strength. It is no accident that progress toward Italian and German unification quickened substantially after both states adopted constitutions following the revolutions of 1848. The formation of the UAE depended upon Abu Dhabi's leadership, but the union would likely have failed without the willingness of the dominant emirate to share its wealth and bind itself to its smaller neighbors.

A similar logic applies to zones of peace that are anchored by supra-state institutions rather than dominant powers. From the outset of the Swiss Confederation, its diets struggled to amass sufficient authority to provide order while preserving the traditional autonomy of the individual cantons. The United States needed to be centralized enough for federal institutions to provide effective governance, but not so centralized that the individual states would have feared tyranny and opted against participation in the union. From the formation of the European Coal and Steel Community through the EU's most recent institutional reforms, European authorities have been careful to balance the power of the Franco-German coalition and the union's collective institutions in Brussels against the political powers of national governments.

How unions have dealt with political control over military forces is illustrative of the importance of striking a balance between the power of union institutions and that of its constituent states. As the last redoubt of autonomy and security, control over the use of force is often the last competence to be handed over to collective authority.[1] Even after the fashioning of a unitary Switzerland in 1848, the individual cantons long maintained their own mili-

[1] The cases reveal notable exceptions to this pattern. The Senegambian Confederation early on created integrated military forces. This exception was in large part a product of the fact that Gambia had no standing military prior to confederation. The UAR established a unified command soon after its founding, and many Egyptian officers were dispatched to Syria to serve in the "First Army." This rapid merging of the armed forces backfired, however, serving as a potent source of Syrian resistance to Egyptian dominance.

tias. The warriors of the separate Iroquois nations at times coordinated their actions, but they were never under the collective control of the confederation. The UAE was to have a union-wide army from the outset, but effective centralization of the forces of the separate emirates took roughly two decades. During the early decades of union, the individual American and German states jealously guarded the autonomy of their separate militias. The EU has yet to arrive at a common foreign and security policy and its member states have thus far refused to embrace union-wide defense planning and procurement, instead retaining national armed forces. Such arrangements are emblematic of the realm of international society—a middle ground between the anarchy of international politics and the single sovereignty of the unitary state.

Several policy implications follow. First, this study constitutes an unambiguous refutation of one of the core principles of neoconservatism. At least as understood by the Bush administration during its first term, the neoconservative school maintains that preponderant power, wielded with unstinting resolve, is a key ingredient of hierarchy and order in the international system. The cases examined in this book point to the opposite conclusion—that the unfettered exercise of power triggers balancing and undermines a rules-based order. Instead, it is the practice of strategic restraint that fosters and sustains international society. Stable peace requires mutual reassurance and respect, not mutual suspicion and resentment. Zones of peace do form around cores of strength, but only when those cores withhold their power and demonstrate benign intent through the exercise of restraint. More generally, the implications of the constellation of power in the international system depend on how preponderant states wield their strength, not just on the distribution of power itself. Structure matters, but so does statecraft.

Second, the cases demonstrate the central role of costly and unambiguous concessions in clearing the way for reconciliation and starting the sequential process that leads to stable peace. Major concessions, not just token gestures, are essential because they are necessary indicators of benign intent. The recent U.S. nuclear deal with India provides a case in point. In negotiating the pact, the United States made major concessions and compromised long-standing nonproliferation policies—primarily as an investment in befriending and building a strategic partnership with India. The complicated politics of accommodation in India initially stood in the way of New Delhi's acceptance of the deal; the Communist Party opposed the pact precisely because it signified partnership with the United States. But a coalitional realignment ultimately enabled India to accept Washington's offer, opening the door to rapprochement and the prospect of dramatic improvement in relations between the United States and India.

Such opening gambits have significant potential with other parties. With Iran, Washington might offer full normalization of relations in return for Tehran's willingness to cease its nuclear program and its support for Islamic extremists. As the preponderant party, the United States is in the best position to take the initial steps toward rapprochement. A rising China is by no means destined to clash with the United States; mutual accommodation holds promise of facilitating a peaceful transition of power. The United States could make way for, rather than seek to arrest, China's emergence as a major power, securing in return Beijing's willingness to practice reciprocal restraint and help fashion the norms and rules that could stabilize relations with the United States and promote a nascent security community in Northeast Asia.[2] Turkey and Greece would have been wise to follow the opening afforded by "earthquake diplomacy" with major concessions on their longstanding grievances. Instead, they allowed reconciliation to stall and those grievances to continue fueling mutual suspicion. Major acts of accommodation may well not be reciprocated—and thus fail to open the door to stable peace. But they are necessary starting points for transforming relationships characterized by suspicion and hostility to ones characterized by mutual confidence and trust.

Third, the cases illustrate the importance of the programmatic practice of strategic restraint, not just its temporary application; zones of stable peace risk unraveling when one or more of their members abandon reciprocal restraint. The Concert of Europe unraveled after Britain and France, prompted by the revolutions of 1848, began to back away from the self-binding and cobinding practices that Concert members embraced after the Napoleonic Wars. Britain's decision in the early 1920s to drop its alliance with Japan extinguished the norm of reciprocity and the mutual reassurance provided by the pact, arguably setting Japan on a unilateral course that culminated in a destructive collision with the Western powers.

These historical lessons underscore the risks associated with America's drift away from the practices of restraint and multilateral engagement which

---

[2] For arguments in favor of containing and impeding China's rise, see John J. Mearsheimer, *The Tragedy of Great Power Politics* (New York: Norton, 2001), chap. 10.

took place after the attacks of September 11, 2001. Especially among the United States' key allies in Europe, elites and publics alike came to view Washington as having reneged on the binding and bounding bargains that it struck after World War II.[3] This perception put significant strain on its relationships around the world, and particularly with its European allies. Were it left unattended, the more unilateral course in U.S. foreign policy would have the potential to put at risk the zone of peace that has formed among the Atlantic democracies. Indeed, the more multilateral inclinations of Bush's second term, as well as the course corrections implemented by President Barack Obama, have made clear Washington's recognition of this danger.

When states abandon the practice of strategic restraint, they no longer appear as benign polities to their partners; behavior can change perception of intent and motivation even as regime type remains constant. Opinion surveys in the wake of the Iraq war in 2003 revealed that publics around the world—even in states that are part of the Atlantic zone of peace—disapproved of U.S. unilateralism and the U.S. "war on terror," prompting them to question the purposes of American power.[4] America's preponderant strength began to lose its ability to attract or group other states, instead reawakening balancing behavior. Indeed, scholars argued that "soft" balancing against the United States took place during Bush's tenure.[5] As countries around the world no longer saw the United States as a benign polity, American power began to exercise centrifugal rather than centripetal force across the international system. The Atlantic zone of peace was subjected to unprecedented strain. Germany and France led the charge to block the invasion of Iraq, breaking with the United States on fundamental questions of war and peace. Russia confronted the United States over NATO expansion, the independence of Kos-

[3] In a public opinion survey from June 2007, 89% of French, 83% of Canadians, and 74% of the British believed that the United States does not take into account the interests of other countries in formulating its foreign policy. See Pew Global Attitudes Project, "Global Unease with Major World Powers," available at http://pewglobal.org/reports/pdf/256.pdf, p. 20.

[4] Pew Global Attitudes Project, "Global Unease with Major World Powers," available at http://pewglobal.org/reports/pdf/256.pdf, pp. 20–23

[5] On the debate over soft balancing, Robert A. Pape, "Soft Balancing against the United States," *International Security* 30, no. 1 (2005); T. V. Paul, "Soft Balancing in the Age of U.S. Primacy," *International Security* 30, no. 1 (2005); Stephen G. Brooks and William C. Wohlforth, "Hard Times for Soft Balancing," *International* Security 30, no. 1 (2005); and Keir Lieber and Gerard Alexander, "Waiting for Balancing: Why the World Is Not Pushing Back," *International Security* 30, no. 1 (2005).

ovo, missile defense, and a host of other issues, in effect challenging the foundations of a U.S.-led Western order.

Domestic reactions to Washington's abandonment of the practice of strategic restraint intensified the sharpness of the international response—in a manner consistent with the historical cases examined in this study. When countries back away from the exercise of strategic restraint, they expose elites in partner states to a domestic backlash—the politics of humiliation—prompting them to abandon cooperative policies, or bringing to power hardliners opposed to accommodation. In the runup to the Crimean War, Britain and France abandoned the practice of strategic restraint. Although Russia made successive concessions to avert a clash with its Concert partners, its moves were not reciprocated. This dynamic embarrassed the Tsar's government and ultimately stiffened Russia's eventual willingness to stand up to Britain and France. Senegal waited patiently for Gambia to honor its pledge to conclude a common market; that the Gambian government failed to do so led to a domestic backlash in Senegal, encouraging President Diouf to back away from the confederation.

A similar dynamic has been taking place in contemporary Russia. From Moscow's perspective, Russia for successive years made a series of concessions to the West, including accommodating NATO expansion, reacting with restraint to democratic revolutions in its "near abroad," and facilitating strategic access for the United States in Central Asia and Afghanistan. More recently, however, Russia has defected from the path of strategic restraint—most notably by sending its forces into Georgia and recognizing the independence of Abkhazia and South Ossetia. Russians—elites and the public alike—have expressed humiliation and resentment stemming from what they see as the West's exploitation of their country's accommodating stance. The result has been Moscow's embrace of a more assertive and nationalistic foreign policy. It remains to be seen whether Obama's call for "resetting" relations and his willingness to compromise on issues such as arms control and missile defense succeed in enabling the politics of accommodation to prevail in Moscow, clearing the way for reciprocal restraint.

A final policy insight stemming from the connection between strategic restraint and stable peace concerns the timing and modalities of restraint. Although bold and costly acts of accommodation are usually necessary to start the process of reconciliation, withholding power does not come naturally to states—even those whose own domestic structures institutionalize political restraint. For reasons that realists identify, states generally let down their guard only slowly and cautiously. Accordingly, strategic restraint is more likely to take hold when practiced incrementally and informally rather than through ambitious and formalized mechanisms from the outset. In virtually all of the cases examined in this book, the onset of stable peace—in particular, the institutionalization of power-checking devices—occurred gradually, enabling the parties in question to adjust their statecraft and its domestic foundations accordingly. The Concert of Europe, the EC, ASEAN, the Swiss Confederation, the Iroquois Confederation, the UAE, the United States—these and other zones of peace began with only loose structures and informal understandings. Had these groupings demanded greater centralization and formality at the outset, they would likely have been stillborn, their members having backed away from unacceptable encroachments on their autonomy. Indeed, unions that form suddenly and aspire to high levels of centralization from the start are prone to failure, as exemplified by the collapse of the United Arab Republic and the dissolution of the Senegambian Confederation.

The lessons for today are amply clear—less may be more when it comes to preserving and expanding stable peace. To borrow insights from the leadership of Franklin Roosevelt, building peace requires "workable minimums," not "impossible maximums."[6] Absent the solidarity engendered by the Soviet threat, the Atlantic zone of peace and its primary institution—NATO— have become more unwieldy, pointing to the need for greater flexibility in decision making. NATO's current reliance on unanimity may be too high a bar, as made clear by the war in Afghanistan, where only a few alliance members are prepared to run the risks of high-intensity combat. Moreover, the Atlantic democracies do not today enjoy a consensus about strategic priorities, diverging, for example, over the nature of the threat of international terrorism and how best to fight it. Simply put, differences in threat perception and capability are far more pronounced than they used to be.[7] Indeed, the United States and its European partners disagreed about how harshly to react to Russia's military actions in Georgia during the summer of 2008 and whether to put Georgia and Ukraine on the path to NATO membership. Accordingly, refashioning a looser and less formal partnership will do more to preserve an

[6] Roosevelt's thinking as described by Forrest Davis after an interview with the president. See "What Really Happened at Tehran," *Saturday Evening Post*, May 20, 1944, p. 44.

[7] See Charles A. Kupchan, "NATO Divided," *International Herald Tribune*, April 10, 2008.

Atlantic zone of peace than clinging to ambitious expectations that will likely go unmet.[8] As the collapse of the Concert of Europe and the Iroquois Confederation revealed, diverging threat perceptions and strategic interests, unless effectively managed, have the potential to lead to the collapse of stable peace.

The same logic applies to zones of peace—whether aspiring or already evolving—in other regions. ASEAN has thrived in no small part as a result of its informal approach to consensus formation. If a cooperative security architecture is to emerge in northeast Asia, it is likely also to be based on the informality of the "ASEAN Way." The same goes for the Middle East, Africa, and Latin America, where zones of stable peace, to the extent they exist, are still in only nascent form. At the global level as well, ad hoc groupings—not the more formalistic UN Security Council—have been the most effective tools of great-power cooperation. The Contact Group in the Balkans, the Quartet in the Middle East, the Six-Party Talks on North Korea, the EU3-U.S. team dealing with Iran's nuclear program—such groupings have become a staple of contemporary diplomacy. At the regional as well as global levels, informal approaches to consensus formation and the practice of reciprocal restraint hold out the most hope of advancing the cause of peace. If successful, these approaches then clear the way over time for the formalization and institutionalization of stable peace.

Societal Integration and Identity Change

One of the most striking findings of this book is the causal *in*significance of economic integration during the early phases of stable peace. Contrary to much of the existing literature on political integration, which stresses the beneficial effects of economic interdependence, the cases examined in this book indicate that there is no causal linkage between commercial ties and the initial steps toward stable peace. This finding constitutes a refutation of the work of Deutsch, Boulding, Rock and others who offer a primarily transactional account of the sources of rapprochement, security community, and union.[9] Of the twenty cases examined in this book, only in the case of Ger-

---

[8] See Charles A. Kupchan, "The Fourth Age: The Next Era in Transatlantic Relations," *National Interest*, no. 85 (September/October 2006).

[9] For further discussion of the impact of international trade on international security and the use of force, see Edward D. Mansfield and Brian Pollins, eds., *Economic Interdependence and In-*

man unification did economic integration play an important role in clearing the way for reconciliation and political integration. Even in the German case, leaders explicitly used economic instruments for political purposes—to enlist the support of the middle class and advance the cause of German unity. In all the other cases, unilateral accommodation and the practice of reciprocal restraint preceded economic integration. Moreover, the advance of reconciliation was driven primarily by geopolitical considerations, not economic incentive.

Economic integration does advance stable peace during later phases, when societal linkages serve to consolidate reconciliation and promote cooperation and trust. Firms that stand to benefit from economic openness and increases in trade and investment become important sub-state agents, calling for the further evolution of commercial and political ties. International society "fills out" as engagement in the process of consolidating stable peace spreads from political elites, to economic elites, to the broader public. Importantly, however, it is politics, not economics, that is in command. Only after political elites succeed in backing away from geopolitical rivalry does economic integration kick in as an important mechanism helping to advance the cause of stable peace; commercial interdependence on its own cannot drive the process forward. Nor can commercial interdependence by itself preserve stable peace in the face of centrifugal political forces. Political decisions can often trump economic considerations, making short shrift of the benefits of interdependence. After Mao and Khrushchev parted ways ideologically, for example, Sino-Soviet exchanges and commerce were broken off with remarkable rapidity.

Although economic integration often plays a role in consolidating rapprochement, security community, and union, it is also the case that economic factors regularly serve as a major obstacle to stable peace. If partner states have incompatible social orders and integration undermines economic elites, the path to stable peace is often blocked. The demise of the UAR and the Senegambian Confederation can be directly attributed to the threat that union posed to the Syrian and Gambian economies. The process of German unification occurred quite slowly, spanning much of the nineteenth century, in large part because the agrarian states of the south resisted the commercialization that would come with economic integration. So too did the United States in the 1860s fall prey to the growing social and economic incompatibil-

---

ternational Conflict: New Perspectives on an Enduring Debate (Ann Arbor: University of Michigan Press, 2003).

ities of its north and south. From this perspective, economic considerations loom larger as a negative than a positive force when it comes to stable peace. On the negative side, economic impediments have the potential to prevent stable peace from taking root—even in the presence of a prior political opening. On the positive side, economic incentives can aid and abet the process—but they do not have sufficient causal weight to bring about stable peace in the absence of a prior political opening.

Important policy considerations follow. When addressing long-standing rivalries, governments, international institutions, and the private sector should no longer labor under the illusion that the advance of economic interdependence will on its own lead to political reconciliation. Trade and investment between China and Japan may mount in the years ahead, but such flows will have little impact on their bilateral relationship unless they are accompanied by accommodation and reciprocal restraint on matters of geopolitics. The international community can encourage trade between Israel and the Palestinian Authority, Kosovo and Serbia, and India and Pakistan. But such trade will yield significant political benefits only in the context of a political accommodation between the parties in question.

A similar logic applies to the preservation of zones of peace. Transatlantic trade and commerce are poised to thrive in the years ahead. But economic interdependence alone will not ensure the durability of an Atlantic zone of peace. As the rift over the 2003 invasion of Iraq demonstrated, disagreements over security issues have the capacity to compromise the character of political ties even amid robust flows of trade and finance. Moreover, globalization and economic integration should by no means be seen only as a source of transatlantic cohesion and interdependence. Economic nationalism is on the rise in the EU as the traditional welfare state is threatened by global competition. In the United States, financial turmoil, outsourcing, de-industrialization, and growing income inequalities have been sapping enthusiasm for globalization and free trade. Protectionist instincts could be the source of new and potent tensions within the transatlantic community. After all, the each-for-his-own attitudes that paralyzed Western cooperation during the 1930s started with the tariffs and economic nationalism that emerged from the Great Depression. Moreover, several of the cases in this book—for example, the collapse of the Sino-Soviet partnership and the U.S. Civil War—make clear that economic separation can be a precursor to geopolitical rivalry.

As for the generation of new narratives and changes in identity, the analysis in this book underscores the causal importance of political discourse. Words and symbols matter, especially when wielded instrumentally by government officials and opinion makers. As political leaders, economic interest groups, and media and cultural outlets deploy new narratives of partner states, they have the ability to alter the deeply held identities that societies hold of each other. The resulting changes in identity play an important role in consolidating zones of stable peace—as well as breaking them apart.

From the Revolutionary War through the middle of the 1890s, Great Britain was the United States' primary enemy. By the early 1900s, societies in both countries were coming to see an Anglo-American war as tantamount to fratricide. British appeasement of the United States and the practice of reciprocal restraint that followed cleared the way for rapprochement. But it was the emergence of a new discourse on both sides of the Atlantic—one that propagated notions such as a "shared Anglo-Saxon race" and an "Anglo-American family"—that produced a compatible identity, consolidated stable peace, and laid the foundation for the strategic partnership that exists to this day. In similar fashion, the Concert of Europe emerged from discrete strategic bargains and elite agreement on a set of ordering norms. But its durability and longevity were also the product of the sense of community generated by political discourse. Regular references to Europe as "a single entity," to "intimate union," and to "Christian brotherhood" helped consolidate a shared European identity. The causal weight of changes in narrative and identity is even more pronounced in cases of unions—the UAE, Germany, the United States—in which the onset of a common identity was critical to legitimating and strengthening the authority of supra-state institutions of governance.

Changes in discourse have as much potential to be destructive as constructive. The demise of Sino-Soviet partnership was triggered by an ideological dispute. Charged rhetorical exchanges followed, with the rift between Khrushchev and Mao spilling out into the public domain. The withdrawal of advisers and the breaking off of strategic cooperation ensued, eventually followed by the militarization of borders and the return of geopolitical rivalry. The onset of civil war in the United States was precipitated by a marked escalation in rhetoric, with northerners and southerners alike deploying oppositional discourse. The South eventually sought to generate its own sense of nationhood, its political and cultural separation symbolized by its own flag and national lore. The Senegambian Confederation did not fall prey to a similar discourse of opposition, but it did suffer from the absence of a discourse of solidarity. Elites in neither Senegal nor Gambia made a concerted effort to construct a common identity. In the absence of societal integration and with opinion makers on both sides failing to deploy a narrative of community, the union effectively atrophied. Both Dakar and Banjul then defected when the opportunity arose.

Today's political leaders and opinion makers should thus take matters of discourse and identity more seriously than they often do. The proliferation of television news channels and the information revolution spawned by digital technology have enhanced the ability of both governments and the media to shape public attitudes. Too frequently, such influence is wielded to effect short-term gains in popularity or market share—without due consideration of the potential impact of discourse on the conduct of statecraft. Moreover, presidential speeches and other forms of public outreach, even if targeted at a domestic electorate, now have a global audience. Accordingly, as political leaders seek to shape public attitudes, they must carefully weigh the potential impact abroad as well as at home.

Within existing zones of peace, elites should ensure that political discourse conveys the need for continued solidarity and the deepening of a communal identity. It is worrisome, for example, that the project of European integration no longer animates national politics and political discourse to the degree that it used to. Indeed, rather than portraying the EU as an essential vehicle for ensuring peace and prosperity, European elites have become regular detractors. Integration, critics charge, is compromising democratic accountability, threatening the welfare state and causing economic duress, and flooding member states with immigrants. A re-nationalization of political discourse has followed, compromising the EU's forward momentum. This elite and popular backlash against globalization, enlargement, and immigration raises the possibility that European integration has reached its high-water mark. That prospect would be less worrisome if the EU's collective institutions and collective identity were sufficiently robust to preclude the possibility of backsliding and unraveling. But history's lessons—the U.S. Civil War, the collapse of the UAR, the unraveling of the Concert of Europe, the breakup of Yugoslavia—these and many other cases counsel against complacency about the EU's durability.

Accordingly, investments in the efficacy of Europe's collective institutions and the sense of commonality needed to legitimate them remain urgent tasks.

The member states must endow EU institutions with sufficient authority to govern effectively, while avoiding a level of centralization that would trigger a backlash against the union. The EU must also pursue policies, particularly in the economic arena, to demonstrate its direct relevance to the lives of its citizens. Such tasks require not just reforming institutions and policies, but also reclaiming a political discourse that emphasizes solidarity and the EU's concrete contributions to European security and prosperity.

The same goes for the Atlantic zone of peace. As recent transatlantic tensions have made clear, U.S.-EU partnership cannot be taken for granted. Generational change on both sides of the Atlantic complicates the task of preserving international society among the Atlantic democracies. The World War II generation, for whom Atlantic solidarity was an article of faith, is being replaced by younger Europeans and Americans for whom the Atlantic link is of much less salience. Patterns of migration pose an additional challenge to the Atlantic community. The onset of Anglo-American rapprochement and of an Atlantic zone of peace was facilitated by cultural affinity; through much of American history, most Americans hailed from Europe. Migration flows are fast changing these ancestral linkages. Americans of European descent will by mid-century constitute less than half of the U.S. population, replaced primarily by citizens with family ties to Latin America. This change could advance the cause of stable peace in the Western Hemisphere, but potentially at the expense of Atlantic solidarity. Europe's population is meanwhile growing more diverse, with many immigrants hailing from Africa and the Middle East. This change could advance the cause of stable peace in the Mediterranean region, but again at the potential expense of transatlantic ties.

These demographic changes need not jeopardize an Atlantic zone of peace, but they do suggest that it may prove more difficult to sustain. Leaders may want to compensate for greater demographic diversity by focusing discourse on shared values and interests rather than common ancestry and history. At a minimum, they must avoid the heated rhetoric that accompanied the rift over the Iraq war, when Europeans and Americans alike portrayed each other as antagonists. If left unattended, discourses of opposition and rivalry have the potential to become a self-fulfilling prophecy. European enthusiasm for President Obama and his commitment to rebuilding the Atlantic partnership have provided an auspicious antidote to the rancor that ensued over the invasion and occupation of Iraq—as have the pro-American leanings of French president Nicolas Sarkozy and German chancellor Angela Merkel.

Discourse has an important role to play among adversaries as well as among states that have already succeeded in escaping geopolitical competition. Iran and the United States may well not find their way to mutual accommodation any time soon. But Washington's branding of Iran as part of an "axis of evil" and Tehran's branding of the United States as the "great Satan" and of Israel as a "stinking corpse" make it particularly difficult for either side to risk the bold acts of accommodation needed to move rivals toward reciprocal restraint. In similar fashion, it may be politically expedient for American leaders to warn of the looming threat posed by China, and for Chinese leaders to decry the excesses of American power. Nonetheless, such rhetoric has the potential to stand in the way of China's peaceful rise.

Regional rivalries would similarly benefit from efforts to alter antagonistic discourses. In East Asia, for example, the continuing controversy over whether Japan has accepted sufficient responsibility for its behavior during World War II and revised its history textbooks accordingly has more than symbolic importance. By maintaining oppositional narratives among Japanese, Chinese, and Koreans, these issues represent a significant impediment to rapprochement in northeast Asia. So too do textbooks and media coverage in the Middle East polarize public attitudes and impede resolution of the Palestine-Israel conflict. In all these cases, entrenched discourses of opposition create domestic obstacles to the practice of strategic restraint, making it politically difficult for leaders to pursue the policies of accommodation that have the potential to advance reconciliation.

CHOOSING FRIENDS

A second main goal of this book is to identify the causal conditions that lead to stable peace. Exploration of this issue provides insight into where and when zones of stable peace are most likely to form and what attributes favor their durability. The twenty cases examined in this book indicate that institutionalized restraint is a favoring condition for stable peace, but not a necessary condition. Of the twelve successful cases of stable peace, four occurred in the absence of institutionalized restraint—initial rapprochement between Brazil and Argentina, the Concert of Europe, ASEAN, and the UAE.[10] In

---

[10] As discussed in chapter 4, rapprochement between Brazil and Argentina began when both countries were governed by military juntas, but it was not consolidated until both were democracies.

contrast, compatible social orders and cultural commonality appear to be necessary conditions for stable peace. Both conditions were present in all twelve of the successful cases.[11] One or both conditions were absent in all six cases of failure, except the GCC. Incompatible social orders emerge as the most significant and frequent impediment to stable peace, playing a prominent role in all of the cases of breakdown, again with the exception of the GCC. These findings point to the following policy conclusions.

Institutionalized Restraint

This book offers a controversial perspective on the relationship between regime type and stable peace by demonstrating that many different kinds of regimes, including autocracies, are capable of fashioning zones of stable peace. Liberal democracy, although it is a facilitating factor, is not a necessary condition for enemies to become friends. Institutionalized restraint is a more inclusive and accurate categorization of the types of regimes that are best suited to forge zones of stable peace. Moreover, the case studies make clear that the institutionalization of restraint can take many different forms. In some cases, including Anglo-American rapprochement and the unification of the United States, Germany, and Italy, constitutions within and among the partner states were the main vehicles for institutionalizing restraint. In others, such as the UAE and the Iroquois Confederation, tribal traditions of power sharing and consensual decision making were paramount. Traditions of restraint practiced within tribes came to be practiced among them. In the case of ASEAN, village-based social norms that emphasized consultation and deliberation provided an important basis for restraint and consensual decision making at the interstate level, laying a foundation for the establishment of security community.

The cases also point to important outliers—states that practiced strategic restraint in their external relations even though they did not exercise political restraint at home. The Concert of Europe functioned effectively despite its inclusion of three absolute monarchies—Austria, Prussia, and Russia. Admittedly, the operation of the Concert was facilitated by the norms of cooperation that had emerged amid alliance against Napoleonic France. But the practice of strategic restraint held across regime type and despite the pres-

---

[11] See the caveats concerning the Swiss and U.S. cases in the conclusion to the preceding chapter.

ence of three members that staunchly resisted constitutional constraints on monarchic rule. The Soviet Union and China, both governed by autocratic regimes, fashioned a remarkably close partnership during the 1950s. So too did the initial moves toward rapprochement between Indonesia and Malaysia and between Brazil and Argentina occur in the absence of constitutional rule. Military juntas were in control of both Brazil and Indonesia when each embarked down the path of stable peace. The stark turn in policy came not from institutionalized constraints on political power, but from the exigencies of domestic crisis. Redressing economic deterioration in Indonesia and containing the growing power of the security apparatus in Brazil—these were the pressing challenges that triggered a dramatic shift in policy. To be sure, the advance of liberalizing reforms then helped consolidate stable peace in the case of Brazil and Argentina. But ASEAN formed and deepened even while Suharto's power remained virtually unchecked at home.

It is also the case that democracy, although it facilitates the onset of stable peace for reasons spelled out in chapter 2, is hardly a sufficient condition for stable peace—and indeed can militate against it. After the revolutions of 1848, it was the more democratic members of the Concert, Britain and France, which were pushed by popular nationalism to overturn the status quo, ultimately resulting in the Crimean War. During the 1890s, London's decision to appease Washington was motivated in part by its appreciation of war fever among the American public and Congress. American democracy was a cause of alarm, not reassurance. Britain was a democracy when it walked away from the Anglo-Japanese alliance in the early 1920s—pressed to do so by anti-Japanese racism in Britain and among its democratic, Anglo-Saxon allies. The union of Singapore with Malaysia ended when Singapore sought to abide by democratic norms that would have altered the balance of power between ethnic Malays and ethnic Chinese.

This diversity as to the relationship between domestic structure and stable peace suggests that foreign policy behavior—in particular, the practice of strategic restraint—is a more important variable than regime type per se in isolating the causes of peace. The readiness of states to engage in reciprocal restraint may therefore be a better marker of potential partners in peace than a more formalistic codification of regime characteristics. This finding would argue against the prevailing wisdom among scholars and policy makers alike, which holds that the United States and other liberal democracies should weigh heavily regime type in choosing their international partners. Institutionalized restraint is a reliable marker of what types of states are most capable of fashioning zones of stable peace, but the case studies make clear that even regimes that do not embrace checks and balances at home may nonetheless do so abroad.

This finding suggests that it would be unnecessary and unwise for the United States and other democratic countries to classify states according to regime type as they seek to fashion a stable international order. In this respect, recent proposals to establish a league of democracies or turn NATO into a global alliance of democracies make little strategic sense.[12] The United States should not make the mistake of excluding from cooperative institutions non-democratic states that may well be prepared to practice strategic restraint and help tame the international system. Doing so would not only miss opportunities for collaboration, but would also make such opportunities less likely by discouraging non-democracies from remaining open to mutual accommodation and the exchange of concessions—steps critical to advancing reconciliation and programmatic cooperation.

From this perspective, a concert of the great powers is a far better investment in the spread of peace than a concert of democracies. Moreover, pressing major powers to quicken their pace of democratization may do more harm than good in promoting great-power peace. At least for the foreseeable future, political stability in Russia and China is likely to make both states more capable partners than the domestic turmoil and nationalism that would likely accompany rapid democratic change. In addition, as elaborated upon in the next section, if the United States predicates partnership with China and Russia on their willingness to democratize, threatened elite groupings may well react by seeking to block strategic cooperation.

Social Orders

The compatibility of social orders proved to be a far more reliable predictor of stable peace than did regime type. With consistency across the cases, compatibility in social orders was a permissive condition for the onset of stable

---

[12] For sources supporting the proposal to establish a league of democracies, see chapter 1, note 3. For a critique of the proposal, see Charles A. Kupchan, "Minor League, Major Problems: The Case Against a League of Democracies," *Foreign Affairs* 87, no. 6 (November/December 2008). On turning NATO into a global alliance, see Ivo Daalder and James Goldgeier, "Global NATO," *Foreign Affairs* 85, no. 5 (September/October 2006).

peace, while incompatibility was a potent obstacle. Social cleavages manifested themselves along several different dimensions. In the case of Norway
and Sweden, a key impediment to stable peace was the threat posed to the
power and privilege of Sweden's aristocracy by Norway's egalitarian social
order. In other cases—the Soviet Union and China, the Swiss Confederation,
Germany, the United States—the principal divide was between rural/agrar-
ian societies and urban/industrializing ones. In the UAR and the Senegambian Confederation, centralized and closed economies clashed with more decentralized and open ones. In all of these cases, social sectors threatened by
political and economic integration blocked the advance of stable peace. In
some instances, such as the UAR, disunion followed. In other instances, such
as the Swiss Confederation and the United States, differences in social order
led to civil war.

In contrast, when such social cleavages either did not exist or significantly
diminished as a result of political and economic change, the onset of stable
peace proceeded apace. Rapprochement between Brazil and Argentina, the
formation of ASEAN, the establishment of the Iroquois Confederation and
the United Arab Emirates—compatible social orders facilitated the advance
of stable peace in all these cases. The unification of Germany was slowed by
political tensions between the more commercialized states in the north and
the more agrarian ones in the south. The advance of commercialization in
the south and the social convergence that accompanied it then helped clear
the way for union. Social cleavages brought civil war to the Swiss Confederation and the United States, but both unions were eventually consolidated as
economic development closed the social gap between urban and rural Swiss
cantons and between northern and southern American states.

It follows that efforts to build new zones of stable peace are most likely to
yield positive results when they take place among states that enjoy compatible
social orders. From this perspective, globalization and the increased flow of
commerce and finance to the developing world do have beneficial geopolitical
effects. But those benefits stem less from interdependence, as commonly presumed, than from the convergence in social order that commerce should engender. If, for example, North Africa has a large and prosperous middle class,
it would be easier to draw the region into a European zone of peace than if
integration threatens Europe's workforce with a flood of immigrants and dis-
possesses North Africa's traditional elite. In similar fashion, the expansion of
stable peace in the Americas may depend on first closing the income gap

within and between the countries of the Western Hemisphere. Otherwise, the advance of free trade and societal integration may produce political back-lashes of the kind that have taken place in countries such as Venezuela and Bolivia. In the absence of compatible social orders, regional integration may do more harm than good, destabilizing countries whose societies suffer from large income inequalities and fueling tensions between countries with ad-vanced economies and those that are significantly less developed.

The relative importance of social compatibilities in securing lasting inter-national cooperation provides a measure of optimism about great-power re-lations. China, India, and Russia have all been experiencing rapid economic growth and the expansion of their middle classes. They have relatively open economies and elite groupings that are being strengthened, not threatened, by integration into the global economy. China's exports of goods and capital, India's exports of computing expertise and services, and Russia's exports of energy are enriching and empowering key social sectors in all three countries. Whereas important differences in social order still distinguish rising great powers from the industrialized West—differences that could stand in the way of deeper societal integration—social convergence does help provide a foun-dation for great-power peace by diminishing the potential for societal opposi-tion to rapprochement.

Economic liberalization may well induce political liberalization over time, but it would be a mistake to precondition cooperation and the practice of reciprocal restraint with Russia and China on their embrace of liberal de-mocracy. Although China in particular is industrializing and urbanizing, it is far from certain that its economic and political trajectory will track that of the West. China is the rising power that is most closely following the Western model of large-scale industrial development. As in the West during the nine-teenth century, a merchant, entrepreneurial, and professional class is thriving and growing. But also as in the West, the traditional elite—in China's case, the Communist Party—is coopting the rising middle class. As described by the *New York Times*, "the party has absorbed entrepreneurs, urban profes-sionals and university students into an elite class that is invested in the politi-cal status quo."[13] This bargain between ruling elites and the upwardly mobile may well forestall political liberalization for the foreseeable future.

It is by no means clear if or when China will pass through the next stage of

[13] "China's Leaders Are Resilient in Face of Change," *New York Times*, August 6, 2008.

industrial development, one that entails the empowerment of the working class and the onset of liberal democracy. Rural peasants still make up 60 percent of China's population. By means of comparison, when Britain consolidated liberal democracy in the late nineteenth century, roughly 70 percent of its population lived in cities and towns, the same percentage of urban dwellers today in North America and Europe. As middle and working classes in China expand and seek political power commensurate with their wealth, democratization may well come from within. But the process, as it was in Europe, is likely to be slow and incremental.

In the meantime, gradual convergence in social orders between rising powers and today's leading states provides a basis for taking tentative steps to consolidate great-power peace. This book suggests that such convergence will do more to lay a foundation for cooperation than achieving uniformity in regime type. Indeed, were the West to condition the participation of China and Russia in global councils upon their full democratization, political elites in both countries would likely resist due to the threat posed to their hold on power. The Concert of Europe, after all, succeeded in preserving great-power cooperation among diverse regimes in no small part because its members did not seek to interfere in each other's domestic affairs. The Concert of Europe, which regularized cooperation but did not aspire to full societal integration or the complete elimination of geopolitical rivalry, provides an illustrative model for a future concert of the great powers.

Cultural Commonality

Differences in ethnicity, race, and religion pose potent barriers to stable peace. In only one of the twenty cases examined in this book—Sino-Soviet relations in the 1950s—did cultural factors not play an important role in either the ascent or demise of a zone of peace. Communist ideology and its focus on transcending cultural and national divides is the best explanation for this anomaly. In all the other cases, cultural commonality was a key facilitator of stable peace, and cultural difference a key obstacle. Anglo-American rapprochement, the outbreak of peace between Norway and Sweden, the Concert of Europe, the amalgamation of the UAE, the Iroquois Confederation, the unification of Italy—each of these instances of stable peace benefited from an underlying cultural affinity. In contrast, the demise of Anglo-Japanese rapprochement, the expulsion of Singapore from Malaysia, the exclusion of Australia and New Zealand from ASEAN—these historical episodes demonstrate the divisive potential of cultural difference.

Interestingly, differences in language do not appear to pose as significant a stumbling block to stable peace as differences in ethnicity, race, and religion. To be sure, a common language does facilitate the onset of stable peace, especially during the phases of societal integration and generation of a communal identity. Anglo-American rapprochement, the formation of the UAE, the amalgamation of the United States, the unification of Germany—linguistic commonality advantaged all of these cases. But a shared language is certainly no guarantor of the durability of stable peace. Despite the common language of member states, the GCC has yet to consolidate as a security community, the UAR collapsed, and war broke out among German-speaking Swiss cantons and between America's North and South.

It is also true that linguistic differences failed to stand in the way of stable peace in many cases. The Concert of Europe, ASEAN, and the EC all exhibited considerable linguistic diversity. Linguistic barriers did not prevent rapprochement between Brazil and Argentina or between China and the Soviet Union. When Sino-Soviet rapprochement ultimately failed, differences in social order and ideology, not language, were the primary cause. At the time of unification, Italians spoke a host of different languages; in addition to numerous dialects of Italian, Latin was spoken in Rome, French in Turin, and Spanish in Naples, Sicily, and Sardinia. In the Swiss Confederation, social order and religion long bedeviled the union—but language differences were not a significant source of political cleavage.

The relative insignificance of language differences aside, the potentially divisive role of ethnicity, race, and religion does provide sobering conclusions about the degree to which cultural dividing lines can impede the onset of stable peace. At the same time, it is clear that such cultural obstacles are not insurmountable. Rather, perceptions of cultural commonality and difference are malleable and open to social and political construction; in the eye of the beholder, what are intractable cultural divides one day can become tolerable or irrelevant the next. The Swiss Confederation was plagued for centuries by rivalry between Protestants and Catholics. This religious cleavage subsided, however, after the arrival of liberal nationalism and constitutional restraint in 1848. A common Swiss identity came to transcend cantonal and religious divides. The same dynamic took place in Germany; loyalty to the separate German states and tensions between Protestants and Catholics waned in step with economic integration, political liberalization, and the spread of nation-alism—evoked in part by a succession of external conflicts. Even in cases in which an underlying cultural commonality was present, it regularly took changes in discourse to bring such commonalities to the surface. Americans and Englishmen, Norwegians and Swedes, Piedmontese and Neapolitans, Mohawk and Oneida—these peoples came to recognize one another as trusted kin only when the cessation of strategic rivalry cleared the way for the generation of a new discourse and the communal identity that followed.

Although this observation is cause for optimism about the ability of prac-tice and discourse to overcome identities of opposition, it is important to be mindful that the process of identity change can also work in reverse. During the Concert of Europe, a shared sense of communal identity helped tran-scend the competitive impulses that had long been sources of bloodshed. The revolutions of 1848, however, awakened nationalism, rekindling the commu-nal cleavages that would again bring war to the continent. The onset of the U.S. Civil War was accompanied by new identities of opposition, with eth-nic, linguistic, and religious commonalities meaningless in the face of polar-ization along sectional lines. For decades, Muslims, Catholics, and Orthodox lived side-by-side in Sarajevo, all embracing a common Bosnian identity. But that sense of commonality proved dangerously vulnerable to manipulation by nationalist elites.

These insights point to the following policy implications. Decision makers should privilege potential zones of peace that enjoy cultural commonality. Such groupings are more likely to form and endure than those that cut across cultural dividing lines. To so acknowledge the importance of cultural bound-aries does *not* constitute resignation to Huntingtonian admonitions about inevitable clashes between civilizations. On the contrary, it is to recognize the potential peace-causing effects of cultural affinity.

It follows that China is more likely to be successfully integrated into an East Asian zone of peace than one that seeks to be more diverse. This con-clusion does not mean that rapprochement between the United States and China is futile, but it does mean that such rapprochement is unlikely to occur as easily and extend as fully as that which occurred between the United States and Great Britain. The United States and China may find their way to stable cooperation, but China's natural partners for the fashioning of a zone of sta-ble peace are its Asian neighbors. From this perspective, the United States should seek a strategic accommodation with China at the same time that it encourages practices of reciprocal restraint and societal integration at the regional level.

In similar fashion, Turkey may find that it has suitable strategic partners among its Muslim neighbors to the east and south as well as among its Christian neighbors to the north and west. This observation by no means constitutes an argument against Turkey's integration into the EU. Indeed, there are compelling strategic and political reasons for Turkey's eventual accession. But it does suggest that Turkey, as a core of strength within the Islamic world, has an important role to play in anchoring a potential zone (or zones) of peace in the Middle East.

This analysis points to the importance of pursuing a global strategy of building peace in parts.[14] Regional groupings of states that enjoy cultural affinity are more likely to cohere as zones of peace than those that cut across ethnic, racial, and religious dividing lines. Such regional zones of peace would then serve as building blocks for more extensive global cooperation, perhaps through the formation of a concert of the world's major powers.[15] As the above analysis makes clear, differences in regime type need not stand in the way of great-power cooperation. Statecraft, societal integration, political discourse—in the right hands and under the right conditions, these instruments have the potential to guide the great powers toward peace.

The most important conclusion of this book is a simple one. Stable peace *is* possible. Enemies *do* become friends. When international societies form, they succeed in transforming the world and enabling states to escape the geopolitical rivalries that have so darkened the course of history. No single regime type, culture, or region has a monopoly on stable peace, meaning that the lessons of this study have potentially universal application. Nonetheless, zones of peace are a rare breed. And when they do form, their durability can by no means be taken for granted. These are inviting prospects, but also sobering admonitions. Accordingly, scholars and policy makers alike need to work ever harder to encourage the preservation and spread of stable peace.

[14] Joseph Nye, *Peace in Parts: Integration and Conflict in Regional Organization* (Boston: Little, Brown, 1971).

[15] For further discussion, see Kupchan, "After Pax Americana: Benign Power, Regional Integration, and the Sources of a Stable Multipolarity."

BIBLIOGRAPHY

Abdelkarim, Abbas, ed. *Change and Development in the Gulf.* New York: St. Martin's Press, 1999.

Abdelkarim, Abbas. "Change and Development in the Gulf: An Overview of Major Issues." In *Change and Development in the Gulf,* edited by Abbas Abdelkarim, 3–24. New York: St. Martin's Press, 1999.

Acharya, Amitav. "Collective Identity and Conflict Management in Southeast Asia." In *Security Communities*, edited by Emanuel Adler and Michael Barnett, 198–227. New York: Cambridge University Press, 1998.

———. *Regionalism and Multilateralism: Essays on Cooperative Security in the Asia-Pacific.* Singapore: Eastern University Press, 2003.

Adler, Emanuel. "The Spread of Security Communities: Communities of Practice, Self-Restraint, and NATO's Post Cold War Transformation." *European Journal of International Relations* 14, no. 2 (2008): 195–230.

Adler, Emanuel, and Michael Barnett, eds. *Security Communities.* Cambridge: Cambridge University Press, 1998.

Albrecht-Carrié, René. *The Concert of Europe.* New York: Walker, 1968.

Alves, Maria Helena Moreira. *State and Opposition in Military Brazil.* Austin: University of Texas Press, 1985.

Anderson, Stuart. *Race and Rapprochement: Anglo-Saxonism and Anglo-American Relations, 1894–1904.* East Brunswick, NJ: Associated University Presses, 1981.

Anthony, John Duke. "The Gulf Cooperation Council." In *Gulf Security into the 1980s: Perceptual and Strategic Dimensions*, edited by Robert Darius, John Amos II, and Ralph Magnus, 93–115. Stanford, CA: Hoover Institution Press, 1984.

Austin, J. L., J. O. Urmson, and Marina Sbisa. *How To Do Things With Words.* Oxford: Oxford University Press, 1976.

Axelrod, Robert. *The Evolution of Cooperation.* New York: Basic Books, 1984.

Ayoob, Mohammed, ed. *Regional Security in the Third World: Case Studies From Southeast Asia and the Middle East.* Boulder, CO: Westview Press, 1986.

Barnett, Michael, and F. Gregory Gause III. "Caravans in Opposite Directions: Society, State, and the Development of Community in the Gulf Cooperation Council." In *Security Communities*, edited by Emanuel Adler and Michael Barnett, 161–197. New York: Cambridge University Press, 1998.

Beale, Howard K. *Theodore Roosevelt and the Rise of America to World Power.* Baltimore: Johns Hopkins University Press, 1966.

Beard, Charles, and Mary Beard. *The Rise of American Civilization.* In *The Coming of the American Civil War*, 3rd ed., edited by Michael Perlman, 23–34. Lexington, MA: D.C. Heath and Co., 1993.

Bedlington, Stanley. *Malaysia and Singapore: The Building of New States.* Ithaca, NY: Cornell University Press, 1978.

Bellquist, Eric Cyril, and Waldemar Westergaard. "Inter-Scandinavian Cooperation." In "Supplement: Contemporary Problems of International Relations: Regional Groupings in Modern Europe," *Annals of the American Academy of Political and Social Science* 168 (July 1933): 183–196.

Bengtsson, Rikard. "The Cognitive Dimension of Stable Peace." In *Stable Peace Among Nations*, edited by Arie M. Kacowicz, Yaacov Bar-Siman-Tov, Ole Elgström, and Magnus Jerneck, 92–107. Lanham, MD: Rowman & Littlefield, 2000.

———. *Trust, Threat, and Stable Peace: Swedish Great Power Perceptions 1905–1939.* Lund, Sweden: Lund University Department of Political Science, 2000.

Best, Antony. "India, pan-Asianism and the Anglo-Japanese Alliance." In *The Anglo-Japanese Alliance*, edited by Phillips Payson O'Brien, 236–248. New York: RoutledgeCurzon, 2004.

Bonjour, E., H. S. Offler, and G. R. Potter. *A Short History of Switzerland* Oxford: Oxford University Press, 1952.

Bonner, Robert. *Colors and Blood: Flag Passions of the Confederate South.* Princeton, NJ: Princeton University Press, 2002.

Boulding, Kenneth. *Stable Peace.* Austin: University of Texas Press, 1978.

Bourne, Kenneth. *Britain and the Balance of Power in North America, 1815–1908.* Berkeley: University of California Press, 1967.

Brooks, Stephen, and William Wohlforth. "Hard Times for Soft Balancing." *International Security* 30, no. 1 (2005): 72–108.

Brooks, Stephen, and William Wohlforth. *World Out of Balance: International Relations and the Challenge of American Primacy.* Princeton, NJ: Princeton University Press, 2008.

Brown, Michael, Sean Lynn-Jones, and Steven Miller, eds. *Debating the Democratic Peace.* Cambridge, MA: MIT Press, 1996.

Bull, Hedley. *The Anarchical Society.* London: MacMillan, 1977.

Bullock, Charles J., John H. Williams, and S. Rufus. "The History of our Foreign Trade Balance from 1789 to 1914." *Review of Economic Statistics* 1, no. 3 (July 1919): 215–266.

Buruma, Ian. *The Wages of Guilt: Memories of War in Germany and Japan.* New York: Meridian, 1994.

Bury, J.P.T. "Great Britain and the Revolution of 1848." In *The Opening of an Era: 1848*, edited by Francois Fejto. New York: Howard Fertig, 1966.

Buzan, Barry. *From International to World Society? English School Theory and the Social Structure of Globalization.* Cambridge: Cambridge University Press, 2004.

Buzan, Barry, and Richard Little. *International Systems in World History: Remaking the Study of International Relations.* Cambridge: Cambridge University Press, 2000.

Campbell, A. E. *Great Britain and the United States, 1895–1903.* London: Longman's, 1960.

Campbell, Charles S. *Anglo-American Understanding, 1898–1903.* Baltimore: Johns Hopkins University Press, 1957.

———. *From Revolution to Rapprochement: The United States and Great Britain, 1783–1900.* New York: John Wiley & Sons, 1974.

Campbell, Robert W. "The Post-War Growth of the Soviet Economy." *Soviet Studies* 16, no. 1 (July 1964): 1–16.

Carter, Susan B., Scott Sigmund Gartner, Michael R. Haines, Alan L. Olmstead, Richard Sutch, and Gavin Wright, eds. *Historical Statistics of the United States.* Millennial Edition On Line. Cambridge: Cambridge University Press, 2006.

Castlereagh, Robert Steward, Viscount. *Correspondence, Dispatches, and Other Papers of Viscount Castlereagh.* 3rd series, vol. 11. London: H. Colburn, 1850.

Chapman, John. "The Secret Dimensions of the Anglo-Japanese Alliance, 1900–1905." In *The Anglo-Japanese Alliance*, edited by Phillips Payson O'Brien, 82–98. New York: RoutledgeCurzon, 2004.

Checkel, Jeffrey. "International Institutions and Socialization in Europe." *International Organization* 59, no. 4 (October 2005): 801–826.

Child, Jack. *Geopolitics and Conflict in South America: Quarrels Among Neighbors.* New York: Praeger, 1985.

Christie, John. "History and Development of the Gulf Cooperation Council: A Brief Overview." In *The Gulf Cooperation Council: Moderation and Stability in an Interdependent World*, edited by John A. Sandwick, 7–19. Boulder, CO: Westview Press, 1987.

Clancy, Tom. *The Hunt for Red October.* New York: Berkeley, 1984.

Collier, Ruth Berins, and David Collier. *Shaping the Political Arena: Critical Junctures, the Labor Movement, and Regime Dynamics in Latin America.* Notre Dame, IN: University of Notre Dame Press, 2002.

Cordesman, Anthony. *The Gulf and the Search for Strategic Stability.* Boulder, CO: Westview Press, 1984.

Craig, Gordon. *Germany 1866–1945.* New York: Oxford University Press, 1978.

Craven, Avery. *The Repressible Conflict, 1830–1861.* Baton Rouge: Louisiana State University Press, 1939.

Crawford, Neta. "A Security Regime among Democracies: Cooperation among Iroquois Nations." *International Organization* 48, no. 3 (Summer 1994): 345–385.

Cress, Lawrence Delbert. "Whither Columbia? Congressional Residence and the Politics of the New Nation, 1776 to 1787." *William and Mary Quarterly*, 3rd Ser., 32, no. 4 (October 1975): 581–600.

Cronin, Bruce. *Community Under Anarchy: Transnational Identity and the Evolution of Cooperation.* New York: Columbia University Press, 1999.

Curtis, John Shelton. *Russia's Crimean War.* Durham, NC: Duke University Press, 1979.

Daalder, Ivo, and James Goldgeier. "Global NATO." *Foreign Affairs* 85, no. 5 (September/October 2006): 105–113.

Daalder, Ivo, and James Lindsay. "Democracies of the World, Unite!" *American Interest* 2, no. 3 (January/February 2007): 131–139.

Darius, Robert, John Amos II, and Ralph Magnus, eds. *Gulf Security into the 1980s: Perceptual and Strategic Dimensions.* Stanford, CA: Hoover Institution Press, 1984.

Davidson, Christopher M. *The United Arab Emirates: A Study in Survival.* Boulder, CO: Lynne Rienner, 2005.

———. "After Shaikh Zayed: The Politics of Succession in Abu Dhabi and the UAE." *Middle East Policy* 13, no. 1 (Spring 2006): 42–59.

Dawisha, Adeed. *Arab Nationalism in the Twentieth Century: From Triumph to Despair.* Princeton, NJ: Princeton University Press, 2003.

Delgado, Christopher and Sidi Jammeh, eds. *The Political Economy of Senegal under Structural Adjustment*. New York: Praeger, 1991

Delzell, Charles. *Unification of Italy, 1859–1961: Cavour, Mazzini, or Garibaldi?* New York: Holt Rinehart, 1965.

Derrida, Jacques. *Of Grammatology*. Baltimore: Johns Hopkins University Press, 1976.

Deudney, Daniel. "The Philadelphian System: Sovereignty, Arms Control, and Balance of Power in the American States-Union, Circa 1787–1861." *International Organization* 49, no. 2 (Spring 1995): 191–228.

———. *Bounding Power: Republican Security Theory from the Polis to the Global Village*. Princeton, NJ: Princeton University Press, 2007.

Deutsch, Karl W. *Backgrounds for Community: Case Studies in Large-Scale Political Unification*. Unpublished manuscript.

———. *Political Community and the North Atlantic Area*. Princeton, NJ: Princeton University Press, 1957.

Dickinson, Frederick R. "Japan Debates the Anglo-Japanese Alliance: The Second Revision of 1911." In *The Anglo-Japanese Alliance*, edited by Phillips Payson O'Brien, 99–121. New York: RoutledgeCurzon, 2004.

Dinan, Desmond. *Ever Closer Union: An Introduction to European Integration*. Boulder, CO: Lynne Rienner, 2005.

Dittmer, Lowell. *Sino-Soviet Normalization and Its International Implications, 1945–1990*. Seattle: University of Washington Press, 1992.

Dolan, Paul. "The Nordic Council." *Western Political Quarterly* 12, no. 2 (June 1959): 511–526.

Dreisziger, N. F. "The Role of War Planning in Canadian-American Relations, 1867–1939." *Canadian Review of American Studies* 10, no. 3 (Winter 1979): 100–106.

Durkheim, Émile. *The Division of Labor in Society*. New York: Free Press, 1984.

Edelstein, David. "Managing Uncertainty: Beliefs about Intentions and the Rise of the Great Powers." *Security Studies* 12, no. 1 (Autumn 2002): 1–40.

Edelstein, Michael. "The Determinants of U.K. Investment Abroad, 1870–1913." *Journal of Economic History* 34, no. 4 (December 1974): 980–1007.

El-Kuwaiz, Abdullah Ibrahim. "Economic Integration of the Cooperation Council of the Arab States of the Gulf: Challenges, Achievements and Future Outlook." In *The Gulf Cooperation Council: Moderation and Stability in an Interdependent World*, edited by John A. Sandwick, 71–84. Boulder, CO: Westview Press, 1987.

Ellis, Joseph. *Founding Brothers: The Revolutionary Generation*. New York: Vintage Books, 2002.

Endy, Christopher. "Travel and World Power: Americans in Europe, 1891–1917." *Diplomatic History* 22, no. 4 (Fall 1998): 565–595.

Ericson, Magnus. "The Liberal Peace Meets History: The Scandinavian Experience." Unpublished paper, Lund University.

———. *A Realist Stable Peace: Power, Threat, and the Development of a Shared Norwegian-Swedish Democratic Security Identity, 1905–1940*. Lund, Sweden: Lund University Department of Political Science, 2000.

Etzioni, Amitai. *Political Unification: A Comparative Study of Leaders and Forces*. New York: Holt, Rinehart and Winston, 1965.

Eyck, Erich. *Bismarck and the German Empire*. London: Unwin University Books, 1968.

Eyck, Frank. *The Revolutions of 1848–49*. New York: Barnes & Noble, 1972.

Fearon, James. "Domestic Political Audiences and the Escalation of International Disputes." *American Political Science Review* 88, no. 3 (September 1994): 577–592.

Feis, H. *Europe: The World's Bankers, 1870–1914*. New York: Norton, 1965.

Fejto, Francois, ed. *The Opening of an Era: 1848*. New York: Howard Fertig, 1966.

Fenton, William N. *The Great Law and the Longhouse: A Political History of the Iroquois Confederacy*. Norman: University of Oklahoma Press, 1998.

Ferris, John. "Armaments and Allies: The Anglo-Japanese Strategic Relationship, 1911–1921." In *The Anglo-Japanese Alliance*, edited by Phillips Payson O'Brien, 249–263. New York: RoutledgeCurzon, 2004.

Fletcher, Nancy McHenry. *The Separation of Singapore from Malaysia*. Ithaca, NY: Department of Asian Studies, Cornell University, 1969.

Foner, Eric. *Politics and Ideology in the Age of the Civil War*. New York: Oxford University Press, 1980.

———. "Politics, Ideology, and the Origins of the Civil War." In *The Coming of the American Civil War*, 3rd ed., edited by Michael Perlman, 169—188. Lexington, MA: D.C. Heath and Co., 1993.

Forsyth, Murray. *Unions of States: The Theory and Practice of Confederation*. New York: Leicester University Press and Holmes & Meier Publishers, 1981.

Friedberg, Aaron L. *The Weary Titan: Britain and the Experience of Relative Decline*. Princeton, NJ: Princeton University Press, 1988.

Fursenko, Aleksandr, and Timothy Naftali. *Khrushchev's Cold War: The Inside Story of an American Adversary*. New York: Norton, 2006.

Gardiner, A.G. *The Life of Sir William Harcourt*. Vol. 2. London: Constable, 1923.

Gelber, Lionel M. *The Rise of Anglo-American Friendship: A Study in World Politics, 1898–1906*. London: Oxford University Press, 1938.

Gellner, Ernest. *Nations and Nationalism*. Ithaca, NY: Cornell University Press, 1983.

Gilbert, Felix. *To the Farewell Address: Ideas of Early American Foreign Policy*. Princeton, NJ: Princeton University Press, 1961.

Gillingham, John. *Coal, Steel, and the Rebirth of Europe, 1945–1955: The Germans and French from Ruhr Conflict to Economic Community*. Cambridge: Cambridge University Press, 1991.

Gittings, John. *Survey of the Sino-Soviet Dispute: Commentary and Extracts from the Recent Polemics, 1963–1967*. London: Oxford University Press, 1968.

Glaser, Charles L. "Realists as Optimists: Cooperation as Self-Help." *International Security* 19, no. 3 (Winter 1995/96): 50–90.

———. "The Security Dilemma Revisited." *World Politics* 50, no. 1 (October 1997): 171–202.

Gleason, John Howes. *The Genesis of Russophobia in Great Britain: A Study of the Interaction of Policy and Opinion*. Cambridge, MA: Harvard University Press, 1950.

Goncharenko, Sergei. "Sino-Soviet Military Cooperation." In *Brothers in Arms: The Rise and Fall of the Sino-Soviet Alliance, 1945–1963,* edited by Odd Arne Westad, 141–164. Washington, DC: Woodrow Wilson Center Press, 1998.

Gonzalez, Guadalupe, and Stephan Haggard. "The United States and Mexico: A Pluralistic Security Community?" In *Security Communities*, edited by Emanuel Adler and Michael Barnett, 295–332. New York: Cambridge University Press, 1998.

Grossman, Bernhard. "International Economic Relations of the People's Republic of China." *Asian Survey* 10, no. 9 (September 1970): 789–802.

Haas, Ernst. *The Uniting of Europe: Political, Social and Economic Forces, 1950–1957.* Stanford: Stanford University Press, 1958.

Haas, Peter. "Introduction: Epistemic Communities and International Policy Coordination." *International Organization* 46, no. 1 (Winter 1992): 1–35.

Hagan, Joe. "Domestic Political Sources of Stable Peace: The Great Powers, 1815–1914." In *Stable Peace Among Nations*, edited by Arie M. Kacowicz, Yaacov Bar-Siman-Tov, Ole Elgström, and Magnus Jerneck, 36–54. Lanham, MD: Rowman & Littlefield, 2000.

Hallberg, Charles W. *Franz Joseph and Napoleon III, 1852–1864: A Study of Austro-French Relations.* New York: Octagon Books, 1973.

Hallerberg, Mark, and Katja Weber. "German Unification 1815–1871 and Its Relevance for Integration Theory." *Journal of European Integration* 24, no. 1 (March 2002): 1–21.

Hamerow, Theodore A. *The Social Foundations of German Unification.* Princeton, NJ: Princeton University Press, 1972.

Hardy, Thomas. *The Dynasts: An Epic-Drama of the War with Napoleon.* London: Macmillan, 1920.

Heard-Bey, Frauke. *From Trucial States to United Arab Emirates.* London: Longman, 1982.

———. "The United Arab Emirates: Statehood and Nation-Building in a Traditional Society." *Middle East Journal* 59, no. 3 (Summer 2005): 357–375.

Hemmer, Christopher, and Peter Katzenstein. "Why Is There No NATO in Asia? Collective Identity, Regionalism, and the Origins of Multilateralism." *International Organization* 56, no. 3 (Summer 2002): 575–607.

Hendrikson, David. *Peace Pact: The Lost World of the American Founding.* Lawrence: University Press of Kansas, 2003.

Herzog, Serge. "Arms, Oil and Security in the Gulf: A Tenuous Balance." In *Change and Development in the Gulf,* edited by Abbas Abdelkarim, 238–259. New York: St. Martin's Press, 1999.

Higgot, Richard, and Kim Richard Nossal. "Australia and the Search for a Security Community in the 1990s." In *Security Communities*, edited by Emanuel Adler and Michael Barnett, 265–294. New York: Cambridge University Press, 1998.

Hirst, Monica. "Mercosur's Complex Political Agenda." In *Mercosur: Regional Integration, World Markets,* edited by Riordan Roett. Boulder, CO: Lynne Rienner, 1999.

Hoeffding, Oleg. "Sino-Soviet Economic Relations, 1959–1962." *Annals of the American Academy of Political and Social Science* 349, no. 1 (September 1963): 94–105.

Holt, Michael. "Party Breakdown and the Coming of the Civil War." In *The Coming of the American Civil War*, 3rd ed., edited by Michael Perlman, 90–113. Lexington, MA: D.C. Heath and Co., 1993.

Hughes, Arnold. "The Collapse of the Senegambian Confederation." *Journal of Commonwealth & Comparative Politics* 30, no. 2 (July 1992): 426–438.

Hughes, Arnold, and Janet Lewis. "Beyond Francophonie? The Senegambia Confederation in Retrospect." In *State and Society in Francophone Africa Since Independence*, edited by Anthony Kirk-Greene and Daniel Bach, 228–243. New York: St. Martin's Press, 1995.

Hughes, Arnold, and David Perfect. *A Political History of the Gambia, 1816–1994*. Rochester, NY: University of Rochester Press, 2006.

Hunter, Janet. "Bankers, Investors and Risk: British Capital and Japan during the Years of the Anglo-Japanese Alliance." In *The Anglo-Japanese Alliance*, edited by Phillips Payson O'Brien, 176–198. New York: RoutledgeCurzon, 2004.

Huntington, Samuel. *The Clash of Civilizations and the Remaking of World Order.* New York: Touchstone, 1996.

Hurrell, Andrew. "An Emerging Security Community in South America?" In *Security Communities*, edited by Emanuel Adler and Michael Barnett, 228–264. Cambridge: Cambridge University Press, 1998.

Huxley, Tim. *Defending the Lion: The Armed Forces of Singapore*. St. Leonards, New South Wales: Allen & Unwin, 2000.

Hyden, Goran, and Michael Bratton. *Governance and Politics in Africa*. Boulder, CO: Lynne Rienner, 1992.

Ibrahim, Jibrin. *Democratic Transition in Anglophone West Africa*. Dakar: Council for the Development of Social Science, 2003.

Iikura, Akira. "The Anglo-Japanese Alliance and the Question of Race." In *The Anglo-Japanese Alliance*, edited by Phillips Payson O'Brien, 222–235. New York: RoutledgeCurzon, 2004.

Ikenberry, G. John. *After Victory: Institutions, Strategic Restraint, and the Rebuilding of Order After Major Wars.* Princeton, NJ: Princeton University Press, 2001.

Ikenberry, G. John, and Charles A. Kupchan. "Socialization and Hegemonic Power." *International Organization* 44, no. 3 (Summer 1990): 283–315.

Ikenberry, G. John, and Anne-Marie Slaughter, Princeton Project on National Security. *Forging a World Under Liberty and Law: U.S. National Security in the 21st Century*. Princeton, NJ: Woodrow Wilson School of Public and International Affairs, 2006.

International Institute for Strategic Studies. "The GCC and Gulf Security: Still Looking to America." *Strategic Comments* 11, no. 9 (November 2005), http://www.iiss .org/index.asp?pgid=8431.

Ion, Hamish. "Towards a Naval Alliance: Some Naval Antecedents to the Anglo-Japanese Alliance, 1854–1902." In *The Anglo-Japanese Alliance*, edited by Phillips Payson O'Brien, 26–47. New York: RoutledgeCurzon, 2004.

Jackson, Patrick Thaddeus. *Civilizing the Enemy: German Reconstruction and the Invention of the West.* Ann Arbor: University of Michigan Press, 2006.

Jankowski, James. *Nasser's Egypt, Arab Nationalism, and the United Arab Republic*. Boulder, CO: Lynne Rienner, 2002.

Jian, Chen, and Yang Kuisong, "Chinese Politics and the Collapse of the Sino-Soviet Alliance." In *Brothers in Arms: The Rise and Fall of the Sino-Soviet Alliance, 1945–1963,* edited by Odd Arne Westad, 246–294. Washington, DC: Woodrow Wilson Center Press, 1998.

Johnston, Alastair Iain. *Social States: China in International Institutions, 1980–2000.* Princeton, NJ: Princeton University Press, 2008.

Jorgensen-Dahl, Arnfinn. *Regional Organization and Order in South-East Asia*. New York: St. Martin's Press, 1982.

Jun, Niu. "The Origins of the Sino-Soviet Alliance." In *Brothers in Arms: The Rise and Fall of the Sino-Soviet Alliance, 1945–1963,* edited by Odd Arne Westad, 47–89. Washington, DC: Woodrow Wilson Center Press, 1998.

Kacowicz, Arie. *Zones of Peace in the Third World: South America and West Africa in Comparative Perspective.* Albany: State University of New York Press, 1998.

———. "Stable Peace in South America: The ABC Triangle." In *Stable Peace Among Nations*, edited by Arie Kacowicz, Yaacov Bar-Siman-Tov, Ole Elgström, and Magnus Jerneck, 200–219. Lanham, MD: Rowman & Littlefield, 2000.

Kacowicz, Arie, Yaacov Bar-Siman-Tov, Ole Elgström, and Magnus Jerneck, eds. *Stable Peace Among Nations.* Lanham, MD: Rowman & Littlefield, 2000.

Kant, Immanuel. *Perpetual Peace: A Philosophical Essay*, translated and edited by M. Campbell Smith. London: Swan Sonnenschein, 1903.

Kennan, George. *American Diplomacy, 1900–1950*. Chicago: University of Chicago Press, 1984.

Kennedy, Paul M. *The Rise and Fall of British Naval Mastery*. London: Macmillan, 1983.

Keohane, Robert. *After Hegemony: Cooperation and Discord in the World Political Economy.* Princeton, NJ: Princeton University Press, 1984.

Khalifa, Ali Mohammed. *The United Arab Emirates: Unity in Fragmentation*. Boulder, CO: Westview Press, 1979.

Kirk-Greene, Anthony, and Daniel Bach, eds. *State and Society in Francophone Africa Since Independence*. New York: St. Martin's Press, 1995.

Kohn, Hans. *Nationalism and Liberty: The Swiss Example*. London: George Allen & Unwin, 1956.

Körner, Axel, ed. *1848—A European Revolution? International Ideas and National Memories of 1848*. New York: St. Martin's Press, 2000.

Koselleck, Reinhart. "How European Was the Revolution of 1848/49?" In *1848—A European Revolution? International Ideas and National Memories of 1848*, edited by Axel Körner, 209–221. New York: St. Martin's Press, 2000.

Kramer, Paul A. "Empires, Exceptions, and Anglo-Saxons: Race and Rule between the British and United States Empires, 1880–1910." *Journal of American History* 88, no. 4 (March 2002): 1315–1353.

Krebs, Ronald, and Patrick Jackson. "Twisting Tongues and Twisting Arms: The Power of Political Rhetoric." *European Journal of International Relations* 13, no. 1 (2007): 35–66.

Kupchan, Charles A. *The Persian Gulf and the West: The Dilemmas of Security*. London: Allen & Unwin, 1987.

———. *The Vulnerability of Empire*. Ithaca, NY: Cornell University Press, 1994.

———, ed. *Nationalism and Nationalities in the New Europe*. Ithaca, NY: Cornell University Press, 1995.

———. "After Pax Americana: Benign Power, Regional Integration, and the Sources of a Stable Multipolarity." *International Security* 23, no. 2 (Fall 1998): 40–79.

———. *The End of the American Era: The Geopolitics of the Twenty-first Century.* New York: Knopf, 2002.

———. "The Fourth Age: The Next Era in Transatlantic Relations." *National Interest*, no. 85 (September/October 2006): 77–83.

———. "Minor League, Major Problems: The Case Against a League of Democracies." *Foreign Affairs* 87, no. 6 (November/December 2008): 96–109.

Kupchan, Charles A., and Clifford A. Kupchan. "Concerts, Collective Security, and the Future of Europe." *International Security* 16, no. 1 (Summer 1991): 114–161.

Kydd, Andrew. "Game Theory and the Spiral Model." *World Politics* 49, no. 3 (April 1997): 371–400.

———. "Sheep in Sheep's Clothing: Why Security Seekers Do Not Fight Each Other." *Security Studies* 7, no. 1 (Autumn 1997): 114–155.

Large, Stephen S. *Emperor Hirohito and Shōwa Japan: A Political Biography*. New York: Routledge, 1992.

Legum, Colin, ed. *Africa Contemporary Record: Annual Survey and Documents*, vol. 18, 1985–1986. New York: Africana Publishing, 1987.

Leifer, Michael. *Indonesia's Foreign Policy*. London: George Allen & Unwin, 1983.

Lieber, Keir, and Gerard Alexander. "Waiting for Balancing: Why the World Is Not Pushing Back." *International Security* 30, no. 1 (2005): 109–139.

Lindgren, Raymond. "Nineteenth Century Norway and Sweden: A Contrast in Social Structures." In *Backgrounds for Community: Case Studies in Large-Scale Political Unification*, edited by Karl W. Deutsch. Unpublished manuscript.

———. *Norway-Sweden: Union, Disunion, and Scandinavian Integration*. Princeton, NJ: Center for Research on World Political Institutions, 1979.

Lloyd Jr., William Bross. *Waging Peace: The Swiss Experience*. Washington, DC: Public Affairs Press, 1958.

Luck, James Murray. *A History of Switzerland—The First 100,000 Years: Before the Beginnings to the Days of the Present*. Palo Alto: Society for the Promotion of Science and Scholarship, 1985.

Lutz, Donald. "The Iroquois Confederation Constitution: An Analysis." *Publius* 28, no. 2 (Spring 1998): 99–127.

Mackie, J.A.C. *Konfrontasi: The Indonesia-Malaysia Dispute 1963–1966*. London: Oxford University Press, 1974.

Madison, James, Alexander Hamilton, and John Jay. *The Federalist Papers*. London: Penguin Books, 1987.

Mainwaring, Scott. "The Transition to Democracy in Brazil." *Journal of Interamerican Studies and World Affairs* 28, no. 1 (Spring 1986): 415–431.

Mann, Michael. *The Sources of Social Power: The Rise of Classes and Nation-States, 1760–1914*. Cambridge: Cambridge University Press, 1993.

Mansfield, Edward, and Brian Pollins, eds. *Economic Interdependence and International Conflict: New Perspectives on an Enduring Debate*. Ann Arbor: University of Michigan Press, 2003.

Mansfield, Edward, and Jack Snyder. "Democratization and War." *Foreign Affairs* 74, no. 3 (May/June 1995): 79–97.

Mansfield, Edward, and Jack Snyder. *Electing to Fight: Why Emerging Democracies Go to War*. Cambridge, MA: MIT Press, 2007.

Manzetti, Luigi. "Argentine-Brazilian Economic Integration: An Early Appraisal." *Latin American Research Review* 25, no. 3 (1990): 109–140.

Martin, William, with additional chapters by Pierre Beguin, translated from French by Jocasta Innes. *Switzerland: From Roman Times to Present*. New York: Praeger, 1971.

Mattern, Janice Bially. "The Power Politics of Identity." *European Journal of International Relations* 7, no. 3 (2001): 349–397.

McCain, John. Lecture. The Hoover Institution, Stanford, CA, 1 May 2007.

McPherson, James. "Southern Exceptionalism: A New Look at an Old Question." In *The Coming of the American Civil War*, 3rd ed., edited by Michael Perlman, 188–203. Lexington, MA: D.C. Heath and Co., 1993.

McRae, Kenneth. *Switzerland: Example of Cultural Coexistence*. Toronto: Canadian Institute of International Affairs, 1964.

Mearsheimer, John J. "The False Promise of International Institutions." *International Security* 19, no. 3 (Winter 1994/1995): 5–90.

———. *The Tragedy of Great Power Politics*. New York: Norton, 2001.

Mehnert, Ute. "German Weltpolitik and the American Two-Front Dilemma: The 'Japanese Peril' in German-American Relations, 1904–1917." *Journal of American History* 82, no. 4 (March 1996): 1452–1477.

Mercer, Jonathan. *Reputation and International Politics*. Ithaca, NY: Cornell University Press, 1996.

Mercer, John. "Emotion Adds Life." Paper presented at the annual meeting of the International Studies Association, Washington, DC, February 1999.

Miller, John C. *The Federalist Era: 1789–1801*. New York: Harper and Brothers, 1960.

Millet, Allan, and Peter Maslowski. *For the Common Defense: A Military History of the United States of America*. New York: Free Press, 1984.

Milne, R. S. "Singapore's Exit from Malaysia: The Consequences of Ambiguity." *Asian Survey* 6, no. 3 (March 1966):175–184.

Milward, Alan S. *The Reconstruction of Western Europe, 1945–1951*. Berkeley: University of California Press, 1984.

Misztal, Barbara. *Trust in Modern Societies: The Search for the Bases of Social Order*. Cambridge: Polity Press, 1996.

Mitchell, B. R. *International Historical Statistics, Europe, 1750–1993*. London: Palgrave Macmillan, 1998.

Moravcsik, Andrew. *The Choice for Europe: Social Purpose and State Power from Messina to Maastricht*. Ithaca, NY: Cornell University Press, 1998.

Morgan, Lewis Henry. *League of the Iroquois*. New York: Corinth Books, 1962.

Nakleh, Emile. *The Gulf Cooperation Council: Policies, Problems, Prospects*. New York: Praeger, 1986.

Narine, Shaun. *Explaining ASEAN: Regionalism in Southeast Asia*. Boulder, CO: Lynne Rienner, 2002.

Neale, Robert G. *Great Britain and United States Expansion: 1898–1900*. East Lansing: Michigan State University Press, 1966.

Neilson, Keith. "The Anglo-Japanese Alliance and British Strategic Foreign Policy, 1902–1914." In *The Anglo-Japanese Alliance*, edited by Phillips Payson O'Brien, 48–63. New York: RoutledgeCurzon, 2004.

Nish, Ian. *The Anglo-Japanese Alliance: The Diplomacy of Two Island Empires, 1894–1907*. London: Althone Press, 1966.

———. *The Alliance in Decline: A Study in Anglo-Japanese Relations, 1908–1923*. London: Athlone Press, 1972.

———. "Echoes of Alliance, 1920-30." In *The History of Anglo-Japanese Relations. Vol. 1: The Political-Diplomatic Dimension, 1600–1930*, edited by Ian Nish and Yoichi Kibata, 255–278. New York: St. Martin's Press, 2000.

———. "Origins of the Anglo-Japanese Alliance: In the Shadow of the Dreibund." In *The Anglo-Japanese Alliance, 1902–1922*, edited by Phillips Payson O'Brien, 8–25. London: RoutledgeCurzon, 2004.

Nish, Ian, and Yoichi Kibata, eds. *The History of Anglo-Japanese Relations. Vol. 1: The Political-Diplomatic Dimension, 1600–1930*. New York: St. Martin's Press, 2000.

Nye, Joseph. *Peace in Parts: Integration and Conflict in Regional Organization*. Boston: Little, Brown, 1971.

O'Brien, Phillips Payson, ed. *The Anglo-Japanese Alliance*. New York: RoutledgeCurzon, 2004.

Oelsner, Andrea. *International Relations in Latin America: Peace and Security in the Southern Cone*. New York: Routledge, 2005.

Oh, John. "The Federation of Malaysia: An Experiment in Nation-Building." *American Journal of Economics and Sociology* 26, no. 4 (October 1976): 425–438.

Omole, Tale. "The End of a Dream: The Collapse of the Senegambian Confederation, 1982–1989." *Contemporary Review* 257, no. 1496 (September 1990): 133–139.

O'Neill, Michael. *The Politics of European Integration*. New York: Routledge, 1996.

Oren, Ido. "The Subjectivity of the 'Democratic' Peace: Changing U.S. Perceptions of Imperial Germany." *International Security* 20, no. 2 (Fall 1995): 147–184.

Ostrom, Elinor. "A Behavioral Approach to the Rational Choice Theory of Collective Action." *American Political Science Review* 92, no. 1 (March 1998): 472–505.

Owen, John M. "How Liberalism Produces Democratic Peace." In *Debating the Democratic Peace,* edited by Michael Brown, Sean Lynn-Jones, and Steven Miller, 116–156. Cambridge, MA: MIT Press, 1996.

———. "Pieces of Stable Peace: A Pessimistic Constructivism." Unpublished paper, Third Pan-European International Relations Conference, Vienna (September 16, 1998).

Owsley, Frank. "The Irrepressible Conflict." In *The Coming of the American Civil War*, 3rd ed., edited by Michael Perlman, 34–39. Lexington, MA: D.C. Heath and Co., 1993.

Oye, Kenneth. *Cooperation under Anarchy*. Princeton, NJ: Princeton University Press, 1986.

Pape, Robert A. "Soft Balancing against the United States." *International Security* 30, no. 1 (2005): 7–45.

Paribatra, Sukhumbhand, and Chai-Anan Samudavanija. "Internal Dimensions of Regional Security in Southeast Asia." In *Regional Security in the Third World: Case Studies From Southeast Asia and the Middle East*, edited by Mohammed Ayoob, 57–94. Boulder, CO: Westview Press, 1986.

Parker, J.S.F. "The United Arab Republic." *International Affairs* 38, no. 1 (January 1962): 15–28.

Paul, T. V. "Soft Balancing in the Age of U.S. Primacy." *International Security* 30, no. 1 (2005): 46–71.

Peck, Malcolm. *The United Arab Emirates: A Venture in Unity.* Boulder, CO: Westview Press, 1986.

Perlman, Michael, ed. *The Coming of the American Civil War*, 3rd ed. Lexington, MA: D.C. Heath and Co., 1993.

Pessen, Edward. "How Different from Each Other Were the Antebellum North and South." *American Historical Review* 85, no. 5 (December 1980): 1119–1149.

Peterson, Erik R. *The Gulf Cooperation Council: Search for Unity in a Dynamic Region.* Boulder, CO: Westview Press, 1988.

Peterson, J. E. "The GCC and Regional Security." In *The Gulf Cooperation Council: Moderation and Stability in an Interdependent World*, edited by John A. Sandwick, 62–90. Boulder, CO: Westview Press, 1987.

Petrov, Victor P. "Some Observations on the 1959 Soviet Census." *Russian Review* 18, no. 4. (October 1959): 332–338.

Pettegree, Andrew. *The Reformation World.* London: Routledge, 2000.

Pflanze, Otto. *Bismarck and the Development of Germany: The Period of Unification, 1815–1871.* Princeton, NJ: Princeton University Press, 1962.

Phillips, Ann. "The Politics of Reconciliation Revisited: Germany and East-Central Europe." *World Affairs* 163, no. 4 (Spring 2001): 171–191.

Phillips, Lucie Colvin. "The Senegambia Confederation." In *The Political Economy of Senegal under Structural Adjustment,* edited by Christopher Delgado and Sidi Jammeh, 175–194. New York: Praeger, 1991.

Pierson, Paul. "The Path to European Integration: A Historical Institutionalist Analysis." Center for German and European Studies, University of California at Berkeley (November 1996).

Pion-Berlin, David. "Will Soldiers Follow? Economic Integration and Regional Security in the Southern Cone." *Journal of Interamerican Studies and World Affairs* 42, no. 1 (Spring 2000): 1–69.

Pleshakov, Constantine. "Nikita Khrushchev and Sino-Soviet Relations." In *Brothers in Arms: The Rise and Fall of the Sino-Soviet Alliance, 1945–1963,* edited by Odd Arne Westad, 226–245. Washington, DC: Woodrow Wilson Center Press, 1998.

Podeh, Elie. *The Decline of Arab Unity: The Rise and Fall of the United Arab Republic.* Brighton: Sussex Academic Press, 1999.

Preston, Richard A. *The Defence of the Undefended Border: Planning for War in North America, 1867–1939.* Montreal: McGill-Queen's University Press, 1977.

Prybyla, Jan S. "Problems of Soviet Agriculture." *Journal of Farm Economics* 44, no. 3 (August 1962): 820–836.

Putnam, Robert. *Making Democracy Work: Civil Traditions in Modern Italy.* Princeton, NJ: Princeton University Press, 1984.

Ramazani, R. K. *The Gulf Cooperation Council: Record and Analysis.* Charlottesville: University of Virginia Press, 1988.

Reid, Brian Holden. *The Origins of the American Civil War.* New York: Longman, 1996.

Resende-Santos, Joao. "The Origins of Security Cooperation in the Southern Cone." *Latin American Politics and Society* 44, no. 4 (Winter 2002): 89–126.

Riall, Lucy. *The Italian Risorgimento: State, Society and National Unification.* New York: Routledge, 1994.

Rich, Norman. *Why the Crimean War? A Cautionary Tale*. Hanover: University Press of New England, 1985.

Richardson, James L. *Crisis Diplomacy: The Great Powers since the Mid-Nineteenth Century*. Cambridge: Cambridge University Press, 1994.

Richmond, Edmun B. "Senegambia and the Confederation: History, Expectations, and Disillusions." *Journal of Third World Studies* 10, no. 2 (1993): 17–194.

Richter, Daniel. *The Ordeal of the Longhouse: The Peoples of the Iroquois League in the Era of European Colonization*. Chapel Hill: University of North Carolina Press, 1992.

Risse, Thomas. "Let's Argue!' Communicative Action in World Politics." *International Organization* 54, no. 1 (Winter 2000): 1–39.

Rock, Stephen R. *Appeasement in International Politics*. Lexington: University of Kentucky Press, 2000.

———. *Why Peace Breaks Out: Great Power Rapprochement in Historical Perspective*. Chapel Hill: University of North Carolina Press, 1989.

Roett, Riordan, ed. *Mercosur: Regional Integration, World Markets*. Boulder, CO: Lynne Rienner, 1999.

Sablonier, Roger. "The Swiss Confederation," In *The New Cambridge Medieval History*, vol. 7, c. 1415–c. 1500, edited by Christopher Allmand, 645–670. Cambridge: Cambridge University Press, 1998.

Sall, Ebrima, and Halifa Sallah. "Senegal and the Gambia: The Politics of Integration." In *Sénégal et ses Voisins*, edited by Momar-Coumba Diop, 117–141. Dakar: Societes-Espaces-Temps, 1994.

Sallah, Tijan. "Economics and Politics in the Gambia." *Journal of Modern African Studies* 28, no. 4 (December 1990): 621–648.

Sandwick, John A., ed. *The Gulf Cooperation Council: Moderation and Stability in an Interdependent World*. Boulder, CO: Westview Press, 1987.

Schimmelfennig, Frank. "The Community Trap: Liberal Norms, Rhetorical Action, and the Eastern Enlargement of the European Union." *International Organization* 55, no. 1 (2001): 47–80.

Schroeder, Paul. *Austria, Great Britain, and the Crimean War*. Ithaca, NY: Cornell University Press, 1972.

———. "The 19th-Century International System: Changes in the Structure." *World Politics* 39, no. 1 (October 1986): 1–26.

Schweller, Randall L. *Deadly Imbalances: Tripolarity and Hitler's Strategy of World Conquest*. New York: Columbia University Press, 1998.

Searle, John. *Speech Acts: An Essay in the Philosophy of Language*. Cambridge: Cambridge University Press, 1969.

Selcher, Wayne A. "Brazilian-Argentine Relations in the 1980s: From Wary Rivalry to Friendly Competition." *Journal of Interamerican Studies and World Affairs* 27, no. 2 (Summer 1985): 25–53.

Shigeru, Murashima. "The Opening of the Twentieth Century and the Anglo-Japanese Alliance, 1895–1923." In *The History of Anglo-Japanese Relations*, edited by Ian Nish and Yoichi Kibata, 159–196. Basingstoke: Macmillan, 2000.

Shimazu, Naoko. *Japan, Race and Equality: The Racial Equality Proposal of 1919*. New York: Routledge, 1998.

SIPRI Yearbook 1995: Armaments, Disarmament and International Security. London: Oxford University Press, 1995.

Skidmore, David, ed. *Contested Social Orders and International Politics*. Nashville, TN: Vanderbilt University Press, 1997.

Smith, Denis Mack. *The Making of Italy, 1796–1870*. New York: Walker, 1968.

Snyder, Jack. *Myths of Empire: Domestic Politics and International Ambition*. Ithaca, NY: Cornell University Press, 1991.

———. *From Voting to Violence: Democratization and Nationalist Conflict*. New York: Norton, 2000.

Solingen, Etel. *Regional Orders at Century's Dawn: Global and Domestic Influences on Grand Strategy*. Princeton, NJ: Princeton University Press, 1998.

Sopiee, Mohamed Noordin. *From Malayan Union to Singapore Separation*. Kuala Lumpur: University of Malaysia Press, 1974.

Sopiee, Noordin. "ASEAN and Regional Security." In *Regional Security in the Third World*, edited by Mohammed Ayoob, 221–231. Boulder, CO: Westview Press, 1986.

Sperber, Jonathan . *The European Revolutions, 1848–1851*. Cambridge: Cambridge University Press, 1984.

———. *A Short Oxford History of Germany*. Oxford: Oxford University Press, 2004.

Sprout, Tuttle. "Mahan: Evangelist of Sea Power." In *Makers of Modern Strategy: Military Thought from Machiavelli to Hitler*, edited by Edward Mead Earle, 415–445. Princeton, NJ: Princeton University Press, 1971.

Spruyt, Hendrik. *Ending Empire: Contested Sovereignty and Territorial Partition*. Ithaca, NY: Cornell University Press, 2005.

Stearns, Peter. *1848: The Revolutionary Tide in Europe*. New York: Norton, 1974.

Steeds, David. "Anglo-Japanese Relations, 1902–23: A Marriage of Convenience." In *The History of Anglo-Japanese Relations, Vol. 1: The Political-Diplomatic Dimension, 1600–1930,* edited by Ian Nish and Yoichi Kibata, 197–223. New York, St. Martin's Press, 2000.

Stepan, Alfred. *Rethinking Military Politics: Brazil and the Southern Cone*. Princeton, NJ: Princeton University Press, 1988.

Stites, Sara Henry. *Economics of the Iroquois*. Lancaster, PA: New Era Printing, 1905.

Suleiman, Ezra. "Is Democratic Supranationalism a Danger?" In *Nationalism and Nationalities in the New Europe*, edited by Charles A. Kupchan, 66–84. Ithaca, NY: Cornell University Press, 1995.

Taryam, Abdullah Omran . *The Establishment of the United Arab Emirates 1950–85*. London: Croom Helm, 1987.

Tate, Merze. "Hawaii: A Symbol of Anglo-American Rapprochement." *Political Science Quarterly* 79, no. 4 (December 1964): 555–575.

Thompson, David G. *The Norwegian Armed Forces and Defense Policy, 1905–1955*. Scandinavian Studies, vol. 11. Lewiston, NY: Edwin Mellen Press, 2004.

Treverton, Gregory F. *America, Germany, and the Future of Europe*. Princeton, NJ: Princeton University Press, 1992.

Vanthoor, Wim F. V. *A Chronological History of the European Union, 1946–2001*. Northhampton, MA: Edward Elgar, 2002.

Varickayil, Robert. "Social Origins of Protestant Reformation." *Social Scientist* 8, no. 11 (June 1980): 14–31.

Velazquez, Arturo C. Sotomayor. "Civil-Military Affairs and Security Institutions in the Southern Cone: The Sources of Argentine-Brazilian Nuclear Cooperation." *Latin American Politics and Society* 46, no. 4 (Winter 2004): 29–60.

Waever, Ole. "Insecurity, Security, and Asecurity in the West European Non-War Community." In *Security Communities*, edited by Emanuel Adler and Michael Barnett, 69–118. Cambridge: Cambridge University Press, 1998.

Walt, Stephen. *The Origins of Alliances.* Ithaca, NY: Cornell University Press, 1987.

Weeks, Jessica. "Autocratic Audience Costs: Regime Type and Signaling Resolve." *International Organization* 62, no. 1 (Winter 2008): 35–64.

Wendt, Alexander. "Anarchy Is What States Make of It: The Social Construction of Power Politics." *International Organization* 46, no. 2 (Spring 1992): 391–425.

———. "Collective Identity Formation and the International State." *American Political Science Review,* 88, no. 2 (June 1994): 384–396.

———. *Social Theory of International Politics.* Cambridge: Cambridge University Press, 1999.

———. "Why a World State Is Inevitable." *European Journal of International Relations* 9, no. 4 (2003): 491–542.

Westad, Odd Arne, ed. *Brothers in Arms: The Rise and Fall of the Sino-Soviet Alliance, 1945–1963.* Washington, DC: Woodrow Wilson Center Press, 1998.

———. "Introduction." In *Brothers in Arms: The Rise and Fall of the Sino-Soviet Alliance, 1945–1963*, edited by Odd Arne Westad, 1–46. Washington, DC: Woodrow Wilson Center Press, 1998.

———. "The Sino-Soviet Alliance and the United States." In *Brothers in Arms: The Rise and Fall of the Sino-Soviet Alliance, 1945–1963,* edited by Odd Arne Westad, 1–46. Washington, DC: Woodrow Wilson Center Press, 1998.

Wiseman, John. "Gambia." In *South of the Sahara—2006*, 35th edition edited by Iain Frame. New York: Routledge, 2005.

Wittfogel, Karl. *Oriental Despotism: A Comparative Study of Total Power*. New York: Vintage, 1981.

Xu, Guoqi. *China and the Great War: China's Pursuit of a New National Identity and Internationalization.* Cambridge: Cambridge University Press, 2005.

Zagoria, Donald. *The Sino-Soviet Conflict, 1956–1961.* New York: Atheneum, 1964.

Zakaria, Fareed. *The Post-American World.* New York: Norton, 2008.

Zhang, Shu Guang. "Sino-Soviet Cooperation." In *Brothers in Arms: The Rise and Fall of the Sino-Soviet Alliance, 1945–1963,* edited by Odd Arne Westad, 189–225. Washington, DC: Woodrow Wilson Center Press, 1998.

Ziblatt, Daniel. *Structuring the State: The Formation of Italy and Germany and the Puzzle of Federalism.* Princeton, NJ: Princeton University Press, 2006.

Zimmer, Oliver. *A Contested Nation: History, Memory and Nationalism in Switzerland, 1761–1891.* Cambridge: Cambridge University Press, 2003.

INDEX

The letters *t, f,* or *n* following a page number indicate a table, figure, or note on that page. If there is more than one note on a page, the number of the note cited follows the *n.*

Abdullah, Crown Prince (Saudi Arabia), 269
Aberdeen, Lord, 243
accommodation, 6, 13, 29, 35, 37–42, 48–49, 390–99, 408; Anglo-American rapprochement and, 74–78, 81–82, 105, 111, 390; Anglo-Japanese Alliance and, 139, 148–49, 150–51; ASEAN and, 223; benign motivation and, 38–39, 46, 391; Brazil-Argentina rapprochement and, 123, 132; China and, 395; Concert of Europe and, 390; consensus formation and, 397–99; costly concessions and, 394–95; cultural commonality and, 53; dispute resolution, power checking and, 391–92; economic integration and, 400; ECSC and, 204; as elite enterprise, 48; GCC and, 390; GRIT and, 42; humiliation versus, 57, 92, 106, 126, 193, 223, 397; Italy and, 371; military forces and, 393–94; motivation assessment and, 41; Norway-Sweden rapprochement and, 114–15, 390; policy implications of, 398–99; political impact of, 391; seats of government and, 392; security community and, 184, 277; Turkey and Greece and, 395; UAE and, 326, 328, 329; UAR and, 390. *See also* restraint, reciprocal; restraint, strategic
Acharya, Amitav, 217, 231
Adenauer, Konrad, 204, 205, 207
Adler, Emanuel: *Security Communities,* 22, 24–25, 44–45, 184
Alexander, Tsar, 191
Alfonsin, Raul, 127
Al-Maktum, Sheik Rashid bin Sa'id (Dubai), 326
Al-Nuhayyan, Sheik Zayed bin Sultan Al-Nuhayyan (Abu Dhabi), 326, 332
Al-Sabah, Sheik Sabah al-Ahmad al-Jabir (Kuwait), 272
Amer, Abdul Hakim, 345
Anderson, Stuart, 97, 98

Anglo-Japanese Alliance, 1902–1923, 134–57; 1911 extension of, 137–38; Anglo-American rapprochement and, 151; assessing intentions and, 139–42, 144–45; Boxer Rebellion and, 136; British elites and, 154–55; China and, 146; communal identity and, 157; cultural commonality and, 153–57; economic ties and, 150; evolution of, 135–38; failure of: how, 138–50; failure of: why, 150–57; first renewal of, 142–44; government instability and, 153; institutionalized restraint and, 151–53; Japanese military growth and, 134–35; Korea and, 136–37, 144; Meiji Constitution and, 151–52; racism and, 154–57; reciprocal restraint and, 139; Russo-Japanese War and, 134, 137; second renewal of, 144–48; social orders and, 153; societal integration and, 139, 148–50; strategic restraint and, 140; terms of, 136–37; transparency and, 152–53; war, likelihood of, and, 148; Washington Naval Treaty of 1923 and, 134, 138, 148; World War I and, 137–38, 145–46
Asquith, Henry, 93
Association of Southeast Asian Nations (ASEAN) from 1967, 217–36; Association of Southeast Asia (ASA) and, 219; bilateral initiatives and, 227; communal identity and, 217; Concert of Europe and, 218, 226, 232–33; conflict between Indonesia and Malaysia and, 217; cultural commonality and, 63, 234–35; decision-making and power-checking mechanisms and, 225–29; dispute resolution, 391; economic interdependence and, 229; economic issues and, 220, 222; enlargement rounds of, 230–31; ethnic Chinese and, 234; great-power withdrawal and, 228–29; institutionalized restraint and, 232–33; *konfrontasi* and, 219–22, 232; Maphilindo and, 219; military cooperation and, 227; Nixon Doctrine